# American Foreign Policy and the Challenges of World Leadership

## POWER, PRINCIPLE, AND THE CONSTITUTION

### Loch K. Johnson

*University of Georgia*

New York   Oxford
Oxford University Press

For August,

*with hopes for a better world.*

Oxford University Press is a department of the University of Oxford. It furthers
the University's objective of excellence in research, scholarship, and education
by publishing worldwide.

Oxford   New York
Auckland   Cape Town   Dar es Salaam   Hong Kong   Karachi
Kuala Lumpur   Madrid   Melbourne   Mexico City   Nairobi
New Delhi   Shanghai   Taipei   Toronto

With offices in
Argentina   Austria   Brazil   Chile   Czech Republic   France   Greece
Guatemala   Hungary   Italy   Japan   Poland   Portugal   Singapore
South Korea   Switzerland   Thailand   Turkey   Ukraine   Vietnam

For titles covered by Section 112 of the US Higher Education Opportunity
Act, please visit www.oup.com/us/he for the latest information about
pricing and alternate formats.

Published in the United States of America by
Oxford University Press
198 Madison Avenue,New York, NY 10016
http://www.oup.com

Oxford is a registered trade mark of Oxford University Press.

CIP data is on file at the Library of Congress
ISBN 978-0-19-973361-3

Printing number:  9 8 7 6 5 4 3 2 1

Printed in the United States of America on acid-free paper

# BRIEF CONTENTS

# CONTENTS

## PART 2: THE INFLUENCES OF HISTORY

## PART 3: INSTITUTIONS AND INDIVIDUALS

## PART 5: FOREIGN POLICY CHALLENGES

# PREFACE

THE ESSENCE OF AMERICAN FOREIGN POLICY resides in the how and why of decision making. A central goal of this book is to examine how foreign policy decisions are made, and to encourage thought and debate about how the United States ought to conduct itself as a world power in the twenty-first century. Criticism of presidentially guided foreign policy has taken on new life today, especially with respect to America's focus on military operations abroad. In contrast to these militant approaches to foreign policy, which are sometimes necessary in self-defense, in this book I explore the value of an executive–legislative partnership that pursues a global perspective extending beyond a reliance on the use of armed force. Whether these methods, which favor constitutional principles and a greater concern for diplomacy and economic statecraft, are superior to a reliance on a powerful presidency and a display of military power around the world is for the reader to decide.

To understand and analyze foreign policy, one must appreciate America's constitutional framework—the country's fundamental blueprint for the making of foreign as well as domestic policy. Important, too, is the story of how US foreign relations have unfolded over the decades, from the earliest days of the new Republic—an era of sailing ships and muskets—to the contemporary world of rapid transportation, instant communications, and the widespread proliferation of powerful weapons. Further, in this book I seek to impart an awareness of how and why Washington officials choose among specific instruments—such as diplomacy, trade agreements, or military force—in their efforts to defend and advance US interests abroad. At the heart of the chapters that follow lie these three aspects of American foreign policy:

1. Its constitutional foundations.
2. Its historical evolution.
3. Its instruments of policy implementation.

The book uses a levels-of-analysis approach for understanding how and why decisions are made by America's foreign policy leaders.[1] This perspective highlights the significance of three levels where foreign policy is shaped:

1. The international setting—the world stage where nations jostle for security and advantage.
2. Domestic politics, where a complex array of interest groups attempt to influence foreign policy at home.
3. The individual level, whether a policy official in high office making a decision or a citizen voting or perhaps writing a letter about foreign policy to the local newspaper.

Foreign policy may be defined as a nation's pursuit of objectives in the world through relationships with other nations, international organizations, and factions (a more formal definition is presented in Chapter 1). As such, it is a far-reaching and complex discipline, and one that is intimately bound to political considerations at the international, domestic (national), and individual levels.

## THE IMPORTANCE OF AMERICA'S CONSTITUTIONAL FRAMEWORK

A primary objective of this book is to examine the advantages and disadvantages for the modern-day conduct of foreign policy that stem from America's constitutional framework. I seek to shed light on the points of friction and cooperation in a system of shared power and to examine the contemporary relevance of the constitutional safeguards put in place by the founders as a protection against the rise of autocratic rule in the United States.

When America's founders wrote the Constitution in 1787, they endorsed an unprecedented institutional design for fashioning foreign and domestic policy. Their genius was to insist on the sharing of authority (legitimate power) across three "departments" of government, as they referred to the executive, legislative, and judicial branches. The overarching purpose of the founders in their adoption of this constitutional framework was to guard against the dangers of tyranny. They had experienced the heavy hand of King George III and had witnessed, as well, the repressive activities of other European monarchs. Consequently, those who wrote the Constitution were determined to avoid the creation of yet another autocratic regime in the new Republic.

Despite the experiences with George III and his unfair decrees (taxation without representation was but one of many grievances that drove the colonies into rebellion), some prominent early Americans flirted with the idea of a monarchy, or at least a chief executive who could dominate over foreign policy. Echoing this concern more than two hundred years later, Vice President Dick Cheney of the George W. Bush administration championed the idea of a unitary presidency, a strong chief executive free to operate largely without the constraints of Congress or the courts when it came to a wide array of policy decisions—especially in the realm of foreign policy.[2]

The founders' prescription for sharing foreign policy powers across the branches—the exact opposite idea of the unitary theory—can be frustrating because of the often foggy boundaries and overlapping jurisdictions that exist among the departments, agencies, bureaus, committees, subcommittees, and individuals involved in determining the proper pathway for the United States in world affairs. Moreover, this dispersal of power can lead to delays in foreign policy making that might be avoided if decisions are made by a single autocratic individual at the top. Yet a constitutional scheme for power sharing produces strong centrifugal, or outward pushing, forces within the government that today, more than two centuries after the Constitutional Convention, continue to prevent the control over the institutions of foreign policy making from becoming too centralized. Creative leadership is required to piece together the fragments of power into support for specific policy initiatives. Persuasion, not coercion, is the order of the day; conflict, not harmony, is the norm.

## ADDITIONAL THEMES OF THIS BOOK

A drama as large as American foreign policy has many subplots. An important secondary theme in this book is the significance of the human dimension in foreign affairs, such as the ambivalence Americans display toward their nation's status as a world power. As a further example, broad historical or institutional ("structural") forces can affect decisions, which are often a function mainly of established bureaucratic norms in various government buildings. Moreover, decisions can stem from the will, and sometimes the whim, of government officials who administer foreign policy.

In this book I also explore the argument that in the modern era the United States has been overly preoccupied with the military as an instrument of foreign policy. Since 1945, the United States has encircled its adversaries with military bases and has spent trillions of dollars on advanced weaponry. Because of this concentration on just one—the most extreme—instrument of foreign policy, critics have lamented that the nation pays insufficient attention to other global concerns beyond war fighting overseas, including everything from environmental pollution and worldwide poverty to gaping holes in America's homeland security and a decline in US economic competitiveness.[3]

## ORGANIZATION AND FEATURES

This book is divided into four Parts:

- In Part One, "Understanding American Foreign Policy," I introduce American foreign policy (Chapter 1); address the approaches pursued by foreign policy officials in Washington, DC (Chapter 2); and offer an analytic framework for the study of foreign policy (Chapter 3), including the influence and continuing role of the Constitution.
- Part Two, "The Influences of History," offers a historical backdrop vital for comprehending the evolution of contemporary foreign policy. I begin by examining the formative years when the United States was relatively isolated and protected from the rest of the world (Chapter 4); then I take up the important era of the Cold War when the United States and the Soviet Union stood preeminent in the world (Chapter 5); and next I explore foreign policy in the more fractured global environment of today (Chapter 6).
- Part Three, "Institutions and Individuals," explores the institutional (Chapter 7) and human dimensions (Chapter 8) of American foreign policy.

～ Part Four, "The Instruments of Foreign Policy," examines how policy makers implement each of the key instruments of foreign policy: intelligence gathering and analysis (Chapter 9), diplomacy (Chapter 10), military force (Chapter 11), covert action (Chapter 12), economic statecraft (Chapter 13), and cultural and moral suasion (Chapter 14). Often these instruments are used together synergistically—a "Black-&-Decker" approach to foreign policy that incorporates every tool in the box.

～ Part Five, "Foreign Policy Challenges," concludes the book with a look at American foreign policy and the ongoing challenges of global leadership (Chapter 15).

Each of the chapters in this book follows a specific format, beginning with a chapter outline, a list of learning objectives, and list of key constitutional questions raised in the chapter. This introductory material is followed by a short vignette that highlights a historical event of significance to the study of US foreign policy. Each chapter then provides an in-depth examination of topics central to an understanding of America's role in the world.

A recurring box feature, called "Perspectives on American Foreign Policy," presents excerpts from key historical documents or revealing observations on the subject from top experts and practitioners.

Each chapter ends with a summary and a set of key terms and study questions to aid the reader in reinforcing a chapter's most important concepts. A list of additional readings are also provided in each chapter for those who wish to explore these concepts further, with an expanded listing in the Website that supports this book.

The Website also includes an Appendix of "Key Foreign Policy Passages from the Constitution of the United States" and a listing of America's secretaries of state and defense since the end of World War II. The end materials include a complete glossary of key terms and chapter notes that provide sources and comments for key ideas.

## ACKNOWLEDGMENTS

Few topics are as complex as American foreign policy, dealing as it does with over two hundred nations in the world; even larger numbers of international factions, parties, and nongovernmental organizations; an intricate decision-making process in Washington, DC; and an ever changing global setting that is characterized by uncertainty, ambiguity, and, all too often, hostility. No one is an expert in every aspect of this subject; but I have had the benefit of studying this topic for over forty years, as well as serving in the legislative and executive branches of the federal government with responsibilities for foreign policy. Along the way, I have had several outstanding mentors who helped me understand more about US relations with the rest of the world. I take this opportunity to thank them: President Jimmy Carter of Georgia; Vice President

Walter F. Mondale of Minnesota; Senators Frank Church of Idaho, Wyche Fowler of Georgia, and Gary Hart of Colorado; Representatives Les Aspin of Wisconsin, Jonathan B. Bingham of New York, and Edward P. Boland of Massachusetts; Secretary of State Dean Rusk; intelligence leaders James Angleton, James R. Clapper Jr., William E. Colby, John M. Deutch, Robert M. Gates (who also served as secretary of defense), Richard Helms, James R. Schlesinger (another secretary of defense), George J. Tenet, Adm. Stansfield Turner, and R. James Woolsey; US Ambassadors Martin Hillenbrand, Karl F. Inderfurth, and Don Johnson; German Ambassador Dieter Kastrup; and Senate staff colleagues Frederick A. O. Schwarz Jr., Gregory F. Treverton, and Garry V. Wenske.

I also owe a debt to several colleagues in the academic and think-tank worlds, especially David M. Barrett, Jeffrey D. Berejikian, Gary Bertsch, Charles S. Bullock III, Arthur C. Campbell, Francis M. Carney, Ralph G. Carter, Kiki Caruson, I. M. "Mac" Destler, Paul F. Diehl, Louis Fisher, John Lewis Gaddis, Michael J. Glennon, Glenn P. Hastedt, Michael Herman, Steven W. Hook, Charles W. Kegley Jr., William W. Keller, Michael Leonard, Mark M. Lowenthal, David S. McLellan, Joseph S. Nye Jr., Han Park, Vernon Puryear, Harry Howe Ransom, Jerel Rosati, David Shambaugh, Harold L. Sims, Robert Swansbrough, Brock Tessman, L. N. Wenner, H. Bradford Westerfield, Howard J. Wiarda, and James J. Wirtz. The bibliographic and footnote entries throughout this book are further testimony of my indebtedness to a wide range of scholars.

Finally, I would like to express my heartfelt appreciation to President Jere W. Morehead of the University of Georgia for his friendship and constant support for my research, teaching, and public service endeavors; to my college dean, Thomas P. Lauth, and my department head, Markus Crepaz, for their backing; to my students at the University of Georgia—particularly, Lt. Col. Jim Borders, Rocky T. Cole, Larry Lamanna, Marie Milward, Virginia S. Newman, Allison M. Shelton, Harriera Siddiq, and Megan White—for their assistance with fact checking and their insights into foreign policy; to my darling wife, Leena S. Johnson, for providing unfailing support and editorial guidance while keeping the Johnson family happy and close; to our daughter, Kristin E. Swati, and her husband, Jamil Swati, for their guidance, inspiration, and thoughts about world affairs; and, last but not least, to Peter M. Labella and Niko Pfund at Oxford University Press for their friendship and encouragement over the years, as well as to acquisitions editor Jennifer Carpenter, development manager and editor Thom Holmes, and development editor Elsa Peterson, for their first-rate efforts, steady enthusiasm, and wise counsel. Much gratitude also goes to associate editor Maegan Sherlock, development intern Sam Power, copy-editor Deanna Hegle, senior production editor Theresa Stockton, and director of design Michele Laseau.

LOCH K. JOHNSON
*Athens, Georgia*

# MANUSCRIPT REVIEWERS

I HAVE GREATLY BENEFITED from the perceptive comments and suggestions of the many talented scholars and instructors who reviewed the manuscript of *American Foreign Policy*. Their insight and suggestions contributed immensely to the published work. I thank them most sincerely and underscore that no one bears any blame for the interpretations that I have settled on in these pages or for any errors of fact.

# ABOUT THE AUTHOR

LOCH K. JOHNSON is the Regents Professor of Public and International Affairs at the University of Georgia. He is the author of over 200 articles, as well as the author or editor of twenty-nine books on U.S. national security and foreign policy, including *National Security Intelligence: Secret Operations in Defense of the Democracies* (Polity, 2012); *The Threat on the Horizon: An Inside Account of America's Search for Security after the Cold War* (Oxford, 2011); *The Oxford Handbook of National Security Intelligence* (editor, Oxford, 2010); *Seven Sins of American Foreign Policy* (Longman, 2007); *Handbook of Intelligence Studies* (editor, Routledge, 2007); and *Strategic Intelligence*, 5 vols. (editor, Praeger, 2007). He has served as special assistant to Chairman Les Aspin on the Aspin–Brown Commission on Intelligence (1995–1996); as the first staff director of the Subcommittee on Intelligence Oversight, House Permanent Select Committee on Intelligence (1977–79); and as special assistant to the chair of the Senate Select Committee on Intelligence (1975–76). He has won the Certificate of Distinction from the National Intelligence Study Center, the Studies in Intelligence Award from the Center for the Study of Intelligence, and (with Charles S. Bullock III) the V.O. Key Prize from the Southern Political Science Association. He has served as secretary of the American Political Science Association, as well as president of the International Studies Association, South; and he is the senior editor of the international journal *Intelligence and National Security*, published in London.

Born in Auckland, New Zealand, Professor Johnson received his PhD in political science from the University of California, Riverside. At the University of Georgia, he has won the Josiah Meigs Prize, the University's highest teaching honor, as well as the Owens Award, its highest research honor in the social sciences. He also led the founding of the new School of Public and International Affairs at the University in 2001. The Southeast Conference selected Professor Johnson as the inaugural "Professor of the Year" in 2012, and the Intelligence Studies Section of the International Studies Association chose him for its "Distinguished Scholar Award" in 2014.

### CHAPTER 1

# The Objectives and Instruments of American Foreign Policy

## AMERICA UNDER ATTACK

It was a typical balmy and clear New England summer morning as American Airlines Flight 11 lifted off from Boston's Logan International Airport at 7:59 a.m. on Tuesday, September 11, 2001. The destination was Los Angeles. Among the passengers assigned to business class were Mohamed Atta and four other men from the Middle East. They believed fervently that the United States was a mortal enemy of Islam and that Americans deserved to be punished for stationing troops in Saudi Arabia close to Islamic holy grounds, as well as for providing Israel with advanced military weaponry over the years.

The South Tower of the World Trade Center in New York City begins to collapse on September 11, 2001.

With Captain John Ogonowski at the controls, the Boeing 767 soon climbed to an altitude of 26,000 feet. Just before 8:14, the flight had its last normal communication with air traffic control; when instructed to rise to 35,000 feet, the pilot did not respond. Approximately five minutes later, as air traffic control continued trying to reach the captain, flight attendant Betty Ong used an airphone on board to call American Airlines personnel on the ground. "I think we're getting hijacked," she reported. Two flight attendants had been stabbed and the hijackers, whom she identified by their seat numbers, had forced their way into the cockpit. While Ong maintained contact with an agent on the ground, her fellow flight attendant Amy Sweeney also telephoned American Airlines personnel on the ground and relayed additional details. As she reported, the airplane began to fly erratically, lurching southward toward New York City, circling in a wide arc and going into a steep descent. At 8:46, Flight 11 slammed into the North Tower of the World Trade Center in lower Manhattan.

Another aircraft, United Airlines Flight 175, had also set off for LA from Boston. Hijacked as well, it turned to the south, circled back toward Manhattan, and plunged toward the city's skyscrapers. The plane struck the South Tower of the Trade Center at 9:03, about fifteen minutes after the North Tower impact.

Two other teams were part of the plot later traced to Al Qaeda, a terrorist group sheltered by the Taliban regime in Afghanistan. They flew their hijacked airplanes

---

**LEARNING OBJECTIVES AND CONSTITUTIONAL QUESTIONS**

**By the end of this chapter, you will be able to:**

- *Define "foreign policy" and explain why the study of American foreign policy is important.*
- *Describe the basic objectives of American foreign policy.*
- *Describe the instruments for conducting foreign policy.*
- *Describe some basic philosophies of foreign policy.*

---

**THIS CHAPTER RAISES THE FOLLOWING CONSTITUTIONAL QUESTIONS, WHICH ARE EXPLORED IN GREATER DEPTH THROUGHOUT THIS BOOK:**

- The Constitution arranges for foreign policy to be guided chiefly by both the executive and legislative branches of government, and over the years the judicial branch has occasionally stepped in to arbitrate disputes between the two. Which of the branches is best equipped to set priorities for American foreign policy? Can power be shared among branches, as the founders proposed, even in times of crisis? What if the government is divided by party control and polarized by deep-seated ideological differences between the parties?

- Should the extent of foreign policy involvement by each of the branches depend on the type of policy objective under consideration: security, economic prosperity, quality of life, or human rights?

- In choosing foreign policy instruments, such as the use of military force versus diplomacy, which branch should prevail—or can these decisions be made by Congress and the presidency working together, with the judiciary acting as a referee?

- To what extent are the various philosophies of foreign policy presented here compatible with the idea of the separation of powers embraced by the nation's founders?

toward Washington, DC. At 9:27, American Airlines Flight 77 smashed into the Pentagon traveling with the velocity of a missile at 530 miles an hour.

Terrorists took over the fourth plane, United Airlines Flight 93, bound from Newark to San Francisco, and turned it back toward Washington, DC. From telephone calls made by their families back home, the passengers had already learned about the fate of American 11 and United 175. At 9:57, several of the passengers decided to rush the hijackers in a desperate attempt to prevent the plane from reaching its target— perhaps the Capitol or the White House. Their brave struggle lasted for several minutes before the hijacker who had seized control of the cockpit rolled the aircraft over on its back and United 93 fell from the sky, crashing in a rural field in Pennsylvania.

In New York City, the tragedy was not over. The Twin Towers continued to burn; then, without warning, first the South Tower and then the North buckled and collapsed, sending office workers, tourists on the observation deck, and firefighters and police officers in a fall to their deaths. By the end of the day, 2,669 American citizens and 310 foreign nationals had perished in New York City, at the Pentagon in Virginia, and on a smoldering farmland southeast of Pittsburgh. The United States had suffered its worst attack ever, surpassing the British burning of Washington in the War of 1812 and the Japanese bombing of Pearl Harbor in 1941.[1] ⌣

## THE IMPORTANCE OF AMERICAN FOREIGN POLICY

The terrorist attacks against the United States on 9/11 underscore, vividly and tragically, the importance of foreign policy. Threats that seemed far away, beyond the Atlantic and Pacific oceans, could suddenly arrive on America's doorstep. The Age of International Terrorism had dawned in the United States. The 9/11 attacks would lead the United States into war against Afghanistan, as well as against the regime of Saddam Hussein in Iraq, who foreign policy advisers in the administration of President George W. Bush decided (incorrectly) had been complicit in the attacks. The number of American soldiers who died in these wars would surpass the civilian carnage in the strikes against New York City and Washington, DC; and the great financial costs of the wars— upward of two trillion dollars—contributed (along with widespread banking mismanagement) to the Great Recession of 2008 that sent the US economy reeling. Terrorists from the Middle East had drawn the United States into unplanned and expensive interventions overseas, emphasizing the reality that no nation stands alone in the world: all are subject to influences emanating from abroad, including violence capable of striking directly at the homeland.

Over the past hundred years, the nations of the world have grown closer together. The result has been both positive and negative. On one hand, improved economic, social, and cultural ties among nations have encouraged the spread of literacy worldwide, improved global health care, spurred technological advances, and increased the speed and frequency of international communications; on the other hand, rivalry among nations has led to outbreaks of war on a global scale. World War I (1914–1918) and World War II (1939–1945) yielded a staggering toll of mass destruction as well as millions of casualties among soldiers and civilians. The instant deaths resulting from America's dropping of atomic bombs on Japan changed the rules of warfare forever. With 78,150 people killed instantly in Hiroshima on August 6, 1945, and another 35,000 three days later in Nagasaki, history's message was clear: now everyone—civilian or military, man, woman, or child—stood in the crosshairs of advanced weaponry. The 9/11 attacks six decades later signaled the further harsh reality that, even in times of relative peace, foreign enemies could commit mass murder against noncombatants in the United States. On the occasion of these terrorist attacks, the weapons used were hijacked commercial airliners; the next time, the weapons could be nuclear, biological, chemical, or radiological weapons ("dirty bombs"), inflicting casualties in the hundreds of thousands, perhaps even millions.

America's economic relations with the rest of the world have also undergone significant evolution since the end of World War II. New economic powers have come into their own in recent decades, including some nations (such as South Korea) that were once considered poor. In the 1980s, expanding market opportunities around the world led to a much larger volume of global commercial activities. Barriers that once impeded the flow of capital, goods, services, information, and technology across borders have given way to new trade alliances. One outcome has been greater competition for the United States in the buying and selling of goods worldwide. As long ago as 1988, one authority observed, "The American economy is increasingly tied to a world economy over which the United States exercises progressively less control."[2] In the twenty-first century, America remains an economic behemoth and accounts for a quarter of the world's gross domestic product (GDP); however, it has lost much of its economic strength relative to its status even in the late 1990s when the US economy accounted for one-third of the world's GDP. These closer economic ties among states have been accompanied by a rise in the number of shared communications, along with films, television, music, and clothing fads. College students today have greater access to information through the Internet than did presidents of the United States just two decades ago; moreover, in some remote parts of Africa and Asia, young people gather around the single computer in their village to learn from online courses taught by top-flight professors at Harvard and Stanford Universities. Professor Joseph S. Nye Jr. of the Kennedy School of Government at Harvard has defined this evolving **globalization** as "*the growth of worldwide networks of interdependence.*"[3]

## THE OBJECTIVES OF AMERICAN FOREIGN POLICY

As these forces of globalization expand, no nation can remain apart. Each has to learn to function in this new, highly interdependent setting. **Foreign policy** may be defined as *a nation's pursuit of objectives in the world through relationships with other nations, international organizations, and factions.* National governments aspire to translate their objectives into realities through the use of various instruments of power, such as military force or diplomatic negotiations. Foreign policy is influenced by a nation's system of values—its political and economic norms as well as cultural and moral beliefs. These values shape a nation's grand strategy: its global objectives (ends) and its choice of instruments of power (means) to pursue those objectives.

Foreign policy is responsive to changing economic, social, political, and military conditions. In 1945 when World War II ended, America stood as a global colossus, much admired for its role in bringing the war to an end and respected, too, for its benevolent use of military power and for its robust economy. The United States was mighty but not imperial; prepared to use force against renegade nations and other "peace-breakers" but with no interest of its own in conquests for the sake of new land and riches. Over time, however, the war-torn nations of Europe, Asia, and the Soviet Union rebuilt their societies and became America's competitors. With the onset of globalization, rivalry among nations has grown fierce in every aspect of life, especially in the search for economic markets abroad. On the education front, for example, nations are now judged on how well they compare in the development of a well-trained workforce. With billions of people in India and China now a part of the global economy, President Barack Obama observed that nations with the most well-educated workers will prevail. "As it stands right now," the President reported in 2010, "America is in danger of falling behind."[4]

In this competition, few nations are content to stand by passively and accept whatever fate their adversaries may deal them. Instead they actively try to shape their destiny, as best they can, in the quest for national objectives. The primary American **foreign policy objectives** include *the physical protection of the nation, its citizens, and its allies; economic prosperity; improvements in the quality of life, such as clean air and water; and the advancement of human rights for its own citizens and people around the world.* These goals are more easily stated than achieved, and discussions about what degree of emphasis should be placed on each can lead to heated debate among Americans. The Constitution's establishment of strong legislative and judicial branches of government ensures that policy debates in Washington, DC, take place across a broad spectrum of actors, not just those within the inner sanctums of the executive branch.

The data presented in Figure 1.1 capture the views of Americans about foreign policy in 2012. Public opinion polls conducted over the past fifty years have consistently indicated widespread support for America's pursuit of security and prosperity; however, the goals of quality of life and human rights have attracted less unanimity.

## Maintaining Peace and Security

A senior State Department official in the Democratic administration of Jimmy Carter (1977–1980) observed that "our first and most important foreign policy priority is peace—for ourselves and for others"; and during the Republican administration of Ronald Reagan (1981–1989), the State Department emphasized the importance of "seeking to protect the security of our nation and its institutions, as well as those of our allies and friends."[5] Barack Obama, elected in 2008, similarly emphasized in a speech at the United States Military Academy that his foremost responsibility was "to forge an America that is safer, a world that is more secure. . . ."[6]

So far, humanity's record for establishing peace and security has been checkered. Most of the time, a majority of nations have been at peace with one another—a remarkable, but seldom remarked on fact. Yet, throughout the roughly 5,500 years of

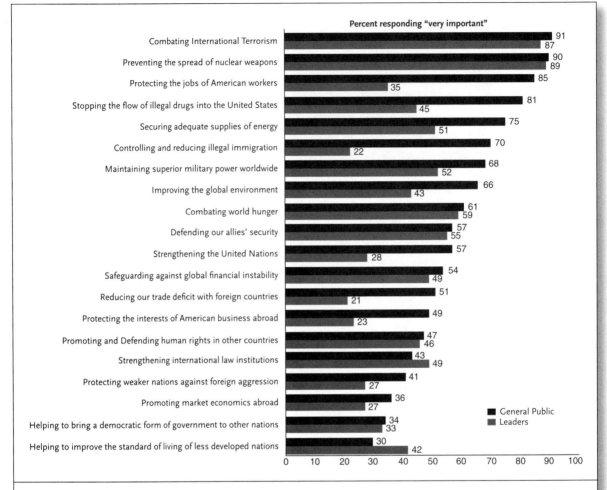

Percent responding "very important"

| | General Public | Leaders |
|---|---|---|
| Combating International Terrorism | 91 | 87 |
| Preventing the spread of nuclear weapons | 90 | 89 |
| Protecting the jobs of American workers | 85 | 35 |
| Stopping the flow of illegal drugs into the United States | 81 | 45 |
| Securing adequate supplies of energy | 75 | 51 |
| Controlling and reducing illegal immigration | 70 | 22 |
| Maintaining superior military power worldwide | 68 | 52 |
| Improving the global environment | 66 | 43 |
| Combating world hunger | 61 | 59 |
| Defending our allies' security | 57 | 55 |
| Strengthening the United Nations | 57 | 28 |
| Safeguarding against global financial instability | 54 | 49 |
| Reducing our trade deficit with foreign countries | 51 | 21 |
| Protecting the interests of American business abroad | 49 | 23 |
| Promoting and Defending human rights in other countries | 47 | 46 |
| Strengthening international law institutions | 43 | 49 |
| Protecting weaker nations against foreign aggression | 41 | 27 |
| Promoting market economics abroad | 36 | 27 |
| Helping to bring a democratic form of government to other nations | 34 | 33 |
| Helping to improve the standard of living of less developed nations | 30 | 42 |

SOURCE: The Chicago Council on Foreign Relations and The German Marshall Fund of the United States. American Public Opinion and U.S. Foreign Policy, 2002 [Computer file]. ICPSR03673-v1. Ann Arbor, MI: Inter-university Consortium for Political and Social Research [distributor], 2004. doi:10.3886/ICPSR03673

*Figure 1.1*
The Opinions of American Leaders and the Public on Key Foreign Policy Goals, 2002

recorded history, the world has enjoyed only about 300 years (off and on) in which no state has been at war anywhere on the planet. During World War II, over 60 million people perished; and nearly 30 million have died in armed conflicts since then. More recently, just in the First Persian Gulf War alone (which only lasted six weeks in 1990–91), well over 20,000 Iraq soldiers perished—some estimate as many as 100,000 or more.[7] During the administrations of George W. Bush and Obama, the use of a new form of warfare—US drones armed with Hellfire missiles—rose sharply against suspected terrorist targets in Afghanistan, Pakistan, and Yemen.[8]

Some historians have labeled the Cold War as "the long peace" because the two superpowers—the United States and the Soviet Union—avoided World War III. Yet, this period was anything but peaceful for many people around the planet. According to one estimate, as the Cold War began to wind down in 1989, one out of every four countries was at war. In that year, when the Berlin Wall was finally dismantled, about 500,000 people lost their lives in violent conflicts in Central America, Sudan, Eritrea, the Middle East, Northern Ireland, Southern Africa, and Sri Lanka.[9]

Whether in the form of terrorist attacks or formal battlefield confrontations, war remains the chief nemesis of the human race. "No diseases, no pestilence, no plagues have claimed as many lives as war," observed Bernard Lown, a Nobel Peace Prize recipient from the United States; and in an address to the United States Military Academy, General Douglas MacArthur reminded his audience of these words from the ancient philosopher Plato: "Only the dead have seen the end of war."[10] The Earth is serene in mountain and lake, a paradise among the uninhabitable orbs that circle the sun; but, at the same time, it is smitten with violence and bloodshed—even though most of its people long for peace and few wish to die prematurely on a killing field. This dilemma is paramount because it is related to the core objective of American foreign policy—the security of the United States and its citizens—and can be achieved only if this nation and others learn how to resolve their international disputes through nonviolent means.

The history of the United States is riven with political and legal disputes over the proper role of Congress, the presidency, and the judiciary in determining how best to defend the nation and advance its global interests. In 1973, lawmakers addressed the question of foreign military interventions by the United States in pursuit of its self-defense; frustrated by the ambiguities of the Constitution on this subject, they attempted to define the roles of Congress and the presidency in war making and ended up passing a War Powers Resolution (discussed in Chapter 11).

## Securing Economic Prosperity

The economic well-being of the American people is another core objective of American foreign policy. In 1993, Warren M. Christopher, Secretary of State in the Clinton administration, stressed during his Senate confirmation hearings that "practitioners of statecraft [must not] forget that their ultimate goal is to improve the daily lives of the American people."[11] Providing physical safety is one dimension of this obligation, but another is the guarantee of bread-and-butter security, which in turn is tied into global economic conditions. As the Carnegie Endowment for International Peace has pointed out, "Today foreign policy can also raise or lower the cost of your home mortgage, create a new job or cause you to lose the one you've got."[12] The high unemployment rates that ravaged the economy of the United States beginning with the recession of 2008 have been, in part, a function of the world's slumping economy.

The success of US goods in foreign marketplaces translates into jobs across America. Yet globalization can also have troubling consequences for the nation. The spiraling cost of oil imports down through the years has led to a hemorrhaging of US national wealth to oil-rich sheikdoms in the Middle East—often the same regimes that give aid and comfort to terrorist organizations that vow to kill Americans in a global *jihad* or "holy war" fought by Islamic extremists against the rest of the world. The United States has also seen the loss of more and more jobs moving overseas to low-wage countries. Many of these countries suffer from environmental pollution and unsafe working conditions, and the abuse of child labor is common. A setback in Washington's political relations with Moscow can cost the American farmer dearly through the loss of grain sales to Russia. Economic woes in Argentina or Mexico can lead to hand-wringing among international loan officers within the US banking community. Money flows across international boundaries like water, with banks in the United States insuring European and other foreign banks—and suffering the consequences if they fail. American warships continue to patrol the waters of the Persian Gulf, at considerable cost to the US taxpayer, to protect the access of Western industrial states to Middle East oil (although today the United States imports more oil from Africa than from the Persian Gulf). Ironically, the nation that may benefit most from this armada, as well as America's recent wars in Iraq, is an economic competitor of the United States: Japan, which obtains over 77 percent of its petroleum from the Persian Gulf but contributes nothing to US military costs in securing this waterway.[13]

Ongoing tensions between rich and poor nations are another troubling feature of globalization. If only as a matter of self-protection, rich states can benefit from assisting less affluent states achieve basic levels of economic well-being. Some Islamic men and women choose to join terrorist cells for purely ideological or religious reasons. These recruits may include well-to-do physicians and engineers who oppose the presence of US troops in the Middle East and its support for Israel or who view Western life as hedonistic and anathema to teachings in the Koran. Others, though, become terrorists because they face a life without work or any hope for the future. Their squalid living conditions breed resentment, especially when they see in magazines or on television people living in the lap of luxury in the Western industrial nations, whereas their lot each day consists of grinding poverty. In this era of globalization, the United States must be concerned not only with its own economic well-being but with how the rest of the world is faring—or suffer the consequences of resentment.

As with the war power, lawmakers and officials in the executive branch have jockeyed over the proper distribution of authority in the US government for the making of international economic policy. Congress has demanded a greater say in the approval of global trade agreements (Chapter 10) and in the review of economic statecraft as carried out by the executive branch (Chapter 13).

## Improving the Quality of Life

A third objective of American foreign policy, less uniformly embraced by the American public, has been to find solutions to a cluster of lifestyle issues that threaten the future of the United States and every other nation. For most people around the globe, adequate health care, housing, and education—themselves important sinews of national strength—are sadly lacking. For example, 1.1 billion people who live mainly in developing countries are without clean water to drink. Impurities in water sources lead to a majority of the diseases that haunt poor countries.[14] Just a short distance from the United States, more people in Belize, Guatemala, Honduras, and Nicaragua died during the 1980s of enteritis and diarrheal disorders, a result of polluted drinking water, than from any other cause.[15] International health experts have estimated that for an expenditure of about $300 billion—a fraction of what states spend collectively each year on weaponry—the planet's water supplies could be made pure and most diseases could be eradicated.[16]

Further, the world's rain forests are vanishing at a rapid rate, largely because of inept management. By 1992, nearly two-thirds of this valuable resource had disappeared in Central America. In Costa Rica, the rain forests are depleted at a rate of 360 square miles annually; and further south in Brazil, the world's most magnificent rain forest—the Amazon—has shrunk from 140,000 square miles to just 4,000 in the past two centuries.[17] Research has shown that over the past decade deforestation has occurred on a larger scale than reforestation in this part of the world.[18] Across the globe, urban growth has swallowed up over two million acres of forested land in just the past twenty years; and today, the rate of rain forest decline around the world is estimated at 50,000 square miles per year, an expanse larger than the state of Pennsylvania. Similarly, arable land in North Africa is being suffocated by spreading deserts.[19] Desertification can lead to the incapacity of rural areas to support the populations that live there, resulting in mass migrations to urban centers. This outcome translates into rising unemployment in the cities of poor nations, with the migrants often forced to live in slums.[20]

The loss of rain forests and the buildup in the atmosphere of chemical pollutants, especially $CO_2$, contribute to the greenhouse effect—a blanket-like layer that reflects thermal heat back to the earth instead of allowing it to dissipate into outer space. This heat-trapping gas in the atmosphere has increased about 41 percent since the beginning of the Industrial Revolution. Global emissions of carbon dioxide reached a record high in 2011 and made another jump in 2012. China is now the largest emitter, although the United States is chiefly responsible for the current high levels, given that its citizens have been consuming fossil fuels at a high rate for far longer than the Chinese.

The result is the warming of the Earth's surface, where the temperature has already increased about 1.5 degrees since 1850.[21] One illustration of the negative effects of global warming is the retardation in the growth of selected farm crops in some countries. Research reported in *Science* concludes that because of climate change, "southern Africa could lose more than 30% of its main crop, maize, by 2030. In South Asia losses of many regional staples, such as rice, millet and maize, could top 10%."[22] (In other instances, though, certain crops might benefit from a shorter, less frigid winter season, such as the growing of grapes for wine production.) To combat global warming, the Obama administration pledged to achieve a 17 percent reduction in the level of 2012 warming gas emissions by 2020—a goal already half met by 2013. As people around the world are slowly coming to appreciate, just as the world's economic systems are interconnected, so is the global environment, as further displayed by the contaminating affect on the quality of air in the Rocky Mountains from unfiltered coal burning in Asia.

The periodic television images of starving children on the horn of Africa, flies crawling across their unblinking eyes, are a grim reminder of the quality-of-life challenges that face many nations. These shocking pictures, and the widespread expressions of sympathy they elicited from across the United States in op-eds and opinion polls, contributed to President George H. W. Bush's decision in the waning days of his presidential tenure to intervene with military force to help feed the hungry in Somalia. Although this intervention in 1992, discussed in Chapter 6, ultimately failed in the face of armed resistance by local warlords, it has been described as "the first substantial military operation that the United States has ever mounted on solely moral grounds."[23]

In this quality-of-life policy domain, the executive and legislative branches have often been at odds again. Currently the Obama administration seeks remedies to control global warming, for example, while Republicans in Congress (who control the House of Representatives) tend to vote against environmental measures, on grounds that further government regulation might lessen America's industrial competitiveness in the world.

### Upholding Human Rights

A fourth foreign policy objective focuses on the elimination of global injustices, notably the violation of human rights around the world. As with quality-of-life challenges, this subject lacks the widespread support that Americans accord to the goals of physical and economic security; nonetheless, human rights has achieved a higher profile in world affairs during recent decades. The Carter administration elevated this concern to a premier position in its foreign policy agenda; and, among a list of international objectives issued by the Reagan administration, at the top stood a similar commitment to "uphold the principles of freedom, the rule of law, and observance of fundamental human rights."[24] Both the first and second Bush administrations also spoke of the importance of human rights; and the Obama administration became a supporter of the Arab Spring in 2011—a movement toward democracy and improved human rights in several nations of North Africa and the Middle East (examined in this chapter). President Obama also established an Atrocities Prevention Board in 2012, based in the Department of State and initially focused on how to halt a wave of anti-Muslim violence in Myanmar as well as politically motivated clashes in Kenya and in Central Africa.

The nurturing of an expanding community of democracies in the world presents an even greater challenge to the United States and its allies than the goal of raising the levels of employment, health care, housing, and education within poor countries. Yet it is a worthy objective, encouraged by the widely accepted **democratic peace hypothesis**, which states that *democracies rarely use armed forces against one another*. The tendency toward friendly relations among the democracies holds out a promising prescription for world peace—if enough nations adopt this form of government. Since the end of the Cold War, many countries have tried to embrace democracy but few have achieved much success because democracies are difficult to create and even harder to sustain.

When a woman in Philadelphia asked Benjamin Franklin at the close of the Constitutional Convention if the founders had established a republic or a monarchy, he replied, "A Republic, if you can keep it."[25]

Despite the difficulties, a large number of Americans would probably agree with an official in the Carter administration who observed that "there is a simple moral imperative at the heart of our national identity. . . . Every individual has inherent rights and a special dignity. This belief has shaped our national purposes throughout our history."[26] President George W. Bush put the case more simply. "I believe that God wants everyone to be free," he said. "That's what I believe. And that's part of my foreign policy."[27] For many people around the globe, freedom from government repression ranks high on their hierarchy of personal hopes.

The spirit of a commitment to human rights and democracy was evident in the spring of 2011 when revolutionaries took to the streets in Tunisia, followed by uprisings in Egypt, Libya, Yemen, Bahrain, and Syria. This "Arab Spring" witnessed efforts to throw off the mantel of tyranny and allow democracy a chance to succeed in these countries. The starting point for the unanticipated revolutions was the self-immolation of Mohamed Bouazizi, a fruit-cart vendor in the Tunisian village of Sidi Bouzid.[28] Bouazizi was a poor man driven to suicide by his frustration with his own impoverishment as well as his nation's heavy-handed government that maintained its rule through the torture of opponents. His death stirred widespread anger among the people of Tunisia, who rose up and swept aside the nation's high-living dictatorship. In turn, the unrest in this nation soon ignited additional uprisings in North Africa. Within months, Egypt's autocracy was also swept aside, replaced by open elections that handed the Muslim Brotherhood—an Islamic fundamentalist party—majority rule and the presidency. In Syria, ironfisted dictator President Bashar al-Assad launched a brutal counteroffensive against the insurgency within his country.

At first unsure which side to support in Egypt—the insurgents or the pro-American dictator, President Hosni Mubarak—the United States soon decided that history was on the side of the rebellion and Washington officials began to work behind the scenes diplomatically to aid the uprising. With respect to another North Africa nation, Libya, President Obama decided to undertake a more direct response. He ordered US military backing in support of a French-led NATO initiative aimed at deposing the nation's autocrat, Col. Muammar el-Qaddafi. In a new form of American warfare, the President opted to "lead from behind." He avoided the placement of US ground troops in harm's way and instead provided NATO with intelligence on targeting and had the US Air Force fly roughly a quarter of the total number of air sorties during the battles against Qaddafi—all without a single US casualty during these military skirmishes.[29] Europeans (chiefly the French) and some Arab countries carried the brunt of the fighting by outsiders, while courageous Libyan insurgents—often armed with only knives and old rifles—fought door-to-door against government and mercenary troops in Tripoli and elsewhere throughout the country, notably in the key port city of Misrata. Within seven months, the pro-democracy forces had taken control of

Libya, and Col. Qaddafi lay dead on a road east of Tripoli after being apprehended by rebel soldiers.

In Tunisia, Egypt, and Libya now came an equally difficult challenge: building democracies from scratch in a region marked by a history and political culture of authoritarianism. Much unrest continued, as riots broke out against the Muslim Brotherhood in Egypt when the new president, Mohammed Morsi, attempted during 2012 to aggrandize his powers; and in Libya, pro-Al Qaeda gunmen murdered U.S. ambassador J. Christopher Stevens and three American companions, also in 2012. In 2013, mass protests in the streets of Cairo against the insufficiently democratic rule of the Muslim Brotherhood led the Egyptian army to topple this regime. Whether the army intended to rule Egypt or just clear the way for a new try at democracy remained unclear.

The government of the United States displayed a divided reaction to the Arab Spring. Although Washington officials encouraged the rebellions in Tunisia, Egypt, and Libya, they were careful not to back some democracy movements aimed at uprooting strong American allies in the region, including the authoritarian rulers of Saudi Arabia—a prime supplier of oil to the West. The Obama administration looked the other way when Bahrain experienced its own uprising. In this instance, America's national interest (and the interests of the Saudi regime, which feared a spreading insurrection across its borders) was to keep Bahrain under the control of the existing ruling family. This family was friendly toward the United States and Saudi Arabia and provided the US Navy with rare basing rights in the Persian Gulf. The passivity of Washington, DC, with respect to this uprising brought dismay from the rebels. "Bahrainis will keep demanding the very values—human rights and democracy—that the United States claims to stand for," wrote one of them. "It is an outrage that America continues to back a regime that tramples them."[30]

As for the fighting in Syria, the Obama administration similarly kept the conflict at arm's length. The rebellion's chances for success were uncertain; and, more troubling still, Syria enjoyed (at least initially) a long-standing alliance with both Russia and China—not powers the United States wished to provoke by the intervention of American or other NATO forces into the civil war. Further, the rebellion had some factions within it that were decidedly unfriendly to the United States and quite possibly aligned with Al Qaeda.

Whatever the outcome of these uprisings, the fact remains that the United States has not been well liked in the region—either before or after the Arab Spring. A Pew Research poll showed, for instance, that 27 percent of Egyptians held favorable attitudes toward America, as did 25 percent of Jordanians surveyed before the Arab Spring revolts; in 2012, after the uprisings, those numbers dropped even lower to 19 percent and 12 percent, respectively.[31]

Often, though, the United States has a clear stake in helping other countries address the problem of human dignity. When the Clinton administration failed to intervene in a genocide that took place in Rwanda in 1994—one that led to the deaths of over a million people—the President later said that it was his greatest foreign policy failure. Yet, for the most part, the United States has been a leader in humanitarian interventions, which have become a new international norm. With modern advances in communication, transportation, and weaponry, the world has simply grown too small and dangerous for Americans to ignore the festering wounds of foreign people in distress. As journalist Thomas L. Friedman cautioned in 2003, "In today's globalized world, if you don't visit a bad neighborhood, it will visit you."[32]

Constitutionally based tensions have arisen as well over human rights policy. Sometimes the executive branch will opt to intervene overseas to ameliorate a deteriorating situation, as when President Bill Clinton carried on an initiative begun by his predecessor, George H. W. Bush, to help the poor in Somalia in 1993. Lawmakers were wary, however, of a US military presence on the Horn of Africa and interceded to close down the initiative and bring the troops home. The separation of powers doctrine embedded in the Constitution frequently pits one branch against the other, engendering the kind of public debate that the founders viewed as a healthy check against government by executive fiat.

## Reviewing American Foreign Policy Objectives

These primary objectives of American foreign policy—physical safety, economic prosperity, quality of life, and human rights—are not easy to achieve. Indeed, American citizens have profound disagreements about how to achieve these goals. Did physical protection of the United States depend on fighting a war on the Korean peninsula from 1950 to 1953 to protect South Korea against authoritarian domination by North Korea, at the cost of 35,000 dead American soldiers? How important to the United States was intervention in the jungles of Vietnam from 1964 to 1973 to protect South Vietnam, with another 58,000 GIs lost? Was it important to engage in covert warfare in Nicaragua in the 1980s, which led to the illegal covert actions known as the Iran-*contra* affair? Was it necessary to invade tiny Grenada in 1982 or Panama in 1989? Did the United States need to repel the Iraqi invasion of Kuwait in 1990 or invade Iraq again in 2003? Should the second Bush and the Obama administrations have sent thousands of troops into Afghanistan?

Today, should the United States secretly dispatch drones armed with Hellfire missiles on aerial missions above Pakistan, Yemen, and elsewhere to strike down suspected Islamic extremists (with civilians inevitably caught up in the destruction)? Should the United States sell drones to other countries, as Washington, DC moved toward doing with South Korea in 2012 (with a profit to the US arms manufacturer Northrop Grumman of $1.2 billion)? Does America's security continue to depend on having large numbers of US troops stationed in Europe (70,000, mostly in Germany) and Japan (37,000), where they have been since 1945, and in South Korea since 1950 (another 27,500)? How many of the 700-plus US military bases around the world, which are costly to maintain, are vital to America's security? Is the ongoing development of an expensive ballistic missile defense (BMD) system money well spent for protection against enemy rockets aimed at the United States or a waste of resources because these rockets would be impossible to shoot down?

Beyond these difficult military questions, many of America's other foreign policy objectives can be controversial as well. Has the Obama administration been tough enough toward China in establishing a better trade balance? Should the United States become more involved in European efforts to stabilize the euro currency as means of warding off the failure of US investments in Europe? Should the United States be more actively engaged in combating global climate change? In fighting the spread of diseases around the world, such as malaria in Africa and gastroenteritis in Latin America? In coming to the assistance of individuals and groups suffering human rights abuse in Africa and elsewhere—even if intervention might mean the loss of American lives?

A poll taken in 2012 plumbed the views of college-age Americans about specific domestic and foreign policy challenges. The results revealed considerable anxiety about economic issues at home, especially the need to create jobs and lower the unemployment rate in the United States. (As many as 77 percent of the respondents thought this was an important issue.) Foreign policy objectives, however, garnered less support.[33] Here are some of results regarding what percentage of those polled thought a particular foreign policy objective was important:

> Preventing the spread of terrorism: 54%
> Preventing Iran from acquiring a nuclear weapon: 52%
> Withdrawing from Pakistan: 51%
> Combating the impacts of climate change: 37%
> Promoting a peaceful resolution to the Israel–Palestine issue: 34%
> Countering China's rising influence: 31%
> Promoting stable democracy in the Middle East/North Africa: 31%
> Solving the European debt crisis: 28%
> Reintegrating North Korea into the world community: 22%

Recall, as well, Figure 1.1, which provides another insight into the question of which objectives are most desirable to American citizens in the conduct of America's foreign policy.

When the Cold War ended in 1990-1991, the Carnegie Endowment for International Peace commissioned a prominent group of Americans to examine the state of US foreign policy and report on recommended new directions. Their sixteen policy proposals, organized according to the four overarching foreign policy objectives presented earlier in this chapter, are displayed in *Perspectives on American Foreign Policy* 1.1. As you read them, consider these questions:

- How valid do the recommendations remain today?
- Are they realistic objectives for America or hopelessly idealistic?
- What would you add to, or subtract from, the list?
- How would you rank each proposal in terms of your own priorities?
- How expensive do you think the accomplishment of these objectives would be?
- Could America afford the costs as the very time the nation is struggling to overcome a lingering recession, deficit spending, and a mounting national debt?

---

## PERSPECTIVES ON AMERICAN FOREIGN POLICY 1.1

**Foreign policy recommendations from the CARNEGIE ENDOWMENT FOR INTERNATIONAL PEACE at the end of the Cold War:**

**Physical Security**

For a *safer* planet we must

- Remain the leading military power even as we significantly reduce our defense spending and overseas deployments;
- Realign North Atlantic Treaty Organization (NATO) and Conference on Security and Cooperation in Europe (CSCE) to deal with the new security problem in Europe;
- Strengthen the peacekeeping capacities of the United States and regional organizations;
- Promote collective leadership by adding Japan and Germany as permanent members of the U.N. Security Council; and
- Strive for a less militarized world by cutting, in this decade, global defense expenditures to half of their 1988 peak, reducing weapons of mass destruction, and halting their proliferation.

**Economic Prosperity**

For a more *prosperous* America and a more prosperous world we must

- Adopt an aggressive strategy for an economic revival at home that favors investment in the future over consumption for the moment;
- Overhaul the international system of trade and finance, moving toward effective collective leadership by the major industrialized countries;

- Renew our commitment to help poor states; and
- Invest in the future of former Communist countries.

**Quality of Life**

For a more *livable* planet we must

- Increase our energy efficiency by significantly raising energy prices, lifting our performance toward that of other industrialized countries;
- Give high priority to improving the environment through sustainable economic growth and ecological agreements;
- Resume decisive American leadership in world population policy;
- Develop a stronger multilateral approach toward humanitarian crises and migration; and
- Combat our drug problem where it counts—at home.

**Human Rights**

For a *freer* world we must

- Practice at home what we preach abroad about liberty and justice; and
- Build democracies through multilateral pressures and incentives.

*SOURCE:* Adapted by the author from Carnegie Endowment for International Peace National Commission, *Changing Our Ways: America and the New World* (Washington, DC: Carnegie Endowment for International Peace, 1992), pp. 4–5.

---

# THE INSTRUMENTS OF AMERICAN FOREIGN POLICY

Perhaps nothing captures the frustrations of foreign policy so well as the realization that no nation is able to fully achieve its international objectives. The United States and every other country is forced to accept a gap between their aspirations and what can actually be accomplished in a world of competing nations and factions. No nation has a monopoly on oil, on technological innovation, on control of the seas or space. None has impermeable borders resistant to pollution, global warming, pandemics, illicit drugs, or illegal immigrants. None has a foolproof system of defense against foreign military or terrorist attacks.

Still, large and wealthy nations like the United States do enjoy a great advantage over less developed countries in their ability to achieve foreign policy goals. The United States, Russia, and China, for example, possess great armies, sophisticated weaponry, sizable populations, dynamic economies (however sluggish from time to time), and vast intelligence-collection capabilities that, say, poverty-stricken Zimbabwe—or even wealthy but small Luxembourg—can only dream about. In determining a grand strategy, each nation gauges its capabilities and develops approaches to foreign affairs that are designed to help advance its interests in the world while avoiding bankruptcy and decline. These approaches are referred to in this book as **foreign policy instruments**, an umbrella term that includes *intelligence gathering, diplomacy, the use of military force, covert action, economic statecraft,* and *cultural and moral influences.* Together, these instruments make up a nation's **power**, that is, its *ability to persuade other nations and factions to accept its policy objectives—or, at least, not to oppose them.*

In this section of the book, I introduce these key instruments, beginning with national security intelligence. A state's intelligence capabilities are one of its most important instruments of foreign policy because success in international affairs usually depends on making rational choices about ends and means (the essence of grand strategy). In turn, such choices require a clear and accurate understanding of global risks and opportunities. Information matters.

## National Security Intelligence

*The gathering and analysis of information about global events and conditions, as well as the views and personalities of worldwide leaders and other individuals of significance to the United States,* can be referred to as **national security intelligence**.[34] Policy makers in Washington, DC, who must choose among the various foreign policy instruments as they pursue the nation's international objectives, will increase their chances for success if their decisions are based on an accurate knowledge of world affairs and the intentions of foreign leaders. When forced to make decisions in a fog of ambiguous and incomplete information, as is often the case—or with no information at all—a nation's decision makers are placed at a great disadvantage. "Creating Decision Advantage" is the motto inscribed on the wall at the headquarters of America's Director of National Intelligence (DNI), located at Liberty Crossing ("LX") in northern Virginia.

National security intelligence is presented here as the first instrument of American foreign policy because all of the other instruments rely on having reliable information about the world. For example, when the Obama administration decided to use a secret operation to capture or kill Al Qaeda leader Osama bin Laden in 2011, the first step was to gather intelligence about his suspected hideaway compound in Abbottabad, Pakistan. America's intelligence agencies resorted to a wide arrange of intelligence collection procedures to confirm or deny his presence at the compound, including telephone tapping, satellite surveillance, and spies on the ground.[35] The findings were never conclusive.

In fact, some intelligence officers predicted a 50–50 chance or less that Bin Laden was at the compound. Nevertheless, enough telltale signs of his presence in Abbottabad existed for President Obama to order a night raid against the hideaway, led by the Navy's elite SEAL Team 6 and backed by the US intelligence agencies.

The mission was a remarkable success. The SEAL team killed Bin Laden, sacked the compound for valuable intelligence, and escaped in helicopters back to a US military base in Afghanistan. The raid's violation of Pakistani air space led to lingering diplomatic tensions between officials in Washington and Islamabad, but the world had been rid of its most notorious terrorist. In the attack against Bin Laden, the gathering of intelligence—the first instrument of foreign policy—had preceded the adoption of a more aggressive instrument: a secret military operation.

Both the Japanese attack at Pearl Harbor in 1941 and the 9/11 attacks sixty years later stand as troubling reminders that a lack of timely and reliable intelligence can endanger a country's physical safety and perhaps even the very survival of its cities in this era of WMDs (weapons of mass destruction). Pearl Harbor and the 9/11 attacks are the most disastrous intelligence failures in the history of the United States. The Japanese bombardment resulted in the destruction of an important part of America's Pacific fleet, moored in Hawaii. Although America's intelligence agencies had broken the Japanese military code (known as "Magic") and knew that Pearl Harbor might be bombed, this information was never forwarded up the chain of command to President Franklin D. Roosevelt or other top officials. The government lacked the necessary organizational channels to assure a careful coordination of intelligence and its dissemination to the White House. This is one of the main reasons why in 1947, when World War II was over and he had a chance to focus on reform, President Harry S. Truman established a *Central* Intelligence Agency (CIA, known by insiders as "the Agency"). Truman hoped that such an organization would be able to bring about a more integrated intelligence effort by the United States, especially in light of a new threat on the horizon: the growing power of the Soviet Union.[36]

Although the US intelligence community made steady progress toward improving its capabilities throughout the Cold War (examined in Chapter 9), these agencies proved unable to warn citizens about the terrorist attacks of 9/11. A year before the attacks occurred, the CIA was aware of, and had conducted surveillance against, a meeting of terrorists in Kuala Lumpur, Malaysia. Two of these terrorists, who ended up being part of the group of nineteen that would carry out the 9/11 hijackings, subsequently traveled to San Diego, California; but the CIA failed to alert the Federal Bureau of Investigation (FBI) of their presence in the United States until early 2001. Once notified, FBI agents were subsequently unable to locate the two terrorists, even though they remained in San Diego. Other mistakes were made, including a failure by the FBI to investigate reports from their field agents in Minneapolis and Phoenix that some men from the Middle East were enrolled in flight training centers in the United States and were acting strangely. One of the men, for instance, told a flight instructor that he didn't want to know how to take off or land a commercial airline, just how to handle the plane in midair.[37]

After the 9/11 attacks, reformers proposed changes to improve the performance of the intelligence agencies; however, many of these reforms remained mired in bureaucratic disputes and battles over turf protection in Washington, DC. Above all, lawmakers were unwilling to endorse a major proposal advanced by reformers in 2004: the creation of a Director of National Intelligence with budget and appointment powers as leverage to bring the US secret agencies into a more cohesive working alliance. The Pentagon lobbied against the creation of a strong civilian intelligence leader, fearing that a new DNI might not support tactical military intelligence operations well enough (an unlikely outcome because any DNI would be dedicated to protecting US fighting forces in the field). As a result of the Pentagon's lobbying efforts, starting in 2005 the United States had a new DNI, but the nation remained without a true national intelligence director; the Congress, responding to Pentagon pressures, had failed to provide the office of the DNI with meaningful budget and appointment powers over all of America's sixteen intelligence agencies.

These agencies continue to display an unwillingness to share information with one another, even though improved sharing would provide the president and other leaders with better coordinated intelligence about world affairs from all parts of the intelligence community ("all-source fusion," in the patios of spy talk). In reality, the intelligence "community" continues to lack cohesion, like a barrel with sixteen staves but no hoop binding them together. Institutional fragmentation has trumped the efforts of reformers to advance institutional integration.

Despite its imperfections, national security intelligence nonetheless provides an important means for deciding which of the other, more action-oriented instruments of foreign policy should be selected to advance national objectives. Based on what America's leaders *know,* derived in large part from intelligence gathered by the nation's secret agencies, they can decide how to *act*, relying on diplomacy, military force, covert action, economic statecraft, or cultural and moral suasion (soft power)—or, most likely, some combination of these instruments. Although the ability of America's intelligence agencies to provide reliable, properly integrated and disseminated information about the world still cries out for further reform, this nation's capability to understand global affairs has come a long way since the Second World War. The observations of former Secretary of State Dean Rusk attest to this in *Perspectives on American Foreign Policy* 1.2. As you read this *Perspective*, ask yourself the following questions:

- Could the United States have ended World War II more quickly—for example, the naval battles in the Pacific—with the kind of sophisticated intelligence gathering available today through satellite surveillance?
- To what extent do you think that lower US casualties in combat today, compared to World War II, the Korean War, and the Vietnam War, is a function of improved American intelligence capabilities?
- Why do you think the United States stills suffers intelligence failures, despite spending some $80 billion a year on satellites, reconnaissance aircraft, and other sophisticated means of intelligence collection?

---

### PERSPECTIVES ON AMERICAN FOREIGN POLICY 1.2

**SECRETARY OF STATE DEAN RUSK on the importance of information to foreign policy decision making:**

The ghost that haunts the policy officer or haunts the man who makes the final decision is the question as to whether, in fact, he has in his mind all of the important elements that ought to bear upon his decision or whether there is a missing piece that he is not aware of that could have a decisive effect if it became known.

I think we can be proud of the extraordinary improvement in our intelligence- and information-gathering activities in the last twenty years. The need for it has been multiplied many times by the fragmentation of the world political structure, and the breadth, character, and depth of the information we need mounts steadily.

When I was assigned to G-2 [U.S. Army Intelligence] in 1941, well over a year after the war had started in Europe, I was asked to take charge of a new section that had been organized to cover everything from Afghanistan right through southern Asia, southeast Asia, Australia, and the Pacific. Because we had no intelligence organization that had been giving attention to that area up to that time, the materials available to me when I reported for duty consisted of a tourist handbook on India and Ceylon, a 1924 military attaché's report from London on the Indian Army, and a drawer full of clippings from the *New York Times* that had been gathered since World War I. That was literally the resources of G-2 on that vast part of the world a year after the war in Europe that started.

We have greatly improved our ability to gather relevant information.

*SOURCE:* Dean Rusk, testimony, *Hearings*, Government Operations Subcommittee on National Security Staff and Operations, U.S. Senate (December 11, 1963), p. 390.

---

## Diplomacy

**Diplomacy** is the *art of adjusting disputes between nations and factions through formal and informal negotiations.* This approach relies on talking instead of fighting and is a common means for achieving US objectives in the world. There are multiple types of diplomacy (discussed at length in Chapter 10), including special missions that focus on a specific dispute, such as efforts to gain the release of an American citizen taken hostage in a foreign state; summit meetings between heads of state; shuttle diplomacy, whereby US officials fly back and forth frequently between Washington and a foreign state as negotiations proceed; and public diplomacy, the attempt to attract adherents by broadcasting information around the world about the United States, its goals, and its values.

Global competition over automobile sales provides an illustration of a prolonged diplomatic negotiation. During the 1970s and 80s, the number of automobile exports from Japan to the United States rose sharply and caused severe dislocations in Detroit's car industry. In response, US auto manufacturers lobbied on Capitol Hill and with the Department of Commerce for government relief from the flood of vehicles from Japan. Rather than resort immediately to tough economic sanctions against that nation (a close ally of the United States), Presidents Carter, Reagan, and George H. W. Bush all turned instead to diplomatic negotiations. They sought to achieve a fair deal for US automakers without rupturing America's ties with Japan, a balancing act that called for patience and skillful bargaining—the essential attributes of diplomacy. During the auto negotiations, tension increased between Congress and the executive branch, however, as lawmakers focused on protecting the US car manufacturers while the State Department tried to preserve cordial relations with the Japanese government (though mindful as well of how important US auto sales are for the American economy). Each branch was following its constitutional responsibilities, but the end result was a clash of basic objectives.

In the 1970s, President Carter succeeded in convincing Japan to place voluntary restraints on its shipments of vehicles to America. In the agreement, Tokyo promised to limit automobile exports into the United States to one million a year—a substantial reduction. By 1985, Japanese negotiators had persuaded the Reagan administration to raise the ceiling to 2.3 million cars a year.[38] This remains the current arrangement, despite persistent grumbling from Japan that the ceiling is still too low and represents an unreasonable form of US protectionism. The Japanese consented to this outcome in part because protectionist lawmakers in Congress threatened to advance stiffer economic conditions against Japan if these initial diplomatic efforts collapsed. Moreover, the agreement with the Japanese allowed them to ship higher-priced automobiles to the United States and thus earn greater profits. In return, the Japanese committed to building more Japanese cars and car parts inside the United States, thus mollifying members of Congress who were happy to see these economic advantages come to their constituencies. Auto manufacturing is now global. For example, American companies are in Europe, Mexico, and Russia; and Japanese and South Korean companies are in America—all a result of painstaking diplomatic negotiations.

As is often the case, the legislative and executive branches—despite their institutional separation—proved able to reach agreement about how to handle automobile imports after a series of compromises and accommodations. Negotiations similar to this one occur every day across the range of America's trading opportunities, as leaders in Washington and other capitals around the world seek commercial advantages in the international marketplace.

In another example of diplomacy at work, in 2011 the Obama administration ended a lengthy standoff on stalled free-trade agreements with South Korea, Colombia, and Panama. In the face of partisan bickering in Washington, the President managed nonetheless to unite Democrats and Republicans in Congress behind the first trade agreement to gain the approval of lawmakers since 2007. Negotiations between the President and members of Congress often proved even more challenging than with the foreign diplomats; the end result, though, was a set of international agreements on trade that enjoyed widespread support among lawmakers on Capitol Hill.

The power to make diplomatic agreements with other nations, referred to in the Constitution as the treaty power, can have far-reaching effects. Pacts dealing with military bases or armaments, for example, are sometimes harbingers of sweeping commitments that can draw the United States into war. With their origins in the original power-sharing design of the Constitution, acrimonious struggles have sometimes erupted between lawmakers and presidents over when and how international agreements should be consummated. Diplomacy is anything but a staid and passive activity; it resides at the center of American foreign policy and is almost always accompanied by political conflict at home and abroad, as the White House, the bureaucracy, Congress, the courts, and a wide range of interest groups jockey to gain ascendance over policy making. By spreading power across the institutions of government, the founders wanted to make sure America did not enter into "foreign entanglements" easily—and they succeeded. The example of US domestic wrangling over Japanese auto imports provides a good illustration of this give-and-take over several years.

## Military Force

The power to make, or threaten, warfare—a topic deliberated over at length at the Constitutional Convention in 1787—is the most extreme instrument that can be used by a nation in its pursuit of foreign policy goals. No decision is more fateful or has cost the United States so much in blood and treasure. Diplomacy is often slow and frustrating. Sometimes presidents turn to *the threatened or actual use of overt* military force—the **war power**—to hasten the resolution of an international problem. According to one estimate, the United States has been at war during roughly 20 percent of its history.[39] On occasion, presidents are left with no other choice; war is thrust on them. This was almost the case during the Cuban missile crisis of 1962, before photographs from CIA reconnaissance aircraft (U2s)—intelligence—indicated that the Soviets on the island would need two more weeks to complete the arming of their missiles with nuclear warheads. This gave President Kennedy a window of opportunity to pursue safer, diplomatic negotiations to end the event. (This important crisis is examined in depth in Chapter 5.)

When one thinks of the United States as a superpower, an image comes to mind of large stockpiles of tactical and strategic nuclear weapons. America's bristling arsenal also includes Stealth B-2s and hulking B-52 bombers; "smart" cruise missiles with highly accurate internal electronic mapping circuitry and memories of pinpointed targets based on satellite surveillance; Trident submarines; aircraft carriers; fighter aircraft; and unmanned aerial vehicles (UAVs) or drones equipped with Hellfire missiles—all summing to the most tangible manifestations of America's might, unmatched by any other nation in the world. No doubt, a primary reason why President Kennedy was successful in persuading the Soviet Union through diplomacy to remove its offensive missiles from Cuba in 1962 was the massive military force he had assembled on the southeastern seaboard of the United States. In this instance, Congress and the courts were shut out of the decision making, which was kept "top secret" at the highest levels of the executive branch. On other occasions that are less crisis driven, Congress and the courts have been major players in American foreign policy, as illustrated in subsequent chapters.

Yet America's military prowess was not the only reason for the successful resolution of the Cuban missile crisis. A diplomatic trade-off that involved the removal of US missiles in Turkey in exchange for the removal of the Soviet missiles in Cuba also played a major role. Moreover, the envisioned horror of a nuclear holocaust no doubt gave pause

to the leaders of both countries. The United States certainly held a logistical advantage because Cuba is just ninety miles off America's shoreline. Moreover, America's strategic advantage in Intercontinental Ballistic Missiles (ICBMs, or long-range rockets with nuclear warheads) was an intimidating consideration the Soviet premier, Nikita Khrushchev, must have been aware of at the time. As Secretary of State Dean Rusk recalled, the superpowers had come "eyeball to eyeball" and the Soviets "blinked."[40] The missile crisis of 1962 illustrates how American foreign policy can be a complex blend of military, diplomatic, and geographic (among other) considerations.

The *USS John Paul Jones* leads a formation in a series of close ship maneuvers as part of the *USS Enterprise*'s Battle Group training in the seas off Southwest Asia on September 24, 2001.

## Covert Action

Another approach used by the United States to advance its foreign policy agenda is the carrying out of **covert action** (**secret intervention abroad**) by the CIA and sometimes by military special forces. These operations include *the secret use of propaganda, as well as political, economic, and paramilitary (warlike) activities.* Such means, often highly controversial, are also referred to in the US government as "special activities," "the Third Option" (between diplomacy and sending in the Marines), or "the quiet option"—that is, an approach to foreign policy that is less noisy or visible than landing the US Marine Corps or the 82nd Airborne on a foreign battlefield. This approach sometimes involves concealed partnerships with other nations against a common adversary. In 1953, for example, MI6 (the British counterpart of the CIA) joined with the Agency to install the Shah as the leader in Iran, primarily to ensure the presence in this important Middle East nation of a leader more friendly toward the West. An additional consideration was to promote the sale of inexpensive oil to the United States and the United Kingdom, as well as to prevent the local takeover of US and UK oil companies in the nation. In another instance of covert action, right after the 9/11 attacks, the CIA worked closely with a local antiterrorist faction in Afghanistan known as the Northern Alliance to rout the Taliban regime and Al Qaeda. Often, though, the CIA carries out covert actions on its own or with Special Operations Forces (SOF) in the US military.

Covert action has been a vital part of American foreign policy since the founding of the Republic. Benjamin Franklin secretly purchased arms from the French to supply American rebels in the War of Independence; and in 1803 President Thomas Jefferson secretly arranged a deal with foreign agents to overthrow the Pasha (or Bashaw) of Tripoli, who had interfered with US shipping in the Mediterranean. More recently, the United States has used covert action of various kinds in an attempt to influence the behavior of selected leaders abroad—or eliminate them from the scene altogether.

Although the history of the role of American presidents in directing foreign assassinations remains murky, reportedly during the Kennedy administration Fidel Castro was a target of over thirty CIA assassination attempts, all of which failed.[41] Under apparent orders from the White House (the origins of this authority remain in dispute among historians and practitioners), the Agency carried out the plots, sometimes in an alliance with an unlikely partner for the government of the United States: professional hit men on loan from mobsters in Chicago, Miami, and New York City. In the waning months of the Eisenhower administration, Patrice Lumumba of Congo was another target; he was eventually killed by a rival African faction, but the CIA may have helped to arrange for his death.[42] Salvador Allende of Chile, a freely elected president in a democratic regime, became a target for a coup d'état during the 1970s; the Nixon administration viewed him and his Socialist Party as too friendly toward the Soviet Union, as well as a threat to America's political and business interests in the Western Hemisphere. Covert actions carried out by the CIA in Chile resulted in a 1973 coup during which Allende died (apparently by suicide) and a military junta took over the government. In another covert scheme during the Cold War, an ad hoc CIA Health Alteration Committee directed foreign agents to implement an operation that used chemicals to "incapacitate" an uncooperative Iraqi colonel.[43]

Further, over the years, politicians in a large number of countries have taken money covertly from the CIA in exchange for the adoption of pro-US positions in their councils of government—political covert action. Economic covert action has also been part and parcel of the Agency's secret foreign policy operations ordered by the White House, with the objective of sabotaging the economies of America's adversaries. For example, CIA operatives have blown up foreign electricity grids, mined harbors, and disseminated counterfeit currencies. As well, CIA secret propaganda operations have been used worldwide to advance the interests of the United States, including some misleading disinformation schemes that have wafted back and ended up fooling the American public as much as they have foreign adversaries—a phenomenon known as CIA "blowback" or "replay."[44]

Under presidential orders, the CIA has also undertaken large-scale "secret" wars (as if the din of war could remain secret for long). During the Cold War, the United States embraced paramilitary (PM) operations to counter Soviet interests in, among other places, Asia (Laos, for instance, from 1962–1968), the Middle East (Afghanistan in the 1980s), and Central America (especially in Nicaragua, also during the 1980s). These "overt-covert" conflicts—they didn't remain secret—have been pursued through covert action to avoid the formalities, and the more complicated legal requirements within the United States, that attend the authorization of open warfare (including the evocation of the War Powers Resolution, which provides Congress with a role in war making, as explored in Chapter 11). This secret approach to war making was never addressed by the founders in the Constitution, and presidents and Congress have fought politically over their respective roles in approving such actions, a struggle addressed in Chapter 12.

The Soviet equivalent of the CIA during the Cold War (the KGB, today known as the FSV) was equally energetic in the domain of covert action, which the Kremlin referred to as "active measures." These operations were designed to advance Moscow's global objectives and thwart the foreign policy of the United States. On both sides, covert action—assassination plots, political bribery, economic dislocations, propaganda, "secret" wars—amounted to a subterranean World War III fought by the CIA and the KGB in the back alleys of the world, in lieu of open warfare that might have destroyed both superpowers in a hail of nuclear-tipped missiles. Since the end of the Cold War, the CIA has been focused mainly on tracing the whereabouts and stopping the spread of WMDs and, since the rise of terrorism in the late 1990s, combating a whole range of terrorism organizations—especially through the use of missile-bearing drones to kill terrorists in the Middle East and Southwest Asia.

## Economic Statecraft

*Trade and aid, forms of diplomatic activity that rely on the commercial and financial side of foreign policy* often referred to as **economic statecraft**, have also served as key instruments in America's pursuit of its global objectives**.** Trade has sometimes entailed the use of negative sanctions (punishments or "sticks") or positive incentives (rewards or "carrots"). The United States has at its disposal the negative sanctions of embargoes, boycotts, trade quotas, and blacklists; it can also offer such positive inducements as the reduction of tariffs and the granting of special import licenses (all defined in Chapter 13). During the Carter and Reagan administrations, the granting of favorable tariffs helped thaw American's relations with the People's Republic of China (the PRC—communist mainland China).

Neither economic sticks nor carrots are guaranteed to work. As a form of punishment for its invasion of Afghanistan in 1979, an angry Carter administration refused to sell grain to the Soviet Union, reversing President Carter's long-standing opposition to the use of embargoes because of their harmful effect on America's own economy. This void in Soviet imports was quickly filled by Argentina and Canada, among other nations, who avidly pursued this unexpected opportunity to capture grain sales for their own farmers. The effectiveness of America's attempt to put pressure on Moscow soon waned. In some cases, though, sanctions can be influential, as when Western states—led by California—cooperated to boycott the purchase of goods from South Africa until it ended its domestic policy of apartheid (segregation) in 1990.

At times, economic statecraft may be the only foreign policy option available to the United States, as in the case of relations with Iran today. A primary goal of America and its allies in the twenty-first century has been to prevent Iran from developing nuclear bombs or other WMDs. Diplomacy has failed to stop Tehran's pursuit of these weapons, yet a military invasion would draw America into yet another war in the Middle East—a further drain on the US federal treasury and a move apt to alienate Muslims who fear a permanent American presence in the region. Even if the funding were available for a third war in that part of the world (on the heels of Iraq and Afghanistan), the United States has an insufficient number of soldiers to fight in another major conflict, short of instituting what would be an unpopular draft (last used for the war in Vietnam during the 1960s). Nor do Americans wish to see more GIs killed and wounded overseas, unless war is absolutely vital to the safety of the United States.

In 1981, Israel solved the problem of an incipient Iraq nuclear program by simply dropping bombs on the nascent facility, a clearly visible, above-ground target easily decimated by the Israeli air force. Today, however, the Iranian facilities being used to develop nuclear weapons reside in deep underground tunnels and bunkers, sheltered by warrens of dense rock—over seventy hidden sites spread around Iran's vast territory. A quick military or CIA covert removal of these facilities would be difficult, if not impossible. Robert M. Gates, Secretary of Defense in the second Bush and the Obama administrations, said that at best a military strike against the Iranian facilities would only slow the nuclear program by one to three years and send the program even deeper underground.[45] Because the foreign policy instruments of diplomacy and military force show little hope of success in the Iranian case, the United States has moved more toward a regimen of strong economic sanctions, coupled with economic covert actions designed to disrupt with a computer virus (known as Stuxnet) the construction of reactors in Iran that can produce highly enriched uranium for nuclear weapons.[46] China, which purchases 15 percent of its oil from Iran, has been ambivalent about the use of sanctions against the government of Tehran, as has Russia—another significant consumer of Iranian oil. Moreover, the covert actions have been highly inflammatory operations that have solicited criticism even from America's allies who worry about opening the global Pandora's box of "cyberwarfare."

## Moral and Cultural Suasion

Supreme Court Justice William O. Douglas once observed that the United States was admired abroad not "so much for our B-52 bombers and for our atomic stockpile, but . . . for the First Amendment and the freedom of people to speak and believe and to write, have fair trails."[47] Here, in his view, was the "great magnet" that made America a respected world leader: the power of **moral suasion**, *winning friends abroad by virtue of setting a good example as a vibrant democracy*. An additional magnet has been America's cultural attractions. Youth the world over wear jeans made in the United States, drink Coca-Cola, play video games crafted in Silicon Valley and Los Angeles, marvel at the flying beasts and other special effects in Hollywood action films, rock to the sounds of American popular music, watch sitcoms and dramas on television produced in the United States, and idolize the towering giants of the National Basketball Association (NBA) and other athletic superstars. This **cultural suasion**, *winning friends abroad by way of attractive social attributes*, does not prevent someone wearing American jeans from signing up for the *jihad* against the West; but it does send a message to millions of young people around the world that the United States is a more attractive place than portrayed in terrorist propaganda tracts. Certain aspects of American culture, however—such as the often negative depiction of the United States by Hollywood, as well as some videos games and television shows, as a violence-prone, crime-ridden state—no doubt alienate potential friends abroad.

*Using moral and cultural suasion to encourage others to follow your leadership* is what Joseph S. Nye refers to as **soft power**—a less costly way to lead than through the **hard power** of *military threats and economic incentives or punishments*. What the United States stands for makes a difference. "It is easier to attract people to democracy than to coerce them to be democratic," Nye argues.[48] Those who accept the importance of soft power maintain that the nation's fortunes in the world advance when Americans are seen as champions of freedom and human dignity, as was the case during World War II; when the United States lives up to its constitutional principles of justice and equality; when the nation shows compassion and a helping hand to the poor and dispossessed around the globe; and when America's lifestyle draws widespread emulation. Conversely, according to this school of thought, America's fortunes abroad tumble, as they did in the aftermath of the 9/11 attacks, when officials in Washington, DC, abandon the nation's basic values. Following the attacks, the Justice Department provided questionable authority to the CIA that allowed torture and the "extraordinary rendition" (kidnapping) of suspected terrorists, as well as the establishment of secret prisons abroad. The Department also authorized the prolonged jailing of suspected terrorists—without charges and without the right of legal self-defense—at America's Guantánamo military base on the island of Cuba.

Proponents of soft power believe that, just as with the internment of Japanese Americans during World War II (despite the fact that many Americans of Japanese heritage were fighting in the United States military at that very time), US leaders in the wake of 9/11 overreacted and violated the nation's basic constitutional safeguards of liberty, privacy, and due process that have served as an inspiration for people around the world.[49] According to this view, leaders in Washington—driven by fear—forgot the wise counsel of Benjamin Franklin that "those who would give up essential liberty to purchase a little temporary safety deserve neither liberty nor safety."[50] A remark by *New York Times* columnist Thomas Friedman captures this perspective: "We can't let our country become just The United States of Fighting Terrorism and nothing more. We are the people of July 4th—not just September 11th."[51] In contrast, a "realist" approach, one of the key philosophies discussed in this chapter, would consider soft power as little more than softheadedness—an idealistic approach that fails to understand and deal with the brutality of international affairs.

President Jimmy Carter, a deeply religious man, placed a high premium on moral principle as basic guide for conducting American foreign policy. He criticized unsavory covert actions, and he vigorously advocated global human rights during his presidential campaign in 1976 and while serving in the White House. Carter condemned the immorality of assassination plots and other "dirty tricks" carried out by the CIA at the direction of earlier administrations; and following his inauguration as president he reined in the Agency's use of covert action. He did not abandon this approach altogether, however, especially after the Soviet Union set back his hopes for relaxed tensions (détente) between the superpowers by invading Afghanistan in 1979.

In the aftermath of this invasion, President Carter reluctantly turned to the CIA and covert action as a response against further Soviet encroachments.

Carter also advocated, although inconsistently, diplomatic and economic pressures against regimes engaged in the degradation of human rights. His immediate successors, Presidents Reagan and George H. W. Bush, carried forward this attention to the rights of individuals around the world. For Reagan, the goal of human rights was pursued by way of CIA covert actions to undermine communist regimes—the so-called Reagan Doctrine. Later for President Obama, the use of drones became an important CIA and military counteroffensive in the struggle against global terrorists and their abuse of human rights.

## KEY PHILOSOPHIES OF FOREIGN POLICY

Both analysts and practitioners of American foreign policy usually have an explicit or implicit philosophy that undergirds their orientation toward global affairs. They may be idealists or realists, the most prominent philosophical schools of thought on foreign policy; or they may be guided by some other ideological roadmap to the world. Many government officials in the United States have been drawn to the soft power of moral principle in international affairs, which is part of a tradition of **liberalism** or **idealism** in international affairs.[52] Use of the word "liberalism" in international relations theory is different from the common usage of the word in domestic politics, in which political views are arrayed along a liberalism–conservative continuum, moving from more to less support for federal government programs. In international relations theory, liberals *advocate the resolution of international conflicts by way of international law, negotiations through international organizations, and the promotion of collective security arrangements.* They also place an emphasis on human rights, and they express a sense of optimism about the chances for peaceful interdependence among nations.[53]

A leading proponent of liberalism was President Woodrow Wilson, who called for a more forthright use of diplomacy ("open covenants of peace, openly arrived at," he proclaimed in his famous "Fourteen Points" program for international peace), along with the establishment of measures to encourage global free trade. More recently, scholar Alynna J. Lyon points out that "the events of September 11, 2011, triggered a revival of liberal rhetoric and policy agendas, yet state security priorities trumped liberal commitments. American foreign policy is saturated in the rhetoric of liberalism, yet this does not necessarily suggest that liberal traditions guide American foreign policy in practice."[54]

A related approach is **neoliberalism**, which also *advocates the worldwide development of democracy, open markets, and free trade, but adds the idea that these objectives can be best achieved through the adoption of international regimes.*[55] **Regimes** are *written agreements entered into by states that seek mutual institutional cooperation for the benefit of all signatories,* as in the case of arms control arrangements among nations or the General Agreement on Tariffs and Trade (GATT) that established important international economic relationships among nations in the 1940s (which lasted fifty years until GATT was replaced by the World Trade Organization or WTO in 1995). The neoliberal approach embedded in the GATT initiative was to use negotiated contractual understandings—not just a reliance on formal international organizations with detailed rules and procedures as a liberal theorist would advocate—to advance economic prosperity between nations.[56] The WTO was a triumph of a liberal emphasis on international institutions over neoliberalism reliance on regimes in the domain of international commerce; nevertheless, neoliberalism remains a significant approach to international affairs. Nations have established useful regimes in a number of policy domains, including efforts to curb the spread of nuclear, chemical, and biological weapons.

Another school of thought about international affairs and foreign policy is known as **social constructivism**, which is related to liberalism and neoliberalism in its expression of optimism about the chances for improvements in global integration and peace. Constructivism, though, is more concerned with the basic processes that make up international relations, whereas liberalism and neoliberalism offer theories about the primary interests, motivations, and forces that shape the interaction between nations. The constructivist school *concentrates on the questions of how social norms, ideas, and images can influence international relations, and the importance of how nations think of themselves and their values in comparison with other nations.* The core idea is that the relationship between nations is a social activity and that these relationships can define (and redefine) national identities and interests. Theorists Jennifer Sterling-Folker and Dina Badi put it this way: "Constructivist theory is about the analytical interconnection between interaction, identity, ideas, materialism, social meaning, agency and structure."[57]

As with liberals, constructivists focus on the value of international institutions for enhancing world peace; but, in addition, they believe that a nation's norms and practices can be transformed. Nations are able to change their identities through self-reflection and learning.[58] An example is the "learning" that occurred in the Soviet Union under the guidance of President Mikhail Gorbachev, who introduced fundamental changes in Russia from 1989–1990 that led to the end of the Cold War and improved relations with the United States. Gorbachev's policies sought to transform Soviet self-understanding and, by extension, the social structure of the Cold War, as Russians came to recognize a broader set of common interests with the United States. For constructivists, with their emphasis on a normative analysis of world affairs, a nation's values are of great importance and can undergo transformation. This sense of mutability in international affairs—a capacity for nations to remake themselves and enter into friendlier relations—stands in stark contrast to the views of realists (examined later in this chapter).

Liberals and idealists, neoliberals, and social constructivists are optimists who embrace the goals of international community and a sense of fair play in global affairs, along with the promotion of worldwide egalitarianism and economic prosperity. In this spirit of idealism, a chairman of the prestigious Senate Foreign Relations Committee,

Frank Church (D-Idaho), once reflected on the possibility that extreme CIA covert actions (among them, assassination plots against foreign leaders) may have damaged the reputation for integrity and fair play enjoyed by the United States at the end of World War II. "I suggest we have lost—or grievously impaired—the good name and reputation of the United States," he concluded, "from which we once drew a unique capacity to exercise matchless moral leadership."[59] Near the end of the Cold War, a leading member of the House Foreign Affairs Committee, Representative Stephen J. Solarz (D-New York), similarly stressed that in the conduct of America's relations abroad "the best way to promote our interests is to promote our ideals."[60]

More recently, in the context of revelations about torture of suspected terrorists by CIA and US military intelligence officers in the aftermath of 9/11, President Obama rescinded the permission granted by the second Bush administration for this harsh approach to interrogation (which included "waterboarding" or the pouring of water over the cloth-covered mouth and nose of a prisoner to simulate a sense of drowning, usually leading to vomiting and screaming by the victim). President Obama concluded that the use of such methods violated the fundamental ethical norms of the United States.

Some students of international affairs—most notably the proponents of a school of thought known as **realism**—have displayed a pronounced skepticism about the value of law in international relations, or the utility of international organizations and ethical considerations in world affairs.[61] They believe that *a state's external relations should rest more prudently on a foundation of military and economic strength*—hard power. As Henry R. Nau notes with respect to the approach to foreign policy advocated by the prominent Cold War US diplomat and realist George Kennan, "power mattered more than ideas and institutions" (power in this case meaning military and economic strength).[62]

If the liberals or idealists are optimistic about world affairs, the realists are pessimistic. "Where Liberals see co-operation as the likely outcome [in relations among nations], Realists see the perpetual threat of conflict and war," concludes theorist Oliver Dadow.[63] Further, political scientist Stanley Hoffmann underscores that realism (or realpolitik, in the European phrase), "Looks at the international system as a milieu in which states compete, seek to increased their power, try to prevent the rise of rivals or hegemons through unilateral moves as well as through balances of power, and depend for their survival and success above all on military might and the economic underpinning of it."[64]

The roots of the realist tradition run deep, extending back to the writings of Machiavelli (1469–1527) and even Thucydides (circa 460–400 BC). In the aftermath of World War II, a hard-boiled cynicism characteristic of the realist school enjoyed a resurgence led by political scientist Hans J. Morgenthau, as an alternative to the interwar optimism and moralism of Wilsonian idealists—the devotees of President Wilson who held aspirations for world peace through a League of Nations.[65] The League's failure to keep the peace, followed by British Prime Minister Neville Chamberlain's dashed hopes to satiate Hitler's appetites for conquest through a policy of appeasement, further swelled the ranks of the realists. "The horrors of Hitler's war made a post-war generation of scholars worry about idealism in foreign policy," writes Joseph S. Nye, "and the conventional wisdom in the professional study of international relations since 1945 has awarded the 'realists' a clear victory over the 'idealists.'"[66]

A subsequent generation of scholars, led by Kenneth Waltz, expanded on Morgenthau's writing to develop a philosophy of **neorealism**.[67] As with the realists, this school downplays the importance of morality and retains a pessimistic outlook on human nature; but the neorealists elevate the role of international economic relations in world affairs, and they use more advanced, scientific tools of analysis. Above all, the neorealists place an emphasis on the international level of analysis: the relations among states, in contrast to the levels of domestic politics or individual decision making by policy officials. They view *international affairs as a structured system of interacting nations, with regularities of behavior.* Whereas liberals speak of an "international community" in which nations work together, neorealists speak of an "international system" in which nations may or—more likely—may not engage in community-like cooperation.

All important to the neorealists are the number of "units"—nations—in the system. A bipolar system, in which there are two major powers (such as the United States and the Soviet Union during the Cold War), is likely to yield one set of international dynamics, whereas a multipolar system with many powerful nations (as before the outbreak of World War II) will lead to another set of dynamics. Some observers maintain that today's world is best characterized as unipolar, with the United States the sole remaining superpower since the end of the Cold War. Yet the world is more complicated than this oversimplification. The United States is indeed the most powerful nation militarily; but when it comes to the important domain of international economics, there are other claimants to the mantle of "superpower," such as China and the combined nations of the European Union. At any rate, the neorealist supposition is that the international system will behave in different ways, according to the number of powerful nations on the world scene. Waltz hypothesized that a bipolar system is more stable than a multipolar system because two superpowers would try to keep the status quo that assured their dominance in the world. This notion of an international system suggests, unlike the realist's perspective, that national leaders in this kind of structured setting have only a limited opportunity for the wily exercise of clever diplomacy to achieve national objectives.

The latest wrinkle in realist theorizing is the school of **neoclassical realism**. Its proponents acknowledge the importance of structure in international relations, but they reject Waltz's reductionism. They insist on *a more complex view of the world that takes into account not only the international system of nations—the number and the types of nations—but also the influence of domestic politics inside a nation and the perceptions of world affairs held by its individual leaders.*[68] This school lacks the theoretical elegance and parsimony of Waltz's approach (attributes that are attractive in any scholarly discipline, from physics or international relations); nevertheless, the neoclassical theorists are wise to stress that domestic politics and individual worldviews can hardly be dismissed in calculations about how foreign policy decisions are made. These three levels of analysis—the international system, domestic politics, and individual leaders and citizens—contribute to the basic orientation adopted in this book.

The realists, neorealists, and neoclassical realists all believe strongly in the value of a balance-of-power approach to international affairs—that the existence of a military equilibrium among nations is essential for peaceful diplomacy to work (discussed further in Chapter 2). By themselves and in coalitions, nations have to maintain strong armies as a means for keeping enemies at bay. As critics have noted, however, this concentration on military readiness paradoxically creates a **security dilemma**: *as one nation arms itself defensively, a rival nation grows fearful of this rising threat and, in turn, further arms itself.* The end result is a back-and-forth arms race that spirals upward in a climate of fear, thereby ironically undermining each nation's sense of safety.[69]

During the administration of George W. Bush, a foreign policy based on yet another school of thought about international affairs, known as **neoconservativism**, gripped the White House and the Department of Defense. The "**neocons**" exhibited *a blend of liberalism and realism. As with liberalism, the neocons promoted the spread of democracy; but they parted from liberals in their resort to the use of military force for success*— "Wilsonianism in boots" or "Wilsonianism on steroids," as some political scientists and historians have characterized the neocon philosophy.[70] Scholar Francis Fukuyama outlined the beliefs of neoconservatives: they embrace realism and the use of force for the achievement of moral objectives while distrusting nation building overseas as well as the effectiveness of international law and institutions.[71]

An influential faction of neocons helped persuade President George W. Bush to mount an invasion of Iraq in 2003, using armed force to bring about (they hoped) a democratic regime in place of Saddam Hussein's dictatorship. In this instance, the White House briefed lawmakers on the plans to attack Iraq, and the Congress voted overwhelmingly in favor of the military action. A decade later, the outcome of this experiment in the advancement of democracy—at the point of bayonets—remained up in the air. Iraq continued to wallow in internal strife and potential civil war, despite expenditures by the United States of more than a trillion dollars on the war in Iraq and the stationing of American troops in the country for over seven years (a period longer than World War II). Political scientist and Director of Policy Planning in the State Department during the Obama administration, Anne-Marie Slaughter, expressed skepticism about the neocon distortion of Wilsonian idealism. President Wilson's vision, she stressed, was not about the "forcible spread of liberal democracy."[72]

These are not the only theoretical "isms" with relevance to foreign policy considerations. One could add to the list Marxism, critical theory, feminism, postmodernism, postcolonialism, poststructuralism, green theory, cosmopolitanism, communitarianism, and anarchism, among others.[73] Nevertheless, the theories discussed briefly here are the philosophies that come up most often in commentary about America's relations abroad. Realism and its variants are the preeminent paradigms for Washington officials and international relations scholars alike; but idealism and its related optimistic approaches continue to have a significant following. Even President George H. W. Bush, usually considered a proponent of the realist perspective, became the leading advocate for a Somalia humanitarian intervention during his waning months in office—an operation worth mentioning again because it stands out as an exception to America's reluctance to engage in humanitarian operations overseas. (President Clinton's humanitarian intervention in Serbia during the 1990s is another example of a rare humanitarian intervention.) In one of his final foreign policy speeches, delivered at Texas A&M University on December 15, 1992, the first President Bush asserted that "our country's tradition of idealism" has made us "unique among states."

The foreign policy views of public officials in the United States are commonly a mixture of realism and idealism. Further, America's leaders in both political parties have adopted a mixed use of hard and soft power. As Nye writes, "*The ability to combine hard and soft power into an effective strategy* is **smart power**."[74] This book, too, reflects a blend of the liberal and realist traditions as it probes into the results of America's search for smart power.

## SUMMARY

Foreign policy has become increasingly important for Americans to understand. As an outcome of globalization, citizens of the world are connected to one another as never before, in their politics, their economies, their cultures, their environments, their communications and transportation, and even their illnesses.

The foreign policy of the United States, like that of other nations, has been a composite of ends and means. The ends, or objectives, have included foremost peace and security, economic prosperity, improvements in the quality of life, and the advancement of human rights. How these goals are to be achieved, and the degree to which America's finite resources should be dedicated to each goal, have been matters of intense debate throughout the nation's history.

Contentious, too, has been the question of the means, or instruments, the United States should use in quest of the nation's objectives. Among the most important have been the collection and analysis of information about world conditions (national security intelligence), the treaty power (diplomacy), the war power (extreme hard power), covert action (secret interventions abroad), economic statecraft (trade and aid), and moral and cultural suasion (soft power). Seldom are these approaches advanced separately; rather, policy makers try to incorporate the range of options available to them as they pursue America's interests overseas. How and why each instrument is selected, how well each works, and the political and constitutional controversies that have accompanied their use are subjects that also lie at the heart of American foreign policy.

Foreign policy analysts and practitioners can be classified according to their philosophies or approaches. Among the key philosophies in modern statecraft are liberalism, neoliberalism, social constructivism, realism, neorealism, neoclassical realism, and neoconservativism.

## KEY TERMS

covert action (secret interventions abroad) p. 24
democratic peace hypothesis p. 12
diplomacy p. 21
economic statecraft p. 26
foreign policy p. 6
foreign policy instruments (means) p. 18
foreign policy objectives (ends) p. 7
globalization p. 6
hard power p. 28
liberalism (idealism) p. 29
moral and cultural suasion p. 27
national security intelligence p. 18

neoclassical realism p. 32
neoconservativism (neocons) p. 33
neoliberalism p. 29
neorealism p. 32
power p. 18
realism p. 31
regimes p. 29
security dilemma p. 33
smart power p. 34
social constructivism p. 30
soft power p. 28
war power p. 23

## QUESTIONS FOR DISCUSSION

1. What is your personal hierarchy of objectives for US foreign policy?
2. How would you array the six main instruments of American foreign policy on a "ladder of escalation," climbing from the least to the most intrusive abroad?
3. What are the strengths and weaknesses of the perspectives advocated by realists, idealists, constructivists, and other theories of international affairs discussed in this chapter? What is your assessment of the neocon approach?
4. What foreign policy instruments would you use to try to bring about the end of the nuclear weapons programs in North Korea and Iran?
5. What blend of hard and soft power would you recommend to a president or lawmakers, in the search for "smart power"?

## ADDITIONAL READINGS

Gaddis, John Lewis. *George F. Kennan: An American Life*. New York: Penguin, 2012.

Morgenthau, Hans J. *Politics Among Nations: The Struggle for Power and Peace*. New York: Knopf, 1973 (originally published in 1948).

Nye, Joseph S. Jr. *The Paradox of American Power*. New York: Oxford University Press, 2002.

For further readings, please visit the book's companion website.

### CHAPTER 2

# An Analytic Construct for the Study of American Foreign Policy

## HIROSHIMA AND NAGASAKI

Colonel Paul W. Tibbets pushed the throttles full forward on a B-29 bomber assigned to the 509th Composite Group of the 20th Air Force. Bearing the name *Enola Gay* painted beneath its cockpit in honor of Tibbets's mother, the plane and its crew of twelve lumbered down the runway on Tinian Island in the Pacific, lifted off the tarmac at 2:15 a.m. on August 6, 1945, and headed toward Japan. Its solitary cargo lay in darkness: ten feet long, two feet wide, 10,000 pounds in weight, and packed with enriched uranium. In an ironic misnomer, the crew called the bomb "Little Boy."

Aerial view of the mushroom cloud of smoke as it billows 20,000 ft. in the air following the United States Air Force's detonation of an atomic bomb over the city of Hiroshima, Japan, August 6, 1945.

As dawn began to break, weather planes and two B-29 observer bombers joined the *Enola Gay* over the island of Iwo Jima. The meteorological reports were favorable for each authorized Japanese target: Nagasaki, Kokura, and, the top priority on the list, Hiroshima, located on the island of Honshu. For the umpteenth time, bombardier Major Thomas W. Ferebee studied the briefing map of Hiroshima, with Aioi Bridge at the center of this city famous for its graceful willow trees.

The sky turned bright and clear as the bomber approached Hiroshima. Local time was almost 9:15 a.m. The speed of the *Enola Gay* was 200 miles per hour; altitude: 31,060 feet. The Aioi Bridge moved swiftly into the crossed hairs of the bombsight. Ferebee opened the hatch of the airplane and, fifteen seconds later, he pressed the cargo-release button. The bomber lurched as the heavy weapon fell from the bomb bay.

Colonel Tibbets immediately turned the plane away from Honshu, at a sharp angle of 159 degrees, just as he had practiced the maneuver time and time again in the United States and at Tinian Island. The *Enola Gay* strained, then pulled away, out over the Sea of Japan. Little Boy fell until its altimeter registered the exact height of 1,890 feet above the unsuspecting city. Then came a burst, a blinding flash of light, and heat as

---

**LEARNING OBJECTIVES AND CONSTITUTIONAL ISSUES**

**By the end of this chapter, you will be able to:**

- *Define three important levels of analysis in foreign policy: the international, the national, and the individual.*
- *Understand an orienting "road map" that connects these levels.*

- *Name key elements of the international setting.*
- *Explain the influence that domestic politics has on foreign policy.*
- *Name some psychological traps that await foreign policy leaders.*

---

**THIS CHAPTER RAISES SEVERAL CONSTITUTIONAL QUESTIONS:**

- Among the many considerations that shape American foreign policy, the Constitution is among the most important because this document spells out—though often with ambiguities and opaque passages—the foreign policy authorities enjoyed by each of the branches. Where does the Constitution appear in this chapter's orienting construct for the study of foreign policy?

- When the founders wrote the Constitution in 1787, what was the international level of global affairs like and how does that setting compare with today's? Do these dramatic differences in the international setting negate the value of the separation of powers doctrine advocated by the founders?

- How would you compare the domestic setting at the time of the founders with the situation today in the United States? To what extent, if at all, do the differences in the two eras nullify the merits of Madison's prescription for separate institutions sharing power in the making of foreign and domestic policy?

- Do you think the characteristics of individual foreign policy makers are apt to have changed over the generations since 1787 in a way that calls into doubt the value of the Madisonian constitutional framework?

fiery as the sun. In an instant, an energy force equivalent to 20,000 tons of TNT struck Hiroshima—more power than all the bombs the US Air Force had used during the entire war in Europe. In a microsecond, the city no longer existed. Above the maelstrom of death and destruction, a stately mushroom cloud rose 22,000 feet into the sky, its stem darkened by urban debris, its top a white plume mixed with shades of blue and pink trailing off toward the horizon. Of Hiroshima's 255,000 population, 78,150 died in the detonation and the fires that came in its wake. One hundred thousand more were seriously burned. Another 13,425 were never found.

Three days later, the United States dropped a second atomic bomb ("Fat Man") on Nagasaki (estimated population 240,000), with 35,000 killed or lost and 40,000 injured. In case the government of Japan still refused to surrender, the military brass in the Pentagon had ordered Col. Tibbets to prepare his crew for a third A-bomb mission. The Japanese government did surrender, though, and may have been preparing to give up the struggle even before the annihilation of Nagasaki. At long last, with a stunning use of a physical power that left the world in awe, the United States had brought an end to the agony of war in the island jungles of the Pacific.[1] ∿

## THREE PERSPECTIVES ON FOREIGN POLICY DECISIONS

The conduct of American foreign policy may be thought of as taking place on three levels or in three settings. First, on the international level, policy makers in Washington, DC, face many strong-willed and often well-armed nations, each with foreign policy goals that may or may not coincide with US objectives. Second, on the national level, policy makers must deal with the ups and downs of domestic politics and institutional conflicts within their own government—the latter intentionally fostered by the Constitution as a means of avoiding a concentration of power in the hands of the president. Third, individual policy makers are vulnerable to misperceptions, groupthink, self-delusion, and other psychological distortions of the world around them. Foreign policy decisions are complex and are usually the result of an interplay of people, institutions, and circumstances at all three levels.

With this framework in mind, what were the international, domestic, and individual influences that led to the decision in favor of dropping nuclear bombs on Japan in 1945? At the international level, US intelligence estimates at the time concluded that an invasion of Japan would take eighteen months and cost the lives of anywhere from 40,000 to upward of half a million American GIs and an even larger number of Japanese soldiers and citizens. Moreover, the Soviet Army was racing toward Japan. The possibility was real that the USSR may have been able to capture Japan, an important industrial base for Moscow's rising Communist empire, before American troops could arrive to block the takeover. These were important considerations as President Harry S. Truman weighed whether to use nuclear weapons against the Japanese.

At the domestic level, Americans would probably have strongly denounced a costly invasion once they learned the US military possessed atomic bombs that might have caused Japan's quick surrender and allowed their loved ones at war in the Pacific to return home safely. From a domestic political perspective, failure to order the use of these potent weapons against the Japanese could have led to President Truman's defeat in the 1948 presidential election and severely damaged the credibility of the Democratic Party.

Some who knew about the Manhattan Project argued at the time that the United States should use an atomic weapon initially in a demonstration bombing against an uninhabited Pacific island, informing the Japanese to observe its destructive power and realize that the time to surrender had come or else the next bomb would be dropped on Japan. The United States had only three of these nuclear devices, however, and the military was reluctant to use one in a mock attack—another domestic pressure on the President, this time from the military bureaucracy. Most of the Manhattan Project scientists were also in favor of using the bombs they had constructed. They had labored around the clock to build the weapons, knowing that here was a way scientists could play a major role in ending the world war. Some also hoped that two different types of bombs could be dropped, one uranium based (with Hiroshima the target) and another plutonium based (Nagasaki). In this way, the different results could be scientifically compared.

At the level of the individual decision maker, the head of the Manhattan Project, General Leslie R. Groves, lobbied vigorously to use the bomb. His personal career was tied to the construction and use of this weapon. An even more important figure at this level, though, was President Truman. Ultimately, the decision was his to make. During World War I, Truman had been a young US Army officer on the front lines in Europe. He had seen at firsthand the carnage of war and understood the horror that an invasion of Japan would entail. That possible outcome was even more unsettling, in his view, than the terrible destruction that would fall on the citizens of Hiroshima and Nagasaki. These remembrances of his own battlefield experience likely had an effect on the President's choice of options to end the war. "You break your head and your heart to save one life," he recalled years later, ". . . No man could fail to use the bomb and look his countrymen in the face."[2]

Here are the key dimensions—the international setting, the domestic setting, and the experiences and attitudes of individual decision makers—that intersect in intricate, often baffling, ways to bound and shape the course of US foreign policy. Each can have a significant influence on the degree of success or failure in America's search for an effective grand strategy that will enhance the nation's security and prosperity in a world plagued by violence, disorder, ambiguity, and uncertainty.[3]

The influences on foreign policy decisions that arise at each of the three levels are summarized in Figure 2.1.[4] The purpose of this "road map" is to provide an outline of the complexities that confront the United States in its relations with the rest of the world. It emphasizes the importance of historical and constitutional antecedents, the conflicted and bargaining nature of America's policy-making institutions, and the sundry human conditions that stand between the "rational actor" and the selection of foreign policy instruments.

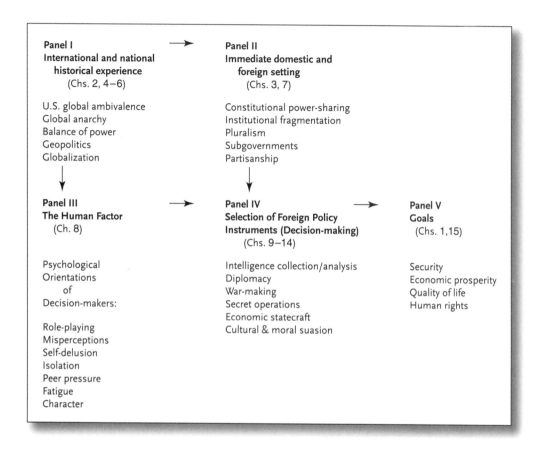

**Panel I**
**International and national**
**historical experience**
(Chs. 2, 4–6)

U.S. global ambivalence
Global anarchy
Balance of power
Geopolitics
Globalization

**Panel II**
**Immediate domestic and**
**foreign setting**
(Chs. 3, 7)

Constitutional power-sharing
Institutional fragmentation
Pluralism
Subgovernments
Partisanship

**Panel III**
**The Human Factor**
(Ch. 8)

Psychological
Orientations
of
Decision-makers:

Role-playing
Misperceptions
Self-delusion
Isolation
Peer pressure
Fatigue
Character

**Panel IV**
**Selection of Foreign Policy**
**Instruments (Decision-making)**
(Chs. 9–14)

Intelligence collection/analysis
Diplomacy
War-making
Secret operations
Economic statecraft
Cultural & moral suasion

**Panel V**
**Goals**
(Chs. 1,15)

Security
Economic prosperity
Quality of life
Human rights

*Figure 2.1*
An Analytic Construct
for the Study of American
Foreign Policy

Historians and social scientists have long debated the question of which is more important in the momentous decisions that shape the course of world affairs: the presence of a "great leader"—say, a Washington, Napoleon, or Lenin—or the special circumstances of the time that forced action, such as the British tyranny perpetrated against the American colonists. As the arrows in Figure 2.1 are meant to indicate, decisions—large and small—are the result of a complex interplay between the psychological orientations and personal attributes of individual decision makers *and* the historical and institutional situation at the time.

As displayed in Figure 2.1, the pressure of events—along with human perceptions about these events—lead to a reaction: a decision. Using the jargon of their academic discipline, two political psychologists sum up this relationship: "Social background works on physiological raw materials to engender psychological orientations that mediate the specific situational stimuli that lead to political behavior."[5] Using the simpler language of Figure 2.1, it can be said that international and national historical experiences (among them, the provisions of the Constitution) influence the personal development and worldview of individual decision makers. In turn, as these decision makers pursue a grand strategy, they operate in a bargaining environment and interact with multiple governmental institutions and societal groups as they select the various instruments of foreign policy in their pursuit of the nation's foreign policy objectives.

Behind this diagram lies a highly intricate reality. Analysts have stressed this complexity by contrasting foreign policy decisions with a game of chess. In chess, there are only six distinct pieces, a handful of rules, and a board that is just eight-by-eight units square. Yet even in this game, the number of possible sequences of moves is incredibly large: some $10^{120}$—essentially, infinity. Chess is simple, however, compared to the sequence of possible moves available to policy makers in real-life situations. Take the interaction between two naval forces at war. As political scientists Bendor and Hammond have pointed out, there are far more than six distinct "pieces" to move in a naval operation. The SOPs—the standard operating procedures, or bureaucratic rules—for moving just one destroyer are far more involved than for a chess piece, and the topographical "board" of the world's oceans is far more vast and difficult to assess than an eight-by-eight chessboard.[6] Figure 2.1 offers not a theory or even a model of foreign policy making but rather a construct or framework, helpful for illustrating some important foreign policy relationships. Central to the construct are the three levels of foreign policy analysis.

## THE INTERNATIONAL SETTING

On one point most scholars of foreign policy stand in agreement: the world is essentially anarchical in the sense that "no central government exists with a range of authority compared to that found in contemporary states."[7] Or, to put it more succinctly, we live in "a world of egoists without central authority."[8] This fragmented international setting makes cooperation among nations difficult, to say the least.

Although factions (terrorist groups, for instance), international and regional organizations like the UN and NATO, and multinational corporations (MNCs) have become increasingly important entities in the world, the nation remains the basic organizational unit in international affairs, as fundamental to an understanding of foreign policy as the atom is to physics. A **nation** may be defined as *a gathering together of individuals under a common leadership, or government, in control of a well-defined territorial space.*[9] Normally, the citizens of a nation *share a cultural identity as well, including a common language and an allegiance to a distinctive flag and national anthem.* A nation, thus, has both territorial and psychological dimensions.

If the existence of a gathering of people into a new nation is widely recognized by other established nations, the geographical entity is considered sovereign. **Sovereignty** is *"the legal capacity of an independent state to regulate its affairs, as it pleases, without permission from any outside source."*[10] To establish the sovereignty of the United States, free from British rule, the founders of this nation led a revolution and by force of arms removed its thirteen colonies from the empire of King George III. New nations, or the reconfiguration of old regimes, are periodically born in blood, torn from some existing sovereign territory by the violence of revolution. If *a nation exercises control over another* *sovereign territory or territories*, it is said to have established an **empire**. If the *control is less sweeping, but still strongly influential*, a nation is considered a **hegemon**.

In 1990 when the United States led a UN invasion of Iraq as a punishment for its conquest of Kuwait, the national sovereignty of Iraq was at stake. Against Iraqi protests, UN weapons inspectors (backed by America's military and intelligence presence in the Persian Gulf region) entered the nation and carried out searches for hidden caches of weapons. Although the Iraqi regime, led by Saddam Hussein, had no fully constructed nuclear weapons, inspectors discovered that its WMD program was five years ahead of where Western intelligence had predicted. In 1992, the UN further eroded Iraqi sovereignty by establishing no-fly zones in the south and north of Iraq and took steps to limit the scope of Saddam's air force operations within his own country. In 2011, the leaders and the people of Pakistan looked on a US Navy Seal team attack against the Al Qaeda leader Bin Ladin—without privately notifying leaders in Islamabad beforehand—as a regrettable violation of their national sovereignty. The Obama administration calculated, however, that the mission required utmost secrecy that prevented a prior briefing.

Sovereign nations are joined on the international stage by various intergovernmental and nongovernmental organizations (NGOs), such as, respectively, the World Health Organization (WHO) and Amnesty International, a human-rights group. As a result of cross-national (or "transnational") ties among their individual chapters around the globe, some of these organizations help reduce the tensions endemic in a system of competing nations.

This understanding of the terms "nation" and "sovereignty," combined with the discussion of US global objectives in the previous chapter, yields the following formal definition of **American foreign policy**: *those decisions and actions taken by the sovereign nation of the United States with respect to other sovereign nations, as well as various international factions, groups, and organizations, in the protection of America's citizens and allies, along with the advancement of their goals and values.*

Attempts to explain why nations behave as they do toward one another have been widely diverse and often contradictory. No single theory of American foreign policy stands preeminent. Some explanations, though, have wider currency than others, and because the purpose of this chapter is to provide a further orientation to the complexities of foreign policy, I introduce them briefly here (and explore them in more detail in subsequent chapters). At the international level of analysis, among the most influential explanations of foreign policy behavior have focused on the balance of power between nations; on their geographical opportunities and constraints (geopolitics); and, more recently, on the growing interdependence of nations in the contemporary world (globalization).

## Balance of Power

Central to the realist's view of foreign policy is the idea of **balance of power**. According to this perspective, *if one nation becomes too dominant militarily, it will attempt to* *manipulate—or even conquer—other nations; therefore, vulnerable nations will form co-alitions among themselves to prevent a threatening outsider from achieving military domi-nance over them.* Western nations have been unwilling to allow any individual country to have dominion over the European continent, with its great industrial capacity for weapons production. In 1939, when Hitler's appetite grew even larger after his initial takeover of Austria and Czechoslovakia and he sent Germany's tanks rumbling into Poland, Great Britain and France reacted by declaring war on the Third Reich. The British and the French understood that this further expansion of Germany would make Hitler's regime a grave threat to their sovereignty. When the Nazi war machine then turned against Britain and France, astute Americans realized that the United States would soon have to join in resisting this attempt to disrupt the power equilib-rium in Europe; otherwise, America might well be the next target of an expansionist Third Reich wielding the industrial might of the entire European continent.

A balance-of-power approach to foreign policy also shaped America's response to the global challenge of Marxist-Leninist ideology promulgated during the Cold War by communists in the Soviet Union and China, along with their allies. Their totalitar-ian collectivist ideology was in obvious conflict with America's fundamental beliefs in democracy, individual rights, and free enterprise. As a check against the spread of communism, US policy makers embraced "the central preoccupation of postwar na-tional security policy—the idea of containment."[11] The containment policy rested on a conviction that the leaders of the USSR were determined to disrupt the international equilibrium, that they wished to dominate the globe just as the Nazis had intended. Sometimes the Soviets used force, as in Eastern Europe and Mongolia; but more often they adopted subtler techniques involving secret propaganda operations and other covert actions to support Marxist "wars of liberation" in the developing world, as in Vietnam during the 1960s and 1970s and Angola during the 1970s and 1980s.

To counter the communist threat, the Truman administration vowed a steadfast resistance to Soviet aggression in Greece, Turkey, and, by implication, throughout the world. (See *Perspectives on American Foreign Policy* 2.1.) Important, as well, was the building of alliances for collective security, most notably NATO, established in 1949 and comprised of the United States, Canada, and key European nations. The resulting Cold War was sustained by the core belief in Washington and other Western capitals that the Soviets, though once a valued ally of the West in World War II, were really no better than the Nazis in their desire for global domination. The Soviet totalitarian state had to be walled in by a coalition of democratic nations prepared to use political and economic pressures as well as covert action and—if necessary—overt military force to stop the communist advance.

With the end of the Cold War in 1990, the world changed dramatically from a bipolar standoff between the two superpowers to what many commentators viewed as a unipolar world with the United States as the most prominent nation on the planet. Efforts to counter US influence, as predicted by the balance-of-power theory, failed to

---

### PERSPECTIVES ON AMERICAN FOREIGN POLICY 2.1

The *TRUMAN DOCTRINE*, from a speech by President Truman before Congress on March 12, 1947, in which he requested $400 million for aid to Greece and Turkey to help them resist Soviet-backed guerrilla warfare—the most important early manifestation of America's commitment to the policy of containment:

At the present moment in world history nearly every nation must choose between alternative ways of life. The choice is too often not a free one.

One way of life is based upon the will of the majority, and is distinguished by free institutions, representative government, free elections, guarantees of individual liberty, freedom of speech and religion, and freedom from political oppression.

The second way of life is based upon the will of a minority forcibly imposed upon the majority. It relies upon terror and oppression, a controlled press and radio, fixed elections, and the suppression of personal freedoms.

I believe that it must be the policy of the United States to support free peoples who are resisting attempted subjugation by armed minorities or by outside pressures.

I believe that we must assist free people to work out their own destinies in their own ways.

I believe that our help should be primarily through economic and financial aid which is essential to economic stability and orderly political processes.

SOURCE: *Public Papers of the Presidents*, Harry S. Truman, 1947 (Washington, DC, Office of the Federal Register, National Archives, 1952), pp. 178–179.

---

materialize in any concerted manner. Only the nations of Europe had the capacity to coalesce against the United States; but, correctly, they looked on America as a friend, not a threat, and saw no need to rally against this country with a military defense pact. The Europeans did, however, take steps to form a stronger economic alliance: a European Union with a common currency, the euro, which was phased in over several years in the late 1990s and early 2000s. Further, in Asia the nations on the border of an increasingly powerful China have displayed no signs of behaving in a traditional balance-of-power manner. Vietnam and Cambodia, for instance, have adjusted to their positions within the Chinese sphere of influence, in the manner that Mexico and other nations of Central America have resigned themselves to standing in the long shadow of the United States. Rather than seeking balances, these nations have attempted to establish reasonably cordial relations with the giants in their neighborhoods.

## Geopolitics

Foreign policy scholars generally agree that geography can play a significant role in the relationships between and among nations. In the late 1800s, understanding the importance of a strong US presence in the Atlantic and Pacific Oceans, Admiral Alfred Thayer Mahan wrote persuasively about the need for a "blue-water" (far oceangoing) US Navy. In the early twentieth century, the English geographer Halford Mackinder and the Yale University professor of international affairs Nicholas J. Spykman also authored (separately) widely read works on the significance of geography in foreign affairs. For Mackinder, the world's most pivotal geographic area—the "Heartland"—resided in central Europe. His most famous dictum was

> Who controls East Europe commands the Heartland;
> Who rules the Heartland commands the World Island;
> Who rules the World Island commands the World.[12]

In contrast, Spykman focused on what he called the "Rimland," which included the European coastland and other regions between the Heartland and the marginal sea powers of the world. In response to Mackinder, his mantra was

> Who controls the Rimland rules Eurasia;
> Who rules Eurasia controls the destinies of the world.[13]

Spykman's focus on drawing a circle around Eurasia—of which the Soviet Union occupied tracts—made him appealing to Cold War strategists looking for a way to defend against the communist empire. As a result, Spykman is often regarded as an important theorist for the later development of the containment doctrine.

A basic tenet of US geopolitics has been to maintain a divided Eurasia, for fear that control of that vast region by any one country would pose a danger to the United States. More recently, American geostrategist Thomas P. M. Barnett has focused on globalization, noting that nations that have benefited economically from this interdependence (reaching a per capita income of $3,000 or more a year) tend to be less violence prone. In Barnett's terminology, these nations constitute the "Core," while poorer nations are left in the "Gap."[14]

A geographical determinist, Spykman no doubt overstated the case when he argued that geography was "the most fundamentally conditioning factor" in foreign affairs. Nonetheless, **geopolitics**—that aspect of *foreign policy influenced by the number, size, strength, location, and topography of nations*—is a prominent feature in the writings of scholars, the planning of government leaders, and the unfolding of historical events. This perspective stands as a significant corollary to the concept of balance of power in international relations.

"Poor Mexico," observed an unhappy President Porfirio Diaz (1830–1915) on the plight of his country's location, "so far from God and so close to the United States." Large nations with imposing arsenals have often insisted on a "sphere of influence" reaching out from their borders, into which other nations might tread only at the peril of triggering a military response. Since the proclamation of the Monroe Doctrine in 1823, the United States has claimed the Western Hemisphere as its sphere of influence. During the Cold War, the Soviet Union seemed to view practically every weak nation on its perimeter as within Moscow's sphere of influence. Finland, Estonia, Latvia, and Lithuania, along with most Eastern European and Central Asian nations, found themselves in the ominous shadow—and sometimes under the foot—of the Soviet military behemoth. In the twenty-first century, China's attempts to claim exclusive control over the South China Sea and its three island groups have been hotly contested by the Philippines, Japan, Vietnam, and Indonesia, among other nations that have used this waterway for centuries without interference. These Chinese claims worry the United States, as well, for its ships—commercial and military—frequently ply these waters.

During the Cold War, Western geostrategists warned that communism could move steadfastly from one contiguous regime to another around the world: a dread widely referred to as the **domino theory**. According to this notion, *first one domino would fall under the weight of a communist onslaught, then the next and the next, toppling one after another as in the child's game until, at last, the chain reaction reached the last standing domino: the United States.* Central to this viewpoint are the concepts of resolve and credibility: if the United States failed to back its allies, as well as neutral countries, those countries might be bullied into joining the communists out of fear of no other place to turn. In a revealing response to a correspondent's query in 1954, President Dwight D. Eisenhower gave expression to his own geopolitical angst about "falling dominoes" (see *Perspectives on American Foreign Policy* 2.2). Within the President's remarks may be found the key arguments that, a decade later, would pave the way for a major—and disastrous—military intervention by the United States into Southeast Asia.

The chief weakness of the domino theory lies in its assumption that somehow the toppling of one domino will somehow lead inevitably to the toppling of others. History would suggest, on the contrary, that there is nothing preordained about anything, and that nations can be quite resistant to outside threats. The next "domino" may well have a strong economy, a potent military defense, or simply a robust belief in nationalism, often born in response to Western colonialism, which finds utterly repugnant the prospect of renewed colonialism or foreign domination of any sort—Marxism or any other "ism" that seeks to topple them. Even when Cuba tried, with Soviet assistance, to establish a communist beachhead in Angola, the relatively weak nations bordering on the African nation were able to resist further communist expansion; they no more wished to be under Cuban or Soviet rule than they did the European colonial powers whom they had finally shed.

Some geopolitical analysts concerned about the future of the United States have pointed over the years to the importance of maintaining access to strategic mineral resources abroad, such as nickel and zinc in Canada; tin in Bolivia; rubber in Indochina; cobalt in the Democratic Republic of the Congo; bauxite in Jamaica and Guinea; platinum, industrial diamonds, and chromate in South Africa; manganese ore in Brazil; lithium in Afghanistan; titanium in Russia (where the US airplane company Boeing plans to spend $18 billion in titanium purchases in the coming decades); the so-called rare earth minerals, like dysprosium and yttrium, which are essential for electric cars, smartphones, computer components, and military weapons and are mined almost exclusively in China; and, above all, oil in the Middle East, Nigeria, and Venezuela to fuel America's industry as well as its automobiles and trucks. Although the administration of George H. W. Bush framed its 1990 military intervention in the

## PERSPECTIVES ON AMERICAN FOREIGN POLICY 2.2

**A news conference with PRESIDENT DWIGHT D. EISENHOWER *(April 7, 1954)*:**

Q. *Robert Richards, Copley Press:* Mr. President, would you mind commenting on the strategic importance of Indochina to the free world? I think there has been, across the country, some lack of understanding on just what it means to us.

A. *President Eisenhower:* You have, of course, both the specific and the general when you talk about such things.

First of all, you have the specific value of a locality in its production of materials that the world needs.

Then you have the possibility that many human beings pass under a dictatorship that is inimical to the free world.

Finally, you have broader considerations that might follow what you would call the "falling domino" principle. You have a row of dominoes set up, you knock over the first one, and what will happen to the last one is the certainty that it will go over very quickly. So you could have a beginning of a disintegration that would have the most profound influences.

Now, with respect to the first one, two of the items from this particular area that the world uses are tin and tungsten. They are very important. There are others, of course, the rubber plantations and so on.

Then with respect to more people passing under this domination, Asia, after all, has already lost some 450 million of its peoples to the Communist dictatorship, and we simply can't afford greater losses.

But when we come to the possible sequence of events, the loss of Indochina, of Burma, of Thailand, of the Peninsula, and Indonesia following, now you begin to talk about areas that not only multiply the disadvantages that you would suffer through loss of materials, sources of materials, but now you are talking really about millions and millions and millions of people.

Finally, the geographical position achieved thereby does many things. It turns the so-called island defensive chain of Japan, Formosa, of the Philippines and to the southward; it moves in to threaten Australia and New Zealand.

It takes away, in its economic aspects, that region that Japan must have as a trading area or Japan, in turn, will have only one place in the world to go—that is, toward the Communist areas in order to live.

So, the possible consequences of the loss are just incalculable to the free world.

*SOURCE: Public Papers of the Presidents,* Dwight D. Eisenhower, 1954 (Washington, DC: Office of the Federal Register, National Archives, 1960), pp. 382–383.

Persian Gulf in terms of restoring the sovereignty of Kuwait, an essential reason for the use of US military force was to halt Iraqi aggression that could have led to a takeover of oil fields throughout the region, including quite possibly Saudi Arabia, an American ally and a prime supplier of petroleum to the West. Many analysts believe that the First Persian Gulf War was more about oil than about liberty in Kuwait.[15]

In the twenty-first century, sweeping changes in transportation and communications, as well as faster means for delivering military strikes across national borders, have diminished the significance of geopolitical influences. Nevertheless, considerations of geography and natural resources continue to enter into the picture when the United States weighs its interests and options abroad. When an earthquake of 7.0 magnitude on the Richter scale hit nearby Haiti in 2010, Americans responded quickly to help. Since 2010, several devastating quakes have also plagued Pakistan and again Americans helped—though at a slower pace and with far less financial and personal involvement. Part of the reason for America's limited response in the Pakistani rescue activities had to do with Islamabad's restrictions on the presence of foreigners in the country—the issue of national sovereignty once more. Still, proximity matters in foreign affairs. Had Pakistan been a next door neighbor like Haiti, America's presence would have been easier and more substantial.

## Complex Interdependence

Some theorists underscore the importance of **complex interdependence** during the Cold War and globalization today: *the entire intricate range of interactions among modern nations*, which has made transnational forces ever more important. Globalization, facilitated by common worldwide transportation carriers and channels of communication, is evident in the business and economic sphere. The growth of multinational corporations has been dramatic, along with the movement of jobs offshore, increasingly interwoven commercial transactions across borders, and a shared concern about the rippling effects of recession and inflation around the globe. It is seen, as well, in cultural and academic exchanges that foster a rising sense of common identity among groups in different nations, such as Russian and American scientists issuing joint statements against nuclear weapons or the youth of the world united in devotion to the same rock bands, movie stars, hair styles, and fashion trends. It is seen further in the widespread concern around the planet about environmental hazards and the transmission of global diseases.

As long ago as 1970, political scientist (and later national security adviser to President Carter) Zbigniew Brzezinski observed that a "new pattern of international politics is emerging. . . . The world is ceasing to be an arena in which relatively self-sustained, 'sovereign,' and homogeneous nations interact, collaborate, clash, or make war. . . . Transnational ties are gaining in importance, while the claims of nationalism, though still intense, are nevertheless becoming diluted."[16] Globalization is not just about the weaving together of national economies around the world (Chapter 13); international television broadcasts and the Internet, as well as the "social media" consisting of blogs, twittering, text messaging, and social networking sites like Facebook, are also a central part of the trend toward international integration.

Television, for example, brought the Vietnam War into the lives of millions of Americans, who from the comfort of their homes viewed the slaughter with a growing revulsion in the 1960s and 1970s. Television also brought into their homes images of the peace marches in cities across the United States and the skeptical hearings on the Vietnam War held by the Senate Foreign Relations Committee in 1966, raising serious questions in the public mind about the wisdom of further involvement in this remote Asian battlefield. The pictures of combat that flickered across the TV screen revealed that America's enemies in Indochina—the North Vietnamese and their guerrilla allies in South Vietnam, known as the Viet Cong—were far stronger than the public had been led to believe by the Johnson administration. Television had clearly become an important foreign policy influence. "If there had been live television coverage of the [American] Civil War," political scientist Austin Ranney suggested, "it would have ended in 1862 with the establishment of the Confederacy, because it was a terribly bloody war and the North was losing most of the early part of it."[17]

Today, when suspected terrorists are apprehended in New York City, Washington, DC, Boston, or Detroit; when US Marines are killed in Iraq or Afghanistan; when an earthquake levels buildings in Haiti, Pakistan, New Zealand, or Turkey; and when crippled pelicans wash ashore in Louisiana drenched in oil from a broken rig in the Gulf, television, Internet news, blogs, text messaging, twittering, and e-mailing inform the public immediately, often with disturbing photographs and video footage. *The speed by which televised images of international events enter the White House Situation Room and other government offices, and well as living rooms across America*, is sometimes referred to as the **CNN effect**, stemming from the 24/7 coverage of world affairs by the Cable News Network.

Powerful media images from overseas can shape ("frame") debates about US foreign policy. When Americans view an injustice somewhere overseas via CNN or other television and Internet news sources—say, the self-immolation of the street vendor in December of 2010, which gave rise to the Arab Spring in Tunisia the next year, with unrest spreading to Egypt and elsewhere in the Middle East—their instinct may be to support US intervention abroad as a means for setting things right. This was the response when the first President Bush sent in troops to feed starving children in Somalia. Then the next set of powerful images may be of America's soldiers dying in the remote place they have been sent, at which point the instinct back in the United States may be to bring the soldiers home (as happened in Somalia and in Lebanon in 1983)—a pushing and pulling of American foreign policy driven by media images. Horrifying media images of regime brutality in Syria in 2012 and 2013 brought expressions of sympathy from Americans and their government; nevertheless, the Obama administration resisted sending direct military support to the insurgents in a setting that was much more complicated for the United States than the Libyan example had been, given Syria's close alliance with Russia and China, as well as the fact that many of the insurgents in Syria had ties to Al Qaeda and other terrorist organizations. The developments in Tunisia in 2010, the spread of the Arab Spring revolutions after that, and the murder of the US Ambassador J. Christopher Stevens in Libya in 2012 along with three of his companions are sobering reminders of how limited America—or any other country—is in controlling world events.

Journalist Diane Sawyer reports from Camp Phoenix in Kabul, Afghanistan, June 2011.

Often it is difficult to know how accurately the media images portray reality overseas, especially in battle zones where the Pentagon controls what reporters can see and report. The military may even manipulate images to conjure a more favorable view of the US war fighting. In the First Persian Gulf War (1991), for example, the Pentagon provided the media with videos of Patriot missiles that seemed to destroy every Iraqi target with great precision; only after the war, when more complete data were available, did it become clear that in reality the missiles frequently missed their designated targets. The American war dead from the recent conflicts in Iraq and Afghanistan battlefields have been flown home to the United States under the cover of darkness to conceal from reporters the number of causalities, just as occurred during the Vietnam War.

Nor are foreign events given much coverage by the US media today. Political scientist Steven W. Hook counted nearly four times as many newspaper articles on health care than on the war in Afghanistan in 2009.[18] Even when abundant and accurate news is available in the media about foreign events, surveys repeatedly find that Americans don't follow these events closely. Doris Graber, a leading media expert, writes that Americans "do not seek out foreign policy news."[19] In 2012, *Time* magazine correspondent Joe Klein reported as he traveled the Midwest that foreign policy was almost nonexistent as an issue in the presidential campaign, with the exception of some concern about China as a trading rival.[20] Rising health care costs and unemployment at home have a much more immediate effect on citizens than seemingly remote circumstances abroad, although thoughtful citizens realize that problems overseas can soon wash onto American shores as the 9/11 attacks tragically demonstrated.

Despite low media coverage of international events and conditions, television, the Internet, and social media nonetheless hold the potential for infusing a global population comprised of distant and untrustworthy strangers with *a strong sense of community in which the world becomes more of a neighborhood*—a **global village**, in media guru Marshall McLuhan's memorable description about the possible effects of TV on international affairs.[21] Some experts anticipate the nurturing of global understanding and cooperation through a worldwide emotional commitment to the same television programs, as well as to social media, soap operas, movies, athletic events, and rock concerts.[22] According to this perspective, world unity might evolve through a spreading visual awareness that human beings around the planet share much in common, from an interest in comedy, sports, music, and television drama to a love for their children and a yearning for peace. The Arab uprisings attracted an international television audience, and the insurgents seemed to draw courage from the fact that they were not alone in their hope for successful democratic reforms throughout the region.

According to media specialist Professor Larry Pintak of Washington State University, today's dissemination of news is often a "one-two punch." First come reports through the Internet and social media from various locations around the world. This reporting is then picked up by the traditional television network news and talk shows and transmitted around the globe. The postings of "citizen journalists" have added significantly to the media coverage of some dramatic events overseas, as when an

Iranian video of a young female protestor being killed by paramilitary troops went viral in 2009.[23]

Some "world order" scholars see in this growing global communion of citizens an opportunity for a **new world order**: *the evolution of an integrated international community that could replace the anarchy and warfare common to the current fragmented system of nations.* Their aspiration is to create fresh transnational loyalties and commitments that will eventually bring lasting peace to "spaceship earth." Others remain skeptical and emphasize the more likely endurance of global competition and strife among nations and factions. In between are groups with a hands-on, practical orientation—such as Amnesty International, Oxfam, and Human Rights Watch—that are in action around the world every day, trying to cope with global poverty and injustice. These groups are having an increasingly important influence on the dynamics of world politics.

## THE DOMESTIC SETTING

In addition to the international influences discussed previously, leaders and policy makers are obliged to deal with the pressures that arise from America's national political landscape. Here is a factor that makes American foreign policy unique, or at least unusual, among nations: the United States is blessed—or cursed—with a Constitution that deliberately fosters conflict as a means of preventing power from being concentrated dangerously in just one branch of government. Of special importance among the influences within the United States that affect foreign policy are the nation's historical experiences, the constitutional underpinnings of the polity, a spirit of exceptionalism that infused the rhetoric and actions of early Americans (and lingers on today), America's contemporary institutional arrangement for governance, and the pluralist politics of Washington, DC.

### The Mirror of the Past

The history of the United States in its relations with the rest of the world can be thought of as an ongoing experiment to determine the proper degree of involvement abroad—an experiment marked by a deep-seated sense of ambivalence. This country has alternated between two contradictory impulses: on one hand, **isolationism**, *a detachment from the affairs of other nations*, and on the other hand, **interventionism**, *attempts to influence the affairs of other nations, openly or secretly.* Though often unsure which of these two impulses would best serve the people's interests, the government of the United States leaned for the most part toward detachment from the world during its first 122 years. When it had to, the nation fought foreign powers, including Great Britain, France, the Barbary pirates, and Mexico (see Chapter 4). Not until 1898, however, with the Spanish-American War and territorial acquisitions as far away as the Philippines, did the United States emerge as an international power. Despite an escapist tendency in its early years, America has always been ready to accept assistance from friends overseas in times of military danger. The French, for instance, helped during the Revolutionary War; and in the modern era, the British strongly supported the US invasion of Iraq in 2003.

With the shock of World War II and the rise of the Soviet empire, most Americans concluded that a headlong retreat into isolationism—the nation's response during its early years and then again after World War I—would be a mistake. Nevertheless, public opinion surveys continue to indicate that many Americans still long "to be free from the wrangling world" (Thomas Paine's quaint phrase in 1776). For example, polling consistently reveals a United States sharply divided over the wisdom of further involvement in the war in Afghanistan; and, more recently, Americans have been strongly opposed to intervention in the Syrian fighting between government forces and antigovernment groups. Indeed, in 2013, 58 percent of Americans who responded to a *New York Times*/CBS News poll said no to the question "Should the United States take the leading role among all other countries in the world in trying to solve international conflicts?"[24] Nevertheless, in the decades since 1945, the United States has often intervened overseas, to curb the spread of communism during the Cold War and to fight brutal dictators or terrorists since the end of the Cold War. In sum, the United States since its very beginnings has oscillated between retreat from and involvement with the rest of the world, contradictory impulses that I examine further in Chapters 4, 5, and 6.

## Exceptionalism

Manifest destiny was an idea popular in the United States in the nineteenth century—the view that the United States had a clear mission: first, to conquer the Western territories of the frontier (Washington, DC's "foreign" policy toward Native Americans was to subdue them and take away their properties); and then to export this nation's blessings of democracy and Christianity to the (as yet) unenlightened backwaters of the world, beginning with the establishment of US hegemony in the Western Hemisphere. In a word, early Americans were driven by a sense of **exceptionalism**, *a belief in a mission to disperse this nation's values around the world*. America, many thought, had been looked on by God with special favor to save humanity by spreading this nation's ideals across the latitudes.[25] For Thomas Jefferson, the nation was "the last best hope of mankind." John Adams was sure the United States was "destined beyond a doubt to be the greatest power on earth." An American diplomat gazed toward China and envisioned Americans bringing to that colossus "a shining cross on every hill and in every valley."[26]

At the beginning of the twentieth century, one could continue to see America's pursuit of this mission to bring its brand of civilization to other parts of the world: to Cuba after the Spanish-American War, as well as to Puerto Rico, the Philippines, Hawaii, and other Pacific islands—a brief period of American colonialism, pursued by force when necessary. President Woodrow Wilson, one of the most conspicuous moralists to occupy the White House, was among those to advance the philosophy that the United States should help sow democracy around the world. "We shall fight . . . for the rights and liberties of small nations," he declared in a war message to Congress on the eve of America's entry into World War I in 1917. According to Wilson, the objective of the United States should be to "make the world safe for democracy." In 1940, Senator Kenneth S. Wherry (R-Nebraska) intoned, "With God's help, we will lift Shanghai up and up, ever up, until it is just like Kansas City." In World War II, a prime reason for America's entry into the fray was to assist Great Britain in its struggle against the totalitarian forces of Nazi Germany, a battle between democracy and tyranny, good and evil.

In the 1960s, President Lyndon B. Johnson viewed the sending of US troops to South Vietnam as an antidote to a communist-totalitarian assault from North Vietnam against a struggling democracy in the south—or, at any rate, a non-communist regime. As a college student writing in his campus newspaper, he had extolled the virtues of Wilson's crusade to spread democracy and now, as President, he was determined not to reward aggression with the same policy of appeasement that Prime Minister Chamberlain of Britain had naively offered Hitler. "We will stay until aggression has stopped," said President Johnson in 1966, "because in Asia and around the world are countries whose independence rests, in large measure, on confidence in America's word and in America's protection."[27] An influential member of the House of Representatives, Mendel Rivers (D), chairman of the Armed Services Committee during the Vietnam War, stated the matter in starker evangelical terms. For the South Carolinian, the global struggle between democracy and communism was nothing less than "a fight between Jesus Christ and the Hammer-and-Sickle."[28] This sense of global mission has not disappeared in more recent times. In the aftermath of the 9/11 attacks, for example, President George W. Bush declared, "We did not ask for this mission, but we will fulfill it . . . We defend not only our precious freedoms, but also the freedom of people everywhere to live and raise their children free from fear."[29]

## The Constitution

The blueprint for government drafted by the American founders has had a profound influence on the conduct of foreign policy as well. The venerable phrase usually invoked to describe this framework is the "**separation of powers**." Political scientist Richard E. Neustadt provided a more accurate description, however, based on the idea of **power sharing**. He depicted *American government as an array of separate institutions required by the Constitution to share authority and power.* Put another way, the *government of the United States distributes foreign (and domestic) policy powers, as well as the authority to use them, across three branches of government* and, within these branches, across a wide array of agencies, bureaus, courts, committees, and subcommittees (as examined further in Chapter 7). The power to make war or to approve treaties, for example, requires participation by both the legislative and executive branches. Article I gives Congress the power to declare war, yet Article II names the president as the commander-in-chief. Disputes between the two are periodically arbitrated by the judiciary. "We rely on the courts to enforce what the Constitution promises," Anthony Lewis of the *New York Times* once noted.[30]

When such powers are shared, tensions and ambiguities arise within the government. Who ultimately will assume the responsibility to commit the nation to war, or to enter into a binding agreement with another country? By spreading the authority for such decisions across governmental institutions, the Constitution pitted one branch against another—precisely what the most influential founders had in mind as a check against any one branch (especially the presidency) from becoming too strong and threatening. "Ambition must be made to counteract ambition," James Madison wrote in *Federalist Papers* No. 51. Although this sharing of authority had the virtue of keeping power under better control, this approach also carries with it a recipe for conflict and inefficiencies.

The Iran-*contra* scandal provides an extreme example of institutional conflict arising from the separation of powers. During the 1980s, in frustration over having to share foreign policy decision making with a recalcitrant Congress, officials in the Reagan administration chose to bypass the legislative branch altogether, the Constitution notwithstanding, when it came to US policies in Iran and Central America. The staff of the National Security Council (NSC) arranged secretly to sell missiles to Iran in exchange for its influence over the release of US hostages in Beirut. Further, the NSC staff used the profits from this sale to support the anti-Marxist *contras* in Nicaragua—even though covert action in Nicaragua had been prohibited by law (the Boland Amendment, named after its sponsor, Edward P. Boland, D, Massachusetts). To manage this sleight of hand foreign policy outside the purview of Congress and the American people, the NSC staff established a hidden organization known as "The Enterprise." It operated beyond the boundaries of the regular government in what one of the conspirators later described as "an off-the-shelf, stand-alone, self-sustaining" secret entity.[31] Article I, Section 8, of the Constitution lodges the power to spend in the hands of Congress, not the executive branch, let alone semiprivate organizations like "The Enterprise." The Reagan administration also violated the Hughes–Ryan Act of 1974, which requires reports to Congress on important covert actions. These violations of the law precipitated the Iran-*contra* scandal in 1987.

The clandestine machinations pursued by the NSC staff were a dangerous blow to constitutional government, carried out by misguided, self-professed patriots who, in the words of a leading Republican US Senator, Warren Rudman (New Hampshire), a participant in a bipartisan investigation of the affair, "wrapped themselves in the flag and go around spitting on the Constitution."[32] More recently, members of Congress criticized the Obama administration for using military force against Libya without proper congressional authorization. The War Powers Resolution of 1973 requires participation by lawmakers in decisions to use military force. The importance of a constitutionally based foreign policy is a core theme in this book and the struggle between the Congress and the Presidency over the war power is taken up in Chapter 11.

## Institutional Fragmentation

The constitutional idea of sharing authority across separated institutions means, in day-to-day policy making, that a great many entities and individuals have a say in deciding the ends and means of American foreign policy: whether this nation will tilt toward isolation or involvement in world affairs, and what instruments—dispatching diplomats, infiltrating spies, relying on foreign aid officials and trade negotiators, sending in the Marines—will be used in the pursuit of specific objectives. Some observers believe the institutional arrangements for foreign policy in the United States have led to excessive **institutional fragmentation**: *the dispersal of power too broadly across America's government.* Critics who are appalled by the involvement of Congress in foreign affairs complain about the 535 would-be secretaries of state on Capitol Hill; too many investigative subcommittees and congressional hearings, each carrying a heavy surcharge on the time of the real secretaries of State and Defense, as well as other officials appointed to key foreign policy posts by the president; and too many new statutes that require timely executive-branch reports to Congress on a vast array of plans and operations.

Others look upon the Constitution's insistence on legislative involvement in foreign affairs more positively. Those suspicious of power lodged too exclusively with the executive branch—the point of view adopted by the founders and in this book— complain about undue secrecy resorted to by presidents and bureaucrats as a means for concealing from Congress and the American people the faulty premises of misguided relations abroad. They complain, further, about slippery grants of authority passed from the White House to the CIA, the Department of Defense, and other agencies in an elusive shell game within the executive branch that prevents lawmakers—and even presidents—from tracking the formulation of policy. They lament, as well, attempts by the executive branch to detour around Capitol Hill by using groups outside the government as a means for achieving foreign policy goals—the illegal "Enterprise" during the 1980s, for example, and, in more recent years, various legal but often unaccountable private organizations to whom foreign policy is "outsourced." An illustration of the latter is the quasi-military North Carolina company initially known as Blackwater (later called Xe and now Academi), hired by the US government to provide security and assistance for secret operations in Iraq and Afghanistan.

The excessive friction and wear that result from too many movable parts in the policy-making machinery have become a sore point for opponents of Madisonian government. In Congress, a proliferation of subcommittees jostle over legislative jurisdiction and compete for the same witnesses from the executive branch for their hearings. Junior members of Congress sometimes travel abroad to barter with heads of state over policy while professional diplomats in the Department of State look on in bewilderment. Similarly, inside the executive branch, officials at times appear to be conducting their own foreign policies, not only beyond the purview of lawmakers but outside the supervision of the president as well. The bureaucracy is inclined to cherry-pick orders, obeying the ones it likes and ignoring the others, under the assumption that the president and lawmakers are too busy to check up on the implementation of policies. A recent example of the executive branch going its own way is the use of torture and extraordinary rendition by US intelligence officers against suspected terrorist detainees, without the knowledge of Congress and in violation of long-standing American norms.[33]

## Pluralist Politics

As if the institutional fragmentation of America's government were an insufficient complication, the nation also has an open, pluralist society that further diffuses the number of groups and individuals able to influence foreign policy decisions. The term **pluralism** is used to characterize *the existence of multiple centers of power* within the United States. These power centers are found not only within the government but across the wide land—a bewildering assortment of organizations of various stripes and colorations, some with strong foreign policy beliefs that they press on decision makers with marked success. Among the most prominent are the two major political parties, the Democrats and the Republicans, who frequently—and, since 1992, often shrilly—disagree with one another (and among themselves) on foreign policy objectives. Joining in the fray are interest or "pressure" groups, like the American-Israeli Public Affairs Committee (AIPAC); and occasional mass demonstrations, such as the anti-Vietnam War protests of the 1960s or the "nuclear freeze" movement of the 1980s that called for a cessation of nuclear-weapons production and fielded even larger crowds than recorded during the era of Vietnam dissent.

Critics argue that the influence of these power centers has become too great, as they provide campaign funds to officeholders in exchange for favorable foreign policy decisions. According to this argument, *the number of power centers has become excessively large, leading to policy gridlock in Washington, DC*—a condition sometimes referred to as **hyperpluralism**. Coming on top of the proliferating number of official government agencies involved in foreign policy, the accumulation of influential outside groups and organizations raises the danger of institutional paralysis. I explore the merits of this view—that the nation suffers frequently from foreign policy deadlock—in Chapter 7.

## THE IMPORTANCE OF THE INDIVIDUAL DECISION MAKER

The acclaimed American diplomat George F. Kennan lamented in 1951 that foreign policy scholarship had been distorted by an "underestimation of psychological and political reactions —of such things as fear, ambition, insecurity, jealousy, and perhaps even boredom—as prime movers of events."[34] In a similar vein, some twenty-five years later a seasoned Washington reporter wrote in reference to Congress that "the central truth about this place is that the chairman—whoever he is—of the committee—never mind which one—did not do that thing strictly and clearly for some ideological or partisan purpose. Five will get you ten that there was also at play a personal ambition, a head cold, a desire to catch a plane, a trade-off, a girl—or some combination of all the above."[35]

Influences of this kind are difficult, indeed often impossible, for researchers to discern or document. The tendency in academic circles is simply to assume the existence of clearheaded decision makers working together in harness, engaged in dispassionate analysis, with access to perfect or near-perfect information. Yet, the emotions, personal idiosyncrasies, distorted or false information, and other psychological vulnerabilities of individuals in high office also play a part in the making of foreign policy. They can hardly be ignored, even if they are difficult to research and understand. Some of these influences are discussed below.

### Role-Playing

The core idea behind the concept of **role-playing** is that *the particular type of office occupied by a decision maker will cause him or her to hold and implement views traditional to that office.* Illustrations of the interplay between the office and the officeholder are widespread. If you were a dogcatcher, for instance, you would probably believe that the streets should be cleared of all unrestrained hounds. If you were in the business of catching foreign spies (counterintelligence), most likely you would have a highly negative view toward policies that permitted an increase in US ports of call by Russian and Chinese ships, with their numerous "sailor" spies on board; or policies that allowed an increase in the number of Russian and Chinese "diplomats"—many of whom are actually intelligence officers—permitted to serve in Washington, DC, or at UN headquarters in New York City. An experienced government official once bemoaned the way in which role-playing engenders a "curator mentality" at the Department of State. According to this critique, when State Department officials inherit the job of a country desk officer, they are expected to keep existing US policy toward that particular foreign nation intact, just as they find it—regardless of their personal views and expertise—carefully protected "under glass, untampered with, and dusted," as if the officials were little more than museum curators.[36]

The nature of a given office, coupled with peer expectations about how the job ought to be managed, become critical influences on foreign policy behavior. As Senator Hubert H. Humphrey (who served in the Senate before and after his position as Vice President in the Johnson administration) liked to say, "How one stands depends upon where one sits."[37] Role-playing is hardly an infallible predictor of how officials will act, though. During the Reagan administration, for example, the Department of State often advocated military intervention to achieve US goals, while the Department of Defense—stung by defeat in Vietnam less than a decade earlier—was apt to encourage a diplomatic approach to America's problems abroad. During the Obama administration, Secretary of Defense Robert M. Gates extolled the virtues of having a stronger Department of State, along with more of an emphasis by the United States on diplomacy instead of military force.

### Past Experience

Skill in a job usually depends on **prior experience**: *the training one has had for a foreign policy job.* Those who value a professional diplomatic corps maintain that the skills needed for the effective conduct of foreign policy through negotiations require special training. "The art of diplomacy, as that of watercolors, has suffered much from the fascination which it exercises upon the amateur," wryly observed the seasoned British diplomat Harold Nicolson.[38]

Such criticism notwithstanding, the United States has often sent abroad to key foreign countries neophyte ambassadors who have not had the benefit of rising through the State Department Foreign Service and developing expertise over the years, but rather are political appointees selected by a president because of partisan connections. Often such people are chosen as a reward for fund-raising in the presidential election. One study of US diplomatic delegations concluded that major posts are sometimes filled overseas with Americans "trained in such dubiously relevant specialties as manu-facturing, scientific research, teaching, singing, or organizing civil clubs."[39] President George W. Bush's appointee as ambassador to Austria spoke no German; President Obama's ambassador to Japan, a wealthy California industrialist and presidential fund-raiser, spoke no Japanese. Neither knew much about the history and culture of their respective assignments overseas before being selected. The United States has had fewer professionals rise to the rank of ambassador and more inexperienced political appointees at this level than any other democracy.[40]

The clash between diplomatic **professionals** and **amateurs**—*long-term careerists versus temporary "in-and-outers" (academicians, businesspeople, military personnel) who serve for only a few years before returning to their previous jobs*—has produced additional friction in foreign policy planning. The careerist diplomat brings to decision councils a longer time perspective on America's relations with other nations, as well as the training to analyze foreign policy disputes dispassionately and, for better or worse, a tendency to maintain the status quo (the curator phenomenon). Temporary political appointees, in contrast, are frequently guided by the political and ideological perspectives of the president and the White House staff, and they have a short-term time perspective and seek to achieve results before the president's term expires.

Commenting on the coming and going of amateurs in high positions throughout the government, political scientist Hugh Heclo suggested that policy making in the United States often resembles "a sandlot pick-up game, with a variety of strangers, strategies, and misunderstandings."[41] America's allies have expressed confusion over this ebb and flow of policy officials, with the disjointedness it lends to this nation's international affairs. Other nations are more accustomed to leaving foreign policy to the "pros"—the professional diplomats.

The place of the amateur in American foreign policy has its defenders, though. "The executive branch of our government is populated with specialists and experts," argued a chairman of the Senate Foreign Relations Committee. He continued:

> These men [sic] have added greatly to the government's skill in conducting foreign relations, but they have also shown a certain arrogance, purveying the notion that anyone who is not an expert, including Congressmen, Senators, and ordinary citizens, is simply too uninformed to grasp the complexities of foreign policy. . . .

> This view is patently false. Clemenceau said that war was too important
> to be left to the generals; similarly, the basic decisions of foreign
> policy are too important to be left to the diplomats.[42]

In the same spirit, the historian Ruhl Bartlett concluded that "there are no experts in wisdom concerning human affairs or in determining the national interest, and there is nothing in the realm of foreign policy that cannot be understood by the average American citizen."[43]

Amateurs present another advantage from the perspective of the White House: presidents often like to place trusted friends and political allies at the controls of the bureaucracy to ensure the policies preferred by the president are honored and carried out by Washington's "permanent government"—the bureaucracy. Individual bureaucrats enjoy strong ties on Capitol Hill and among interest groups. In a 1971 Senate hearing, former Secretary of Health, Education, and Welfare John W. Gardner commented on these **iron triangles** (or subgovernments)—*an unofficial permanent government composed of interest groups, bureaucrats, and lawmakers* that has frustrated many a president of both parties:

> Questions of public policy . . . are often decided by a trinity consisting
> of (1) representatives of an outside body [interest groups], (2) middle
> level bureaucrats, and (3) selected members of Congress, particularly
> those concerned with appropriations. In a given field these people
> have collaborated for years. They have a durable alliance that cranks
> out legislation and appropriations on behalf of their special interests.
> Participants in such durable alliances do not want the department
> secretaries strengthened.[44]

The hopes and plans of individual decision makers at lofty perches within the executive branch—department secretaries, agency directors, even presidents—are frequently dashed in the national political arena by the counterforces of these enduring iron triangles.

## Distorted Perceptions

As psychologists have long understood, how one perceives reality can be more important than reality itself. Foreign policy officials have often erred because of **distorted perceptions**: *a failure to accurately comprehend events and conditions in the world* around them. This happened to politicians—and even intelligence professionals—during the second Bush administration, with their misperceptions about the likely presence of WMDs in Iraq. Three important agencies in the US intelligence community (the Bureau of Intelligence and Research in the State Department, the US Air Force, and the Energy Department) prepared reports that questioned the likelihood of WMDs in that nation; yet the president never examined these reports or invited representatives of these agencies to the Oval Office before making his decision to launch an invasion of Iraq in 2003.[45] A variety of psychological orientations contribute to this common pathology of the policy process, including the following problems.

### Self-delusion

One important source of misperception is **self-delusion**, as officials *brush aside or bend facts that fail to conform to their preconceived worldview.* Looking back at the critical years 1964 and 1965 in the escalation of the Vietnam War, a high-ranking American intelligence officer rued the fact that "the policymakers did not better exercise their own power to listen," because the evidence against a quick US victory in Indochina was readily available and compelling—but ignored.[46] A former chief of CIA analysis, Dr. Ray S. Cline, remembered that by 1966 American policy makers started to "lose interest in an objective description of the outside world and were beginning to scramble for evidence that they were going to win the war in Vietnam." By 1969, Cline recalled, the pathology had reached disease proportions, lasting through 1974, when "there was almost total dissent from the real world around us."[47]

### Leadership isolation

Sometimes *leaders are cut off from reality because they are removed from vigorous debate and outside opinions.* A clear example of **leadership isolation** occurred in the lead-up to the Bay of Pigs disaster under President John F. Kennedy. Before the CIA's secret invasion of Cuba in 1961, Agency analysts (as opposed to its operatives) expressed skepticism in their reports about the possibility of overthrowing Fidel Castro. The Cuban leader was "likely to grow stronger rather than weaker as time goes by," summed up a top-secret CIA Estimate prepared for the Agency's director at the time. The study warned that Castro "now has established a formidable structure of control over the daily lives of the Cuban people."[48]

President Kenney evidently neither saw this study nor spoke with a single CIA analyst about the Bay of Pigs invasion plans. Ambitious, persuasive, a member of the Georgetown set that dined privately with the President and sailed with him on Chesapeake Bay, Richard M. Bissell Jr., the CIA operations officer in charge of the covert action to invade Cuba, assured Kennedy that Castro could be easily removed by a swift paramilitary action. This was happy news for the moment, but the advice proved disastrously wrong. The Agency invaders, mostly Cuban exiles, were quickly defeated as they landed at the Bay of Pigs. A trained analyst from the CIA—or from the Department of State, whose Cuban specialists were also excluded from the NSC and CIA planning sessions—would have warned the President about Castro's deeply entrenched power and that, among other things, the envisioned escape route through the Escambray Mountains after the invasion was blocked by the impenetrable marshlands of the Zapata Swamp.[49]

### Groupthink

Moreover, reality can be distorted within the individual mind by a phenomenon of interaction displayed by small groups, labeled **groupthink** by Yale University psychologist Irving L. Janis. Groupthink refers to *a tendency for individuals in some groups to cast aside a realistic appraisal of alternative courses of action in favor of high cohesiveness among the group's members.* It becomes more important for members to conform to group expectations—peer-group pressure—than it is to be correct. On the basis of his study of the Bay of Pigs invasion, Janis concluded that "the failure of [President] Kennedy's inner circle to detect any of the false assumptions behind the Bay of Pigs invasion plan can be at least partially accounted for by the group's tendency to seek concurrence at the expense of seeking information, critical appraisal, and debate."[50]

This concurrence seeking works against openness in decision making. An organizational expert commented on this tendency within the government's intelligence agencies during the Cold War years. "Like other bureaucrats, intelligence analysts have to conform to the regime's basic views, about the nature and morality of international relations, if they wish to be treated as 'responsible' and 'serious,'" the expert suggested. "Therefore, they refrain from asking the really 'tough' but crucial questions [about] the aggressiveness of the Soviet Union, the morality of the Vietnam War, and the validity of the 'domino theory.'"[51] A lack of opinion diversity (a desirable "competitive intelligence") can lead to unfortunate results, as organizations drift farther and farther away from the moorings of reality.

### Executive fatigue

The higher up the organizational ladder, the more harried an official is apt to be. This condition can have an effect on perceptions as well. A secretary of defense in the Reagan administration was reportedly "swamped," "overwhelmed," "left with not enough time to think forward."[52] Similarly, a study of American policy makers during the war in Vietnam pointed to **executive fatigue** as a significant influence on decision making. Fatigue, resulting from too many responsibilities and not enough time to carry them out, has *a deadening effect on "freshness of thought, imagination, a sense of possibility and perspective* . . . The tired policymaker becomes a prisoner of his own narrowed view of the world and his own clichéd rhetoric."[53]

### Character

*A policy maker's basic personality traits,* his or her **character** as evolved from childhood, can also have a profound, if often subtle, influence on foreign policy decisions. One study reports, for instance, that a willingness of some individuals in high office to use military force as a policy option is tied to their "high-dominance" personalities. Individuals with this type of personality insist on "running the show," imposing their will forcefully on subordinates, berating them, and often ignoring them altogether as they set policy directions by themselves. One might contrast the aggressive and curt behavior of Henry Kissinger against the more affable and passive William P. Rogers, both of whom served as secretary of state for President Nixon.[54]

This book offers these glimpses into the importance of the individual in foreign policy only to suggest the many pressures that come to play on officeholders, which sometimes undermine their capacity to cope rationally and realistically with foreign policy challenges. The linkages between policy and psychology remain murky, in part because systematic research on this relationship is still in its infancy (see Chapter 8).

For day in, day out policy making, the effect of the individual decision maker on foreign policy is likely to be less significant than institutional fragmentation and bureaucratic bargaining. As political scientist Fred I. Greenstein has noted, though, under certain conditions individual personality traits may become quite important, as when a person in a position of authority faces ambiguous, novel, complex, or contradictory situations.[55] The student of foreign affairs who ignores or rejects these influences of the mind risks the danger of overlooking strong undercurrents in the shaping of America's relations abroad.

## SUMMARY

American foreign policy can be understood by way of a three-part framework. As US officials determine their grand strategy objectives (ends) and consider what instruments (means) to adopt for their fulfillment, they confront many obstacles in three domains: in the world, at home, and within their own minds.

On the international setting, the nation's goals may be affected at one time or another by the influences of, among other forces, balance of power considerations, geography and geopolitics, and the growing trend toward interdependence and globalization.

A second category of influences flows from America's own history and traditions—the domestic setting. These influences include the Constitution and laws, which often pit the Congress against the executive branch for control over the direction of foreign policy; an exceptionalist zeal that can turn foreign policy into a crusade; the large number of institutions involved in the conduct of international relations, leading to friction and a certain amount of disjointedness; and the wide range of interest groups in American society, many of which attempt to mold the country's international dealings to advance their own self-interest.

Finally, within the setting of the individual decision maker, one finds such forces at work as role-playing; the effects of past experience and the lack thereof; and psychological distortions such as misperception, isolation, groupthink, and fatigue. All of these influences can result in an undermining of rational decision making. American foreign policy is more than global interactions and domestic politics; at the leadership level, it can involve internal battles of the psyche as well.

The founders of the United States did not wish this country to fall easily into war, treaty commitments, or other foreign entanglements. That is why they shared the powers for war and diplomacy, among others, between the Congress and the president.

The pursuit of America's foreign policy is complex not only because the modern world is intricate but because the founders intentionally designed a government in which powers would be checked and used only after thorough deliberation by the legislative and executive branches working together, with further arbitration when necessary by the judicial branch.

Did this early fear of centralized authority—a concern reinforced in the modern era by the experiences of the Vietnam War, Watergate, CIA domestic spying, and the Iran-*contra* scandal—lead to an excessive fragmentation of control over the instruments of American foreign policy? If Madisonianism is a shorthand term for dispersing power in a political system as a guard against tyranny, has this approach to governance run amok? Can the United States maintain its unique form of democracy and still compete successfully in a world of more hierarchically organized and tightly disciplined authoritarian adversaries? A central question throughout this book is whether, in the face of grave dangers from abroad, the constitutional arrangements designed more than 225 years ago in an era of schooners and covered wagons can continue to serve the purposes of this nation in an age of nuclear weapons and ruthless terrorists.

## KEY TERMS

American foreign policy p. 43
balance of power p. 43
character p. 62
CNN effect p. 50
complex interdependence p. 49
distorted perceptions p. 60
domino theory p. 47
empire p. 43
exceptionalism p. 53
executive fatigue p. 62
geopolitics p. 46
global village p. 51
groupthink p. 62
hegemon p. 43
hyperpluralism p. 57

institutional fragmentation p. 56
interventionism p. 52
iron triangles p. 60
isolationism p. 52
leadership isolation p. 61
nation p. 42
new world order p. 52
pluralism p. 57
power sharing p. 54
prior experience p. 58
professionals and amateurs p. 59
role-playing p. 58
self-delusion p. 61
separation of powers p. 54
sovereignty p. 42

## QUESTIONS FOR DISCUSSION

1. On the basis of your knowledge of a significant foreign policy decision—say, the Cuban missile crisis of 1962, the escalation of the war in Vietnam in 1965, the US invasion of Iraq in 2003, or America's recent war fighting in Afghanistan—how would you explain what happened using the framework for foreign policy analysis presented in this chapter?

2. Did the sudden demise of the Soviet Union in 1990 accelerate or retard the growth of "complex interdependence"? Is this "globalization" likely to facilitate, or set back, harmony among nations? Is the world today more or less dangerous for the United States than during the years of the Cold War? Is the United States a hegemonic power?

3. How would you contrast the statements by Presidents Truman and Eisenhower in the *Perspectives on American Foreign Policy* presented in this chapter? How do they compare with recent foreign policy remarks and actions by President Obama?

4. How well does the word "anarchy" describe the world as it is today?

## ADDITIONAL READINGS

Brzezinski, Zbigniew. *Strategic Vision: America and the Crisis of Global Power*. New York: Basic Books, 2012.

Shultz, George P. *Turmoil and Triumph: Diplomacy, Power, and the Victory of the American Ideal*. New York: Scribner's, 1993.

Waltz, Kenneth N. *Man, the State, and War*. New York: Columbia University Press, 1954.

For further readings, please visit the book's companion website.

### CHAPTER 3

# A Constitutional Framework for American Foreign Policy

### CONFLICT OVER PRESIDENTIAL WAR POWERS

In August of 1990, Iraq invaded and annexed the adjacent small but strategically important Persian Gulf state of Kuwait. In response, the George H. W. Bush administration rallied a UN coalition force prepared to oust the Iraqi occupiers and liberate Kuwait. During the crisis, the President made questionable assertions about his war-making authority, fluctuating from claims of inherent presidential war powers all the way to reliance on a UN grant of presidential authority for war making.

The painting *Signing the Constitution of the United States*, by Thomas Pritchard Rossiter.

Senate Armed Services Committee Chairman Sam Nunn (D-Georgia) held hearings into the danger of a wider war erupting in the Middle East. He expressed concern that the Bush administration was rushing toward military intervention when economic sanctions might achieve the same goal. Just as Congress began to rally behind Nunn's doubts about the President's use of the war power, the UN Security Council passed Resolution 678, which authorized the United States and other members of the anti-Iraq coalition to use "all necessary means" against the regime of Saddam Hussein if the Iraqi leader failed to remove his army from Kuwait by January 15, 1991. Unimpressed by this UN declaration, some lawmakers insisted that Congress—not the United Nations—would have to give its "affirmative approval" before the President could launch an attack against the Iraqi troops. The Nunn position in favor of sanctions first, then force later (if necessary), gathered increasing steam in both legislative chambers.

Within days, the congressional debate on Kuwait reached the decisive arenas: the floors of the House and the Senate. The President had forced the issue by sending Congress a letter, dated January 8, 1991, in which he asked for a resolution of support to repel the Iraqi aggressors by force of arms. With the passage of UN Resolution 678,

**LEARNING OBJECTIVES AND CONSTITUTIONAL ISSUES**

**By the end of this chapter, you will be able to:**

- List several key points of contention between the branches of government in the conduct of foreign policy.
- Describe the evolution of the use of the war power by the executive branch.
- Describe the evolution of the use of the treaty power by the executive branch.
- Explain why Congress relinquished much of its constitutional authority over foreign policy—until the 1970s.
- Identify attempts by lawmakers to regain these lost powers.

**THIS CHAPTER RAISES THE FOLLOWING CONSTITUTIONAL QUESTIONS:**

- The Constitution shares powers for war making between the executive and legislative branches. Is Congress too cumbersome a body to handle decisions concerning when the United States should use military force?
- What virtues, if any, does Congress bring to the table in debates over the use of military force abroad?
- Should Congress still have a role to play in treaty making and other diplomatic activities, or are lawmakers insufficiently expert in international negotiations to participate effectively in this process?
- What stirred lawmakers to restore an institutional balance in the making of foreign policy during the 1970s?
- What recourses are available to members of Congress who believe that a president has overreached his (or, one day, her) authority in foreign policy?

Bush informed Congress that he did not really need congressional authorization to act. His letter, he underscored, was more of a courtesy to lawmakers than a requirement. Behind the scenes, the President's aides also referred lawmakers to the "inherent" war powers of the commander in chief, supposedly lodged in Article II, Section 2, of the Constitution. A trio of congressional resolutions soon materialized: one backing the President and Resolution 678, and two variations of Senator Nunn's antiwar, pro-sanctions stance. In the ensuing floor action on the resolutions, some lawmakers endorsed the notion that the president should be trusted to make the right decisions, as one lawmaker put it, in "matters of our national security and relations with other nations." In rebuttal, others argued for caution and restraint: sanctions first, and war later only if necessary—and if authorized by Congress.

On January 21, 1991, lawmakers delivered their verdict. The House sided with the President by a lopsided margin of 250-to-182. So did the Senate, but by a much closer vote of 52-to-47—a rare defeat for Senator Nunn on a debate about military affairs. Two days later, President Bush signed the joint resolution that, in essence, authorized him to use military force as he saw fit. The military, however, was already in action: on January 17, two days past the UN deadline imposed on Iraq to withdraw its troops from Kuwait and with no sign of an Iraqi retreat, Bush had ordered a ferocious airborne US-UN counterattack against the Iraqi occupation army in Kuwait and targets throughout Iraq that lasted five weeks, including heavy bombing of Baghdad. On February 23, the allied ground counterattack began. It quickly routed the Iraqi troops from Kuwait. The enemy fled back to Baghdad and, after a four-day ground war with only 148 US battlefield deaths, President Bush declared victory on February 27. He called for a halt of the American advance short of the Iraqi capital, rather than being accused by world opinion of piling on a defeated enemy. Besides, the UN mandate did not include a regime change in Baghdad, nor had the coalition (whose members included the Arab nations of Egypt and Syria) signed on for a regime change. The purpose was to punish Iraq for its violation of internationally recognized borders by invading Kuwait. That purpose had been achieved. The war was over, but not the debate about the President's claim of a constitutional—and even a UN-backed—right to initiate warfare, with or without congressional approval. ⁓

## SHARED POWERS

As described in the opening chapters of this book, the US government consists of separate institutions sharing power. America's early leaders were "imbued with antipower values."[1] Their central philosophical point is worth reiterating: by distributing power across institutions, they hoped to limit its potential for abuse. With responsibilities and prerogatives spread across the executive, legislative, and judicial branches of government, the constitutional framers reasoned that no branch would grow so mighty as to dwarf the others or dictate to the American people.

Justice Louis Brandeis eloquently expressed the spirit of the American founders in a case that came before the Supreme Court in 1926:

> The doctrine of the separation of powers was adopted by the [Constitutional] Convention of 1787, not to promote efficiency but to preclude the exercise of arbitrary power. The purpose was, not to avoid friction, but by means of the inevitable friction incident to the distribution of governmental powers among three departments, to save the people from autocracy.[2]

The absence of language in the Constitution that gives the judiciary an explicit role in foreign policy has encouraged the courts to abstain from this domain most of the time, deferring to the executive and legislative branches. As a consequence, the foreign policy battleground in the founding document essentially involves two political branches: Congress and the presidency—especially with respect to the war power—and thus they are the focus of this chapter.[3]

From time to time, though, the judiciary has handed down decisions that have had a strong bearing on the conduct of US foreign policy. One of the most widely discussed cases is *United States v. Curtiss-Wright Export Corp.* (233 U.S. 304), decided in 1936. This case involved a question about the constitutionality of a joint resolution authorizing President Franklin D. Roosevelt to halt the sale of arms to Bolivia and Paraguay, if he found that it would contribute to peace between these nations. An opinion in the case written by Justice George Sutherland advanced the notion that the president was the "sole organ" of American foreign policy. This "doctrine" has been thoroughly debunked, however, by scholars who point out that Sutherland drew on—and badly misconstrued—an argument presented by an earlier Supreme Court Justice, John Marshall, in a speech given in 1800. Marshall did say that "the President is the sole organ of the nation in its external relations, and its sole representative with foreign nations." He never promoted the view, however, that the president had inherent, plenary, exclusive, or independent powers; rather, Marshall was merely stating that the president is the rightful person to *communicate* to foreign powers—but certainly not to formulate or develop policy on his own, as Sutherland twisted the meaning of Marshall's words to mean. Sutherland's opinion in 1936 implied far more than Marshall intended.

Nevertheless, Sutherland's misinterpretations have been embraced by those seeking to aggrandize the powers of the American presidency. During the Iran-*contra* hearings, for example, the conspirators behind the scandal pointed to the *Curtiss-Wright* case as a justification for bypassing the congressional appropriations process. More recently, the Justice Department during the second Bush administration attempted to justify its violation of a wiretap law requiring judicial warrants for national security wiretaps (the Foreign Intelligence Surveillance Act of 1978) by referring to Southerland's views. The activities of the National Security Agency (NSA, which conducts national security wiretaps) were, the Department opined, "supported by the President's well-recognized inherent constitutional authority as Commander in Chief and sole organ for the Nation in foreign affairs." This same idea provided shelter, as well, for the administration's involvement in the extraordinary rendition program that kidnapped suspected terrorists and delivered them to foreign countries for interrogation that often included torture. In other recent cases, the courts have usually bowed down to the so-called state secrets privilege, evoked by the second Bush and the Obama administrations to convince judges that they should disallow court proceedings on supposedly sensitive national security cases. As Louis Fisher points out, this passivity by the courts has had the effect of rendering the judicial branch "largely supine" as a check against abuses of power by the executive branch.[4]

James Madison noted when he presented the Bill of Rights to Congress that the role of the courts would be to serve as "guardians" of the Bill of Rights and as an "impenetrable bulwark" against abuses of power by the other branches of government.[5] As examined later in this book, sometimes the courts have intervened as bulwarks against abuse (as in the Supreme Court "Prize Cases" of 1892 and the *Youngstown v. Sawyer* case of 1952, both of which reasserted the right of Congress, not the executive branch, to initiate war); but on other occasions, often in more recent war-power disputes, the courts have normally opted to stay out of conflicts between lawmakers and the executive branch.[6]

"The greatest insight of our Founding Fathers," concluded a member of the Senate Foreign Relations Committee during the Vietnam War era, "was their recognition of the dangers of unlimited power exercised by a single man or institution. Their greatest achievement was the safeguards against absolute power which they wrote into our Constitution."[7] But how could one coordinate and integrate these intentionally dispersed units of government, each with formidable powers? Would separate entities really share power and work together for the good of the nation? The answers remained in doubt, particularly because the very Constitution that gave the three branches their authority presented—with all of its silences and ambiguities—"an invitation to struggle," in Professor Edward S. Corwin's memorable phrase.[8]

A well-known example of silences and ambiguities comes in Article II, Section 2, of the founding document, which discusses the role of the president as commander in chief (see the Appendix for key portions of the Constitution related to foreign policy). Left largely unstated is a precise understanding of how extensive the president's powers should be when it comes to war making. A reading of the constitutional drafting notes and correspondence among the founders, though, provides insights into their intent. They wanted the president to serve as the manager of wars that had been first approved by lawmakers in Congress. Political scientist David Gray Adler writes, "The Constitutional Convention severed the authority to decide for war [the responsibility of Congress] from the power to conduct it [the responsibility of the executive branch]."[9] Both branches generally accepted this prescription throughout most of the nation's history, but presidents began to interpret their war powers more expansively beginning with the administration of Franklin D. Roosevelt in the early 1940s.[10]

Those who drafted the Constitution were prudent to concern themselves with the dangers of concentrated power. Few observers of history would deny the truth of **Lord Acton**'s aphorism concerning power: *"Power corrupts, and absolute power corrupts absolutely."*[11] Reflecting on the challenge facing America's founders, Edward A. Kolodziej observed, "An effective and legitimate central government had to be strong enough to deter and defend against external depredations, yet be limited in its power to preclude the tyranny of its own people."[12]

In their headlong flight from tyranny, however, had the founders embraced another serious threat to democracy: an institutional paralysis resulting from a government that was overly fragmented and prone to deadlock? If at one end of a power continuum stood the dangers of absolute power, at the other end stood anarchy. My purpose in this chapter is to examine the foreign policy strains that have evolved from this constitutional blueprint devised by America's early leaders. At the heart of this chapter, and indeed the entire book, is the question of governability: Do America's institutions permit the making of sound foreign policy decisions? Can collaborative government work, especially when dealing with the often tangled and perilous challenges of international affairs?

Sometimes the institutions of American government appear to be chaotic and unmanageable. "The executive branch," observed presidential scholar Grant McConnell in 1967, "is so divided, so fragmented, and its parts are often so autonomous that the President's power of command over them is often little more than a fiction."[13] Have the precautions against the abuse of power adopted by the founders led to a government that, more than two centuries later, lacks sufficient centralized authority to react to contemporary global threats with requisite speed and coherence? Or are the concerns and remedies of the nation's founders with respect to safeguarding against the abuse of power as valid today as they were in the eighteenth century?

To explore these vital questions, in this chapter I probe into the challenges associated with power sharing between Congress and the executive branch, especially with respect to the use of military force (the war power) and the making of international agreements (the treaty power—diplomacy). These two instruments of foreign policy have produced the most friction between the branches, as different parts of the government have gone about interpreting their constitutional responsibilities in different ways. First, though, in the chapter, I look broadly at the Constitution's foreign policy provisions.

## FOREIGN POLICY AND THE CONSTITUTION

Although the phrases "foreign policy" or "foreign affairs" appear nowhere in the Constitution, America's founding document does spell out the basic authorities of the president and the Congress in carrying forth the nation's responsibilities in international relations. The president's powers are addressed in Article II, Section 2. They are relatively meager. "The Executive Power shall be vested in a President," states this Article, and "he shall take Care that the Laws be faithfully executed." The president has the authority to make treaties, but these international agreements have to be based on the "Advice and Consent of the Senate" and approved by two-thirds of the senators present and voting. Further, the president can appoint US ambassadors, as well as "receive Ambassadors and other public Ministers" from other countries; but this remains a rather limited duty, except when controversy brews over whether a new nation should be officially recognized by the United States.

More empowering was the president's designation as "Commander in Chief of the Army and Navy of the United States." It was up to Congress, however, "To provide for the common Defense . . . To declare War . . . To Raise and support Armies . . . To provide and maintain a Navy." As a leading constitutional authority has noted, "Nothing in the text or in the history of its promulgation suggests that the Commander in Chief was to have authority to deploy the armed forces for political purposes determined by him."[14]

The Constitution spells out the powers of the legislative branch chiefly in Article I. Preeminent among them is the power of the purse: "No money shall be drawn from the Treasury, but in Consequence of Appropriations made by Law." The president is unable, constitutionally, to spend one thin dime without a congressional authorization and appropriation. If lawmakers wish to curb a presidential action, they can withhold funding. Further, they have the authority to remove a president from office by impeachment. Congress was also expected to "To regulate commerce with foreign nations," and to "make all Laws which shall be necessary and proper."

Much has changed in the world since the writing of the Constitution in Philadelphia. The American government now has a mammoth bureaucracy; Congress has grown into a complicated warren of committees and subcommittees, each with its own staff. The United States has expanded vastly, both in territory and population; and scores of new nations have come into existence. Weapons of mass destruction have been invented. News now travels at near lightning speed, as do missiles and stealth bombers. Humanity has been faced with global wars, numerous smaller wars, a great depression, and periodic worldwide recessions. Throughout these changes, though, one principle has remained constant: in a constitutional government, important decisions are supposed to rest on the consent of both the legislature and the president, each democratically elected by the nation's citizens. This principle has been sorely tested with respect to the contentious issues of war making and treaty making.[15]

## THE WAR POWER

The Constitution divides the treaty power (discussed later) equally between the executive and legislative branches. In contrast, the war power—defined in Chapter 1 as the actual or potential use of overt military force in the conduct of foreign policy—is lodged primarily in the hands of lawmakers (Article I, Section 8).[16] It is here that the founders gave Congress the right to declare war; to raise and support armies; to provide and maintain a navy; to make rules for the government and regulation of the armed forces; to provide for calling forth the militia to execute the laws, suppress insurrections, and repel invasions; to provide for the organizing, arming, and disciplining of the militia; and to make all laws necessary and proper for executing the foregoing powers. Only subsequently, in Article II, Section 2, did the authors of the Constitution address the role of the executive during war, designating the president as commander in chief.

The founders were more concerned about the war power than any other constitutional provision. As colonists, they had viewed with great alarm how easily King George III could commit Great Britain—and, therefore, the American colonies—to war. In the new Republic, James Madison and most of his colleagues were determined to remove the momentous decision of war making from the dictates of a single individual. Even Alexander Hamilton, a champion of executive power, remained wary of concentrating the war making authority into the hands of one person. In *The Federalist Papers,* Hamilton wrote:

> The President is to be commander in chief of the army and navy
> of the United States. In this respect his authority would be nominally
> the same with that of the king of Great Britain, but in substance
> much inferior to it. It would amount to nothing more than the
> supreme command and direction of the military and naval forces, as
> first General and Admiral of the Confederacy, while that of the British
> king extends the *declaring* of war and to the *raising* and *regulating*
> of fleets and armies—all which, by the Constitution under consideration would appear to the legislature.[17]

The Constitutional framers worried further that the widespread predisposition toward monarchy throughout the world was a malady that might afflict their own nation. The prospect of a large standing army in America, with its potential for military defiance of republican rule, troubled them deeply. They had no interest in turning over the weapons of war to the discretion of a solitary leader, even someone as admired as George Washington. It would be wiser, they reasoned (and Washington agreed), to keep this power harnessed within a popular assembly. "We have already given in example one effectual check to the Dog of war" wrote Thomas Jefferson to Madison in 1789, "by transferring the power of letting him loose from the Executive to the Legislative body, from those who are to spend to those who are to pay."[18]

## Defensive and Offensive Warfare

A misinterpretation of Article II, Section 2, of the Constitution sometimes leads to the unwarranted conclusion that the president enjoys preeminent authority over the war power. As the correspondence of the founders makes clear, this section gives to the president the right and obligation as commander in chief to *repel* sudden attacks against the United States, when a delay to consult with Congress would be foolhardy, even suicidal.[19] As commander in chief, the president is responsible as well for leading the armed forces in ways specified by Congress. The president is not expected, however, to *initiate* hostilities. A celebrated constitutional authority, Senator Sam Ervin Jr. (D-North Carolina), has emphasized the difference:

> A distinction must be drawn between **defensive warfare** and **offensive warfare**. There is no doubt whatever that the President has the authority under the Constitution, and, indeed, the duty, to use the Armed Forces to *repel sudden armed attacks on the Nation*. But any *use of the Armed Forces for any purpose not directly related to the defense of the United States against sudden armed aggression*, and I emphasize the word "sudden," can be undertaken only upon congressional authorization.[20]

During the first hundred years of the nation's history, presidents for the most part honored this original understanding between the two branches. An illustration is President Jefferson's handling of the Barbary pirates, who jeopardized American shipping in the Mediterranean Sea. He dispatched a naval squadron to protect US commerce in these waters. On deciding that defensive action was insufficient, however, the President turned to Congress for permission to employ offensive measures against the pirates. Jefferson acknowledged that he was "unauthorized by the Constitution, without the sanction of Congress, to go beyond the line of defense," and he requested permission to "place our force on an equal footing with that of its adversaries"—an offensive warfare decision, he noted, that was "confided by the Constitution to the legislature exclusively."[21]

In an exhaustive analysis of the war power's early use, the Senate Foreign Relations Committee observed in 1969 that even President James Monroe, well known for his aggressive foreign policy views, drew a careful distinction between, on one hand, the enunciation of his major statement on foreign policy (the Monroe Doctrine of 1823), and, on the other hand, its implementation. The latter required authority from Congress. His Secretary of State, John Quincy Adams, replied with this prudent notice to an inquiry from Colombia in 1824 regarding what steps the United States would take against possible European intervention in Latin America: "With respect to the question, 'in what manner the Government of the United States intends to resist on its part any interference of the Holy Alliance for the purpose of subjugating the new republics or interfering in their political forms' you understand that by the Constitution of the United States, the ultimate decision of this question belongs to the Legislative Department of the Government."[22]

The Foreign Relations Committee further noted a speech given by Abraham Lincoln when he was a member of Congress from Illinois and critical of presidential power. (The Committee chose to overlook President Lincoln's subsequent disregard for the prerogatives of Congress during the Civil War.) In 1846, at the time of President James Polk's war against Mexico, Lincoln was convinced that the president had acted unconstitutionally when he dispatched American forces into disputed territory along the Rio Grande without the permission of Congress. Wrote Representative Lincoln:

> Allow the President to invade a neighboring nation, whenever *he* shall deem it necessary to repel an invasion, and you allow him to do so *whenever he may choose to say* he deems it necessary for such purpose—and you allow him to make war at pleasure. Study to see if you can fix *any limit* to his power in this respect, after you have given him so much as you propose. . . .
>
> The provision of the Constitution giving the war-making power to Congress, was dictated, as I understand it, by the following reasons. Kings had always been involving and impoverishing their people in wars, pretending generally, if not always, that the good of the people was the object. This, our convention undertook to be the most oppressive of all kingly oppressions; and they resolved to so frame the Constitution that *no one man* should hold the power of bringing this oppression upon us.[23]

Such distinguished protests to the contrary notwithstanding, the erosion of legislative control over the war power accelerated, slowly at first and then in the twentieth century with increasing speed. Encouraged by congressional acquiescence, presidents during the late 1800s used military force abroad for limited—although sometimes clearly offensive—purposes, including the "hot pursuit" of criminals across international borders, as well as operations against piracy and the slave trade. Presidents confined this use of force chiefly to missions involving individuals or bands of renegades, not other sovereign states. In the twentieth century, however, presidents would claim constitutional authority to direct military force against other nations. Although presidents like Theodore Roosevelt, William Howard Taft, and Woodrow Wilson never declared the right to launch full-scale wars on behalf of the United States, they nonetheless did use the military to intervene repeatedly into the affairs of Mexico and other nations in Central America and the Caribbean. Again, Congress either stood by passively or sometimes enthusiastically cheered this use of the war power. These precedents, and accompanying temptations, led presidents to exalt the commander in chief clause of the Constitution (Article II, Section 2) over those passages that spell out the right of Congress to declare war and raise armies (Article I, Section 8).

Early in the twentieth century, the twin catastrophes of the Great Depression and World War II arrived on the international scene, both powerful catalysts for a further concentration of power in the White House. In this time of great risk for the nation, the American people were prepared to accept, and indeed demanded, aggressive leadership from the White House. This suited the temperament of Franklin D. Roosevelt. In the worthy battle against the Axis powers, not only was he willing to usurp the treaty power through his destroyers-for-bases deal with Britain (discussed later in this chapter), but he also sought a more exclusive control over the war power than any other president since Lincoln.

In the waning months of 1940 and during the early months of 1941, at a time when the American people held strong isolationist sentiments, Roosevelt offered—strictly on his own authority and without meaningful consultation with Congress—US forces for the protection of Greenland and Iceland against a Nazi invasion; assigned warships to accompany, all the way to Iceland, American convoys loaded with supplies for Britain; and announced, after an American destroyer assisted in a British military operation and was fired on by a German submarine, that American naval ships would shoot on sight against any German or Italian vessels discovered in the western Atlantic. With these decisions, the executive branch by itself had done nothing less than draw the United States into undeclared naval warfare against the Germans in the Atlantic Ocean. While few would dispute the merits of the President's cause against repressive regimes, by circumventing the constitutional authorities of Congress he had established a dubious precedent for war making that his successors could tap into for more questionable purposes.

## Inherent Presidential Authority

Each of the presidents since World War II, from Harry S. Truman to Barack Obama, has tended to view the war power more from the vantage point of Franklin Roosevelt than of Thomas Jefferson and his contemporaries, although the degree of presidential claims over prerogative (exclusively presidential) powers has varied widely. For both schools of thought, the belief has endured that only Congress has the authority to declare war formally; nevertheless, many presidents and their aides have believed that—short of a formal declaration of war—the president as commander in chief enjoys the right to use the military option as the White House sees fit, as though America's soldiers and sailors were so many chess pieces and the president the grandmaster.

In 1950, President Truman made the decision to commit American troops to the war in Korea—a "police action," in the administration's phrase—without congressional authorization. This undeclared war resulted in the death of over 30,000 American soldiers. The administration's only public explanation regarding its use of the war power appeared in the *Department of State Bulletin*. "The President, as Commander in Chief of the Armed Forces of the United States, has full control over the use thereof," stated a State Department memorandum prepared on the President's authority, adding sweepingly that there existed a "traditional power of the President to use the Armed Forces of the United States without consulting Congress."[24]

In the institutional struggle over the war power, the Truman administration had evoked a novel doctrine that claimed an **inherent constitutional right** of presidential dominance over the decision to make war. *The president's designation as commander in chief, and the constitutional injunction that "he shall take Care that the Laws be faithfully executed," allowed him*—so went the claim—*the implicit right to use US troops as he alone wished.* Once more, lawmakers allowed this accretion of presidential power to pass with hardly a murmur from Capitol Hill, although by 1951 a leading conservative senator, Robert Taft of Ohio ("Mr. Republican," as the GOP leader of the Senate was often called), lamented that "the President simply usurped authority, in violation of the laws and the Constitution, when he sent troops to Korea to carry out the resolution of the United Nations in an undeclared war."[25]

Truman's Secretary of State, Dean Acheson, rejected Taft's interpretation out of hand. He found the Senator's reference to constitutional matters entirely inappropriate. "We are in a position in the world today where the argument as to who has the power to do this, that, or the other thing, is not exactly what is called for from America in this very critical hour," he chided the Senator, then concluded magisterially: "Not only has the President the authority to use the Armed Forces in carrying out the broad foreign policy of the United States and implementing treaties, but it is equally clear that this authority may not be interfered with by the Congress in the exercise of powers which it has under the Constitution."[26] In this same spirit, an aide to President Reagan would argue much later (in 1987) that laws passed by Congress to bar US aid to the Nicaraguan counterinsurgency known as the *contras* failed to affect the president's "constitutional and historical power" to manage American foreign policy as he saw fit.[27] Further, in 2011, President Obama would invoke his rights as president to provide support for a NATO coalition that was fighting against the dictator of Libya, as long as the president did not use US ground troops—a new and woolly wrinkle in the "inherent authority" argument.

## War by Blank Check

Perhaps mindful of Senator Taft's views on the misuse of the war power by the Truman administration, President Dwight D. Eisenhower, a fellow Republican, proved to be shrewder than either Franklin Roosevelt or Truman about executive claims to broad, inherent war powers. Eisenhower requested from lawmakers permission to use military force by way of **congressional resolutions,** requiring *a majority vote in both legislative chambers in support of a policy initiative.* Eisenhower asked on several occasions for congressional authority to use the armed forces in various parts of the world, and lawmakers readily complied. In fact, they provided broad grants of authority to employ force "as [the President] determines necessary." Caught up in the exigencies of the moment, the legislative branch had lost sight of its own constitutional standing, leaving the impression that members of Congress were willing to accept the concept of presidential discretionary authority over the use of military force and that the role of lawmakers was largely to rally behind the White House and express a sense of national unity as the president strove to protect America's "vital interests" abroad. In its 1969 review of these presidential initiatives, the Senate Foreign Relations Committee expressed concern that "an authorization so general and imprecise amounts to an unconstitutional alienation of its war power on the part of the Congress."[28]

The specific resolutions deemed so repugnant by the Foreign Relations Committee had been passed by Congress at the request of President Eisenhower to defend the islands of Formosa (Taiwan) and the Pescadores (located between Formosa and mainland China) in 1955, as well as nations in the Middle East in 1957. Equally objectionable, according to the Committee's study, were subsequent resolutions sought by President Kennedy for Cuba and Berlin in 1962 and by President Johnson for Vietnam in 1964. Written with a broad brush, these congressional grants of authority steadily evolved toward an advance approval by lawmakers for practically any military operation the president might see fit to undertake.

At first, the Eisenhower administration was cautious in its dealings with Congress on foreign policy. When Chinese communists shelled the Pescadores island of Quemoy in 1955 and an invasion from mainland China against Formosa seemed imminent, President Eisenhower asked Congress "to participate now, by specific resolution, in measures designed to improve the prospect of peace," including "the use of the Armed Forces of the United States if necessary to assure the security of Formosa and the Pescadores." A senior Senator asked Secretary of State John Foster Dulles if it would be "fair to describe this resolution as a predated declaration of war." Dulles replied cautiously: "The president does not interpret this as a declaration of war, and if there were a situation to arise which in his opinion called for a declaration of war, he would come back again to the Congress."[29]

Calmed by these assurances, Congress quickly approved the Formosa Resolution-with little thought to the shift in constitutional prerogatives it implied. As historian Arthur M. Schlesinger Jr. has written, *unlike prior resolutions in American history, the* **Formosa Resolution** *failed either to order a specific action or even to name an enemy*: "Rather it committed Congress to the approval of hostilities without knowledge of the specific situation in which the hostilities would begin."[30]

Two years later, in 1957, the Eisenhower administration came to Capitol Hill to propose another resolution on foreign policy, this time aimed at the Middle East where US strategists feared that a recent British withdrawal from the region had created a power vacuum the Soviet Union might find enticing. In January, President Eisenhower asked Congress for *authority to use American armed force, if necessary, to protect the national sovereignty of nations in the Middle East against Soviet encroachment.* Once more, a Senator posed the question of whether such a resolution would amount to a "predated declaration of war." Secretary Dulles adroitly turned the question on its head: "I would call it a declaration of peace rather than a declaration of war, because I think that without this we are in great danger of getting into war."[31]

The Secretary soon discovered, however, that important lawmakers were now prepared to match his brazen attitude with their own equally strong dose of skepticism. The Formosa Resolution had slipped through Congress with relative ease; but now this Middle East Resolution, dubbed the **Eisenhower Doctrine** by the press, faced considerable opposition in the Senate. (The House remained content to ally itself with the President, at least for the time being.) The floor debate revealed new misgivings among senators who had supported the Formosa Resolution two years earlier. For example,

J. William Fulbright (D-Arkansas), Chairman of the Foreign Relations Committee, complained that there had been

> no real prior consultation with Congress, nor will there be any sharing of power. The whole manner of presentation of this resolution—leaks to the press, speeches to specially summoned Saturday joint sessions, and dramatic secret meetings of the Committee on Foreign Relations after dark one evening before the Congress was even organized, in an atmosphere of suspense and urgency—does not constitute consultation in the true sense. All this was designed to manage Congress, to coerce it into signing this blank check.[32]

The transcript of closed hearings (since made public) on the Middle East Resolution, held jointly by the Committees on Foreign Relations and Armed Services, indicates that Fulbright's views were shared by other stalwarts of the Senate leadership. "In my opinion," said Richard B. Russell (D-Georgia), widely regarded at the time as the most influential member of the Senate on military issues, "the Congress of the United States is being treated as a group of children, and very small children, and children with a very low IQ at that, in the manner that this resolution has been presented to us. . . . I think that the Congress, if it is going to preserve its own self-esteem, ought to have more information than we have on it." Russell said the resolution left the legislative branch "as an appendage of the executive branch in dealing with this very vital and important matter," and predicted that if the Senate passed the resolution (as it finally did on March 12, 1957): "It may be going for the next twenty-five or thirty years, and the Congress will never regain control of it. It will from here on out be in the hands of the executive branch of the Government."[33]

Senator Wayne Morse (D-Oregon) concurred. "You have got a resolution here which, for the first time, suggests that the President of the United States can exercise discretion to proceed to protect the territorial integrity of some other country somewhere in the world attacked by some Communist country, because he thinks that eventually that may involve the security of the United States," he said, "and I think that is an absurd stretching of that alleged emergency power on the part of the President, and I think it would be a clear violation of the constitutional power of the president."[34] Backing up his colleague, Senator Sam Ervin observed further that the Constitution

> contemplates that the Armed Forces of the United States will not be put into an offensive war . . . without the consent of Congress; and here this first part of this resolution says that the president can put our Armed Forces against some enemy which has not yet been selected, in the Middle East. The resolution is not directed against Russia; it is directed against the nations which we fear will become Communist in the Middle East . . . and it is a perfect invitation for

another Korea, with Russia furnishing arms, and us furnishing the
boys to do the dying.[35]

For several weeks, senators agonized over the language of the resolution, stumbling around in what Senator Russell referred to as the "shadowland" that fell between the commander in chief and the declaration-of-war clauses of the Constitution. At last they decided to strike from the resolution the concept of legislative authorization; instead, the language would simply represent a statement of American policy on the Middle East. The effect was a lesson in unintended consequences. According to historian Schlesinger, President Eisenhower became convinced "less of the need for serious consultation with Congress than of his inherent authority to employ armed forces at presidential will."[36] When the President sent American troops into Lebanon later in the year, he neither invoked the Middle East Resolution nor requested authority from Congress; he merely pointed to his authority as commander in chief.

The most fateful of the foreign policy resolutions passed by Congress, however, was the **Gulf of Tonkin Resolution**, approved in August of 1964. Reacting to intelligence reports provided by the executive branch claiming that American naval vessels off the coast of Vietnam had come under enemy fire, lawmakers hastily declared in this resolution that "*the Congress approves and supports the determination of the President, as Commander in Chief, to take all necessary measures to repel any armed attack against the forces of the United States and to prevent further aggression.*" During the legislative debate, a colleague asked Senator Fulbright (a leading sponsor of the resolution, willing on this occasion to give the president the benefit of the doubt) whether "looking ahead, if the President decided that it was necessary to use such force as could lead into war, we will give that authority by this resolution?" Responded Fulbright, "That is the way I would interpret it."[37] Despite this worrisome admission by Senator Fulbright, the resolution passed 533-to-2.

I examine the aftermath of this fateful vote later in this book (Chapter 5). Suffice it to note here that the erosion of legislative control over the war power had reached an apex; Congress seemed to acknowledge practically unlimited control to the White House over the use of military force. Subsequently, the Johnson administration's Undersecretary of State, Nicholas Katzenbach, would point to the Gulf of Tonkin Resolution as the "functional equivalent" of a declaration of war by Congress—even though, according to a senior member of the Foreign Relations Committee who participated in the original debate, "Congress neither expected nor even considered at the time of the debate on the resolution that the President would later commit more than half a million American soldiers to a full-scale war in Vietnam."[38] (See *Perspectives on American Foreign Policy* 3.1.) As the war in Vietnam unfolded, pressures on Capitol Hill would mount to revisit the war-powers authority presented in the Constitution. These pressures would lead to the most important debate on these powers since the drafting of the founding document, culminating in passage of the War Powers Resolution in 1973 (examined in Chapter 11).

## PERSPECTIVES ON AMERICAN FOREIGN POLICY 3.1

**SENATOR FRANK CHURCH (D-IDAHO), a member of the Senate Foreign Relations Committee (and later its chairman), commenting in 1970 on the aggrandizement of presidential power over the use of overt military force:**

One hears it argued these days—by high officials in the Executive Branch, by foreign policy experts, and by some political scientists—that certain of our Constitutional procedures, including the power of Congress to declare war, are obsolete in the nuclear age. This contention, in my opinion, is without merit. Nothing in the Constitution prevents—and no one in Congress would ever try to prevent—the President from acting in a genuine national emergency. What is at issue is his authority to order our military forces into action in foreign lands whenever and wherever he judges the national interest calls for it. What is at issue is his right to alter Constitutional processes at his option, even in the name of defending those processes.

I do not believe that the Constitution is obsolete; I do not believe that Congress is incapable of discharging its responsibilities for war and peace; but, if either of these conditions ever should arise, the remedy would lie in the amendment process of the Constitution itself. As George Washington said in his farewell address, ". . . let there be no change in usurpation; for though this in one instance may be the instrument of good, it is the customary weapon by which free governments are destroyed."

*SOURCE: Congressional Record* (April 30, 1970), p. 13566.

## THE TREATY POWER

The struggle between the branches over the control of foreign policy has extended into the domain of diplomacy as well. By virtue of the Constitution, the Congress and the executive branch share the authority to establish America's diplomatic commitments abroad. The only explicit reference to international agreement making in the Constitution is the **treaty power** in Article II, Section 2, which states that *the president "shall have power, by and with the advice of the Senate to make treaties, provided two-thirds of the Senators present concur."* These words convey the idea of a partnership between the legislative and executive branches. As one prominent legal analyst of the treaty clause concludes: "The Founders made it unmistakably plain their intentions to withhold from the President the power to enter into treaties all by himself."[39]

The executive branch obviously plays a central role in the treaty procedure, including the final right of ratification (a word often attributed wrongly in the media and textbooks to the Senate's approval vote).[40] In 1953, Professor Hollis W. Barber offered these observations about the president's involvement:

It is on his initiative and responsibility that the treaty-making process is undertaken; he determines what provisions the United States wishes to have embodied in the treaty; he decides whether reservations or amendments that the Senate attaches to a draft treaty are acceptable to him and should be submitted to the other parties to the treaty; and, even if the Senate by two-thirds vote approves a treaty that he has negotiated, he may, influenced by change of heart or political conditions, decide not to ratify it and at the last minute file it in his wastebasket.[41]

Despite the president's considerable powers, the wording of Article II, Section 2, undeniably also gives the Senate a central role in decisions regarding foreign diplomatic commitments. Nonetheless, the historical record reveals that presidents, and often even middle-rank officials in the executive bureaucracy, have involved the United States in major obligations abroad without the requisite advice and consent of the Senate (or a vote in the House). The practice of the modern executive branch has drifted far away from the original treaty-making principles of the nation's founders.

Thomas Jefferson argued that "on the subject of treaties, our system is to have none with any nation, as far as can be avoided."[42] His advice has come close to being honored; treaties are rarely used anymore as instruments of American foreign policy. Although there are a few important exceptions (such as the North Atlantic Treaty Organization based on a treaty ratified in 1949), the executive branch has simply chosen on many occasions to bypass this constitutional procedure. In its place have arisen two additional forms of international agreement making: either *loosely worded statutes that grant permission to the executive branch to move ahead on an agreement*, known as a **statutory agreements** and that at least have the merit of legislative involvement through a majority vote in both chambers; or *transactions carried out by the executive branch without any meaningful consultation with either chamber of Congress and sometimes hidden altogether from all lawmakers*, known as **executive agreements**. Originally designed to be the solemn means by which the United States would enter into accords with other countries, a scant 6 percent of America's international agreements were approved through the formal treaty process during the early stages of the Cold War (for which the data are most thorough).[43] This pattern has remained constant in more recent years, even though every now and then presidents have negotiated a few treaties of substantial importance, such as the Panama Canal Treaties of 1978.[44]

## The Destroyers Deal

As with the war power, the erosion of the constitutional treaty authority accelerated in the modern era during the administration of President Franklin Roosevelt. In the summer of 1940 Great Britain faced imminent invasion by the Nazis. France had already fallen, and the English Channel no longer seemed a protective moat in light of the formidable military prowess displayed by the German general staff. The hour was late, the fate of Britain dark. To assist a fellow democracy in trouble, President Roosevelt sent envoys to England for the purpose of entering into a major agreement with British government officials in Whitehall (a counterpart of America's Defense Department, dealing with foreign and security policy). *The United States would lend the United Kingdom fifty somewhat antiquated navy destroyers for the British defense against the Germans in*

Several old American destroyers among a total of 50 crossing the Atlantic as part of the US Lend Lease agreement to aid Great Britain against Germany and the Axis powers.

*exchange for US leasing rights to certain naval bases in the Western Hemisphere that belonged to the British.* The President would have liked to have gone even further in his assistance to the British, but Congress and the Neutrality Act of 1937 blocked him.

This **"lend-lease"** agreement had far-reaching implications, providing legal grounds for a possible German declaration of war against the United States. Whereas one might expect that American government officials would enter into such a serious commitment only by way of the constitutionally based treaty procedure, President Roosevelt instead resorted to an executive agreement. He simply signed an understanding with London, without the slightest nod to Congress—let alone a request for a two-thirds vote of approval within the Senate. Only later would he seek and win the approval of lawmakers for the Lend-Lease program. The President's motives in first using an executive agreement with the British were no doubt of the highest order. He quite properly wished to help turn back the Nazi assault against a leading Western democracy and to move quickly before it was too late. A debate in Congress might have prolonged an American response; the British Isles could have succumbed before London received the ships it needed.

Critics have subsequently contended, however, that the President dangerously exceeded his constitutional authority by failing to use the treaty procedure. In 1969, the Senate Foreign Relations Committee made special note of the destroyers deal in its assessment of the treaty powers:

> More serious in the long run than the President's action [the lend-lease agreement] was the preparation of a brief by the Attorney General contending that the action was constitutional. Had the President publicly acknowledged his incursion on the Senate's treaty power and explained it as an emergency measure, a damaging constitutional precedent would have been averted. Instead, a spurious claim of constitutionality was made, compounding the incursion on the Senate's authority into a precedent for future incursions.[45]

The destroyers agreement ushered in an era that witnessed many other international commitments arrived at outside the stipulations of the Constitution, as the treaty process was largely pushed aside and replaced by the use of executive and statutory agreements. (I examine the specific differences among these forms of agreement making, and their frequency of use, in depth in Chapter 10.) For example, during the Cold War executive agreements were signed with South Korea to establish major US military installations inside that nation; and statutory agreements authorized most of America's economic pacts around the world.[46] Roosevelt's deal with the British, reached in a time of emergency, came to be seen by the executive branch as a precedent to draw on even in the peacetime that followed World War II.

## Creeping Commitments

In 1962, Secretary of State Dean Rusk joined with the Foreign Minister of Thailand to issue a statement in which Rusk announced "the firm intention of the United States to aid Thailand, its ally and historic friend, in resisting Communist aggression and subversion." This pledge went far beyond the language of the treaty that established the Southeast Asia Treaty Organization (SEATO), ratified in 1954. That document required only that member nations would "consult" in times of military peril and act to meet the common danger in accordance with their own "constitutional processes." The collective security arrangement established under SEATO was suddenly transformed by this joint communiqué into a bilateral US–Thai defense pact.

Under the new relationship, the US Military Assistance Program (MAP) for Thailand rose from $24 million in 1960 to $88 million in 1962. This dramatic leap upward in funding required congressional approval; but, under the provisions of MAP, the approval only had to come from the House and Senate Armed Services Committees. These panels have the authority granted by Congress to disguise, for purposes of national security and secrecy, specific military requests within the overall annual Pentagon budget. So, for some programs like MAP, all the executive branch had to do was persuade two committees in Congress, not a majority in each chamber; and often the lawmakers on these committees have deferred to the committee chairs and their minority-party counterparts in the handling of such requests.

Through this approach, the executive branch was able in 1962 to avoid a full-fledged debate in Congress on the merits of the Thai relationship, relying instead on support from a few strategically located and sympathetic lawmakers at the helms of the House and Senate Armed Services Committees. By the end of the Johnson administration in 1969, the United States—or, more accurately, the executive branch—had assured the Thai government through a secret joint-contingency agreement that America would intervene in the event of a conventional military attack against Thailand. The secret agreement also established the payment of special bonuses to Thai troops in Vietnam—in essence, hiring mercenaries to fight on behalf of the United States in the Vietnam War.[47]

During this period, the executive branch never requested from Congress either treaty or even statutory approval (which requires a majority vote in both chambers for passage, in contrast to a two-thirds Senate vote for treaties) to authorize the stationing of 5,000 US combat troops in Thailand, a portion of whom were actively engaged in counterinsurgency operations in the jungles. Yet the executive branch did manage to forward to the Senate for approval a far less significant tax treaty with Thailand. This and similar experiences led frustrated members of the Senate Foreign Relations Committee to conclude that "In some instances we have come close to reversing the traditional distinction between the treaty as the instrument of a major commitment and the executive agreement as the instrument of a minor one."[48] Whether or not the military pacts with Thailand were in America's best interests is a separate question; what concerned constitutional experts was the procedural method used to arrive at the commitments. The original intent of SEATO, a military alliance that had been approved through the rigorous and solemn treaty procedure laid out in the Constitution, had been altered by communiqué and a series of secret executive agreements.

In 1966, Secretary Rusk cast his net more widely still. As the war in Vietnam heated up and threatened to boil over into Thailand, he warned that "no would-be aggressor should suppose that the absence of a defense treaty, congressional declaration, or U.S. military presence grants immunity to aggression." Again, as with Franklin Roosevelt and the lend-lease deal, the Secretary's motives may have been laudable enough; but members of Congress saw the declaration as still another blow to their constitutional prerogatives. It "put Congress on notice," remarked a prominent Senator, "that, with or without its consent, treaty or no treaty, the Executive will act as it sees fit against anyone whom it judges to be an aggressor. . . . It is indeed nothing less than a statement of intention on the part of the Executive to usurp the treaty power of the Senate."[49]

Under international law, executive agreements carry the weight of treaties, as do statutory agreements. All three forms of agreement making represent official commitments by the United States to other nations. For this reason, the realization that these agreements are sometimes made in secret—without congressional perusal or debate— has made them a subject of controversy. Lawmakers accept the usefulness of the executive agreement method when used openly and for minor commitments; good management sense would argue against congressional involvement in the hundreds of routine understandings reached each year between the United States and other nations, on everything from trade in strawberries with Mexico to the protection of migratory birds whose flight carries them across international borders from Canada into the United States. Members of Congress balk, though, when new and far-reaching commitments are pursued through this less accountable instrument of diplomacy, as occurred in the 1960s with the establishment of US military bases in Spain by way of executive agreements.

It was Secretary Rusk, again, who laid the groundwork for this set of secret commitments, beginning with a joint declaration signed in 1963 with the Spanish minister for foreign affairs. The document, which read like a treaty, asserted that

> The United States Government reaffirms its recognition of the importance of Spain to the security, well-being and development of the

Atlantic and Mediterranean areas. The two governments recognize that the security and integrity of both the United States and Spain are necessary for the common security. A threat to either country, and to the joint facilities that each provides for the common defense, would be a matter of common concern to both countries, and each country would take such action as it may consider appropriate within the framework of its constitutional processes.

On top of this public pronouncement came a series of secret understandings, including a memorandum signed between high-ranking military officers in both nations that committed the United States to defend Spain against third countries. Another memorandum, written by the Chairman of the Joint Chiefs of Staff to his Spanish counterpart, offered the assurance that US troops stationed on Spanish soil represented "a far more visible and credible security guarantee than any written document."[50] For the Senate Committee on Foreign Relations, these pronouncements epitomized yet again the penchant of the executive branch for commitment by accretion and an abandonment of constitutional procedure. "The making of such a commitment by means of an executive agreement, or a military memorandum," the Committee argued, "has no valid place in our constitutional law, and constitutes a usurpation of the treaty power of the Senate." The Committee referred to the Spanish bases agreement as a "quasi-commitment, unspecified as to exact import but, like buds in springtime, ready, under the right climatic conditions, to burst into full bloom."[51]

Although aware of these agreements, the full Congress remained unwilling to join the Senate Foreign Relations Committee in a challenge to the executive branch on either the Thai or Spanish military arrangements. The agreements stuck and Congress provided the necessary funding. Within the next few years, however, attitudes toward executive agreements would change sharply on Capitol Hill. Fed by disillusionment over the Watergate scandal and the souring war in Vietnam, a legislative rebellion against executive dominance in foreign affairs erupted during the 1970s. Presidential insensitivity to the constitutional underpinnings of the war power, coupled with a growing concern among members of Congress about the demise of the treaty power, released pent up congressional grievances toward the executive branch. A key objective in this congressional resurgence was the restoration of a meaningful involvement for lawmakers in the making of American commitments abroad, examined more closely in Chapter 10. (See *Perspectives on American Foreign Policy* 3.2.)

## THE SEEDS OF ACQUIESCENCE

If the war and treaty powers rightly belong to Congress, as claimed by the Senate Foreign Relations Committee and other critics at the height of the Vietnam War, why had they been abdicated by lawmakers in the first place? In the early days of the Republic, the answer to this question of **legislative acquiescence** can be found in *a willingness of lawmakers to give presidents free rein*: first, in chasing pirates and bandits

---

### PERSPECTIVES ON AMERICAN FOREIGN POLICY 3.2

**The SENATE FOREIGN RELATIONS COMMITTEE in 1972 on the importance of keeping Congress informed about international agreements:**

The principle of mandatory reporting of agreements with foreign countries to the Congress is more than desirable; it is, from a constitutional standpoint, crucial and indispensable. For the Congress to accept anything less would represent a resignation from responsibility and an alienation of an authority which is vested in the Congress by the Constitution. If Congress is to meet its responsibilities in the formulation of foreign policy, no information is more crucial than the fact and content of agreements with foreign nations.

*SOURCE:* "Transmittal of Executive Agreements to Congress," *Senate Report No.* 92–591, 92nd Cong., 2d Sess., January 19, 1972, p. 3.

---

who threatened US interests, and second, in defending the Monroe Doctrine and its corollaries. In more recent times, passage of the Gulf of Tonkin Resolution was a result of lawmakers responding too quickly to a perceived emergency, without anticipating President Johnson's later interpretation of their temporary grant of authority as a "blank check" to expand the war in Vietnam through a massive, secret troop buildup. The failure of lawmakers to anticipate Johnson's reversal is understandable. After all, the President had promised audiences around the country during the 1964 presidential election that "we are not about to send American boys 9,000 or 10,000 miles away from home to do what Asian boys ought to be doing for themselves."[52]

The Senate Foreign Relations Committee had trusted the Johnson administration during its early years. The President and Committee Chairman Fulbright, from the adjacent states of Texas and Arkansas, respectively, had been friends and voting allies in the Senate for over a decade. That trust backfired, however, initially over the US invasion of the Dominican Republic in 1965. The President had promised Fulbright he would never send troops into the Dominican Republic, then reneged on that promise. Subsequently, Johnson escalated the war in Vietnam, viewed by Fulbright and many of his colleagues as another breach of trust. "In adopting the [Gulf of Tonkin] resolution with such sweeping language," concluded the repentant and wiser Committee in 1969 (still under Senator Fulbright's leadership), "Congress committed the error of making a *personal* judgment as to how President Johnson would implement the resolution when it had a responsibility to make an *institutional* judgment, first, as to what *any* President would do with so great an acknowledgment of power, and, second, as to whether, under the Constitution, Congress had the right to grant or concede the authority in question."[53]

Because congressional acquiescence to the White House in foreign affairs began long before the Johnson administration, however, one must search for deeper explanations. One important contributing factor in the modern era is what historians call the ghost of the Versailles Treaty. Some lawmakers continued to feel a sense of guilt because the Senate had failed to approve that treaty in 1919, bringing World War I to an end. Had the treaty been accepted by senators, the League of Nations might have functioned properly with American membership and World War II might have been avoided—questionable "mights" about the potential capabilities of the League, in light of the UN's inauspicious record of peacekeeping around the globe since 1945. Whatever the validity of this causal linkage between the failure of the Versailles Treaty and the 1930s outbreak of totalitarian aggression led by Japan, Germany, and Italy, this memorable story line had the effect of inhibiting some members of Congress who otherwise may have urged a greater involvement by lawmakers in key matters of foreign policy.

Important, too, was the preoccupation of Congress with the dangers of the Cold War in the decades after 1945. Just as the Depression and World War II had the effect of centralizing power in the government, so, too, did the enduring conflict between the United States and the Soviet Union. Some lawmakers expressed the belief that Americans would have to live in a constant state of war readiness. The two heavily armed camps that faced each other throughout the Cold War—the United States and its NATO allies, on one side, and the USSR and its Warsaw Pact allies, on the other side—nurtured this fortress view of the world. During an exchange between senators at a hearing in 1975, for example, Frank Church of Idaho argued that CIA intelligence operations that infringed on US civil liberties should be prohibited in peacetime. In response, John Tower (R-Texas) objected to Church's distinction between "war" and "peace." This exchange took place:

> *Church:* I think that we should recognize the distinction between war and peace. It poses the question whether this country in peacetime wants to live always under the customs of war. . . .
> *Tower:* I think that we cannot draw this in strict terms of war and peace, in terms of whether or not the United States is actually at war. We are in effect in a war of sorts. That is a war of the preservation of the climate in this world where national integrity will be respected.[54]

Some lawmakers use this same logic of constant threat today to justify massive defense spending and restrictions on civil liberties—only substituting terrorists for the Soviet bugbear. Members of Congress have been reluctant to question the president and his aides on matters of foreign policy, for fear their criticism might be misinterpreted as a lack of patriotism or proper support for the nation in an age of ever-present global dangers. A careful consideration of constitutional issues has often been abandoned in the face of emergencies, as during the Cuban missile crisis in 1962 or with the attempted rescue of the merchant ship *Mayaguez* in 1975—instances in which Congress was excluded from important foreign policy deliberations. In their rush to stand with the president against the communist threat during the Cold War or the terrorist threat today, lawmakers have often failed to weigh the effects of their uncritical support for presidential actions on the constitutional obligation of the legislative branch to serve as an independent check on the use of power by the executive branch in the conduct of foreign policy.

Moreover, the pressures of **bipartisanship** have intimidated some lawmakers. "Politics stops at the water's edge" is a venerable adage in the lore of US foreign policy. According to this rallying cry, Congress is supposed to eschew partisanship when it comes to foreign affairs and *fall in behind the president for the sake of national unity*. The world had become too threatening to reveal foreign policy fissures at home before the eyes of adversaries abroad; politics would have to be reserved for disputes about domestic policy. While this argument has some obvious merit, members of Congress began to realize during the 1960s that one of its end results was to concentrate foreign policy powers further into the hands of the president by stifling dissent on Capitol Hill. The pill of "bipartisanship" became, all too often, merely a soporific to lull the "loyal opposition" in Congress.

The war in Vietnam provided a rude awakening for the legislative branch. "The myth that the Chief Executive is the fount of all wisdom in foreign affairs today lies shattered on the shoals of Vietnam," proclaimed a leading member of the Foreign Relations Committee at the height of the war.[55] The unpopular uses of presidential power in Vietnam, and the still more blatant manifestation of presidential arrogance in the Watergate scandal, would turn the attention of lawmakers back to forgotten questions of constitutional authority—especially the treaty and the war powers. I examine the chief measures adopted by Congress to restore its eroded powers in later chapters on the diplomatic and the military instruments of foreign policy (Chapters 10 and 11, respectively).

The interests of lawmakers in maintaining robust congressional powers would ebb and flow in the decades that followed the Vietnam War and the Watergate scandal. When the legislative branch perceived that the executive branch was becoming too assertive and robbing the Congress of its foreign policy authority, lawmakers would stand up for their prerogatives (as when the second Bush presidency ignored the provisions of the 1978 Foreign Intelligence Surveillance Act and carried out wiretaps without required warrants, or when the Obama administration refused to provide documents for legislative hearings on Department of Justice activities).[56] And when the executive branch was less assertive, or when the nation faced a crisis (as with the 9/11 attacks), lawmakers displayed less concern about their own powers and tended to support the White House.

## MONEY AND OTHER CONSTITUTIONAL DISPUTES

As we have seen throughout this chapter, the question of the proper distribution of power between the legislative and executive branches of government has been a source of ongoing debate, fueled by the ambiguities and omissions of the Constitution.

The war and the treaty powers have produced the most frequent and acrimonious disagreements, but other constitutional provisions have led to conflict, too. Chief among these is the power of the purse.

## The Purse Strings

The Constitution places the power to spend directly in the hands of Congress. Recall that Article I, Section 9, reads, "No Money shall be drawn from the Treasury, but in Consequence of Appropriations made by Law." The importance of funding for foreign and domestic policy is self-evident; virtually everything a country might wish to do at home or abroad requires financial resources. So ubiquitous is the spending power that, rather than being considered separately, I examine this aspect of American foreign policy throughout this book. A few initial examples are offered here, though, to provide a sense of how the power of government spending has been a further source of tension inside America's government.

Although the Constitution places the spending power in the hands of the legislative branch, executive officials have established methods to evade the intentions of lawmakers. Presidents have sometimes opposed specific weapons procurements proposed by Congress in favor of their own shopping list; but, rather than veto congressional recommendations, the White House has taken the less visible (and therefore easier) course of simply never spending the funds appropriated by lawmakers. This technique is known as **impoundment**: *the freezing of funds in the federal treasury, despite the passage of an appropriations law requiring expenditure of the funds.* For example, Presidents Truman, Eisenhower, and Kennedy (among others) all refused to spend monies appropriated by Congress for various weapons systems.[57] The rationale used by the executive branch to justify impoundment has often been that conditions had changed between the passage of a law and its implementation. Inflation, for example, may suddenly spiral upward, making additional spending unwise. Further, the lack of presidential authority for a line-item veto presents the White House with the choice of either vetoing a popular omnibus bill just to delete a single weapons proposal within it or else accepting the weapons as a bitter pill lodged within the larger and more palatable statute. Impoundment becomes a tempting alternative.

In 1974, Congress passed the **Budget and Impoundment Control Act** in *an effort to tighten its reins over the executive use of impoundment.* Now the executive branch must openly report its intention to impound funds, providing lawmakers with an opportunity to accept or reject its rationale. Although a significant piece of legislation, this 1974 budget law is sufficiently ambiguous, according to one authority, to allow "the executive ample room for interpretations."[58] Institutional jockeying over the nature of permissible impoundments continues.

Secret spending by the executive branch has caused friction as well. Burying secret appropriations requests in the Defense Department's annual budget bill, with the cooperation of just the two Armed Services Committees in Congress (or only their leaders) is another way of bypassing legislative debate, as mentioned earlier. This approach may be legitimate at times because vital, clandestine military missions may necessitate special handling on Capitol Hill; but such legerdemain can be abused, as critics contend was exactly the case with funding to Thai mercenaries in the Vietnam War and with the hidden escalation of funding for US forces in Southeast Asia from 1964–1966.

Appropriations for the CIA and America's fifteen other intelligence agencies (examined in Chapter 9) are also handled in secrecy. Although this is understandable, the practice leads to a situation of limited accountability, with reliance again on only a few lawmakers and staff to monitor the spending. In the early days of the CIA, established in 1947, members of Congress allowed the Agency to handle its financial affairs with minimal congressional involvement. In retrospect, it is clear that closer legislative supervision might have raised important questions about—and possibly have prevented—the channeling of resources to the Bay of Pigs operation and other misfortunes. Moreover, in the past, administrations have sometimes diverted funds from one foreign policy account to another without legislative approval—or even awareness—as when funds for foreign aid to Laos were used for CIA paramilitary warfare against communist guerrillas in its northern region.[59]

Since 1975, controls over intelligence funding have improved; but, as the 1986–1987 Iran-*contra* scandal reminds us, an administration can still seek support from outside (nongovernment) sources when Congress shuts off the money spigots for a particular program. The staff of the National Security Council during the Reagan administration sought to finance a covert war in Nicaragua with money from private citizens and foreign governments—a troubling "privatization" of American foreign policy. The administration secretly raised private monies from wealthy conservatives at home and rich potentates aboard (such as the Sultan of Brunei and the King of Saudi Arabia) to finance covert actions in Nicaragua led by American mercenaries—all in violation of the Boland Amendment of 1983, whereby Congress prohibited US covert actions in Nicaragua. (This important case is explored further in Chapter 12.) The adoption of this approach to foreign policy would have, as constitutional authority Louis Fisher has stressed, "destroy[ed] the system of checks and balances. Executive use of funds obtained outside the appropriations process would create a government the framers feared the most: union of sword and purse."[60] This is why the Iran-*contra* affair was so alarming and led to a major congressional inquiry. (See *Perspectives on American Foreign Policy* 3.3.)

## Diplomatic Recognition, Confirmation, and Accountability

As mentioned at the beginning of this chapter, the Constitution grants to the president the power to receive foreign diplomats. As the nation's first president, George Washington relied on this section of the founding document to bestow **diplomatic recognition** on *foreign nations that otherwise Congress might have failed to acknowledge as legitimate*, as in the case of revolutionary France. He successfully converted a seemingly

---

## PERSPECTIVES ON AMERICAN FOREIGN POLICY 3.3

**LAURENCE H. TRIBE, professor of constitutional law at Harvard University, on the Reagan administration's attempts to privatize American foreign policy during the Iran-*contra* episode:**

The carefully crafted requirement of Article I, Section 9 [of the Constitution], that all funds raised by the Government or its agents must enter and leave the Federal Treasury, and must do so only pursuant to laws passed by Congress, would be rendered utterly meaningless if the President, seeing himself not as an agent of the Government but as an outsider, could preside freely over the

creation of a shadow treasury designed to aid his shadow intelligence network in pursuit of his private schemes.

Congress's control over the purse would be rendered a nullity if the President's pocket could conceal a slush fund dedicated to purposes and projects prohibited by the laws of the United States.

*SOURCE:* Laurence H. Tribe, "Reagan Ignites a Constitutional Crisis," *New York Times* (May 20, 1987), p. 31. © Laurence H. Tribe, Carl M. Loeb University Professor and Professor of Constitutional Law, Harvard Law School.

---

insignificant constitutional clause into a sometimes important executive prerogative in foreign affairs.

On the legislative side of the constitutional ledger, the Senate possesses a **confirmation power** to either *accept or reject selected presidential appointments*. This can be a powerful instrument used by lawmakers to cross-examine candidates for high office in the executive branch, to see if they are fit for a position of authority and are willing to cooperate with Congress. From time to time, the Senate Foreign Relations Committee has rejected an ambassadorial candidate who displayed during confirmation hearings an appalling ignorance about the country where he or she was about to serve. In 2007, for example, the Senate turned back President Bush's nominee to be the US Ambassador to the United Nations, John Bolton, on grounds that he had made derogatory statements about the UN; and, in 2008, the Senate rejected President Obama's ambassadorial nominee to Iraq, Brett McGurk, questioning his judgment and managerial competence. Most of the time, though, the Senate has confirmed presidential nominees for ambassadorships.

The Senate Select Committee on Intelligence has also rejected proposed candidates to lead America's intelligence agencies, including President Clinton's nominee: Anthony Lake, the national security adviser at the time. Along with its anti-impoundment provisions, the 1974 Budget and Impoundment Control Act established the right of the Senate to confirm the president's budget director. Some lawmakers have further proposed the passage of a statute that would require confirmation hearings for a president's national security adviser.

Moreover, Congress has taken up—if inconsistently—the duty to provide **accountability** over the executive branch—an activity often referred to as "**oversight**" by political scientists. Lawmakers have realized the importance of *monitoring and* *reviewing the executive branch's implementation of existing laws.* In this capacity, the legislative branch serves as the watchdog that James Madison envisioned. In *Federalist Paper* No. 51, he wrote:

> If men were angels, no government would be necessary. If angels were to govern men, neither external nor internal controls on government would be necessary. In framing a government which is to be administered by men over men, the great difficulty lies in this: you must first enable the government to control itself. A dependence on the people is, no doubt, the primary control on the government; but experience has taught mankind the necessity of auxiliary precautions.[61]

Discussions with officials in the executive branch, field inspections, legislative hearings, budget reviews, and full-scale investigations provide the "auxiliary precautions" that Madison advocated. These methods are imperfect, however, and all too often lawmakers fail to devote adequate time to their oversight responsibilities.[62] Moreover, sometimes Congress has abused its role as an overseer, as during the McCarthy era in the 1950s when Senator Joseph McCarthy (R-Wisconsin) used his powers as chairman of a special investigative committee to charge the Truman and Eisenhower administrations—without clear evidence—of harboring communists within their bureaucracies. Here was legislative "accountability" run amok, resting more on innuendo than a fair and open review of the charges.[63] This time the checks on McCarthy came from his more levelheaded colleagues on the Hill, as well as push back from the executive branch. President Eisenhower criticized McCarthy's approach; and the US Army hired one of the nation's leading prosecutors, Joseph Welch of Boston, to defend the military in public hearings. By the time the sharp-tongued and witty Welch had finished verbally sparring with McCarthy in hearings, the Senator had been revealed to the public as the buffoon he was. One branch of government counteracting another—just as Madison had in mind.

## CONFLICT AND COMITY

Although disputes over power sharing have always been a central feature of American foreign policy, not all the relations between the executive and legislative branches are conflicted. Widespread agreement exists among lawmakers, presidents, and bureaucrats on some topics, despite the current political polarization between Republicans and Democrats in Washington, DC. Examples include consensus on the need to combat terrorism and drug trafficking, although debate over the appropriate methods to adopt can lead to disagreements. Moreover, the president will always have some vocal supporters on Capitol Hill, especially from fellow party members and other lawmakers who believe it is their duty for the sake of national unity to accept the president's position on foreign affairs. Moreover, Congress will continue to have a greater say on some matters than others—international trade, for example, which sometimes touches constituents directly, as opposed to security issues, a subject lawmakers generally know less about.

Institutional strife will continue to be a hallmark of American government. What else would one expect from a system willfully fractured by the nation's founders to thwart the concentration and potential abuse of power? As Madison further argued in *Federalist Papers*, No. 51, "The great security against a gradual concentration of the several powers in the same department consists in giving to those who administer each department the necessary constitutional means and personal motives to resist encroachments of the others. . . . Ambition must be made to counteract ambition."[64] The founders embraced this prescription and the result, doubtless, is a government less prone to tyranny; but critics argue that the costs may be too steep, that the United States is unable to compete in the global arena against adversaries more streamlined and autocratic in their decision making.

According to this anti-Madisonian argument, the world is too small, events move too quickly, secrecy is too important, and weapons have become too dangerous for the luxury of traditional constitutional checks and balances—for Congress to do anything more than support executive decisions on foreign affairs. I examine this perspective in subsequent chapters, where I take a closer look at the nation's institutional arrangements for the conduct of foreign policy.

## SUMMARY

The Constitution established a government in which power was spread across the three branches of government in an attempt to guard against its dangerous concentration into the hands of one person or institution. "Ambition would be made to counteract ambition," reasoned James Madison, one of the most influential of the nation's constitutional architects. This sharing of power, however, has led to acute tensions among the branches—a result of the explicit intention of the drafters to establish internal institutional opposition, as well as from ambiguities and silences in the Constitution.

Chief among the sources of tension have been disagreements over the war and the treaty powers. Through the years, the executive branch has gained dominance over the war power. This has been controversial, particularly when a president initiates offensive warfare, based on an assumed inherent constitutional right of the commander in chief or on authority stemming from resolutions passed by an outside body (such as the United Nations or NATO). Controversial, too, is the use of openended congressional resolutions, passed in times of perceived emergency and subsequently used by presidents to escalate military conflicts beyond the original intent of lawmakers. Critics point to the Gulf of Tonkin Resolution, approved by Congress during the early days of the Vietnam War, as a classic example. The executive branch has also largely discarded the treaty procedure in favor of other forms of international agreement making.

Although the executive and legislative branches sometimes work together co-operatively, particularly during national emergencies, jockeying for advantage in the sharing of power is built into America's form of government. Whether or not the world has become too dangerous a place for this power sharing, pluralistic approach to foreign policy making is a matter of debate, explored throughout this book.

## KEY TERMS

accountability (oversight) p. 93
bipartisanship p. 90
Budget and Impoundment Control Act (1974) p. 91
confirmation power p. 93
congressional resolution p. 78
defensive warfare and offensive warfare p. 75
diplomatic recognition p. 92
Eisenhower Doctrine (1957 Middle East
    Resolution) p. 79
executive agreements p. 83

Formosa Resolution (1955) p. 79
Gulf of Tonkin Resolution (1964) p. 81
impoundment p. 91
inherent constitutional right p. 77
legislative acquiescence p. 87
lend-lease agreement (1940) p. 84
Lord Acton (on power) p. 72
statutory agreements p. 83
treaty power p. 82

---

## QUESTIONS FOR DISCUSSION

1. What foreign policy authorities does the Constitution give to the executive and legislative branches of government?
2. Evaluate the argument that questions of war making ought to be decided jointly by the president and the leaders of Congress in ongoing consultations.
3. Is the treaty procedure as devised by the founders too cumbersome in the modern era?

4. Should politics "stop at the water's edge," as an old saying admonishes in favor of a bipartisan approach to international affairs?
5. What could be done to improve relations between Congress and the presidency in the conduct of foreign policy?

## ADDITIONAL READINGS

Corwin, Edward S. *The President: Office and Powers.*
    New York: New York University Press, 1957.
Fisher, Louis. *Defending Congress and the Constitution.*
    Lawrence: University Press of Kansas, 2011.

Henkin, Louis. *Foreign Affairs and the United States
    Constitution.* Oxford, UK: Clarendon, 1996.

For further readings, please visit the book's companion website.

### CHAPTER 4

# The Formative Years of American Foreign Policy

## THE SINKING OF THE *MAINE*

Bristling with 250-mm guns, the *USS Maine* steamed toward Cuba on January 25, 1898. With a displacement of 6,682 tons and a length equal to a football field, America's first true battleship—built at a cost of over $2 million—vividly displayed the nation's military might. On board, the crew of 363 officers and men understood their mission: display the flag, signaling that the United States would protect its commercial and geopolitical interests in Cuba.

Lifeboats rescue surviving crewmen of the wrecked *USS Maine* after an explosion destroyed the battleship on the night of February 15, 1898, as it was anchored in Havana Harbor, Cuba.

A few years before, a rebellion in Cuba had broken out against the island's Spanish rule. The strategy of the insurgents was to ruin Cuba's economy through a campaign of burning the sugarcane fields and destroying the sugar mills that earned robust profits for the colonial power. Once the island no longer had any commercial value, Spain would withdraw—so ran the theory. Spain, however, responded to the rebellion by dispatching 200,000 troops to Cuba with orders to stop the wave of destruction. In the fighting that ensued, Spanish soldiers herded peasants from the countryside into camps in the cities, hoping to remove the rebels' primary source of support. Although this might have been effective to a point, the Spanish military authorities underestimated the difficulty of providing food and sanitation for several hundred thousand displaced farmers and agricultural workers, and the relocation sites soon became riddled with malnutrition and disease. By the time the *Maine* sailed into Havana harbor, some 200,000 civilians had died in the camps.

President William McKinley had hoped to avoid US military intervention, but the steady drumbeat of sensationalist newspaper stories—known as "yellow journalism"—about the plight of those in the camps made neutrality increasingly difficult. Further, in January of 1898 rumors grew among leading Spanish officers headquartered in Havana

**LEARNING OBJECTIVES AND CONSTITUTIONAL ISSUES**

**By the end of this chapter, you will be able to:**

- *Identify the early foreign policy decisions made by the United States.*
- *Describe how the United States emerged as a world power in the decades between the Civil War and World War I.*

- *Explain how the two global wars of the twentieth century affected American foreign policy.*
- *Describe how the United States donned the mantel of world leader after the Second World War.*

**THIS CHAPTER RAISES THE FOLLOWING CONSTITUTIONAL QUESTIONS:**

- Although the Constitution set up separate institutions of government, America's early domestic objectives—especially Westward expansion and the development of trading relations with Europe—helped to bring a common sense of purpose to the nation's leaders across the three branches of government. Unresolved constitutional issues about race and states' rights, however, tore the nation in two in 1861. Did President Abraham Lincoln's aggrandizement of authority during the Civil War set a dangerous precedent leading to a less justifiable concentration of power in the White House in subsequent administrations?

- Did the Senate's vote against the League of Nations proposal suggest that lawmakers should not be trusted with a major role in the making of American foreign policy or, at the time, was this a wise decision by a Senate majority?

- It is sometimes said that in the crucible of war the Constitution takes on malleable proportions. Should Congress have deferred to the executive branch in the use of the war power during the decades examined in this chapter? Should Congress have played a greater role in important diplomatic initiatives, such as the Louisiana Purchase from France?

that the government of Spain was considering a grant of independence to the island. Opposed to this outcome, Spanish officers and their soldiers rioted in the streets of Havana and elsewhere on the island. This development pushed even the reluctant McKinley toward taking action and, without formal authority from Congress (but with considerable behind-the-scenes encouragement), he sent the *Maine* to Cuba. On entering the Havana harbor, the *Maine* dropped anchor and began a peaceful vigil. Three weeks after its arrival, however, a devastating explosion on board obliterated the forward third of the ship. Within minutes the *Maine* sank to the bottom of the harbor, with 274 of its crew perishing.

The immediate suspicion in the United States—fomented by yellow journalism and US business interests in Cuban sugar—was that Spain was to blame. "Remember the *Maine*! To hell with Spain!" became the battle cry across the United States. McKinley continued to seek a diplomatic resolution to the Cuban problem, but he was being outraced by angry public opinion. Increasingly, Americans pressed for military intervention; and lawmakers, worried about the next election, tried to outdo one another with jingoistic speeches. In April of 1898, McKinley reluctantly supported a congressional declaration of war against the Spanish, as advocated by arrant "war hawks" and expansionists in Congress. The President set up a US naval blockade placed around the island and a series of quick victories over the Spanish in Cuba, Puerto Rico, and in the faraway Philippine Islands led to an early peace settlement— although the treaty that ended the conflict passed the Senate by only a single vote. Suddenly, in the flush of victory, the United States found itself as a global power. As historian Ernest May has observed, "Some nations achieve greatness; the United States had greatness thrust upon it."[1]

With the advent of the Spanish-American War, the nation's century-long efforts to remain isolated changed dramatically. The narrow aperture through which America looked at the world opened up. "There can be little question that the year 1898 is a landmark in the development of American foreign policy," concludes historian Dexter Perkins, ". . . roughly, it can be said that up to 1898 the United States looked inward; after 1898 she looked outward."[2] The United States had become a fledgling world power and its leaders gazed across the Pacific Ocean with a growing appetite for colonial possessions, trading opportunities, and missionary work. To understand the extent to which 1898 was a stunning watershed year in the evolution of American foreign policy, it is necessary to review the young Republic's earlier years of introspective nation building, then to consider as well key the events that occurred after the war with Spain in 1898. ⁓

## NATION BUILDING, 1776–1898

Operating under a novel and untested constitutional framework, as well as militarily weak and weary of much more powerful countries on the European Continent, the new Republic moved cautiously in its conduct of foreign affairs. America's goals in the world consisted chiefly of staying clear of European conflicts and, in search of greater prosperity, developing trading relations overseas. Yet conflict with the powers of Europe sometimes proved hard for the United States to avoid: run-ins with France in an on-again, off-again relationship; with the British, who also alternated between amity and enmity toward the erstwhile colonies and, in 1812, humiliated the Americans with in a devastating attack against the nation's capital; and with constant skirmishes involving Spanish soldiers along America's eastern seaboard. Now and then, the United States broke its rule of detachment from foreign engagements and sought out policy advantages abroad. For example, President Thomas Jefferson viewed the Louisiana Purchase of 1803 as an opportunity to expand the United States; and, in 1846, war with Mexico held out the prospect of gaining land on the American frontier. For the most part, however, the founders and those who followed in their footsteps pursued a policy of isolation from political and military entanglements abroad. Nevertheless, the young nation's leaders were always on the lookout for beneficial economic ties and were pleased to accept military assistance from France against England and vice versa.

In America's early years, diplomacy was in ascendance as the nation's leaders dispatched State Department negotiators to Europe and Latin American capitals in search of trade deals and, for the same purpose, welcomed diplomatic representatives to the United States from overseas. More than anything else, America's initial diplomatic forays overseas were on behalf of business enterprises at home. This remains an important mission for US diplomats today. (For highlights in the evolution of US foreign policy from 1776 to 1945, see Figure 4.1.)

Contemporary American foreign policy has important antecedents in the nation's early history. Whether the American experiment in constitutional democracy would

*Figure 4.1*
Highlights in the Evolution of American Foreign Policy, 1776–1945

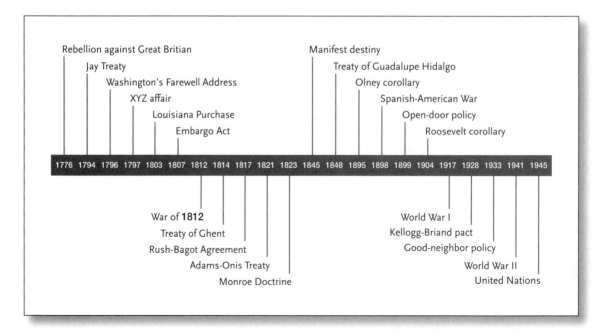

work in these early years, allowing the new nation to compete securely in a world of dangerous rivals who were unencumbered by the constraints of public accountability, was in doubt and is still a subject of debate over two centuries later. Another ongoing dispute from these early years is the extent to which the United States should return to a posture of political and military isolation or, instead, turn to a more open-throttled internationalism. Over the years, Americans have displayed an uneasy vacillation between indifference and attraction toward the rest of the world, depending on the perceptions held at any given time by leaders and the public about the possible risks and rewards of foreign involvement.

A chairman of the Senate Foreign Relations Committee observed during the Cold War that America's "belief in freedom and popular government once made us a beacon of hope for the downtrodden and oppressed throughout the world." He urged the United States to embrace again a foreign policy that "whether openly or secretly pursued, conformed once more to our historic ideals."[3] These remarks sound reasonable enough, even noble; but what are America's "historic ideals"? In this chapter I examine the evolution of the nation's bedrock principles as they matured from early beginnings in 1776 to the dawning of the nuclear age in 1945.

## Apart from the World

In the nation's infancy most citizens and certainly their leaders had little, if any, interest in being a beacon of hope for anyone overseas, however downtrodden or oppressed they might be. Devoid of a strong army and navy, groping for an identity, facing an uncertain future, Americans were chiefly concerned about protecting the fragile tendrils of the new democracy established by the writing of the Constitution in 1787. Survival and protection of this new form of government was the foremost value. The ongoing aspiration was to distance the United States from the dangers posed by powerful and bellicose European nations, with their muscular armies as well as warships that boasted twenty-eight guns capable of firing three broadsides in ninety seconds—not to mention the legendary battlefield skills of Napoleon I (Napoleon Bonaparte), the ambitious general and Emperor of France who sought territorial expansion; or Lord Horatio Nelson and the Duke of Wellington, British military commanders determined to halt the French aggression. (Wellington finally defeated Napoleon at the Battle of Waterloo, near a village south of Brussels, Belgium, in 1815.)

The Revolutionary War against Great Britain had been exhausting enough in blood and treasure; the inexperienced nation did not seek further embroilment in the violent machinations of the Old World (including the French Revolution, which sent the King and Queen of France to the guillotine in 1793). What it needed was rest, a breathing space, time to put its house in order, time to sort out its unique rules of democratic governance, time to see if the Constitution actually worked—a document so starkly different from the ruling edicts of other regimes of the time, with its emphasis on free and open elections; its dispersal of powers among three departments of government; its freedom of speech and religion; and its startling promise to ensure the preeminence of the people over their rulers. Concerned chiefly with self-preservation, the new nation struck a posture of aloofness, at least to the degree possible as avaricious powers overseas eyed the riches of the Western Hemisphere.

In this hope for a separation from the maelstrom of European and other foreign dangers, a policy later generations would refer to as isolationism, the United States was blessed by good fortune. The foremost advantage was geographic: protection afforded by the wide moats of the Atlantic and Pacific Oceans—what one contemporary wag referred to as "America's greatest liquid assets."[4] Europe was six weeks away by even the fastest of warships, and potential Asian adversaries farther still. Moreover, no strong rivals existed within the Western Hemisphere, although a number of European powers had well-established footholds in the New World. English explorers and well-armed adventurers prowled the northwest territory; and Canada was of great interest as well to Europeans and Americans, with its rapidly developing society (Quebec City predated the Plymouth Colony, for example). This land to the north displayed considerable hostility toward the United States and its expansionist ambitions, however, fueled by the presence of loyalists from the thirteen American colonies who had fled to Canada after the American Revolution. Moreover, France had recently repossessed New Orleans, formerly a French colony, along with the rest of the Louisiana territory (by treaty with Spain in 1800); and the Spanish considered Florida part of its dominion. Russia peered longingly across the Bering Strait into Alaska and the Pacific Northwest.

Despite these looming threats, those who lived among the warring powers of Europe and the Far East looked upon America's relatively tranquil setting with envy. "North and south, you have weak neighbors," sighed a French diplomat. "East and west, you have fish!"[5]

A historical circumstance was important, too: the reigning powers of Europe were distracted by troubles on their own turf. Napoleon was on the march and the nations of Europe had little time or inclination to deal with a small, upstart regime in North America. Like human beings and animals, nations obey a survival instinct—the fundamental law of man and nature. They are threat oriented (see Chapter 9). A nation's leaders want to know how many army divisions and how many warships an adversary has. To what extent does another country endanger one's own territorial integrity and one's right to exist, free from foreign control? In this regard, George Washington and his ragtag army (America had no navy at the time)—even though victorious over the British in the Revolutionary War, ended by the Treaty of Paris in 1783—paled as a threat to the Europeans, who faced great political and military upheavals lacerating the continent in the late eighteenth century.

America did benefit, though, from skillful diplomatic representation in European capitals, including the services of Benjamin Franklin (in Paris as America's first ambassador to France from 1776 to 1785) and Thomas Jefferson (also in Paris, from 1784–1789, before he became the nation's first secretary of state in 1790). Their personal charm and acumen proved a boon for US efforts to establish commercial ties in

Europe while avoiding "as little political connection abroad as possible"—the prescription for America's diplomacy advocated by President Washington in his Farewell Address of 1796. Among the diplomatic initiatives of this early period were treaties to normalize relations with Great Britain and Spain and to settle disputes over fisheries and trade with all the European powers. The skill of the young nation's diplomatic corps helped compensate for America's anemic arsenal at home. Six of the early secretaries of state were held in such high regard by their fellow Americans that they were elected to the presidency: Jefferson, Madison, James Monroe, John Quincy Adams, Martin Van Buren, and James Buchanan.

## Ambivalence Toward Europe

America would cautiously seek out commercial opportunities overseas through a series of treaties in the 1840s and 1850s with the contentious powers of European. These treaties dealt with everything from fishing rights to import and export duties; but the nation would continue to avoid political and military "entanglements," a favorite expression of both Washington and Jefferson whenever they wrote about America's relations with Europe. As Washington observed in his celebrated Farewell Address

> Europe has a set of primary interests, which to us have none, or
> a very remote relation. Hence, she must be engaged in frequent
> controversies, the causes of which are essentially foreign to our
> concerns. Hence, therefore, it must be unwise in us to implicate
> ourselves by artificial ties, in the ordinary combinations and collisions
> of her friendships or enmities . . . Why, by interweaving our destiny
> with that of any part of Europe, entangle our peace and prosperity in
> the toils of European ambition, rivalship, interest, humor or caprice?

America and its diplomats honored this policy of keeping an arm's length distance from Europe; however, they practiced Washington's advice only inconsistently, even in the case of those who basically agreed with the first president's sentiments. As the leader of the rebellious colonial forces, Washington himself had wooed France into an alliance against England during America's Revolutionary War; French troops played an indispensable role in assisting the colonies' defeat of the numerically superior British forces. Following the War of Independence, Washington—as president— pushed the French away and issued a Proclamation of Neutrality in 1793, to avoid being caught up in the latest political storms gathering on the European horizon. In his second term in office, Washington signed the **Jay Treaty** of 1794, deftly negotiated by America's first Supreme Court chief justice, John Jay of New York, who managed to *restore by way of this pact robust commercial ties with America's erstwhile archenemy, Great Britain.* Jay had served as "Secretary of Foreign Affairs," a precursor to the secretary of state position created in 1790, during the Washington administration. His subsequent service as a diplomat and Chief Justice is a conspicuous (and rare) example of a prominent role for a member of the judiciary in American foreign policy. As war raged on in Europe, merchants in the new nation profited by selling goods to both the French and the British.

Although President Washington would advise in his Farewell Address that the United States should "hold an equal and impartial hand" in its relations with other nations, Francophiles in Congress and across the thirteen states bitterly resented what they perceived as his ungrateful tilt away from France—the very nation that had helped secure the freedom of the colonies from the British monarchy. Anglophiles, in turn, supported American efforts at **rapprochement**—*the establishment of cordial relations*—with Britain through additional diplomatic overtures to heal breaches between the nations over shipping rights and trade tariffs. As much as the United States might have wished to seal itself off from entanglements overseas, foreign policy even at this early stage had demonstrated a capacity to inflame domestic constituencies and upset the best attempts at steering an open course between warring European factions. In the wake of the Jay Treaty, an undeclared war broke out between the United States and France, beginning with the French navy's practice of halting American merchant vessels and roughing up their sailors.

John Adams followed Washington as president and, in 1797, he sent a diplomatic envoy to Paris in hopes of soothing relations with the French. A beautiful Parisian woman and three mysterious gentlemen, identified only as Messieurs "X," "Y," and "Z," approached the American envoy and attempted to extort a cash payment from him in return for a negotiated resolution of hostilities between the two governments. Worse, this improper proposal turned out to be secretly backed by the French Foreign Minister, Talleyrand. Outraged, President Adams revealed the *French covert action* (the **XYZ affair**) to the public, further agitating many Americans against the French.

Despite public sentiment to the contrary, the United States needed commercial markets abroad if it were to prosper and grow as a nation; yet attempts to establish trading partnerships ineluctably led to political and even military entanglements, however much Washington, Jefferson, and other early leaders tried to keep trade and politics separated. The evolving rule of thumb for America's nascent dealings with the world was isolationism, yes, except when a timely military alliance might benefit the nation, as with the French during the War of Independence; isolationism, yes, except when commercial opportunities abroad might help entrepreneurs in Boston, New York, and Savannah sell their furs, fish, grain, tobacco, and textiles, thereby buoying the nation's economy.

In his inaugural address, the nation's third president, the cerebral Thomas Jefferson, spoke in a spirit reminiscent of Washington's Farewell Address. He advocated "peace, commerce and honest friendship with all nations, entangling alliances with none." Jefferson, though, was no more a purist on the idea of keeping America apart from the rest of the world than Washington had been. Even though Jefferson was personally a Francophile, he was entirely prepared to join England in a war against France if Napoleon Bonaparte refused to sell New Orleans to the United States in

1803. Here was a domestic objective of territorial expansion that helped to unite the constitutionally separated Congress and presidency.

Jefferson displayed, as well, a penchant for an aggressive use of secret agents to achieve US foreign policy objectives. For example, in a scheme to overthrow the Bashaw (or Pasha, in modern parlance) of Tripoli, who had from time to time disrupted American commercial shipping in the Mediterranean, Jefferson authorized the provision of a few artillery pieces and assorted small arms to the Bashaw's older brother, who promised to assume the role of head of state and treat the Americans more favorably. Thus was launched America's first major covert action, a paramilitary operation.

As historian Robert Wallace relates, "In Washington, [William] Eaton, the US Consul in Tunis, laid before Jefferson a scheme that had been developing among Americans in the Mediterranean for a couple of years." Wallace continues:

> The Bashaw of Tripoli was a usurper, having stolen the throne from an older brother who was now wandering forlornly somewhere in Africa. Eaton proposed to find the brother, give him sympathy and support, and install him as rightful head of state. Jefferson approved the idea and thus was launched the first, although not the last, American effort to overthrow an objectionable foreign ruler and put a cooperative one in his place. Jefferson also chose to have that plot proceed quietly, in twilight. He would send the would-be Bashaw, through Eaton, a few artillery pieces and 1,000 small arms. Eaton himself was to be given a vague title—'Navy agent of the United States for Barbary regencies'—and placed under the jurisdiction of the commodore of the Mediterranean squadron. If he could accomplish something, fine. If not, small loss.[6]

This use of covert action by the United States failed when the Bashaw's troops managed to capture and exile the aspiring US-sponsored ruler.

## Expansionist Stirrings

The first attempt to throw Europeans out of the Western Hemisphere, America's War of Independence, had succeeded. The second attempt—the Louisiana Purchase—was a success as well, and without shedding a drop of blood. In 1803, Jefferson simply placed $15 million on the barrelhead and bought out the French interests in New Orleans and the Louisiana Territory. Some members of Congress questioned, though, whether he had exceeded his constitutional powers with this purchase. Lawmakers had granted him budget authority to spend $10 million—not $15 million. Yet, in the bargaining with the French, Jefferson permitted his emissary to pay the extra amount demanded by Napoleon.

The President worried privately that, in this most consequential act of his administration, he might have overstepped his constitutional bounds.[7] Members of Congress grumbled about Jefferson's freewheeling check writing; after all, recall, the Constitution provides that "No money shall be drawn from the Treasury but in consequence of appropriations made by law." Nonetheless, the vast land acquisition was so attractive to Americans and their representatives that Congress agreed after the fact to enact a supplementary appropriation to cover the additional costs.[8] Fortunately for the United States, Napoleon needed the money; he was content to relinquish the land in North America and concentrate his efforts on conquering the rest of Europe and Russia. Although the price paid by Jefferson for the purchase strained the nation's financial resources, this approach to Westward expansion was infinitely less expensive than the potential costs of a war against Napoleon for control over this vast, rich, and fertile tract of territory.

As Napoleon set forth on his ill-fated conquests on the Continent, the United States again found itself caught up in the eddies of European warfare, hopes to the contrary notwithstanding. Angered by America's burgeoning trade with France and in need of sailors to fight Napoleon on the seas, British ships resorted to the **impressment** of US merchant marines—*naval recruitment by force: the kidnapping of Americans to serve as sailors on British warships* against the French fleet. More than 6,200 American sailors were victims of impressment between 1803 and 1811.[9] When in 1807 the British fired on the American frigate, the *USS Chesapeake*, killing three crew members, President Jefferson responded by persuading Congress to legislate an **Embargo Act** in 1807 *against the export of American goods to Britain*. This policy was deeply unpopular among New Englanders, who were largely pro-British and depended for their livelihoods on foreign trade with the "motherland." Members of Congress from that region managed to have the embargo law overturned in 1809—the constitutional separation of powers manifesting itself to the detriment of Jefferson's foreign policy objectives. The New Englanders pointed out that the French had been as treacherous as anyone toward the new Republic, marauding America's vessels at sea at least as frequently as the British. Although at least the French had refrained from impressment, it was true: they were not shy about capturing American ships and selling them to the highest bidder while imprisoning the crews indefinitely.

Outside of New England, though, the British were considered far more objectionable than the French, especially among the ultranationalist "War Hawks" who supported the next president, James Madison—the architect of the Constitution's separation of powers doctrine—and who longed for another war against Great Britain. The time had come, they argued, to put an end to England's insulting attempts to dominate shipping across the Atlantic Ocean and its conscription of American sailors. "Embargoes, nonintercourse, and negotiations are but illy [badly] calculated to secure our rights," a War Hawk faction proclaimed at a Fourth of July celebration in Kentucky in 1811. "Let us now try old Roman policy, and maintain them with the sword."[10] This rise of the War Hawks is an important early illustration of the influence that interest groups in the United States can exert on foreign policy, if they are well organized, well funded, and know how to make noise—the same requirements for interest-group success in foreign policy today.

A further annoyance to the War Hawks was the British presence in Canada, a region brimming with His Majesty's gunboats and column after column of red-coated soldiers. More troubling still, the British were interfering with America's march Westward. As pioneers began to roll their wagons across the Alleghenies, they encountered resistance from Native Americans, armed with muskets provided by the British. The Native Americans were understandably resentful of the intrusion into their homelands, and were further encouraged by their British arms suppliers to resist takeover by the Americans.[11] Pressures mounted for US infantrymen to throw the British out of Canada and stop the flow of weapons to Native Americans. Even though the American Army had only around 11,000 troops, the infantry was the only viable military option since America's Navy remained an unworthy adversary (at only seventeen ships strong) against the sizable flotilla of British warships on the Great Lakes. It was hoped that because Napoleon had so easily surrendered his Louisiana stakes in the New World, perhaps the British might also decide to leave Canada.

Thus was America riven with debate over who most warranted an attack: the British (a policy supported by Francophiles, mostly rural Jeffersonian Republicans) or the French (a policy supported by the Anglophiles, mostly New England Federalists). One conclusion was certain: the United States did not have the resources to take on both challenges at the same time. Britain eventually received the honors, with impressment the first article of offense to justify the bellicose tilt by the young Republic in its direction. Another, far less glorious, war of independence against the British was about to begin.

Even though the United States survived the ordeal intact at least and retained its independence, the War of 1812 with Great Britain was something of a disaster—indeed, a historian has called it "the greatest disgrace ever dealt to American arms."[12] Another scholar, Thomas A. Bailey, further notes that the war "was a rash departure from the judicious policy of Washington, Adams, and Jefferson—of playing for time and letting America's booming birthrate and Europe's recurrent distresses fight the nation's battles."[13] The United States—still in its formative years, disorganized, and divided in allegiances toward Britain and France—was unable to repel the British military this time around. A recalcitrant Congress refused to appropriate monies for President Madison (who was possibly having reservations about his separation of powers theory) to combat the red coats' siege against Washington, DC. Admiral Sir George Cockburn of the Royal Navy torched the Capitol and the White House as the President fled on horseback into the Virginia countryside. Cabinet members hid in their home states, federal lawmakers adjourned, Anglophiles in New England denounced "Mr. Madison's war," and Massachusetts went so far as to seek a separate peace with the British crown. American infantrymen sought to rout British and Canadian forces and a rout is what they got, but they were the victims. Only Andrew Jackson's spirited victory at New Orleans and Admiral Oliver Hazard Perry's triumph in the Battle of Lake Erie provided occasions for national pride.

At last, on Christmas Eve of 1814, both British and American leaders—war weary, tax burdened, bloodied—decided they were fed up with the conflict. Luckily for the United States, Napoleon had attracted greater attention in London than the unruly colonialists across the Atlantic. The British needed to marshal their resources for a final push against the French Emperor, who more directly threatened the British way of life than the faraway, obstreperous Republic in the New World. American and British diplomats signed the **Treaty of Ghent**, *bringing this second war between America and Britain to an end in 1814.* The treaty proved tremendously popular throughout the American states, even though the peace treaty delicately sidestepped any mention of freedom on the high seas or curbing the evils of impressment—the original causes of the war.[14] The Duke of Wellington would go on to defeat Napoleon's armies the next year; and, with Napoleon out of the picture, the British no longer needed to engage in the impressment of American sailors for war against France.

In the **Rush-Bagot Agreement** of 1817, *America's first significant arms control pact, the British and the Americans contracted to remove their naval ships from the Great Lakes,* defusing an explosive situation. Though humiliated in the War of 1812, the Americans had demonstrated additional success at diplomacy, again thanks in large part to Britain's greater interest in maintaining its military strength on the high seas in defense of the British Isles against the French and other European rivals.

Rebuffed in their efforts to annex Canada, America's leaders looked toward Florida where Spanish armies and their indigenous allies often disrupted the flow of commerce from farmers in Georgia and Alabama to eastern seaboard ports for shipment to Europe. In 1817, and without approval from Congress, President James Monroe sent troops—led by the indomitable "hero of New Orleans," General Andrew Jackson—into the Florida territory to protect US interests. With questionable authority but unquestioned brio, Jackson swiftly deposed the Spanish governor, executed suspected British spies who got in his way, and announced that henceforth America held legal jurisdiction over the entire Florida territory. In response, Spain entered into protracted negotiations with Secretary of State John Quincy Adams that resulted in a tradeoff set down legally in the **Adams-Onís Treaty** of 1821: *the Florida territory in exchange for assurances from the United States that the Spanish could enjoy unfettered rule over Texas and the southwest.* At the time, some Americans questioned the wisdom of the bargain, but most were happy to have Spain permanently out of the nation's southeast corner.[15]

## Monroe Delivers a Lecture

America's main foreign policy interests in these early days—securing the territorial integrity of the world's first constitutional democracy and protecting its commercial activities—were underscored in President James Monroe's 1823 State of the Union Address. In this most heralded of all American foreign policy pronouncements, subsequently labeled the **Monroe Doctrine**, the President warned the capitals of the Old World that *the nations of the Western Hemisphere were "henceforth not to be considered as subjects for future colonization by any European power."* Speaking brashly on behalf of a weak nation that not long before had been sent reeling by a stronger opponent in the War of 1812, Monroe said further

> In the wars of the European powers in matters relating to themselves we have never taken any part, nor does it comport with our policy so to do. It is only when our rights are invaded or seriously menaced that we resent injuries or make preparations for our defense. With the movements in this hemisphere we are, of necessity, more immediately connected. . . . We owe it, therefore, to candor, and to the amicable relations existing between the United States and those powers, to declare that we should consider any attempt on their part to extend their system to any portion of this hemisphere as dangerous to our peace and safety. . . . It is equally impossible, therefore, that we should behold such interposition, in any form, with indifference.

This message from Monroe—a "lecture" to Europe, observed Adams (it was not considered a "doctrine" until the 1850s)—amounted to a second declaration of American independence. Or a third, if one wishes to count the feeble efforts of 1812, when the new Republic was saved by the British need to withdraw and concentrate on Napoleon's armies. Monroe put the Europeans firmly on notice: America would resist further attempts by them to colonize the Western Hemisphere. It was also a signal from the United States that it had a special interest in its neighbors to the south as future friends and allies (although America's "friendship" would periodically take the form of intervention by the US Marines or the CIA). An additional theme in Monroe's address was a familiar repudiation of American involvement in European politics. Although this stance has been discarded as a modern principle of American foreign policy, at the time it was a natural continuation of the isolationism heralded in Washington's farewell address and largely supported by the legislative branch of government.

Monroe's remarks had a strong effect on many who read them, including retired president Thomas Jefferson. "This sets our compass and points the course which we are to steer through the ocean of time opening on us," he wrote. Looking back on the "doctrine" decades later, the first Chancellor of the German empire, Otto von Bismarck (who was eight years old at the time the doctrine was announced), dismissed the speech as nothing more than an "international impertinence." In one of those odd twists of history, President Monroe enjoyed the backing of a strong-armed ally who quickly supported the President's desire to preserve the Americas for the Americans: none other than its recent foe, Great Britain. The British sought to counter rumors (false as it turned out) regarding French and Spanish economic designs on the Americas and, at least for the moment, leaders in London were delighted to stand with the United States.

His Majesty's Government even offered to issue a joint US-UK statement of warning to the Continental Europeans. Secretary of State John Quincy Adams advised the President, however, that the United States should take a stance on its own and avoid leaving the impression to other nations that the nation was merely a "cockboat in the wake of the British man-of-war."[16] Even though the President's address had little immediate influence in world capitals, nor with Bismarck near the end of the 1800s, the prestige of Monroe's famous name and the aura of antiquity association with his declaration would lead subsequent presidents to invoke the principles of the Monroe Doctrine as if they were a hallowed American tradition.

## Westward Ho!

The sense of American "exceptionalism" discussed in Chapter 2 bolstered the nation's belief in a global calling to lead and uplift the rest of the world. Initially, in the name of democracy and commerce, that mission was to tame the Western frontier—foreign territory at the time and, like the Louisiana Purchase and other distant land acquisitions in the West that followed, a matter for American foreign policy. The nation turned to this task with gusto during the Monroe administration (1817–1825). As newspaper editor John L. O'Sullivan would later proclaim in 1845, the United States had a **manifest** [that is, self-evident] **destiny** *"to overspread and to possess the whole of the continent which Providence has given us."*[17] A rapidly rising number of ambitious farmers and trappers ventured into the continental heartland, soon followed by merchants who dreamed of harbors on the Western seaboard and sea-lanes to the markets of Asia. The advance toward the Pacific coast was in motion, as Americans envisioned unlimited possibilities for themselves and their progeny. By dispensing generous land grants and cheap financing, the federal government provided much of the impetus for this opening up of the Great Plains and the Westward expansion. The Central Pacific and Union Pacific railroads, for example, were government-chartered companies encouraged by the incentives of large land grants and huge government loans.[18]

The Westward march was costly not just in terms of depleting the federal treasury (as the Louisiana Purchase had clearly demonstrated), but in the blood spilled in wars with Native Americans. The tragedies visited on the Cherokees, herded from their ancestral lands in the southeast along the Trail of Tears into Oklahoma, as well as on other Native Americans, are wretched episodes in America's early history. Moreover, in the name of further expansion, the nation seemed prepared in 1846 to fight the British yet again, this time for land in the Pacific northwest. The rallying cry became "54°–40° or Fight" for presidential candidate James K. Polk and his supporters, who insisted the United States dissolve its 1818 pact with the British that established joint control over the region and take over the northwest territory through 54 degrees, 40 north latitude. Once elected president, Polk managed to avoid war by negotiating a compromise urged by the Senate that allowed US control of the territory through the 49th parallel. The episode was an illustration of Congress and the President working together toward a successful resolution of a diplomatic standoff. Heated debate often erupted between the branches, with give-and-take on both sides, and—by an overwhelming vote—the Senate advised the President to accept the latest British bargaining position. When Polk finally agreed, the Senate passed the treaty decisively. The end result: "Expansionism thus carried the nation to the far reaches of the Pacific Northwest and did so without armed conflict."[19]

Next on the young nation's real estate list was the prospect of more land in the southwest and along the Pacific coast. Expansionist aspirations had contributed to the war against Britain in 1812 and the efforts to drive the Spanish out of Florida. Now the nation would declare war against Mexico in 1846, *acquiring in the peace treaty of 1848—the* **Treaty of Guadalupe Hidalgo**—*all of New Mexico, California, and an extension of the Texas boundary to the Rio Grande.*

Moreover, across the Pacific Ocean, Asia beckoned to the restless spirit of southern cotton growers, Western fur trappers, business entrepreneurs, adventurers, and missionaries. Two years before the Mexican War, the United States had sent an emissary to China for the purpose of negotiating access to markets for American goods, as well as to establish the right of **extraterritoriality**. *The purpose behind this legal doctrine was to seek the extension of US law to cover American citizens in foreign nations.* This right would allow US citizens accused of crimes in China to be tried before an American consular official rather than face unpredictable Chinese judicial procedures that sometimes included torture. The claim of extraterritoriality can create tensions between nations because a host nation prefers to honor its own laws rather than turn over alleged criminals to their native countries. Although the number of cases was few and no single incident precipitated this request to China, Washington officials found it prudent to seek this authority. Extensive negotiations between the State Department and the Chinese foreign ministry led to the signing of a treaty in 1844 that endorsed the legal arrangement between the nations. Enticing commercial opportunities smoothed the bargain for both sides. Today, Washington officials have requested extraterritoriality in Afghanistan as a condition of leaving a small force of US troops in that country after the bulk of America's army departs in 2013 and 2014. The Afghan President said he would consult with his legislative assembly about the acceptability of this request.

In 1854, Commodore Matthew C. Perry steamed into the Bay of Yedo (now Tokyo) with an armada of US naval ships worthy of a major power—*an intimidating display of military force* sometimes referred to as **gunboat diplomacy**. Perry carried a letter of friendship from President Franklin Pierce addressed to the Emperor of Japan and, while in the region, the Commodore visited China as well, nudging this market of (at the time) a half-billion consumers further toward a trading relationship with the United States. America was hardly the only nation to dream of commercial profits in Asia; European rivals had their own merchant and warships plying the waters off the Chinese and Japanese seaboards. The long history of isolationism practiced by China and Japan was beginning to erode. Further, on the missionary front, the hearts of American Christians swelled at the prospect of converting untold millions of Asian heathens to their faith.

Defending US interests in the Philippines, a Senator from Minnesota would soon maintain that "we come as ministerial angels, not as despots."[20] And, demonstrating the persistence of this feeling in the nation, decades later at the turn of the century President William McKinley further argued that it was the duty of Americans in the Philippines to "uplift and civilize and Christianize."[21] Here was another matter on which the executive and legislative branches of government could agree—a policy lubricant for the complex machinery of government established by the Constitution. It was sorely needed in light of the rising tensions in the nation over states' rights and a southern economy based on slavery. In 1807, the federal government passed the Act Prohibiting Importation of Slaves that outlawed the shipment of slaves into the United States—a move that bridged foreign and domestic policy and contributed to growing resentments between the nation's North and South.

At mid-nineteenth century, the United States had established two quite different stances toward the world: keeping Europe at a distance while reaching out to Asia; isolation, on one hand, involvement, on the other hand. "Americans did not feel that a vigorous and far-reaching policy in the Pacific contradicted their basic isolationist premise," noted the historian Charles O. Lerche Jr., "even though great-power intrigue complicated their every move."[22]

## Civil War

While America had in mind Westward expansion and missionary work abroad, as well as trade in such commodities as cotton and furs in exchange for Asian tea and spices, challenges closer to home soon began to dominate the nation's agenda. Indeed, the "United" States stood on the brink of disintegration, its constitutional principles about to be tested as never before or since. President Lincoln essentially set the Constitution aside and adopted quasi-dictatorial powers for the purpose of preserving the Union. He did so not by claiming inherent presidential powers but by conceding openly that he was going beyond his rightful authorities in response to the nation's tragic breach—a state of national emergency. Lawmakers in the North largely agreed with the need for special presidential authorities, although they—and the President— made it clear that this aggrandizement of executive powers was both extraordinary and temporary.[23]

Nothing since the War of Independence so turned the nation inward as the War Between the States (or, for Southerners, the "War of Northern Aggression"), which erupted in 1861. As the nation split in half over the question of slavery and secession, it now had dual foreign policies: both the North and the South reached out to Europe for help in their cause. Great Britain came close to making a formal alliance with the South, the source of 80 percent of the cotton used in British textile mills. "We do not like slavery," said British Prime Minister Lord Palmerston, "but we want cotton."[24] After the North's impressive victory at Antietam, however, strategists in London had second thoughts about tilting toward the South and chose the more prudent course of neutrality. Important, too, was President Lincoln's willingness to work tirelessly with diplomats in the State Department toward the goal of ensuring that European nations rejected recognition of the Confederacy.

In the midst of President Abraham Lincoln's internecine woes, France spied an opportunity: perhaps the Americans would be too distracted by their own civil strife to worry much about defending the principles of the Monroe Doctrine. French troops invaded Mexico and, in alliance with Mexican monarchists, placed a reliable puppet, the Austrian archduke Ferdinand Maximilian, on its throne. The government of Napoleon III had calculated correctly: officials in Washington, DC could manage nothing more than a verbal protest of the invasion. Yet, when the Civil War ended in 1865, the United States sent a stern warning to France to cease and desist from its Mexican venture or face the consequences. The French withdrew, perhaps in part because of the military might demonstrated by the United States in the Civil War, but probably even more so because the people of France were enraged by the costly Mexican gamble. Further considerations included the French fear of rising German militarism, along with a concern about the mounting guerrilla war fought by Mexican Republicans against the French interlopers. Left in the lurch was poor, handsome Maximilian (cynically known as the "Archdupe"), who for all his troubles soon found himself standing before a Mexican firing squad.[25]

The American Civil War represented a low ebb in this nation's evolving foreign policy; the nation had been forced to turn dramatically inward to resolve its own domestic problems related to Southern secession, ignoring relations with most of the outside world even more than usual. Still, paradoxically, the war had a significant influence on US relations with the world. The firepower and battlefield skill displayed by the North and the South sent a message around the globe that the United States was now a mature military power with legitimate claims of global eminence. The apparent determination of America's leaders to push the French out of Mexico, at the point of a bayonet if necessary, revealed a tenacious adherence to the principles Monroe had enunciated in 1823. No foreign power would seriously challenge the Monroe Doctrine again until the Soviet precipitation of the Cuban missile crisis in 1962.

## A Nation Grown Bolder

When the Civil War formally ended at Appomattox in 1865 after four years and a staggering number of casualties on both sides (over 775,000 killed or wounded), Americans returned to the task of nation building, further Westward expansion, and trying to make their separate institutions of government work together in the nation's capital. In the most significant territorial acquisition since the Louisiana Purchase, at the behest of Secretary of State W. H. Seward—a zealous expansionist—the newly reunited America in 1867 purchased the Alaskan territory from the Russians for $7.2 million (about two cents an acre). Those who failed to share the Secretary's enthusiasm for these icy fields referred to the Alaskan purchase as "Seward's Folly" or "Seward's Icebox" (a view shared by the Russians and, thus, their willingness to unload the property at a bargain rate).

Despite pockets of opposition on the Hill, Seward proved a masterful negotiator, both with the Russian foreign ministry and with the members of the US Senate whose support he needed to move this and his many other treaties forward toward approval.

Although the Alaskan Purchase in 1867 was his most famous diplomatic accomplishment, by the end of his tenure Seward had managed to negotiate more treaties with other nations than had all of his predecessors combined.[26] His record is all the more remarkable in light of how politically weak President Andrew Johnson was at the time on Capitol Hill—a function of his own limited leadership abilities and the still smoldering resentment over the Civil War exhibited by members of Congress from the South. A combination of Seward's persuasiveness, along with a belief among most lawmakers in the goal of territorial expansion, yielded a dynamic burst of successful diplomatic activity during this post-Civil War period.

Seward had his failures, though, including an attempt to annex Hawaii. Key members of Congress—reflecting the views of many Americans—had grown uneasy about the costs and long-term burden of constantly adding new territory to the nation. Further bucking the executive branch on some diplomatic initiatives, lawmakers also voted against efforts to buy the Virgin Islands and to establish a protectorate over Haiti. As with earlier generations, Americans in 1865 were of two minds about the involvement of their country overseas. "The nation lunged into the future at breakneck speed," writes Lerche, "but with constant nostalgic glances to the simpler past it was leaving behind."[27] That ambivalence would persist.

Near the end of the nineteenth century, the United States displayed a strong self-confidence based on its rising military and economic strength. The nation's impressive military firepower had been demonstrated during the Civil War, and its commercial ties abroad were rapidly mushrooming as the US diplomatic presence expanded around the world. Thus when a diplomatic dispute between the United Kingdom and Venezuela arose in 1895, the administration of President Grover Cleveland felt self-reliant enough to inform the British that Washington, DC, would arbitrate the matter. Magisterially, *Secretary of State Richard Olney informed London that "the United States is practically sovereign on this continent, and its fiat is law upon the subjects to which it confines its interposition."* As Gaddis Smith noted, "this blustering affirmation quickly became known as 'the **Olney corollary**'—the first of many expansions and interpretations of the original [Monroe] Doctrine."[28]

Olney's hubris aside, the United States resumed its core, long-standing policy of standing largely apart from the powers of Europe—again something that all the branches of government could agree on. There was much work to be done at home: a bountiful continent to cultivate and lace together with roads, rails, and canals; factories to build; farmlands to seed. Yet, at the same time, Americans understood the importance of some degree of international diplomacy to ward off or settle disputes with other nations. Moreover, they were enjoying the prosperity that came from global trade, and many had an ongoing interest in foreign missionary work. Americans were, just as they always had been, ambivalent about foreign "entanglements." Regardless, the world would soon intrude on their preoccupations at home, as the sands of isolationism ran quickly through the hourglass. The events of 1898 would cast aside the idea of a United States apart from the world.

## EMERGENCE AS A GREAT POWER, 1898–1920

America's plunge into world affairs was a result of the Spanish-American War. This conflict, examined briefly at the opening of this chapter, also marked the beginning of concern in Washington, DC about questions of global human rights.

### The Spanish–American War

When the mysterious explosion sank the US battleship *Maine* in Havana harbor in 1898, lost beneath the waves, too, were McKinley's hopes for a diplomatic settlement. Prodded by the war-mongering journalism of newspaper titans Joseph Pulitzer and William Randolph Hearst, the American public demanded revenge. In Spain's eyes a diplomatic settlement began to look more attractive, but it was too late. Congress declared war in April and the United States quickly defeated the Spanish. "The United States had the opportunity to conquer and occupy Mexico, Cuba, and islands in the Caribbean," Amos Perlmuter wrote, "but doing so was always rejected and unacceptable to the American people."[29] The McKinley administration did take over the Philippine Islands in the Pacific, however, and a few other island possessions from Hawaii to Puerto Rico.

Historian John Lewis Gaddis has justified America's expansion at home and abroad with this argument: ". . . for the United States, *safety comes from enlarging, rather than from contracting, its sphere of responsibility*."[30] The relevance of this maxim for today's world has been questioned, however, because critics see an important difference between pursuing hegemony from Maine to California, on one hand, as America did in its early history, and, on the other hand, seeking hegemony practically everywhere around the world. It is one thing to take on Mediterranean pirates and North American natives in the old days (or, even today, in the case of pirates off the coast of Somalia) and quite another to have over seven hundred military bases around the world and to be engaged simultaneously in three major wars, as the United States has been recently in Iraq, Afghanistan, and against global terrorists. A successful grand strategy in support of American foreign policy requires a balance between ends and means, the central message in Gaddis's popular "Grand Strategy Seminar" at Yale University. Critics of his justification for US expansion wonder, though, if America can keep its ends within its means while supporting armies and wars around the world. One of these critics, Paul Kennedy, a seminar colleague of Gaddis at Yale, suggests that America's grand strategy has been out of balance, suffering from an "imperial overstretch" likely to bankrupt the nation while also generating fear (however unjustified) among other nations about the military, political, and economic global intentions of the United States.[31]

### Spreading Democracy and Opening Markets

One thing was clear at the beginning of the twentieth century: most of the world had begun to see the United States as a new colonial power—and, for some, an imperial hegemon. The maturing Republic now had far-flung interests stretching across the

Pacific Ocean, along with a world-class military establishment prepared to defend those interests. The United States had also adopted an inspiring mission that would figure more prominently in its foreign policy calculations than any other theme: "the repeated presidential calls to promote the creation of democratic government abroad."[32]

This startling expansion in the watershed year of 1898, however, "did not constitute so sharp a departure from the isolationist tradition as has often been assumed," maintains historian Foster Rhea Dulles. "For the United States made no commitments to foreign nations as it emerged upon the international scene." In the spirit of its founding principles and with over a century of experience as a nation, "it entered upon no entangling alliances with other powers."[33] Nevertheless, something had changed profoundly. Between the end of the Civil War and the beginning of the twentieth century, US exports increased from about $200 million to almost $1.5 billion; and, in defense of these trading interests, the US Navy expanded by thirty new battleships and cruisers between 1832 and 1900. When President Theodore "Teddy" Roosevelt became president in 1901, he made it clear that "more and more the increasing interdependence and complexity of international political and economic relations render it incumbent on all civilized and orderly powers to insist on the proper policing of the world." He said that the United States would be in the forefront of "civilized" nations ready to police and intervene abroad to maintain global order.[34] Other nations now understood that America had arrived on the world stage, with a worldwide presence and a willingness to back up its diplomacy with armed force.

To believe that a nation could be a world power and still remain free of "entangling alliances" was naive; nevertheless, such was the thinking in Washington, DC at the beginning of the twentieth century. As the United States gathered more experience abroad in its dealing with well-armed rivals in the Far East, this naïveté would become tempered with a stronger sense of realism.

The United States decided that the Philippines and Guam were especially attractive as "stepping stones" to China—islands where Americans could establish a base of operations for developing commercial inroads into the populous marketplaces that beckoned on the Asian mainland.[35] The McKinley administration confronted a situation, though, in which Europe and Japan seemed intent on creating their own spheres of influence in China, regardless of what the Chinese may have wished. With America's entrepreneurs providing access to capital, President McKinley vowed to compete aggressively for business opportunities on the Asian mainland, *an approach to foreign policy based on advancing private US commercial interests* and known at the time as **dollar diplomacy**. His Secretary of State, Jay Hay, argued in 1899 for an **open door policy** in China, *whereby each major power—including the United States—would have a sphere of trading influence that had to be honored by other nations.* The leaders of Europe and Japan, however, essentially ignored Hay's unilateral proclamation and conducted business as they wished.

As for the Chinese, a zealous faction of xenophobes among them strenuously opposed the plans of foreigners to divide up their nation for economic gain. Known as the "Boxers" ("Righteous Harmony Society" or Yehequan in China), they instigated a resistance movement in 1900 against the interlopers from Japan and the West. The modus operandi of the **Boxer Rebellion** was simple: kill the foreign "invaders." The secret society set about murdering hundreds of Western businesspeople and missionaries. In a show of America's first efforts at major multinational diplomatic leadership, Secretary Hay proposed that the trading powers work together to defuse the rebellion by assuring China of its territorial integrity, by emphasizing the commercial benefits that would be made available to the Chinese, and by displaying Western muscle. The Secretary of State's call for an "open door" was now taken more seriously by the Europeans and the Japanese; and even the Boxers calmed down, in part because European and American iron-hulled steamships, powerful artillery, and the placement of 15,500 soldiers (among them 2,500 Americans) in China projected greater strength than the delusional Boxers had anticipated.[36]

The negotiations were largely a success, but the Japanese felt affronted by America's interference in what they viewed as their own exclusive geopolitical sphere of influence, namely, all of China. Hay's bold practice of diplomacy in China led to a simmering resentment in Tokyo that would later mingle with other grievances and fears about the West to boil over into a Japanese attack against Pearl Harbor in 1941. Especially vexing to Tokyo was the unwillingness of the United States during these intervening years to allow unfettered Japanese expansion throughout Asia.[37] Americans insisted on clear sea-lanes in Asia for US Navy and merchant shipping. To emphasize the point, Teddy Roosevelt sent sixteen battleships on a world cruise—the "Great White Fleet," it was dubbed by journalists—with the unambiguous message that, if necessary, America's military might would back up its diplomatic efforts to keep Asian markets open to US goods.

Even though Roosevelt played a key role in negotiating an end to the Russo-Japanese War in 1905, tensions between the Japan and the United States persisted off and on during the early decades of twentieth century, fueled in America by anti-Japanese sentiment in California (where "Oriental" students were segregated from "Americans"). Other points of contention between the two nations included US immigration restrictions against the Japanese promulgated by officials in Washington, DC; and, on the Japanese side, anti-US articles in Tokyo newspapers. Relations continued to deteriorate all the way through the administration of the next Roosevelt president: FDR. Franklin Delano Roosevelt grew so concerned about Japanese threats of expansion in Asia that, in 1940, he increased US aid to China and instituted a complete embargo on American iron and steel scrap—war materials—headed for Japan.

Immigration disputes between Japan and the United States were particularly heated, as had often been the case in American foreign policy long before the acrimony arose over quotas for Japanese during the years between the tenures of Teddy and Franklin Roosevelt. Until 1880, the United States had no federal immigration policy to speak of; each state decided how many newcomers to admit. When the flow of immigration began to rise dramatically at the end of the nineteenth century, Congress decided to step in and set country quotas. This policy domain became another battleground between the executive and legislative branches and, acting on behalf of the State Department and its quest for better diplomatic relations with foreign nations, American presidents occasionally vetoed legislative quotes. With respect to the Japanese during these decades, American workers' groups lobbied Congress to ban cheap laboring coming into the United States from Japan; while the executive branch tried—often unsuccessfully—to convince lawmakers about the inadvisability of damaging US-Japanese relations by restricting immigration. Today's hot-button immigration issue is the debate over illegal migrants from Mexico; and, again, lawmakers have sought to defend American workers while the State Department (though not unmindful of unemployment figures in the United States) has fretted about harming relations with Mexico.

Teddy Roosevelt's role in the completion of the Treaty of Portsmouth (signed near Portsmouth, New Hampshire) that brought the Russo-Japanese War to an end further signaled America's emergence on the world scene. For this and other diplomatic initiatives, Sweden awarded the President with the Nobel Peace Prize in 1906. Not wanting to turn either Russia or Japan against the United States, Roosevelt had to exhibit careful neutrality between the two warring nations during the peace negotiations. Through extensive talks at the highest levels, the President was able to use the rising prestige of his office to serve as a trusted mediator. When the talks stalled, he grew frustrated and went on a hunting trip to Colorado. This seeming aloofness to the negotiations convinced the Russians and the Japanese that Teddy Roosevelt was sufficiently above the fray to serve as an unbiased peacemaker. The President invited the disputants to the United States for a conclusive peace conference (Portsmouth was cooler in the summer than humid Washington, DC) and, after protracted bargaining over territorial disagreements related to the war, the Russian and Japanese diplomats at last settled on acceptable treaty language. Roosevelt had provided the venue for peace negotiations, as well as a patient, steady hand that eventually moved the contending parties together. As one of his biographers concluded, peace had come by virtue of Roosevelt's "sheer force of moral purpose, by clarity of perception, by mastery of detail and benign manipulation of men."[38]

The interest of the United States in the Far East was not fueled by economic considerations alone; the concern for human rights that had surfaced during the Spanish-American War proved to have strong legs. American foreign policy was now shot through with a new strain of idealism that sought to carry home-grown, constitutionally based concepts of freedom and civil liberties to other parts of the globe. Despite this rising interest in human rights, power politics (or **realpolitik**, in the language of the Europeans) remained preeminent in the strategic planning of leaders in Washington, as was true in every other major capital of the world. According to this perspective, *international affairs were to be based not on theoretical or ethical considerations but rather on practical and material objectives.* No one demonstrated this approach more vividly than the intervention of the indefatigable Teddy Roosevelt into Central American affairs. An equestrian hero of cavalry charges in Cuba during the Spanish-American War, he sided early in his presidency with insurgents in a Colombian civil war. Successful in their rebellion, they established a new land—Panama—where Roosevelt was allowed to carry out his vision of building a canal to connect the Atlantic and Pacific Oceans, a triumph for American commercial shipping interests as well as for US military strategists.

To ensure that Europeans got the message that America's interest in Latin America was still alive and well, Teddy Roosevelt issued an amendment to the Monroe Doctrine in 1904. According to this **Roosevelt corollary**, henceforth

> Chronic wrongdoing, or an impotence which results from a general loosening of the ties of civilized society, may in America, as elsewhere, ultimately require intervention by some civilized nation, and in the Western Hemisphere the adherence of the United States to the Monroe Doctrine may force the United States, however reluctantly, in flagrant cases of such wrong-doing or impotence, to the exercise of an international police power.

The United States was not (yet) policing the whole world, but Roosevelt had laid claim to this role in Latin America. One of his favorite expressions was the West African proverb, "Speak softly and carry a big stick."[39] The Roosevelt corollary was a classic expression of **big stick diplomacy**: *brandishing the military instrument of foreign policy to persuade adversaries toward an acceptance of the American point of view.* A cousin of gunboat diplomacy, this big-stick approach was periodically coupled with dollar diplomacy. Favored particularly by Roosevelt's successor, William Howard Taft, the objective frequently was the exercise of unbridled government support for US corporate interests in Latin American and elsewhere. Military muscle and corporate money, with an occasional interest in questions of religious proselytizing and the advancement of democracy and human rights abroad—these were the driving forces behind America's foreign policy at the dawn of the twentieth century.

## Wilsonian Idealism

With the advent of the Wilson administration (1913–1921), the United States continued to work diligently to keep its traditional distance from affairs in Europe. Isolationism, the nostalgia of turning the clock back to a happier, more peaceful era when America could concentrate on its internal development, again became the order of the day. President Woodrow Wilson, though, did not allow this introspection to weaken the hold of the United States over its self-proclaimed sphere of influence in Latin America. The otherwise dovish Wilson ordered military expeditions into Mexico in

1914, and again in 1916, to subdue rebels in the countryside who were resistant to the idea of bowing to the United States as a hegemonic guardian over the Western Hemisphere.

Yet in spite of the nation's overall isolationist sentiments, just as the sinking of the *Maine* had drawn American into war, so in 1915 did the sinking of the British liner *Lusitania* by a German submarine—with the loss of 128 US citizens along with 1,070 other passengers—stir impassioned anti-German sentiments. At first resisting these public passions, Wilson the idealist received thunderous applause from Democratic Convention delegates in 1916 for his pledge to keep the United States far removed from worn-ravaged Europe. Yet soon the Germans began to engage in unrestricted submarine warfare against any ship entering the Atlantic Ocean, including those flying an American flag. Adding to the insult, in 1917 German Foreign Secretary Arthur Zimmermann sent a secret telegram to his envoy in Mexico, which was intercepted by British naval intelligence and passed along to Washington officials. The telegram *ordered the envoy to seek a pact of aggression with Mexico against the United States, should the Americans enter the war against Germany.* The payoff to Mexico—in another display of realpolitik in world affairs—would be a return of Texas, New Mexico, and Arizona to the Mexicans. Disclosure of the **Zimmermann telegram** by the American press was equivalent to throwing kerosene onto the flames of anti-German sentiment.[40]

The bellicose behavior of the Germans was too much even for Wilson. He urged war against Germany in a speech before Congress on April 2, 1917; and, when that body obliged with a declaration of war, the President sent two million American soldiers overseas to help tip the scales against the Kaiser. In Wilson's words, this would be a "final war for human liberty."

After the death of six million soldiers, including 116,516 in American uniform, the conflict finally came to an end on November 11, 1918. President Wilson turned to the daunting task of preventing all future wars through the establishment of his cherished **League of Nations**, listed as the crowning glory of the "Fourteen Points" he presented to Congress in 1919. At last, an international "league" would be able *to exercise collective action by the civilized nations of the world for the purpose of preventing future wars.* Among the other provisions in Wilson's famous Fourteen Points declaration was independence for Poland, Austria, Hungary, and the Balkans, as well as a renouncement of secret diplomacy (see *Perspectives on American Foreign Policy* 4.1).

The major powers of Europe and, indeed, senators in Wilson's own government, viewed the prospects for enduring peace in the world through a more jaded lens. "God gave us his Ten Commandments and we broke them," observed French Foreign Minister Georges Clemenceau. "Wilson gave us his Fourteen Points—we shall see."[41] Brushing aside such cynicism, Wilson sailed for France—thus becoming the first American president to set foot in the Old World—to negotiate the *terms for the end of the war* through the **Treaty of Versailles** (1919). The brilliant British economist John

---

## PERSPECTIVES ON AMERICAN FOREIGN POLICY 4.1

**WILSON'S FOURTEEN POINTS, January 8, 1918.
In a speech before the Congress, President Woodrow Wilson announced his plan for the peace to follow World War I. The Fourteen Points, especially number 14, represented what Wilson called "the moral climax of this . . . final war for human liberty."**

1. Abolition of secret diplomacy
2. Freedom to navigate the high seas in peace and war
3. Removal of economic barriers among the nations
4. Reduction of armaments
5. Adjustment of colonial claims in the interest of both the inhabitants and the powers concerned
6. Restoration of Russia and a welcome for her in the society of nations
7. The return of Belgium to her people
8. Evacuation and restoration of French territory, including Alsace-Lorraine, taken by the Germans in 1871
9. Readjustment of Italian frontiers "along clearly recognizable lines of nationality"
10. Free opportunity for "autonomous development" for people of Austria-Hungary
11. Restoration of the Balkan nations and free access to the sea for Serbia
12. Protection for minorities in Turkey
13. An independent Poland
14. "A general association [the League] of nations" to secure "mutual guarantees of political independence and territorial integrity to great and small states alike"

*SOURCE:* Summary drawn from Thomas A. Bailey, *A Diplomatic History of the American People*, 9th ed. (Englewood Cliffs, NJ: Prentice-Hall, 1974), p. 598.

---

Maynard Keynes sketched a profile of Versailles's key negotiators with these elegantly phrased, if damning, words:

> These were the personalities of Paris—I forbear to mention other nations or lesser men: Clemenceau, aesthetically the noblest; the President [Wilson], morally the most admirable; Lloyd George [the British Prime Minister], intellectually the subtlest. Out of their disparities and weaknesses the Treaty was born, child of the least worthy attributes of each of its parents, without nobility, without morality, without intellect.[42]

During the course of the negotiations, Wilson was forced to barter away thirteen of his fourteen points in exchange for support for his prized League of Nations. On returning to the United States, the President discovered that the toughest negotiations still lie before him, as senators began to openly express disapproval of the League. The GOP leader and chairman of the Senate Foreign Relations Committee, Henry Cabot Lodge of Massachusetts, disliked the President on a personal level and would probably have sought to block the League proposal on those grounds alone—an example of the influence exerted by individual personalities in world affairs.[43] But he also opposed the notion of involving the United States in an international alliance of any kind, preferring a unilateral American foreign policy—Washington, DC, calling its own shots in the world. The separation of powers doctrine was now running at full tilt, as the leader of the executive branch (Wilson) locked horns with a prominent lawmaker (Lodge) over the future of American foreign policy.

Supported by the mesmerizing orator Senator William E. Borah (R-Idaho) and other "irreconcilables," Lodge stalled the League proposal in committee. This forced President Wilson to take his case to the American people in 1919. In an exhausting series of speeches across the nation that would break his health and lead to a severe stroke, he presented to the public the merits of the League proposal. Lodge, Borah, and their colleagues in the Senate remained unimpressed. The Foreign Relations Committee Chairman proceeded to amend the proposal beyond recognition. Disgusted by the sweeping revisions and by Lodge's haughtiness toward him, Wilson withdrew presidential support for the transfigured document and the Senate quickly voted down the treaty.

In the end, several other major nations embraced the League of Nations (at least on paper), but the United States would not become a member—even though America's own President had put forth the initiative. Echoing the Senate's position against foreign involvement, the voters turned against the Democrats in 1920 (who continued to cling to the idea of a League). They voted into the White House the Republican candidate Warren G. Harding, who promised a return to "normalcy." In the constitutional system of divided institutions sharing power, the legislative branch had won out and appeared to be more in tune with the isolationist sentiments of the American people.

## AMERICA AS A RELUCTANT LEADER, 1920–1945

The world, though, was becoming increasingly difficult to ignore. Further, thanks in part to Wilson's advocacy of international involvement, many Americans now had a greater interest in global affairs; they shared his longing for peaceful relations among nations, even if they may have been skeptical about the idea of a League of Nations. In this spirit, US diplomats and the leaders of fifteen other leading nations met from 1922 to 1928 to negotiate *a major agreement: the* **Kellogg-Briand Treaty**, which *renounced war "as an instrument of national policy."* Eventually, sixty-two nations endorsed the proposal. Nonetheless, even though the Senate approved the treaty and Republican President Herbert Hoover signed it on July 24, 1929, officials in both branches of government studiously avoided entering the United States into any kind of permanent international organization necessary to enforce the document's underlying principle of peaceful conflict resolution. The solemn treaty became little more than a dash of Wilsonian-inspired internationalism in America's isolationist stew. At least, however, the pact had the virtue of underscoring the importance of settling global conflicts by way of peaceful negotiations. This legacy "has stood as an ideal in international relations to this day."[44]

The Great Depression that began in 1929 turned the United States inward as the nation attempted to cope with its most severe unemployment and financial dislocation ever. Overseas, only Latin America received much concentrated attention from the highest levels of the government. President Hoover swept aside the Roosevelt corollary, viewed by some US neighbors to the south as an arrogant expression of Yankee imperialism, and declared in 1930 that nothing in the Monroe Doctrine justified intervention by the United States into the internal affairs of Latin American nations. His successor, Democrat Franklin D. Roosevelt (a distant cousin of Theodore Roosevelt), carried this benevolent departure from the philosophy of "Washington knows best" a step further. He *removed all US troops south of the Rio Grande, with the exception of those stationed in the Panama Canal Zone*, and in 1933 proclaimed a new "**good neighbor policy**" toward Latin America. Mostly, though, President Franklin Roosevelt concentrated his energies on restoring the US economy while keeping a watchful eye on the totalitarian regimes in Germany, Italy, and Japan—all cynical signatories of the Kellogg-Briand peace pact—as they began to build up their arsenals.

## The Fascist Threat

The United States was about to be rudely awakened from its isolationist slumber by the greatest challenges Americans had faced from abroad since the early wars against Great Britain: the rise of fascism and communism, twin threats that would dominate foreign policy for the greater part of the twentieth century. Japan was the first of the "Axis" powers to display an alarming militancy, invading Manchuria in 1931 and Shanghai the next year. The League of Nations proved too feeble to halt the aggression. Critics were quick to blame the absence of the United States from the League's membership as the chief cause of its failure. No nation—member of the League or not—did anything to reverse the Japanese military advances; their passivity set a match to the parchments on which the League and the Kellogg-Briand had been written. An admiring and opportunistic witness to the ease with which Japan took over Manchuria and Shanghai, Italy's Benito Mussolini sent his military into Ethiopia in 1936 and joined a fascist alliance with Adolf Hitler's Germany. Japan allied itself with these Axis powers in the same year and turned toward its major objective, overrunning China with troops in 1937.

Still the United States and the rest of the world did nothing, looking away as the Japanese slaughtered the Chinese people on a grand scale.[45] Americans and their leaders, regardless of which branch of government, did not like what was happening; but they disliked even more the idea of involving their own citizens in expensive combat on a distant continent. Disillusioned by the First World War, viewed by many Americans as an unfortunate involvement by the United States in Europe's petty bickering, isolationists tried to avoid the same mistake again.

Hitler ordered German troops to occupy Austria in 1938. Again, America, Great Britain, Russia, and France stood by passively. Then, with seven divisions massed along the borders of Czechoslovakia, Hitler issued threats demanding the return to

Neville Chamberlain met Adolf Hitler at Berchtesgaden on September 15, 1938, when they discussed the Czech crisis for nearly three hours. Subsequently, they met in Munich to sign the fateful pact that doomed Czechoslovakia. Left to right: Neville Chamberlain, British premier; Adolf Hitler; Joachim von Ribbentrop, German foreign Minister; and British ambassador Sir Nevile Henderson taking tea during the conference at Hitler's mountain retreat near Munich.

Germany of the Sudetenland, a northwestern section of the country where a majority of the populace was of German descent. British Prime Minister Neville Chamberlain led a diplomatic rescue attempt, meeting in Munich with Hitler and Mussolini. Backed by the French Premier Daladier, Chamberlain offered Hitler a policy of appeasement: Germany could have the Sudetenland in exchange for a promise not to take over all of Czechoslovakia—as if the British and French somehow had the right to authorize the dismemberment of another nation.

Following this fateful meeting in Munich, Chamberlain returned to London and beamed triumphantly as he descended the stairs from his airplane on September 30, 1938, with the agreement signed by Hitler. The British Prime Minister proudly held the agreement aloft in his hand and assured the crowd that Europe would have "peace in our time." The document proclaimed "the desire of our two peoples never to go to war with one another again." Six months later Nazi tanks moved across the borders to seize the rest of Czechoslovakia, a nation that had a larger and better equipped army than Germany, but whose leaders felt weakened by the loss of the Sudetenland and demoralized by the willingness of the British and the French to turn their backs on its sovereignty. In Bailey's felicitous phrase, the pact with Hitler and Mussolini proved to be "merely surrender on the installment plan."[46] The site of the surrender, Munich, became a location forever synonymous with **appeasement** and the futility of *attempting to satiate fanatics by yielding to their demands.* The policy of appeasement came to mean "a lack of backbone in foreign affairs."[47]

Hitler next signed a nonaggression pact with the Russians, a people widely popular in the United States at the time. This surprise alliance opened the way for a German invasion of Poland by promising Kremlin leaders the eastern half of the territorial spoils. On September 1, 1939, German Panzer tanks crushed the brave but poorly armed Polish resistance, many of whom rode into battle on horseback. The German Foreign Minister, Joachim von Ribbentrop, recklessly advised Hitler that the British—ever spineless, in Ribbentrop's estimation—would continue to remain on the sidelines.[48] Two days after the German invasion, the British and the French honored a defense treaty with Poland and declared war against the Nazis. The Second World War had begun.[49]

Despite these chilling events in Europe, isolationist opinions remained strong among Americans. For example, at Harvard University—the President's alma mater—the *Crimson* student paper declared in an editorial: "We refuse to fight another balance-of-power war." The President said repeatedly that the United States would remain neutral. Even when rumors of genocide against German Jews filtered out, the Roosevelt administration issued expressions of concern and protest but took no action. This was an internal German problem, concluded the Department of State; America's hands were tied. Besides, two major European powers—Britain and France—were already responding to the Nazi threat; therefore, intervention by the United States was unnecessary.[50] This illusion quickly shattered, however, as France fell before the German blitzkrieg in early 1940 and, a few months later, the British barely escaped a tightening Nazi noose in a desperate evacuation from the European Continent at the port of Dunkirk. His ambition swollen now by a sense of invincibility, Hitler brazenly, treacherously opened a second front in 1941 against his erstwhile ally, Russia.

These disheartening Nazi military successes gave Roosevelt a new perspective on the danger facing the United States. Although the American people were still unwilling to enter into the European war, the President began to take steps toward aiding the British. "We must be the great arsenal of democracy," he declared as 1940 came to a close, adding that the United States would support the Allied Powers "by all means short of war." He failed in his attempt to persuade Congress to repeal the Neutrality Acts, enacted by Congress during the 1930s to keep the United States out of war—the core feature of American foreign policy from 1935 to 1941. Nevertheless, undeterred, he proposed a Lend Lease Act to assist the British struggle against the Nazis. The United States would lend or lease military supplies to the United Kingdom and others fighting Germany, setting aside the inability of the Allied Powers at the time to pay cash for arms. As the President explained to the American people, the United States was reacting like someone who would lend a garden hose to a neighbor whose house was on fire. Isolationists in Congress opposed the measure, fearing a slide toward war and too much power in the hands of a liberal president. America's constitutional blueprint again set the stage for members of Congress to oppose a foreign policy advocated by the executive branch. Nonetheless, the President's Lend Lease Act passed in March of 1941, providing formal legislative authority to backup Roosevelt's lend-lease executive agreement.

The President had already introduced conscription—a military draft—in 1940, which he implemented by way of an executive order. Both actions signaled an end to neutrality. So did Roosevelt's use of an executive agreement (another unilateral executive branch option—in essence, a foreign policy executive order) to aid the British by way of exchanging fifty US warships for American naval base rights in British-owned Bermuda, as discussed in Chapter 3. These initiatives profoundly angered the isolationists on Capitol Hill. "We have torn up 150 years of traditional foreign policy," opined their leader in Congress, Senator Arthur H. Vandenberg (R-Michigan). "We have tossed Washington's Farewell Address into the discard. We have thrown ourselves squarely into the power politics and power wars of Europe, Asia and Africa. We have taken the first step upon a course from which we can never hereafter retreat."[51] Then came December 7, 1941, and the Japanese attack on Pearl

Harbor—a day that, in Roosevelt's lasting words, would "live in infamy." America's insistence that Japan withdraw from China, coupled with a US ban against the sale of aviation fuel and scrap metal to the Japanese, anti-Japanese immigration policies in the United States, and the lingering, irrational fear of the Japanese that it was only a matter of time before the American "imperialists" attacked their homeland, all summed to a humiliation in Tokyo that led to the surprise bombing at Hawaii.[52] At this point, even the staunchest isolationists in Congress were ready to fight. "The only thing now to do is lick hell of out them," declared one of their prominent leaders, Senator Burton K. Wheeler (D-Montana).[53] On December 8, the President asked the Congress to declare war on Japan, which it did immediately; then on Germany, three days later (following a Nazi declaration of war against the United States).

## Embracing Internationalism—Gingerly

Four years of global warfare that sent 60 million people to premature graves and left Europe, Russia, and Japan in smoldering ruins finally ended in 1945, in a victory for the United States and its allies in Europe and the Pacific. The war ushered in the nuclear age with the US bombing of Hiroshima and Nagasaki, revealing how atomic weapons could destroy whole cities in an instant. The war led as well to a new era of international cooperation, one in which the United States was the acknowledged leader. In a revival of Wilsonism spurred by the horrors of the war, most of the world's nations gathered in San Francisco in July 1945 to establish a **United Nations**—"the *boldest experiment in international organization yet adopted by man.*"[54] From the beginning, though, the UN exhibited a fatal flaw. Just as with the League of Nations, it had no workable international police force to halt military aggression by rogue nations. Still, hopes remained high among internationalists that the creation of the UN would be an important step toward Wilson's vision of a lasting world peace.

Peace, however, was not to come easily. No sooner had the United States demobilized its troops after the victory over fascism than yet a new threat emerged on the horizon: a "Cold War" between the Western democracies and the Soviet-led communist nations of the world. "Within six months after war's end all pretense at friendship was being dropped," writes political scientist David S. McLellan. "Henceforth each side would interpret all moves as basically hostile and therefore would act accordingly. The Cold War had begun."[55] The Soviet leader, Joseph Stalin, appeared to be increasingly hostile toward the United States and aggressive in his rhetoric about communist expansion around the globe, not to mention shockingly cruel to his own people and domineering over contiguous nations.

In 1946, British Prime Minister Winston Churchill described the new world in a speech at Westminster College in Fulton, Missouri:

> From Stettin in the Baltic to Trieste in the Adriatic, an iron curtain has
> descended across the continent. Behind that line lie all the capitals
> of the ancient states of Central and Eastern Europe. Warsaw, Berlin,

Prague, Vienna, Budapest, Belgrade, Bucharest and Sofia, all these former cities and the populations around them lie in the Soviet sphere and all are subject in one form or another, not only to Soviet influence, but a very high and increasing measure of control from Moscow.

Every president throughout the Cold War, from Truman to George H. W. Bush, would place the Soviet Union at the top of their lists of foreign policy threats to the United States—and rightly so since the Soviets had acquired the capacity to strike North America with atomic warheads delivered by bombers as early as 1950 and, soon thereafter, by swift intercontinental ballistic missiles. In the chilling and all too accurate acronym of the era, *each of the two "superpowers" had a capacity to retaliate against an attack with a massive counterresponse: a condition known as* **mutual assured destruction**. Its appropriate acronym was MAD, as a deadly rain of nuclear bombs would leave each civilization in radioactive ruins.

Despite a lingering admiration in many nations around the world for all the good things Americans had achieved, from the establishment of a laudably democratic form of government in 1787 and an embrace of civil liberties and civil rights over the years (however slowly), to its victories in Europe and the Pacific in 1945, many in foreign lands were beginning to express doubts about the leadership of the United States. Some feared its intentions as an armed colossus, a hegemonic power, with an army, navy, and air force fanned out across the globe. In the next two chapters I explore the roots of this shift in affection and trust toward America.

In the decades that followed World War II, the United States moved dramatically away from its long-held isolationist leanings toward a posture of greater global involvement. By the end of the twentieth century, thanks to US commercial ventures around the world, "you could buy a Coke in deepest Africa or stay at a Holiday Inn in Urumqi in northwestern China."[56] Nonetheless, many Americans remain ambivalent about foreign entanglements (only one in three adult Americans hold passports),[57] fearful that the resources of the United States might be diverted away from pressing needs at home.

## SUMMARY

From its beginnings, American foreign policy has been like a roller-coaster ride, with occasional heady peaks of intervention abroad to quick rushes down into longer stretches of isolationism. Though often ambivalent about which part of the ride has been the most gratifying, Americans have felt more secure for the most part when distanced from the rest of the world—although never to the point of overlooking the need for profitable commercial relations overseas or turning away allies in times of military danger, as with the assistance of the French during America's revolutionary war.

On the whole, a plunge back into the kind of isolationism that preceded the Second World War is, however, an option that most US citizens believe the nation can no longer afford. America is the world's only superpower, like it or not, and many countries around the globe look to Washington, DC, for guidance and support. As I relate in the next two chapters, the responses of the United States to these expectations of global leadership during and after the Cold War have resulted in both success and failure.

## KEY TERMS

Adams-Onís Treaty (1821) p. 110
appeasement p. 126
big stick diplomacy p. 121
Boxer Rebellion (1900) p. 119
dollar diplomacy p. 118
Embargo Act (1807) p. 108
extraterritoriality p. 113
good neighbor policy (1933) p. 125
gunboat diplomacy p. 113
impressment p. 108
Jay Treaty (1794) p. 105
Kellogg-Briand Treaty (1928) p. 124
League of Nations (1919) p. 122
manifest destiny p. 112

Monroe Doctrine (1823) p. 110
mutual assured destruction (MAD) p. 129
Olney corollary (1895) p. 116
open door policy (1899) p. 118
rapprochement p. 106
realpolitik p. 120
Roosevelt corollary (1904) p. 121
Rush-Bagot Agreement (1817) p. 110
Treaty of Ghent (1814) p. 110
Treaty of Guadalupe Hidalgo (1848) p. 113
Treaty of Versailles (1919) p.122
United Nations (1945) p. 128
XYZ affair (1797) p. 106
Zimmermann telegram (1917) p. 122

---

## QUESTIONS FOR DISCUSSION

1. To what extent do the instincts of the nation's early leaders against global "entanglements" continue to provide a prudent note of caution for today's foreign policy decision makers?

2. Does the Monroe Doctrine remain relevant today? Should the United States extend this doctrine of American hegemony to other parts of the world, such as Southwest Asia (comprised chiefly of Pakistan, Afghanistan, India)?

3. Are there signs of dollar diplomacy and gunboat diplomacy today? To what extent should the needs of the US business community dictate America's foreign policy choices?

4. Do you admire Woodrow Wilson's struggle for a League of Nations, or was he foolishly idealistic? In what ways, if any, has the United Nations been more successful than the League?

5. What are some explanations for the ebb and flow of America's involvement with the rest of the world since 1787? Can you craft a set of hypotheses about the likely course of US foreign policy in the twenty-first century?

6. Why is 1898 considered such an important benchmark in the history of American foreign policy?

## ADDITIONAL READINGS

Bailey, Thomas A. *A Diplomatic History of the American People*, 9th ed. Englewood Cliffs, NJ: Prentice-Hall, 1974.

Kennan, George F. *American Diplomacy: 1900–1950*. Chicago: University of Chicago Press, 1951.

Perkins, Dexter. *The Evolution of American Foreign Policy*. New York: Oxford University Press, 1948.

For further readings, please visit the book's companion website.

MEDIUM RANGE BALLISTIC MISSILE B

SAN CRISTOBAL

LAUNCH POSITION

### CHAPTER 5

# The Cold War and the Doctrine of Containment

## HIGH NOON IN CUBA, 1962

During the Kennedy administration (1961–63), the CIA carried out close surveillance of Cuba, the location of the only socialist revolution that had succeeded in Latin America during the Cold War. The Agency also carried out sabotage and assassination plots against Cuba's leader, Fidel Castro.[1] Reports from US intelligence sources in 1962 pointed to the Soviet shipment of large cylindrical objects onto the island. In response, the CIA stepped up its U-2 surveillance flights. Bad weather, however, prohibited reconnaissance throughout most of August 1962. Even more important, the State Department opposed further U-2 reconnaissance over Cuba. Secretary of State Dean Rusk and national security adviser McGeorge Bundy thought the flights were too risky, not to mention being in violation of international law; moreover, they doubted the presence of nuclear weaponry in Cuba. Analysts at the CIA shared these

A CIA U-2 aerial reconnaissance photo taken over San Cristobal in Cuba in late October, 1962, showing Soviet missile erectors.

doubts (although DCI John McCone thought the Soviets might well try such a gambit). Rusk and Bundy worried, further, that a conventional surface-to-air missile (SAM) on the island might be able to down one of the aircraft, revealing America's questionable surveillance operations to the world. (The Chinese had recently shot down a U-2 over their territory.) Not until mid-October did the U-2s begin to fly again, after McCone and the CIA successfully protested the State Department's position and won approval for renewed flights from the President.

The images from the U-2 cameras were rapidly analyzed by photo-interpreting experts at the CIA. The black-and-white pictures provided unmistakable—and shocking—information: the Soviets were constructing nuclear missile bases in Cuba. The images also made it clear that, fortunately, the missiles would not be armed for at least another two weeks. As a result, President John F. Kennedy could resist pressures from a trigger-happy Pentagon for a quick invasion. Reflecting back on these tense days, former Secretary of Defense Robert S. McNamara expressed his belief that an invasion would have triggered a nuclear war in Cuba, which would have spiraled rapidly into a thermonuclear World War III between the superpowers.

The President instituted a naval blockade against further shipment of missiles to Cuba and insisted that the Soviet leader, Nikita Khrushchev, remove the missiles that were already on the island. The crisis seemed to escalate toward a possible Armageddon. Behind the scenes, though, both sides kept channels of communication open and a

---

**LEARNING OBJECTIVES AND CONSTITUTIONAL ISSUES**

**By the end of this chapter, you will be able to:**

- *Describe how the advent of nuclear weapons changed the nature of American foreign policy.*
- *Understand how the United States and allied democracies countered the threat of global communism during the Cold War.*

- *Recount how the two superpowers—the United States and the Soviet Union—managed their often dangerous relationship.*
- *Explain why détente—the relaxation of tensions between the superpowers during the Cold War—sometimes succeeded and sometimes failed.*

**THIS CHAPTER RAISES THE FOLLOWING CONSTITUTIONAL QUESTIONS:**

- Even though open military combat never erupted between the superpowers during the Cold War, was this era sufficiently dangerous to treat it as a time of quasi-warfare requiring special powers for the president and the executive branch? Who should decide what special powers a president should have? Should such powers be spelled out clearly in law? How should the president's use of such powers be monitored?

- Could the executive branch have benefitted from greater consultation with the legislative branch during the Bay of Pigs planning? The Cuban missile crisis? The lead-up to the wars in Korea, Vietnam, Iraq, and Afghanistan?

- Are the Constitution's foreign policy powers dependent on circumstances, such as crisis versus noncrisis? On the pressure of fast-moving events? On the need for secrecy at any given time?

- Can constitutional governments compete effectively against hierarchically organized autocracies?

compromise arrangement came into view: if America would remove its fifteen Jupiter missiles from Turkey and promise not to invade Cuba, the Soviets would remove its missiles from the island. Not wanting to appear as though he were caving in to Khrushchev, which Congressional Republicans would have denounced as a policy of appeasement, Kennedy managed to keep the deal a secret at the time.

Officials in Washington, DC, remained concerned, however, because Soviet ships bearing missiles continued on course toward Cuba. Nerves frayed in the nation's capital. As Rusk remembers, the United States and the USSR were "eyeball-to-eyeball."[2]

Then, suddenly, the Soviets blinked. Khrushchev agreed to remove the missiles, and the Soviet ships bound for Cuba reversed course. The two-week crisis that had carried the superpowers to the rim of a nuclear holocaust had ended. Quietly, Kennedy would later keep his word about removal of the US missiles in Turkey, which were of dubious military value anyway.

The Cold War lingered on, punctuated by a number of dangerous events in the coming decades. Tensions rarely relaxed, kept alive by a steady, subterranean struggle between the secret agencies of both sides, spearheaded by the CIA and its Soviet counterpart, the KGB. Famously characterized as a "long peace" by historian John Lewis Gaddis, the Cold War was, true enough, a period when no shooting occurred between the superpowers. More accurately, however, it was a long and mostly hidden struggle between the intelligence services of the two superpowers, accompanied by diplomatic maneuvering for the allegiance of countries around the globe. The year 1945 had ushered in not only the nuclear era but a time of intense clandestine conflict between superpower spies. It was the coming of age of America's secret foreign policy. ⌒

## THE NUCLEAR ERA

American foreign policy from 1945 (the end of World War II) to 1990 (the end of the Cold War) had to cope with a world more complicated and dangerous than ever before—more complicated because the United States was now a major world power, and more dangerous because the era of nuclear weapons held out the prospect that a regional war could spread to engulf the superpowers, leading to the extinction of the human race. In psychologist Erik Erikson's chilling assessment, Homo sapiens had become "a species mortally dangerous to itself."[3]

Several events were important in defining international affairs during the Cold War: the invention of nuclear weapons with their massive powers of instant destruction; the emergence of the United States and the Soviet Union as superpowers; the global confrontation between these two nations—the essence of what we mean by "the Cold War"; the splintering of the globe into some 170 nations, as the old colonial empires disintegrated; and, finally, the collapse of the Soviet Empire at the end of this period. The Cold War was a time of significant peril for the United States. For these forty-six years, Americans faced an adversary capable of reducing US cities to a pile of rubble—the same condition that would have visited the Soviet Union when the United States returned fire. The superpowers were like "two scorpions in a bottle" (in nuclear

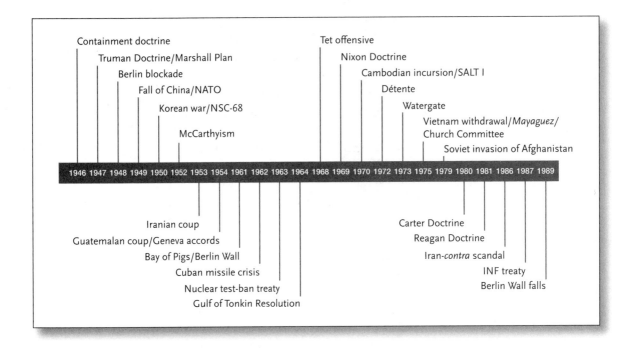

*Figure 5.1*
Highlights in the Evolution of American Foreign Policy, 1945–1990

scientist J. Robert Oppenheimer's famous analogy), fearful of attacking one another because the end result would be death for both.[4] With the dawning of the nuclear age in Hiroshima, humanity confronted the prospect of self-inflicted extinction if nuclear war had erupted between the superpowers. Highlights in the evolution of American foreign policy during the Cold War are presented in Figure 5.1.

## Containment and the Cold War

"The predominant characteristic of international affairs [since World War II] has been competition and confrontation between the United States and the Soviet Union," observed political scientist John Mueller during the end stages of the Cold War.[5] The US-Soviet alliance against the Axis powers during the Second World War quickly unraveled as the war wound down and jockeying for global influence began between the two nations. Unlike the USSR, the United States demobilized its troops after the war. Americans sought again to remove themselves from the world. These isolationist sentiments were not as extreme as they had been in the aftermath of World War I; nonetheless, as officials in Washington, DC, made clear, Americans were now going to concentrate on priorities at home. Despite lobbying by domestic political groups to create the United Nations in 1945 (an initiative based on a proposal from Senator J. William Fulbright of Arkansas) and who expressed a willingness to have the UN's headquarters building located in New York City, the United States displayed little inclination toward a deep involvement in foreign affairs.[6]

Meanwhile, Soviet leaders consolidated their control over the nations of Eastern Europe, as well as Mongolia, by forcing these once-free countries to become satellites.

Attacked too often in the past by armies form Europe, and with the loss of twenty-six million soldiers and civilians in World War II (almost 15 percent of the Soviet population), communist leaders in Moscow viewed their conquests by intimidation in Eastern Europe as a vital step toward the establishment of a buffer zone against future threats from abroad. For Western Europeans and their American allies, however, this projection of Soviet power—accompanied by rhetoric from Moscow boasting that the Marxist-Leninist way of life would soon overshadow democracy and capitalism—represented an unsettling turn of events in global relations. The true intentions of the Soviets were largely a matter of speculation, with few definitive answers available at the time—or even now, with Soviet archives still closed for the most part. The personal idiosyncrasies of the Soviet leadership seemed to be all important, though, in another illustration of the significant role that the individual can play in foreign policy and international affairs. The heavy hand of Moscow's suppression in Eastern Europe and the manner in which the brusque leader of the Soviet Union, Joseph Stalin, broke one treaty promise after another with the United States and other nations, indicated to the West that an erstwhile friend and ally had become a foreboding adversary.

Stalin had declared the outbreak of World War II "the inevitable result of the development of world economic and political forces on the basis of modern monopoly of capitalism . . . The capitalist system harbors elements of general crises and armed conflicts and . . . hence the development of world capitalism proceeds . . . through crises and military conflicts."[7]

After the war, President Harry S. Truman was not about to crater under rhetorical intimidation from Stalin. Nor was he going to back down in the face of aggressive actions taken by the Soviet leader against the West. For example, the USSR was involved in covert actions to undermine free elections in Italy and France, beginning in 1946, while at the same time they secretly funded the communist Parties in both of these (and other) NATO nations. "I do not think we should play compromise any longer," Truman told his Secretary of State, Dean Acheson. "I'm tired of babying the Soviets."[8] One of the President's decisions was to order the CIA to conduct covert actions in Italy and France—the first major use during the Cold War of this secret instrument of American foreign policy—as a means of counteracting the clandestine influence of the Soviet Union.

Recall Professor McLellan's observation (Chapter 4) that within six months after the end of World War II the United States and the Soviet Union would view one another as hostile adversaries and "would act accordingly."[9] This rude thump of reality compelled the United States to abandon its semi-isolationist cloak and adopt a new global leadership role. No other nation in the West could stand up to the Soviets. The United Kingdom and the European Continental powers had been devastated by the war, their far-flung colonial empires in a state of financial ruin, their armies shattered.

Soon to be one of the most influential voices in this recognition of America's new place in the world was a young US diplomat stationed in Moscow by the name of George F. Kennan, author of what would become the **containment doctrine**, *America's grand strategy for the growing conflict with the Soviets.* The doctrine took shape initially in a lengthy (over 5,000 words) classified cable, which Kennan sent to the Department of State in 1946, on the subject of Soviet foreign policy motivations. The ideas in the cable came to the public's attention a year later, when Kennan published an article under the pseudonym "X" for the journal *Foreign Affairs*. "At the bottom of the Kremlin's neurotic view of world affairs," he wrote, "is the traditional and instinctive Russian sense of insecurity."[10] Kennan warned that Soviet power "is a fluid stream which moves constantly, wherever it is permitted to move, toward a given goal. Its main concern is to make sure that it has filled every nook and cranny available to it in the basin of world power." To counter Soviet aggressiveness, Kennan recommend in a key passage, "a long-term, patient but firm and vigilant containment of Russian expansive tendencies." Although only a mid-level official, Kennan's viewpoint acquired authority because he was one of the few Americans in Russia, engaged in firsthand observations. Moreover, his arguments and writing were compelling, and his article in *Foreign Affairs* was widely respected. Forty years later, the editors of the journal would look back on the Kennan article as a landmark event, signifying "the final collapse of nostalgia for prewar isolationism."[11]

This strategy of patience and firmness, with what soon became an emphasis on the latter, was most evident in what became known as the **Truman Doctrine:** *President Truman's proclamation of a Greek-Turkish foreign aid package in March of 1947.* The United Kingdom, still reeling from the costs of war, decided early in the year to withdraw its military and economic support for Greece and Turkey. The United States moved with alacrity to fill this power vacuum before the Soviets had a chance to rush into "the basin" themselves. As Truman told Congress on March 12, it would be the policy of the United States "to support free people who are resisting attempted subjugation by armed minorities or by outside pressures." The phrase "armed minorities" was a reference to communist insurgents around the world financed by the Kremlin (the "outside pressures").

Truman's ringing declaration that the United States would come to the support of free peoples seemed to promise an expansion of American commitments far beyond Greece and Turkey. As historian John Lewis Gaddis has observed, the President's statement implied "a world-wide commitment to resist Soviet expansionism wherever it appeared."[12] This was, at any rate, the general perception of those who read or heard Truman's remarks at the time. In reality, the Truman administration remained ambivalent about the extent to which the United States should bear the responsibility for shoring up the perimeter around the Soviet Union. While the President's proclamation appeared to have no bounds, Secretary Acheson reassured a concerned Senate a week later that the Greek-Turkish aid package carried no precedent for future policy. Subsequent needs would be examined individually, on a case-by-case basis, said Acheson, to see "whether the country in question really needs assistance, whether its request is consistent with American foreign policy, whether the request for assistance is sincere, and whether assistance by the United States would be effective in meeting the problems of that country."[13]

Some of the confusion over the proper direction of American foreign policy during this period stemmed from a misinterpretation by the Truman administration of Kennan's views on containment. Kennan had advocated neither the use of military force to contain communism—except as a final resort—nor resistance to communism everywhere in the world. In the first instance, he believed that the United States could successfully employ political, economic, and, especially, psychological pressures on the Soviets to change their behavior. As Gaddis writes, "the very purpose of 'containment' had been to change the *psychology* of the Soviet leadership."[14] Toward this end, Kennan urged the United States to align itself with the strongest of all anticommunist forces on the globe: nationalism.

In the second instance, not all regions of the world were of equal importance to the United States. For Kennan, the freedom of Western European countries and Japan, both great industrial centers, was crucial to America's own security. If the weapons-production capabilities of these nations were to fall into the hands of an adversary, the outcome could be disastrous for the United States. Kennan urged officials in Washington to help these nations defend themselves; but he cautioned against the belief that the United States could guarantee the protection of every place in the world. Financially, the United States could ill afford such a universal approach. Effective grand strategy meant maintaining a balance between ends and means. As Kennan put it, practically every leader around the planet would show up on America's doorstep "with his palm out and saying, 'We have some communists—now come across.' . . . That obviously won't work."[15]

The pursuit of US foreign policy objectives in the aftermath of World War II reduced to two central concerns: first, the appropriate means—military force, diplomacy, covert action, and the other instruments of foreign policy—and, second, the selection of geographic locations where these powers should be targeted. For Kennan, the United States was better off emphasizing nonmilitary resistance to Soviet expansionist aspirations. He thought, further, that America should carefully direct its resistance to communism in just a limited number of places in the world. In his view, the Soviet challenge was basically political and concentrated against Europe. Kennan was only one person, however, and here were great issues that could lead to differences of opinion as others weighed in to shape America's grand strategy in the aftermath of World War II. President Truman and Secretary Acheson soon began to view the Soviet threat more in military terms than Kennan had counseled.

## A New Militancy

Complicating this debate was the ongoing ambivalence toward the broader role of the United States in world affairs. Undecided which way to turn, the nation continued to feel the tug of isolationists, on one hand, who wished to retreat from the entanglements of external relations, and of internationalists, on the other hand, who argued for US global leadership against the new threat to world peace presented by the Soviet Union. Another significant group—the one-worlders—also hoped for US global leadership, but its members were dedicated to establishing a single world government instead of a fresh round of hostility threatened by a Cold War with the Soviet Union.

Senator Robert A. Taft (R-Ohio) led the isolationists and Henry Wallace, Truman's Secretary of Commerce (and former vice president under Franklin Roosevelt), led the much smaller group of one-worlders. Though miles apart on most issues, these two camps both looked on the prospects of a superpower Cold War with dismay. For Taft and the isolationists, it meant a continuation of twin evils: a large, spendthrift federal government to direct America's course in the Cold War, and a further drain on American resources by foreign nations lined up for aid. (Among the numerous World War I allies of the United States, only Finland had fully repaid its debts.) "Don't be Santa Claus!" was a popular isolationist slogan.

For Wallace and the one-worlders, a Cold War meant a continuation of rivalries among nations that could lead to yet another world war. At every opportunity, Wallace criticized Truman's new "get tough on the Russians" policy, overlooking the fact that he was Secretary of Commerce, not Secretary of State, and that Harry Truman was at the helm of the administration. Truman finally asked for his resignation, and, in 1948, Wallace ran ineffectually against his former boss for the presidency on the Progressive Party ticket.

Taft and Wallace represented minority opinions, however; most Americans supported the idea of containment, especially after the Truman administration presented its case for economic assistance to Turkey, Greece, and (soon thereafter) the rest of Western Europe in stark, Cold War terms: the world had to choose between the United States or the USSR, freedom or enslavement. Truman and his successors continued to carry the concept of containment far beyond what George Kennan had originally espoused. The careful nuances in Kennan's State Department cable and *Foreign Affairs* article lost their refinements in the hands of high-level strategists, backed by lobbyists for the burgeoning military-industrial complex. They viewed Kennan's writings as a convenient point of departure for a philosophy of armed opposition to communism wherever it raised its ugly head. "In effect, containment came to be equated with constructing military alliances around the entire Soviet periphery over two continents," recalled former Secretary of State Henry Kissinger, who was a student of political science at Harvard University at the time.[16] Cultural historian Louis Menand has summed up the situation at the time with this succinct observation: "The Cold War became an arms race, exactly what Kennan had hoped to prevent."[17]

Historian Gaddis writes that "by presenting aid to Greece and Turkey in terms of an ideological conflict between two ways of life, Washington officials encouraged a simplistic view of the cold war which was, in time, to imprison American diplomacy in an ideological straitjacket almost as confining as that which restricted Soviet foreign policy." He continues: "Trapped in their own rhetoric, leaders of the United States found it difficult to respond to the conciliatory gestures which emanated from the Kremlin following Stalin's death and, through their inflexibility, may well have contributed to the perpetuation of the cold war."[18] The sense of trust in the Russian people expressed by the American public in opinion polls before and during World War II declined precipitously in the postwar period.[19] On the eve of the Japanese surrender, 54 percent of the US respondents to a national public opinion poll indicated a willingness to trust the Russians in international affairs; just two months later, the figure dropped to 44 percent; and by the end of February 1946, it plummeted to 35 percent.[20]

The communist takeover in Czechoslovakia (1948); the Berlin blockade (1948), and other US-Soviet confrontations in this divided city; the loss of China to communists in a civil war that drove the anticommunist Chinese offshore to Taiwan (1949); the successful Soviet testing of a nuclear bomb (1949), several years ahead of the CIA's estimated date; and, a major turning point, the war in Korea (1950–1953), would convert most of the isolationists (if not all the one-worlders) into Cold War supporters. These international events led most initial doubters to embrace Truman's more militant view of the Soviet threat over Kennan's softer reliance on diplomacy, trade, and propaganda.

The red-baiting at the height of the McCarthy era (1952–1954), when Senator Joseph McCarthy (R-Wisconsin) made a national reputation by blaming, with flimsy evidence, the nation's foreign policy woes on unnamed phantom communists engaged in treason within the US government, had a further stifling effect on those who might have questioned the bellicose form the containment doctrine had assumed. McCarthy was right to an extent: there were some communists who had infiltrated America's government, including the high-level British spy Klaus Fuchs in the Manhattan Project; but the Senator's unfair *tactics of smear and innuendo*, along with his overreach—**McCarthyism**, as this slanted approach came to be known—eventually discredited his allegations and destroyed his reputation.[21]

By 1950, the Truman administration was prepared to state, in its most important decision document on national security—the top secret **National Security Council Memorandum No. 68** or simply **NSC–68**—that *"the assault on free institutions is worldwide now, and in the context of the present polarization of power a defeat of free institutions anywhere is a defeat everywhere."*[22] The Cold War had morphed into a zero-sum game in which any communist gain was seen as an American loss. All Marxist, communist, and even many socialist nations in the developing world, regardless of how small their strategic importance or how weak their allegiance to Moscow, were considered adversaries of the United States.

Subsequently, the Eisenhower administration (1953–61) preached the same gospel, only with more fire and brimstone. "As there is no weapon too small, no area too remote, to be ignored, there is no free nation too humble to be forgotten," declared President Eisenhower.[23] His Secretary of State, John Foster Dulles, a champion practitioner of inflamed rhetoric against the communists—unmatched until the Reagan administration in its first term, three decades later—warned that "already one-third of the world is dominated by an imperialist brand of communism; already the free world has been so shrunk that no further substantial parts of it can be lost without danger to the whole that remains."[24]

## PERSPECTIVES ON AMERICAN FOREIGN POLICY 5.1

**Top Secret Recommendation of the GENERAL DOOLITTLE COMMITTEE, part of the Hoover Commission, 1954:**

It is now clear that we are facing an implacable enemy whose avowed objective is world domination by whatever means at whatever cost. There are no rules in such a game. Hitherto acceptable norms of human conduct do not apply. If the U.S. is to survive, longstanding American concepts of "fair play" must be reconsidered. We must develop effective espionage and counterespionage services. We must learn to subvert, sabotage and destroy our enemies by more clever, more sophisticated and more effective methods than those used against us. It may become necessary that the American people will be made acquainted with, understand and support this fundamentally repugnant philosophy.

*SOURCE:* "Foreign and Military Intelligence," *Final Report*, Senate Select Committee on Intelligence (the Church Committee), April 26, 1976, p. 9.

Neither the Truman nor the Eisenhower administrations carried out these pronouncements to the point of initiating open warfare against the Soviet Union or attempt to block Red Army military interventions in countries on the Soviet perimeter. For example, despite some blustering, Truman took no military action to assist Czechoslovakia when the Soviets invaded this country in 1948. Dulles often spoke with passion, too, about the "liberation" of the Soviet satellite states in Eastern Europe, although (as Gaddis has noted) this posturing was motivated "more by determination to lure East European voting blocs [such as the vocal and politically active colonies of Estonian exiles in New York City and Los Angeles] away from the Democrats than from any realistic expectations of 'rolling back' Moscow's sphere of influence."[25] The United States did little to assist the anticommunist uprisings in East Berlin (1953), Hungary (1956), or Czechoslovakia (1968) other than to encourage the efforts from the sidelines and provide some secret CIA funding and weaponry in support of the rebellions.

Nevertheless, the escalation in rhetoric was accompanied by more than mere shadowboxing. As *Perspectives on American Foreign Policy* 5.1 illustrates, a special panel on foreign policy (the Hoover Commission) advised the Eisenhower administration to take off its gloves in this struggle against the communists after the Korean War. This is exactly what officials in Washington did, with the vigorous use of the CIA to topple regimes in Iran (1953) and Guatemala (1954) viewed by the Eisenhower administration as insufficiently pro-American; and with the dispatch of US combat troops to quell unrest and discourage Soviet intervention in Lebanon (1958).

## PERIL POINTS

The most significant early response by the United States to the perceived Soviet threat was the establishment of NATO as a collective Western defense (discussed later in this chapter). Leading up to the creation of this political and military alliance was the

**Berlin blockade,** implemented by the Soviets in 1948. During the blockade, *the Soviets cut off all supply routes to Berlin except for a narrow air corridor*, clearly signaling that Moscow was prepared to take extreme measures against the West. Roads, bridges, tunnels, railway corridors, and canals were all blocked; further, Soviet troops halted a military supply train and sent it back to the West. This left only the air space as a possible route to counter the Soviet attempt to isolate Berlin. "The American people will not allow the German people to starve," declared an American colonel, one of the top commanders in Berlin.[26] Onlookers—and even senior officers in the US Air Force— were skeptical, however, that the Western powers could supply enough necessities to sustain over two million Berliners by air alone.

In this instance, the President demonstrated an ability to move the bureaucracy in the desired direction. Gloomy predictions notwithstanding, Truman ordered the Air Force to carry out the airlift. The British Royal Air Force joined in the dramatic intervention, and, together, the two nations managed to deliver more than 4,000 tons of food and fuel a day to Berlin. The courageous pilots continued to fly their round-trips, despite several fatal crashes. Ten and a half months later the Soviets abandoned their policy of blockade. It was a heroic moment for the Americans and the British working in harness, made possible by brave pilots and crews that endured danger and enormous hardships.[27]

Reluctant to send troops and arms back to Europe so soon after World War II—and flying in the face of America's traditional isolationist instincts—officials in Washington nonetheless turned to a policy of remilitarization to bolster the European nations against the communist threat. The fear in Washington, Gaddis observes, was that the Europeans, demoralized by the devastation of World War II, "might simply have allowed their own communists to take power by constitutional means, much in the way the Germans had voted in the Nazis in 1933." Out of exhaustion and disillusionment, the new governments of Europe would simply open the door to communist leaders (who were secretly funded by the Soviet Union) within their own nations. "That was the threat," Gaddis concludes.[28]

The initial step taken by the United States to thwart this outcome was to *strengthen the European economy through the infusion of billions of dollars in economic aid*—a policy known as the **Marshall Plan** or, more formally, the European Recovery Program (ERP). Named after Secretary of State George C. Marshall, who had served with distinction as Army Chief of Staff during the war, this program of assistance was designed to bolster the sagging economies of Europe, thus making them resistant to communist influence. Moreover, America's business titans, seeing the possibility of profits in a healthy European marketplace and aware of the need to prop up Europe against the anticapitalists of the Soviet bloc, rallied behind the Marshall Plan, which began in 1948 and lasted until 1952. As McLellan observes, "The isolationists like Robert Taft and [former GOP president] Herbert Hoover and extreme laissez-faire opponents of foreign 'give-aways' were hopelessly outnumbered."[29]

Thoughtful strategists were aware, though, that economic strength for Europe was a necessary but insufficient condition for thwarting communist influence. Secretary of

State Acheson, among others, remained convinced that the only sure way to prevent Soviet encroachments into Western Europe was to place a barrier of American military might in the way of Kremlin leaders. "Acheson believed," McLellan writes, "that a workable American deterrence to Soviet seizure of Western Europe depended upon the emplacement of American ground forces and the American strategic bomber wings as close to the Soviet industrial heartland as strategy would permit."[30] Throughout Western Europe, US military bases began to proliferate. Further, the United States, as well as France and the United Kingdom, developed arsenals of nuclear weapons (including hydrogen bombs—far more powerful than the atomic bombs dropped on Japan) and a range of conventional weaponry to keep the Soviets at bay.

In 1949, the United States joined with Canada and Western Europe in the establishment of NATO, *America's first peacetime military alliance* since the early days of the Republic. Formally labeled the **North Atlantic Treaty Organization**, this pact—approved by the Senate as a rare formal treaty—committed the United States to the placement of soldiers in Europe on a permanent basis. The combined forces of NATO would provide the muscle to protect the economic recovery in Europe. In 1953, the Soviet Union responded by testing a hydrogen bomb and by forming, two years later, a Moscow-led security alliance known as the **Warsaw Pact,** *comprised of the Soviet Union and the nations of Eastern Europe.*

## The Korean War

The most extreme outward probes by the communists came not in Europe, however, but in Asia (particularly in Korea) and then in America's own neighborhood (Cuba). Korea had been ruled by Japan since the early twentieth century as a consequence of the Russo-Japanese War. On Japan's surrender in 1945, both Russian and American troops advanced to liberate the peninsula. A decision had to be made as to which country should occupy what territory, and the 38th parallel was agreed on as the dividing line between the Soviet and the Western—primarily American—zones of occupation. In 1948, the Allied powers held elections in Korea as a means for ending the military occupation and restoring self-rule to the Koreans. South of the 38th parallel, the United Nations supervised an open election and the people of the newly named Republic of Korea elected Syngman Rhee as their president. In the Soviet zone north of the 38th parallel, though, UN officials found themselves barred from observing "elections" that brought a communist regime to power in the Democratic People's Republic of Korea. Dashed were Western hopes for a free and democratic government to serve all of Korea. In place of one government stood two, each claiming authority to rule throughout the peninsula.

The government in the north was a Soviet and Chinese satellite, whereas the government in the south was recognized by the UN and supported by the United States. Two years later, in June of 1950, the Soviet- and Chinese-backed army of the Democratic People's Republic of Korea, led by Kim Il Sung, suddenly advanced southward across the demarcation line. An invasion of South Korea was under way—perhaps unintentionally encouraged by Secretary Acheson's failure to include South Korea in a speech he had given earlier about America's vital interests around the globe.

Though geographically distant from the United States, the Korean peninsula was seen as a possible strategic stepping-stone to Japan for the communists. Moreover, Korea had taken on added importance in light of President Truman's vow that no nation was too remote in America's struggle against global communism. In a history of the Cold War, McLellan summed up the reasons why the United States decided to enter into this struggle, so far away, to help a country that was not much of a democracy under President Rhee:

> The Korean aggression was immediately interpreted in the light of Britain's experience at Munich [in 1938; see Chapter 4]. Dictators' appetites grow with eating and if allowed to get away with one aggression, they will be encouraged to perpetrate another. The integrity of America's pledge to defend its European allies would be judged by the resolution with which it acted to stem aggression in Korea. And it was felt that the strategic balance already shaken by the loss of China would be irretrievably upset should the United States fail to respond.[31]

Strategist (and Nobel laureate in economics) Thomas C. Schelling stated the case even more bluntly: "We lost 30,000 dead. . . . *to save face* . . . [that is, to prove to the Western world that the United States would be a resolute leader in resisting communist expansion] and it was undoubtedly worth it."[32]

As these statistics on fatalities indicate, the fighting in Korea was intense and always carried the possibility of a widening war. Soviet pilots flew aircraft for the North Koreans in 1950 and a showdown in the skies between the superpowers, perhaps leading to a nuclear confrontation, greatly worried officials in Washington.[33] Regardless of the risks, the United States steadfastly held to its conviction that it had to demonstrate resolve. If Americans failed to take a stand against communist aggression in Korea, the West would be without leadership and the communist nations could march relentlessly forward from one vulnerable nation to another, toppling each domino as they went. So was the feeling at the time among most of America's foreign policy makers. The memory of Neville Chamberlain's failed efforts to appease Hitler in 1938 lingered ominously as a historical analogy.

Even today, that dark moment in history—Munich—remains a powerful argument against those who would retreat or compromise in the face of aggression. In contemporary world affairs, a key question is whether the United States should negotiate with Taliban factions in Afghanistan, in hopes of achieving peace in Southwest Asia, or would that amount to appeasement? What about negotiating with Al Qaeda in Pakistan, Yemen, Somalia, and elsewhere? Some politicians and talk-show personalities would pounce on anyone suggesting such ventures, labeling them appeasers (if not traitors) and calling for their electoral defeat or immediate resignation from office.

The Korean War was important because of the opportunity it presented for a display of Western, chiefly American, determination to resist the spread of communism. Fought for almost three years to a stalemate, the war was unpopular at home; but it had the tangible effect of forcing the communists to retreat behind the 38th parallel, the demilitarized zone or DMZ that bisected the Korean peninsula at the time (and still does today). The Western nations demonstrated to the dictators in Russia, China, and North Korea that the spread of communism would be fiercely resisted.

The war in Korea proved, too, that armed conflict between the superpowers could be kept limited, without an inevitable escalation to a third world war. The United States would begin to move away from the idea of **massive retaliation,** *a counterattack strategy based on using America's full nuclear arsenal—a theory of deterrence central to the Eisenhower administration.* (In Chapter 11, I address the concept of deterrence and the characteristics of nuclear weapons.) A new school of thought began to emerge during the Kennedy administration, called **flexible response.** It emphasized the importance of preparations *to fight at every level of combat, from guerrilla insurgencies to all-out nuclear warfare.* As in Korea, the United States might be required to join battle against the communists in remote regions of the world, from the jungles of Asia and Africa to the deserts of the Middle East. As part of its flexible response to global challenges, the Kennedy administration strengthened Special Forces units within the military. Popularly known during the 1960s as the "Green Berets," these elite teams of highly trained combat personnel were prepared to wage tactical warfare in virtually any part of the world. The administration also strengthened other nontraditional responses to Moscow-sponsored guerrilla insurgencies in the developing world, including a reinforced CIA capability for paramilitary operations and other covert actions.

Subsequent administrations and America's experiences in the Vietnam War further advanced strategic thinking about approaches to *limited or low-intensity conflicts,* also known as *"irregular wars," "asymmetric wars,"* or in today's military terminology, **counterinsurgency warfare** (**COIN**, in the Pentagon acronym). At the core of US fighting methods in Iraq and Afghanistan since the advent of the Obama administration has been the strategy of counterinsurgency. (The second Bush administration rejected this approach, which it found redolent of the failed methods tried in the Vietnam War.) A counterinsurgency strategy is based on *trying to identify possible allies among foreign locals, then working with them through the use of civic programs (such as building schools and health clinics)—not just armed conflict—to turn the tide against the recalcitrant, main enemies in the target nation.*[34] Home building would trump home destruction. Opinion is divided on how well this approach has worked in Iraq and Afghanistan, and General David H. Petraeus was rotated out of his assignments in the war zones before his COIN efforts had reached fruition—if, indeed, they ever would in two nations that remained in a state of semi-chaos despite the best efforts of Western nations to defeat local antidemocratic forces.

## Crises in Cuba

Throughout most of the Eisenhower presidency, Cuban guerillas had been fighting against the pro-American regime of Fulgencio Batista. When they succeeded in overthrowing Batista in 1959, officials in Washington greeted the outcome with a sense of ambivalence. Batista had been a cruel dictator, but had welcomed US businesses and tourists to Cuba; in contrast, the goals of the new Cuban leader, Fidel Castro, were unclear, as was his level of friendship toward the United States. He soon proved hostile toward American interests, making speeches about the evils of US hegemony in Cuba and moving to expropriate large American land holdings on the island. As relations deteriorated, Castro reached out to America's enemy—the Soviet Union—for assistance in developing a socialist state. From the point of view US government officials, this made Cuba an enemy.[35]

### *Bay of Pigs*

Among the anticommunist paramilitary operations carried out during the Kennedy years (although the planning began in the final years of the Eisenhower administration) was an *ill-fated attempt in 1961 to overthrow the Castro regime by landing a team of CIA-backed Cuban exiles on the island's beaches* at the **Bay of Pigs**. The Eisenhower and the Kennedy administrations initiated the secret planning without seeking approval from the Congress, which was kept thoroughly in the dark about the risky covert invasion. The operations side of the Agency anticipated that the people of Cuba would greet the "liberators" with open arms and join them in a counterrevolution. In reality, however, most Cubans remained loyal to Castro, whose soldiers easily defeated the small expeditionary force. The CIA invaders anticipated air cover from the US Air Force during the operation, if it became necessary; but, at the eleventh hour, the Kennedy administration rejected this overt use of force when the invasion faltered. Following the advice of Secretary of State Dean Rusk, the President decided that he did not wish to have the role of the United States acknowledged publicly, out of concern that an air attack represented a clear violation of international law.

The new range of military capabilities provided by the Kennedy administration doctrine of flexible response placed the United States in a better position to respond to military situations around the globe, without escalating precipitously to the level of nuclear weaponry. These capabilities would soon be put to use in one of America's longest and most tragic foreign conflicts, the Vietnam War. First, though, the administration faced a deepening chill in US-Soviet relations. On August 13, 1961, the Soviet-supported East German regime erected the Berlin Wall—a high concrete barrier built by the East German government between East and West Berlin in 1961 to prevent emigration by its citizens to a more appealing lifestyle in the West. The wall stood as a conspicuous symbol of the Cold War. Then, in the next year, the Soviets forced the United States into *the most perilous confrontation that occurred between the superpowers during the Cold War*: the **Cuban missile crisis** of 1962.

## Cuban missile crisis

This chapter opened with a sketch of the Cuban missile crisis. It is such an important event in the Cold War that it warrants some elaboration. What follows places the confrontation into historical context and provides added details about its course. In 1957, the Soviet Union lifted into space on the back of a powerful rocket a shiny satellite about the size of a basketball. Called *Sputnik 1*, the satellite went into orbit around the Earth and continued circling the planet for almost three months, transmitting research data to Soviet scientists all the while. This feat demonstrated to the world impressive Soviet scientific advances in the field of rocketry, with all the implications that spelled out for the ability of the Soviet Union to reach the United States accurately and swiftly with ICBMs carrying nuclear payloads. The long-range-missile race was on between the superpowers. In response, and with a sense of panic, America poured enormous resources into its space and missile programs and took steps to improve the teaching of basic science in its schools. The effort paid off most visibly as the United States beat the Soviets in the race to land an astronaut on the moon; moreover, America soon moved ahead of the Soviets in the number and accuracy of its long-range (strategic) missiles.

In hopes of offsetting the American missile advantage, and also to help protect Fidel Castro, his only Marxist ally in the Western Hemisphere, against another Bay of Pigs covert action or an outright overt US invasion of Cuba, the Soviet leader Nikita Khrushchev (who rose to power in 1958) ordered the placement of Soviet nuclear missiles on Cuban soil in October of 1962. The move took US intelligence analysts by surprise; the Soviets had never before deployed nuclear missiles outside their own homeland. Further, the CIA's analysts estimated that neither the Soviets nor the Cubans had much to gain from the missile venture.

Once CIA reconnaissance aircraft (the U-2) spotted the missiles, the implications were clear: as soon as they were operational, the missiles had the capacity to strike the United States quickly with nuclear warheads—a frightening prospect for President Kennedy to ponder as the nation's commander in chief and the person who would ultimately have to decide how to respond to the threat. In times of crisis, the Constitution takes on a certain elasticity and the president is expected to provide dynamic leadership to protect the United States. In some instances, lawmakers can provide consultation or may even seek to participate more aggressively in deliberations (as when some members of Congress strenuously objected to President Truman's entry into the Korean War without formal legislative approval). In the case of the 1962 crisis, however, even the basic knowledge about the Soviet missiles in Cuba was so closely kept within the executive branch that lawmakers were excluded from involvement in the decision making. President Kennedy convened a group of national security officials, known as the "Executive Committee" or Ex Comm, to advise him on a course of action. The Ex Comm's initial recommendation to the President, strongly supported by its military representatives, was to hit Cuba immediately with an air strike against the sites where the missiles were located.

The majority of the nonmilitary members of the Ex Comm, though, expressed reluctance to adopt this drastic option as a first step. Inevitably, Soviet troops and technicians would be killed in an air strike. As part of the argument against the use of military force made by nonmilitary officials during the Ex Comm meetings, Attorney General Robert Kennedy introduced a moral and political consideration into the debate. The use of force against Cuba, he reminded his colleagues, would be viewed as reprehensible in the eyes of world opinion: a giant Uncle Sam smashing a fist down on a small developing nation off the American shoreline.

In rebuttal, the Pentagon brass argued that an air strike could "surgically" remove the Soviet missile threat, although the option would have to be exercised immediately—before the missiles were ready for launching. Recall from the introduction to this chapter, fresh intelligence from U-2 photography gave the President more time to consider other approaches. As a deputy director of the CIA remembered:

> In the final analysis, war was avoided because President Kennedy had time to consider and carefully weigh his political and military options. The Intelligence Community [as America's secret agencies are called, collectively] spotted the missiles before they became operational, and throughout the crisis, we were able to inform the President—with great precision—about the operational status of each and every site. This meant that the President didn't need to rush into a hasty military solution—such as the quick all-out air strike against Cuba that several of his advisors had recommended. He realized that he had the time to pursue more measured policies that would not cause an uncontrolled escalation and quickly draw us into a nuclear war.[36]

This U-2-based intelligence was immensely helpful to the President, yet more recent studies reveal that the CIA had failed to realize the missiles may have been ready for launch more quickly than the ten to fourteen days reported to Kennedy. Nor did the Agency know about the over 200 tactical nuclear weapons on the island; the A-bombs cradled inside Russian bombers (IL-28s) on Cuban runways that a US invasion force would have faced; or even how large the Soviet military presence was in Cuba. The Pentagon had mustered a 180,000 invasion force along the Eastern seaboard of the United States. If the President had accepted the guidance of his generals and admirals and ordered an invasion during the early days of the crisis, Castro and the local Soviet commanders would probably have resorted to the use of tactical nuclear weapons in response, even if the longer-range missiles were not yet operable. In turn, this could well have led to a nuclear exchange between the superpowers, annihilating Washington and Moscow as well as many other cities in both nations. The immediate death toll would have been astronomical, not to mention the long-range effects of lingering radiation. In the judgment of Robert S. McNamara, Secretary of Defense during the crisis, "We all would have been history."[37]

Nonetheless, because of the CIA's U-2 photography, President Kennedy at least believed at the time that he had some leeway for further deliberation. The Ex Comm accelerated its search for additional options. Some advisers, including McNamara, argued that no military response was necessary because Americans already lived under the shadow of Soviet strategic missiles, including some close by on submarines in the Atlantic Ocean. A few more in Cuba did not change things that much. Besides, they reasoned, the United States had encircled the Soviet Union with comparable missiles in Turkey and West Germany and expected Moscow to accept that situation; it was logical to assume, and accept, that Moscow would seek some parity. Others argued for a diplomatic settlement, perhaps swapping the US missiles in Turkey for the Soviet missiles in Cuba. The President explored this possibility behind the scenes, at the same time as he listened to other advice. The missile swap was the course he eventually adopted, along with a US naval blockade around Cuba. While these less extreme approaches were being analyzed in the Ex Comm meetings, some participants in military uniform were spoiling for a fight with the Cuban dictator—a second Bay of Pigs, only this time backed up by the US military with the full support of air power. "Go in there and take Cuba away from Castro," argued a short-fused Ex Comm member in uniform.[38]

As the tense days of the crisis flew by, the Ex Comm and the President leaned toward a decision that combined a show of strength and determination with a measure of prudence. In the manner of President McKinley in 1898, the United States established a "quarantine" around Cuba to keep out further shipments of Soviet missiles to the island. (The Ex Comm decided the word quarantine sounded less belligerent than McKinley's use of a "naval blockade," although it amounted to the same thing.) At the last minute President Kennedy did manage to "consult" with a few members of Congress, stretching the meaning of that word, because in fact he merely informed a few key lawmakers about the crisis hours before the naval action. Most lawmakers accepted the President's approach, because this was a secretive, highly dangerous situation and one of a defensive nature.

Congress often reacts differently when a president takes offensive action overseas—initiating a war somewhere without their participation. An illustration is the First Persian Gulf War against Iraq in 1990, which the first President Bush was about to undertake without the approval of lawmakers—until they loudly complained and he finally asked for a vote on Capitol Hill (and, recall from Chapter 3, received approval, albeit by a narrow margin in the Senate). Secrecy, time constraints, crises—all matter in determining the constitutional balance between the Congress and the presidency at any given time. On October 22, 1962, a week after he first learned of the missile threat, President Kennedy told the American people about the situation in a television address: "The 1930s taught us a clear lesson," he said, evoking the memory of Munich. "Aggressive conduct, if allowed to go unchecked and unchallenged, ultimately leads to war."

The question now was whether the Soviets would turn back their missile-laden freighters, or perhaps use their submarines armed with nuclear warheads to punch a hole through the blockade. A sense of crisis spread and deepened across the United States, but good news came at last on October 28: Khrushchev had decided to turn back all the Soviet freighters and dismantle the missiles under construction in Cuba. The Kremlin had stepped away from the abyss. The back-channel deal on Turkish missiles for Cuban missiles had had its desired effect. In addition, the Soviet leader probably found sobering the fact of a 5,000-to-300 ICBM advantage enjoyed by the United States at the time, along with America's massive military strength poised along the coastline in Florida, Georgia, South Carolina, and Virginia. Nevertheless, the superpowers had come close to Armageddon, more so than either fully realized at the time.

## Vietnam

A year after the Korean War ended in stalemate in 1953, events in Indochina would again test how far the United States was prepared to go in the pursuit of its policy of global containment through military means. In 1954, the French army suffered a humiliating defeat in its attempt to maintain colonial rule over Indochina (which included the territory now called Vietnam) against indigenous communist revolution-aries. Operating out of the region that is now Laos, the Vietnamese communists under the leadership of Ho Chi Minh sought to expel the French and unite all of Vietnam under their rule. After months of fierce jungle combat, the communists surrounded the French forces at Dien Bien Phu, a city in northern Vietnam.

The Eisenhower administration refused a request from the government of France to provide its desperate soldiers with air cover from American aircraft carriers and, if necessary, ground troops—perhaps even the use of atomic bombs against the com-munists (as advocated by Secretary of State John Foster Dulles). Despite having made a number of aggressive remarks underscoring the "domino theory" (that Soviet and Chinese communist leaders were intent on toppling noncommunist regimes around the world), President Eisenhower proved reluctant to enter into this war. (See *Perspec-tives on American Foreign Policy 2.2* in Chapter 2.) At his request, the CIA provided the President with an intelligence prediction—an "Estimate"—about the situation in Vietnam in 1954. The Agency reported that the use of a nuclear weapon by the United States in Indochina would probably bring the Chinese and the Soviets into the con-flict, resulting in World War III. Eisenhower also asked for the advice of senior mem-bers of Congress and they, too, counseled against US involvement, especially because America's other European allies appeared unwilling to help the French out of their predicament.[39] "You boys must be crazy," President Eisenhower ended up telling those aides in his administration who continued to advocate dropping nuclear bombs on the Vietnamese communists. "We can't use those awful things against Asians for the second time in less than ten years."[40]

The constructive role of lawmakers in this important foreign policy decision cannot be emphasized enough. The Secretary of State had advocated US entry into a war in Vietnam using nuclear weapons; opposing this rash idea, key members of

Congress helped persuade President Eisenhower that this initiative would be foolish and extremely unpopular around the world. In this instance, genuine consultation between the President and members of Congress experienced in foreign policy led to a wise decision and demonstrated that, inherent constitutional tensions notwithstanding, the executive and legislative branches of government could work together toward a favorable outcome. President Eisenhower displayed the maturity, self-confidence, and good judgment to seek insights from congressional leaders, many of whom (such as Richard B. Russell, D-Georgia) had been involved in foreign policy deliberations in Washington for decades as lawmakers.

The foreign policy experts in the Eisenhower administration had peered into the swampland of Indochina and, admonished by President Eisenhower, drew back— although the Chairman of the Joint Chiefs of Staff joined Secretary Dulles in urging the White House to charge ahead. In the next decade, the United States would take the fatal plunge and enter into war in Vietnam. In the interim, high-level government negotiations in Switzerland produced the **Geneva Accords** of 1954, as *diplomats "temporarily" divided Vietnam at the 17th parallel and scheduled general elections for Vietnam in 1956.* Instead, as had occurred earlier in Korea, civil war broke out between the communists concentrated in the north and the anticommunists in the south. Within two months following the Geneva negotiations, the Eisenhower administration knitted together SEATO, along with several other formal anticommunist alliances around the world, in a rush of containment-driven international agreements that led some critics to charge Secretary Dulles with "pactomania." The purpose of SEATO and similar alliances was to strengthen defenses against further communist expansion in Indochina and elsewhere in Southeast Asia.

Breaking from the modern norm, SEATO and several other formal alliances during this period were consummated by way of the formal treaty process, with the Senate weighing in with its advice and consent. This was a relatively brief burst of commitment to constitutional procedure, again displaying President Eisenhower's willingness to work closely with Congress on some matters—despite his controversial pursuit of dubious open-ended "resolutions" from lawmakers on other occasions (discussed in Chapter 3).

Though less overheated in his public rhetoric than Secretary Dulles, President Kennedy was, if anything, often tougher in his responses to the communists than the Eisenhower administration had been. (See his inaugural address in *Perspectives on American Foreign Policy* 5.2.) The Kennedy team approved and implemented the Bay of Pigs operations; and the administration led the United States to the brink of a nuclear war during the missile crisis, before a secret diplomatic compromise was reached between the superpowers. Moreover, during the Kennedy years, the CIA attempted to assassinate Fidel Castro, among other targets (America's assassination plots are examined in Chapter 12).

This toughness of the Kennedy administration resulted, in part, from the pressure of circumstances. Khrushchev's rash move to place nuclear missiles in the Western

## PERSPECTIVES ON AMERICAN FOREIGN POLICY 5.2

**Inaugural Address of PRESIDENT JOHN F. KENNEDY, January 20, 1961. This excerpt from the President's address reveals that his foreign policy represented a continuation of America's militant commitment to the doctrine of containment.**

I have sworn before you and Almighty God the same solemn oath our forebears prescribed nearly a century and three quarters ago.

The world is very different now. For man holds in his mortal hands the power to abolish all forms of human poverty and all forms of human life. And yet the same revolutionary beliefs for which our forebears fought are still at issue around the globe—the belief that the rights of man come not from the generosity of the state, but from the hand of God.

We dare not forget today that we are the heirs of that first revolution. Let the word go forth from this time and place, to friend and foe alike, that the torch has been passed to a new generation of Americans—born in this century, tempered by war, disciplined by a hard and bitter peace, proud of our ancient heritage—and unwilling to witness or permit the slow undoing of those human rights to which this Nation has always been committed, and to which we are committed today at home and around the world.

Let every nation know, whether it wishes us well or ill, that we shall pay any price, bear any burden, meet any hardship, support any friend, oppose any foe, in order to assure the survival and the success of liberty.

Hemisphere took place during President Kennedy's watch, for example, not Eisenhower's. The toughness, though, was an attempt as well on the part of the inexperienced President to compensate for his sense of political and personal insecurity.[41] Kennedy had narrowly won the presidency in 1960, and he brought little foreign policy expertise to the job (much like another senator elected to the presidency, Barack Obama). He had backed the Bay of Pigs scheme, according to an authoritative study, because he was afraid he would be labeled "chicken" by the Republican Party if he refused. This could have led to nasty political repercussions for the President: a "Who lost Cuba?" debate like the "Who lost China?" one that harmed the Democrats during the Truman years.[42] Kennedy and, subsequently, President Lyndon B. Johnson hoped to avoid accusations from vocal right-wingers in the GOP that they were weak in the struggle against global communism; the Democrats would prove they could be as resolute as the Republicans—an insight into the importance of psychological and domestic political considerations in foreign affairs. At the same time, both political parties also engaged from time to time in some attempts at US-Soviet cooperation. In 1963, for instance, President Kennedy signed a **Limited Test Ban Treaty** with Moscow, which *required nuclear-weapons testing to be conducted underground*—"the first substantial step toward arms control in the nuclear age," recalled a Kennedy aide.[43]

When SEATO members began to feel the strains of communist insurgencies in Southeast Asia during the Kennedy years, the President—true to the themes of his inaugural address—responded to the challenge by bolstering the American military presence in that part of the world. Less willing than his predecessor to seek congressional advice (even though Kennedy had been a member of Congress), the President sent additional US troops to Vietnam without debate on Capitol Hill, relying on his own interpretation of the authority permitted him by the commander-in-chief clause of the Constitution. This was a slippery slope that his successor, President Lyndon B. Johnson, would also follow, leading eventually to a congressional rebellion against a presidential overreach of war-making authority. "Eisenhower could stand the political consequences of Dien Bien Phu and the expulsion of the west from Vietnam in 1954," Kennedy told a confidante, political scientist Walt W. Rostow, "because the blame fell on the French. I can't take a 1954 defeat today."[44]

In consultation with his national security advisers, President Kennedy decided to expand the role of US military personnel advisers in South Vietnam. They would sometimes fly sorties against the Vietcong (the VC, who were South Vietnamese communists allied with their comrades in the North); and they also returned ground fire while on patrol throughout South Vietnam. About 1,000 American "advisers"—mostly military personnel—were stationed in South Vietnam during the early months of the Kennedy years; by 1963, that figure had jumped to 11,000.[45] The Kennedy administration found itself deeply embroiled in the political machinations of internal South Vietnamese politics, even condoning a military coup against President Ngo Dinh Diem, who was murdered along with his brother by rival South Vietnamese generals friendly toward the United States. At the time of President Kennedy's death in November of 1963, the number of US military advisers had swollen to some 16,500. Passed along to the next president, Lyndon B. Johnson, the conflict would become a Bay of Pigs in slow motion.[46]

President Johnson came into office as a highly experienced and much admired lawmaker, having served as Senate majority leader before assuming the vice presidency. His interests lay in domestic politics, however; his dream was to rebuild the decaying cities of America and establish a "Great Society" founded on a life of justice and well-being for all citizens. Instead, he soon found himself consumed by events in Vietnam. Here was the tragedy of Lyndon Johnson: the President was so well prepared to advance his Great Society programs on Capitol Hill, yet dragged down by a distant war that increasingly robbed him of resources, personal energy, and, ultimately, his standing with the American people.

Recall from Chapter 3 that Congress precipitously passed the Gulf of Tonkin Resolution in August of 1964 and Johnson interpreted this congressional support as a blank check to do whatever was necessary to protect America's military advisers in Vietnam, as well as US warships in the South China Sea. He began an escalation of the conflict in Vietnam, both in rhetoric and in the number of US troops sent to the battlefield. What was at first supposed to be a limited operation meant to shield American military advisers and warships soon became in the President's speeches a fundamental test of America's will to halt communist expansion in Southeast Asia. The small number of American troops initially shipped to South Vietnam under Johnson in 1963 and 1964 were joined in the spring of 1965—without public knowledge or congressional debate—by thousands more, rising to a total of over 128,000 by the end of the year.

In 1933, Dean Rusk—Secretary of State for Kennedy and Johnson, throughout the build-up of US troops in Vietnam—had studied at Oxford University in England as a Rhodes Scholar. At the time, he witnessed a debate by the student members of the Oxford Union, which resulted in a vote of 275-to-153 in opposition to fighting "for King and country" against the Nazis—or anybody else. He sharply disagreed with this tally and the policy of appeasement it endorsed. The aggressive behavior of Adolf Hitler would soon prove him correct. From this experience, Rusk carried back to the United States and into his diplomatic career a conviction that aggression had to be stopped wherever it occurred, a principle he would apply to Vietnam during the Johnson years.[47]

The war went badly for the United States. American soldiers found the jungle terrain alien; and "irregular" guerrilla warfare was still something of a novelty for Americans—not at all like the head-on clashes and distinguishable fronts in World War II and Korea. Here was combat where an innocent-looking elderly woman in a rice paddy might be hiding a hand grenade tucked beneath her black robes, where every turn on the jungle trail could hold a booby trap, where VC appeared and disappeared like deadly phantoms in the thick underbrush. To make matters more difficult still, America's South Vietnamese allies in the Army of the Republic of Vietnam (ARVN) were virtually indistinguishable in physical appearance from the Vietcong and their communists allies in the North.

For almost ten years the fighting in Vietnam went on. Over 57,000 Americans lost their lives, nearly 3,000 were taken prisoner or missing in action; another 200,000-plus required hospitalization from battle wounds. The question of prisoners of war and those missing in action (POW/MIA, in the shorthand language of the Pentagon) would lead to protracted negotiations between the United States and Vietnam after the war ended. The United States properly demanded more information about these soldiers and the Vietnamese provided only incomplete responses. A strong lobby grew in Washington to seek better information from the Vietnamese, and concern over the fate of these individuals continues today. Among those American soldiers who returned from the war, thousands and thousands were badly maimed forever, physically and mentally. Moreover, many soldiers returned home with serious drug addictions, for the strain in Vietnam was great and drugs were plentiful.[48]

Fearful, on one hand, that dramatic escalation might bring in the Chinese or even the Soviet armies, yet unwilling, on the other hand, to retreat and incur the political wrath of those who would blame the Democrats again for being soft on communism, the Johnson administration opted for a middle course. As in Korea, the United States would attempt to contain communism but steer clear of a global war with the Chinese and the Soviets. Two thoughtful analysts, Leslie Gelb and Richard K. Betts, have argued that this was exactly the course preferred by most Americans; therefore, "the system worked."[49] Yet did the system really work when America entered into the fighting without a meaningful debate or a year-by-year review and reappraisal by Congress of the war effort? When the reality of the failing war was kept from the American people? The essence of democracy is an informed electorate, but both the Johnson and Nixon administrations were notorious for refusing to discuss the war candidly with lawmakers or the public. Nixon's national security adviser, Henry Kissinger, wrote in his memoirs, with specific reference to the military operations carried out by the Nixon administration against Cambodia as part of the Vietnam War effort: "We were wrong, I now believe, not to be more frank with congressional leaders."[50]

The end result was a bloody war of attrition leading first to a stalemate (as occurred in the Korean War) and then a slide toward outright defeat, with a steady continuation of dead American soldiers shipped home in pine boxes, often under the cover of darkness (a Pentagon innovation at the time) to avoid media reporting on the numbers who had perished. Accompanying these tragic losses came a growing public alienation toward the conflict. Virtually every evening, television news carried gruesome images of death and destruction in Vietnam: villages burning and engulfed in napalm; wounded GIs evacuated by helicopter, their faces contorted in pain; the rag-doll figures of men, women, and children massacred at the village of My Lai—a mass murder of Vietnamese civilians by overzealous American soldiers; the profusion of bomb craters that became the pockmarks of the distress that infected Vietnam; the chaos of Saigon, with the bodies of protesting Buddhist monks aflame in self-emulations. On television, too, came the seemingly incessant count of American soldiers killed each week, along with US Army generals speaking of victory just around the corner—with always another corner. And images of demonstrations on the college campuses and streets of America that often erupted into violent clashes with police and members of the National Guard in various states.

Media and congressional criticism of the Johnson administration spiraled upward, and serious political opposition to Lyndon Johnson's reelection plans arose within his own party. In the 1968 presidential contest, Senator Eugene McCarthy (D-Minnesota) entered the New Hampshire primary against the incumbent President. McCarthy lost, but recorded a sufficiently impressive second-place finish to reveal the weakness of the incumbent. These results encouraged Robert Kennedy, at the time a US Senator (D-New York), to enter the presidential race as a more well-known and formidable foe than McCarthy.

This opposition from Kennedy and McCarthy, coupled with Johnson's decline in the public opinion polls, led to an unexpected political decision on March 31, 1968. In a stunning television address to the nation, the President announced that he would not seek a second term. Kennedy and McCarthy immediately moved their campaigns into high gear. In June, on the night of Kennedy's impressive victory in the pivotal California primary, an assassin shot him dead in a Los Angeles hotel. Hubert H. Humphrey, vice president in the Johnson administration, went on to capture the nomination over McCarthy, as antiwar protesters—mainly college students from around the country—clashed violently with police in the streets of Chicago outside the meeting place of the national nominating convention. The Republican nominee, Richard M. Nixon, narrowly won the general election, in large part because of Humphrey's identification with the failing war in Vietnam and the unwillingness of antiwar Gene McCarthy and Robert Kennedy Democrats to support him. Rarely had foreign policy played such an important role in the outcome of an election.

Prominent in Nixon's campaign rhetoric was a promise to end the war in Vietnam, just as Eisenhower (for whom Nixon had served as vice president) had promised to end the war in Korea during the 1952 election. Nixon's much heralded "secret plan" to bring the conflict to a close worked poorly. The negotiations between his top foreign policy aide, Secretary of State Henry Kissinger, and the North Vietnamese failed. Neither did the ongoing US bombing of Hanoi and other cities in North Vietnam result in any success, nor the mining of North Vietnamese harbors and an invasion of Cambodia in May of 1970 to close down this enemy sanctuary.

The Cambodian invasion in May of 1970, which Nixon tried to soften by calling it an "incursion," served only to incite further public rage against the fighting in Indochina—more so than any other single event during this turbulent era. Soon after the invasion, members of the National Guard in Ohio gunned down antiwar students protesting at Kent State University, as did police at Jackson State University in Mississippi. An avalanche of antiwar mail fell on Congress from an incensed citizenry; constituents came to Washington in unprecedented numbers and flooded the halls of Congress and the grounds of Capitol Hill with protest demonstrations against the war. In 1973, the initial year of the President's second term, the Nixon administration finally decided to bring America's soldiers home.

While President Nixon wrestled with how to end the war—during his presidency an additional 20,000 American soldiers died in Vietnam—he was caught up in the Watergate scandal in 1973. Newspaper reports in the *Washington Post* disclosed the President's attempt to cover up criminal evidence that implicated his White House aides in a burglary of the Democratic Party's national headquarters offices in the Watergate Hotel in Washington, nestled next to the Potomac River near Georgetown. Members of Congress investigated the charges and, in August of 1974, Nixon resigned in the face of a seemingly inevitable impeachment conviction in the Senate against him. The final retreat from Vietnam fell to his vice president and successor, Gerald R. Ford, a former member of the House of Representatives from Michigan. In April of 1975, as VC and North Vietnamese troops surrounded South Vietnam's capital, Saigon, some Americans still in the city waited nervously (along with a few lucky South Vietnamese chosen for rescue) on the roof and grounds of a building at the US Embassy compound for evacuation by helicopter to US Navy ships anchored in the South China Sea. America's Dien Bien Phu had arrived.

Other, less fortunate Americans and South Vietnamese officials were caught up in the chaos of the North Vietnamese assault on the city and did their best to find a way out of the country by way of the sea. The lucky ones were later picked up by US naval vessels, while many others went to watery graves on overloaded small boats. Some failed to escape Saigon; the city's expanding cemeteries became their final destination.[51] Looking back, one of America's most esteemed diplomats, George F. Kennan, referred to the Vietnam War as "the most disastrous of all America's undertakings over the whole 200 years of its history."[52]

For the first time, the United States had lost a war overseas. The cost in blood and treasure had been staggering, and the long conflict tore America asunder like nothing else since the Civil War. Never had the United States experienced such massive street protests. In demonstrations against the war, groups of students burned American flags and attacked banks thought to be implicated in the financing of the war, as well as campus and private labs with government contracts to produce napalm and other chemicals used by the US military in Vietnam. Young men fled to Canada rather than be drafted into a war they viewed as immoral and illegitimate. A few joined radical antiwar groups, like the Weathermen (later called the Weather), resorting to violent attacks against the government and any other organization known to support the war in Vietnam.

At the height of the protests, the Nixon administration sought to protect the White House by surrounding the compound with a fleet of DC city buses, like early settlers circling the wagons against an Apache attack. The CIA, the FBI, and military intelligence agencies carried out—in violation of various laws—Orwellian espionage operations to monitor the domestic unrest. This spying by the nation's intelligence organizations against the very people they had been created to defend led to major investigations in 1975, as lawmakers and the Ford White House sought to establish better safeguards against the abuse of secret power.[53] Frank Church (D-Idaho) led the most extensive of these inquiries, *a sixteen-month Senate probe that uncovered a wide array of improper spying operations within the United States carried out by the CIA and its companion agencies.* The **Church Committee** uncovered, as well, *a record of CIA assassination plots attempted overseas.* For several years America was in a state of distress, a product largely of the war in Vietnam, setbacks in the civil rights movement, the Watergate scandal, and revelations about the CIA's spying at home and murder plots abroad.

## DÉTENTE

The Vietnam experience also called into question the most fundamental tenet of American foreign policy during the Cold War. As Gelb and Betts observed, it "brought an end to the consensus on containment."[54] In fact, long before the fighting was over, the street protests, the burning of draft cards, and the chaotic election of 1968 had made apparent the need for a new approach to foreign policy. During his first month in office, Nixon announced in a press conference what came to be known as called the **Nixon Doctrine**: a policy stipulating that *nations in the developing world would be expected to use their own—not America's troops—to defend themselves.* The United States, though, would continue to sell arms to these countries, or sometimes provide them weapons for free if their cause struck a strong chord with America's interests, too. Moreover, observing a widening of the schism between China and the Soviet Union, which began to yawn in 1962, Nixon and Kissinger skillfully set out to *edge China farther away from Moscow's influence*, a policy known as the **opening to China**.

## A Thawing in the Cold War

America's icy relations with the USSR underwent a remarkable thaw during the Nixon years, an ironic outcome since Nixon had built his political reputation as a devoted Soviet basher. Nudged in this friendlier direction by Secretary Kissinger, Nixon ushered in *a period of relaxed tensions between the superpowers, known as* **détente** *and punctuated by arms control accords and increased trade agreements.* Nixon turned to the foreign policy instruments of diplomacy and economic statecraft at a time when Americans had become skeptical about the power of war making and CIA covert actions—intrusive instruments of foreign policy that had been unable to win the war in Vietnam. The ongoing, periodic experiment in détente, which reached a high point in the years from 1972 to 1974, made the harsh rhetoric of the Eisenhower/Dulles era seem antediluvian. The purpose of the thaw was to attempt, by way of civil dialogue and trade induce-ments, a calmer management of US-Soviet relations. The objective was to find, as po-litical scientist John Spanier has written, *"a lower level of tension and lower cost than those required by the policy of cold war confrontation and frequent crisis."*[55] Among the break-throughs was progress toward equitable arms reductions, agreed to by both superpowers in the Strategic Arms Limitation Talks I (SALT I), signed in 1972.

The war in Vietnam had demonstrated that the policy of containment would not work as intended everywhere. General Maxwell D. Taylor, once a strong proponent of US involvement in Indochina, stated after the retreat from Saigon, "Until we know the enemy and know our allies and know ourselves, we'd better keep out of this kind of dirty business. It's very dangerous."[56] Senator Gary Hart (D-Colorado) viewed the year 1973 as a significant turning point in American foreign policy. "Nixon proved that big govern-ment is not necessarily a benign government [a reference to the Watergate scandal]," he noted, adding, "OPEC [the Organization of Petroleum Exporting Countries] proved that our economy was vulnerable to international influences; and the Vietnam War proved that we couldn't have our way in the world."[57] In each case, it was a rude awakening.

## Fresh Conflicts

The attempts at détente with the Soviet were a disappointment for many Americans. From the viewpoint of Washington, DC, the Soviets continued to be obstreperous, sponsoring surrogate warfare in the African nation of Angola and engaging in a number of other provocations around the world. Of these, most worrisome was Moscow's preparation to enter (so it seemed at the time) the Israeli-Egyptian Yom Kippur War of 1973, which led to the placement of US forces on their first major nu-clear alert since the Cuban missile crisis. From Moscow's point of view, the United States appeared to be dragging its feet on trade agreements, as well as moving slowly on arms control and, in 1974, turning inward as the nation became transfixed on the Watergate scandal. For both sides, détente lost its glitter.

Even though the Nixon administration downplayed human rights in its foreign policy and maintained close ties to anticommunist Latin American dictators, military juntas in Greece, and South Africa's white leaders who practiced apartheid, both Nixon and Kissinger began quiet negotiations on what became known as the **Helsinki Accords**. Eventually signed by President Ford in 1975, the accords consisted of three "baskets," which many observers have concluded played a major role in the fall of East European communism in 1989. The baskets, or separate declarations, *encouraged "respect for human rights and fundamental freedoms," improved economic and technical cooperation among the signatories, and "freer movement of people, ideas, and information" between the East and the West.*

On the whole, though, President Ford turned out to be less attracted to the use of diplomatic initiatives, so central to détente, than his predecessor Nixon had been. With the ignominious defeat in Vietnam fresh in mind, Ford—advised by the ongoing Secretary of State Kissinger and White House chief of staff Dick Cheney—responded quickly with military force when Cambodian communists stopped and boarded an American merchant vessel, the *Mayaguez*, off their coast a few weeks after America's evacuation from Saigon in 1975. This rescue mission, which cost the lives of forty-one Marines, occurred *after* the American merchant sailors had already been released and were steaming homeward even as the Marines landed on Cambodian soil—a tragic failure of intelligence.[58] The Ford administration was ready for battle in Africa, too, in this case to counter Soviet adventurism in Angola. The President requested funding for a CIA covert action in the West African nation designed to assist pro-Western forces in the south against Moscow-backed local Marxists and Cuban soldiers in the north. The Congress balked at the President's request, however, displaying both its new assertiveness in the post-Watergate period and wariness about more "Vietnams" now popping up elsewhere in the developing world. This new *restraint with respect to the military instrument of foreign policy, as well as the use of covert action*, has been referred to as the **Vietnam syndrome**—a dangerous flirtation with global appeasement, in the eyes of critics.

Regardless of his administration's frequent demonstrations of bellicosity abroad, President Ford did cooperate with the Soviet Union in the pursuit of additional arms-control diplomacy, beginning with negotiations on a SALT II pact with Moscow in 1974. These arms accords with the Soviets had such a high profile that the administration understood the necessity of using the constitutional treaty procedure, rather than the more common use of executive or statutory agreements; senators would not tolerate being left on the sidelines during important diplomatic initiatives that involved arms control and the two superpowers. Ford's presidency enjoyed only a short life span, though (1974–1976), and the Carter administration that followed displayed a more complex approach to foreign policy.

President Carter, less experienced in international affairs than John Kennedy—or, in fact, than any president since Calvin Coolidge (who came to office in 1923)—seemed prepared to resume the experiment in détente with the Soviets. He expressed concern about the dangers of nuclear war and dedicated himself to winning Senate approval of

SALT II, as an extension of Nixon's SALT I, both crafted to place caps on the number of strategic weapons in the US and Soviet arsenals. The SALT II accords would have been "another baby step toward halting the arms race," according to arms control expert Barry Blechman.[59] The Senate never approved the treaty, however, chiefly because of a Soviet invasion of Afghanistan in 1979. Still, the SALT II provisions were honored less formally by both nations until 1986, when the Reagan administration decided to exceed the existing arms ceiling. President Carter also advocated—more than any president since Woodrow Wilson—a moral approach to American foreign policy that emphasized human rights, a reflection of his personal experience as a born-again Christian.

Carter's Secretary of State, the Wall Street attorney Cyrus Vance, enthusiastically supported the President's embrace of détente as well as his human rights initiatives. In contrast, the President's national security adviser, political scientist Zbigniew Brzezinski (born in Warsaw, Poland), was more of a conservative hard-liner on relations with the Soviet Union. In this sense, the Carter administration had a split personality. Vance's devotion to diplomacy could be seen in the Carter administration's pinnacle of foreign policy achievement, the **Camp David Accords**. *Negotiated in 1979 by the President and his Secretary of State at the Camp David presidential compound in Maryland with the leaders of Israel and Egypt, the purpose of the agreements was to bring peace between these warring nations.* In contrast, the Brzezinski stamp on foreign policy was clear in what became known as the **Carter Doctrine,** announced in 1980 following the Soviet invasion of Afghanistan. This policy stated that *"any use of outside force to try to gain control of the Persian Gulf oil area will be regarded as an assault on the vital interests of the United States and will be repelled by American military force."* Here was an application of the Monroe Doctrine to the Persian Gulf, a region of the world rather more difficult to defend than America's close neighbors in the Western Hemisphere.

The outcome of the awkward staff arrangement that pitted Vance against Brzezinski was a periodic vacillation by President Carter between the conflicted grand strategies of the dovish Secretary of State and the hawkish national security adviser. This internal confusion spilled into the public arena as the two aides appeared on television talk shows to speak on behalf of the administration, or at any rate to present their own views on what the President ought to be doing. When the Soviets invaded Afghanistan with 85,000 troops in December of 1979 to assist its new and teetering Marxist puppet regime, Carter's foreign policy perspectives shifted more toward Brzezinski's hawkish worldview. Brzezinski had already gained some ascendency over Vance in November of 1979, when American diplomats were taken hostage by Islamist revolutionaries in Iran. Brzezinski recommended use of the military instrument to rescue the hostages, while Vance maintained that diplomacy was the best route. When President Carter sided with Brzezinski, Vance resigned quietly in protest. The operation failed at the outset because of the collision of US rescue helicopters in the Iranian desert and other mistakes of military coordination and execution.

With respect to the Soviet entry into Afghanistan, the President said that he had changed his "opinion of the Russians . . . more dramatically in the last week than over the previous two and one-half years"—revealing, critics contended, an astounding naiveté about the merits of détente in the first place. Carter embargoed grain shipments bound for the Soviet Union, imposed a boycott of the 1980 Moscow Olympics, and stopped the shipment of high-technology exports to the Soviet bloc. "Cold War II had begun," concluded an experienced American diplomat.[60] In the next presidential election, the newly militant Carter—now sharply critical of the Soviets—was no match for the Republican nominee, former California governor Ronald Reagan, who had been on the belligerent far right when it came to the USSR for most of his political career. Slumping economic indicators at home; stalled hostage negotiations with the government of Iran; an aggressive Soviet Union; and a political opponent with a winning, upbeat personality provided the *coup de grace* to the President's campaign. After winning only six states, Carter limped home to Georgia in defeat.

## The Cold War Revived

Under President Reagan, the Cold War took on new life. The Soviet Union was an "evil empire," the President declared as he dramatically increased spending on military weaponry and, in the process, drove the national deficit to unprecedented heights. The easygoing President was immensely popular among voters and this enthusiasm could be seen in Congress as well. Lawmakers went along with Reagan's anti-Soviet rhetoric and dramatic spending increases, although Democrats on Capitol Hill periodically grumbled about this new foreign policy truculence and the unprecedented peacetime military spending.[61] Covert actions by the CIA proliferated around the world, wherever Marxists and Communists posed or appeared to pose a threat to the United States or its allies. This **Reagan Doctrine,** less a formal policy statement than an appellation applied by the media to the Reagan administration's new aggressiveness against the Soviets, envisaged *the robust use of CIA covert action to assist nations in their resistance to communist influence.*

This revival of harsh relations between the superpowers, in the style of the Cold War's early years, led to the excesses of the Iran-*contra* scandal that came to light in 1986. In contravention to the will of Congress, which enacted the Boland Amendment of 1983 to prohibit covert action in Nicaragua, the Reagan administration carried out such operations anyway, relying on a supersecret organization called "The Enterprise" and receiving money for its operations from Iran, the King of Saudi Arabia, the Sultan of Brunei, and a few conservative American millionaires—all sworn to secrecy. A leak (in a Middle East magazine) revealed the illegal covert actions, which in turn led to major congressional and executive branch inquiries. During the Reagan years, the United States seemed to return to the 1950s in both rhetoric and action, although this time with a divided consensus in the nation as lawmakers who were worried about a renewed Cold War sometimes rejected funding for the President's combative approach to foreign relations.[62]

After the embarrassment of the Iran-*contra* scandal—it cost the President twenty-one percentage points in the popularity polls—Reagan softened his views about the struggle against global communism and turned the United States toward another try at détente. He had already allowed low-level arms talks with the Soviets to proceed in 1982. The administration preferred to use the designation START (Strategic Arms Reduction Talks) rather than SALT, highlighting largely for public relations purposes the goal of reductions in the number of existing weapons, not just limitations on new weapons. In 1985, Reagan agreed to meet in Geneva with the surprisingly reform-minded Soviet leader, Mikhail S. Gorbachev. The meeting yielded a lively exchange of good will on the prospects for the reduction of nuclear armaments.

A second gathering occurred the next year in Reykjavik, Iceland, where—to the astonishment of Reagan's aides—both men openly expressed a desire to abolish all nuclear weapons. "Give up all nuclear weapons?" President Reagan asked rhetorically. "I've been in favor of that for a long time."[63] Then, in 1987, Gorbachev traveled to the United States and the two leaders agreed on a bold **INF Treaty** *to remove all intermediate-range nuclear forces from West and East Europe.* The Senate approved the pact, and Reagan's signature ratified it the next year.

President Reagan visited the Soviet Union in 1988 and, just five years after his "evil empire" speech, he embraced President Gorbachev in the streets of Moscow like an old political ally. Historian Gaddis commented on the irony: "Both men worked the crowd, shaking hands and kissing babies, while their respective military aides—holding the briefcases containing the codes and target lists for annihilating each other's country—tried to remain inconspicuously in the background." Gaddis's constructivist conclusion was: "Leaders of great states, like most other people, learn from experience."[64]

In 1988, Gorbachev announced that he would withdraw within the next year all 115,000 Soviet troops in Afghanistan, winding down Moscow's Vietnam. The Reagan administration had successfully used CIA covert action in Afghanistan to support local efforts designed to drive out the Soviet Army (an important secret foreign policy initiative I explore in Chapter 12). President Gorbachev kept his word about the troop withdrawal; and he also proposed significant cuts on both sides in the number of European conventional forces, a step endorsed by President George H. W. Bush in

US President Ronald Reagan, left, and Soviet leader Mikhail Gorbachev sit down for a summit talk in Reykjavik, Iceland, on October 11, 1986.

1989. By the end of the Reagan administration, the START negotiations had culminated in a 30 percent reduction in strategic armaments in each superpower's arsenal. Moreover, the thaw in relations between Washington and Moscow would lead—amazingly, unpredictably—to the end of the Cold War itself, beginning with the fall of the Berlin wall in November of 1989.

By this time, the Soviet economy had deteriorated to the point where reformist President Mikhail Gorbachev realized his empire could no longer sustain the costs of arms competition with the United States.

The crumbling Soviet economy, coupled with the willingness of Gorbachev to allow change (which went farther than he had anticipated), rang the death knell for the old communist regime. By 1990, the superpower rivalry had come to an end—yet this danger was soon followed by new threats on the global horizon.

In January of 1993, President George H. W. Bush (Reagan's successor) and Russian President Boris Yeltsin (Gorbachev's successor) signed far-reaching arms control treaties growing out of the START II negotiations that further reduced the number of strategic nuclear weapons on both sides. As Bush observed at the end of the Cold War, now perhaps all nations could enjoy a "New World Order."[65] It was an attractive vision, but short lived.

## SUMMARY

Ideological, political, economic, and military competition with the Soviet Union—a rivalry known as the Cold War—was the dominant preoccupation of US foreign policy during the first forty-five years of the nuclear era. In the protection of America's global interests, the response of officials in Washington to this rivalry was primarily a reliance on nuclear deterrence and the containment doctrine. Combined, these approaches provided a longer epoch of great power stability than the world had seen before in this century, and one of the longest in history. Although the superpowers avoided direct warfare, they fought limited, secret intelligence wars against one another in various developing countries: the CIA against the KGB. The United States also engaged in costly overt conflicts in a desire to curb communism, most notably in Korea and Vietnam. Further, in Cuba conflicting foreign policies led the superpowers to the brink of nuclear war in 1962.

Occasionally, the United States and the Soviet Union attempted to accommodate one another's needs through less severe forms of foreign policy, embracing diplomatic negotiations (especially in the domain of arms control) and economic trade agreements. The period of détente during the Nixon administration, lasting from 1972 to 1974, is a notable illustration. This effort led to disappointments on both sides, however, and a new round of bickering began between the superpowers. When the Soviet Union invaded Afghanistan in 1979, relations plummeted and led to a return of Cold War animosities. Under President Reagan, superpower relations cooled further still, at least at first. Then, ironically and unpredictably, during the final years of the Reagan administration and throughout the first Bush administration, the world witnessed breakthrough efforts in both Washington and Moscow to ease—and then erase—the Cold War.

## KEY TERMS

Bay of Pigs (1961) p. 147
Berlin blockade (1948) p. 143
Camp David Accords (1979) p. 161
Carter Doctrine (1975–1976) p. 161
Church Committee (1975–1976) p. 158
containment doctrine p. 137
counterinsurgency warfare (COIN) p. 146
Cuban missile crisis (1962) p. 147
détente p. 159
flexible response p. 146
Geneva Accords (1954) p. 152
Helsinki Accords (1975) p. 160
INF Treaty (Intermediate-Range Nuclear Forces Treaty, 1987) p. 163
Limited Test Ban Treaty (1963) p. 153

Marshall Plan (European Recovery Program, 1948–1952) p. 143
massive retaliation p. 146
McCarthyism (1950–1956) p. 141
National Security Council Memorandum No. 68 (NSC–68), 1950 p. 141
Nixon Doctrine (1969) p. 158
North Atlantic Treaty Organization (NATO, 1949) p. 144
Reagan Doctrine (1981–1989) p. 162
opening to China (1962) p. 159
Truman Doctrine (1947) p. 138
Vietnam syndrome p. 160
Warsaw Pact (1955) p. 144

---

## QUESTIONS FOR DISCUSSION

1. From the Soviet point of view, do you think the placement of nuclear missiles in Cuba in 1962 was justified, given the presence of US nuclear missiles in Turkey?
2. Should the United States have fought the Korean War? The war in Vietnam? What differences do you draw between these two conflicts, if any?
3. In retrospect, what were the major points of dispute between the United States and the Soviet Union that fueled the Cold War?
4. Why do you think the Cold War finally ended?
5. What are the chances that another Cold War could breakout between the United States and Russia? The United States and China?

---

## ADDITIONAL READINGS

Hook, Steven W. and John Spanier. *American Foreign Policy Since World War II*, 18th ed. Washington, DC: CQ Press, 2010.

Karnow, Stanley. *Vietnam: A History*. New York: Viking, 1983.

Rusk, Dean, with Richard Rusk and Daniel S. Papp. *As I Saw It*. New York: Norton, 1989.

---

For further readings, please visit the book's companion website.

### CHAPTER 6

# American Foreign Policy in a Fractured World

### DEATH IN SOMALIA

The Black Hawk helicopter lay crumpled near the center of Mogadishu, Somalia, brought down by a rocket-propelled grenade (RPG) fired by local warriors in 1993 opposed to the US military presence on the Horn of Africa. A well-armed and angry mob approached the crash site. What is known as the Battle of Mogadishu, a struggle between Somali warlords and the US military over control of the capital city, was about to reach fever pitch. The motley but battled-tested and determined fighters in Mogadishu managed to shoot down two other Black Hawks that day. Furious crowds surrounded the downed crews at each crash site.

Inside the wreckage of his Black Hawk, pilot Mike Durant lay dazed but clearheaded enough to realize his right leg was broken. Durant's copilot was sprawled next to him, unconscious. The rest of the crew looked in even worse shape, but they were all still alive.

The wreckage of an American Blackhawk helicopter in Mogadishu, Somalia, October 14, 1993, shot down by Somali warlords.

A team of Delta airmen, a special military branch stationed at a US Army Headquarters base three miles away on the shores of the Indian Ocean, soon arrived in hopes of rescuing Durant and his crew. The mob thickened and surrounded the crippled chopper. Durant came out of his stupor and fired at the locals with a pistol to keep them away as the Delta rescuers worked to free the injured crew. Return fire from the gathering crowd increased. Within a few minutes, Durant could no longer hear any firing by his crew or members of the rescue team. They had all perished under a fusillade of bullets from the local fighters. The frenzied mob pulled Durant from the cockpit, ripping his clothing and shouting: "Ranger, Ranger, you die Somalia!" Miraculously, Durant survived. One of the mob leaders decided he might be valuable in a swap for US-held Somalia fighters and so he called off the killers. They turned to the other Americans who had died and, rejoicing over their conquest, stripped some of the airmen of their clothing.

This urban combat on October 3, 1993—the longest sustained firefight involving US troops since the Vietnam War—led to the deaths of eighteen American soldiers and the wounding of seventy-five more. The television cameras of CNN and other

**LEARNING OBJECTIVES AND CONSTITUTIONAL ISSUES**

**By the end of this chapter, you will be able to:**

- *Identify the circumstances that brought the Cold War to an end.*
- *Discuss the reasons why the United States entered into military conflicts after the Cold War, as well as the consequences of these conflicts.*
- *Explain how international terrorism became the central foreign policy concern of the United States in the twenty-first century.*

**THIS CHAPTER RAISES THE FOLLOWING CONSTITUTIONAL QUESTIONS:**

- To what extent did the decisions to enter into various wars since 1991 follow the prescriptions spelled out in the Constitution, with Congress declaring—or at least authorizing—warfare by a majority vote in both chambers and the president responsible for carrying out the war on a day-to-day basis?

- Was the George H. W. Bush administration on firm constitutional ground in claiming these two sources of authority for entering into the First Persian Gulf War: the inherent powers of the presidency and authority from the United Nations?

- If the Clinton administration had decided to send US ground troops into the Balkans, would that action have required—constitutionally—a majority approval in both houses of Congress? Should a president be allowed to use the US Air Force in combat without congressional approval (as Obama did in Libya), but be required to obtain legislative authority for more intrusive interventions (as with the use of ground forces)?

- Is it permissible for a president to bypass existing law in times of national emergency, as George W. Bush did when he set aside the Foreign Intelligence Surveillance Act requirement for national security wiretap warrants? What other options did Bush have? Did he act in the same manner as President Lincoln had during the Civil War? What were the essential differences, if any, between these two presidents in their approach to their constitutional authorities and in the crises they faced?

international media at the scene relayed back to the United States and around the world images of Somali clans dragging the naked bodies of Black Hawk crew members through the dirt alleyways of Mogadishu.[1]

Earlier, in August of 1992, President George H. W. Bush had unilaterally (that is, without a congressional debate or vote) ordered some 25,000 American troops into Somalia. The purpose was to buttress a failing UN-sponsored humanitarian relief operation designed to airlift food to the famine-ravaged Horn of Africa. Less than a year later, the Clinton administration expanded the mission, again unilaterally, to include the disarming of the warring Somali clans. For congressional critics, this escalation looked more like a high risk gamble in support of nation building than a traditional UN relief operation. Other members of Congress, though, called for an increased American presence in the region to curb the senseless killings.

The sophisticated firepower displayed by the Somali warriors took the US military by surprise. Sickened by the news video footage of American soldiers being dragged through the streets of Mogadishu, lawmakers introduced legislation to halt funding for further US military operations in Somalia, unless President Clinton explicitly requested additional monies and obtained congressional approval.[2] The administration chose to withdraw the troops.

In just two years, America had moved from a sense of joy over the end of the Cold War to a fresh set of international woes. Osama bin Laden, head of the Al Qaeda terrorist group based in Afghanistan that would later attack the United States on 9/11, is said to have viewed the retreat in Somalia as a telltale sign of US weakness.[3] America's erstwhile grand strategy of communist containment was now a thing of the past, as the George H. W. Bush administration first hoped for a New World Order and found instead an international scene plagued by terrorism and failing nations like Somalia. Presidents Bush and Clinton would set the United States on a course to bolster democracies around the globe as a defense against these new threats and the rise of autocracies in the Balkans, Africa, and elsewhere. For the Clinton administration, the awkward phrase "Democratic Enlargement" replaced "Containment" as a rallying banner for the foreign policy of the United States.  ⁓

## A FRACTURED WORLD

In the years following the Cold War, more nations than ever before—indeed, a majority—experimented with democratic forms of government. In this sense, it was a time of opportunity and a time to embrace new or revived forms of collective security, as displayed by NATO's impressive role in the Bosnian and Kosovo wars. It was a time, as well, to rise above the fighting that had scarred the earth for so long. Yet the United States soon found itself at war in two of the most volatile regions of the world: the Middle East and Southwest Asia. Moreover, people around the globe continued to look toward the United States for leadership, at a time when Americans groaned under the strains of costly foreign wars, a sluggish economy, spiraling debt, and intense partisan wrangling at home.

The startling collapse of the Soviet Union as a global power during the period from 1989 to 1991 altered the nature of world politics. An era of binary thinking—the US versus the USSR—had come to a close. Throughout four decades of Cold War, the Soviet Union was Priority No. 1 in the calculations of Washington's foreign policy officials; now, with the Soviet empire fallen, the focus of American foreign policy shifted and broadened. As a Director of Central Intelligence (DCI) put it, the Soviet dragon had been slain, but the United States now confronted "a jungle filled with a bewildering variety of poisonous snakes."[4]

Ethnic and tribal disputes suddenly flared into violence around the globe. In Yugoslavia, unrest burst into a full-blown civil war that tore apart the loosely threaded seams of unity that had held this nation together out of fear that the Soviets would otherwise intervene. In Africa, tribal warfare in Somalia grew more intense, with hundreds of civilians caught in the crossfire and thousands more starving as drought continued to plague the land and tribal bandits stole food from the UN and other international relief agencies. In January 1993, Czechoslovakia broke in two—peacefully at least—along an ethnic fissure, creating separate Czech and Slovak republics. The trash bins of harried cartographers filled with outdated drawings of national boundaries that seemed to shift almost month to month. (The highlights of US foreign policy since the end of the Cold War are presented in Figure 6.1.)

## A NEW WORLD DISORDER

The administration of George H. W. Bush was understandably elated when the Soviet Union collapsed during its watch. The President spoke of a **New World Order,** *a time of global peace that would replace the strife that darkened the era of the Cold War.*[5] Proclamations from the White House notwithstanding, however, the world had become anything but orderly; rather, a new world *dis*order seemed to take the place of the previous superpower standoff. For the first time, the United States soon found itself engaged in wars in the volatile Muslim regions of the Middle East and Southwest Asia. In 1993, terrorists tried to bomb the Twin Towers in New York City, followed by attacks against Americans in Kenya, Tanzania, and Yemen from 1998 to 2000. Then came 9/11.

### Disintegration of the Soviet Union

The most spectacular event of the years since 1945 was a second Russian revolution. The first, in 1917, had brought communism to power; the second, in 1989–1991, saw communism overthrown. The beginning of the end to this long reign of tyranny came in 1985, when the Russian elite chose Mikhail S. Gorbachev as General Secretary of the Politburo. The first Soviet leader born after the Russian revolution, the 54-year-old Gorbachev realized that the Marxist-Leninist experiment of a state-controlled society had failed; indeed, without reform the Soviet Union seemed on the brink of economic collapse. He introduced the dual policies of *glasnost* (more openness in government affairs), as well as *perestroika* (a reduction in the government's grip on the economy). These reforms amounted to an unprecedented embrace

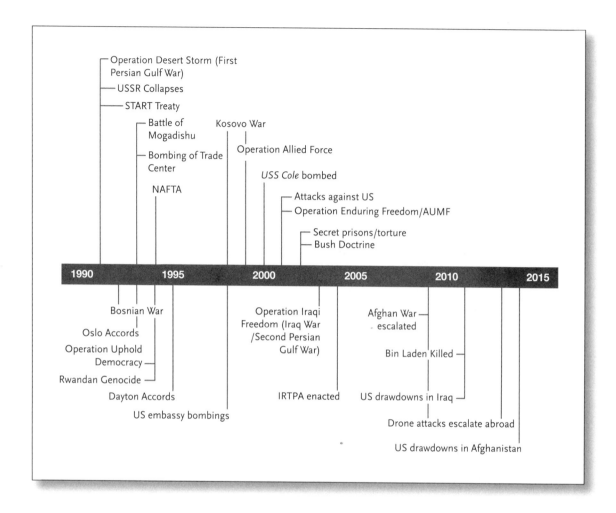

of democracy and free enterprise, at least to a degree never before seen in that part of the world.

*Figure 6.1.*
Highlights in the Evolution of U.S. Foreign Policy, 1991-2014

Although many Soviet citizens welcomed the changes with great hope, the old guard viewed Gorbachev as a dangerous threat to their established positions of power. Despite their resistance behind the scenes, Gorbachev bravely pushed forward his reforms. By August of 1991, following revolutions in East Germany, Poland, and other nations in East Europe, he was prepared to grant the fifteen Soviet republics (Estonia, for example) virtual autonomy. This was too much for the old guard. Led by Soviet Vice President Gennadi I. Yanayev, a twelve-man State Committee for the State of Emergency ordered Gorbachev arrested. The State Committee also planned to apprehend another key reformer, Boris N. Yeltsin, just elected president of the Russian Republic.

What the State Committee failed to anticipate was the courage that the taste of freedom had given Gorbachev, Yeltsin, and the Russian people. Upward of 100,000 protesters poured into the streets of major Russian cities and refused to accept Gorbachev's incarceration. Russians, young and old, set up barricades in the streets of Moscow and Leningrad, surrounded Red Army tanks at great risk to their own lives, and unfurled banners declaring their opposition to the coup against Gorbachev. The protesters demanded his release from house arrest. With impressive bravado, Yeltsin clambered onto a tank in downtown Moscow, sent to intimidate reformist Russian officials in the Parliament. With television cameras from around the world recording his astonishing act of defiance, Yeltsin declared the military coup "reactionary" and "unconstitutional." A vast sea of supporters applauded his leadership and formed their own human chains surrounding other Russian tanks. These internal events in Russia had a profound effect on American foreign policy. The central villain in the Cold War—the USSR—was dissolving before the eyes of stunned leaders in Washington and other democratic capitals around the world. These leaders, including President Bush, expressed outrage at the coup attempt against Gorbachev and refused to recognize the actions of the State Committee.

The Soviet military found itself split. The ardor of the demonstrations had given many Russian army officers pause. Persuaded by the pleas of protesters, military commanders in Moscow refused to fire on the peaceful pro-Gorbachev crowds, although early in this tense confrontation two courageous students were crushed by a tank as they stood their ground in its pathway. In the face of rebellion by their own troops, members of the State Committee experienced a failure of nerve and backed down from ordering a bloody battle against Gorbachev, Yeltsin, and their followers that would have left the streets of Moscow awash in blood and might have led to a Russian civil war.

Within a few days, Gorbachev was restored to the presidency of the Soviet Union; Yeltsin had become a bona fide national hero; and the old military guard found itself thoroughly discredited, along with the crumbling communist system it had tried to defend. The attempted coup was among the last throes of a dying establishment, though ultranationalists would try again—and once again fail—to oust the reformers in 1993. In place of state repression now stood a new system based on a devolution of power and an embrace of some democratic forms of government and market economics. It was the end of an important era in American foreign policy and, as observed George F. Kennan, "a turning point of the most momentous historical significance."[6]

Gorbachev had brought reform to the Soviet Union, but the public's zeal for democracy and free enterprise raced far beyond what he had envisioned for his country. During the aftermath of the coup attempt against him, Gorbachev lost control of the careful, incremental steps toward reform he had proposed. Instead, the increasingly bold Boris Yeltsin pushed for faster, more far-reaching reforms—a popular stance among Russians frustrated by their stagnant economy and lack of political freedoms. The newly free, former Soviet Republics also displayed resistance to Gorbachev's plans for preserving the political and economic bonds of the old USSR federation. In December of 1991, for example, voters in Ukraine—a former Soviet Republic second only to Russia in military and economic power—overwhelming endorsed a referendum to separate altogether from Moscow's rule. Proving to be a clever political infighter, Yeltsin managed to outmaneuver Gorbachev, his erstwhile ally for reform, and, as the Republics debated the best type of union—if any—with Russia, Yeltsin rapidly became the dominant political figure in Moscow and the primary individual with whom America's foreign policy leaders had to deal in relations with Russia.

The fifteen former Soviet Republics settled on the idea of a Commonwealth of Independent States (CIS) to allow some form of mutual cooperation for defense and economic development, but the glue failed to hold as some former Soviet Republics began to request (and received) permission to join NATO. In 1994, Lithuania became the first to request admission, followed by Estonia and Latvia soon after. In response to these initiatives, NATO decided to expand eastward and admitted to membership the Czech Republic, Hungary, and Poland in 1996, and would soon bring in the Baltic nations—in each case over the strong protest of Kremlin leaders.

In some of the former Soviet Republics, ethnic fighting broke out. The pro-communist Dnestr region of Moldova, for example, joined in battle against the new Moldovan government. In Georgia, rebellious Azeris enjoyed the support of right-wing elements in the Russian army, which was suspected of supplying them with weapons. Subsequently, separatist rebellions would flare up in the Abkhazia and South Ossetia regions of Georgia. In Armenia, the dominant Armenians drove nearly all the Azeri ethnic group out of their Republic. The world seemed to be fragmenting and, in the process, creating a host of new complications for American foreign policy.

A central debate in Washington, DC during this period, and one that continues still, is how much support—especially financial—the United States should lend to the former Soviet Republics. For some observers, American resources expended in these new states would be so much taxpayer money down the drain; the Republics would simply waste the funding, so ill-equipped were they to create a market economy. This school of thought preferred to see genuine strides toward market reform taken by Russia and the other Republics before Western money was invested. In June 1991, the Bush administration turned down an appeal from Gorbachev for $20 to $30 billion in Western capital. Subsequently, the government of Germany—its East and West sections reunited in 1990—blamed the United States, Britain, and Japan (among other reluctant nations) for having undermined Gorbachev and thereby fermented the coup attempt against him.

*A school of thought in the United States agreed with the Germans that a major infusion of Western capital and known-how, coupled with an insistence that the former Soviet Republics follow Western recommendations on how to revamp their economies,* was the only way to avoid a backslide to the old communist regime or into a civil war. This approach became known in 1991 as the **grand bargain**. It gained little support in the United States, however, in large part because many Americans questioned the affordability of helping the economies of other nations. Still, at the same time, few Americans wished the former Soviet Republics to revert to communism or descend into a civil war that might be dangerous to the whole world in a region that harbored some 27,000 nuclear warheads. Moreover, few wished to see a return to the Cold War. Torn between anxieties about what a Russia in economic free fall might mean for world stability, on one hand, and a reluctance to spend money abroad with America's own fitful economy sputtering along at home, on the other hand, Washington officials in both the executive and legislative branches temporized as conditions in the former Soviet Republics continued to deteriorate.

The United States did appropriate $500,000 in defense funds to Russia in late 1991, with the aim of helping Moscow leaders dismantle the Soviet nuclear arsenal. Moreover, and again obviously in America's self-interest, Congress provided over $1 billion through the **Nunn-Lugar Act** *to improve the security of Russian nuclear warheads and related WMD materials*, out of fear that "loose nukes" might fall into the hands of terrorists.[7] This defense funding proved insufficient, though, to complete the process of Soviet weapons destruction. By 1993, most of the nuclear warheads in the former Soviet Republics remained intact; and vast numbers of sophisticated conventional weapons, filling 40,000 railroad cars in Russia alone, sat in stockpiles—tempting targets for criminals and terrorist cells.

One hopeful note sounded in the final stages of the President George H. W. Bush administration. Bush and Yeltsin signed the **Strategic Arms Reduction Talks (START) Treaty** in July of 1991, which *authorized dramatic cutbacks in the number of strategic nuclear warheads in both nations by some two-thirds.* Even this good news was dampened, though, by the realization that Yeltsin, just returned from China and India, intended to step up Russian arms sales to those nations. The sales of Patriot-style, surface-to-air missiles and advanced fighter-interceptors to China alone would net some $2 to $3 billion annually for Russia, equivalent to all the aid Moscow was receiving from the West.

Its economy in shambles, the sale of weapons abroad—including three Kilo-class submarines for Iran, MIGs and bombers to Syria, and even weapons to the renegade regimes in North Korea and Libya—became an irresistible option for the Russians, whatever instabilities the weapons might render in various regions of the world. In 1992, America sold 150 F-16 aircraft to Taiwan, then criticized Russia for selling two dozen SU–27 fighter-bombers to China. Critics pointed out that the United States, the world's foremost seller of weapons overseas, was not in a strong position to complain about the arms sales of other nations—although at least Washington officials refrained from selling weapons to notoriously bad actors like North Korea.

The optimists who hoped for progress toward a market economy and democratic institutions in Russia received a sharp jolt in 1993 when ultranationalists in the Russian legislature rose up against the Yeltsin regime and barricaded themselves in the Parliamentary building. Via CNN, the world witnessed the spectacle of pro-Yeltsin military forces shelling the high-rise Parliament building with heavy artillery until this latest set of coup plotters finally surrendered. A fresh round of parliamentary elections at the end of the year gave optimists yet another jolt when the ultranationalists won more seats than any other faction. Nerves frayed among those in Washington with responsibilities for US policy toward Russia, with its vast number of nuclear weapons and teetering government.

Over the next decade, Russia's politics and economy began to stabilize. In 2000 Vladimir Putin, a former KGB chief, replaced Yeltsin as the nation's president and tightened control over policy making. Putin got along reasonably well with a new American President, George W. Bush, and signed a **Strategic Offensive Reduction Treaty (SORT)** *in 2002 that cut US and Russian strategic nuclear arsenals to the lowest total in decades, at about 2,000 warheads each.*

Putin backed away from his opposition to the eastward expansion of NATO, initially opposed by the Kremlin as a provocative encroachment into the Russian sphere of influence, as long as he received assurances that Moscow leaders would be brought into NATO discussions more frequently. After the terrorist attacks of 9/11, when Putin offered support for the United States in its fight against terrorism, Washington muted its criticism of Moscow's brutal repression of Chechnya, a Russian province seeking independence but, in Putin's view, just another terrorist movement. The two nations continued to bicker over Russia's friendly trade relationships with Iran and North Korea, which the United States viewed (along with Iraq) as an "axis of evil," in George W. Bush's words delivered during the 2002 State of the Union speech—rogue regimes dedicated to nuclear-weapons programs and regional trouble-making.

When his term of office expired (2000–2008), Putin moved into the seemingly secondary position of prime minister but remained the power behind the scenes as he maneuvered his top aide, Dmitry A. Medvedev, into the Russian presidency. In May of 2012, Putin again won the presidential election, as Russia seemed to slip further away from the moorings of democratic reform. From his obscure retirement, Gorbachev remained hopeful. "It will be difficult, even painful," he said, "but democracy will prevail in Russia. There will be no dictatorship, although relapses into authoritarianism are possible. That's because we, or so it seems to me, have only come halfway."[8] President Putin and President Obama failed to warm to one another and relations between the erstwhile superpowers began to deteriorate in 2013—especially when Russia gave asylum to the US intelligence contractor Edward J. Snowden, who that year stole huge amounts of classified material from the National Security Agency and fled to Hong Kong, then Moscow.

## Bloodbath in the Balkans

Crowding President Clinton's foreign policy agenda, too, were further territorial breakups, this time in Yugoslavia where civil war splintered its former components—especially in the heartland of Bosnia-Herzegovina and Serbia. The President's Ambassador to the United Nations (and later Secretary of State), Madeleine K. Albright, referred to this crisis during her Senate confirmation hearings on July 8, 1997, as "clearly the highest priority of the President in the National Security Council's agenda."

Nowhere was the post-Cold-War revival of atavistic ethnic grievances more apparent than in Yugoslavia. Inside the boundaries of what was, until 1990, a sovereign state where people of Albanian, Bulgarian, Croat, Hungarian, Macedonian, Montenegrin, Muslim, Serb, Slovak, and Slovene descent—not to mention of different religions—lived in uneasy proximity to one another. For generations, many of these ethnic groups had aspired to form their own nations, which often meant confiscating territory from neighboring ethnic groups. During the Cold War, their animosities had been held in check by the prospect of Soviet tanks rumbling across the border to silence any unrest. Now that check had vanished.

As part and parcel of this ethnic fighting, most observers pointed to a revival of nationalism in the world: the same force that had given rise to World War I (which had its origins in the Balkans), as well as to Hitler and to Stalin. As historian John Lukacs defines it, nationalism is "the myth of a 'people,' justifying everything."[9] He labels the post-Cold-War variant of nationalism witnessed in the Balkans and elsewhere in Central Europe and the former Soviet Republics as **populist nationalism**, whereby *people within the same nation who do not seem to agree with some of the populist and nationalist ideology are assigned the status of minorities, suggesting that they cannot belong within the authentic body of the national people.* Each ethnic faction is driven by a vision of dominance over rivals, a lust for revenge for earlier grievances (some as old as decades or even centuries), the desire for territorial acquisition, the raw ambitions of their leaders, and deep religious differences. "If we don't stop Islam now," a Serb soldier told a reporter, "fundamentalism will dominate Europe in ten to twenty years."[10] The end of the Cold War had led to a proliferation of ethnic groups seeking independence.

"Barbarism" is not too strong a word when one examines the civil war in former Yugoslavia. From the war's inception in 1991, triggered by the desire of Serbian leaders to create in the place of Yugoslavia a "Greater Serbia," reports of horrendous atrocities poured out of the region on an almost daily basis. The publicly stated goal of the Serbs, who opened what is known as the **Bosnian War** with *an attack against Croatia in 1992*, was nothing less than **ethnic cleansing**, *a policy of attacks against rival ethnic groups with the intent of ridding the area of them.* The war went on until 1995.

Around 44 percent of the people living in Bosnia were Muslim and 31 percent were Serbs; nonetheless, the Serbian leader, Slobodan Milosevic, joined by the Bosnia Serbs, attempted to expel the Muslims. All of these events were of concern to US foreign policy officials; they worried about the spread of these ethnic wars in the Balkans to ignite war in Europe, as happened at the outbreak of World War I. European nations and Russia had long-standing ties with different groups in former Yugoslavia and might be persuaded to come to their assistance. What may have seemed to some a distant civil war had the potential to sweep Europe into the fighting, with all the implications that would carry for the United States—heavily invested in the European markets and politically tied to these nations through NATO.

Among the widely reported Serb atrocities were over 20,000 rapes of Muslim women by Serbian soldiers. As a further atrocity, the Serbs kept the impregnated women in captivity until an abortion was no longer feasible, thereby bringing lifelong shame to the mother and the child—rape used as a weapon of war, a visible manifestation of enduring ethnic rage and revenge. The Serbs also engaged in mass murders, including over 200 hospitalized Croats who were taken from their beds in 1992 and shot point-blank in a nearby field. The Serbs fired artillery shells at Sarajevo, the capital of Bosnia-Herzegovina, and other civilian targets, resulting in the deaths of thousands of noncombatants. They also used sniper fire against civilians, including international news correspondents, several of whom died from their wounds; and they dragged the deputy prime minister of Bosnia, a Muslim, from a UN escort vehicle and murdered him in cold blood. Such events had a deep influence on the American public, which was increasingly shocked by the violence; they turned to foreign policy leaders in Washington to do something to stop the horrors. Pressures mounted for American intervention.[11]

Whereas Serbian soldiers were the most blatant perpetrators of war crimes, they were hardly the only ones with the blood of innocents on their hands. Each ethnic group involved in the conflict violated the accepted canons of modern warfare. In December of 1992, for example, the *New York Times* reported that Bosnian Muslims killed over sixty Serbs, chiefly civilians, in villages close to the Bosnian town of Bratunac. Here was the New World "Order"—not at all like the time of peace hoped for by George H. W. Bush.

While the Serbs pursued their goal of ethnic cleansing by killing or ejecting all non-Serbs from Bosnia-Herzegovina, Croatia reversed itself and laid claim to the besieged territory. Subsequently, the Croatian battled against Serb militia in this topsy-turvy war of ethnic factions. By 1993, the fight had led to the deaths of thousands of Muslims and a trail of refugees over 1.6 million people long—the largest exodus of war victims in Europe since since World War II. Muslim nations threatened intervention, while elsewhere the leaders of other countries (including some Russian officials) spoke of weighing in on the side of the Serbians. The specter of a spreading war loomed in the Balkans, reminiscent of 1914 when fighting had washed outward from Sarajevo to engulf all of Europe.

For the time being, though, the outside world largely stood by, stunned by the television and newspaper reports of brutality and death, but reluctant to become involved in a civil war where the combatants were heavily armed and where the shifting ethnic loyalties, like the region's mountainous terrain, were complex and foreboding. First, the United Nations issued an arms embargo in September of 1991 against all Yugoslavian territory, a feckless initiative given that the Serbs were already well armed. Then, in 1992, UN negotiators entered the region in search of a peaceful settlement. Relief agencies followed, along with UN administrators and 22,500 UN soldiers (known as "blue helmets" for the color of their headgear)—the largest contingent deployed since 1960, when the UN had sent a peace mission to the Congo.

The Bosnian civil war represented a major test of the UN's role in the post-Cold-War era and raised serious questions in the United States about its proper role in the war.

As the fighting continued throughout 1993, a dismembered Yugoslavia—once a popular vacation spot on the shimmering Adriatic Sea—fell into a prolonged siege. The United States finally entered the fray in 1993. Denouncing Europe for its "abysmal" failure to negotiate a settlement to the conflict in the Balkans, a region where the Europeans had deeper historical roots and experience than did the United States, the Clinton administration vowed to "vigorously pursue concerted action with our European allies and international bodies to end the slaughter in Bosnia." The administration added that the fighting had created "near genocidal conditions or perhaps really genocidal conditions."[12] Unilateral intervention by the United States with ground troops, though, was an option firmly rejected by the administration. The most it would attempt at this time were some largely symbolic humanitarian airdrops of food and clothing into Bosnia, followed by a limited number of air sorties in early 1994.

The fighting in Yugoslavia went on and, by the end of 1995, over 500,000 people had been killed in the conflict. So-called safe areas protected by UN blue helmets were routinely overrun by Serb forces; ethnic cleansing, rape, and the mass murder of civilians continued, primarily but not exclusively carried out by Serbian soldiers. At last, as 1995 came to a close, the United States managed to broker the **Dayton Peace Accords** *among Croats, Bosnian Muslims, and Serbs—diplomatic talks that resulted in a division of Yugoslavia along ethnic lines.* The United Nations ended its deployment in the Balkans and NATO took over the job of enforcing the Dayton Accords. Fighter aircraft and bombers flown by NATO pilots filled the skies above Yugoslavia. Further, NATO deployed an "Implementation Force" (IFOR) to Bosnia that consisted of 20,000 US troops, along with 43,000 more from France and Great Britain, with several thousand additional soldiers joining the effort from other countries (including 2,500 from Russia). In 1997, IFOR became a 30,000-person NATO "Stabilization Force" (SFOR) designed to keep the warring parties at arm's length as well as to map minefields and destroy any heavy armaments that were still on the battlefields. Thanks to NATO, this region of the Balkans began to enjoy peace, however tenuous.

Meanwhile, in 1998, ethnic cleansing and fighting erupted in another region of what was once Yugoslavia. Inside the province of Kosovo, *Albanian Muslims pushed for greater autonomy and eventually took up arms against Serbian soldiers and police stationed in the province. The Serbian leader Milosevic again unleashed the forces of repression and began yet another campaign of ethnic cleansing.* Serbian soldiers murdered more than ten thousand Kosovars, according to prosecutors in the Hague, and the Kosovars did their best to even the score. In 1999, NATO belatedly turned to the **Kosovo War** and launched massive air strikes against the Serbians (Operation Allied Force); but President Clinton again refused to send US ground troops into battle, and lawmakers were also reluctant to push for intervention and the spilling of American blood. Refugees in the hundreds of thousands fled from Kosovo into nearby Albania, Macedonia, and Montenegro, upsetting stability in each of these small, newly created nations. Succumbing to the NATO air raids after three months, Milosevic sued for peace and NATO troops (including many Americans) occupied Kosovo as peacekeepers. The International

Criminal Court in The Hague, Netherlands, tried and convicted Milosevic and several of his military chiefs as war criminals in 2006; however, ethnic tensions remained on edge in Bosnia and Kosovo.[13]

## Fusion in Western Europe

While much of the world seemed to be breaking apart, *East and West Germany moved against the trend and reunited in 1990*—and with astonishing speed, just a year after the dismantling of the Berlin Wall in 1989. This **German reunification** was of great significance to American foreign policy because it marked a consolidation of NATO power through the establishment of a united Germany with a pro-Western orientation and great economic potential. Most analysts had predicted that with the fall of the Berlin Wall and a newly restrained Soviet military under Gorbachev unwilling to use force to retain East Germany as a communist satellite, German reunification would surely become a reality. The problems raised by this integration would be great, however, because East Germany was economically backward. Moreover, the international community—particularly France—might balk at too rapid a reunification; memories from World War II of a strong, united Germany still lingered painfully in the mind of many a French citizen.

When the gates of freedom opened to the West, the attraction of instant democracy and a robust economic system with jobs, venture capital, and a more reliable social welfare net for the poor proved irresistible to East Germans. In large numbers, they packed their belongings and moved across the open borders. Chancellor Helmut Kohl of West Germany was forced to face the reality that much of East Germany would migrate across the artificial border into the west unless he accelerated the plans for reunification and made the eastern region of Germany a more desirable place to live. These stepped-up plans would mean a tremendous drain on the West German treasury, but it was the only way to slow a potential mass exodus from the east. Kohl could hardly erect another wall between the two Germanys, as hateful a symbol as the Berlin Wall had been. This was a time for freedom, not for new barriers. The Chancellor and his governing conservative party braced themselves and moved forward toward reunification, surely mindful, too, of the historic opportunity to bring the people of Germany together again. The economic strains of East–West integration would be trying. Ugly incidents would arise as young neo-Nazi "skinheads," frustrated and disoriented by the dislocations underway, engaged in acts of violence—particularly against "guest workers" from Turkey and other foreign lands who competed with Germans for scarce jobs. Nevertheless, compared to other trouble spots such as Yugoslavia, Germany—with its impressive economic capacities—proved able to cope with the challenges that accompanied the end of Soviet dominance over East Germany and joined the United States as a strong economic and political leader among the world's democracies.[14]

Beyond Germany, there was a further coming together of Western European nations in the wake of the Cold War. In adopting the **Maastricht Treaty**, named after the town in Belgium where it was signed in 1992 and more formally known as the **Treaty of European Union**, the twelve-nation *European Community (EC) pledged to establish a lasting economic and political European Union (EU)*. Britain and Denmark eventually refused to ratify the treaty, fearful that their own national economies might be harmed by joining a new and untested financial arrangement; however, most of Europe adopted the euro as a common currency and moved toward a more unified economic and defense policy for Europe. The outcome remained in doubt, as some member countries like Greece, with its weak economy, seemed to be more of a burden than a help to the Union. By 2012, the economy of Greece appeared on the verge of collapse and its EU membership—as well as the euro itself—were in question. At the last minute, the European Union followed Germany's lead and bailed out Greece with financial loans, at least for the time being.

## Desert Storm

Whereas the fall of communism in the Soviet Union has been the central defining moment in world history since the end of World War II, the first dramatic foreign policy event to affect Americans directly in this new and uncertain era was *the 1991 decision by President George H. W. Bush to repel with massive US-led military force an Iraqi invasion into neighboring Kuwait*, a small oil-rich regime on the Persian Gulf. Known as **Operation Desert Storm**, this *First Persian Gulf War* was a bold manifestation of the President's hope to maintain some semblance of a New World Order by restoring Kuwait's sovereignty—in this case, by force of arms. The United States would attack Iraq again in 2003, under the second President Bush, in what became known as the Second Persian Gulf War or, more commonly, the Iraq War, discussed later in this chapter.

In harness with the United Nations in 1990, America would stand up to the blatant Iraqi aggression, Bush declared, although the First Persian Gulf War was also about ensuring Western access to Middle East oil. If Iraq could so easily overrun Kuwait, would its leader, Saddam Hussein, next eye the even more lucrative oil fields of Saudi Arabia, whose pipelines pumped much of the black blood that gave life to Western industry? In a favorite comparison drawn by the George H. W. Bush administration, Saddam, like Hitler, had to be stopped before his appetite grew out of control. Ironically, Saddam had been an ally of the United States in the 1980s, when Washington, DC, supported his war against a common adversary, Iran, even to the point of looking the other way when Iraqi troops used chemical weapons against Iranian soldiers and civilians. (See *Perspectives on American Foreign Policy* 6.1 for a thoughtful view on the question of when the United States should intervene abroad with military force.)

The new passivity of the Soviet leaders toward external affairs in 1990–1991 influenced the Desert Storm decision. No longer having to worry about the possibility of a Soviet military response if US troops entered the Middle East, the first President Bush was able to unleash America's impressive military might against Iraq, joined mainly by British and French soldiers. Germany's constitution forbade it from sending troops

## PERSPECTIVES ON AMERICAN FOREIGN POLICY 6.1

**CHRISTOPHER C. JOYNER, a professor of political science and international affairs, examines when it is legitimate to invade another nation:**

The critical question to be weighed is an old one: Do the ends justify the means? In the cases of Somalia and of the Kurds [in Iraq], the answers were easy: Yes. The nations intervening sought no territorial change and did not challenge the political independence of those states. They moved because of intense human-rights deprivations, and their actions conformed to the general international legal regulations governing the use of force-economy, proportionality, lawfulness of purpose, and necessity. Based on the experiences in Somalia and Iraq, the principle of *humanitarian intervention* in the so-called New World Order represented the triumph over national sovereignty of international law designed to protect the fundamental human rights of citizens in every state.

Caution is called for, however. In the past, humanitarian intervention was sometimes used by governments as a cover to accomplish political and ideological goals. The U.S. intervention in 1965 in the Dominican Republic, Vietnam's invasion of democratic Kampuchea [Cambodia] in 1978, and Tanzania's use of force against Uganda in 1979 are cases that come to mind. An armed humanitarian campaign loses its meaning and lawfulness when governments become motivated more by political

ambitions than by a genuine commitment to limited intervention to protect basic human rights.

Given that more international interventions like that in Somalia may occur in the future, the need arises for scholars and statesmen to clarify the standards and guidelines for humanitarian intervention under international law. Some standards are readily apparent. For example, there should be evidence of an immediate and overwhelming threat to fundamental human rights, especially if massive loss of human life is involved.

Also, the force employed in interventions must be used with restraint, so as not to trample upon even more human rights. Likewise, intervention should pose only a minimal threat to the authority structure of a state, and there should be prompt disengagement and withdrawal from the country after human rights have been restored. In the post-cold-war era, decisions mandated by the United Nations Security Council have become instruments for legitimizing international actions. Therefore, the U.N. Security Council should be given immediate, full, and direct reports when an operation is under way.

*SOURCE:* Christopher C. Joyner, "Point of View: When Human Suffering Warrants Military Action," *The Chronicle of Higher Education* (January 27, 1993), p. A52. Used with permission of The Chronicle of Higher Education Copyright© 2013. All rights reserved.

overseas, a stipulation that would be widely criticized in the West—ironically in light of the fact that German military might had wrecked such havoc on the West during World War II. The German parliament—the Bundestag—would eventually abandoned this passivist stance and, a decade later (after the 9/11 attacks), authorized the dispatch of German troops to help the United States fight terrorists in Afghanistan.

Beginning on January 17, 1991, the American military led a 270,000-person, 1,500-tank counterattack against the Iraqi army designed to drive it out of Kuwait, and deployed another 270,000 personnel in the theater of war. At the time, Iraq boasted the fourth largest force in the world. Under assault from the most advanced conventional weaponry the West could muster—smart bombs; superior fighter aircraft; night-vision equipment; and elaborate intelligence-gathering platforms in the sky, on the ground, and on ships in the Gulf and other nearby waterways—in six short weeks the Iraqi military cratered like a tinfoil village struck by a meteor. According to some estimates, over 100,000 Iraqi soldiers died in battle, compared with 148 American troops (one fourth of whom were accidentally killed by friendly fire). It was the most lopsided victory in the annals of modern warfare, a result of the superior firepower and intelligence-gathering capabilities of the United States and its allies.

The Operation Desert Storm victory raised President George H. W. Bush to a high pinnacle of popularity at home. His approval ratings soared above 90 percent—the highest point ever recorded. As a former Secretary of the Navy recalls

> The result [of Desert Storm] was to transform America itself, giving the nation a long-overdue tonic that would clear away the Vietnam hangover. As the hugely victorious campaign exorcized the ghost of Vietnam from the military, so presidential, congressional, and public opinion for the war locked the closet on another Vietnam skeleton. The Gulf war would be popular . . . [and] would thus reconfirm American leadership abroad and presidential primacy in foreign policy.[15]

President Bush had been appalled by the Iraqi invasion of Kuwait, not only because it threatened Western access to oil but because it raised once again the memories of Munich. Like Hitler, Saddam Hussein would only understand strong military opposition. British Prime Minister Margaret Thatcher, known as the Iron Lady, had reinforced Bush's instincts at a scholarly conference in Aspen, Colorado, coincidentally held at the time of the Iraqi incursion into Kuwait. "Remember, George, this is no time to go wobbly," she reportedly told the President.[16]

When the President declared an allied victory against Iraq on February 27, 1991, it seemed a significant step toward his goal of a New World Order: the aggressive behavior of bullies would not be tolerated—at least, skeptics may have amended, if Western access to oil were threatened. On the hawkish side, though, onlookers fretted that the United States had missed a golden opportunity by failing to march all the way to Baghdad and finish the job by topping Saddam's regime. Others countered that this would have inflicted many more casualties on allied forces because Iraq's elite troops in Baghdad (the Republican Guard) could have been expected to fight to the death in their nation's capital.[17]

Regardless, Bush had convinced Congress to support the First Persian Gulf War (see the introductory case study in Chapter 3), and he had now achieved his primary objective: Iraq was out of Kuwait. At this point, the United Nations could begin the process of dismantling Iraq's WMD programs, if there were any. In an unprecedented step, the Bush administration (supported by Congress) ordered the government of Iraq by way of State and Defense Department diplomatic communiqués to destroy its program to develop nuclear, chemical, and biological weapons—an order backed up by the veiled threat of a returning US-led invasion force if Saddam Hussein failed to respond properly. The Iraq dictator would survive for the time being; but, in 1991, the Gulf War was a popular victory for the George H. W. Bush administration and the UN coalition that the President and Secretary of State James A. Baker III had so adroitly assembled.

Despite his overwhelming defeat, Saddam Hussein remained an irritant to the international community. A Sunni Muslim, he tightened his internal repression over the Kurdish and Shiite Muslim populations within Iraq. In response, the UN—nudged by the United States—soon established no-fly zones in northern and southern Iraq where most of the persecuted Kurds and Shiites lived; henceforth, Iraq was prohibited from flying its own jets or helicopters into these zones. The job of enforcing the no-fly zones fell to US fighter jets based on aircraft carriers in the Red Sea and the Indian Ocean.

Saddam Hussein complained bitterly about this unprecedented violation of his nation's sovereign rights, and, on occasion, he tested the resolve of the West to police the no-flight rules—suicide missions for his hapless Iraqi pilots against America's greater firepower and intelligence capabilities. Near the end of the George H. W. Bush administration, the President escalated the levels of hostility between the United States and Iraq by unilaterally ordering American jets to bomb any Iraqi missile sites that dared lock onto US planes with their radar or that moved into the no-fly zones. The administration reemphasized that any Iraqi planes sent into a no-flight zone were to be shot down. American pilots carried out these orders and, when President Bill Clinton entered office in 1993, he adopted the same policies. The first foreign policy event of the Clinton years, just a day after he entered the White House, was the firing of US missiles at Iraqi ground missile sites that had locked onto a US warplane with radar, a step preparatory to firing. As is usually the case, the foreign policy challenges in Iraq and soon in the Balkans quickly crowded the new President's agenda, regardless of Clinton's intentions to address domestic issues like the economy, health care, and reform of the welfare system.

## Chaos in Somalia

In contrast to the oil fields of Kuwait and Iraq, the deserts on the Horn of Africa held far less strategic interest for the United States in the aftermath of the Cold War. Nevertheless, as related in the introduction to this chapter, *in November of 1992, the United States sent troops into Somalia to provide protection for the humanitarian relief efforts of the United Nations—the largest purely humanitarian intervention abroad in America's history, known as* **Operation Restore Hope**. Marines took over the streets of Mogadishu and other towns, chasing away or disarming the tribal extortionists and bullies. Food at last flowed unimpeded to the needy—at least in those locations where the Marines were stationed, though not in most of the hinterland where drought, tribal fighting, starvation, and the daily death toll continued unabated.[18]

Television displayed images of children who were once on the verge of death now coming back to life, their emaciated bodies slowly returning to normal, a spark returning to their eyes. Boys and girls played in the streets again, instead of sitting listlessly on stoops and gutters. It seemed a great triumph for American foreign policy and the United Nations, helping people in desperate straits with what they needed most: protection from murderers and bandits, food in their bellies, the hope of a new beginning. Life in Mogadishu and elsewhere in Somalia would not remain peaceful for long, however, as local warlords renewed their theft of UN aid supplies and murdered anyone who tried to get in their way. Soon international terrorists linked to Al Qaeda would make their presence felt on the Horn as well.

The deaths of Black Hawk pilots and crews in 1993 raised important foreign policy questions about the post-Cold-War era. How many other countries in the developing world where people suffered from starvation and civil war would warrant US intervention? Did the concept of a New World Order envision the possibility that anyone with a problem could simply summon a US-UN rescue team? Dial 911 and the 82nd Airborne would be there? How much would it cost the American taxpayer? How much blood of US soldiers would be spilled? Would the United Nations, or perhaps NATO, be able to move in and maintain peace and order after an American withdrawal?

In the waning months of the George H. W. Bush administration, acting Secretary of State Lawrence S. Eagleburger, a Kissinger protégé, hinted at the limits to establishing a New World Order. Foreign policy was more a matter of managing problems rather than solving them, he advised. America had no choice but to provide leadership, but it could not expect to dominate world affairs. His conclusion: "The United States cannot have its own way simply by snapping its fingers."[19] President Clinton's Secretary of State, Warren M. Christopher, sounded a similar cautionary note during his Senate confirmation hearings on February 7, 1993. He expressed a belief in the "discreet and careful" use of force abroad by the United States but without responding to "every alarm." The blood and treasure of the American people was decidedly not "an open account for use by the rest of the world."

## WOLVES IN THE WOODS

Historical developments at the end of the Cold War were a great disappointment to those who had dreamed of "the end of history"—a lasting time of tranquility that seemed to be at hand, now that the titanic struggle between communism and democracy was well along toward a resolution in favor of the open societies.[20] The Cold War had ended, yes; but despite his heralding of a New World Order, President George H. W. Bush understood that, as he said in his 1992 nomination acceptance speech at the GOP national convention: "There's still wolves in the woods."

### Weapons Proliferation

In the immediate aftermath of the Cold War, the most serious risk to America's security was the global proliferation of *nuclear, biological, and chemical armaments* (so-called **NBC weapons**), along with radiological devices and the spread of high-powered conventional arms. High on the list of worries was the status of Russia's nuclear warheads. Were they well secured? What were the odds they might be stolen by criminals or terrorists, or sold to them by poorly paid and disgruntled Russian military personnel? Further, North Korea flatly rebuffed a request by the International Atomic Energy Agency (IAEA) in 1993 to inspect sites within its borders that had been identified by Western intelligence services as nuclear weapons facilities, fueling speculation that leaders in Pyongyang had ordered the development of atomic bombs by North Korean scientists. The world would learn in the next few years that the North Koreans had in fact built a small arsenal of nuclear weapons and long-range missiles.

## Counternarcotics

In the opening year of his presidency, George H. W. Bush had declared drug trafficking "Public Enemy No. 1," although he designated less than 1 percent of America's GDP to combat the drug lords inside the United States and in other countries. Two decades later, the United States continues to lose the battle against the illicit drugs that stream across its borders. Tracking the flow of narcotics presents a challenge of enormous proportions. Colombia, Peru, and Bolivia, the main suppliers of drugs to the US market, together occupy a land mass almost half as large as the United States. Every year some 6,000 ships traverse the waters between the Andean counties and US ports, each carrying 300 or so containers; every year a comparable number of airplanes make the trip. Efforts to inspect this traffic for contraband are a heavy burden. So far, America's law enforcement and intelligence officials have largely failed to stem the flow, with an estimated 70 percent of the drugs slipping through US defenses. Experts have concluded that trying to attack the supply side of the problem through drug interdiction—a foreign policy approach—is doomed to failure; a better solution lies on the demand side—a domestic politics approach, especially improving antidrug education efforts in the United States. This would require an expansion of the "Just Say No" campaign adopted with some success by the Reagan administration in its efforts to educate Americans about the physiological dangers of using narcotics.[21]

## Immigration

The United States is a nation of immigrants, going back thirteen generations to the arrival of the Pilgrims at Plymouth Rock. Over the years, the nation became a "melting pot" of individuals arriving in New York City, New Orleans, San Francisco, and other US ports of entry. These men and women were of different skin colors and spoke a wide assortment of foreign languages. As they assimilated into American society, they provided the hands, the backs, and the brains that allowed the United States to become an agricultural and industrial power in the world. After World War II, Latin Americans accounted for the largest number of immigrants coming to America, summing to over half of the 35 million people living in this nation in 2007 who had been born abroad (according to US Census Bureau figures). Of these, about a third were living in America illegally as "undocumented workers." They tend to be employed in jobs that entail hard labor (crop picking and landscaping, for example), or involve undesirable working conditions (such as poultry factories) that most Americans eschew. Their pay is typically low.

Some Americans welcome these laborers, especially American farmers who need their crops harvested, cheaply and in a timely manner. So do those who understand that, as the US population ages, new and younger workers from abroad will be necessary to sustain economic growth. Others rail against the violation of law that undocumented workers represent. Further, they point to the danger of porous borders, especially in an era of terrorism; and they criticize what they see as the stealing of jobs once held by legal citizens and the lowering of wages around the country caused by the cheap labor from (chiefly) Mexico.

Foreign governments benefit from having workers in America because the workers send home a percentage of their wages to family members—a valued flow of foreign capital into their countries of origin. Less interested in this outcome than they are about pressure from constituents to curb the tide of illegal immigrants from Mexico, lawmakers in Congress passed the REAL ID Act in 2005 that gave the executive branch increased authority to fortify the border between the United States and Mexico. The next year—and against the wishes of President George W. Bush—lawmakers enacted a "Secure Fence" law that allowed the construction of a wall along the border, further defended by drones and beefed-up security patrols. The cost was some $1.2 billion. In 2012, a presidential candidate in Mexico (who would go on to win the presidency) drew a contrast to the Berlin Wall and called the project "shameful."[22] Nonetheless, the government of the United States funded even larger sums in 2013 to complete the wall, and to increase the number of security personal and drones guarding America's border with Mexico. Not all of America's foreign policy problems were far away in the Middle East and Southwest Asia.

### The Micro-States

Washington officials became aware during the final stages of the Cold War that they knew little about *the smaller nations of the world*, the **micro-states,** some of which proved to be significant to American foreign policy. So lacking was US intelligence on Grenada, for example, that when the Reagan administration ordered an invasion of the Caribbean island in 1983 to subdue an alleged communist threat, American soldiers had to obtain maps of the local terrain from gas stations. In Panama four years later, the US commander was shocked to discover that his supposedly weak adversary, the army of Panama, had 50,000 sophisticated automatic weapons—another sobering intelligence gap stemming from a slighting of espionage in the micro-states during the Cold War in favor of expensive satellite surveillance of the Soviet Union.[23] Grenada and Panama were in America's neighborhood; Washington officials knew even less about faraway places like the Persian Gulf, where US troops would be fighting within a decade after the Cold War. Or events in North Africa leading to the Arab uprisings in 2011, which took the United States and other nations by surprise. Much uncertainty remains about how these uprisings will play out, especially in Egypt and Syria.

At least, though, Presidents George H. W. Bush and Clinton took a strong interest in economic conditions in nations close to the United States and made strides *toward improving trade ties among Canada, Mexico, and the United States.* In 1994, Clinton ratified the **North American Free Trade Agreement (NAFTA)**, initiated by Bush and passed by the House and the Senate. This statutory agreement further reduced commercial barriers among these trading partners. Here were markets close at hand, with reduced foreign-trade shipping costs and millions of consumers that promised greater prosperity for all three nations. Clinton had further diplomatic success in moving Israel and its neighbors closer to peace by way of the **Oslo Accords** in 1993, facilitated by the Norwegian government. *With this agreement, the Palestine Liberation Organization (PLO) renounced terrorism and its call for the destruction of Israel in return for Israel's promise to withdraw from the Gaza Strip and the West Bank town of Jericho.*

The next year, the Clinton administration confronted another test of its diplomatic skills as unrest boiled over in Haiti, sending thousands of refugees in rickety boats toward Florida. The President decided that a *US military intervention in Haiti was necessary to stem the flow of refugees and to restore order on the poverty-stricken island.* In 1994, **Operation Uphold Democracy** thrust the United States into the difficult role of nation building, a mission in which it has mostly failed (as in South Vietnam, Somalia, Iraq, and Afghanistan). Haiti remains mired in poverty; but at least some semblance of order was restored there in 1994, thanks to the presence of US and UN soldiers. America's response to the **Rwanda genocide** in 1994 was less successful. The *Clinton administration vacillated and 800,000 people were slaughtered in tribal warfare in this African nation before assistance arrived from the United States and other nations.* Once burned by Somalia, the administration was twice shy about entry into further African turmoil. Clinton later apologized to the people of Rwanda for America's slow response in trying to end the killing; yet words, however sincere, could not restore the lives that had been lost.

## Other Transnational Challenges

On November 15, 1991, President George H. W. Bush signed **National Security Review No. 29 (NSR-29)**, which *directed America's secret agencies to compile the most exhaustive list of intelligence priorities since the end of World War II.* The NSR-29 document called for the increased collection and analysis of information on ethnic and territorial disputes around the world; on global water, food, and energy supplies; on the spread of AIDS and other diseases, which were undermining the political stability of some nations; on foreign nuclear-safety problems; on immigration trends; on the international technology race, including telecommunications breakthroughs and trading in semiconductor devices (important for manufacturing smart bombs); and on a range of macroeconomic and microeconomic issues. Terrorism was also on the list, but without any special sense of urgency. The United States would soon find out that here was the greatest immediate danger of all, one that would draw Americans into three wars: in Iraq and Afghanistan, and against the global terrorist organization known as Al Qaeda.

The United States would follow the Arab uprisings with great interest, too, when they began in December of 2010. Since the end of the Cold War, aiding the spread of democracy worldwide had become the rally cry for foreign policy officials of both parties in Washington, displacing the earlier grand strategy of communist containment. President Obama rejected the advice of those who wanted to stand by the faltering dictatorships in the Middle East and North Africa.[24] He was properly sensitive, though, to the damage that American involvement could incur if it were too blatant; these were local revolutions, not to be shaped by outside forces. Still, rebels in Libya and Syria asked for help; and NATO responded to the first by aiding the Libyan rebellion (as discussed in Chapter 1). With Syria, though, the conditions were more knotted when it came to outside assistance because the United States supported the rebels and Russia and China supported the Syrian dictator Bashar al-Assad (though Moscow began to back away from this support in 2013). Complicating matters further was the realization that several of the rebel groups in Syria were zealous Islamic fundamentalists with ties to Al Qaeda.

The Syrian moral dilemma continued to grow: how long could the United States and other democracies stand by on the sidelines as genocide-like attacks by government-backed militia occurred across Syria, with massacres taking place in rebel strongholds that involved the widespread killing of noncombatants—even the use of sarin gas in 2013? The representatives of fifty-five countries gathered in Washington, DC, in the summer of 2012 to explore ways of ending the violence; and the UN and Arab League sent an envoy, former UN Secretary General Kofi Annan, to Syria in pursuit of peace talks. America's Treasury Secretary, Timothy F. Geithner, who hosted the Washington gathering, urged the use of stronger economic sanctions against Syria. "Strong sanctions make clear to the Syrian business community and other supporters of the regime that their future is bleak so long as the Assad regime remains in power," he said. "And strong sanctions can help hasten the day the Assad regime relinquishes power."[25] Geithner hinted at the possible use of a UN military intervention in Syria if all else failed, but polls of American citizens in 2013 regularly indicated the unpopularity of US intervention in the Syrian civil war.

## THE RISE OF GLOBAL TERRORISM

Since the 9/11 attacks, the most pressing foreign policy priority of the United States has been global terrorism. Soon after the end of the Cold War, America became the prime target of *a new terrorist movement, centered in the Afghan-based organization* **Al Qaeda** *("The Base," or "The Foundation," in Arabic) and led by Osama bin Laden,* who had fought alongside CIA operatives during the 1980s in a paramilitary war supported by the United States against the Soviets after their invasion of Afghanistan.[26] During its formative stages in the early 1990s, Al Qaeda was comprised chiefly of veterans from this earlier US-backed Afghan insurgency against the Soviets (examined in Chapter 12).

Bin Laden, a son of a Saudi construction billionaire, had become disaffected toward the United States and other Western democracies because of their support for Israel (seen as an enemy of Islam); their stationing of troops in Saudi Arabia near Mecca and other Muslim holy sites; the US attack against the regime of Saddam Hussein (a fellow Sunni Muslim) during the First Persian Gulf War, as well as the enforcement of the no-fly zones over Iraq; and what he viewed as a decadent Western life style: the consumption of alcohol, the revealing dress of women, the raucous rock music and lurid films. All of these societal attributes summed to a way of life alien to Muslims, at least in the view of Bin Laden and other militant Islamists. The ultimate aspiration of Bin Laden and his top lieutenants, recruited mostly from Egypt where they had been members of the group known as the Muslim Brotherhood, was to win a global *jihad* ("holy war") against the Western Judeo-Christian infidels and to establish an Islamic world order or "caliphate."

More recently, Al Qaeda has evolved into a decentralized global network of affiliates, often just individuals filled with hatred toward Israel, America, and the West, and inspired by Bin Laden and the 9/11 attacks he sponsored. Al Qaeda has branches in some seventy countries; but its most well-known cells abroad are in Afghanistan, Iraq, Kenya, Somalia, Tanzania, Mali, Nigeria, and Yemen, all of which have loose connections with one another. The Qaeda group in Yemen, known as Al Qaeda in the Arab Peninsula or AQAP, has been especially active in planning attacks against the United States, which so far have been thwarted by US intelligence operations. "Al Qaeda offers these groups a powerful brand," notes a recent study, adding that in return "the groups offer Al Qaeda an expanded platform."[27]

## The 9/11 Attacks

The signs of terrorist danger long preceded *the infamous Qaeda assaults against the American homeland on September 11, 2001*, referred to commonly as the **9/11 attacks**— the "day of fire," as President George W. Bush recalled the episode in his memoirs. Al Qaeda had claimed responsibility for attacks against US embassies in Kenya and Tanzania in 1998, as well as against the *USS Cole* anchored off the coast of Yemen in 2000. More ominously, Osama bin Laden implied in US television interviews in 1997 and 1998 that he was inspired by Islamic extremist Ramzi Yousef's attempt to blow up the World Trade Center in New York City in 1993 by detonating explosives in a van parked in the building's lower deck. The ineptly executed explosion caused only limited damage, but Bin Laden vowed to follow this example and "bring the fighting to America."[28]

Even earlier, in 1995, the CIA's Counterterrorism Center (CTC) cautioned the Clinton White House that US cities could become primary Qaeda targets. According to the CTC, "**aerial terrorism** seems likely at some point—*filling an airplane with explosives and dive-bombing a target*."[29] The warning erred only in its failure to understand that hijacked commercial aircraft, with their volatile jet fuel, would be powerful enough missiles in their own right without added explosives.

Yet the CTC never provided Washington officials with precise information about the timing or location of the anticipated hijackings. Such "actionable intelligence" would have given US authorities the ability to intercept the terrorists before they boarded the commercial airliners that they would soon fly into the World Trade Center and the Pentagon on 9/11. Moreover, the US intelligence agencies flooded officials with dire warnings about other potential threats, from trucks filled with dynamite exploding in urban tunnels to attacks against the nation's railroad system, harbors, nuclear reactors, crops, livestock, computer infrastructure, and water supplies. Missing in these reports was a sense of probability and priority about the dangers, as well as the degree of specificity necessary to take timely protective measures. Despite all these warnings (or perhaps paralyzed by the scope of so many threats), the Clinton and George W. Bush administrations failed to take significant steps toward establishing stronger homeland defenses—until after 9/11. Even then, while creating a Department of Homeland Security, the Bush administration spent most of its defense funding on wars in Iraq and Afghanistan rather than strengthening facilities at home. An important aspect of foreign policy is to protect the United States against foreign threats; and in the judgment of many, these administrations came up short.[30]

Further, government inquiries have discovered that the intelligence agencies failed to coordinate and act on the few shards of specific information they did possess regarding the Qaeda operatives of September 11.[31] For instance, the agencies proved unable to track two of the nineteen 9/11 terrorists, despite warnings given by the CIA to the FBI about their arrival in San Diego. Intially, these warnings were handled too slowly at the CIA; and, once forwarded to the FBI, the Bureau's agents proved inept at tracking down the terrorists in San Diego. In addition, the FBI neglected to respond to reports from its own agents in Phoenix and Minneapolis about suspicious flight training undertaken by foreigners in those cities. At a deeper level, the United States was taken by surprise on 9/11 because the CIA had no agents within Al Qaeda; the National Security Agency had fallen far behind in translating its interceptions of terrorist telephone conversations; and all of America's intelligence agencies lacked sufficient language skills and a basic understanding about developments in the Middle East and Southwest Asia to anticipate the likely motivations and operations of Al Qaeda cells.[32]

September 11th was more than an intelligence failure, however; it was also a policy failure. Despite the CIA's red flags about aerial terrorism, neither the Clinton nor the George W. Bush administrations took meaningful steps to tighten airport security, caution pilots, seal off cockpits, field air marshals, or alert top officials in the Department of Transportation (which screens airport passengers) about the possibility of terrorists hijacking aircraft and flying them into skyscrapers. Each of these preventive measures would have cost money and policy makers are reluctant to spend finite funds to guard against dangers that may well never materialize. In New Orleans, engineers knew that a strong hurricane could wreck the dikes around the city and cause havoc; yet the chances of a Level 5 hurricane were low and the costs of reinforcing the dikes high. Then mighty Hurricane Katrina struck in 2005, causing deaths and a clean-up that was much more expensive than bolstering the dikes against such a storm would have been. The problem is: how does one evaluate the risk of not taking preventive actions?

Sometimes the issue is not so much the costs of protection as it is ignorance about a potential threat. The government's top counterterrorism expert during these years, Richard A. Clarke, recalls strongly cautioning the new national security adviser, Dr. Condoleezza Rice of the George W. Bush administration, in January of 2001, about the danger that Al Qaeda presented to the United States. He urged her to hold a National Security Council meeting on this threat as soon as possible. Rice finally got around to scheduling an NSC planning session devoted to Al Qaeda nine months later, on September 4, 2001—by then, too late.[33]

In the aftermath of the 9/11 attacks, the Bush administration implemented **Operation Enduring Freedom** in 2001, *a counterattack against Bin Laden and the other Qaeda leadership in Afghanistan, targeting as well the* **Taliban regime** *that had provided a safe haven for the organization throughout the 1990s and during the attacks on the United States in 2001.* The counterattack employed an effective mix of CIA para-military officers and military Special Operations Forces, supported openly by B-52 bombers. This combination, aided by the assistance of anti-Taliban tribesmen on the ground in Afghanistan (known collectively as the Northern Alliance), toppled the government and sent Qaeda members and the Taliban into full retreat. Before the United States could round up Bin Laden and his followers, they vanished like ghosts into the mountains of Afghanistan and Pakistan. Rather than pursue them, the administration turned its attention to another enemy, claiming (despite overwhelming intelligence to the contrary) that Saddam Hussein had been supportive of the 9/11 attacks, and that he was constructing WMD (here the intelligence was mixed).[34] Iraq would become the next target in the war against terrorism. It provided a much more target-rich environment, argued deputy secretary of defense Paul Wolfowitz at a Camp David meeting with President Bush on September 15, 2001—far more promising (however irrelevant) than a difficult hunt for Al Qaeda in the inhospitable terrain of Afghanistan and Pakistan.[35]

Within the first two months after the 9/11 attacks, President George W. Bush signed the USA PATRIOT Act, which allowed the FBI and other intelligence agencies to increase their surveillance of domestic terrorist suspects. The President also created the Office of Homeland Security, which became a cabinet-level Department in 2002. More controversially, the administration allowed individuals captured in Afghanistan to be placed in secret ("black") CIA and military prisons abroad—most notoriously in the Abu Ghraib prison, located in Baghdad.[36] Additional "detainees" were sent to the American base known as Guantánamo on the island of Cuba. These suspects languished in prison without legal counsel, the right to habeas corpus (that is, to know the reason for being detained), or a trial.

The Bush administration authorized the use of "renditions" (kidnappings) against suspected terrorists, along with torture (such as waterboarding) against some of the prisoners. These harsh measures stained the reputation of the United States, known for its fair play and support for the rule of law. Moreover, the administration ignored the Foreign Intelligence Surveillance Act (FISA), which requires a court warrant for national security wiretaps, and allowed unauthorized—warrantless—telephone taps against American citizens suspected of terrorist activities or ties. Fear generated by the 9/11 attacks had the immediate effect of pushing aside the law and the Constitution. The President chose simply to bypass the FISA requirement for a judicial review of wiretap requests—a law passed by bipartisan majorities in Congress in 1978 after three years of debate; and the Justice Department issued orders to the CIA that are still classified, allowing harsh interrogation techniques (such as waterboarding) even though they violated international law.[37]

In 2004, President George W. Bush signed the **Intelligence Reform and Terrorism Prevention Act (IRTPA)** *to bring greater cohesion to the nation's sixteen intelligence agencies, which would now be led by a Director of National Intelligence or DNI.* The Pentagon lobbied against the creation of a strong civilian spy chief, however, on grounds that it might weaken military intelligence (which is unlikely, because any DNI will want to provide the best intelligence possible for America's fighting men and women—or the director would be fired by the president). Congress succumbed to the lobbying and diluted the proposed reform, with the result that the IRTPA legislation failed to provide the new intelligence chief (the DNI) with sufficient authority over intelligence budgets and appointments to bring about the integration of the sixteen secret agencies. The United States continues to lack strong leadership that could bring about more cohesive intelligence reports for the president on world affairs. In the first five years of the DNI, the office had four different incumbents, all soon leaving because of their frustration over the spy chief's lack of authority to lead and better coordinate America's intelligence agencies (a topic taken up further in Chapter 9).[38]

### "Preemptive" War in Iraq

A little over a year after 9/11—on September 17, 2002—President George W. Bush released a report entitled *The National Security Strategy of the United States of America*, which outlined what became known as the **Bush Doctrine**. As historian John Lewis Gaddis sums up, the doctrine stated that "*the United States will identify and eliminate terrorists wherever they are, together with the regimes that sustain them.*"[39] America would no longer wait to be hit by terrorists; according to the President, *leaders had an obligation to strike first against foreign threats, even when they may not represent an immediate threat.*

This approach to the use of force abroad, based on the notion that an enemy may attack the United States at some future time—though not imminently—is known by political scientists as **preventive war;** it was mislabeled by the Bush administration, however, as **preemptive war**. In political science theory, the concept of *preemption is reserved for the rapid use of force against an adversary who is about to attack at any moment.* Some find the approach of preventive war rash because it invites regimes to use military force prematurely and quite probably with insufficient evidence that an adversary may be planning an attack. Others argue that one cannot afford to wait until an enemy strikes, especially in an age of nuclear weapons; one has to take the initiative—or possibly lose millions of citizens in an eventual surprise attack by that enemy.[40] Most everyone agrees, though, that the Bush Doctrine and the notion of preventive warfare set the stage for **Operation Iraqi Freedom**, *the Second Persian Gulf War, which became known as the Iraq War.*

Launching the attack against Iraq in 2003 was the most consequential decision of the George W. Bush administration, and perhaps also the most controversial. The President did seek and receive authority from Congress to invade Iraq, but the intelligence briefings on the need for war erred badly, misleading lawmakers and the American people. The connection between Saddam Hussein and Osama bin Laden, suspected by Vice President Dick Cheney, was highly conjectural; all the evidence the CIA had gathered pointed toward no ties at all that related to the 9/11 attacks. *The Bush administration soon shifted to another argument, namely, that an* **Iraqi WMD program** *that could be dangerous to the United States was probably under way.* National security adviser Rice, and even the President, began to speak in public about the possibility of "mushroom clouds" appearing on American soil as a result of an Iraq nuclear attack; or they tried to inflame fear that Baghdad might provide WMDs to Al Qaeda for future use against the United States.[41]

A National Intelligence Estimate (NIE) of October 2002, prepared hastily by the US intelligence agencies at the request of lawmakers (not the administration) concluded that Iraq was likely to have developed WMDs since the end of the Gulf War in 1991. This assessment, however, proved to be based on several inaccurate sources of information.[42] The intelligence agencies had been unable to recruit any significant human agents in Iraq since the American troops pullout in 1991 after the First Persian Gulf War; thus, its analysts were forced to extrapolate from what they knew when the United States last had "boots on the ground" there. At the time, in 1991, the CIA had discovered that it was about five years behind in estimating how far along Iraq's nuclear weapons had advanced. As a result, analysts compensated for their earlier error by this time *overestimating* the probability of Iraqi WMDs. The intelligence analysis about WMDs also suffered from a false report provided to the CIA by German intelligence, based on an incompetent Iraqi defector (codenamed "Curveball") that such weapons existed.

At the eleventh hour before the invasion of Iraq in March of 2003, President Bush questioned CIA Director George Tenet directly about his confidence in the October 2002 NIE that supported the Iraqi WMD hypothesis. Tenet assured the President that the presence of WMDs in Iraq was a "slam dunk."[43] Other intelligence analysts were less certain: the odds favored the presence of WMDs, they concluded; but they inserted caveats into the estimate that warned about the "softness" of the data, including dissents from experts in the State Department, the Energy Department, and the Air Force. The softness of the data, critics observe, is precisely what Tenet—America's senior intelligence officer at the time—should have underscored. He had an obligation to emphasize that the NIE was not a definitive report; indeed, that it was written in only three weeks (estimates usually require seven months to prepare, on average), and that additional fact-finding was needed.[44]

These deliberations over the necessity of an invasion against Iraq rested on the assumption that the Bush administration wanted to go to war for the purposes of destroying a WMD threat. Many critics argue, however, that weaponry and intelligence had little to do with the invasion plans. A national intelligence officer (NIO) for the Middle East, Paul Pillar, recalls that the administration never asked him for an assessment until a year after the war began. He concludes: "What is most remarkable about prewar US intelligence on Iraq is not that it got things wrong and thereby misled policymakers; it is that it played so small a role in one of the most important US policy decisions in recent decades."[45]

Sundry members of the administration's national security team wanted Saddam Hussein toppled for reasons beyond the issue of WMDs: the Al Qaeda and Taliban targets had evaporated into the mountains and the American public wanted some tangible results after the 9/11 attacks; democracy could be forced on the Iraqis and perhaps then spread to other countries in the region; Iraqi oil could be guaranteed for the West and tapped into to pay for the invasion; America could establish military bases in a key Middle East country; the President could finish the work that his father had left short in 1991, battling all the way to Baghdad and overthrowing the Saddam Hussein regime; US military power could be demonstrated to the world, as a warning against future 9/11 attacks—"Don't mess with the US"; and, of particular importance to the neoconservatives high in the administration (or "neocons"—see Chapter 2): a bellicose Iraq—a major irritant to the Israelis—could be removed. In his memoirs published in 2010, George W. Bush wrote that revenge for Saddam's assassination attempts against his parents when they visited to Kuwait to celebrate the First Persian Gulf War victory also played a part in his deliberations about going to war against Iraq.[46]

The invasion enjoyed successes at first, as US troops overran one Iraqi city after another; but it soon bogged down. The war lost its original mantel of legitimacy when no WMDs were found. Further, insurgency warfare against US troops, and between Sunni and Shiite Muslims in Iraq, prevented a quick victory. President Bush's boast of "Mission Accomplished" on May 1, 2003, quickly proved hollow. Moreover, as predicted by the CIA, Qaeda forces gravitated to Iraq as a place to kill American soldiers. Only an escalation in the number of US troops (a "surge") damped down the outbreak of a full-blown civil war. As Bush left office in 2009, some 140,000 US troops remained in Iraq.

While lowering America's military presence from this battlefield in 2009, the Obama administration dramatically escalated the number of US soldiers in Afghanistan. The purpose was to capture or kill Qaeda members and extremist Taliban who continued to operate in Afghanistan and Pakistan, with spidery connections in Yemen,

Somalia, and other locations primarily in the Muslim world. In 2010, America's intelligence agencies traced the likely whereabouts of Osama bin Laden to the city of Abbottabad, near the Pakistani capital of Islamabad. In a daring mission, Navy Seals succeeded in killing the Qaeda leader on May 1, 2011, and they confiscated his terrorist operational files from the compound. It was Obama's most significant foreign policy success.[47]

In October of 2010, President Obama stepped up his withdrawal of America's fighting forces in Iraq as his administration shifted its attention to Afghanistan and the Taliban—the original hosts of the Qaeda terrorists who attacked the United States on 9/11. The President sent 30,000 additional troops to Afghanistan in 2010 (another "surge") to combat the Taliban extremists and members of Al Qaeda, even though this part of the world was widely known as a "graveyard of invaders."[48] British and Soviet armies suffered major defeats there in the twentieth century, and skeptics doubted that the United States would have any greater success. In 2012, President Obama spoke publicly about removing most of America's troops from Afghanistan by 2014.

An undated image of a man identified as Osama Bin Laden in front of a television, obtained from video seized by US Navy Seals when they stormed a walled compound in Abbottabad, Pakistan, in May of 2011 and killed the Al Qaeda leader.

## Drone Warfare

To hunt down Qaeda and extremist Taliban fighters in Afghanistan, as well as in Pakistan, President Obama ordered a dramatic increase in the number of drone sorties against their suspected encampments, initially begun by the preceding Bush administration. The frequency of these remote-control attacks rose even more after seven CIA officers in Khost, Afghanistan, near the Pakistani border, were killed by a suicide bomber in December of 2009. The drones—the Predator and the larger Reaper—carried surveillance cameras as well as Hellfire missiles, a dangerous combination for America's enemies. These aircraft killed enemy combatants on an almost daily basis following the CIA's loss, without any American pilots having to risk their lives. The number of drone attacks climbed steadily throughout 2011 and 2013 (I present data on the drone attacks in Chapter 12), as the United States became "the first nation to regularly conduct strikes using remotely piloted aircraft in an armed conflict."[49]

Unfortunately, the drones sometimes miss their intended targets and end up killing civilian noncombatants. This has made US drone attacks highly unpopular in Pakistan, even though most Pakistanis dislike the extremist Taliban who have moved into the northwest territories of their country. In 2011, President Obama rejected a drone attack against the compound where Osama bin Laden was hiding in Pakistan in favor of a more precise assault by a small team of Navy Seals.[50]

Most of the time, though, the Obama administration has supported the use of drones as its leading paramilitary instrument of counterterrorism around the world. By 2013, however, pressure was grown stronger to pull back on the frequency of drone attacks abroad—especially in Pakistan. Critics of the drone program worried about the callousness of this form of robotic fighting. Would America come to find "arcade warfare" all too easy and tempting, leading to the dispatch of CIA drones around the world wherever terrorists might be? Another important question was how the targeting would be carried out. In 2012, it became clear in newspaper reports that the President himself reviewed the drone target selections, which included some American citizens living in Yemen—four of whom have been killed by drone strikes. Doubts lingered about how legitimate it was to have targeting based on the authorization of the president alone. Reformers called for the creation of a special FISA-like court that would review warrant requests from the executive branch for specific assassinations against American citizens before they could be carried out.[51]

Congress also demanded to know more about the decision pathway for the approval of drone attacks. Ron Wyden (D-Oregon), a member of the Senate Select Committee on Intelligence, formally requested from the Obama administration a copy of the classified legal documents in the Department of Justice (DOJ) that dealt with drone attacks. Wyden stated in a letter to the Department that only by reviewing the precise language in the administration's legal opinions could he know "whether the president's power to deliberately kill American citizens is subject to appropriate limitations."[52]

Some moderate Muslim critics in Pakistan believe that US drones should be removed from the battlefield or handed over to the Pakistani military to conduct the operations in their own country. Others think that US troops and intelligence officers in Iraq, Afghanistan, and Pakistan should return home altogether. That, instead, the United States should field small teams—ideally, international in membership—of special forces and paramilitary officers to track down, arrest, and, if necessary, kill terrorists, one by one, wherever they are hiding. This policy would be carried out in a close working relationship with the Afghan and Pakistani armies and police. Still others argue that the best solution for undermining the influence of Qaeda and Muslim extremism is to win over the affections of people living in this part of the world by stepping up the limited efforts by the Western powers to build health clinics, schools, roads, and other infrastructure services.[53]

One thing was certain: the struggle against terrorism promised to be anything but easy. A major concern was *the protection of America's computer systems against attack*: **cybersecurity**. To develop defenses against what some feared could be an "electronic Pearl Harbor"—a terrorist shutdown of US communications and computer facilities—President Obama established a Cyber Command within the Pentagon in 2009. (This Command also had responsibilities for aggressive cyberattacks by the United States against its adversaries, a topic explored in Chapter 12.) The Obama administration experimented as well with various approaches for protecting the nation against Muslim extremists, including counterinsurgency warfare in Afghanistan (however ineffectual this approach had been in Vietnam) to augment the use of drones, diplomacy, and economic assistance.[54] For the most part, though, the counterterrorism policies of Presidents George W. Bush and Barack Obama were strikingly similar, despite their ideological divergences on domestic policies.

## SUMMARY

With the ending of the Cold War in 1991, expectations rose that the world might live in peace under a New World Order, free from the tensions of two rival superpowers armed with nuclear weapons. In place of the US-Soviet standoff, however, emerged several new challenges to American foreign policy. A proliferation of ethnic, religious, tribal, and terrorist factions fragmented the former Soviet Union and adjacent satellite nations into many new entities pursuing their own domestic and foreign policy agendas, which sometimes put them into conflict with the United States. At the same time, the decades-old partition of Germany ended, and Western Europe coalesced into the European Union and adopted a common currency, the euro.

The post-Cold-War world presented other challenges. Weaponry spread around the globe as nations with a record of hostility sought to develop WMDs. Illegal drugs continued to pour across US borders, as did illegal immigrants. Various micro-states, despite their small size, also created dangerous situations for US interests abroad, as illustrated by how Iraq's conquest of the small nation of Kuwait gave rise to the First Persian Gulf War in 1990. The failure of a humanitarian mission to Somalia in 1992–1993 made the United States cautious about other foreign involvements, damping enthusiasm for acting as the international enforcer of peace.

Terrorism became a primary threat to the United States, first through a bombing of the World Trade Center in 1993; then by attacks on US embassies and a Navy ship abroad; and finally with the horror of 9/11. The United States responded to 9/11 by striking back at Al Qaeda and its host in Afghanistan, the Taliban regime. Then, citing various foreign policy goals as justification—especially the risks of Iraqi WMDS—the United States turned its attention to another invasion of Iraq in 2003. American soldiers found no WMDs. Under the Obama administration, the American troop presence in Afghanistan increased, at the same time that the number of US soldiers in Iraq was drawn down, followed in 2012–2014 with drawdowns in Afghanistan as well. The sophisticated technology of military drones made unmanned robotically controlled aerial attacks possible thousands of miles away from the United States—and increasingly common, as well as highly controversial.

## KEY TERMS

aerial terrorism p. 189

Al Qaeda p. 188

Bosnian War (1992–1995) p. 176

Bush Doctrine (2002) p. 192

cybersecurity p. 196

Dayton Peace Accords (1995) p. 178

ethnic cleansing p. 176

German reunification (1990) p. 179

grand bargain (1991) p. 173

Intelligence Reform and Terrorism Prevention Act (IRTPA, 2004) p. 192

Iraq War (see Operation Iraqi Freedom) p. 193

Iraqi WMD program p. 193

Kosovo War (1998–1999) p. 178

Maastricht Treaty (Treaty of European Union, 1992) pp. 179–80.

micro-states p. 186

National Security Review No. 29 (NSR-29), 1991 p. 187

NBC weapons p. 184

New World Order p. 170

9/11 attacks p. 189

North American Free Trade Agreement (NAFTA, 1994) p. 187

Nunn-Lugar Act (1991) p. 174

Operation Desert Storm (First Persian Gulf War, 1990–1991) p. 180

Operation Enduring Freedom (Afghanistan, 2001–2014) p. 191

Operation Iraqi Freedom (Iraq War or Second Persian Gulf War, 2003–2011) p. 193

Operation Restore Hope (Somalia, 1993) p. 183

Operation Uphold Democracy (Haiti, 1994) p. 187

Oslo Accords (1993) p. 187

populist nationalism p. 176

preemptive versus preventive war p. 192

Rwanda genocide (1994) p. 187

Strategic Arms Reduction Talks (START) Treaty, 1991 p. 174

Strategic Offensive Reduction Treaty (SORT), 2002 p. 175

Taliban regime p. 191

---

## QUESTIONS FOR DISCUSSION

1. Some commentators predicted the "end of history" when the Soviet Union disintegrated. Why did their prediction fail to come true?

2. How would you describe the differences in the reasons and methods for US interventions in Iraq (twice), Somalia, the Balkans, Afghanistan, and Pakistan since the end of the Cold War?

3. What are the greatest foreign policy challenges facing the United States today?

Which time period was a safer global setting for the United States: the Cold War or now?

4. What is your evaluation of the Bush Doctrine in favor of preventive war against America's foes?

5. How do you think the United States should pursue its war against global terrorists?

6. Can the United States aggressively defend itself against foreign adversaries without trampling on the constitutional protections of American citizens?

## ADDITIONAL READINGS

Bush, George, and Brent Scowcroft. *A World Transformed.* New York: Knopf, 1998.

Mayer, Jane. *The Dark Side: The Inside Story of How the War on Terror Turned into a War on American Ideals.* New York: Doubleday, 2008.

Mondale, Walter F. *The Good Fight.* New York: Scribner, 2010.

———————————

For further readings, please visit the book's companion website.

### CHAPTER 7

# Institutional Conflict and Cooperation

**THE PRESIDENT, THE CONGRESS, AND DIEN BIEN PHU**

In 1954, a shabbily uniformed but well-armed Vietminh military slowly closed the noose around the French colonial army at Dien Bien Phu in Vietnam. The Vietminh placed howitzers, supplied by Communist China, on the hills surrounding the city. This enabled them to control the only airstrip in the valley, preventing the delivery of armaments to the surrounded French soldiers and blocking any attempted evacuation. Bad weather barred the French use of aircraft to strafe the enemy or parachute reinforcements into the war zone. Further, the terrain at Dien Bien

Captured French soldiers are marched through the fields after their surrender at Dien Bien Phu, Vietnam, in 1954.

Phu—thick bush flooded by monsoon rains—proved inhospitable for tank movements, the primary military strength of the French military. Outnumbered by a ratio of about five to one (50,000 Vietminh to 13,000 French fighters), the French saw defeat as all but inevitable unless the United States came to the rescue.

Secretary of State John Foster Dulles, a strong proponent of the domino theory who feared the collapse of Western containment in Indochina, proposed a rescue plan to President Dwight D. Eisenhower. The Secretary recommended sending US troops into Vietnam immediately, along with using atomic bombs if necessary, to free the French army from certain annihilation. The Chairman of the Joint Chiefs of Staff, Admiral Arthur Radford, supported the proposal.

Before making a final decision, President Eisenhower told Dulles to consult with leading members of Congress on how the United States should proceed. The President also solicited the opinions of other members of the Joint Chiefs of Staff, and he asked the CIA to prepare an estimate on the possible effects of dropping atomic bombs at Dien Bien Phu. He consulted with America's allies as well.

Invited to the White House for a meeting with Dulles and other top officials, the members of Congress asked probing questions about the proposed operation. The answers from White House officials revealed division inside the military over support for the intervention. In unison with several other leading officers in the Pentagon, General Matthew Ridgway, the Army chief of staff, recoiled from the notion of a US military presence on mainland Asia. So did leading State Department foreign service

---

**LEARNING OBJECTIVES AND CONSTITUTIONAL ISSUES**

**By the end of this chapter, you will be able to:**

- Identify the limitations on the foreign policy powers of the president.
- Describe the role of the National Security Council and its adviser.
- Describe the role of the State and Defense Departments, as well as that of the other major bureaucracies involved in foreign policy.
- Explain the place of Congress in foreign policy.
- Explain the relevance of the judicial branch in foreign policy.

---

**THIS CHAPTER RAISES THE FOLLOWING CONSTITUTIONAL QUESTIONS:**

- Which of the models of foreign policy decision making discussed in this chapter did the founders implicitly adopt when they wrote the Constitution?
- In what ways does the Constitution limit the institutional powers of the presidency in foreign policy?
- In what ways has the rise of a modern foreign policy bureaucracy affected the nation's constitutional framework?
- In what ways does the Constitution limit the institutional powers of Congress in foreign policy?
- What are examples of how the judicial branch has tried to clarify some ambiguities in the Constitution related to foreign policy?

officers, who believed that governments throughout the free world would condemn the military action. The CIA, led by the Secretary's brother, Allen Dulles, prepared an intelligence estimate. Its conclusion was that the use of even one atomic bomb at Dien Bien Phu would probably bring China and the Soviet Union into the conflict and ignite a third world war. Next, the President sent John Foster Dulles to London for consultation with the British on the plight of the French army. Prime Minister Winston S. Churchill refused to participate with the United States in any joint operations in Vietnam.

In light of these developments, key lawmakers—many of whom were strong administration supporters—advised the President to back away from an American intervention. Swayed by the voices of dissent, Eisenhower rejected Secretary Dulles's recommendation. On the afternoon of May 7, 1954, the red flag of the Vietminh waved in the wind over the French command post at Dien Bien Phu.[1]  ⌒

# FRAGMENTS OF POWER

As illustrated by President Eisenhower's approach to foreign policy during the 1954 crisis in Vietnam, a president can provide strong, effective leadership while at the same time taking the time to consult with lawmakers, top bureaucrats, and other stakeholders in American foreign policy. In this instance, Eisenhower's broad consultation had a sobering effect. The President turned away from the counsel of his Secretary of State and the Chairman of the Joint Chiefs of Staff when it became clear that other thoughtful experts on foreign policy opposed military involvement so far away from home—and especially the use of nuclear weapons. Eisenhower skillfully managed to blend his authority with a healthy respect for the Madisonian philosophy of power sharing with lawmakers (discussed in Chapter 2).

## Efficiency versus Freedom

Constitutional specialist Laurence H. Tribe has noted that "the framers were unwilling to give the President anything resembling royal prerogative."[2] By rejecting royal prerogative, however, the founders created a decentralized government that often displays signs of sluggishness, parochialism, and disarray. The framers had crafted precisely what Winston S. Churchill once said a democracy would always be: the worst possible form of government—except for all the others that have been tried from time to time. In this chapter I examine how leaders in Washington seek to make effective foreign policy decisions while coping with the problem of fragmented power and the inefficiencies it can produce.

## Presidents versus Lawmakers

A central issue of American foreign policy—and a central concern of this book—is the degree to which the nation's relations abroad ought to be an executive branch responsibility or whether, as in domestic policy, the United States should have a wide range of participants involved, especially representatives of the American people in Congress. Presidents are sorely offended when lawmakers see fit to criticize their foreign policy. But that is exactly what the founders had in mind: an activist, critical legislative branch that could contribute to, and thereby improve, policy making. One can imagine a presidential model of foreign policy in which global decisions would be left exclusively to the White House and senior bureaucrats; or a legislative model, in which key decisions would be left to Capitol Hill. (The judicial branch is seldom a part of day-to-day foreign policy decision making, although its legal judgments about foreign policy decisions can sometimes have lasting consequences, as will be explored later in this chapter.)

The presidential model enjoys widespread support in some quarters for reasons of urgency and secrecy—in a word, efficiency. Moreover, a strong sense exists in this school of thought that, to be taken seriously in world affairs, the nation must speak with one voice: the president's. Some lawmakers have adopted this view, happily passing along responsibility to the White House for tangled problems overseas that might spell trouble in the next election. For example, a leading conservative Republican legislator, Barry Goldwater (Arizona), often expressed his preference for foreign policy run by the executive branch because participation by Congress would harm the ability of the president to act quickly.[3]

Not everyone, though, has been enthusiastic about foreign policy by executive fiat. Even before Vietnam and Watergate raised serious doubts about an uncritical reliance on presidential power, a pro-Congress viewpoint was well established, especially on the conservative side of the American political spectrum (Senator Goldwater notwithstanding). Economic conservatives lamented the centralism that Franklin Roosevelt had brought to the marketplace; and states rightists fretted that international agreements negotiated by presidents might lead indirectly to the strangling of local government. In the 1950s, lawmakers from the South worried that the federal government might initiate civil rights reforms by way of binding agreements with African nations.[4] Further, isolationists looked on the presidency as the agent of interventionism abroad, leading to a drain on American resources—or even the selling out of American interests altogether, as conservatives were certain Roosevelt had done in 1945 by way of secret agreements reached with Joseph Stalin at Yalta.[5]

More recent generations of conservative Republicans (like Goldwater) have often sung a different tune. They have favored broad authority for the president in foreign affairs—at least if the president is a Republican. During the Reagan administration, for example, GOP conservatives on Capitol Hill advocated giving the White House leeway to carry out whatever policies were necessary to halt communist aggression around the world. They argued that laws passed by Democratic majorities in Congress to place limits on military assistance to the CIA-backed anticommunist *contras* in Nicaragua were unconstitutional (a proposition never tested in court, as the judicial branch shied away from taking up this dispute between the executive and legislative branches). A member of the Senate declared at the time: "It's another example of Congress trying to take away the constitutional power of the President to be Commander in Chief and to formulate foreign policy."[6]

More recently, both the George W. Bush and Obama administrations have claimed the right when signing bills into law to issue **signing statements** that *highlight provisions in a statute that the White House believes can be disregarded because they supposedly amount to unconstitutional restraints on executive power.* Presidents since the nineteenth century occasionally issued signing statements to this effect; but George W. Bush adopted this procedure with gusto, twice as many as all previous presidents combined. Bush instructed officials to view the law as merely advisory in one instance—a controversial form of presidential "veto" without the opportunity for Congress to override the action.[7] According to the *New York Times*, "Mr. Bush routinely and contemptuously disregards laws that he himself signed, most famously stating that he was not bound by the ban on torturing prisoners."[8]

In 2013, President Obama attached a controversial signing statement to a defense bill that imposed restrictions on the authority of the executive branch to transfer detainees out of military jails in Afghanistan and Guantánamo Bay. Lawmakers—notably conservative Republicans—sought to restrict the ability of the administration to wind down the detention of terrorists around the world. In his signing statement, Obama claimed that the president had the constitutional right to override the limits in the law. The American Bar Association responded by calling on Obama and other presidents to stop using signing statements. The ABA found the practice "contrary to the rule of law and our constitutional system of separation of powers."[9]

Regardless of political leanings, some students of democratic theory have felt that lawmakers are closer to the grass roots and, as a result, they have a better understanding of what citizens from Pocatello to Tuscaloosa expect in their nation's foreign policy. According to this perspective, members of Congress are like raw nerve endings reaching into each of the fifty states and the 435 congressional districts across the land, gauging the likely public response to vital issues of foreign policy. Whereas the president cannot realistically visit each district, lawmakers typically do so every week—some each day, if their districts are close to Washington, DC. This makes Congress a unique, continuous forum of timely public opinion.

The US Capitol Building, Washington DC.

During his second term when he began to focus more on international trade issues, President Reagan was initially inclined to resist on ideological grounds the subsidized shipment of American wheat to the Soviet Union. Lawmakers complained, however, that he ought to spend more time listening to the plight of farmers out in the congressional districts and less time playing Cold War politics. In response to this criticism, the President allowed the wheat sales to go forward. This episode underscores how complex foreign policy can be: by authorizing the wheat sale, the President mollified members of Congress from agricultural states, but he irritated the hawkish right wing of the GOP that frowned on any trade deals that might aid the Soviet economy. Moreover, the President's decision undercut the sale of Australian wheat to the USSR, triggering angry protests by Australian farmers in front of the US embassy in Canberra.

## A Foreign Policy Compact

In between the presidential and legislative models of foreign policy making lies another approach, which might be called the model of institutional power sharing. In this model the emphasis is on cooperation between coequal legislative and executive branches of government: an engine with all its cylinders at work. The response of President Eisenhower to the crisis at Dien Bien Phu is a classic illustration of constructive interbranch cooperation. More recently, George H. W. Bush demonstrated the value of a common effort between the branches. During his first months in office, he patiently negotiated an agreement with Congress that favored nonlethal aid for the *contras* in Nicaragua, successfully defusing the most controversial foreign policy issue of the 1980s. As another example, in 1989 when Chinese troops attacked pro-reform students in Beijing, George H. W. Bush immediately called key lawmakers to the White House and worked out with them a strategy of public criticism and economic sanctions as a punishment for the slaying of peaceful demonstrators.

President Carter's Undersecretary of State, Warren M. Christopher (who would later serve as Secretary of State in the Clinton administration), framed the argument for interbranch cooperation in terms of an **executive-legislative compact**. "As a fundamental precept," he wrote, "the compact would *call for restraint on the part of the Congress—for Congress to recognize and accept the responsibility of the Executive to conduct and manage foreign policy on a daily basis.*" In return, the executive branch would *have to be prepared to provide Congress with "full information and consultation.*" He went on: "Broad policy should be jointly designed and only in rare extreme circumstances should Congress attempt to dictate or overturn Executive decisions and actions."[10] Employing different imagery, Senator J. William Fulbright, Chairman of the Foreign Relations Committee from 1959 to 1974, often suggested that lawmakers and the president should jointly chart the desired routes for the American ship of state. Then it would be up to the president to take command as an able captain and steer the ship safely to port, making periodic adjustments as necessary in consultation with the experienced deckhands in the Congress.[11]

As one looks at the institutional side of foreign policy, each of these models—or, at least, approximations of them—can be observed at different times. Sometimes the president is able to gather together enough fragments of power to achieve ascendancy over a decision, especially in times of perceived emergency to the nation's security; sometimes Congress shapes foreign policy; and sometimes the two branches work together toward a policy decision. No single model is sufficient to explain decisions made at home regarding America's relations with other countries.

# THE PRESIDENCY AND LIMITS TO PRESIDENTIAL POWER

The powers of the president are often exaggerated. A researcher once examined high school and college texts on government and discovered an image of *the president as someone who can do no wrong, who has all the information and skilled advisers needed to make wise decisions.*[12] Even the astute journalist Theodore H. White lapsed into unfettered praise of the presidency. "So many and so able are the President's advisors of the permanent services of Defense, State, Treasury, Agriculture," he wrote, "that when crisis happens all necessary information is instantly available, all alternate courses already plotted."[13]

In contrast to this distorted **textbook presidency** stands a starkly different reality. Despite the fabled red telephone on the president's desk that could prevent or initiate a third world war, despite the president's guaranteed access to the people of the United States through television and radio, and despite a common belief that the president is—as the GOP leader Nelson Rockefeller once put it in overstatement—"the unifying force in our lives," scholarly studies of the presidency show that *nothing so defines the nation's highest office as its limitations.*[14]

One of the primary **limitations on presidential power** is the international setting. Regardless of how skilled a chief executive may be, the events a president faces can be unmanageable. Reflecting on the setbacks of the Carter administration, national security adviser Zbigniew Brzezinski expressed dismay at the inability of officials in Washington to control events abroad. Particularly vexing had been the fate of fifty-two American hostages held in Tehran by Iranian insurgents from November of 1979 until the day when Carter, having lost his campaign for a second term, vacated the White House—fourteen months. "History is much more the product of chaos than of conspiracy," concluded Brzezinski. "The external world's vision of internal decision-making in the Government assumes too much cohesion and expects too much systematic planning. The fact of the matter is that, increasingly, policy makers are overwhelmed by events and information."[15] The Carter administration's ill-fated military mission attempting to free the hostages is replete with further examples of circumstances that defied careful planning, including the crash of rescue helicopters in the Iranian desert and a series of military communications snafus.

## Information and Time

Brzezinski's emphasis on the problem of information is warranted. Government leaders find that they have either too much or too little information about world affairs. They can be inundated by data. The early warning predicting a Japanese attack on Pearl Harbor in 1941 illustrates the point. American intelligence agencies had intercepted coded Japanese messages about the impending attack, but this information was lost in the "noise" of several conflicting reports from other sources. The key messages floundered in the lower realms of the bureaucracy and President Roosevelt never received the warning.[16] The opposite phenomenon, insufficient information, is even more common and vexing. Research on surprise military attacks makes it plain that nations are often caught unprepared because of a lack of information about their enemies.[17] In the months leading up to the 9/11 attacks, the United States knew little about Al Qaeda and its plans for aerial terrorism against the American homeland. Improvements in intelligence gathering have reduced this danger (Chapter 9), but no administration has a crystal ball. Inevitably, unexpected events will continue to occur.

Time is another limitation faced by all decision makers. Sometimes a president can stall for more time to examine a wider range of foreign policy options. The Cuban missile crisis provides a vivid example. "If we had had to act in the first twenty-four hours," reflected President Kennedy, "I don't think . . . we would have chosen as prudently as we finally did."[18] On other occasions, the sands seem to be racing ineluctably through the hour glass. George W. Bush argued in 2002 that the United States had to invade Iraq quickly, before Saddam Hussein developed WMDs.

## Permissibility

Theodore C. Sorensen, a top aide to President Kennedy, underscored the further limits on presidential power of permissibility, available resources, and previous commitments.[19] The Constitution, statutes, court decisions, and international law all define what the president is allowed to do (although ambiguities certainly exist). Presidents are further hemmed in by what others within the government, and in other nations, are prepared to let them do. Kennedy's use of a naval quarantine during the Cuban missile crisis was facilitated by formal support from the Organization of American States (OAS), a union of most governments in the Western Hemisphere that voted to endorse the military blockade. This endorsement gave added legitimacy to Kennedy's decision in the eyes of world opinion; it was now sanctioned by international law through the required two-thirds vote of the OAS for such actions. When President George H. W. Bush and his son, President George W. Bush, invaded Iraq at different times (1990 and 2003, respectively) both were able to point to a coalition of nations that had joined with the United States in the war efforts, providing added legitimacy for the use of military force.

Sometimes presidential objectives are seen as impermissible. This was the congressional attitude toward President Truman's proposal to woo Yugoslavia away from the Soviet bloc early in the Cold War by offering it economic incentives to turn toward the West. Lawmakers rejected the idea on grounds that it was inappropriate to provide economic help to any Soviet satellite. More recently, President George W. Bush sought to work out immigration issues with the President of Mexico through diplomatic channels; Congress, however, was unwilling to wait for protracted negotiations and insisted on the construction of a wall between the two nations as a means for dealing with illegal aliens. "What is clear is that a President's authority is not as great as his responsibility," concludes Sorensen, "and that what is desirable is always limited by what is possible or permissible."[20]

## Resources

Sorensen noted that the director of the Office of Management and Budget (D/OMB), the top financial officer in the executive branch, is one of the most important officials in the executive branch. Almost all government programs cost money. Yet a president inevitably faces limits on how much funding is available, or the extent to which taxes can be raised without wreaking havoc on the economy or stirring a taxpayer rebellion. For each foreign policy program, a president will have to consult closely with the budget director and will always feel the pressure to control spending. Lyndon Johnson's attempt to rebuild the cities of America and fight a war in Vietnam simultaneously proved too costly, fueling inflation and leading to the unpopularity that drove him from office. Today, the expenditure of some $2 trillion in the Iraq and Afghanistan Wars has kept Presidents Bush and Obama from adequately funding many programs at home, whether the repair of America's decaying infrastructure—interstate highways and bridges—or a host of educational and health care programs.

Money is only one governmental resource. Others include the number of soldiers available to fight a war, the quantity and quality of weapons in a nation's arsenal, the will or determination of a populace to pursue a difficult course overseas, the credibility of a president, and a nation's industrial output as well as its supply of brilliant generals and civilian advisers. Presidents are unlikely to feel they ever have enough of these resources. During the Johnson years, media experts concluded that the President used television appeals too often in his efforts to muster support for the Vietnam War. The media saturation, combined with the President's lack of candor about the poor progress of the war, led the public either to tune him out or to view his remarks with increasing skepticism. A "credibility gap" arose between the White House and the American people. Today, without a national draft, the United States has been sorely pressed to field armies in Iraq and Afghanistan while still maintaining a readiness for the possible outbreak of conflict in other parts of the world, such as on the Korean Peninsula.

## Previous Commitments

Sorensen reminded us, too, that "no President starts out with a clean slate before him."[21] A president must honor many initiatives put in place by his predecessors. It would be difficult for an incoming president to decide suddenly to withdraw from NATO. Too many previous administrations have promised America's commitment to this defense pact, which continues to provide a sense of US-Canadian-European unity even today, more than twenty years after the end of the Cold War. Nor could a new president easily abandon a major weapons system already in production; such a decision would prove difficult to justify, in light of the funds that had already been invested in the development of the prototype. President Obama could not have pulled out of Iraq and Afghanistan precipitously, even if he had wanted to; the United States had invested too much money and sent too many troops to the region for a new administration to hastily abandon the effort.

## Formal Powers

Even the formal powers of the presidency are less potent than frequently believed by the public. Truman's classic prediction about the experience that his successor, General Eisenhower, would have in the Oval Office serves as a poignant reminder of this fact. "He'll sit here," Truman predicted, "and he'll say, 'Do this! Do that!' And nothing will happen. Poor Ike—it won't be a bit like the Army. He'll find it very frustrating."[22] Expressing his own sense of exasperation about foreign policy, President Johnson once exclaimed, "Power? The only power I've got is nuclear—and I can't use that."[23] As commander in chief, President Obama found that he had to spend much of his time in the White House adjusting his own personal views about troop surges and withdrawals in Iraq and Afghanistan in light of what the Pentagon thought was proper military strategy; and the President's use of drones to kill terrorists overseas drew much attention at home and required him to enter into a dialogue with lawmakers and outside critics about the scope of the targets—especially when American citizens in Yemen were placed on the kill list.[24]

In another example from the days of the Cuban missile crisis, President Kennedy decided it would be prudent to move his naval blockade closer to Cuba. This would give the Kremlin more time to evaluate the danger as Soviet ships sailed across the Atlantic toward the island. The US Navy, though, had a different idea about how to conduct the operation, as Secretary of Defense Robert S. McNamara soon discovered. McNamara and his aide drove to the Pentagon from meetings at the White House to inquire about the blockade plans. Inside a heavily guarded section of the sprawling building, he confronted Navy officials with incisive questions about their management of the operation. Finally, an angry chief of naval operations waved the *Manual of Navy Regulations* in the Secretary's face and shouted: "It's all in there!"

"I don't give a damn what John Paul Jones would have done!" McNamara snapped back. "I want to know what you are going to do, now."

At the end of this angry exchange, the chief of naval operations concluded brusquely, "Now, Mr. Secretary, if you and your Deputy will go back to your office the Navy will run the blockade."[25]

Bureaucrats often have their own agendas and standard operating procedures, which may be quite distinct from White House objectives. A Secretary of the Navy in the Reagan administration remarked on the difficulty of ensuring Pentagon responsiveness to presidential programs: "No matter who is Secretary of Defense, it is not a rational decision-making organization. It is too big. It is big, big, big . . . it makes any management person laugh out loud."[26]

The powers of the presidency are few in number and largely outmatched on most occasions by the limitations on the office, even when coupled with the advantage of ready access to the media enjoyed by the chief executive. John F. Kennedy put it as well as any president just a few months before his death: "The President . . . must wield these powers under extraordinary limitations—and it is these limitations which so often give the problem of choice its complexity and even poignancy."[27] President

Obama would no doubt be sympathetic to this perspective; the Arab Spring uprisings in the Middle East and North Africa were clearly beyond his control to shape, even if he were the most powerful leader in the world. A look at the executive bureaucracy further corroborates this reality of limited presidential power.

# THE FOREIGN POLICY BUREAUCRACY

The Department of State has a seemingly endless number of windows in its many-storied complex; and the Department of Defense, the giant of them all, is a honeycomb of corridors that can stymie the most accomplished orienteer. These are merely two of the huge government buildings devoted to foreign policy that dominate the streets of Washington like so many feudal fortresses, none with moats but all difficult to coordinate toward the goal of integrated policy outcomes. To improve the integration of these departments and agencies, the Congress enacted the National Security Act of 1947, which established a National Security Council.[28]

## National Security Council

The **National Security Council (NSC)** is *the most important organization in the federal bureaucracy when it comes to foreign policy.*[29] It consists of three primary groups of people: the principals (the president, the vice president, the secretary of state, and the secretary of defense), the advisers (the director of national intelligence and the chair of the joint chiefs of staff, with others invited to attend NSC meetings from time to time), and their lower-level staff aides. The NSC's professional staff has ranged in size from only a few people in the early days to upward of 100 in more recent years. All but a handful of these aides serve on loan from various executive agencies.

### From executive secretary to NSC adviser

The bridge that joins all three NSC groups is the "special assistant to the president for national security affairs," a job title established during the Eisenhower administration to designate that individual who would be the overall director of the NSC's staff activities. The cumbersome formal title was shortened under President Nixon to "the assistant for national security affairs" or, in common parlance, "the national security adviser." Initially with the passage of the National Security Act of 1947, Washington officials viewed the post as little more than a neutral coordinator of information prepared for the president by the government departments and agencies with foreign policy responsibilities. Within a few years, though, this office came to reside "at the center of the system for making foreign and defense policy."[30]

By the 1960s, the adviser position had evolved into a number of complicated and sometimes contradictory roles. As Colin Powell, who served as national security adviser under President Reagan, once put it, "I was to perform as judge, traffic cop, truant officer, arbitrator, fireman, chaplain, psychiatrist, and occasional hit man."[31] The job had stretched from the original task of paper coordinator to one of policy advocacy on behalf of the president. Twenty-two men and two women have served as either executive secretary during the Truman and Eisenhower years (three) or, beginning with Robert Cutler, as national security adviser during and since the Eisenhower years (twenty-two). Their names and years of service are displayed in Table 7.1.

According to Samuel ("Sandy") R. Berger, who held this office during the Clinton administration, the adviser's principal role is to provide the president with information that "he *needs to know* in addition to what he *wants to know* . . . and to keep the process moving in a direction that he wants it to move." Berger stressed that the objective of the NSC, and therefore its adviser, is "to have a coherent decision-making process," as well as "determining what [the] priorities are and what is important for the rest of the government to focus on."[32] Another former national security adviser, Walt W. Rostow from the Johnson administration, emphasized that the adviser's "number one duty [is] to give the president the facts."[33]

### The NSC adviser as honest broker

Powell stressed that the adviser exists "to help the president manage foreign policy," especially by ensuring that the chief executive receives "full, objective, coherent, and balanced recommendations on issues he must decide," and that decisions are forced forward, "not allowing the bureaucracy to sit and spin its wheels and fail to move issues forward for decision."[34] The president must hear "the strongest views as well as the weakest views." Moreover, Powell added, it is imperative for the adviser to make the secretaries of state and defense "look good." As he emphasized, "It is in the best interest of the United States for the secretary of state and the secretary of defense to be seen as the principal players in the execution of the president's foreign policy." Further, the adviser is often called on to be a crisis manager. Powell continued: "When something happens in the world—a military action in the Persian Gulf, a crisis in a foreign land, any kind of crisis that is going to be a major international event—there is only one place that crisis can be managed from, and that is the West Wing of the White House, and it immediately flows into the National Security Council staff and the national security adviser."

Above all else, the office of the NSC adviser has evolved into the role of an **honest broker** to *mediate disputes among the cabinet departments, and especially to mollify as much as possible the institutional tensions between State and Defense, serving as a bridge between the two.* Brent Scowcroft, considered by many the quintessential honest broker when he served as adviser under Presidents Ford and George H. W. Bush, observed, ". . . if you are not the honest broker, you don't have the confidence of the other members of the NSC. If you don't have their confidence, then the system doesn't work, because they will go around you to get to the president and then you fracture the system."[35]

### The counselor's role prevails

From the National Security Act of 1947 through today, the history of the NSC advisor's performance has swung between passive and more active roles. As political scientists Crabb and Mulcahy observe, on the passive side advisers act as "administrators" and "coordinator*s*," helping to move paper between the bureaucracy and the White House but staying away from policy initiation.[36] In contrast, as "counselors" and

| THE NSC EXECUTIVE SECRETARIES | |
|---|---|
| **Truman Administration** | |
| Sidney W. Souers | 1947–1950 |
| James S. Lay | 1950–1953 |
| **Eisenhower Administration** | |
| Robert Cutler | 1953 |
| **THE ASSISTANTS TO THE PRESIDENT FOR NATIONAL SECURITY AFFAIRS** | |
| **Eisenhower Administration** | |
| Robert Cutler | 1953–1955 |
| Dillon Anderson | 1955–1956 |
| William Jackson | 1956–1957 |
| Robert Cutler | 1957–1958 |
| Gordon Gray | 1958–1961 |
| **Kennedy and Johnson Administrations** | |
| McGeorge Bundy | 1961–1966 |
| Walt W. Rostow | 1966–1969 |
| **Nixon and Ford Administrations** | |
| Henry A. Kissinger | 1969–1975 (also Secretary of State in 1973–75) |
| Brent Scowcroft | 1975–1977 |
| **Carter Administration** | |
| Zbigniew Brzezinski | 1977–1981 |
| **Reagan Administration** | |
| Richard V. Allen | 1981–1982 |
| William P. Clark | 1982–1983 |
| Robert C. McFarlane | 1983–1985 |
| John M. Poindexter | 1985–1986 |
| Frank C. Carlucci | 1986–1987 |
| Colin Powell | 1987–1989 |
| **George H. W. Bush Administration** | |
| Brent Scowcroft | 1989–1993 |
| **Clinton Administration** | |
| W. Anthony Lake | 1993–1997 |
| Samuel R. Berger | 1997–2001 |

*Table 7.1*
The National Security
Advisers, 1947–2013

*(continues)*

*Table 7.1*
The National Security
Advisers, 1947–2013
*(continued)*

| George W. Bush Administration | |
| --- | --- |
| Condoleezza Rice | 2001–2004 |
| Stephen Hadley | 2004–2008 |
| **Obama Administration** | |
| James Jones | 2009–2010 |
| Thomas A. Donilon | 2010–2013 |
| Susan E. Rice | 2013— |

"agents" the advisers become increasingly more assertive in the policy-making process. The counselor is much more involved in the substance of policy than the administrator or coordinator, serving as the personal adviser to the president on foreign policy issues; and the agent goes a big step further, becoming a vigorous public advocate for specific foreign policy positions. Crabb and Mulcahy point to a fifth role as well: the adviser as "insurgent," someone who takes the NSC staff into an aggressive operational role, as did Robert C. McFarlane and John Poindexter during the Iran-*contra* scandal, based more on the adviser's "assessment of the president's *intentions* rather than on expressed presidential policies."[37]

Throughout the NSC's first two decades, the adviser's role moved steadily toward a more assertive stance, as measured by the office's internal managerial responsibilities and advocacy of policy, especially in public forums. This trend surged upward under Henry Kissinger, as depicted in Figure 7.1. In reaction to Kissinger's dominance over the policy-making process, the level of activity in initiating policy and "going public" fell back toward a more behind-the-scenes approach under Scowcroft during the Ford administration. The role of adviser began to rise again under the aggressive personality of Brzezinski, then experienced another decline with the more passive Allen and Clark, followed by a disastrous turn upward on the aggressive scale with the controversial covert operations carried out under McFarlane and Poindexter—the Iran-*contra* affair. The strong personalities of advisers Carlucci and Powell no doubt helped to retard a full plunge back into a mere administrator or coordinator role in the wake of the Iran-*contra* excesses. More recently, the role of adviser has leveled off in the activist "counselor" mode under President Obama's second and third national security advisers, Thomas E. Donilon and Susan E. Rice (his first, Marine Corps General James L. Jones, adopted a low-profile, passive approach to the job). Vice President Joseph R. Biden Jr. described Donilon as "the most important person" on the Obama administration's national security team; and Rice, his successor, also enjoyed close ties to the President.[38]

This narrowing oscillation of **National Security Council adviser roles**, between the extremes of *administrator* and coordinator on one hand, and *insurgent* on the other hand, settling on the preferred job description of *counselor*, is a result of a long and sometimes painful process of trial and error. The fact that the counselor role has prevailed reflects a learning experience regarding the dysfunction of extremes,

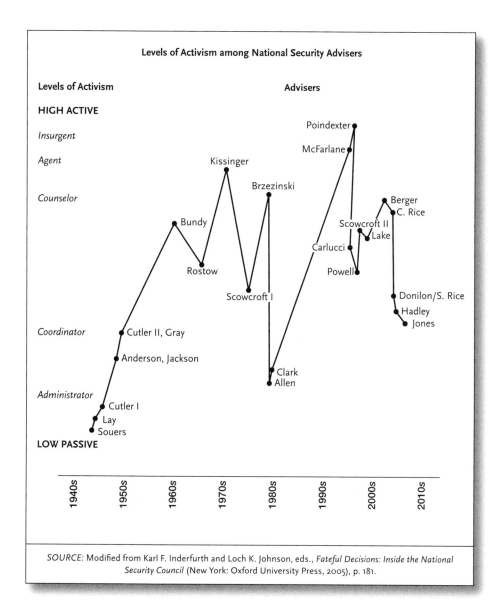

**Levels of Activism among National Security Advisers**

Levels of Activism

Advisers

HIGH ACTIVE

Insurgent

Agent

Counselor

Coordinator

Administrator

LOW PASSIVE

Poindexter

McFarlane

Kissinger

Brzezinski

Bundy

Rostow

Scowcroft I

Berger
C. Rice

Scowcroft II

Lake

Carlucci

Powell

Donilon/S. Rice

Hadley

Jones

Cutler II, Gray

Anderson, Jackson

Clark
Allen

Cutler I

Lay

Souers

1940s  1950s  1960s  1970s  1980s  1990s  2000s  2010s

SOURCE: Modified from Karl F. Inderfurth and Loch K. Johnson, eds., *Fateful Decisions: Inside the National Security Council* (New York: Oxford University Press, 2005), p. 181.

*Figure 7.1*
Levels of NSC Adviser Activism in Policy Initiatives and Public Advocacy, 1947–2012

whether too passive or too active. Further, presidents have understood that the complex issues of foreign and security policy since the Cold War demand an activist adviser—although not an independent, out-of-control insurgent.

The goal is have an adviser who can serve as an honest broker, in the model of Scowcroft, faithfully representing the views and recommendations of NSC principals, while sharing his or her own thoughts with the president; an adviser who keeps information flowing into and out of the Oval Office; and an adviser who can assist the administration in explaining its foreign policy initiatives to an increasingly demanding public and media. Even with the best of national security advisers, though, a president can find it difficult to guide the large foreign policy bureaucracy, among them the Departments of State and Defense, where tribalism not cooperation is often the ruling premise.

## The Departments of State and Defense

The two oldest departments in the government are the Departments of State and Defense (the latter known as the Department of War until 1947). Both stretch back to the very beginnings of the nation's history. They are also the most influential of the foreign policy departments. Their organizational structures illustrate the intricacy of the bureaucracy that sprawls beneath the president.

### The Department of State

The first of America's cabinet-level departments to be established, the Department of State is the organization through which the president guides the nation's foreign policy, officially at least. In reality, the State Department faces a number of bureaucratic rivals for this job: including not only the national security adviser and the NSC staff, but the Department of Defense when it comes to political and military matters; along with the Office of the Special Trade Representative, the Commerce Department, and the Treasury Department when it comes to international economics. Nevertheless, the State Department is generally viewed as the formal manager of America's foreign policy. When high-level disputes arise among these departments, agencies, and offices, the president must arbitrate them, often seeking counsel from the national security adviser and other White House aides.

The secretary of state is the first-ranking cabinet member and is widely considered the chief foreign policy adviser to the president. That role is sometimes wrestled away from the secretary by activist national security advisers, who since the 1960s have had the advantage of proximity—occupying an office just down the corridor from the Oval Office in the West Wing of the White House. Whether the secretary is able to serve as the president's top foreign policy person depends on the personal chemistry between the two, as well as how talented and aggressive the secretary is.

On Washington's scale of organizational size, the State Department is a rather modest bureaucracy. In recent years, it has employed around 10,000 personnel who work inside the United States, mostly at Foggy Bottom—the nickname of the neighborhood in the District of Columbia where the Department's headquarters building is located near the Potomac River. Another 7,000 people serve overseas. Within this grand total are about 6,500 Foreign Service officers, who are the elite of America's diplomatic corps—less than the number of sailors attached to an aircraft carrier group.[39] Small as the Department of State is when compared with other behemoths in the American government, no other nation in the world comes close to approximating the size of the US diplomatic establishment. Yet within the domain of Washington politics with its intense competition for scarce resources and the ear of the president, the State Department (usually just referred to as "State," in Washington talk) finds itself at a distinct disadvantage. Unlike other cabinet departments, it lacks a constituency across the nation. The Department of Agriculture, for example, can rally farmers to help with lobbying for funds on Capitol Hill; and the Defense Department can rely on the potent assistance of weapons manufacturers and military personnel on bases located in congressional districts. In contrast, diplomats, who serve much of their careers overseas, must largely fend for themselves in the government's budget and policy hearings.

The secretary of state is assisted by a deputy secretary and four undersecretaries: one each for political affairs; economic affairs; security assistance, who handles the overall coordinator of the US military aid program; and management. The secretary also has on call one or more ambassadors at large, sometimes referred to as envoys, who may be dispatched to conduct special negotiations anywhere around the world. After his retirement as secretary of state in 1976, Henry Kissinger was subsequently tapped by GOP presidents for special envoy missions abroad, especially to the Middle East. Another famous envoy is George J. Mitchell, a former Senate majority leader (D-Maine) who has served as President Obama's leading negotiator in efforts to resolve core disputes in the Middle East.

At the heart of the State Department is the **Foreign Service**, which is *responsible for the day-to-day conduct of America's relations with other countries.* The men and women of the Foreign Service, selected through the most rigorous screening examinations in the government, serve overseas in 134 embassies, 10 missions, 68 consulates general, 47 consulates, and a few other offices, as well as within the State Department's headquarters building.[40] Their reports provide valuable information for the shaping of foreign policy decisions. The United States Agency for International Development (USAID) is also located within the Department of State. Its job is to guide America's economic assistance programs for the less developed countries of the world.

The *top American official in a US embassy overseas* is the **ambassador**, who in about two-thirds of the cases since 1950 have been career State Department officers. The other one-third are political appointees. Some of the political appointees have served with distinction and some have been a flop, displaying little knowledge about their country of assignment. A few of the embassies, including the prize postings of London and Paris, require a wealthy American at the embassy helm because in these countries the ambassador is expected to entertain often and well—far beyond the government-allotted expense account.

Overseas, life for ambassadors and their staff has become much more complicated than in the old days when State dominated American foreign policy. Traditional Foreign Service diplomacy proved unable to handle on its own the growing number of transnational issues that America confronts in the world, such as global pollution, destruction of rain forests and coral reefs, trafficking in drugs and human beings, pandemics, and shortages of energy and water. International and nongovernmental organizations have joined the State Department on the world stage to address these challenges, including such international entities as the World Health Organization (WHO), the International Labor Organization (ILO), and the International Atomic

*Figure 7.2*
Organization Chart
for the Department
of State

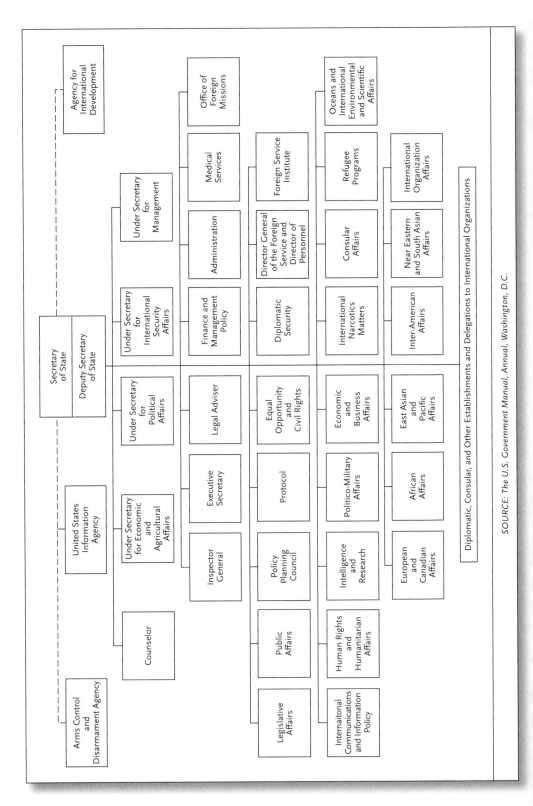

SOURCE: *The U.S. Government Manual, Annual, Washington, D.C.*

Energy Agency (IAEA); and, on the NGO side, the Catholic Relief Services, CARE, Amnesty International, and Doctors Without Borders, among many others. State Department officials have sometimes found it difficult to establish good working ties with these organizations. Life for ambassadors has become more dangerous, too, as the murder by terrorists of the US ambassador to Libya, J. Christopher Stevens, underscored in 2012—the first American ambassador to die in a violent assault since 1979.[41]

Inside the State Department in Washington reside the **country desk officers**, *the men and women (over 100 serve in this capacity) who keep daily watch over all the major countries around the globe, reading the secret and nonsecret communications that stream into the State Department from US embassies.* Although low on the organizational totem pole, the country desk officer plays a vital role as the person with first contact between the Department and its ambassadors and other diplomatic representatives abroad. He or she must make the initial response to incoming information.

## The Department of Defense

The most imposing of all the organizations involved in American foreign policy is the Department of Defense (DOD). Within its institutional framework are large standing military forces. The Department of Defense has more than three million employees, 750 military bases in 130 countries, and secretive Special Forces in 125 countries. Several of the bases are new and located in the Middle East and Southwest Asia, in places like Bahrain, Kyrgyzstan, United Arab Emirates, Qatar, and, of course, Iraq and Afghanistan.[42] In 2012, the United States had 90,000 soldiers stationed in Afghanistan alone, joined by 40,000 NATO troops. With an annual budget of over $600 billion, the DOD secretary (who by law must be a civilian) is the mightiest of the cabinet officers who deal with foreign and security policy—often jokingly (and with envy) referred to in Washington as an eight-hundred pound gorilla. The annual DOD budget dwarfs the spending of the State Department ($50 billion). For example, funding for public diplomacy—the State Department program to advertise American values and interests around the world—amounts to barely more than $4 million a year, while the Pentagon spent $167 million *a day* in Afghanistan during 2012.[43] With worldwide leadership aspirations and global interests come high costs, not just in money but in lives. Over 6,600 US military personnel have died in Iraq and Afghanistan since the 9/11 attacks.

Because America is periodically at war, the Defense Department is often the most prominent organization in the government when it comes to the foreign policy preoccupations of the president and Congress. For the same reason, it looms large as well when it comes to media coverage. In the initial term of the George W. Bush administration, Defense Secretary Donald H. Rumsfeld garnered vastly more daily media coverage than Secretary of State Colin Powell, as did Robert M. Gates over Hillary Clinton during the first years of the Obama administration.

The "wiring diagram" in Figure 7.3 hints at, but fails to capture fully, the staggering complexity of the DOD organization. Not until 1986 did the Defense Department achieve genuine unification among the military services and an effective administration structure, by way of the **Goldwater-Nichols Act**. This statute made the chairmanship of the **Joint Chiefs of Staff (JCS)** a much stronger position, backed by a large professional staff. *The JSC chair was given wide authority over the separate armed services, including the right to discipline officers who failed to participate professionally in joint-duty responsibilities assigned to them by the JSC.* The Goldwater-Nichols Act also explicitly emphasized important new roles for each of the **CINCs**, *the four-star "commanders in chief" of the separate services who head the joint specified and unified commands in the military,* such as the CINCPAC or commander in chief for the Pacific theater of operations. They would now work unequivocally for the DOD secretary and the JSC chair and not for their parent services. The long sought-after goal of military unification in the United States had come closer to reality than ever before. As one authority observes, "That streamlined and efficient arrangement contrasted sharply with the almost thirty levels of authority before reaching the field operation commander that existed in October 1983, when the marine barracks in Beirut, Lebanon, were blown up and 241 marines were killed."[44]

The Pentagon has also played a vital role in the development of America's domestic and international economic prowess. In alliance with the Congress, it has been responsible for funding some of the largest US export companies, such as the commercial and military aircraft industries as well as computer businesses. Dramatically influencing the commercial world, the DOD's Defense Advanced Research Projects Agency (DARPA) invented the Internet and continued to operate it until 1990. Further, the Department has been the key client for several giant US industries, including Boeing, Lockheed, and Honeywell. As John Cassidy notes, "No other government department comes close to exerting the commercial sway of the Pentagon."[45]

In the twenty-first century, the DOD has taken over activities that were once considered the State Department's domain, such as nation building, bilateral negotiations with other nations, and peacekeeping. As *Washington Post* journalist Dana Priest noted in 2005, an imbalance of resources had begun to grow in recent years, to the point where "the military took on many of the jobs that the State Department had, and they still have them today."[46] An American historian has observed that in the age of globalization, "American military proconsuls—generals with immense power and support staff larger than that of the White House—control the four corners of the world."[47]

In 2005, the Pentagon promoted a global counterterrorism plan that would permit Special Operations Forces to move inside a foreign country for covert activities without informing the US ambassador, weakening the long-standing "chief of mission" authority enjoyed by the State Department. In 2006, an ambassador reported to the Senate Foreign Relations Committee "that his effectiveness in representing the United States to foreign officials was beginning to wane, as more resources are directed to special operations forces and intelligence." He continued: "Foreign officials are 'following the money' in terms of determining which relationships to emphasize."[48]

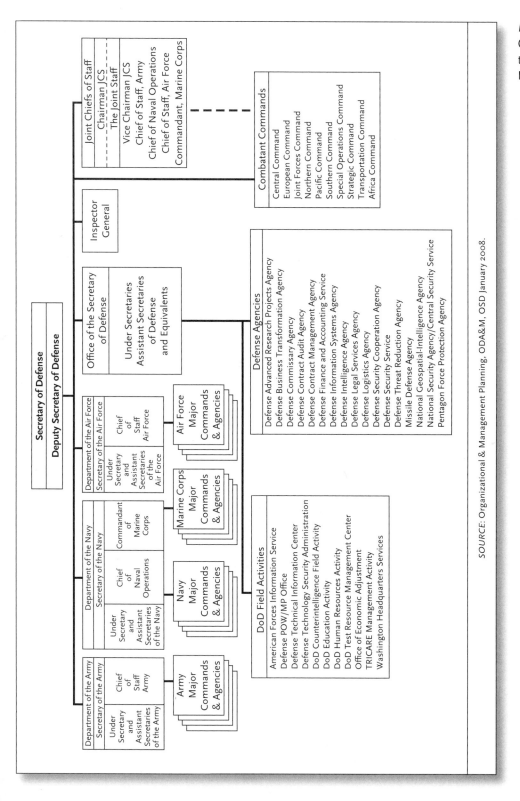

*Figure 7.3*
Organization Chart for the Department of Defense

SOURCE: Organizational & Management Planning, ODA&M, OSD January 2008.

Nor would the CIA necessarily know about the covert military operations.[49] In the halls of the DOD, the State Department is sometimes referred to derisively as the Department of Nice; when it came to achieving America's foreign policy objectives, the tougher Defense Department would get the job done. Aware of the declining role of the State Department in foreign affairs, Secretary of State Hillary Clinton of the Obama administration vowed to strengthen America's diplomatic corps. She announced in 2010 that she would invigorate the US Agency for International Development and build up State's staffing after its 38 percent decline since 1990. She also traveled abroad more during her tenure than any of her predecessors.[50]

### Differing departmental perspectives on foreign policy

As if their institutional complexities alone were insufficient management challenges, the Departments of State and Defense make life all the more challenging for presidents by sometimes advocating quite separate views on how to respond to foreign threats. Traditionally, State has been predisposed to advocate the power of diplomacy; Foggy Bottom is the home of the peacemakers. The DOD, not surprisingly, has tended to gravitate toward the war power. The Cuban missile crisis is illustrative. The pressures for an immediate air strike against Cuba came chiefly from the DOD; the Department of State advocated a more cautious approach, relying on diplomatic channels in the United Nations and elsewhere. More recently, the Pentagon displayed enthusiasm for the invasion of Iraq in 2003, while the State Department was more skeptical—especially about the plausibility of the WMD argument as a rationale for going to war.[51]

During the Reagan years, however, these departmental views were periodically reversed, with State advocating the use of force and Defense moving more cautiously. The DOD stance appeared to be a reaction by the armed services to the loss of the Vietnam War and a resulting unwillingness to become involved in military ventures abroad, at least without the full and clear support of America's political leaders in both the executive and legislative branches. Under President Obama, Secretary of Defense Robert M. Gates surprised some observers by consistently advocating a greater role for State in a partnership with DOD to help counter the success of anti-American insurgents in Iraq and Afghanistan.

During the Cold War, the State Department often served as a greenhouse for the nurturing of détente with the Soviet Union, whereas the Department of Defense was notorious for its "worst-case" analysis of Soviet military intentions and projected a more negative view of superpower relations. These different perspectives became all the more divisive in the Carter and Reagan administrations because of personality conflicts between the two Departmental secretaries (explored in Chapter 8). During the Obama years, though, Secretary Gates argued for a significant reduction in DOD spending, in light of the severe recessionary pressures confronting the United States. Relying on stereotypes for predicting the likely policy positions of State and Defense has become increasingly problematic.

## Turf Battles

The magnitude and number of foreign programs and operations conducted by the Departments of State and Defense would alone be enough to keep a conscientious president burning the midnight oil. Yet these behemoths represent only a fraction of the foreign policy leadership challenge. Almost every major agency in the government has an international component involved in negotiations of one kind or another with other nations, frequently with little or no guidance or control from the White House or the State Department. As one observer wrote, "With over 700 international conferences a year, transnational collegiums of professionals in agriculture, atomic energy, meteorology, satellites, and health tend to work directly with one another with little supervision by the foreign-policy agencies (basically State) in staffing conferences, drawing up technical guidelines or reaching consensual decisions."[52] Those numbers keep rising as globalization expands America's relations abroad. James Madison was right: the president needs help from the Congress in supervising the conduct of American foreign policy—especially as the number and scope of bureaucratic agencies has proliferated.

Worrisome, too, from the viewpoint of democratic controls over foreign policy is the phenomenon of "subgovernments" and "iron triangles." President Eisenhower famously warned the nation about the dangers of one of these subgovernments—the **military-industrial complex**—in his famous Farewell Address of 1959, perhaps the most important valedictory remarks in the modern era. This *alliance of the Pentagon, the weapons industries, and the armed services and appropriations committees in Congress has led to an almost consistent rise in military spending by the United States every year since Eisenhower's warning*, regardless of whether the nation was at war or which political party was in control of the White House or Congress. Author James Ledbetter concluded, "It is not a stretch to believe that this armaments industry—which profits not only from domestic sales but also from tens of billions of dollars in annual exports—manipulates public policy to perpetuate itself."[53]

---

### PERSPECTIVES ON AMERICAN FOREIGN POLICY 7.1

A notorious example of an iron triangle is the so-called *military-industrial complex*. In a passage from his Farewell Address of 1960, PRESIDENT DWIGHT DAVID EISENHOWER warned:

This conjunction of an immense Military Establishment and a large arms industry is in the American experience. The total influence—economic, political, even spiritual is felt in every city, every statehouse, every office of the Federal Government. We recognize the imperative need for this development. Yet we must not fail to comprehend grave implications. Our toil, resources, and livelihood are all involved; so is the very structure of our society.

In the councils of government we must guard against the acquisition of unwarranted influence, whether sought or unsought, by the military-industrial complex. The potential for the disastrous rise of misplaced power exists and will persist.

SOURCE: *Public Papers of the Presidents*, Dwight D. Eisenhower, 1960–1961 (Washington, DC: Office the Federal Register, National Archives, 1961), p. 1038.

Bureaucrats, in short, are often resistant to the charms and blandishments of presidents. And they are supposed to be on the president's side—or, at any rate, they are in the same branch of the government. More forbidding still to the White House are those institutions in Washington that have a constitutional obligation to be skeptical about the president's goals and methods: Congress and the courts. By virtue of the Constitution, the law, and historical tradition, these institutions stand separate from the presidency and sometimes engage in a more open form of resistance than practiced by bureaucrats.

## THE CONGRESS

"Congress looks more powerful sitting here [in the White House] than it did when I was . . . one of a hundred in the Senate," President Kennedy said. "From here I look . . . at the collective power of the Congress . . . there are different views, different interests [and] perspectives . . . from one end of Pennsylvania Avenue to the other. . . . There is bound to be conflict."[54] Presidents spend a good deal of time expressing exasperation about the legislative branch of government. Eisenhower went so far as to refer once to its members as "those damn monkeys on the Hill."[55] Most presidents may think that—or worse—from time to time, but usually keep it under their hats to avoid retaliation against their programs by aggrieved lawmakers with their hands on the budgetary purse strings.

Presidents find members of Congress difficult to deal with because there are so many of them. Moreover, they have powerful, constitutionally based authorities over war making and treaty passage; and all of them seem to have an opinion on foreign policy. To boot, lawmakers view themselves as sovereign entities, answerable neither to the president nor even to congressional leaders, but rather to the voters on election day in each of their constituencies. "This is a Senate; a Senate of equals; of men of individual honor and personal character, and of absolute independence," declared Senator Daniel Webster in 1830, adding, "We know no masters; we acknowledge no dictators."[56] That spirit of independence has ebbed and flowed over the years, sometimes giving way to deference to the president on foreign policy and sometimes being erased by the demands of party loyalty. Nonetheless, members of the Senate and the House often insist on the constitutional prerogative to be counted in the making of America's foreign policy. Moreover, since the early 1990s, Democrats and Republicans have displayed stronger than usual partisanship, with a rise in the frequency of heated debate between the parties and even uncivil relations displayed on the floor and in hearings. Congress has also become far more fragmented that was the case in the 1950s.

### Minnows and Whales

"When I was a young assistant secretary of state," recalled Dean Rusk, who served in that capacity during the 1950s, "the Department had only to consult five 'whales' on the Hill to gain an accurate reading on how the Congress would react to our foreign policy initiatives." The five whales included Senators Everett Dirksen, the minority leader (R-Illinois); Lyndon B. Johnson, the majority leader (D-Texas); Hubert H. Humphrey (D-Minnesota); and Richard B. Russell (D-Georgia); and, in the House, Speaker Sam Rayburn (D-Texas). "Today," Rusk concluded, with all the devolution of power, "you have 535 minnows."[57] In 1961 Lyndon Johnson left the Senate to become vice president in the Kennedy administration; Rayburn died that same year. Then, with the profusion of new subcommittees in the post-Watergate reformist era, the spawning of the minnows ran wild. Lobbying five individuals on behalf of the president's foreign policy is clearly a much easier task than trying to lobby virtually the entire congressional membership—the expectation of lawmakers today.

Another complication in executive-legislative relations has been the recent Senate practice of requiring a 60-vote margin to pass almost all legislation, the number necessary since 1974 to halt a filibuster (before, the rule was a two-thirds vote for cloture). The culture in the Senate once permitted the passing of most laws by a simple majority vote for all but the most controversial proposals. In earlier years, Southern Democrats periodically resorted to the filibuster (a practice never intended by the founders) as a method to block civil rights legislation; more recently, Republicans have used the filibuster rule to curb, or at least slow, routine Democratic legislative initiatives—more than 360 times between 2007 and 2012, a historical record.[58] The filibuster option remains an important safeguard for the airing of minority views, but the privilege can be abused as an instrument of partisan delay and sabotage. In a 2011 *New York Times* editorial, former senator Walter F. Mondale recommended reducing the number of votes needed to end a filibuster, perhaps to fifty-five, so that lawmakers could more easily bring debate to a close, then vote and move on with their business.[59]

In 2013, Republicans and Democrats in Congress struck a deal to eschew filibusters on presidential nominations. This was just a temporary measure, however, that failed to clearly reinstate the traditional—and constitutional—principle that simple-majority votes should determine the confirmation of executive appointments and other legislative business, except in the most extraordinary of circumstances when a monumental issue might warrant longer debate.

## Legislative Watchdogs

Other features of the legislative branch make it a natural rival for the executive branch on matters of foreign policy. Even though presidential powers are more limited than generally acknowledged, presidents and their aides have been able from time to time to aggrandize unwarranted powers, as Americans learned from the experiences of Vietnam and Watergate, and, most recently, President George W. Bush's bypassing of the wiretap provisions in the Foreign Intelligence Surveillance Act (among other examples). Understanding the dangers of centralized authority, the nation's founders *required* Congress by the language of the Constitution to watch the executive branch closely, especially when it came to the treaty and the war powers. In more recent times, lawmakers have passed a raft of *statutes that mandate executive branch reporting to various committees and subcommittees on a range of policy proposals*. Since the mid-1970s, members of Congress have been no longer willing to tolerate being kept in the dark; and these **reporting requirements** are designed to inform Congress about the intentions of the White House and the bureaucracy.

In a rare attitude of defiance at the time (early in the Cold War), Representative Carl Vinson (D-Georgia), chairman of the House Armed Services Committee, informed the Secretary of Defense in 1949 that "Congress won't be bypassed, and we will be conversant with what goes on."[60] Today, this spirit of independence has been expressed by many members of the legislative branch in the wake of Vietnam, Watergate, the CIA domestic spy scandal in the mid-1970s, the questionable arguments for war against Iraq in 2003, the CIA's use of torture and the establishment of CIA secret prisons overseas (also during the Bush years), and the hazy authority for killing suspected American terrorists abroad during the Obama years. Although this congressional ardor for a copartnership in foreign policy has cooled somewhat as the wars in Iraq and Afghanistan have wound down, many lawmakers continue to insist on respect from the executive branch for the constitutional prerogatives of the legislative branch. A recent illustration is the insistence of some members of Congress that the executive branch provide them with more information about the controversial scope of domestic wiretaps by the National Security Agency (a program leaked in 2013 by a private-sector government contractor, Edward J. Snowden, who then fled to Russia).

In another recent example of robust congressional oversight, Dianne Feinstein (D-California), chair of the Senate Select Committee on Intelligence, led the preparation of a major inquiry into CIA torture practices that resulted in a 6,000-page classified report used by the panel to evaluate how the Agency came to engage in methods of "harsh interrogation" (torture) against suspected terrorists. Although the report remains classified, several senators with access to the findings told newspapers about the conclusion: torture was unproductive, as well as a terrible stain on the good reputation of the United States.[61]

At the insistence of the Congress, the CIA now provides over 1,000 briefings and more than 7,000 intelligence reports to Capitol Hill each year.[62] During congressional hearings one is likely to find a staff aide whispering to a lawmaker, "That testimony is wrong, and you can cite CIA document such-and-such." According to one report, Secretary of State George P. Shultz of the Reagan administration testified formally before Congress twenty-five times in 1983, or about once every other week; and other senior State Department officials appeared an additional 375 times in that same year.[63] During formal investigations of the CIA by the Senate and the House in 1975 on charges of domestic spying, the Agency's director, William E. Colby, recalled spending at least half of his time preparing for hearings; he testified thirty-five times on Capitol Hill that year—although this was during an unusually stressful time for the intelligence agencies.[64] Proponents of an active role for Congress in the making of foreign policy maintain that this time devoted to **congressional accountability (oversight)**—*the ongoing review of public policy initiatives by lawmakers*—is well spent; lawmakers can hardly be expected to fund multibillion-dollar programs without a serious review of how well the executive agencies are operating and spending taxpayer money.

Those less sanguine about this congressional involvement are likely to embrace the quite different view offered by Zbigniew Brzezinski in *Perspectives on American Foreign Policy* 7.2. Certainly Congress has sometimes abused its power to investigate the executive branch, as demonstrated most vividly by the McCarthy hearings in the 1950s that charged the Truman and Eisenhower administrations—on flimsy evidence—of harboring agents for the Soviet Union within the US government. Even earlier, journalist Walter Lippmann had attacked "that legalized atrocity, the Congressional investigation, where Congressmen, starved of their legitimate food for thought, go on a wild and feverish manhunt and do not stop at cannibalism."[65]

Despite some occasional excesses, congressional inquiries have become one of the chief means used by lawmakers to review the foreign policy initiatives of the executive branch. The investigative findings frequently lead to new legislation meant to make the government work more effectively. Senate and House committees in 1975, for example, uncovered several instances of wrongdoing in the intelligence agencies. As a result of this evidence, Congress created permanent intelligence oversight committees in both chambers, with a mandate to watch more attentively the future operations of the CIA and its companion services. Ever since, America's intelligence agencies have operated with a better sense of their legal and ethical boundaries—although even with these new guidelines they succumbed to the Iran-*contra* affair, as well as questionable practices of warrantless wiretapping, prisoner interrogation, and rendition in the past few years.[66]

"You see the way a free government works," President Truman remarked, "there's got to be a housecleaning every now and then."[67] This is a central purpose of congressional inquiries—a vital part of the "auxiliary precautions" to safeguard democracy recommended by Madison in *Federalist Paper* No. 51. When it becomes clear that the government's house has fallen into disarray, members of Congress react in an effort to restore lawfulness and propriety.

---

### PERSPECTIVES ON AMERICAN FOREIGN POLICY 7.2

Political scientist and national security adviser in the Carter administration, **ZBIGNIEW BRZEZINSKI** comments on what he perceives to be an excessive involvement of lawmakers in foreign policy decisions:

Today, the decision-making process at the very top [the presidency] is institutionally more fragmented than at any point since World War II. . . . This condition is made worse by the continuing and expanding intrusion of Congress into the tactics of foreign policy. Almost every congressman sees himself as a putative secretary of State, surrounded by personal staffers who make it their business to make the life of the secretary of State as miserable as possible. . . .

SOURCE: Zbigniew Brzezinski, "Reagan May Be a Great Leader, but His Foreign Policy Is a Shambles," *The Washington Post*, National Weekly Edition (October 20, 1986), p. 23. Dr. Zbigniew Brzezinski is a Counselor and Trustee of the Center for Strategic & International Studies. He was National Security Adviser to U.S. President Jimmy Carter.

Sometimes well-intended oversight can lead to meddlesome second-guessing by members of Congress in the day-to-day conduct of international affairs by the executive branch. This *excessive involvement in the details of policy implementations* is referred to by critics as **micromanagement**, a damning word that has become a favorite of bureaucrats opposed to virtually any congressional participation in foreign policy decisions. An example—and a legitimate complaint by critics—was the practice by some lawmakers in the Senate of placing a "hold" on foreign policy personnel nominated by the Obama administration. In 2010, Senator Richard Shelby (R-Alabama), for example, warned that he would use the "hold" privilege unless the White House awarded certain defense contracts to his home state. This is a form of parochial obstructionism, fed by a poisonous partisanship that can paralyze the government. Most of the time, though, the Senate has confirmed presidential cabinet members; throughout history, there have been such 579 nominees, and only seven have been rejected (and just two since 1959).[68]

At the other extreme from micromanagement, Congress frequently proves unable or unwilling to engage in serious oversight at all. A seasoned Hill observer once described the House of Representatives as a modern dinosaur, "a large, slow-witted, thin-skinned, defensive composite that wants to stay out of trouble. Its real passion is reserved for its creature comforts: salaries, recesses, office space, allowances, and ever more staff to help it reach its timid decisions."[69] One Congressional observer wrote recently that, when it comes to reviewing the use of the war power by the executive branch, "Congress generally sits there silently, except for the occasional clapping."[70] At their best, though, lawmakers can play an indispensable role in protecting democracy and improving America's foreign policy decisions—as with the constructive Senate probes into CIA spying at home (1975) and the Iran-*contra* scandal (1987).

Political scientist Stephen K. Bailey stated the possibilities decades ago and his observation remains just as valid today:

> Congress defends freedom by asking rude questions; by stubbornly insisting that technology be discussed in terms of its human effects; by eliciting new ideas from old heads; by building a sympathetic bridge between the bewildered citizen and the bureaucracy; by acting as a sensitive register for group interests whose fortunes are indistinguishable from the fortunes of vast numbers of citizens and who have a constitutional right to be heard. Congress defends freedom by being a prudent provider; by carefully sifting and refining legislative proposals; by compromising and homogenizing raw forces in conflict; by humbling generals and admirals—and, on occasion, even Presidents.[71]

The capacity of Congress to test the programs and proposals of the executive branch through independent means, coupled with its grip on the purse strings, subpoena powers, and the authority to impeach, makes it the strongest legislative branch not only in the world today but at any time in history—with the possible exception of a brief period during the Roman Empire when its Senate was all powerful. A strong legislative branch is exactly what Madison and the other founders had in mind to help preserve freedom.

## THE COURTS

The judiciary is often overlooked in books on foreign policy, largely because its involvement has been relatively infrequent. Indeed, the Supreme Court had little to say on this subject for the first 150 years of the nation's existence. Yet beginning with the administration of Franklin Roosevelt, the courts occasionally have had a profound influence on foreign policy.

One well-known instance in which the Supreme Court curbed presidential powers involved work stoppage in the steel industry during the Korean War: the Steel Seizure case of 1952, known more formally as the *Youngstown Sheet & Tube Co. v. Sawyer* (343 U.S. 579, 583). The Court decreed that President Truman had improperly engaged in lawmaking—a constitutional prerogative given to Congress alone—when he issued an executive order that directed the Secretary of Commerce to take charge of steel mills closed by striking workers. What is most famous about the *Youngstown* case is the concurring opinion written by Justice Robert Jackson. His rejection of "inherent" presidential powers and his reference to the will of Congress are important statements regarding the proper demarcation in the exercise of powers by the legislative and executive branches.

Jackson offered this tripartite distinction:

1.  When the President acts pursuant to an express or implied authorization of Congress, his authority is at its maximum.

2.  When the President acts in absence of either a congressional grant or denial of authority, he can only rely upon his own independent powers, but there is a **zone of twilight** *in which he and Congress may have concurrent authority, or in which its distribution is uncertain.* Therefore, congressional inertia, indifference or quiescence may sometimes, at least as a practical matter, enable, if not invite, measures of independent presidential responsibility.

3.  When the President takes measures incompatible with the expressed or implied will of Congress, his power is at its lowest ebb, for then he can rely only upon his own constitutional powers minus any constitutional powers of Congress over the matter . . . Presidential claim to a power at once so conclusive and preclusive must be scrutinized with caution, for what is at stake is the equilibrium established by our constitutional system.

Jackson concluded that "only Congress itself can prevent power from slipping through its fingers."

Historically, the Supreme Court has observed a wide zone of twilight in foreign policy and has tended to stand clear of interbranch disputes over the ambiguities in this realm. But the Court's usual dormancy in foreign affairs, with an occasional decision usually in favor of the executive branch, may now be a relic of the past.

## Tilt Toward the President

The judiciary's first major venture into the foreign policy field in the modern era came with the celebrated case ***United States v. Curtiss-Wright Export Corporation*** (1936). The case gained further attention half a century later, in 1987, because a principal in the Iran-*contra* scandal—Lieutenant Colonel Oliver L. North, top aide to national security adviser Admiral Poindexter—invoked *Curtiss-Wright* as a justification for the NSC staff's secret operations that bypassed the Congress. In the *Curtiss-Wright* case, a lower court *convicted Curtiss-Wright (an American weapons-manufacturing company) for the improper sale of machine guns to Bolivia.* The conviction was based on grounds that the weapons sale violated a presidential embargo of arms and munitions to both Bolivia and Paraguay, who were at war against one another at the time. Franklin Roosevelt had based his embargo on authority derived from a congressional joint resolution, which permitted this trade sanction at presidential discretion if such action might "contribute to the reestablishment of peace between [the warring] countries." On appeal to the Supreme Court, the Curtiss-Wright Corporation argued that the wording of the resolution was too vague and represented an unconstitutional delegation of legislative power to the president.

*Curtiss-Wright* is often misconstrued as an affirmation of presidential eminence in America's external affairs. "The power at issue was legislative, not executive," however, emphasizes the constitutional authority Louis Fisher.[72] Nor did *Curtiss-Wright,* in the opinion of another expert, have "anything to do with 'plenary' presidential power— the authority of the President to act in the face of congressional disapproval."[73] What has confused the issue and allowed the *Curtiss-Wright* case to be used selectively by those attempting to advance the independent powers of the executive branch are the pages of *obiter dicta* (a legal term from the Latin, meaning incidental comments and, therefore, not binding) added by Justice George Sutherland. His opinion went far beyond the scope of the decision before the Court. In these *dicta,* Sutherland opined that the president had an inherent right to exercise authority in foreign affairs, over and above existing statutory inhibitions—a position the Court had never dared to propose with respect to domestic policy. As another Supreme Court justice would later emphasize, the most that Sutherland's opinion could mean was that "the President might act in external affairs without congressional authority, but not that he might act contrary to an Act of Congress"[74]

In recent years, Supreme Court justices have sometimes taken strong positions in favor of the presidency. One illustration comes from President Carter's decision in 1979 to end, without Senate consultation, a mutual defense treaty with Taiwan. Initially, a federal district court came close to siding with Congress ("the power to terminate treaties is a power shared by the political branches of this government," said the presiding judge, "namely the President and the Congress"), but ultimately declined on technical grounds.[75] The Supreme Court, which heard the case on appeal, proved unsympathetic to the belief of many senators that President Carter should have sought the Senate's advice and consent. By a vote of 7-to-2 the Court held, in ***Goldwater* v. *Carter*** (1979), that *the president had the authority to terminate the Taiwan defense pact.*

Lawmakers suffered another setback in 1983 when *the Supreme Court declared the legislative veto unconstitutional* in ***U.S. Immigration and Naturalization Service v. Chadha*** (1983). Ruling on an obscure immigration statute that contained a legislative-veto provision, a majority on the Court struck a blow against this provision in hundreds of laws, including some highly important ones like the War Powers Resolution of 1973. The legislative veto embedded in the War Powers Resolution allowed Congress to terminate US military involvement abroad by a concurrent resolution, that is, by a bicameral majority vote, free of a possible presidential veto. The **Chadha case** made the use of this controversial legislative veto null and void.

## Curbing Presidential Excess

Now and then, the judicial branch has trimmed back the president's authority. For example, the so-called **Pentagon Papers case** (***New York Times Co. v. United States***, heard by the Supreme Court in 1971) came out *against the president's request to prevent the* Times *and other papers from publishing the Pentagon's classified, in-house history of the Vietnam War.* This attempt by the Nixon administration to quash the public release of this history was the first time ever the federal government had sought to censor a newspaper in advance of publication (a legal step known as "prior restraint," discussed in Chapter 9). In the opinion of the Court's majority (a 5-to-4 vote), nothing within these papers would have led to "irreparable harm" to the United States if published. Congress and the American people were allowed to read these documents about America's conduct in the war in Vietnam—a signal from the Court that the executive branch could not cover up questionable decisions simply by classifying documents "top secret" and hiding them from the public.

During the George W. Bush administration, the Supreme Court entered the thicket of how combat detainees from the war in Afghanistan should be dealt with legally. In ***Hamdi v. Rumsfeld (2004)***, for instance, the Court *rejected the Administration's argument that detention was a purely presidential matter above review by the courts.*[76] Four years later (2008), in ***Boumediene v. Bush***, the Court gave Guantánamo prisoners a "meaningful opportunity" to challenge their detention by filing habeas corpus petitions in court. Justice Anthony Kennedy wrote for the 5-to-4 majority: "the framers decided that habeas corpus, a right of first importance," had to be an integral part of America's legal framework. Yet since then, the Court has backed away from hearing additional cases on the plight of the 174 detainees who, by the time President Obama was elected for a second term, were still being kept in Guantánamo cells.

## FOREIGN POLICY POWER: A STUDY IN CUBISM

The key institutions involved in American foreign policy resemble more a study in cubism than a harmonious and pleasantly arranged landscape portrait, for in truth the various parts of the US government hold but fragments of power and are often set one against the other. Participants in the democratic process within the United States are faced with the difficult task of piecing together these fragments in an effort to build coalitions that support their policy objectives. Leadership in Washington, DC relies primarily on the skills of persuasion and bargaining, and only rarely on simple command. "Presidential power is the power to persuade," wrote political scientist Richard E. Neustadt.[77] This was President Truman's view as well. "All the President is," he wrote in a letter to his sister, "is a glorified public relations man who spends his time flattering, kissing, and kicking people to get them to do what they are supposed to do anyway."[78]

Sometimes, though, presidents do find themselves in a position of command, especially in times of foreign policy crisis. They may even find it necessary to elevate themselves above the law, or so some presidents have argued. Abraham Lincoln's eleven-week "dictatorship" during the Civil War is a case in point. Historian Clinton Rossiter summarizes:

> He called out the militia, clamped a blockade on the South, enlarged the regular army and navy beyond their statutory limits, advanced public moneys to persons unauthorized to receive them, pledged the credit of the United States for a sizable loan, closed the mails to "treasonable correspondence," authorized the arrest of potential traitors, and, in defiance of all precedent, suspended the writ of habeas corpus along the line of communication between Washington and New York.[79]

In a message to Congress dated July 4, 1861, Lincoln justified these actions in terms of an obligation to exercise the power of self-preservation for the government of the United States, even if that meant breaking the law. "Are all the laws but *one* to go unexecuted, and the Government itself go to pieces lest that one be violated?" he asked. "Even in such a case, would not the official oath be broken if the Government should be overthrown when it was believed that disregarding the single law would tend to preserve it?"[80] Richard Nixon also expressed his beliefs regarding the prerogative of presidents to violate the law in their "higher" calling to protect the nation's security. His response, which glosses over the important distinction made by Lincoln between times of war and peace, is presented in *Perspectives on American Foreign Policy* 7.3.

The examples of Lincoln and Nixon suggest that the ability of presidents to exercise power will depend on the role they are playing, as well as the level of crisis faced by the nation. Presidents wear different hats from time to time. As political scientists Tatalovich

---

### PERSPECTIVES ON AMERICAN FOREIGN POLICY 7.3

*Former president* **RICHARD M. NIXON** *on presidential power and the rule of law:*

It is quite obvious that there are certain inherently governmental actions which if undertaken by the sovereign in protection of the interests of the nation's security are lawful but which if undertaken by private persons are not. . . . [I]t is naive to attempt to categorize activities a president might authorize as "legal" or "illegal" without reference to the circumstances under which he concludes that the activity is necessary. Assassination of a foreign leader—an act I never had cause to consider and which under most circumstances would be abhorrent to any president—might have been less abhorrent and, in fact, justified during World War II as a means of preventing further Nazi atrocities and ending the slaughter. Additionally, the opening of mail sent to selected priority targets of foreign intelligence, although impinging upon individual freedom may nevertheless serve a salutary purpose when—as it has in the past—it results in preventing the disclosure of sensitive military and state secrets to the enemies of this country.

In short, there have been—and will be in the future—circumstances in which presidents may lawfully authorize actions in the interests of the security of this country, which if undertaken by other persons, or even by the president under different circumstances, would be illegal.

*SOURCE:* "Supplementary Detailed Staff Reports on Foreign and Military Intelligence," Appendix, Book IV, *Final Report of the Select Committee to Study Governmental Operations with Respect to Intelligence Activities* (the Church Committee), Report No. 94–755, US Senate (April 23, 1976), pp. 157–158.

---

and Daynes note, when acting as commander in chief, the president is most powerful—especially when the nation is threatened from abroad.[81] Next, in the role of chief diplomat, the president's powers remain considerable, for the Constitution and custom give the president clear prerogatives in this area. Presidential authority becomes progressively weaker, however, in the roles of chief executive, legislative leader, and, the least powerful of all, public opinion and party leader. These roles rely less on constitutional or statutory authority than on the president's abilities to persuade. In matters of power in Washington, DC circumstances are vital, too. "If Lincoln had lived in a time of peace," Theodore Roosevelt once observed, "no one would have known his name."[82]

## SUMMARY

American foreign policy is guided by a host of different structures within the government, including the presidency; a large array of bureaucratic agencies; a proliferation of legislative committees and subcommittees; shifting coalitions of subgovernments beneath the patina of official organizational charts; and, occasionally, the courts. At the top of this vast empire sits the president, whose hand ostensibly guides the ship of state through safe passage in the treacherous seas of international affairs. In reality, the powers of the president are limited by inadequate time and information for thoughtful decision, by disagreement over what is permissible public policy, by a lack of resources, by the bonds of previous commitments, and—except in times of acute national emergency—by fewer grants of formal authority than often supposed.

The president must contend with a bureaucracy that is huge and complex. These departments, agencies, bureaus, and offices frequently have their own tribal mores, as well as closer ties with outside interest groups and individual lawmakers than with the president. Sometimes the executive agencies devote more attention to the protection of their own interests than to the policy agenda set by the president and lawmakers.

Members of Congress have a major part to play in the making of foreign policy, as with the war and the treaty powers spelled out in the Constitution. Further, the practice of congressional accountability or oversight—the monitoring of the executive branch by lawmakers—has evolved from an implicit constitutional duty into a formal and extensive scrutiny of the presidency and the bureaucracy through the use of hearings, reporting requirements, and investigations, supported by a large corpus of law. Post-Watergate reforms on Capitol Hill in the 1970s dispersed authority over lawmaking and oversight, which has further complicated the foreign policy duties of the president. Since the mid-1970s, some members of Congress have no longer been content to passively follow leadership from the White House; they have demanded a legislative-executive partnership in the charting of the nation's international directions. The courts, too, have become more actively engaged in the review of foreign policy decisions, with an inclination toward favoring the presidency but occasionally with major judgments against the excesses of executive power.

The complex institutional arrangements for arriving at foreign policy decisions within the United States present a picture far different from the one suggested by simplistic organizational charts. Officials in Washington must work with the fragments of power provided by custom and the Constitution. It is up to their ingenuity to assemble these pieces into workable policy initiatives. Much depends on circumstances facing the nation. In crisis, greater deference is shown to the president. As well, the skills and initiative of officeholders are important—made all the more difficult by the deep-seated acrimony between the major political parties that has spread across the nation's capital and the country in recent decades.

## KEY TERMS

## QUESTIONS FOR DISCUSSION

1. How did the Vietnam War, the Watergate scandal, and investigations into illegal CIA activities affect the historical tendency of lawmakers to defer to the president on matters of foreign policy?

2. How would you evaluate the effectiveness, and the consequences, of congressional efforts to become more involved in foreign policy since the late 1960s, when the Vietnam War raised doubts about presidential infallibility? Has it led to micromanagement by lawmakers, or to healthy interbranch debates on policy? What have been the effects on executive-legislative relations in foreign affairs resulting from the mistakes made by the George W. Bush administration about WMDs in Iraq? From the revelations about CIA torture and rendition abuses? From violations of the Foreign Intelligence Surveillance Act of 1978, revealed by the *New York Times* in 2005?

3. In the period since the end of the Iraq War in 2012, how would you characterize the foreign policy powers of the presidency? Of Congress? Of the courts?

4. Can you envision a future scenario in which an American president might make an argument in favor of his or her right to rise above the law, as expressed (in profoundly different ways) in earlier eras by Presidents Lincoln and Nixon?

## ADDITIONAL READINGS

Inderfurth, Karl F., and Loch K. Johnson, eds. *Fateful Decisions: Inside the National Security Council.* New York: Oxford University Press, 2004.

Kalb, Marvin. *The Road to War: Presidential Commitments Honored and Betrayed* (Washington, D.C.: Brookings Institution, 2013).

Schwarz, Frederick A. O. Jr., and Aziz Z. Huq. *Unchecked and Unbalanced: Presidential Power in a Time of Terror.* New York: The New Press, 2007.

For further readings, please visit the book's companion website.

### CHAPTER 8

# Foreign Policy and the American People

## A VICTORY FOR CONGRESSIONAL ACCOUNTABILITY

On December 6, 1977, the House Permanent Select Committee on Intelligence (HPSCI, pronounced "hip-see") convened to hear Admiral Stansfield Turner, the DCI under President Carter, present his first secret briefing to the panel on a presidential covert action approval. The Committee's chairman, Edward P. Boland (D-Massachusetts), a close confidante of the Speaker and a senior member of the House Appropriations Committee, was a force to be reckoned with.

Turner drew a prepared statement from his attaché case and took only five minutes to summarize the president's statement in support of the covert action, a briefing required by law since passage of the Hughes-Ryan Act in 1974. When Turner stopped, silence filled the room.

Jordan's King Abdullah meets with members of the Senate Appropriations Committee at the US Capitol on April 24, 2013.

The lawmakers at first assumed he was simply pausing for a sip of water. The Admiral slowly looked at each of the Committee members and grinned. "That's it," he said.

Representative Roman Mazzoli (D-Kentucky), a junior member of the Committee, cleared his throat and began to pick apart the covert action; in his view, the target was an insignificant country, the operation cost too much, and the admiral's briefing had been vague. Turner stared at the notebook in front of him. When Mazzoli finished, Turner offered a spirited rebuttal. Mazzoli remained skeptical, however, and initiated another round of questions.

Chairman Boland interrupted Mazzoli. "I don't want any adversary proceedings between this Committee and the intelligence agencies," he said and abruptly adjourned the meeting. Turner left the room wreathed in smiles.

A few weeks later the DCI returned for another covert action briefing, only to find on the Committee premises a "recorder." This individual, a stenographer who held a security clearance like everyone else in the room, was present to record everything said by the DCI. Turner eyed the man for a minute; then, to everyone's surprise, he asked Boland to dismiss the recorder from the room. Turner wanted no "outsiders"

**LEARNING OBJECTIVES AND CONSTITUTIONAL ISSUES**

**By the end of this chapter, you will be able to:**

- *Evaluate the relevance of public opinion in the shaping of American foreign policy.*
- *Explain how lawmakers decide what foreign policy options to support.*
- *Describe the influence of interest groups in determining foreign policy outcomes.*
- *Describe the role of individuals in foreign policy making and how psychological pressures can affect their deliberations.*
- *Explain the value of operation codes as a means for understanding foreign policy decisions.*

**THIS CHAPTER RAISES THE FOLLOWING CONSTITUTIONAL QUESTIONS:**

- The Constitution begins with the words "We, the People of the United States," but public opinion is nowhere directly mentioned in the document. Nevertheless, the founders embraced democratic principles far beyond what any other country at the time was willing to accept. In what ways did their adoption of a Madisonian system of checks and balances, as well as separated institutions, aid or hinder the ability of citizens to make their views known in the conduct of foreign policy?

- Madison placed great stock in the idea of multiple centers of power in government, which he discussed at length in *Federalist Paper* No. 10. Has this led to an excessive number of power centers—a proliferation of interest groups—that hinder the careful fashioning of foreign policy by experts in the bureaucracy? Are the poor, bereft of the resources needed to organize and lobby, left out of this system of influence?

- Individuals in high office often interpret the Constitution and foreign policy powers in different ways. To what extent should presidents and other key officials be allowed to engage in interpretations that may enhance their own constitutional authorities? Does the rule of law, along with judicial decisions made since 1787, limit—or even exclude—individual interpretations? Should they?

privy to his briefing. For what seemed like a full minute, only the hum of neon lights on the ceiling disturbed the tomb-like silence of the room.

"All right," Boland said at last. "We'll dispense with the recorder."

Les Aspin (D-Wisconsin), another fearless junior member, immediately objected to Boland's decision, insisting that the DCI's statement alone was insufficient. More important would be his follow-up responses to questions, which needed to be recorded verbatim. "I would like a roll-call vote on this, Mr. Chairman," Aspin concluded. A crisp "second" came from Mazzoli. Aspin and his sidekick had just picked a fight with a House heavyweight. Boland's face turned crimson, angered by this challenge to his authority; but he ordered the Committee clerk to poll the members present.

When the tally ended, Aspin had won the right for HPSCI to have a recorder present—by the margin of a single vote (6-to-5). Against his will, Chairman Boland had been forced into a more serious form of intelligence oversight, one that would allow lawmakers the opportunity to monitor the ongoing performance of the secret agencies in light of promises made by the DCI during Committee briefings.[1] As the confrontation with Chairman Boland illustrates, individuals can make a difference in the drama of American foreign policy—in this case, Aspin and Mazzoli holding the President and the CIA more accountable for covert actions. Personalities matter.

"Political science without biography," observed political scientist Harold Lasswell, "is a form of taxidermy." A pioneer in the analysis of personality and politics, he understood that although a knowledge of political institutions was important to the study of public policy, so was the behavior of individuals, whether in public opinion polls, in the voting booth, as members of pressure groups, or in high office.  ∼

# PUBLIC OPINION AND AMERICAN FOREIGN POLICY

It has been said that public opinion is like the castle ghost: no one has ever seen it, but everyone is scared of it. Although indeed often ghostlike in its elusiveness, the public does express itself with a palpable voice on election day. Elections seldom turn on issues of foreign policy, though, unless the nation is at war. Voters are usually most concerned about the state of the domestic economy: basic pocketbook issues, such as the level of unemployment or inflation. While the ballot box remains the most crucial means of public expression in a democracy, few successful politicians have been prepared simply to ignore voters in between elections.

## Democracy versus Demoscopy

Sometimes elected officials, who may have access to secret information unavailable to the general public, must make foreign policy decisions that they believe are best for the country—even if these decisions may be unpopular. "Democracy is not equivalent to demoscopy [the scientific analysis of public opinion polls]," declared West German chancellor Helmut Kohl in defending his government's acceptance of American intermediate-range nuclear missiles on German soil in 1983, despite the fact that polls indicated overwhelming public opposition in his country toward hosting these weapons.[2] Political leaders in the United States have found this distinction valid as well. "Men of integrity find it necessary, from time to time, to act contrary to public opinion," wrote John F. Kennedy. "The true democracy . . . puts its faith in the people—faith that the people will not condemn those whose devotion to principle leads them to an unpopular course."[3] In deciding on foreign policy, how have presidents and lawmakers coped with this tension between devotion to principle and a healthy respect for the opinions of constituents?

## The President and Public Opinion

Most of the time, the American people remain in a state of ignorance about the details of international affairs.[4] Important US-Canadian trade negotiations, for example, pass virtually unnoticed by most citizens. Only 35 percent of Americans possess a passport (compared to 80 percent in the United Kingdom); and in the 2012 presidential election, only 4 percent of the American public indicated in a national survey that foreign policy was important in the election.[5] Even when the public is aroused, as when the Nixon administration expanded the Vietnam war into Cambodia in 1970, opinion can be so diverse and conflicting that no clear signal emerges from the public. Public opinion was divided, too, on the wisdom of US involvement in a Libyan civil war in 2011 during the Arab Spring uprisings. As a result of such opinion diversity, policy makers are usually free to rely on their own personal judgments.

Although most voters have little specific information about foreign affairs, from time to time they express meaningful views on "overall policy directions."[6] In 1968, for example, Americans made plain enough their dislike for President Johnson's Vietnam War policies. Johnson's precipitous decline in the polls contributed heavily to his decision that year to withdraw his bid for a second term. With the beginning of a recession in 2008, the attention of the American public was riveted on economic issues, including concern about the effects on US prosperity of foreign economic developments (especially the fairness of Chinese trade practices). Political scientist V. O. Key Jr. reached the conclusion that the nation's electorate is in fact "responsible," in the sense of being able to follow international and domestic affairs closely enough to evaluate the nation's overall policy directions.[7]

Two conditions are most likely to stir an awakening of public opinion in the United States: first, prolonged military conflict with no victory in sight; and second, bleak economic news—inflation, rising interest rates, a dramatic plunge in the stock market, high unemployment (which hovered between 8 and 10 percent during Barack Obama's first term in office), an unfavorable Consumer Price Index (CPI), and above all a depression or recession. The lives of US soldiers overseas and the family checkbook—peace and prosperity: these are the matters that count the most in the public eye. War-induced inflation, coupled with the spiraling loss of American lives in Vietnam, cost Lyndon Johnson the presidency in 1968. Confronted by wars in Iraq and Afghanistan, as well as a deep recession, Obama's standing in the public opinion polls began to slide soon after he entered office. He was criticized for failing to offer an "overarching narrative" of reform, or to knit together the country with a "powerful vision" of how to pull America out of the recession. In response, the President quickly ended America's involvement in Iraq, bolstered the US presence in Afghanistan to stabilize the situation there before drawing down the troop numbers in 2013–2014, and focused on a strategy of leaving a "light footprint" elsewhere in the world.[8]

A question of particular interest to students of international affairs is how the public responds, as indicated by opinion polls, to the most extreme form of foreign policy power: the use of overt military force. The **rally-round-the-flag hypothesis** provides one answer. This hypothesis states that *a perceived threat to the United States and its citizens will result in a display by the American public of strong patriotic support for the president, sending the standing of the chief executive sharply upward in opinion ratings on job performance.* This rallying response seems to occur, though, only during certain kinds of events. They must be international in nature (domestic political events remain too divisive in most cases for a clear rally phenomenon, even in times of crisis); they must directly involve the United States and, therefore, the president; and they must be "specific, dramatic, and sharply focused."[9]

Six types of international events meet these criteria. They must involve one or more of the following conditions: a rapid military intervention by the United States abroad—say, in Korea in 1950, Grenada in 1983, and Afghanistan in 2001; significant military developments in an ongoing war, such as the Gulf of Tonkin incident in 1964; major diplomatic initiatives, as with the Truman Doctrine in 1947; startling new technological developments abroad that threaten the United States, such as the launching of the Soviet satellite "Sputnik" in 1957; a summit conference among leading nations because of wide media coverage such high-level meetings attract; and a major terrorist attack against Americans at home or abroad.

Instances of the rally response are abundant (see the examples in Table 8.1). Among the most conspicuous is the military confrontation in Cambodia in 1975. Use of the Marines in an abortive rescue attempt of American sailors aboard the *Mayaguez* led to an eleven-point rise in President Ford's standing in the polls. The shooting down of the American U-2 plane by the Soviets in 1960 pushed President Eisenhower three points upward in the polls. The presidentially ordered landing of Marines into Lebanon in 1958, and into the Dominican Republic in 1965, stimulated a rise of six percentage points each for Presidents Eisenhower and Johnson, respectively. The Grenada invasion in 1983 boosted President Reagan's standing in the polls by four percentage points.

In 2003, the public expressed approval of President George W. Bush's invasion of Iraq by a margin of about 2-to-1. Two years later, though, when more information about the war's planning became available to the public, a majority of the respondents to a Gallup poll expressed a belief that the Bush administration had deliberately misled the public into thinking Iraq possessed WMDs that might be used against the United States.[10] What researchers find most intriguing about the rally hypothesis is its apparent validity regardless of how poorly the president handles a crisis. Why is it, asks a researcher, that "invariably, the popular response to a president during [an] international crisis is favorable, regardless of the wisdom of the policies [the White House] pursues"?[11] After all, the *Mayaguez* "rescue" could hardly be considered a successful use of force by President Ford in 1975: thirty-eight Marines died, fifty more were wounded, and no one was rescued.

Unwilling to accept the rally hypothesis at face value, or the argument that the rally response is simply an outpouring of patriotic sentiment from the public, political scientists have examined the phenomenon more closely. Skepticism toward the conventional explanations grew out of a series of events that fit the assumed rally criteria but led to a *decline* in presidential standing in the polls. For example, the *Pueblo* incident of January 23, 1968, when North Korea captured a US spy ship off its coastline, has some similarity to the *Mayaguez* incident; however, the public displayed no rallying response in support of President Johnson during the *Pueblo* crisis. Moreover, contrary to the US military interventions in Lebanon (1958) and the Dominican Republic (1965), the Cambodian intervention in 1970 afforded Nixon only a modest rise in the polls (barely one percentage point, as displayed in Table 8.1).

## Opinion Leadership

Of sixty-five instances of "rally events" examined by researchers between 1947 and 1986, forty-two led to an increase in presidential popularity, as the rally hypothesis would predict.[12] But what about the other twenty-three cases, which were clearly significant events—six involved major military encounters in an ongoing war? The missing ingredient in the rally hypothesis, according to the **opinion-leadership hypothesis**, may be the availability of information to the public that could call into question the merits of a presidential decision.[13] Until technological advances—CNN, YouTube, twittering, text messaging—introduced the 24-hour news cycle, it was often the case that in many crises overseas, the inattentive public and, for that matter, even attentive public opinion leaders in Congress and elsewhere, had little access to information about fast-breaking events. In the *Mayaguez* rescue, for instance, most people remained unaware of the details of the operation until it was well over.

*Without reliable information, individuals who might be critical of the president—say, congressional leaders in the opposition party—are in a weak position to offer a persuasive critique; therefore, they are inclined to be supportive, or at least they remain quiescent.* And when these opinion leaders remain silent, the general public has no alternative source of information or guidance—cues—from respected officials as to why they should question a presidential decision. Safe from criticism, for the time being at any rate, the White House decision gains public support, thanks to its monopoly over information about unfolding events. "A lack of critical opinion leadership can outweigh even relatively unambiguous evidence of policy failure and hence pave the way for positive evaluations of presidential performance," conclude Brody and Shapiro. They add: "A corollary of this hypothesis is that when opinion leadership is both divided and vocal such that it offers contradictory evaluations of presidential performance, the public's

| PRESIDENT AND EVENT | PERCENT CHANGE IN APPROVAL |
|---|---|
| *Eisenhower* | |
| U.S. Marines land in Lebanon (July 1958) | +6 |
| U-2 shot down by Soviets; Paris summit (May 1960) | +3 |
| *Kennedy* | |
| Bay of Pigs incident (April 1961) | +5 |
| Cuban missile crisis (October 1962) | +12 |
| *Johnson* | |
| Gulf of Tonkin incident (August 1964) | −5 |
| Invasion of Dominican Republic (April–May 1965) | +6 |
| *Pueblo* incident (January 1968) | −7 |
| Tet Offensive; U.S. embassy invaded (January–February 1968) | −7 |
| *Nixon* | |
| Invasion of Cambodia (May 1970) | +1 |
| *Ford* | |
| *Mayaguez* incident (June 1975) | +11 |
| *Reagan* | |
| Bombing of Marine compound in Beirut; invasion of Grenada (October 1983) | +4 |
| Iran-*contra* affair (November 1986) | −21 |

*Table 8.1*
Selected Rally Events in American Foreign Policy, 1958–1986

SOURCE: *Drawn from Richard A. Brody and Catherine R. Shapiro, "A Reconsideration of the Rally Phenomenon in Public Opinion," in Samuel Long, ed.,* Political Behavior Annual, *Vol. 2 (Boulder, CO, and London: Westview, 1989), pp. 85–86.*

response will be tied in greater measure to the indications of policy success or failure *evinced by the events* themselves."[14] The digital age and access to instantaneous information from around the world facilitate the ability of the public to know about what is going on in the world—often displayed in vivid YouTube and Twitter pictures—and, therefore, to reach their own judgments without awaiting delayed cues from policy elites. In this sense, Facebook and other social networks have helped to "democratize" foreign policy.

## Congress and Public Opinion

Over the past several decades, Congress has been more involved in decisions of foreign policy than was the case before the Vietnam War. What can be said about the relationship between lawmakers and public opinion on foreign policy? Political theorists often discuss this subject in terms of a classic dichotomy: on the one hand, a member of Congress may be a "trustee" reaching decisions strictly on the basis of his or her own judgment; or, on the other hand, the lawmaker may behave as an "instructed delegate" who attempts to mirror the opinion of constituents back home. While in the Senate, John F. Kennedy (D-Massachusetts) wrote derisively about those lawmakers content simply to *serve as "a seismograph recording shifts in popular opinion."*[15] Centuries earlier, the British conservative Edmund Burke, in a speech to his constituents at Bristol in 1774, also dismissed this **instructed-delegate model of representation** with a famous rebuke: "Your representative owes you, not his industry only, but his judgment; and he betrays, instead of serving you, if he sacrifices it to your opinion."[16]

Despite the acclaim for this *independent stance that rises above the whims of public opinion*, often referred to as the **Burkean model of representation**, most elected officials in the United States read the tea leaves of public opinion as best they can. Lawmakers on Capitol Hill, as well as White House officials, try to gauge "en masse" or "grass roots" opinion on foreign policy in a variety of ways, including a close reading of communications from constituents (whether old fashioned mail or new social media), visits from citizens, travels around their respective districts or states, op-eds and letters to the editor in the state newspapers, and opinion polls.

Public opinion polls usually rank last as a source of constituency opinion. Part of the problem is the broad focus of polls. With some exceptions (such as the statewide Field Poll in California), they are national or regional in scope; therefore, members of Congress must make a considerable extrapolation to assume the opinions on foreign affairs expressed in these surveys reflect the views held by citizens in their smaller constituencies. Some representatives conduct their own polls; but because accurate, scientific surveying is expensive, most simply send out unsophisticated questionnaires to a small percentage of citizens on their mailing lists. The response rates are uniformly low and unreliable. Although lawmakers and presidents do keep track of available polls—even if they are inclined to be skeptical about their validity for their constituency—researchers consistently confirm that most members of Congress believe that "their mail provides them with the single best indicator of constituent attitudes on legislative issues." The use by constituents of e-mails, text messaging, and twittering has added to this inflow of digital age "mail" that remains so important for lawmakers in gauging opinion from back home.[17] The question of how members of Congress measure the will of their constituents may be irrelevant most of the time, though, since "the people" seldom articulate their policy views in the mail or any other way.[18]

In the 1960s, political scientists Miller and Stokes suggested an updated twist to the Burkean model: a **presidential deference model of representation**. Writing in the era before the Vietnam War, they argued that *in the case of foreign policy, lawmakers are freed from constituent pressures because on such matters the public is ill informed and inattentive. Yet, rather than exercise their own judgment in a Burkean fashion, lawmakers* *were inclined to defer to presidential leadership*—a kind of "father knows best" approach to foreign policy.[19] According to the Constitution, US senators are expected to give their "advice and consent." Yet, as James M. Lindsay observes, the 1950s and 1960s were "a time of 'consent without advice,' as a Senate largely followed the president on foreign policy."[20] So did the House.

In the decades since it was proposed, this model of presidential deference has remained alive and well under some circumstances, as in 2013 when a narrow majority of lawmakers in the House of Representatives supported the controversial broad gathering of data by the National Security Agency on the telephone contacts of US citizens. Yet members of Congress have grown far less trustful of White House leadership since the failed war in Vietnam, along with the Watergate scandal, domestic spy scandals, the Iran-*contra* affair, and the controversial wars in Iraq and Afghanistan. Lindsay views this decline in presidential deference as a trend more in line with the philosophy of the Constitution. The intuition of the founders, he points out, "was not that giving the Senate a say would guarantee that the country would always choose wisely. It was instead that it would decrease the chances that the country would choose unwisely. They have yet to be proven wrong."[21] These words apply to the House as well. This pooling of policy knowledge and responsibility by the presidency and the two chambers of Congress is the genius of power-sharing governance envisioned by James Madison and his colleagues.

Some lawmakers have recently turned to another method for making decisions on foreign policy: the **party loyalty model of representation**, whereby they simply *vote along party lines*. For more than two centuries, such voting was rare in the US Congress; but, starting in the early 1990s, partisanship became more shrill on Capitol Hill and members have increasingly voted with their party colleagues. Republicans in Congress are especially inclined to emphasize the importance of party loyalty, indeed to the point where they have been charged by two leading experts on Congress, Mann and Ornstein, with making politics on Capitol Hill rigid and ideological.[22] Strictly enforced voting by this model—a kind of tribal warfare in Congress along party lines, in lieu of the bargaining and compromise that once characterize the legislative process in the United States—would sound the death knell for negotiating between Democrats and Republicans and make it almost impossible for a president of one party to work amicably with congressional chambers controlled by the other party, as the Democratic president Obama discovered in his dealings with a GOP-led, strongly ideological House.

President Woodrow Wilson leaving the Quai d'Orsay at the start of the Paris Peace Conference known as the Treaty of Versailles. At these talks, diplomats signed a peace treaty ending the First World War and establishing the League of Nations. Wilson appealed to American public opinion for support of the League, but failed.

### Vox Populi

In light of the inattention paid by most citizens to international affairs, one might be tempted to dismiss public opinion—the "voice of the people" (or *vox populi* in Latin)—altogether as an inconsequential influence on American foreign policy. The influential journalist Walter Lippmann scoffed at the notion that the public ought to play a role in *US foreign policy deliberations*; such delicate matters, he argued, *should be left to the pros—the professional diplomats and the national security experts.*[23] In contrast to this **Lippmann school of thought on public opinion**, which has been widely supported by realists like George Kennan, idealists believe in the value of public opinion as a restraint on leaders, especially when it comes to checking their appetites for war.

Everett C. Ladd, who specializes in the study of public opinion, concludes that the realists tend to overstate their case. "The point isn't that the heads of 'We the People' are full of Jell-O and that they should be ignored," he writes. "The public brings to the controversy some basic values and expectations that are firm enough."[24] Here is the hard lesson that President Johnson learned from the war in Vietnam. Most of the time, the public's views on foreign affairs will be as invisible as the castle ghost; but, when officials go beyond the boundaries of what the people find acceptable, here is a ghost that can become quite real for officials who hope to stand for reelection.

Since the end of the Cold War, public opinion on foreign policy has risen in importance. White House manipulation of information is less easily managed with the many nonmilitary issues that now crowd the foreign policy agenda, such as international trade balances, global impoverishment, environmental degradation, and immigration flows in a world of porous boundaries. As political scientist Ole Holsti noted more than twenty years ago, "Not only are the latter typically resolved over a longer time period—providing greater opportunities for the public, pressure groups, the media, and Congress to play a significant role—but they also tend to be more resistant to claims that the needs for secrecy, flexibility, and speed of action make it both necessary and legitimate for the executive to have a relatively free hand."[25] In the same era, Richard J. Barnet anticipated this rise in the importance of the public in foreign policy decisions. "Unlike traditional war planning and war-prevention strategies, the national security tasks of the new century call for much greater decentralization," he maintained, "and much greater participation of the population of the whole."[26] The existence of the Internet and other modern forms of communication has accelerated this participation.

Bruce W. Jentleson adds another wrinkle to the debate over the relationship between the public and foreign policy decisions. He argues that public support for the use of military force abroad depends on "the principal policy objective for which force is used." Sometimes the United States employs military force to coerce restraint by an adversary; at other times, the goal is to bring about internal political change within another nation, either in support of a friendly regime or faction or in opposition to an unfriendly regime of faction. Setting aside the quick-strike military operations like Grenada and Panama during the Reagan and George H. W. Bush years, toward which the public almost always responds favorably, Jentleson maintains that "the American public is much more likely to support the use of force for the restraint rather than the remaking of other governments."[27] He questions "the traditional view of the public as boorish, overreactive, and generally the bane of those who would pursue an effective foreign policy." Instead, he continues, "Americans do appear to have a much more pragmatic sense of strategy than they are given credit for—an approach to the world that is actually 'pretty prudent' when it comes to the use of military force . . . a very different portrait than the 'know-nothingist' portrayal found in much of the literature on public opinion and foreign policy."[28]

In the twenty years since Jentleson made these observations, the American public has continued to display prudence in their opinions on foreign policy. For example, they supported the invasion of Iraq in 2003 when told by the second Bush administration that the United States was threatened by WMDs in the hands of Saddam Hussein; then when it was discovered after the invasion that no WMDs existed, the public began to turn against the war. Similarly in Afghanistan, the public supported the hunt for Al Qaeda terrorists behind the 9/11 attacks, but cooled on the war after the host of the terrorists—the Taliban regime—was routed and Al Qaeda vanished into the mountains of Afghanistan and Pakistan.[29]

## INTEREST GROUPS AND AMERICAN FOREIGN POLICY

On most occasions, though, the foreign policy views of the general public are less likely to be taken into account day by day than are the views of citizens who have organized themselves into pressure groups for promoting their interests. Here are "the people" I examine next.

An astonishing array of interest (or pressure) groups in the United States attempts to influence foreign policy. They enjoy the constitutional right to advocate their interests in the councils of power; the First Amendment to the Constitution grants Americans the privilege "peaceably to assemble, and to petition the Government for a redress of grievances." Sometimes the goals of a group receive disproportionate attention through the activism of high-profile individuals, including Hollywood stars. In 2012, for example, Washington, DC police arrested actor George Clooney in front of the Sudanese embassy as he protested a hunger crisis in that North African nation. In 2003, actress Angelina Jolie traveled to war-torn Afghanistan and other nations in the Middle East and Southwest Asia, speaking as a UN Goodwill Ambassador on behalf of peace and human rights. The United Nations Correspondents Association presented her with its inaugural "Citizen of the World Award" and the International Rescue Committee named her the recipient of its Freedom Award.

A review of citizen groups with foreign policy objectives reveals that every conceivable interest seems to be represented, including such organizations as Amnesty International; International League for Human Rights; Women's International League for Peace and Freedom; Council for a Livable World; and the Committee for a Sane Nuclear Policy. Also included are oil companies, textile industries, veterans, peace movements, trade associations, shipping interests, airline interests, farmers, human rights activists, animal rights advocates—the list goes on.

These groups hope to convince decision makers to embrace the goals of their members, say, American farmers who seek assistance in selling their surplus wheat, corn, and potato crops overseas. Or groups may seek to fulfill political and ideological objectives, such as support for the existence of Israel, independence for Tibet, or freedom for political dissidents in China. The range of goals and the lobbying methods are as diverse as the groups themselves. Not only do legitimate lobbyists and the people they represent have a right to be heard, but many of them bring to the government useful information and opinions that can elevate the quality of policy deliberations and decisions. For decades, scholarly studies on lobbying in Washington have concluded that they are an excellent source of facts and ideas for policy makers who seek to understand the problems confronting the nation and their constituents.[30]

Yet definite inequities exist in the system of American foreign policy lobbying. Most of the time, well-heeled corporations—with their high-profile lobbyists (often former members of Congress and former ambassadors), large expense accounts, and sizable treasure chest of campaign funds—enjoy far greater success in bringing their case to top officials in Washington than small groups operating on a shoestring budget. A Supreme Court case known as *Citizens United v. Federal Election Commission* made it possible, as President Obama noted unhappily in his State of the Union address in 2010, "for special interests—including foreign companies—to spend without limit in our elections." In contrast, Republican lawmakers praised the Court decision, viewing the case as a victory for free speech and corporate rights against excessive government regulations.[31]

Sometimes even rich corporations are unsuccessful in lobbying, as was Westinghouse International's efforts to obtain government subsidies for constructing nuclear reprocessing plants at home and abroad. During the Carter administration, the corporation lobbied the government to fund a plant in South Carolina, but the President decided the proposal was too expensive. He was also against letting Westinghouse build reprocessing plants overseas, even though the company would have reaped high profits. The White House argued that the reprocessing of spent fuels would encourage the proliferation of nuclear weapons. When the United States turned down Brazil's request for a reprocessing plant, Germany stepped into the void, promising to put in place safeguards against misuse of the spent fuel for weapons building. The George W. Bush administration initially proposed a resumption of US corporate involvement in reprocessing at home and abroad. The administration retreated from this position, though, when the National Research Council reported that going in this direction was not economically justifiable. The Obama administration scrapped the Bush proposal altogether.[32]

## Foreign Lobbies

Some of the lobbyists that descend on Washington with foreign policy demands represent the interests of other nations. A brief look at a few of the major foreign policy lobbying groups in the United States provides a sense of their diversity. The American

Jewish community has been successful in lobbying the US government for large sums of foreign aid earmarked for Israel, indeed funding levels "without precedent in international philanthropy," as Zbigniew Brzezinski noted during the 1980s.[33] Large caches of weapons are also sold at special rates to the Israelis—one of the grievances enumerated by Al Qaeda for its attacks against the United States in 2001.[34] The Jewish community's chief lobbying arm is the **American Israel Public Affairs Committee (AIPAC)**, which *works with forty-seven allied organizations around the country under the umbrella of the Council of Presidents of Major American Jewish Organizations.* These organizations are in alliance with a dozen other groups with a pro-Israeli agenda. The AIPAC staff numbers over one hundred; its membership includes some 55,000 households; and its budget exceeds $15 million.[35] The organization does not provide campaign funding to members of Congress directly; however, its reports on the voting records of lawmakers strongly influence Jewish donors. Most of the pro-Israel groups skillfully channel campaign contributions directly to key members of Congress, especially those on the foreign affairs, armed services, and appropriations committees, and to the president; and, in presidential election years, to those pro-Israel political candidates who seem to have a good chance of winning the White House.

This careful nurturing of the powerful by AIPAC and its allies pays off. The American aid package to Israel is worth over $3 billion annually, the largest for any country until Afghanistan took precedence in recent years.[36] When Egypt agreed to a peace treaty with Israel in 1979, it found itself amply rewarded by becoming second on the list of US aid recipients at the time, to the tune of $2.3 billion annually. In 1984, the United States decided to provide outright economic and military grants to Israel instead of loans, so that Israel would not have to pay back anything. Again, in 1990, lobbyists pushed a reluctant Bush administration into providing a $650 million grant to Israel, on grounds that support for Operation Desert Storm in the Persian Gulf had cost the Israelis that much. Not all this success is attributable singularly to the lobbying prowess of AIPAC, considerable as that may be. Policy makers are pleased to have a pro-US stalwart like Israel in the Middle East. Moreover, most Americans are sympathetic to the claim of Israel—a fellow democracy—for the right of self-determination in a region of hostile nations; Americans are prepared as a matter of fairness to help this small country protect itself with sophisticated US weaponry against opponents vastly superior in number.[37]

Even so, Israel sometimes loses its bid for favorable treatment in Washington's corridors of power. Occasionally US officials, sensitive to the dependence of America and its allies on Arab oil and appreciative of the help from nations like Saudi Arabia and Jordan in maintaining peace in the Middle East, will sell advanced weaponry to Israel's opponents despite AIPAC's loud objections. An example involved the sale of AWACS (Airborne Warning and Control System), a modern radar-equipped intelligence aircraft, to Saudi Arabia in 1980. The Saudis told American officials they wished to use the plane as part of their defense against a Soviet attack, but Israelis feared it might be used some day in a war against them. In 1985 and 1986, however, AIPAC was instrumental in blocking congressional support for the sale of forty F-15 jet fighters and 800 Stinger missiles to the Saudis, who then took their $25 billion shopping list to the United Kingdom, where the pro-Israeli lobby is weaker.[38]

American sympathies for the Israeli cause diminished somewhat near the end of the Cold War, as US television news cameras revealed instances of brutality directed toward Palestinians (including women and children) by Israeli soldiers attempting to quell rock throwing and other manifestations of unrest in disputed territories. By and large, though, Israel has remained the most important ally of the United States in the Middle East—although relations became strained in 2010 when, under the Obama administration, the United States completed one of its largest arms deals in history by selling Saudi Arabia $60 billion worth of military equipment. The package included eighty-four new F-15 fighter jets, upgrades to 70 existing Saudi F-15s, 190 Apache Black Hawk, and Little Bird attack helicopters, as well as bomb and delivery systems. Israeli officials were "not pleased," reported the Associated Press.[39] One could understand why: the deal threatened to shift the region's balance of power in the Saudi direction.

The fortunes of AIPAC have been helped by Jews in important political positions in the American government, such as the late Jacob Javits (D-New York), who served with distinction on the Senate Foreign Relations Committee for years; Senator Joe Lieberman (D-Connecticut), the vice presidential candidate for the Democrats in 2000 (who later became an Independent); Senator Dianne Feinstein (D-California), Chair of the Senate Select Committee on Intelligence; and, among others, Chuck Schumer (D-New York), another influential senator.

The Greek-American lobby has proven to be effective as well and Greece is ranked consistently among the top three or four recipients of US foreign aid over the years. It has benefitted by having Greek Americans in high office, such as one of the most important members of the Foreign Relations Committee from the 1980s until 2007, Senator Paul Sarbanes (D-Maryland), and, more recently, Senator Olympia Snowe (R-New Hampshire). Another Greek American of prominence was DCI George Tenet (1997–2004). Not to be outdone, Turkey—often a bitter rival of Greece in Europe and in Washington, DC—has established an impressive lobbying effort of its own in the United States. The Turkish embassy, a magnificent building along Embassy Row in Washington (built at the turn of the 20th century by the inventor of the bottle cap), is the site of sumptuous feasts hosted by Turkish diplomats as part of their effort to win friends among the powerful in the nation's capital. The Indian embassy is famous, as well, for its lavish banquets for lawmakers and their aides.

The Washington skies have been further brightened by additional constellations of foreign lobbies that, until the end of the Cold War in 1990, had been only a distant twinkle. Both China and Taiwan have stepped up their attention to Washington lobbying. Arab nations, as well, have hired well-connected former government officials who are able to open the right doors—and the public purse strings—on their behalf. By paying former members of Congress substantial salaries for providing access to their erstwhile colleagues on Capitol Hill and in the executive branch, these and other foreign countries have been able to gain face time to promote their policies before highly placed American decision makers. Former chairs of the Foreign Relations Committee and other key foreign policy panels on the Hill, as well as former cabinet secretaries, CIA directors, and ambassadors, are prepared to help outsiders enter the inner sanctums of Capitol Hill, the White House, and the Departments of State, Defense, Treasury and other places where these former government officials have maintained lucrative contacts.

## A Kaleidoscope of Domestic Pressures

Several groups that are thought of as pressure groups with a domestic agenda can also have an effect on foreign policy. The National Rifle Association (NRA), for example, is concerned mainly with protecting the rights of Americans to bear arms; yet its success in loosening gun laws in the United States has made it easier for Mexican bandits to purchase weapons in Arizona, causing strife south of the US border and weakening the government of one of America's leading trade partners. The Religious Right has been a potent domestic force, too, especially in swaying the outcome of elections in the southern part of the United States; but, again, its agenda goes beyond domestic cultural and social issues to include the targeting for defeat of any lawmaker who fails to display an appropriately conservative view on American foreign policy objectives, such as those members of Congress who supported détente with the Soviet Union, endorsed the "give away" of the Panama Canal during the Cold War, or opposed the invasion of Iraq in 2003.[40]

Some altruistic groups within the United States are less concerned about the fortunes of a particular interest at home or helping a foreign government lobby in Washington than they are promoting the well-being of needy people everywhere in the world. The group known as Advancing Human Rights, for example, is composed of "cyberactivists" who use the Internet to advise online insurgents abroad about how to throw off the shackles of authoritarian governments.[41] At times, the humanitarian goals of some groups can run counter to the official policy of the US government. Such a conflict occurred in 1986 with the Boston-based, private relief organization Oxfam America. This group wanted to ship to nongovernment organizations in Nicaragua some $41,000 worth of supplies, including hammers, chain saws, water pipes, shovels, wrenches, rakes, seeds, and books on agriculture. The purpose, according to the group's director, was to alleviate food shortages in a country ravaged by civil war. A year earlier, however, the Reagan administration had instituted a trade embargo against Nicaragua as part of its squeeze on the supposedly Marxist-oriented Sandinista regime. The administration refused permission for Oxfam to ship the materials. "We are dealing with the politics of hunger," complained an Oxfam official. "This is a clear example of the government playing politics with the poor overseas."[42]

In 2012, a polio vaccination team sent into Pakistan had more than a dual purpose. It also spied for the CIA in hopes of discovering where Osama bin Laden was hiding. This espionage may have helped confirm his whereabouts in the city of Abbottabad (near the capital city of Islamabad); however, locals discovered the ruse and chased away legitimate vaccinators in the area, accusing them of further espionage. On one hand, the CIA operation may have helped the US government confirm the location of the Al Qaeda leader; but, on the other hand, an unfortunate result was to undermine the efforts of American and other humanitarian groups in their efforts to eradicate polio from Pakistan.[43]

A *long-established organization in the United States with foreign policy interests* is the **Council on Foreign Relations (CFR)**, an association of well-educated, affluent, and mainly east coast members. Founded in 1921 and supported by leading US foundations and corporations, the CFR has become a significant recruitment reservoir for top-level foreign policy officials of both major parties. It also publishes the widely read journal *Foreign Affairs*, as well as numerous reports and studies, several of which are commissioned by the government. With its publications and study groups, the Council attempts to lobby decision makers through the art of intellectual reasoning. The CFR has been criticized by outsiders, and an occasional insider, for its tepid writings and its often hawkish outlook.[44] During the Vietnam war, its members were largely in support of a strong US combat role, down to the last gasp of retreat, although in recent years its membership has been younger and somewhat less tied to the status quo. Its president, Richard N. Haass, has been a regular on television talk shows, where he has criticized Democrats and Republicans alike for failing to address what he views as America's most important foreign policy challenge: putting the US economic house in order so the nation will have the funding necessary to conduct relations abroad.[45]

Significant as lobbying interests, too, have been the proliferation of so-called **non-state actors**, that is, various *global corporations and international organizations operating outside the framework of national governments*. In the 1960s, the US corporation International Telephone and Telegraph (ITT) demonstrated its clout at the White House by applying strong direct pressure on the Nixon administration to intervene on its behalf in Chile. The corporation wanted the government to overthrow the socialist leader, Salvador Allende, who might have nationalized its holdings in Chile. As a means for encouraging adoption of an anti-Allende policy by the Nixon administration, ITT offered a satchel filled with $1 million of its own funds for use by the CIA in carrying out the operation, an extreme form of "lobbying."[46]

Individual American states sometimes appear intent on adopting their own foreign policies. The California State Assembly, for instance, passed a statute in 1986 that required the state's pension system to divest itself of stocks in companies conducting business with South Africa. At the time, this law represented one of the strongest blows against apartheid delivered by any organization within the United States, involving some $11.3 billion worth of investments. Seventeen other states had already taken modest steps toward divestiture but, as the *New York Times* reported, "in the scope of its divestment legislation and the amounts involved, California's action dwarfs any previous effort in this country to use economic pressure on multinational corporations as a lever to persuade South Africa to change."[47] More recently, in 2012 Arizona and Mississippi enacted harsh immigration statutes that seemed to be in conflict with federal laws. When states formally craft their own foreign policies, the door swings open toward a defiance of the federal system of government outlined in the Constitution.[48]

Even mayors of American cities can be found pursuing their own foreign policies. Richard Barnet reported in 1990 that "more than one thousand cities in the United States are now establishing their own relations with local communities in foreign countries, including those designated as adversaries, making it possible to deal city to city on issues of trade, technical assistance, immigration, and refugees. . . . The radical reduction in the costs of transportation and communication is democratizing international relations."[49] Sam Yorty, a colorful mayor of Los Angeles, spent much of his time traveling abroad in search of markets for goods produced in his city; and Andrew Young also traveled abroad frequently when he was mayor of Atlanta, dabbling in foreign policy. In August of 1986 on a visit to Angola, for example, he hoped to find a new market for Georgia goods and he proclaimed his undying friendship to the Marxist regime there. This caused conservative interest groups in Washington, DC, to ask the mayor in newspaper letters to the editor, "Which side are you on?"[50]

Another Georgia politician, President Jimmy Carter, also discovered the potency of aroused interest groups. Conservative organizations, spurred to new heights of Cold War rhetoric by the Soviet invasion of Afghanistan in 1979, pounded away at what they perceived to be deficiencies in the President's conduct of foreign policy. Among the chorus of critical voices heard from the right during this period were the "Madison Group," a coalition of conservative lawmakers who met weekly at the Madison Hotel in Washington; the Committee for the Survival of a Free Congress; the Committee on the Present Danger; the Advanced International Studies Institute at Bethesda, Maryland; the Ethics and Public Policy Center in Washington; the Institute for Foreign Policy Analysis in Cambridge, Massachusetts; the National Strategy Information Center in New York; and the Institute for Contemporary Studies in San Francisco.[51] Several of these organizations remain alive and well, with a new object of scorn: the Obama administration.

Accompanying these groups with their focus on one foreign policy issue or another are others that are essentially domestic in their orientation but whose objectives, nonetheless, have definite implications for America's relations abroad. High on this list is the military-industrial-intelligence complex. The manufacturers of expensive weaponry and spy machines (satellites, piloted reconnaissance aircraft, drones), along with the network of consultants, think tanks, and laboratories that surround them, have a clear economic stake in maintaining a strong budget for national defense. So do politicians, labor unions, and a host of other beneficiaries in many states. The Saudi arms deal lost to Britain, referred to earlier, carried with it some 50,000 new jobs for the US weapons-manufacturing sector.

Weapons like the laser-beam shield (ballistic missile defense or BMD), advocated by the Reagan administration (the Strategic Defense Initiative, or "Star Wars") and pushed chiefly by GOP administrations since, can mean large sums of federal funds for a state's economy. Specialists at a Harvard-MIT roundtable held in 1985 agreed that laboratories engaged in the designing of a BMD—the Livermore labs in California and the Los Alamos labs in Nevada, for instance—may well represent a stronger influence in Washington over increased military expenditures than even the defense corporations.[52] The roundtable participants concluded, though, that these components of the military-industrial intelligence complex were of secondary importance for understanding the government's embrace of large US defense budgets. The more fundamental driving force during the Cold War was, in their view, the ongoing attitude of unalloyed fear and distrust toward the Soviet Union held by the American public and, at the time, fueled by the rhetoric of the Reagan administration.

Today, a driving force is the fear of terrorism, which has led to the wars in Iraq, Afghanistan, and against Al Qaeda around the world, along with record-breaking defense spending. The munitions manufacturers (for example, the companies that build drones) and the weapons laboratories (busy designing new drone missiles) have a self-interest in persuading lawmakers and presidents to spend more money to fight whatever is the latest threat to the United States, with terrorist jihadists currently in the forefront.

### A Diversity of International Pressures

In addition to the formidable array of pressure groups within the United States, the world has some 245 **intergovernmental organizations (IGOs)** and nearly 30,000 **international nongovernmental organizations (INGOs)**, many of which have an effect on the conduct of US foreign policy.[53] *Examples of IGOs include the UN, NATO, OAS, the League of Arab States (LAS), the European Economic Community (EEC), the World Health Organization (WHO), the International Labor Organization (ILO), and the International North Pacific Fisheries Commission.*

*The INGOs, which comprise about 90 percent of all international organizations, include organizations such as the International Olympic Committee, terrorist organizations, religious groups (the Roman Catholic Church, for one), professional associations (such as the global network of Doctors Without Borders), and a wide range of groups established to foster commercial relations between nations. They also include political parties,* such as the Social Democrats in Western Europe. The Social Democrats have separate parties within many of the nations of Western Europe, but they also reach across national boundaries in an attempt to maintain financial and policy ties with one another based on shared ideological interests.

## THE INDIVIDUAL AND AMERICAN FOREIGN POLICY

Often more important to foreign policy than public opinion or group opinion are the beliefs of individual decision makers. This microlevel of foreign policy analysis focuses on the behavior of individuals in high office, what international relations scholar J. David Singer referred to as the "psycho-political process" in foreign affairs.[54] "Character is a man's guiding destiny," emphasized the Greek historian Heraclitus.[55] But how is character formed? In an effort to comprehend the effects of an individual's experience and personality on decision making, scholars have turned to a wide variety of approaches and produced a rich lode of findings and hypotheses.[56]

## The Lasswellian Hypothesis

The eminent twentieth-century political scientist Harold Lasswell was sensitive to the influence that early, private events in the life of a political leader could exert on his or her later public decisions. He defined "political man" (*homo politicus*) as a power seeker, driven primarily by a desire to overcome feelings of inferiority engendered by unpleasant experiences in early life. "Power," Lasswell wrote, "is expected to overcome low estimates of the self."[57] With obvious Freudian antecedents, he attempted to *link the low self-esteem of the youth to power seeking in the adult.* The causal chain of the **Lasswell hypothesis** is depicted in Figure 8.1.

Employing this hypothesis, studies have explored the life of Woodrow Wilson, tracing back his intransigence with senators over the League of Nations proposal to his early childhood relationship with his father, a prominent clergyman in Virginia.[58] In odd emotional outbursts, Wilson refused to compromise with the Senate and especially with Henry Cabot Lodge (R-Massachusetts), the Chairman of the Foreign Relations Committee. Searching through his early record, scholars find evidence of low self-esteem in the young Wilson. Cowed by a domineering father, Wilson seemed stymied in his maturation, fearful that he might be unable to reach the lofty expectations his father had set for him.

According to this research, Wilson later sought political power as a means for proving his worthiness to himself and to his father. When confronted by opponents like Lodge, Wilson lashed out irrationally at what he perceived to be a manifestation of attempts to dominate him, just as his father had done. Through Lodge and other enemy "fathers," Wilson—now a powerful adult figure—had the opportunity to settle the score, indirectly, with his real father. This "victory," as Lasswell predicted, gave Wilson only a fleeting sensation of euphoria before the more deeply seeded feelings of inferiority once again flooded his psyche. This cycle would begin anew, as Wilson set out to prove his worth against the next manifestation of that source of his childhood frustration and anxiety: the domineering father figure. As Lasswell observed, in an approving comment on this line of research, "[It calls] attention to the significance of Wilson's relationship to his father, noting the inner necessity for over-reacting against any subsequent authority figure who reawakened incompletely resolved unconscious conflicts."[59]

A physical impairment also can be a source of low self-esteem. For example, the candid autobiography of Kurt Schumacher, a German Social Democrat in the 1930s, spoke about his sense of inferiority that resulted from a physical loss, a battlefield amputation of a limb during the First World War. In his memoir, he testified about his

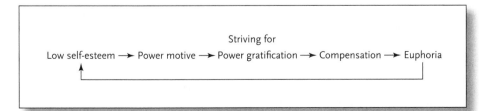

Striving for

Low self-esteem → Power motive → Power gratification → Compensation → Euphoria

*Figure 8.1.*
The Lasswellian hypothesis on leadership motivation

subsequent attempts to gain political power as a means of compensating for his perceived loss of manliness inflicted by the amputation—a startlingly frank affirmation of the Lasswellian hypothesis.[60]

Lasswell's Freudian approach lacks appeal to many students of political behavior. A major objection is the theory's unscientific nature, in the sense of failing to provide an opportunity for testing and disproving ("falsifying," in philosopher Karl Popper's famous methodological prescription) the central hypothesis, as one can, for instance, Einstein's equations on relativity.[61] The Freudian explanation requires a leap of faith. One can only evaluate whether this kind of theory appears to fit the available facts and trumps alternative explanations—a less satisfying test than the rigors of modern scientific empiricism demand.

Moreover, this Freudian-based form of analysis can be far-fetched. Commentator Dinesh D'Souza offered this "analysis" of the relationship between President Obama and his father, who was a citizen of Kenya and met his wife while studying in the United States: "Incredibly, the US is being ruled according to the dreams of a Luo tribesman of the 1950s. This philandering, inebriated African socialist, who raged against the world for denying him the realization of his anti-colonial ambitions, is now setting the nation's agenda through the reincarnation of his dreams in his son." This bizarre theory found a receptive audience in former House Speaker and Republican presidential candidate in 2012, Newt Gingrich of Georgia, who quoted it widely on TV talk shows.[62]

Looking at an earlier president, filmmaker Oliver Stone—widely criticized for his loose interpretations of history—has argued that Harry S. Truman was "bullied by other boys who called him 'Four Eyes' and 'sissy' and chased him home after school." Stone continues: "When he arrived home, trembling, his mother would comfort him by telling him not to worry because he was meant to be a girl anyway." *New York Times* writer Andrew Goldman slams Stone for leaving the impression in his film *Untold History* (2012) that Truman "suffered from a gender confusion that led to mass murder" [at Hiroshima and Nagasaki, as the President] "dropped bombs on Japan not to end the war but to flex his muscles and intimidate Stalin, as he himself had been intimidated as a boy." Goldman, and historian Douglas Brinkley, scoff at this fanciful theorizing about Truman's behavior.[63]

Despite the Wilson and Schumacher examples that seem to fit Lasswell's theoretical framework, critics of *psychoanalytic and psychological theory*—sometimes referred to as **psychohistory** *when applied to historical biography*—would readily agree with Stanley Hoffman that "it partakes of the fascination of adventure stories: it is the search for the missing clue and the missing link, a search in which everything revealed is treated as a sign of something concealed, and things expressed are deemed the revelation of things repressed."[64] In contrast, Hoffman prefers to emphasize the centrality of politics and **statecraft**: *"the way in which the leader conceives of and carries out his role as statesman, his relations with and impact on his followers or opponents."* From this perspective, the League of Nations failure can be explained in the simpler terms of inept lobbying on Capitol Hill by Wilson and his aides, coupled with an isolationist political tide running against the President for a variety of political and international reasons having nothing at all to do with his relationship with his father during adolescence. Foreign policy leaders are ruled far less by inner demons than by external reality, according to Hoffman's point of view.

## Psychological Pressures on Foreign Policy Leaders

Nevertheless, Washington officials engaged in foreign policy sometimes display individual psychological vulnerabilities, such as a tendency toward isolation from objective facts about the world. In contrast to murky Freudian and Lasswellian antecedents of behavior, these vulnerabilities spring from more immediate and apparent pressures on leaders. Presidents Johnson and Nixon are classic examples. Both men possessed incredible stamina and had high-energy personalities, arguably an admirable embodiment of the work ethic revered in American culture. Both men, though, were often downcast and felt isolated, as if the world had turned against them.[65]

In the conduct of the Vietnam War, both presidents were accused of shutting themselves off from information regarding the conflict that failed to conform to their preconceptions. In response to outside criticism, they closed themselves off from a hostile environment, choosing to rely on the loyal band of staffers surrounding them—several of whom were all too ready to provide them with comforting reassurances. Other scholars reject this characterization of President Johnson, though, pointing to instances where he was highly involved in reaching out for opinions beyond the White House.[66]

The phenomenon of personal isolation appears to have occurred during the Reagan administration, too. The President's immediate advisers urged him to take steps—trading weapons for hostages in Iran and failing to report this covert action to Congress, among others—that a less sheltered and compliant president might have realized would lead to widespread criticism outside the confines of the White House and, eventually, to a major scandal (Iran-*contra*). President George W. Bush also isolated himself from advisers outside his immediate entourage—the presentation of views that would have called into question his belief in the existence of WMDs in Iraq on the eve of the US invasion of that country in 2003. Intelligence analysts in the Energy and State Departments, as well as the US Air Force, had serious reservations about the WMD hypothesis, but were kept away from the White House by CIA Director George Tenet and other advisers to the President; and the President displayed no inclination to reach outside the Oval Office for wider expert opinion.[67] In contrast, writes the conservative columnist David Brooks, "When President Obama makes a decision, you can be sure that he has heard and accounted for every opposing argument. If he senses an important viewpoint is not represented, he will stop the proceedings and demand that it gets included."[68]

A former press secretary to President Johnson commented on the danger of leadership withdrawal from the world outside the White House. "The President, needing 'access to reality' in order to govern effectively, too often has access, instead, only to a self-serving court of flunkeys," he wrote, adding that a president's aides prefer to avoid uncomfortable truths: "Every effort must be made to relieve [the president] of the irritations that vex the average citizen . . . no one ever invites him to 'go soak your head.'"[69]

Why? Because, like Iago's "knee-crooking knaves" in *Othello*, *no one wants to upset his or her access to the Great Leader*. Other seasoned Washington observers have similarly criticized this **sycophancy trap,** whether in foreign or domestic policy. "In a thousand conference rooms, where the smell of moral sterility is as strong as ether in a hospital corridor," wrote journalists Russell Baker and Charles Peters in 1971, "the new courtiers dance to their minuet each day and [government] organizations slip further and further from reality."[70] The end result can be a foreign policy based less on fact than on fantasy.

## Operational Codes

More readily researched than these various psychological approaches is a leader's **operational code ("op-code")**, a helpful research tool for exploring individual attitudes and behavior related to foreign policy. As explained by political scientist Alexander L. George, the op-code approach provides a framework for the *systemic investigation of a "political leader's beliefs about the nature of politics and political conflict, his views regarding the extent to which historical developments can be shaped, and his notions of correct strategies and tactics."*[71] For George, a leader's answers to basic philosophical and instrumental (ends-means) questions can provide important clues to how he or she "may perceive different types of situations and approach the task of making a rational assessment of alternative courses of action."[72] The explanation and prediction of leadership behavior are improved by understanding the political beliefs of those in high office.

Each leader's operational code is made up of several fundamental philosophical and instrumental dimensions. Among the most significant are those dealing with his or her views on the nature of politics and political conflict. Does the leader approach political goals from a moralist-ideological, or a pragmatic and problem-solving, perspective? Does he or she look on foreign adversaries in "zero-sum" terms (that is, as a life and death struggle with only one winner), or in "positive sum" terms with a more cooperative attitude and a willingness to bargain (a belief that nations can work together)? In the pursuit of global objectives, does the leader believe in the use of armed intervention or in less intrusive instruments of foreign policy? These are vital questions, the answers to which can provide insights into the fundamental beliefs and likely decisions of an official. A look at the contrasting belief systems of a few important foreign policy decision makers provides a sense of the operational code methodology.

The op-code approach can be demonstrated by looking at the beliefs of a prominent chairman of the Foreign Relations Committee, Senator Frank Church, a leading spokesman for a noninterventionist philosophy of international affairs during the Cold War.[73] The first dimension in his code is philosophical and the second is instrumental; each consists of a cluster of basic foreign policy beliefs:

### Image of the opponent (philosophical)

Belief 1: Neither the Russians nor the Chinese are inherently evil.
Belief 2: Nationalities do not differ markedly one from another.
Belief 3: Communist nations have shown no greater tendency toward aggression than the United States.

Belief 4: Under certain circumstances and certain leaders, nations will be carried into adventures of aggression.

Belief 5: Moral judgments must be discounted on many questions of international relations, because spheres of influence and the hegemony of large nations over their smaller neighbors have been historical facts of life.

One of the most important principles to remember about relations between nations, the Senator believed, is that "big countries have always tended to behave aggressively toward their smaller neighbors." When the Russians have acted in this manner in East Europe, Westerners called it "naked aggression"; yet the United States has insisted at the same time on maintaining a large hegemony in its own region of the world, the Western Hemisphere. The Monroe Doctrine was only the beginning. As the United States grew in power, it was no longer content (in Church's view) with a limited hegemony: "In the years following the Second World War, we extended our sphere of influence to the middle of Europe, incorporating the whole of the Atlantic and Pacific Oceans; and not content with Pacific Ocean—the widest moat on earth—we extended our hegemony on to the mainland of Asia." Church looked on Asia as China's "natural sphere of influence." He saw no chance for good relations with the most populous nation in the world until adjustments were made in global politics "that will give to China what large nations are accustomed to demanding for themselves."

The instrumental dimension of an operation code consists chiefly of a leader's thoughts on how to conduct foreign policy:

## Utility of means (instrumental)

Belief 6: The United States must abandon its propensity to intervene in the affairs of other nations around the globe.

"We not only can live with a great deal of ferment and change," Senator Church argued, "but there is no reason why we cannot allow a relationship to develop between countries that we need not dominate." He pointed to Asia as an illustration, observing that were it not for the intervention of US military power in this region following World War II, a "natural equilibrium" would have developed there between Russia, China, and Japan in the north (the "triangle of power") and India and Indonesia in the south, both bulwarks of resistance against foreign adversaries. "The smaller countries were really incidental," he reasoned, "and would develop relationships with the larger countries as was natural to their situation, as they had done historically through the ages." The unnatural element injected into Asia was the American presence, with its insistence on establishing alliances that made no sense and depended on the presence of US military forces. Church believed that the Vietnam War was viewed by most Asians as "the last gasp of Western imperialism." Above all, he thought that the United States must "live with the world and not try so feverishly to control it." Throughout his career, he emphasized that "nationalism—rather than preference of the great powers—is the engine of change in modern history." He cautioned against overseas involvement "except when the national security of the United States was under clear and present danger."

As a way of placing Senator Church's views in a broader context, they are contrasted in Figure 8.2 (Church is designated by "C") with the operational codes of some other leading spokesmen of American foreign policy during the Cold War: Secretaries of State Dean Acheson, 1949–1953 ("A"), John Foster Dulles, 1953–1959 ("D"), and Dean Rusk, 1961–1969 ("R"), as well as two other chairmen of the Senate Foreign Relations Committee: Arthur H. Vandenberg, 1946–1948 ("V") and J. William Fulbright, 1959–1974 ("F"). The placement of these individuals on the two key belief dimensions—image of opponents and utility of means—is based on the findings of several op-code studies and represents an approximate "center of gravity" for the worldview of each leader.[74] As illustrated in the figure, the foreign policy philosophies of Church and Fulbright differed markedly from the secretaries of state. Both senators displayed a much stronger belief in the possibility of cooperation with US adversaries. Instrumentally, Church, Fulbright, and (to a lesser extent) Vandenberg also stood apart from the secretaries in their greater reluctance to intervene abroad with overt military power. On both dimensions, Church and Fulbright exhibited more affinity for one another's beliefs that for those held by the secretaries, with Vandenberg in the middle—though leaning toward his colleagues in the Senate.

The contrast between the belief systems of Church and Dulles is dramatic. According to an op-code analysis prepared by Ole Holsti, Secretary Dulles saw a "world dominated by bold strokes of black and white," a zero-sum outlook that pitted communism against Christianity, atheism against spiritualism, Marxist economic

*Figure 8.2.*
A comparison of operational codes among leading foreign policy officials

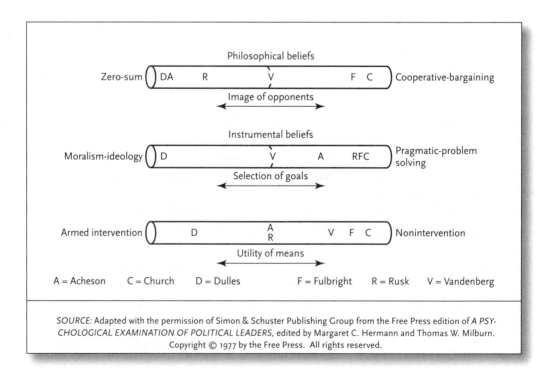

doctrine against the free enterprise system.[75] The United States faced, in Dulles's view, a titanic struggle against evil, where physical power—not diplomatic persuasion—was the only argument the Soviets would understand and respect. Victory would require, in the Secretary's words, a "crushing spirit" in defense of America's spiritual and economic values. The United States had to do whatever it could to sow dissension within the USSR. Moreover, in the Korean War, China would have to be given "one hell of a licking." No wonder he advised Eisenhower to use atomic bombs at Dien Bien Phu.

Dulles would probably have considered Church and Fulbright naive and immoral practitioners of appeasement in their willingness to try negotiation and compromise— the instrument of diplomacy—with the Soviets and the Chinese during the Cold War. As this comparison between Church and Dulles suggests, a leader's philosophical views may have a marked effect on how he or she approaches the practical problems of foreign policy. This is why the operational code approach, which concentrates on the policy maker's fundamental set of beliefs, can be a useful tool of analysis.

## The Worth of the Individual

Foreign policy decisions reflect not only the forces of history, constitutional principles, institutions, and the other influences examined earlier in this book, but the influence of individuals as well. Political man is driven by private motives displaced onto public objects and rationalized in terms of the public interest—so argued Harold Lasswell in his classic formulation about the effect that private battles of the psyche can have on public decisions.[76] For example, in a more recent confirmation of the importance of individuals in decisions regarding the use of the military instrument in foreign affairs, Graham H. Shepard reports that high-dominance personalities are more likely than low-dominance personalities to advocate the use of force.[77]

Who can deny the importance of private motives, even though the attempts of researchers to understand them remain primitive? Consider for a moment the importance of individual emotions in the following descriptions of relations between high-ranking officials in the Reagan administration. "Think of someone you really hate," said a foreign policy specialist during the Reagan years. "Multiply that by twenty and raise the answer to the fourth power. Then you will have an idea of how Shultz and Weinberger [the Secretaries of State and Defense, respectively] feel toward one another."[78] According to a senior official in the Reagan administration, the assistant secretary of state for Latin American affairs and a key NSC staff aid "fought like cats and dogs and would not speak to each other."[79] Another Reagan administration observer reported that Secretary Shultz "had come to loathe [DCI William J.] Casey."[80]

During the second Bush administration, Vice President Dick Cheney and Secretary of State Colin Powell similarly had running political battles over the shaping of foreign policy, with Cheney eager to use force in Iraq and Afghanistan and Powell—a former chairman of the Joint Chiefs of Staff—wary about excessive unilateral military intervention abroad by the United States. "Cheney and Powell went at each other in a blistering argument [at an NSC meeting]," reported *Washington Post* journalist Bob

Woodward. "It was Powell's internationalism versus Cheney's unilateralism."[81] How well individuals relate to one another, and how well they cope with the stresses of their own psychic civil wars, can influence the quality of policy making.

Government is in large part a matter of personal relations and bonds of trust. Presidents, lawmakers, diplomats, bureaucrats, lobbyists—all are made of flesh and blood. They are moved by the often contradictory emotions of trust and suspicion, love and hate, altruism and avarice, toughness and charity, fatigue, anger, idealism, fear, ambition, pride, zeal, restraint, and all the other feelings that give humanity its character and complexity. How these emotions are balanced by foreign policy officials can be a matter of consequence to the United States. As John Stuart Mill understood, "The worth of a state, in the long run, is the worth of the individuals composing it."[82]

## SUMMARY

Individuals have an effect on American foreign policy, as members of the general public, in smaller groups, and in their capacity as officials in government office. As one moves from the macrolevel to the microlevel—that is, from broad public opinion to the individual decision maker—the significance of the individual is magnified. At the macrolevel, the foreign policy views of individuals as aggregated into "the public" are frequently discounted by policy makers. Presidents and lawmakers normally prefer to think of themselves as "trustees" when it comes to foreign policy, exercising their best judgment on behalf of their electors, rather than mere "instructed delegates" registering the ups and downs of popular whim.

In foreign policy, this trustee form of representation is encouraged by the lack of instructions from the electorate. Knowledge about foreign affairs tends to be low among the general public. What instructions or opinions do exist are often difficult for leaders to gauge; accurate barometers of "en masse" sentiment are rarely available.

As with domestic policy, organized groups within the broad public have learned that with foreign policy, too, the government of the United States responds to pressure from those who band together to make their needs known. Individuals who pool their resources—money, advertising, organizational skills, the threat of votes against uncooperative elected officials—have a better chance of gaining the attention and favor of decision makers in the United States than do those who remain just part of a faceless and fragmented mass. Large corporations with foreign policy interests have honed their approaches to lobbying into a high art form, as have groups concerned about the fate of specific countries abroad, such as AIPAC.

The destiny of the nation depends in part on the character of its individual leaders, a central lesson of government carried down from the days of the ancient Greek philosophers. The character of American foreign policy makers is shaped by many influences during a life span. Scholars with Freudian antecedents stress the importance of low self-esteem as a significant influence on leadership behavior, a condition hypothesized to trigger emotional responses and feelings of paranoia. Researchers skeptical about Freudian and other psychological approaches have preferred to analyze the influence of the individual foreign policy official in the more straightforward terms of statecraft, that is, the acquired leadership skills of the individual and how skillfully they are directed against foreign policy challenges. Others have found it useful to probe the official's system of beliefs or "operational code," particularly a leader's basic views about the Soviet Union during the Cold War or terrorism today.

## KEY TERMS

American Israel Public Affairs Committee
   (AIPAC) p. 249
Burkean model of representation p. 244
Council on Foreign Relations (CFR) p. 252
instructed-delegate model of representation p. 244
intergovernmental organizations (IGOs) p. 254
international nongovernmental organizations
   (INGOs) p. 254
Lasswell hypothesis p. 255
Lippmann school of thought on public opinion p. 246

non-state actors p. 252
operational code (op-code) p. 258
opinion-leadership hypothesis p. 242
party loyalty model of representation p. 245
presidential deference model of representation
   p. 244
psychohistory p. 256
rally-round-the-flag hypothesis p. 241
statecraft p. 256
sycophancy trap p. 258

## QUESTIONS FOR DISCUSSION

1. President George H. W. Bush enjoyed a substantial increase in popularity during the First Persian Gulf War (Operation Desert Storm). Explain the President's surge in the polls, using the rally-round-the-flag hypothesis and the opinion-leadership hypothesis.
2. Of the various models of legislative representation, which would you adopt if you were a member of Congress dealing with foreign policy issues?
3. What are the pros and the cons of interest group involvement in the making of American foreign policy?
4. What can be done about the problems of sycophancy and self-delusion in the White House?
5. How would you describe your "operational code" with respect to contemporary US foreign policy?

## ADDITIONAL READINGS

Brody, Richard A. *Assessing the President: The Media, Elite Opinion, and Public Support.* Stanford, CA: Stanford University Press, 1991.
George, Alexander L, and Juliette L. George. *Woodrow Wilson and Colonel House: A Personality Study.* New York: Dover, 1956.

Hermann, Margaret G., ed. *A Psychological Examination of Political Leaders.* New York: Free Press, 1977.

For further readings, please visit the book's companion website.

### CHAPTER 9

# Intelligence Collection and Analysis

## INTELLIGENCE TO THE RESCUE

Early one morning in October of 1994 in his spacious office at the Pentagon, Secretary of Defense (SecDef) William J. Perry—a tall, thoughtful man with a PhD in mathematics—greeted Chairman of the Joint Chiefs

This undated image shows a film canister from the Hexagon program parachuting to Earth before being snagged by a plane for recovery. Dubbed "Big Bird," it was the most successful space spy satellite program of the Cold War era. From 1971 to 1986, the United States launched a total of 20 satellites, each containing 60 miles of film and sophisticated cameras that orbited the earth snapping vast panoramic photographs of the Soviet Union, China, and other potential foes. The film was shot back through the earth's atmosphere in buckets, which were caught with grappling hooks by C-130 Air Force planes as they dropped by parachute over the Pacific Ocean.

of Staff General John Shalikashvili. Under his arm, the General carried a portfolio of satellite photographs of Iraq. He spread the imagery across a conference table. Using a pointer, Shalikashvili directed Perry's attention to a disturbing set of pictures. Improbable as it might have seemed, coming just three-and-a-half years after a US-led coalition had knocked Saddam Hussein's army to its knees in the First Persian Gulf War, elements of the Republican Guard (Saddam's elite troops), supported by mechanized infantry, armor, and tank units, were moving at a rapid clip southward toward the Iraqi city of Al Basrah, a mere thirty miles from the Kuwaiti border. The force was aimed like an arrow at the Al Jahra heights overlooking Kuwait City, in an apparent repeat of the same maneuver that led to the Iraqi conquest of Kuwait in 1990.

Perry quickly ordered a US armored brigade stationed in Kuwait to the Iraqi border. With a mounting sense of uneasiness, the SecDef and the top Pentagon brass waited as captains and lieutenants brought new batches of satellite imagery into Perry's office over the next twenty-four hours. Upward of 10,000 Iraqi troops had amassed in an area near Al Basrah. Steadily the number rose to 50,000, some camped within twelve miles of the border. The American brigade had arrived, but consisted of only 2,000 lightly armed Marines.

## LEARNING OBJECTIVES AND CONSTITUTIONAL ISSUES

**By the end of this chapter, you will be able to:**

- *Explain why national security intelligence is fundamental to the making of American foreign policy decisions.*

- *Describe the scope and structure of the US Intelligence Community (IC), especially its premier organization: the Central Intelligence Agency (CIA).*

- *Describe how important foreign policy information moves, by way of an "intelligence cycle,"* *from the field where it is collected to the high councils of government where it illuminates decision making.*

- *Explain why intelligence sometimes fails to warn US leaders of impending danger.*

- *Explain why democracies must try to balance the twin needs of secrecy and transparency, security and liberty.*

### THIS CHAPTER RAISES THE FOLLOWING CONSTITUTIONAL QUESTIONS:

- The Constitution says nothing about secret government agencies, yet they have grown to become a significant part of America's government. Have these agencies given undue power to presidents and upset the constitutional balance between the executive and legislative branches envisioned by the founders?

- In light of the large size and hidden nature of America's intelligence agencies, can lawmakers carry out their constitutional duties of accountability in this shadowy domain?

- Given the Constitution's philosophy in favor of a strong Congress, not just a strong executive, should the intelligence agencies be expected to provide lawmakers with timely information on an equal basis with the president? Or perhaps just the leaders of Congress and the House and Senate Intelligence Committees?

- Even though democracy depends on an informed citizenry and an informed Congress, are some types of information so sensitive that they should only be held by the executive branch?

President Bill Clinton ordered 450 more warplanes to Kuwait, along with the 24th Mechanized Infantry Division and a Marine contingent from Camp Pendleton in California. The aircraft carrier *George Washington* steamed at maximum speed toward the Red Sea from the Indian Ocean. It would be impossible, though, for these forces to arrive in time to block what appeared to be an imminent invasion of Kuwait.

Perry and Shalikashvili waited nervously for the next set of satellite photographs. When they arrived, the two men breathed an audible sigh of relief. The Iraqi troops had suddenly stopped and some elements were already turning back toward Baghdad.

The good news was that imagery intelligence (know today in the world of spies as geospatial intelligence) may have prevented the outbreak of another war in the Persian Gulf. Using these timely photographs to pinpoint the location of Iraqi troops, Perry had been able to place an American brigade as a barrier against Iraqi aggression. "Had the intelligence arrived three or four days later, it would have been too late," he told the Aspin-Brown Commission on Intelligence in 1995. The episode, though, revealed troubling weaknesses in America's spy system. "Had we analyzed the data better from techint [technical intelligence collection, such as geospatial intelligence]," said Perry, looking back at the crisis, "we could have had a seven-to-ten-day earlier alert. Better humint [human intelligence—spies on the ground] might have given this alert, too."[1] ⌣

## INTELLIGENCE AND THE FOUNDATIONS OF FOREIGN POLICY

I n this opening chapter of Part 4, I examine the instruments of American foreign policy, beginning with the subject of **national security intelligence** The primary purpose of this instrument is to *gather and analyze information about world events.* (Another core mission of national security intelligence is covert action, treated separately in Chapter 12.) The collection and analysis of information from around the globe is fundamental to the successful pursuit of US foreign policy objectives. Without an accurate understanding of the world around them, policy makers are forced to make decisions about international affairs while essentially blindfolded. Every modern president has acknowledged his reliance on intelligence—the nation's first line of defense. As President Clinton put it, "Every morning I start my day with an intelligence report. The Intelligence I receive informs just about every foreign policy decision we make."[2]

While reliable information can improve the vision of decision makers, the planet is too vast and the governments of most nations are too secretive to expect a completely unfettered view into the capabilities and intentions of America's foes, or even its friends. This wish for global transparency remains beyond human grasp, even though the United States spends almost $80 billion a year in search of this objective. Many shadows—ambiguous data, misperceptions, and secrecy among them—fall across the latitudes and longitudes, dimming the chances of 20/20 vision for the CIA and America's other secret agencies responsible for intelligence collection.

Vexing, too, is the question of who should receive what information from the secret agencies, and when—yet another constitutionally based friction between the legislative and executive branches. Institutional ill feelings in the domain of intelligence stem chiefly from attempts by the executive to monopolize information about global events, sometimes in an effort to avoid congressional criticism of its policy plans. When this hoarding of intelligence succeeds, as is frequently the case, Congress is left in the dark and America's constitutional framework of checks and balances is knocked out of kilter. Further, because an informed electorate is the very anchor of democracy, constitutional government suffers when the public is kept in the dark. At the same time, though, not all government secrets can be revealed; some are legitimate and contribute to the protection of US citizens against threats, such as the names of CIA agents abroad.

In this chapter I explore these problems: first, the difficulties of gathering, analyzing, and disseminating intelligence to key American decision makers; and second, the conflict that has arisen between the branches over secrecy and the sharing of information. In subsequent chapters, I examine what policy makers do with the information they are provided—the action that follows knowledge. In their pursuit of US foreign policy ends, how do officials go about choosing the appropriate means from among those at their disposal: chiefly, diplomacy, the overt use of armed force, covert action, economic statecraft, and cultural and moral suasion? As anticipated in the earlier chapters of this book, and by the analytic construct for the study of American foreign policy presented in Chapter 2, these choices are shaped by a collision of events, institutions, and personalities.

## THE ORIGINS OF AMERICA'S MODERN SPY AGENCIES

America's leaders in the War of Independence were well aware of the vital role intelligence would play in a successful revolutionary struggle. In 1776, the Continental Congress established the nation's first intelligence service, the Committee of Secret Correspondence; and General George Washington, who had his own secret code (711), made use of an effective network of spies led by Paul Revere.[3] Perhaps the most famous officer in this network was Nathan Hale, a young graduate of Yale University whom the British hanged for espionage in 1776. Hale is remembered for his declaration, uttered moments before his execution: "I only regret that I have but one life to lose for my country."[4] A statue of his imagined likeness (no pictures are available of Nathan Hale) stands at the entrance to the CIA Headquarters Building in Langley, adjacent to the township of McLean in northern Virginia.

The interest of the constitutional founders in matters of intelligence went well beyond **espionage**, *the secret collection of information by spies.* They were also concerned with the *interpretation of information* gathered by the spies and combined with more openly derived information—what modern practitioners call **analysis**, bringing insight to raw data. Benjamin Franklin, among others, energetically encouraged the use of secret operations for yet another objective: to influence nations toward a favorable regard for America's foreign policy objectives—covert action, in current parlance (Chapter 12). For example, when the thirteen colonies declared their independence from Britain,

Franklin urged the government of France to supply military aid to the rebels through a secret conduit. To conceal this relationship from the British, a front or proprietary was formed, the Hortalez Company, ostensibly a private commercial enterprise. The founders were concerned, too, about protecting their army and the new nation from the invidious activities of foreign spies, an important and difficult responsibility known today as counterintelligence.[5]

Aerial view of the CIA Headquarters, Langley, Virginia.

The intelligence mission known as collection and analysis has been drastically revamped in the modern era as a result in part of the surprise attack by the Japanese against Pearl Harbor on December 7, 1941.[6] Enemy aircraft hit all eight battleships moored in Hawaii, sinking five along with two destroyers and several other ships. Over 200 US planes were damaged and many totally destroyed. Luckily, the two aircraft carriers in the Pacific fleet happened to be at sea and escaped the attack; less fortunate were the 2,330 service personnel killed and the 1,145 wounded, along with 100 civilian casualties.

The blow stunned the nation. It was the most disastrous intelligence failure in American history (later surpassed by the 9/11 attacks). The United States had failed to appreciate both the capabilities and the intentions of the enemy. American officials were unaware that the Japanese had developed aerial torpedoes. When dropped into the sea, they could navigate in the relatively shallow waters of Pearl Harbor. The greatest damage to US warships came from these weapons.[7] Officials had also thought that a Japanese attack at the Philippines was infinitely more likely. Moreover, policy makers failed to stitch together and examine thoroughly the fragments of data that were available regarding the possibility of an attack against Hawaii, or to distribute in a timely fashion the information that was known to key Naval officers. Lower officials kept vital data bottled up, for fear that Operation Magic (the US intelligence program that cracked the Japanese military codes) might be revealed—compromised, in spy lingo—if shared too widely.[8]

## The Coordination of Intelligence

This poor sharing and coordination of intelligence in 1941 was a serious flaw that Truman, who succeeded Roosevelt as president in April of 1945, vowed to address. The exigencies of war delayed his intentions to reform America's approach to intelligence—not that much existed to overhaul. "On the eve of Pearl Harbor the United States had no strategic intelligence system worthy of the name," conclude two experts.[9] At the time, funding for intelligence was only about $3 million a year. America had to make do throughout World War II with a loosely defined intelligence apparatus called the Office of Strategic Services, created by President Franklin Roosevelt via an executive order. The OSS had a good reputation. Less highly regarded were America's Army and Navy intelligence units; they were often in competition with one another and suffered from a lack of coordination as well as a duplication of efforts.

After the war, President Truman decided to do something about this organizational fragmentation. Still fresh in his memory, too, was the lack of information about Japanese activities available to the White House in the months leading up to the Pearl Harbor disaster—another reason for reform. Moreover, and most important, the Soviets were beginning to look like a genuine threat to the global interests of the United States and the President wanted a more sophisticated intelligence capability to monitor the activities of this rising superpower. Finally, Truman was perturbed by the downpour of intelligence reports that fell on his desk from different parts of government, sometimes directly in contradiction to one another. He preferred to have a single report from one central organization. "So I got a couple of admirals together," Truman told an interviewer, "and they formed the Central Intelligence Agency for the benefit and convenience of the President of the United States." As a result, Truman continued, "instead of the President having to look through a bunch of papers two feet high, the information was coordinated so that the President could arrive at the facts."[10]

On July 26, 1947, the National Security Act—whose main purpose was to create a modern Department of Defense with more reliable interservice cooperation—gave statutory authority as well to the idea of *improved intelligence coordination through the leadership of* a **Central Intelligence Agency (CIA).**[11] This law placed the CIA under the control of a new White House structure that would coordinate American foreign policy: the National Security Council or NSC. The CIA failed, however, to achieve undisputed dominance over matters of national intelligence, as its advocates had hoped it would. One of the early deputy directors of the CIA, Admiral Rufus Taylor, ruefully described the various intelligence agencies in the late 1960s as little more than a "tribal federation."[12] Still, the centrifugal—outward pushing or fragmenting—forces in the intelligence system were now less pronounced than they had been during World War II and previous years.

From 1947 to 2004, a **director of central intelligence (DCI)** *led the intelligence agencies and also served as the director of the CIA (D/CIA).* Wearing the DCI hat, this individual had the primary mission of trying to coordinate information from the different secret agencies for presentation to the principal decision makers in the government—an all-source fusion (in spy lingo), or sharing, of information collected from around the world. Lacking authority to hire and fire agency heads or to shape their budgets, however, the DCI would only be a titular head of the intelligence establishment or "community" (in the accepted mythology of cohesiveness among these agencies, which in reality remain more separate and rival fiefdoms than close partners that share their information freely with one another).

In the wake of the 9/11 attacks, intelligence reformers—the families of the victims who died that day, as well as scholars, op-ed writers, and government committees of inquiry into the attacks—pointed to the ongoing fragmentation of the Intelligence Community as part of the reason why the terrorist attacks against Washington, DC and New York City had taken the nation by surprise. America's secret agencies had inadequately cooperated with one another to prevent the attacks.[13] Reformers attempted to strengthen the DCI by way of the Intelligence Reform and Terrorism Prevention Act (IRTPA), enacted in 2004. The law failed, though, to achieve the goal of reformers. The Department of Defense lobbied against a strong intelligence director, fearful that a civilian intelligence chief might move attention away from military intelligence requirements—an unlikely occurrence since **support to military operations (SMO)** will always remain *the top U.S. intelligence priority* for government officials whenever America is at war. The *office of DCI was given a new name*, the **director of national intelligence (DNI),** but the powers of the office over budgets and appointments remained almost as slim as they had been for the DCI. Today, an enfeebled DNI must plead for intelligence sharing, as more powerful cabinet secretaries—especially the mighty secretary of defense—resist any attempts to erode their authority over intelligence activities within their departments. More than a decade after the 9/11 attacks, the United States still has no true director of intelligence.

## The Structure of Intelligence

As with the DCI earlier, just how difficult the job of the DNI is can be appreciated by a look at the way intelligence is structured in the United States (see Figure 9.1). The goal of reformers to bring cohesion to America's intelligence agencies through the creation of a strong national spymaster has twice failed: in 1947 when the DCI was given few powers over budgets and appointments, and in 2004 when again the new DNI lacked these powers, too.

### The Intelligence Community

Beyond the lack of a strong spymaster at the helm of US intelligence, additional centrifugal forces in the IC come from the sheer number of secret agencies under the DNI's titular leadership—the sixteen major organizations displayed in Figure 9.1. Beneath the DNI on the organizational charts are eight military intelligence agencies; yet they have another boss, too: the secretary of defense, who outranks the DNI in cabinet status. These military intelligence agencies dominate spy spending, absorbing some 85 percent of the total US intelligence budget of $80 billion in 2011 (which exceeded the budget of the State Department, home of America's diplomats, by $30 billion).[14] Much of this spy funding goes toward the collection and analysis of tactical intelligence used by military commanders in the field and admirals at sea, in contrast to broader strategic intelligence used by policy planners in the America's highest decision councils.

A sizable portion of the budget supports the work of America's largest intelligence agency, the military's **National Security Agency**. The NSA has the most floor space, the longest corridors, the most electrical wiring, the most advanced computers, and

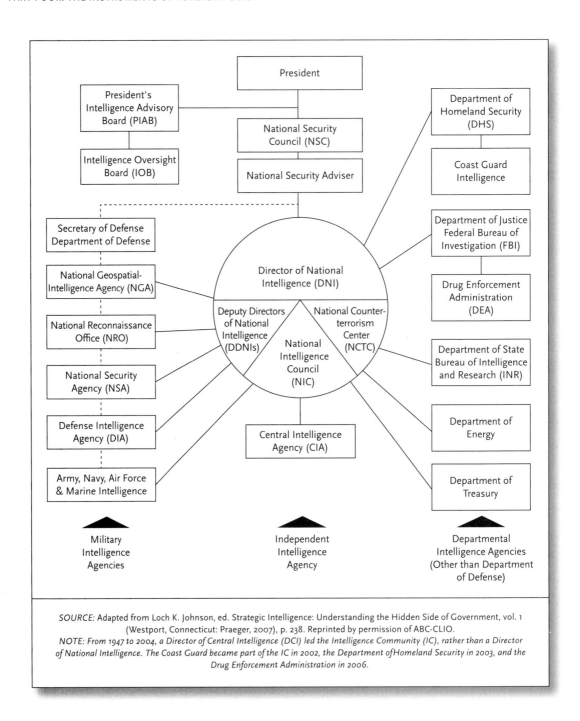

SOURCE: Adapted from Loch K. Johnson, ed. Strategic Intelligence: Understanding the Hidden Side of Government, vol. 1 (Westport, Connecticut: Praeger, 2007), p. 238. Reprinted by permission of ABC-CLIO.
NOTE: From 1947 to 2004, a Director of Central Intelligence (DCI) led the Intelligence Community (IC), rather than a Director of National Intelligence. The Coast Guard became part of the IC in 2002, the Department of Homeland Security in 2003, and the Drug Enforcement Administration in 2006.

*Figure 9.1*
The U.S. Intelligence
Community, 2014

one of the biggest budgets of any agency in the Intelligence Community. In addition to the elaborate antennae atop its headquarters building at Ft. Meade, Maryland, that provide instantaneous communications throughout the world, the NSA has a fleet of eavesdropping satellites in space and ground antennae in foreign countries that are capable of *intercepting international and domestic telephone and e-mail communications.* The NSA is also the nation's cryptological, or *code-breaking, center.* Although the CIA receives more publicity and more funding, in large part because of its involvement in periodic plots to influence—and sometimes overthrow—regimes through covert action (including costly drone attacks), the NSA and other secret military organizations constitute the hidden mass of the intelligence iceberg.

In 2013, the NSA also became the secret agency most embroiled in controversy. The agency hired an outside computer specialist, Edward J. Snowden, to help with some of its work. He stole programs from its computers, leaked some of them to the American public, and fled abroad, eventually gaining asylum in Russia. The leaks revealed that the NSA was gathering data on all the telephone calls made and received by American citizens, both inside the United States and with parties overseas. The NSA was also collecting data on the use of social media by Americans. The appropriateness of this "dragnet" approach to intelligence gathering against US citizens became a topic of heated national debate.[15]

America's other military intelligence agencies include the **National Geospatial-Intelligence Agency (NGA)**, which commands the nation's capacity to *take photographs of enemy targets* by way of sophisticated cameras on satellites and reconnaissance aircraft; the **National Reconnaissance Office (NRO)**, which *administers NSA and NGA satellites, from production and launching to their management in space*; the **Defense Intelligence Agency (DIA)**, which *analyzes global information gathered on military matters*; and four other intelligence units, one in each of the military services engaged in tactical intelligence gathering and analysis (the Army, Navy, Air Force, and Marine intelligence services).

The civilian side of intelligence includes seven agencies that are embedded within various cabinet departments (as is true with the military intelligence agencies as well—the DOD in their case). An independent CIA, which stands outside the policy departments, rounds out the "community." The seven civilian agencies inside departments include the Federal Bureau of Investigation (FBI), located in the Justice Department and responsible for counterterrorism and counterintelligence (as well as its chief duty: law enforcement); the Drug Enforcement Administration (DEA), also in the Justice Department and the newest member of the intelligence community (although the DEA has been located elsewhere in the government for decades); the Bureau of Intelligence and Research (INR) in the State Department; the Energy Department's intelligence unit, which focuses on tracking nuclear materials worldwide and protecting America's nuclear weapons storage sites at home; the Treasury Department's intelligence unit, given the task of tracing the international funding of terrorist organizations; an analytic group within the Department of Homeland Security (DHS); and an intelligence unit within the Coast Guard. The latter two agencies are, along with the DEA, the newest members of the Intelligence Community.

During the Cold War, the CIA resided at the heart of this system and was expected to coordinate the work of the other agencies. Its status has fallen since the

9/11 attacks, however, as much of the blame fell on this agency's shoulders. While the DCI used to have his office at the CIA, now the DNI works in a building outside all of the agencies, in a location near North Arlington, Virginia, known as Liberty Crossing (or "LX"). Nevertheless, the CIA remains in charge of coordinating major analytic reporting as well as the conduct of covert actions. Given its ongoing prominence and large budget, I examine the CIA's structure more closely as an example of how US secret agencies are organized and how they operate.

Combined, the sixteen agencies of the Intelligence Community employ about 200,000 individuals, a large number of whom (some 30 percent) are contract workers in the private sector. No country—or even empire—throughout history has developed an intelligence apparatus as large and as costly as this set of secret organizations.[16]

## Inside the CIA

No longer run by a DCI since the passage of IRTPA in 2004, *the CIA now has its own manager*, the **director of the Central Intelligence Agency (D/CIA)**. During the Cold War, the DCI had his (no women served in this office) hands full just trying to manage the CIA, let alone all the other secret agencies in the US government. Even though "the Agency," as CIA officers refer to their organization, has a D/CIA who doesn't have to worry about community-wide management problems now, the challenge of running the Agency remains daunting enough. Below the D/CIA's office on the seventh floor at CIA Headquarters lies a maze of hallways with warrens staffed by thousands of analysts, scientists, clerical assistants, and computer technicians who attempt to understand and anticipate world events. The Agency is divided into five sections: the Office of D/CIA and four directorates. (See Figure 9.2.) The directorates include the National Clandestine Service (NCS, known as the Directorate of Operations or DO during the Cold War); the Directorate of Science and Technology (DS&T); the Directorate of Support (DS); and the Directorate of Intelligence (DI), the Agency's analytic division.[17]

## The National Clandestine Service

The largest and most controversial of these units is the National Clandestine Service. About two-thirds of the NCS's personnel are engaged in espionage, counterintelligence, and liaison work with intelligence services in allied nations. The rest are assigned to carry out covert action, including (to give two examples) paramilitary operations and the secret financing of friendly politicians overseas. The NCS is subdivided into specialized staffs, such as the Special Operations Group for paramilitary activities, as well as regional divisions (see Figure 9.3). The *top CIA officer in each country* is called the **chief of station (COS)**. He or she is the NCS's country spymaster and the CIA's equivalent of an ambassador. *Beneath the COS serve the Agency's* **case officers** (sometimes referred to as **operational officers**) and their *native agents*, known as **assets**. The COS reports to the country desk housed in one of the geographic divisions of the NCS at CIA headquarters, supposedly without bypassing the US ambassador to

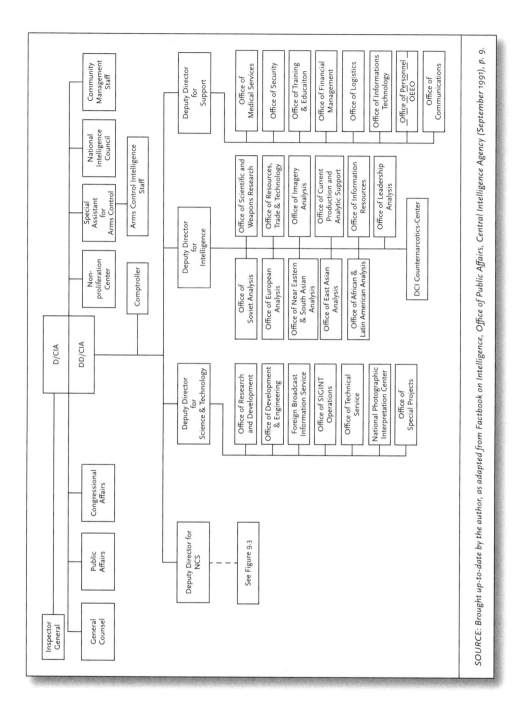

SOURCE: Brought up-to-date by the author, as adapted from Factbook on Intelligence, Office of Public Affairs, Central Intelligence Agency (September 1991), p. 9.

Figure 9.2
Inside the CIA, 2014

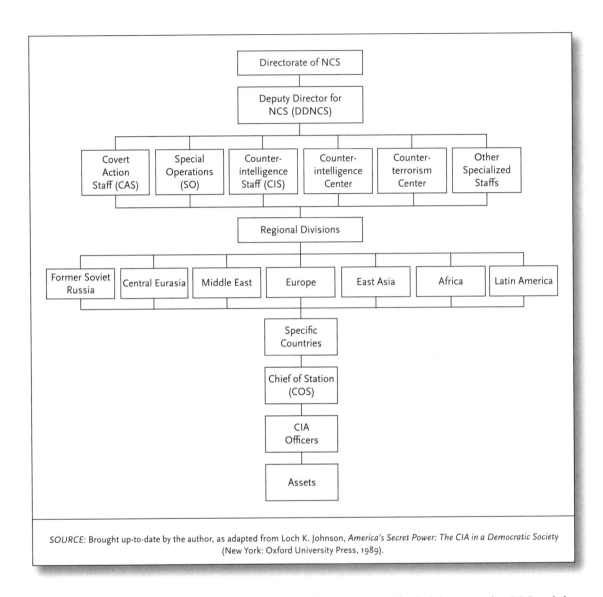

SOURCE: Brought up-to-date by the author, as adapted from Loch K. Johnson, *America's Secret Power: The CIA in a Democratic Society* (New York: Oxford University Press, 1989).

*Figure 9.3*
The National Clandestine
Service, 2014

whom the COS is (in theory at least) subordinate. The link between the COS and the ambassador in the field has often been delicate and has led to tension at times between the CIA and the Department of State. In extreme cases, the Agency may be plotting to undermine a regime while at the same time the unwitting US ambassador is trying to improve America's ties with the government.

The CIA places an emphasis overseas on the recruitment of spies from the so-called hard targets (or "denied areas"), such as North Korea, Iran, and other dictatorships—a daunting task because these closed societies have formidable defenses (counterintelligence) against America's espionage attempts. Over half the time case officers spend abroad is devoted, first, to observing (technically referred to as "spotting and assessing");

gaining access to; recruiting; and, finally, handling an asset inside a target nation or group (such as a terrorist cell).[18] Simply meeting and becoming better acquainted with a potential foreign recruit can be a painstaking endeavor. A CIA manager commented on the asset recruitment process:

> Often, when we target a person and say, 'All right, there is an indi-
> vidual who has access to information we want,' often our case officer
> doesn't have a direct approach to him, so he may have to recruit sev-
> eral 'access agents' in order to finally develop [the relationship] to the
> point where he can engage in a dialogue with that individual and
> hopefully bring him around to recruitment.[19]

Often, after all this preparation, the recruitment pitch will fail. The foreigner may reject the advance, or even hold a press conference exposing the recruitment attempt. Even if the recruitment is successful, the new asset may prove unproductive as a spy—or, far worse, may be a double-agent merely pretending to work for the CIA and using this opportunity to provide the Agency with false information to trick the United States (a deception operation). Now and then, though, well-placed assets can provide a gold mine of information for the CIA about the inner decisions made by a foreign government.

## The Directorate of Science and Technology

The Directorate of Science and Technology, the smallest of the CIA's major divisions, is devoted to applying technology to espionage. The DS&T conducts research and development on gadgetry used by Agency officers and assets in the field. The products include such items as advanced lock-picking tools or disguises of all kinds, as well as fake rocks and trees with hollowed-out spaces for hiding messages, and even mechanical birds that carry listening devices in their bellies or cameras on their wings as they flap around forbidden terrain overseas or alight on the window sills of foreign embassies. The Directorate's scientists also experiment with drugs and other chemicals to find antidotes against concoctions that might be used by enemies against Americans—a program criticized by congressional investigators in the mid-1970s because CIA scientists used the chemicals (LSD among them) in tests against individuals without their permission. Moreover, the Agency continued to store the chemicals even after President Richard M. Nixon ordered them destroyed.[20] This Directorate's sophisticated computers also handle many of the Agency's data processing tasks.

## The Directorate of Support

The Directorate of Support (DS) carries out the Agency's housekeeping chores: hiring, training, computer processing, worldwide communications and logistics, security, and various other administrative duties from hanging art in the hallways of the CIA Headquarters building to sweeping the floors. Although on the surface this directorate may seem innocuous, its support for secret operations abroad has brought it into a close working relationship with the NCS. Further, this Directorate (at the time called the Directorate of Administration) became involved in domestic spying during the Vietnam War era—a central focus of the Church Committee investigations in 1975. Together, the NSC and the DS form, according to former insiders, "an agency within an agency . . . [which] like the largest and most dangerous part of an iceberg, floats along virtually unseen."[21]

### The Directorate of Intelligence

The Directorate of Intelligence (DI) is where the CIA endeavors to make sense of (analyze) the raw information about international events and personalities that America's assets and spy machines have gathered from around the world. Only about 20 percent of the Agency's employees—the analysts—are engaged in this activity, accounting for less than 10 percent of the total CIA budget. In contrast, two-thirds of the Agency's personnel and budget are dedicated to operations overseas, especially intelligence collection and covert action.[22] Still, the DI is a vital center in the US intelligence universe. Its importance becomes more obvious with a closer look at the purposes, or missions, of American intelligence.

## The Intelligence Missions

In 1947, President Truman insisted that a *Central* Intelligence Agency was necessary to collect, evaluate, and coordinate intelligence, and to provide for its proper dissemination within the government. The CIA would serve as a clearinghouse for the various American spy services. It would also be expected, in the words of its longest serving DCI, Allen Dulles (1953–1961), "to weigh facts, and to draw conclusions from those facts, without having either the facts or the conclusions warped by the inevitable and even proper prejudices of the men whose duty it is to determine policy."[23] Espionage and analysis would be the primary responsibility of the Agency. While this was hardly a new venture, President Truman hoped it could be carried out more effectively and efficiently with the CIA serving as a hub for America's espionage activities.

The National Security Act of 1947 placed the CIA under the direction of the NSC and gave the Agency five specific authorities, the last of which gestured—in slippery language—toward duties beyond espionage. The statute charged the Agency with responsibilities to advise the NSC on intelligence activities related to national security; to make recommendations for the coordination of such activities; to correlate, evaluate, and disseminate intelligence within the government; to carry out services for existing agencies that the NSC decides might be best done centrally; and, in an ambiguous catchall phrase, to "perform such other functions and duties related to intelligence affecting the national security as the National Security Council may from time to time direct."[24] Whereas the founding statute overwhelmingly emphasized intelligence collection and analysis, the door was left ajar to use the CIA for "other functions and duties"—an invitation quickly accepted by President Truman and the NSC when the

Cold War heated up, as a means for launching the Agency on a wide range of anticommunist covert actions around the world.

Like covert action, counterintelligence went without specific mention in the 1947 act; but, by the early 1950s, it had also achieved a status of considerable importance as a mission within the CIA. Counterintelligence (CI) specialists soon waged nothing less than a secret war against antagonistic intelligence services around the world. Explaining why this form of covert warfare evolved, a CI specialist points out that "in the absence of an effective US counterintelligence program, [adversaries of democracy] function in what is largely a benign environment."[25] As the Soviets, the Chinese, and others tried to steal America's military and industrial secrets and disrupt its global activities, some organization—the CIA, as it turned out—had to take the lead with countermeasures. Led by James Angleton, an Idaho-born, Yale educated CIA chief of counterintelligence from 1954 to 1974, the CI Staff developed its own global network of assets—spies spying on spies. Rather than merely settle for catching foreign espionage agents as they tried their handiwork against the United States, under Angleton the CI Staff conducted aggressive operations to confuse and thwart hostile intelligence services, as well as to infiltrate the enemy camp with its own penetration agents (moles)—the most important counterintelligence method, for a well-placed mole may be able to report back on operations being run against the United States.[26]

Collection and analysis, covert action, and counterintelligence were soon established as the core missions of the intelligence community in the years following the end of World War II and they remain so today—with collection and analysis considered Mission No. 1.

## COLLECTION AND ANALYSIS

The **collection and analysis** mission is driven by a series of activities known as the **intelligence cycle**. The CIA defines the cycle as *"the process by which information is acquired, converted into intelligence, and made available to policymakers."*[27] It has five phases: planning and direction, collection, processing, production and analysis, and dissemination (see Figure 9.4). As a former Agency analyst notes, the cycle is really less a series of discrete phases, one leading to another, than it is a matrix of steady interactions between producers and consumers of intelligence, with multiple feedback loops.[28] These interactions are simplified here to illustrate in general how information flows from the field to decision councils in Washington.

### Planning and Direction

The first phase of the intelligence cycle entails identifying what kinds of data need to be collected from around the world by America's secret agencies, then assigning specific agencies to harvest the data. The chief responsibilities for collection overseas fall on the CIA, the NSA, and the NGA. The State Department's INR, the DIA, and the CIA are the top analytic organizations in the intelligence community. The example of the CIA is used for purposes of highlighting the key phases of the intelligence cycle, although in reality each of the major agencies has an important part to play in this core mission.

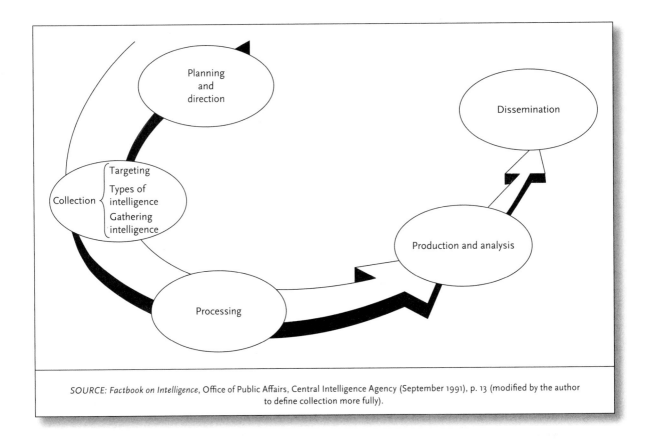

SOURCE: *Factbook on Intelligence*, Office of Public Affairs, Central Intelligence Agency (September 1991), p. 13 (modified by the author to define collection more fully).

*Figure 9.4*
The Intelligence Cycle

Within the CIA, the deputy director for intelligence (DDI) is the chief analyst. More than anyone else, this official deserves the credit or the blame for the quality of the finished intelligence products presented to those who make decisions on behalf of the United States. The purpose of the cycle is to provide useful knowledge to leaders in Washington in advance of their decisions—especially to the president, but also to the nation's top advisers, from the secretaries of state and defense to the scores of assistant and deputy assistant secretaries throughout the executive branch. As the CIA puts it, "Intelligence is knowledge and foreknowledge of the world around us—the prelude to Presidential decision and action."[29] The motto inscribed on the wall at the DNI's headquarters reads: "Creating Decision Advantage."

Major difficulties arise, however, in this seemingly straightforward relationship between the CIA and its companion organizations (the producers of knowledge) and the policy makers (the consumers). At the beginning of each administration, key national security officials gather in the Cabinet Room of the White House to engage in a **threat assessment**, *a priority ranking of the stream of dangers that confront the United States*. These threats are arrayed from the most pressing—Tier 1A targets—to those of lesser immediate concern (although still important), arrayed into Tiers 1B, 2, 3, and 4. During the Clinton years, officials considered WMD proliferation the most important intelligence priority; now that top 1A tier is held by Al Qaeda and other terrorist organizations, as well as nations and groups that engage in cyberattacks aimed at the United States. An example of a 1B target might be Afghanistan, where US troops are still under fire; WMD proliferation, always a concern; or the civil war in Syria. Tier 2 could include political, economic, and military activities in Russia and China; Tier 3, unrest in Tunisia or Egypt; and Tier 4, perhaps anti-US policies in Venezuela.

The establishment of this threat listing helps guide spending on intelligence collection. The sorting out of global risks can be subjective because not everyone will have the same roster of concerns and sometimes the smaller intelligence agencies are muscled aside by the larger ones. For instance, the CIA's concern about Al Qaeda will trump the DEA's request for more funding to interdict the flow of cocaine from Honduras to the United States. The threat assessment is a starting point, though, and the specific targeting continues to evolve throughout the tenure of an administration as world conditions ebb and flow.

Despite this formal review of intelligence targeting, the informational needs of policy makers are sometimes never clearly emphasized; therefore, the intelligence agencies may be uncertain about a key official's hierarchy of foreign policy concerns. Most everyone in Washington agrees that terrorism in the Middle East and Southwest Asia, along with cyberwarfare, are top collection priorities (1A targets), but other targeting requirements may be less obvious. How much interest is there in Washington policy circles about the activities of the terrorist group Boko Haram in Nigeria, for example? In 2013, this radical anti-American faction murdered twenty-nine school children and their English teacher, Mohammed Musa, in Nigeria on grounds that "Western education is sacrilege" (which is the literal translation of the name Boko Haram). Continual dialogues between producers and consumers of intelligence about targeting are vital to ensure that the IC is serving decision makers well. If an analyst is examining data on the subject of vodka consumption among males in Outer Mongolia, whereas the decision maker is focused on learning more about the rebel factions in the Syrian civil war, the work of the analyst will be viewed as irrelevant in policy circles—a self-licking ice cream cone.

Another occasional problem between the producers and consumers of intelligence is that the informational requests of policy makers may exceed the capabilities of the intelligence agencies, such as the question of exactly how many atomic bombs North Korea has hidden in deep underground caverns. The world consists of secrets and mysteries. Secrets may be found out with some luck and a well-placed agent or satellite, say, the number of Chinese nuclear submarines. Mysteries, however, often lie beyond the ken of mere mortals, such as accurately predicting who the Russia leader will be after Putin or when the civil war in Syria will end. Further, even when the proper intelligence is collected, policy makers may choose to disbelieve or ignore it—especially if the new information fails to corroborate the speech they made last month or support the political objectives they have just publicly announced.

The management problems inside the CIA can grow complex, as the Intelligence Directorate attempts, first, to obtain the best information available and, second, to make sure the right people know about it in a timely fashion. What may appear at first glance to be a simple and smoothly flowing stream of intelligence in Figure 9.4, with essential and accurate data swept along from asset to analyst to consumer, is instead a complicated series of interactions among men and women and their organizations that often result in the loss or distortion of vital information.

This planet may be but a tiny speck in the universe from a cosmological point of view, but its dimensions are vast for any spy agency trying to keep up with events in the 200-plus nations of the world. No individual or organization can claim omniscience; and since the United States (like every other nation) has finite resources, targeting priorities must be set. During the formal threat assessment and throughout the rest of each year, the managers of the intelligence cycle must decide in consultation with policy makers on which countries to target, what kinds of information are most important to gather, and what means of collection is likely to be most effective.

### Targeting

"The most obvious and most significant [threat to the United States] is the global challenge posed by the only nation that rivals in military power—the Soviet Union," stated Harold Brown, Secretary of Defense during the Carter administration.[30] Similarly, Casper Weinberger, Secretary of Defense in the Reagan administration, observed, "It's the threat that makes the budget. You've got to build your budget on the Russian budget."[31] In support of this policy emphasis, the Soviet Union steadily attracted most of America's intelligence resources during the Cold War—at times upward of 70 percent of the total. Even during the Cold War, though, America's intelligence interests covered a wide gamut of topics, in step with the broad diplomatic and security objectives of policy makers in Washington, as this excerpt from a CIA memorandum indicates:

> The traditional idea of intelligence is the spy who provides the enemy's war plans. Actually, intelligence is concerned not only with war plans, but with all the external concerns of our government. It must deal with the pricing debates of OPEC [Organization of Petroleum Exporting Countries] and the size of this year's Soviet crop (and here our foreknowledge comes from CIA's pioneering in new analysis techniques). It is concerned with Soviet strength along the Sino-Soviet border, with the intricacies of Chinese politics, with the water supply in the Middle East, with the quality of Soviet computers and its impact on our own export controls, with the narcotics trade in Southeast Asia, even with the struggle for control of Portuguese Timor.[32]

According to Agency officials, Russia and the Republics of the former Soviet Union continued to attract roughly one-half of the US intelligence budget for collection in the early 1990s after the end of the Cold War, but the remaining half was broadly distributed. As the Cold War receded into history, intelligence resources aimed at

Russia and its former allies further diminished, as a host of other targets—less countries than topics, like nuclear proliferation, terrorism, and international crime—crowded in line for budget resources. Clamoring for attention in recent years have been such matters as debt financing in the developing countries; international energy shortages; advances in science and technology around the world; narcotics shipments; immigration trends; human trafficking; global water supplies; population projections; arms control; and, above all, Al Qaeda and other terrorist organizations as well as the security of US troops in Iraq, Afghanistan, and elsewhere overseas. Policy makers have even asked the intelligence agencies to track global environmental developments and to keep an eye open for incipient pandemics.

The *selection of intelligence targets*, known as the setting of requirements or **tasking**, is a job involving many hands, sometimes even the president. "When I became President," recalled Jimmy Carter, "I was concerned, during the first few months, that quite often the intelligence community, itself, set its own priorities as a supplier of intelligence information. I felt that the customers—the ones who receive the intelligence information, including the Defense Department, myself and others—ought to be the ones to say this is what we consider to be most important."[33] The White House, the Department of State, and especially President Carter's DCI, Admiral Stansfield Turner, took a more active role than had recently been the case in assigning intelligence-collection requirements to the CIA and other agencies, especially in shifting attention away from the Soviet Union somewhat and toward the gathering of global economic information and data on developments within the smaller nations of the Third World. When the American four-star Army general and former leader of the US war effort in Afghanistan, David H. Petraeus, became head of the CIA in 2011, he placed an emphasis on gathering intelligence to direct the targeting of drones against terrorists operating in Afghanistan, Pakistan, Somalia, and Yemen.

With their constitutional standing to be defended against the aggrandizement of power in the executive branch, members of Congress have had their own suggestions for intelligence tasking, too; but here the intelligence community tries to draw the line. "We don't seek input from the Hill on collection requirements, but sometimes we get it anyway," a top CIA analyst in the DI complained during the Reagan administration. "We definitely don't want 535 new taskers; serving the executive branch is tough enough."[34] Like it or not, though, the CIA has had to respond to lawmakers—the men and women who approve or disapprove the Agency's annual budget. In the spirit of James Madison, some lawmakers insist that the CIA is there to serve the entire government, not just the White House and the Pentagon. The Agency, mindful that its funding comes from Capitol Hill, has reconsidered its initial hesitancy and now attempts to honor some of this tasking by Congress—at least when so ordered by influential lawmakers. In 2002 on the eve of war, for example, a few members of Congress insisted that the CIA prepare an in-depth study (a National Intelligence Estimate) on conditions in Iraq because President Bush had never gotten around to requesting one.

## Types of intelligence

Policy makers might like to know what has occurred in, say, Northern Mali or Northern Nigeria (hotbeds of terrorism in 2012–2013) in the past two hours, or whether Russia is presently supplying the Syrian regime with attack helicopters to defend itself against insurgents (a charge leveled at Moscow by Secretary of State Hillary Clinton in June of 2012).[35] In the these examples, the policy maker desires **current intelligence**—that is, *up-to-the-minute information that is often vital in times of crisis.*

In contrast, a policy maker might desire instead an extensive *study on a specific subject, accompanied by a long-range prediction.* This form of intelligence reporting is known as **research intelligence,** which can take the form of a National Intelligence Estimate (NIE) like the one on the situation in Iraq in 2002 mentioned earlier; or perhaps a definitive examination of potential leadership succession in China over the next decade; or an exhausting probe into the suspected Iranian nuclear weapons program.

Whereas these are the most common forms of intelligence sought by consumers, many others exist. Sometimes a policy maker will simply ask for a brief response to a query in the form of a memorandum on paper or sent through secure e-mail facilities. In one page, the memo is expected to inform the policy maker about the Nigerian oil industry; about Russian President Putin's agenda for his approaching visit to the United States; about the likelihood that CIA drone attacks against Taliban bases in Pakistan will eradicate Qaeda terrorism. On other occasions, the consumer (decision maker) may prefer a quick oral briefing, perhaps on the run between meetings or in a limousine on the way to the airport. "Policymakers will accept fifteen-minute briefings over the investment of five minutes to read a report," a senior CIA manager has observed.[36] The president and other top officials in the Reagan administration liked to have intelligence reports presented in a videotape format, especially personality profiles of Colonel Muammar Qaddafi of Libya and various Soviet leaders. President Obama enjoys questioning intelligence managers directly during early morning briefings in the Oval Office.[37] Regardless of what form the intelligence takes, the policy makers usually want it *now,* want it perfectly accurate, and want it without too many nuances—demands that can defy the human capabilities and the protective instincts of intelligence analysts.

## Collection

The second phase of the intelligence cycle is intelligence collection. The intelligence community relies on three broad approaches for the gathering of information. Two are covert collection methods: the use of *machines*—especially satellites and drone aircraft (**technical intelligence or TECHINT**), and the use of *spies* (**human intelligence, or HUMINT** in the intelligence acronym). Technical intelligence includes primarily: **signals intelligence or SIGINT,** which consists of *telephone calls, social media, and other forms of electronic transmissions*; **geospatial intelligence or GEOINT (**also known as

**imagery intelligence or IMINT)**, which includes *photographs of targets taken by satellites, reconnaissance aircraft, and, on the ground, hand-held cameras*; and **measurement-and-signatures intelligence or MASINT**, which relies on the placement of *concealed sensory devices to determine the presence of radioactive weaponry, lethal chemicals, and bacteriological materials*. The NSA is the key SIGINT collector; the NGA, the key GEOINT collector; and several intelligence agencies use MASINT.

The third approach to intelligence collection, and entirely overt, is known as **open source intelligence (OSINT)**. Ransom concluded in 1970 that about "80 percent or more of intelligence material in peacetime is overtly *collected from non-secret sources such as newspapers, libraries, radio broadcast, business and industrial reports, or from accredited foreign service officers.*"[38] Today, that figure is more like 90 to 95 percent because places like Russia and China are now more easily monitored through open sources than was the case during the Cold War.[39] An example of OSINT is the CIA's close attention to the public pronouncements of Iran's leaders about that nation's nuclear program.

As valuable as OSINT can be, a well-situated HUMINT asset may be able to steal a vital document from a safe in the middle of the night, download a foreign government computer, or overhear foreign leaders discuss impending military operations. Moreover, GEOINT satellites can photograph the number and location of Russian and Chinese missiles—topics unlikely to be covered in open media reporting.

To assist the efforts of analysts in sifting through open sources, the CIA maintains vast library and computer holdings. Further, the DNI has an Open Source Center (DNI/OSC) that monitors global radio and television programs, then translates and circulates this information to analysts throughout the intelligence community. Although overt collection provides the bulk of information gathered by the CIA, HUMINT and TECHINT often unearth the most important knowledge for US decision making—the golden nuggets hidden by foreign governments and terrorist organizations. The Library of Congress (LC) has vast OSINT holdings the US government can draw on; but often policy makers must go beyond library-based holdings, turning to the secret sources of information gathered by spies and machines to learn what is happening in foreign lands.

An example of HUMINT's importance is Colonel Oleg Penkovskiy, the man who smuggled to the United States and the United Kingdom thousands of documents on Soviet missilery, including the useful insight that Soviet missile bases were often configured in a Star of David design.[40] This blue-chip intelligence led to the uncovering of Soviet rockets in Cuba in 1962. Calculating the cost-effectiveness of HUMINT is difficult, though. For every Penkovskiy, the Intelligence Community may have hundreds of agents who produce little more than snippets of gossip. Often HUMINT reports are unreliable. Prior to the Cuban missile crisis of 1962, intelligence from CIA assets in Cuba proved notoriously inaccurate; of 200 reports about missile sightings, only six proved accurate.[41] Moreover, one always faces the possibility that an asset is actually a double agent through whom deception operations are being conducted by an adversary against the United States, as proved to be the case with *every* CIA asset in East Germany and Cuba during the Cold War.[42]

Another difficulty with HUMINT is that most of the Agency's case officers who recruit and handle local assets are under official cover (OC) inside US embassy overseas. Yet they are unlikely to run into Qaeda operatives at embassy cocktail parties. More useful are nonofficial cover (NOC) case officers out in the local society using one cover or another, such as pretending to be an archeologist or a bartender during the day, then emerging as a case officer prowling for assets when night darkens the streets. The United States is short on NOCs, because it can be dangerous work, not to mention exhausting to hold down two jobs: the cover job and the spy. If a NOC is apprehended by local law enforcement or counterintelligence authorities, he or she is without diplomatic immunity.

Collection is the costliest phase of the intelligence cycle, especially through technical means such as satellites. The managers of the various intelligence agencies engage constantly in a tug-of-war over the distribution of these large dollars. The HUMINT argument is difficult to sell in budget councils. The people who make decisions about national security spending prefer "to concentrate on things that can be 'scientifically' measured."[43] Just as counting missiles, and—the favorite—warheads, became the fascination of strategic planners during the Cold War, so are intelligence planners today drawn to the counting of satellites and other mechanical devices for surveillance, with all their glittering, dazzling technology. A reconnaissance spy plane, including drones carrying high-resolution cameras, is something tangible; it takes pictures that can be examined by lawmakers in close hearings. In contrast, the nameless spy may or may not obtain information of great significance; and, for reasons of security, specifics about the spy's operations can never be discussed, even in closed-door budget meetings; indeed, his or her true identity will be known only to the spy's case officer and one or two other managers at CIA Headquarters.[44]

Moreover, the giant aerospace corporations and laboratories persistently lobby for surveillance-hardware contracts, with skills finely tuned during years of experience with weapons contracting through the Department of Defense. Practitioners of HUMINT have no such external advocates and, despite occasional coups like Penkovskiy, this approach to espionage—"tradecraft"—remains the neglected stepchild of intelligence collection. Yet satellites and aircraft, whether piloted or unpiloted, have their limits. For example, half the world remains cloud covered at any given moment.

When technical methods of intelligence collection are coupled with HUMINT and open-source intelligence, however, the result is an impressive array of data-gathering by the US intelligence agencies that produces a complex network of information. The world will continue to offer up surprises, however, as Americans were reminded painfully with the 9/11 attacks and when the anticipated WMDs in Iraq proved to be a myth in 2003. Neither officials in Washington, DC nor in the capitals of other nations will ever achieve a god-like ability to know everything that is taking place around the globe. Surprises, though, are now fewer in number than during the days when "intelligence" meant occasional newspaper clippings.

## Processing

The next step in the intelligence cycle also presents difficulties. Here the collected information undergoes various refinements for closer study by analysts. Coded data must be decrypted, foreign languages translated into English, photographic material interpreted. The purpose is to make the information readable and understandable for the analyst.[45]

Even with today's computers, the processing procedures can be time consuming. A professional photo interpreter may require four hours to fully decipher a single frame of satellite photography, determining what the black-and-white lines actually mean.[46] (Over four hundred photographs stream into NGA each day.) The recondite art of "cratetology," interpreting the often obscure markings—numbers, letters, symbols—on crates (shipping containers) aboard ocean freighters, can also consume hours of careful study by experts. In 1984, cratetologists at the CIA failed to agree on the meaning of markings on boxes unloaded from a Soviet cargo vessel in Nicaragua. Did the cargo consist of MIG-21s, antiaircraft missiles, attack helicopters, or something more benign? Today, cratetologists worry chiefly about whether a nuclear devise might be hidden aboard a freighter headed for an American harbor and they search for telltale signs on ships at the port of origin and at sea. A reliable HUMINT asset on board ship would be invaluable.

The most significant challenge in the processing phase is to sift out the meaningful "signals" from all the "noise" that is collected by machines and human spies—separating the wheat from the chaff. This is primarily an information technology (IT) challenge. One NSA Director, Admiral Noel Gayler, complained that he felt as though a "fire hose held was held to my mouth," so overwhelming was the deluge of information—useful and useless—gathered by NSA's interceptors.[47] Another NSA Director complained that he had three intelligence problems: "processing, processing, processing."[48] Breakthroughs in computer sophistication are improving the ability of the NSA to process "big data" more rapidly and with finer tuning in the search for important signals.

After processing comes the central purpose of the intelligence cycle: the conversion of raw information into usable intelligence. Here is the marriage of data, overtly and covertly obtained, with thoughtful study—in a word, analysis (what British intelligence officers refer to as "assessment"). The objective is to bring insight to the mountain of data that has been swept in by all the intelligence agencies.

## Analysis

The *individuals responsible for the conversion of raw (unevaluated) information into "finished" (evaluated) intelligence* are called **analysts.** They are highly educated men and women who are experts on a single country, such as Zaire; on broad topics, such as the flow of petrodollars; or on quite narrow—albeit important—topics, such as the efficiency of North Korean rocket fuels. Each analyst, ideally, has the characteristics advocated decades ago by Sherman Kent, a former Yale University historian and for years the dean of analysts at the CIA: "the best in professional training, the highest intellectual integrity, and a very large amount of worldly wisdom."[49] Like students and professors, analysts conduct research—only their work is based on a combination of secret and open sources. The approaches they use are similar to the ones used at universities: library and Internet searches, poring over documents, talking with experts, thinking hard about the connections they are beginning to notice—like archeologists piecing together an ancient ruin shard by shard. The task of the analyst is difficult, to say the least, as illustrated by the challenge of ascertaining Sadam Hussein's intentions on the eve of what had all the hallmarks of another invasion of Kuwait in 1994, examined in the case study at the beginning of this chapter. Or take the failure of CIA analysts to anticipate the fall of the Shah of Iran in 1979. In *Perspectives on American Foreign Policy* 9.1, a senior CIA analyst recalls the complexities of predicting events in Tehran that turbulent year.

The job of analysts is to supply policy makers with accurate and timely interpretations of global threats (as well as opportunities) facing the United States. The intelligence agencies produce hundreds of documents for this purpose, including brief memos, secure e-mails, and even baseball-card sized fact sheets that provide photos and biographical profiles of foreign leaders. For current intelligence, *preeminent among the daily documents produced by the CIA and the other secret agencies is the* **President's Daily Brief (PDB)**. This report is the most tightly held document in Washington. The *PDB* arrives early in the morning via CIA courier in the offices of a dozen or so key individuals. The number varies slightly from administration to administration, but the *PDB* readership always includes the president, the vice president, the secretaries of state and defense, and the national security adviser. This top secret "newspaper" provides officials with the latest information on major political developments around the globe that have occurred in the last twenty-four hours. It often sets the agenda for morning discussions among the recipients and their aides, who often ask the CIA at the time of the PDB delivery and briefing for additional information about articles in the document.

---

### PERSPECTIVES ON AMERICAN FOREIGN POLICY 9.1

**Senior CIA ANALYSTS on predicting the 1979 revolution in Iran:**

We knew the Shah was widely unpopular, and we knew there would be mass demonstrations, even riots. But how many shopkeepers would resort to violence, and how long would Army officers remain loyal to the Shah? Perhaps the Army would shoot down 10,000 rioters, maybe 20,000. If the ranks of the insurgents swelled further, though, how far would the Army be willing to go before it decided the Shah was a losing proposition? All this we duly reported; but no one could predict with confidence the number of dissidents who would actually take up arms, or the "tipping point" for Army loyalty.

*SOURCE:* Loch K. Johnson, interview with senior CIA analyst (August 28, 1984) Washington, DC.

More difficult to prepare are long-range research reports. The key document in this category is the **National Intelligence Estimate**, a type of intelligence analysis mentioned earlier in this chapter. An **NIE** may be defined formally as *"a statement of what is going to happen in any country, in any area, in any given situation, as far as possible into the future."*[50] As with the *PBD*, an NIE may influence high-level discussions among Washington decision makers, as when the Estimate on Dien Bien Phu requested by President Eisenhower in 1954 contributed to his decision against US intervention in Vietnam; or when the 2002 NIE on Iraq led some lawmakers to question the invasion plans of President George W. Bush.[51] The trend, though, has been away from the preparation of Estimates, as analysts respond to the greater interest of consumers in current intelligence: what has happened in the past twenty-four hours. This is a risky trade-off, though, because a nation needs to have a strong reservoir of deep knowledge about the world, not just information about what has happened recently. "CNN intelligence" is the derisive term for current intelligence used by critics concerned about the erosion of NIEs and America's deeper knowledge base for understanding world affairs.

Good intelligence analysis is a demanding responsibility that requires much expertise and sophistication. A well-prepared intelligence report has to be objective, accurate, timely, relevant, well-written, to-the-point, based on all-source fusion, and specific enough to be "actionable." None of these goals is easy in a world of secrets and mysteries. In August of 2013, the United States closed several of its embassies overseas and tightened security at home because of warning intelligence that indicated the likelihood of a Qaeda attack against Americans somewhere. Because the reports from CIA assets failed to name a specific target, the intelligence never became actionable enough to focus America's defensive capabilities. Fortunately, no attack occurred.

Even though the amount of resources devoted to collection and analysis is great, the intelligence community—like every other human enterprise—will never be free of mistakes and will never have a complete picture of dangers in a world of "increasingly complex, fragmented, and ubiquitous information."[52] Recall that in the months before 9/11, the FBI failed to locate two of the hijackers based in San Diego for months as they prepared for their attacks. More broadly, the Intelligence Community knew little about Al Qaeda and its plans for global jihadist battlefield. Subsequently in the lead-up to the 2003 war in Iraq, Intelligence Community had little information about events inside Iraq. As a result, the secret agencies were too quick to accept what proved to be misleading reports about WMDs in the country, including "Curveball's" fabrications. Absent solid information, the CIA extrapolated from its earlier underestimated reports about the progress of the Iraqi nuclear weapons program in 1991 and this time overestimated the chances that Saddam Hussein might have WMDs in 2002.

These disastrous errors have led the intelligence agencies to improve their capabilities, such as placing more assets in places relatively ignored during the Cold War (such as the Middle East)—although the FBI continues to have more agents in New York City than the CIA has assets around the world. The CIA has also expanded its "co-location" experiment begun in the 1990s that placed some operatives and analysts at CIA Headquarters in the same suite of offices, so they could share their field and "library" experiences (respectively). Reforms notwithstanding, political scientist Richard K. Betts has stressed that "some incidence of failure [is] inevitable." He urges a higher "tolerance for disaster."[53]

Even the last phase of the intelligence cycle, dissemination, is replete with chances for error. Indeed, the greatest intelligence hazard of all can occur at this stage: the intentional distortion of information.

## Dissemination

"Being right isn't enough," stresses Donald Gregg, a seasoned CIA officer. "You have to inject that 'rightness' into the policy process. Unless a particular concern is actually raised at the correct moment during one of the key meetings, say, the NSC, the good analysis done by the intelligence community is often lost. The chip must be put in the pot at this stage—and forcefully."[54]

The key to success for the CIA during the dissemination phase may be summed up in one word: "dialogue." Intelligence officers and senior policy makers must talk to each other if the transfer of intelligence is to work properly. Perhaps the toughest assignment for an intelligence agency, notes a senior CIA analyst, is "to give honest assessments and still keep the policymaker reading."[55] Another former senior Agency analyst draws this conclusion: "Many of the consumers are ideologues. It is hard to work with them—especially when we're usually dealing with highly ambiguous data. When consumers criticize our product, it is often on grounds that it fails to support their suppositions."[56]

This *rejection by policy makers of objective intelligence for their own political purposes*, the **politicization of intelligence**, became particularly controversial during the Reagan administration. Intelligence analysts threw doubt on a number of the administration's beliefs: that Syria was a puppet of the Soviet Union; that Nicaragua aggressively exported arms to Marxist guerrillas throughout Central America; that a Soviet oil pipeline to Western Europe would significantly increase the vulnerability of US allies to Soviet pressure; that the shooting down of a South Korean passenger airline in 1983 was not a misidentification by the Soviets of a hostile spy plane but rather an intentional murder of civilians; and, among other examples, that the assassination plot against the Pope in 1984 had been concocted in Moscow.[57]

During the administration of George W. Bush, Vice President Cheney and others cast aside intelligence that questioned White House and DOD conclusions regarding Saddam Hussein: that the Iraqi leader had close ties to Al Qaeda; that he was importing yellow-cake uranium from Niger; and that he had WMDs on hand and would use them against the United States. The DCI at the time, George Tenet, failed in his responsibility to ensure that the President heard dissent from experienced intelligence analysts about the likelihood of WMDs in Iraq, not just rosy reassurances that corroborated White House policy aspirations.[58]

On other occasions, policy makers may like some of the intelligence provided by the CIA; it may agree with their predispositions or political objectives. They will "cherry pick" this supportive analysis and ignore the rest. Yet, according to a former Agency analyst, even the favorable portions of an intelligence report may have a short shelf life. "We always get new information," he notes, "and we may have to change our original assessments."[59] In the meantime, the policy maker may have delivered a widely reported speech or press comment based on the first evaluation. President Carter, for example, spoke strongly in favor of pulling US troops out of South Korea in the early days of his administration, but he had to reverse his position when the intelligence community began to report increases in the number of North Korean fighting forces.

More recently, in 2012, America's Ambassador to the UN, Susan E. Rice, gave a press conference about the murder of America's ambassador in Libya, J. Christopher Stevens, and three other Americans. She duly reported what she had learned from the US intelligence agencies; but it was early in the crisis and some of initial analysis was incorrect. When the CIA came up with a more complete understanding of the circumstances, Rice was left in the embarrassing situation of seeming to have misled the media and the public. She had said in the press conference, based on early CIA reports, that the murders had arisen out of a spontaneous anti-American street protest in Libya; later it became clear that the assassinations were well planned and carried out by Al Qaeda affiliates in the region. This controversy hurt Rice's reputation and led to a withdrawal of her nomination to become secretary of state (although she bounced back and became the administration's national security adviser).[60] No wonder President Johnson compared intelligence to a cow that sticks its dirty hoof into a clean pail of milk.[61]

Moreover, Congress is now part of the dissemination phase and this addition has caused further friction between analysts and policy makers. During the period from 1947 to 1974, when congressional monitoring of the CIA was considerably less systematic and comprehensive, lawmakers asked for little information and little was offered by the Agency.[62] Today, members of Congress have renewed their interest in their constitutional prerogatives to hold the executive branch accountable and now demand a greater share of the intelligence product. "Few intelligence documents went to the Hill before 1976," a top CIA manager reported in 1984. "Now only a tiny percentage of intelligence that goes to the executive doesn't go also to the two Intelligence Committees of Congress."[63] In any given year since the mid-1980s, the Directorate of Intelligence alone will provide Capitol Hill with over 500 briefings. This flow of intelligence to lawmakers provides them with ammunition for reliable critiques of the foreign policy perspectives advocated by the executive branch. This favor to Congress is unlikely to endear the CIA to executive branch officials in any administration, but a robust role for lawmakers in the nation's governance is exactly what the constitutional framers had in mind.

Despite the hazards, intelligence officials have become increasingly sophisticated in the ways of nurturing ties with policy makers in both branches. "We used to throw things over the transom," remembers a senior CIA analyst, "Now we *market*."[64] The top manager of current intelligence in the Agency during the Reagan years emphasized the importance of packaging, timing, and building rapport. "Good packaging is vital," he stated. "You must focus the policy maker's attention. They are busy. They like pictures and graphs."[65]

Regardless how hard they may try, though, intelligence officers can find it difficult—if not impossible—to persuade policy makers that they need to read, or at least listen to, intelligence reports. President Clinton had little interest in intelligence, for instance, and even George W. Bush—the son of a former DCI—displayed a casual concern for the latest news from the CIA.[66] Over the nation's lifetime, the most avid consumers of intelligence have been George Washington, Dwight David Eisenhower, John F. Kennedy, and George H. W. Bush. As former generals, Washington and Eisenhower knew that battlefield victories could be won by good intelligence, and they carried this desire for information into the presidency. Although momentarily angry about the Bay of Pigs fiasco, President Kennedy had a natural interest in spies and devoured all of the James Bond novels, as well as the *President's Daily Brief* and other intelligence reports. The first President Bush came to understand the importance of intelligence firsthand while serving as DCI in 1975.

To improve the chances of access to policy makers, the CIA encourages the nurturing of close personal ties between analysts and policy makers—easier said than done, given the harried existence of the latter. While serving as an assistant secretary in the Defense Department in 1995–1996, Harvard University scholar Joseph S. Nye Jr. recalls having only a few minutes a day to read intelligence reports. He advised the nation's top analysts, National Intelligence Officers (NIOs, located at the CIA), that they needed to brief policy makers orally on key intelligence conclusions "because they're probably not going to have read the written product."[67] The personal chemistry between the producers and consumers of intelligence may be the most important aspect of the intelligence cycle; but even when the chemistry is good, "getting on the policy maker's calendar is hard," lamented a senior DIA manager.[68]

## SECRECY AND FOREIGN POLICY

Despite all of its challenges, intelligence often provides a reliable foundation of knowledge for the making of more thoughtful foreign policy decisions. In a democracy, however, it is not enough to provide solid information to decision makers in the executive branch; it is important, as well, to ensure proper access to information by Congress and the American people whenever possible. Yet secrecy has obvious advantages in the planning and implementation of foreign policy, a viewpoint acknowledged by America's leaders from the earliest days. Commenting on the importance of military intelligence during the Revolutionary War, General George Washington observed: "The necessity of procuring good Intelligence is apparent and need not be further urged. All that remains for me to add is that you keep the whole matter as secret as possible, for upon Secrecy Success depends in most enterprises of the kind, and for want of it, they are generally defeated, however well-planned or promising of favorable issue."[69]

However true this perspective may be, not all secrets are good and bad secrets can corrode democracy (see *Perspectives on American Foreign Policy 9.2*).

## PERSPECTIVES ON AMERICAN FOREIGN POLICY 9.2

**The MOYNIHAN COMMISSION on secrecy:**

Excessive secrecy has significant consequences for the national interest when, as a result, policymakers are not fully informed, government is not held accountable for its actions, and the public cannot engage in informed debates. This remains a dangerous world; some secrecy is vital to save lives, bring miscreants to justice, protect national security, and engage in effective diplomacy. Yet as Justice Potter Steward noted in his opinion in the Pentagon Pagers case, when everything is secret, nothing is secret. Even as billions of dollars are spent each year on government secrecy, the classification and personnel security systems have not always succeeded at their core task of protecting those secrets most critical to the national security. The classification system, for example, is used too often to deny the public an understanding of the policymaking process, rather than for the necessary protection of intelligence activities and other highly sensitive matters.

SOURCE: *Secrecy,* Report of the Commission on Protecting and Reducing Government Secrecy, chaired by Senator Daniel Patrick Moynihan (D-New York), Washington, DC: US Government Printing Office, 1997, p. xxi.

## Secrets Good and Bad

The departure schedules and destinations of American troop transport ships during time of war; the sophisticated technology of the radar-elusive *Stealth* bomber and other advanced weaponry; the names of espionage agents operating on behalf of the United States in foreign lands; the bargaining positions of US diplomats at arms control sessions in Geneva or trade talks in Tokyo—each depends on secrecy. Sometimes, too, secret or "back-channel" diplomatic dialogues with the leaders of other nations can persuade them to change their positions more readily than can public criticism. In the glare of the media, foreign leaders may be unwilling to back down under pressure from the United States, for fear they may lose face with their own people.

At the time of the Carter administration, for example, the leader of South Korea was apparently on the verge of executing his chief political opponent. President Carter moved to intercede, but South Korean diplomats warned Carter's emissary that if the United States made a public issue of the matter, the president of South Korea would order the execution rather than have it seem that he was an American lackey. Carter quietly negotiated a stay of execution through back channels. During the Nixon and Ford administrations, Secretary of State Henry Kissinger maintains that he achieved his greatest successes through private diplomacy with foreign ministers and heads of state. In his memoirs, he aimed his sharpest criticism at Congress for meddling in this private diplomacy and, through publicity, sometimes upsetting finely tuned understandings with foreign officials. Kissinger is especially critical of legislative pronouncements during the Vietnam War that called for a quick US withdrawal, at the same time he was trying to negotiate a peace settlement with North Vietnamese representatives in Paris.[70]

Frequently, though, executive branch officials prefer to conduct foreign policy in secret simply because this approach avoids the necessity for defending their policies before lawmakers, journalists, and the public. Recall how during the investigation into the Iran-*contra* scandal in 1987, lawmakers asked a key witness, Vice Admiral John M. Poindexter (President Reagan's national security adviser), why he failed to inform the congressional intelligence committees of these covert actions—as required by law. Poindexter's response was that he "simply did not want any outside interference."[71] Constitutional checks and balances—lawmakers—were merely a hindrance, to be secretly bypassed. The Admiral said that he believed in tight **compartmentation**, *the practice within the executive branch of maintaining operational security through the establishment of special channels that limit the access of individuals to information*—even though the Senate and House intelligence committees were legally permitted access to the details of covert action by virtue of the Hughes-Ryan Act of 1974 and the Intelligence Oversight Act of 1980.

The cochair of the Iran-*contra* investigative committee, Lee H. Hamilton (D-Indiana), had this response for Poindexter: "You compartmentalized not only the President's senior advisers [neither Secretary of State George P. Shultz nor Secretary of Defense Casper Weinberger knew of the *contra* diversion of funding from the secret sale of CIA missiles to Iran], but, in effect, you locked the President himself out of the process."[72]

The American people and their representatives in Congress have become wary of secret foreign policy because of the many instances when they have been misled by officials in the executive branch. For example, in 2002, the administration of George W. Bush frightened the American people into believing that Saddam Hussein had WMDs, only for the public to learn after the US invasion of Iraq that the dictator did not. The American people were told, too, that Al Qaeda and Iraq shared a 9/11 terrorist connection. They did not. Similarly, during the Cold War, Senate investigators discovered the use of unlawful intelligence operations against American antiwar protesters (Operation Chaos), assassination plots against foreign leaders, and attempts to topple democratically elected officials whom the US government distrusted (Salvador Allende of Chile, among others)—all carried out in utmost secrecy.[73] In the name of national security, open debate has often been abandoned. Regardless of the lessons drawn from recent scandals such as the Iran-*contra* and misuse of wiretap authority by the White House in 2001–2005, secrecy continues to hold an almost irresistible temptation for officials in the executive branch.[74] The periodic evocation of the so-called doctrine of executive privilege is one example of attempts by the executive branch to eliminate the constitutional prerogatives of lawmakers by hiding information from them.

## Executive Privilege

In the eyes of officials in the executive branch, a central attraction of America's intelligence agencies is the opportunity they afford to chart a foreign policy course with little or no public debate. In its covert shipment of arms to Iran during the Iran-*contra* affair, aides in the Reagan administration carried the goal of exclusion to an extreme. They refused not only to inform Congress but kept the operation strictly within the limited ambit of a few NSC staffers, a handful of field operatives, and a narrow slice of the CIA—beyond the purview of even the president and the NSC's other principal members.

More recently, the use of drones by the Obama administration for foreign assassinations has raised questions about the right of presidents to determine how such force will be used overseas, especially when the targets are American citizens. Congress has never debated or taken a vote on the use of drones as instruments of a US secret foreign policy. While the details of drone attacks dribbled out in media leaks in 2012, their value—not to mention judgments about the morality and legality of these operations—remained concealed in the private deliberations of the Oval Office, the CIA, and the upper reaches of the Pentagon.

In 2013, members of the House complained about FBI refusals to provide information to Congress about possible flaws in the Bureau's counterterrorism operations—especially its failure to prevent the Boston terrorist attack earlier that year. "What I am looking to do is identify our security shortcomings and change them," Representative William Keating (D-Massachusetts) wrote in a letter to incoming FBI Director James B. Comey. "Without forthright information from the FBI we are prevented from taking the critical steps needed to protect the American public." In the Senate, lawmakers sought access to Department of Justice legal opinions justifying drone operations, but the DOJ refused to provide full access to these documents.[75]

### The cloak of executive secrecy

Sometimes this goal of congressional exclusion is achieved through the use of **executive privilege**, defined as *an assertion by the president of constitutional authority to withhold information from the legislative and judicial branches of government.* This topic is nowhere addressed in the Constitution but became a source of dispute between the executive and legislative branches as early as the first presidency. George Washington initially refused, then acquiesced, to a request from lawmakers for information about a botched military confrontation with Native Americans.

The confrontation over executive privilege became most shrill, however, in the context of the Watergate scandal. Appearing before the Ervin committee, established by the Senate in 1973 to investigate the Watergate affair and chaired by Sam Ervin Jr. (D-North Carolina), President Nixon's attorney general, Richard Kleindienst, claimed that "the constitutional authority of the President in his discretion" allowed the president to withhold information in his possession or in the possession of the Executive branch, if the president reached the conclusion that disclosure "would impair the proper exercise of his constitutional functions."[76] This implied that Congress could be prohibited from speaking to any of the millions of employees in the executive branch. Kleindienst's statement represented a sweeping extension of the more traditional notion that only the closest White House aides could hide behind the president's

cloak by evoking executive privilege. The Watergate crisis was coming to a head, however, and Nixon soon fired Kleindienst for his inept efforts to head off a legislative
inquiry.

President Nixon went even further in his attempt to use executive privilege as an
escape from the Watergate inquiry. Without precedent, he stated in 1973 that not only
could current members of the president's staff refuse to appear before congressional
committees, but so could past members—a position that senators sarcastically labeled
the "doctrine of eternal privilege."[77] Among other things, Nixon also extended executive privilege to cover "presidential papers," which he defined magisterially as "all
documents, produced or received by the President or any member of the White House
staff in connection with his official duties."[78] In a case that went to the Supreme Court
in 1974, Nixon argued that the doctrine of executive privilege protected sixty-four
Oval Office conversations that had been recorded by the President's own secret taping
system and were being sought by Watergate investigators. *The Court rejected the contention (**United States v. Nixon**) that a president had an absolute executive privilege and
forced the President to yield the tapes to investigators.* The judges, however, did give constitutional stature to executive privilege as a general rule for most confidential communications, noting that great deference would be entitled to the claim if foreign
policy or military secrets were involved.

In response to the Ervin Committee's pointed criticism of the Nixon administration's interpretations of executive privilege, the President's aides eventually consented
to appear in executive (secret) session on Capitol Hill, but not in public hearings.
Chairman Ervin remained unimpressed. "What do they eat that makes them grow so
great?" he asked at a press conference. "I am not willing to elevate them to a position
above the great mass of the American people. I don't think we have any such thing as
royalty or nobility to let anybody come down at night like Nicodemus and whisper
something in my ear that no one else can hear. This is not executive privilege. It is
executive poppycock."[79] As evidence regarding the Watergate break-in began to surface in the media, a refusal to testify in open hearings became an increasingly un-
tenable position for White House aides implicated in the cover-up. This segment of
Nixon's wall of executive privilege began to crumble.

The Ford administration attempted to stretch the cloak of executive privilege to
another extravagant length. At issue was Operation Shamrock, an intelligence program that involved the NSA and private communications companies; it was designed
to intercept all cables and telegrams sent abroad or received by Americans. Initially at
the request of the Truman administration, RCA, Global, and ITT World Communications stored their international message traffic on magnetic tapes, which they turned
over to the NSA. The agency studied the messages for possible hints of espionage activity. The operation may have violated the Federal Communications Act provisions protecting the privacy of communications, so Shamrock became a subject of legislative
inquires. When a House subcommittee called the corporation presidents as witnesses
in 1976, the CEOs turned to the Ford administration for guidance. President Ford,

through his attorney general Edward H. Levi (formerly dean of the University of Chicago School of Law), claimed that the corporations were immune from congressional appearances in this case because Shamrock was a sensitive, top-secret project ordered by the White House. The doctrine of executive privilege was now extended to the private sector.

The chairperson of the subcommittee, Bella S. Abzug (D-New York), expressed dismay over the assertion of executive privilege by a private corporation. Her colleague, Representative E. Moss (D-Utah) put the matter bluntly. "The Attorney General is without any authority," Moss declared. "It is the most outrageous assumption, the most arrogant display by the Attorney General I have ever seen. Some damn two-bit appointee of the President is not the law-making body of this country."[80] The House subcommittee, like the Ervin Committee, was disinclined to accept extensions of executive privilege that blocked what it thought was the constitutional duty of lawmakers to provide a check on power in the executive branch. When the subcommittee called for contempt of Congress citations against the corporate executives if they refused to testify, the CEOs decided that wisdom lie in appearing before the Congress promptly—regardless of President Ford's backing and advice not to appear.

In 2012, President Obama evoked executive privilege—reversing his earlier judgment against this practice—in response to a GOP-led House Oversight Committee request for more documents on a controversial Justice Department operation to trace illegal guns flowing to Mexican drug lords from the state of Arizona. Labeled "Fast and Furious," the operation accidentally resulted in sophisticated weaponry falling into the hands of drug dealers who killed a US border guard with one of the rifles. House Republicans accused the President of resisting their attempts to investigate Justice Department incompetence and hindering the duty of lawmakers to conduct oversight. In return, the White House and the Justice Department claimed the inquiry was a witch hunt to embarrass the administration in the middle of a presidential election campaign.[81]

### Delay and deceit

Usually, though, conflicts between the branches over information are less clear-cut. A more common tactic of the executive branch is simply to **stonewall** and **slow roll** lawmakers, that is, *to delay, delay, and then delay some more in response to congressional requests for information*. "Bureaucrats engage in interminable stalling when asked for information," wrote an expert on executive privilege, Harvard University professor of law Raoul Berger.[82] During investigations into the intelligence failures related to the terrorist attacks on 9/11, the George W. Bush administration constantly sought to delay congressional investigations by refusing access by lawmakers to documents and witnesses relevant to the case.[83] The administration responded in the same manner when lawmakers tried to probe the President's decision to bypass the Foreign Intelligence Surveillance Act of 1978 and allow wiretaps without a warrant—even though a strong coalition of Democrats and Republicans had passed that law to ensure close supervision by the judicial branch over the use of national security wiretaps by executive branch officials. All too often in the past, presidents of both parties had misused wiretaps for political purposes—a blow to American democracy. When the second Bush administration ignored this important statute beginning in 2001 and the violations finally leaked to the media (published by the *New York Times* in 2005), members of Congress initiated a probe that led to a new surveillance law (the FISA Amendments Act of 2008) that required closer adherence by the administration to the wiretap rules established by the original FISA in 1978.[84]

The executive branch will no doubt continue to resist full disclosure of its activities to the Congress. Another disturbing example has been the secrecy surrounding the harmful effects of nuclear waste at government facilities, concealed over the years by officials seemingly more concerned with nuclear weapons production than with public health.[85] Both the George W. Bush and the Obama administrations also resisted attempts by Congress and the public to investigate the origins of torture activities used by the military and the CIA during the war against global terrorism. In 2013, the Senate Select Committee on Intelligence was finally able to complete a (still classified) report on the subject of torture that, according to the panel's chair, Diane Feinstein (D-California), is sharply critical of this harsh approach to intelligence collection.[86]

## Prior Restraint

As a further attempt to bottle up information, officials in the executive branch sometimes attempt to curb the publication of materials deemed too sensitive for public eyes. This *withholding by the government of the right to publish information* is often referred to as **prior restraint**. For the most part, courts have been loath to allow prior restraint, recognizing that the viability of democracy depends on an adequate flow of information from the media to the people on public affairs. Only in this way can voters make informed decisions about the quality of their representatives in the White House and on Capitol Hill. Without good information, elections become a farce; the electorate has no way to evaluate the merits of those who hold office. Truth is the *sine qua non* for a successful democracy, but truth can be arrived at only through transparency. "Any system of prior restraints of expression comes to this Court bearing a heavy presumption against its constitutional validity," stated the Supreme Court in the celebrated case of *New York Times Co. v. United States* (1971), known less formally as the Pentagon Papers case (a legal decision discussed initially in Chapter 7). The Court concluded: "The government thus carries a heavy burden of showing justification for the imposition of such restraint."[87]

Recall that in the Pentagon Papers case, the Nixon administration failed to convince a majority of justices that prior restraint was necessary when the White House sought to prevent publication of a secret Department of Defense history of the Vietnam War. The administration argued that the documents contained information that could be harmful to American foreign policy. The man responsible for the leak, RAND think tank analyst Daniel Ellsberg, believed to the contrary that Americans needed to know the facts about the true course of the war in Vietnam; this knowledge would make public debate over further involvement in Indochina more meaningful and accurate. He was personally convinced, moreover, that no secrets of real significance were in the papers; rather, they were being kept classified because officials wished to conceal from public view a record of the various mistakes that had led the United States deeper into an unwinnable war.[88] Ellsberg's critics viewed his decision to leak the Pentagon documents as treasonable, because he revealed classified information without proper authorization that might have aided the enemy (the North Vietnamese).

By a vote of 5-to-4, the justices decided against the government. Justice Potter Stewart joined the majority and explained his reasoning in this manner: "We are asked, quite simply, to prevent the publication by two newspapers [the *New York Times* and the *Washington Post*] of material that the Executive Branch insists should not, in the national interest, be published. I am convinced that the Executive is correct with respect to some of the documents involved. But I cannot say that disclosure of any of them will surely result in *direct, immediate, and irreparable damage* to the Nation or its people. That being so, there can under the First Amendment be but one judicial resolution of the issues before us. I join the judgments of the Court."[89] This decision was a high-water mark for freedom of the press, but was by means an end to future government efforts at prior restraint.

In 2010, a similar controversy arose over an unorthodox media organization called WikiLeaks, which elected to publish—often in close cooperation with the mainstream media, including the *New York Times*—classified documents from the Pentagon and the Department of State. Some of the WikiLeaks papers included the names of CIA assets in Afghanistan as well as highly personal remarks about foreign dignitaries made by American diplomats in embassy cables meant for the eyes of top State Department officials only. The White House, along with the leaders of Defense and State, were livid over the disclosures and sought to take legal action against WikiLeaks. In 2013, the WikiLeaks case was still up in the air, but apt to land in court as well.

Senator Daniel Patrick Moynihan (D-New York), who led a major commission inquiry into secrecy in the 1990s, once spoke about the relationship of secrecy (in the context of the Iran-*contra* scandal): "[The scandal] could not have happened without the secrecy system. Millions on millions of secret documents every year—some seven million to be semi-exact, for the number itself is a secret. The effect is to hide things from the American people that they need to know. And within the executive branch to hide things from each other . . . It's over, you could say. But it's not. A set of captains and kings has departed. Issues are different. But the secrecy system is still in place: the oldest, most enduring institution of the Cold War.[90] And it continues today, with the secrecy surrounding warrantless wiretapping, CIA renditions and prisons, the torture of detainees, the scope of NSA domestic intelligence gathering, and the escalating use of drones against foreign targets—including the assassination of suspected terrorists, even Americans—without sufficient accountability from Congress or the courts.

On the broad subject of secrecy, many lawmakers share the conclusion reached by Professor Berger: "At bottom, the issue concerns the right of Congress and the people to participate in making the fateful decisions that affect the fortunes of the nation. Claims of presidential power to bar such participation or to withhold on one ground or another the information that is indispensable for intelligent participation undermine this right and sap the very foundations of democratic government."[91] Yet, paradoxically, the Republic itself could be endangered by foreign threats if all of America's secret foreign policy activities were conducted in the open. The challenge for democracy is to maintain a proper balance between the necessity, on the one hand, of protecting some secrets that might be used by enemies of the United States and, on the other hand, the desire for government transparency and open debate—the lifeblood of democracy.

## SUMMARY

Since America's War of Independence, intelligence has been an integral part of US foreign policy. At the heart of the collection and analysis mission is the intelligence cycle, which consists of five major phases: planning, collection, processing, production and analysis, and dissemination. Each phase holds the potential for human mistakes, especially the dissemination phase in which policy makers (the consumers of intelligence reports) sometimes cherry pick or otherwise distort the findings of the intelligence analysts (the producers) on ideological grounds, or fail even to consider intelligence for lack of time or interest.

Although intelligence has long been a vital part of American foreign policy—most notably in its capacity to keep an eye on US adversaries through satellites, reconnaissance aircraft, and human agents—the question of control over intelligence has led to bitter political disputes between the branches of government. Secrecy in the pursuit of American foreign policy has been attractive to executive officials since the nation's earliest days and, indeed, some "good" secrets need to be kept closely guarded; but other secrets are indefensible, such as efforts to conceal mistakes within the government and attempts to bypass constitutional procedures like the formal appropriations process (as happened during the Iran-*contra* affair). Other forms of obfuscation used by the executive branch to avoid public debate over its policies have included the use of executive privilege, delay and deceit, and prior restraint. In accord with their constitutional mandate, Congress and the courts have sought greater openness.

## KEY TERMS

analysis p. 268
assets (agents) p. 274
case officers (operational officers) p. 274
Central Intelligence Agency (CIA) p. 270
chief of station (COS) p. 274

collection and analysis p. 279
compartmentation p. 294
current and research intelligence p. 284
Defense Intelligence Agency (DIA) p. 273
director of central intelligence (DCI) p. 270

# QUESTIONS FOR DISCUSSION

1. Why does Part 4 of this book begin with a chapter that examines intelligence collection and analysis?
2. What are the challenges associated with each phase of the "intelligence cycle"?
3. Why has current intelligence driven out attention to Estimates in the intelligence community?
4. What can be done to mitigate the "fire hose" problem in intelligence processing?
5. What might be done to improve the producer–consumer relationship in the dissemination phase of the intelligence cycle?
4. What are the most significant intelligence-collection requirements (targets) for the United States today, in your judgment?
5. How could the Office of the DNI be strengthened? If too strong, could the office become a danger to democracy in America—an Intelligence Czar?

# ADDITIONAL READINGS

Barrett, David M. *The CIA and Congress: The Untold Story from Truman to Kennedy.* Lawrence: University Press of Kansas, 2005.

Johnson, Loch K. *The Threat on the Horizon: An Insider Account of America's Search for Security After the Cold War.* New York: Oxford University Press, 2011.

Lowenthal, Mark M. *Intelligence: From Secrets to Policy,* 5th ed. Washington, DC: CQ Press, 2012.

For further readings, please visit the book's companion website.

### CHAPTER 10

# Diplomacy

## THE ATTACK OF THE BRICKERITES

John Bricker, a leading Republican Senator from Ohio in the 1950s, feared that a president might enter into executive agreements with other nations that would bypass the Senate, despite Article II, Section 2, of the Constitution. "The power of the executive agreement has resulted in such catastrophes as Yalta, Potsdam, and Tehran," railed the Wisconsin State Republican party, in 1953, in support of Senator Bricker's concern.[1] The Brickerites were setting the stage for an important constitutional drama.

In 1954, Senator Bricker introduced *a constitutional amendment to curb the president's power over international agreement making.* Critics of the **Bricker Amendment**, a long list that included President Dwight D. Eisenhower, were profoundly dismayed that the proposal might actually become law. The President considered the proposal an unacceptable restraint on his ability to conduct diplomacy through the use of executive agreements. Senator J. William Fulbright (D-Arkansas) stood with the

This impressive building in New York City standing alongside the East River has been the UN's official headquarters since June 17, 1952.

President. "It was never intended by the Founding Fathers," he declared, "that the President of the United States should be a ventriloquist's dummy sitting on the lap of the Congress."[2] Nor was the constitutional authority Professor Edward S. Corwin much impressed with Bricker's handiwork. He observed magisterially, "No such mayhem on the Constitution is required to meet existing perils . . . The Anti-Genocide Convention . . . and the like are undoubtedly ill-considered proposals, but the Senate itself has the power, has it but the intestinal fortitude to use it, to administer the *congé* to all such utopian projects."[3]

The Brickerites, however, were not easily dissuaded. On February 26, 1954, after Senator Bricker's own tougher measure went down in defeat, they rallied behind a substitute constitutional amendment offered by Senator Walter George (D-Georgia). The Bricker Amendment would have required implementing laws passed by state legislatures for all international agreements touching on questions of states' rights—a crippling blow to the day-to-day foreign policy activities of the executive branch. The **George Amendment**, if successful, would still have represented a significant victory for the Bricker movement. It, too, aimed at blocking the hated use of executive agreements with these key provisions:

**LEARNING OBJECTIVES AND CONSTITUTIONAL ISSUES**

**By the end of this chapter, you will be able to:**

- *Define and describe the foreign policy instrument known as diplomacy.*
- *Discuss the effects of recent government leaks about how American diplomats report on world events and personalities.*
- *Describe the scope of US diplomatic challenges around the world.*

- *Identify the forms of formal international agreement making.*
- *Assess the efforts by lawmakers to ensure a role for Congress in America's global diplomatic initiatives.*

**THIS CHAPTER RAISES THE FOLLOWING CONSTITUTIONAL QUESTIONS:**

- The Constitution refers to the treaty as America's instrument for international agreement making, but two other forms have evolved since the founding: the statutory agreement (involving both chambers of Congress) and the executive agreement (which bypasses Congress). Why did the treaty process prove inadequate to deal with US relations abroad?

- What has been the view of some senators toward including the House in the approval process for international commitments via the statutory agreement? What has been the view of House members toward the Constitution's treaty provision?

- Is the executive agreement a procedure of concern from a constitutional perspective, or merely a routine method for dealing with minor international negotiations?

- To what extent should members of Congress be included in US diplomatic negotiating missions abroad as a means for honoring the constitutional principle of power sharing between these co-equal branches of government?

> Section 1. A provision of a treaty or other international agreement
> which conflicts with the Constitution shall not be of any force or effect.
> Section 2. An international agreement other than a treaty shall become
> effective as internal law in the United States only by an act of Congress.[4]

On February 27, 1954, the George Amendment came to the Senate floor in a tense confrontation between the Brickerites and those who rallied behind President Eisenhower. "The last moments of the debate were both bitter and emotional," reported the *New York Times*.[5] When the smoke cleared, the tally was yeas 60, and nays 31. By a single vote, the President and his allies in the Senate had halted the Bricker movement.[6] 〜

## TALKING INSTEAD OF FIGHTING

The demise of the Brickerites was an important episode in efforts to define in the modern era how America's relations with other nations would be conducted: strictly by the treaty process, as spelled out in the Constitution, or by some other means? The Bricker debate was about the role of each branch of government in determining how, when, and with whom the United States would commit its good name and resources abroad through diplomatic pacts. What might seem an arid subject—the Constitution's treaty power—had led to a lively dispute within the government in the early 1950s, one that would endure into later decades and remain a controversial topic today.

International agreements carried out by executive fiat (devoid of legislative consultation) would ignite another "revolution" on Capitol Hill in the 1970s, this time led by Senator Fulbright—an ironic turn of events, given Fulbright's earlier stance in support of President Eisenhower. Once again, as with the Bricker movement, these rebellious lawmakers favored a greater role for Congress in determining the proper instruments of US diplomacy. This time, though, the attack was led by a liberal faction in Congress. Along with the war power, the Constitution's treaty power—diplomacy—has resided at the heart of American foreign policy since the nation's founding and has frequently taken center stage in the "invitation to struggle" among the branches of government.

Introduced initially in Chapter 1, the concept of diplomacy (from the Greek word *diplomata*, meaning "folded documents") may be further described as "the process of representation and negotiation by which states customarily deal with one another in times of peace." Stated more simply by George Kennan, diplomacy is "the business of communicating between governments."[7] Former Secretary of State Henry Kissinger embellished: "[The statesman's] instrument is diplomacy, the art of relating states to each other by agreement rather than by the exercise of force."[8] The thoughtful Israeli minister of foreign affairs, Abba Eban, added that diplomacy attempts to achieve national goals "by persuasion, eloquence, inducement, threat or deterrence, and not only by physical domination and war."[9]

For the prominent international relations scholar Hans J. Morgenthau, a leader of the realists in the 1960s, diplomacy was far and away the most important power possessed by a nation. Defining the concept broadly, Morgenthau considered diplomacy to be "the formation and execution of foreign policy on all levels, the highest as well as the subordinate." It was an "art" whose purpose was nothing less than to bring "the different elements of national power to bear with maximum effect upon those points in the international situation which concern the national interest most directly." When carried out with competence, diplomacy managed to "bring the ends and means of foreign policy into harmony with the available resources of national power"[10]—the essence of a nation's grand strategy.

As experienced US Foreign Service officer and former ambassador David D. Newsom emphasized, once a sound foreign policy is crafted by a nation's leaders, "diplomacy can then add the needed skills of implementation in the knowledge of other cultures, the skill of negotiation, the art of persuasion, and the power to observe and report." He continued: "The policies the United States pursues . . . must, to be acceptable, be expressed and explained and defended to skeptical, distracted, and occasionally unfriendly governments and peoples abroad. This becomes the task of the American diplomat who, in a mediating role, must also explain the realities that confront America to those in Washington who may be unready to accept the anomalies of an outside world."[11]

Although the job description sounds straightforward enough, the actual practice of diplomacy is immensely complicated, with often far-reaching ramifications for a nation—however bland this approach to foreign policy may seem in comparison to sending in the Marines or unleashing the CIA. As the distinguished British statesman Lord Salisbury (1830–1903) once observed, the victories of the diplomat "are made up of a series of microscopic advantages: of a judicious suggestion here, of an opportune civility there, of a wise concession at one moment and a farsighted persistence at another; of sleepless tact, immovable calmness and patience that no folly, on provocation, no blunders can shake."[12] These small steps and intricate compromises, while usually lacking in drama, can move a nation toward momentous and sometimes dangerous commitments abroad. And, of course, one person's "wise concession at the one moment" may be another's unacceptable "appeasement."

Few individuals have the requisite patience, training, and genius to match the skills in "statecraft" of history's most famous diplomats: France's Richelieu, Mazarin, Talleyrand, and Cambon, to give some examples; or Great Britain's Cardinal Wolsey, Castlereagh, and Canning; Germany's Bismarck; Italy's Cavour; and America's Franklin, Jefferson, Madison, Jay, and the Adams', in the early days, and Kennan, Kissinger, and James A. Baker III (of the George H. W. Bush administration) more recently. Rather than hope for the occasional Bismarck to guide a nation's external affairs, Morgenthau urged a "dependence upon tradition and institutions." America's institutions of diplomacy have been largely inept, in his view, with the exception of the nation's earliest years; but its traditions, especially as embodied in Washington's Farewell Address and the Monroe Doctrine, have provided guidance to "protect a poor diplomacy from catastrophic blunders and make a mediocre diplomacy look better than it actually was."[13]

Part of the ineptitude of American diplomacy has come from questionable presidential choices for top ambassadorships. About 30 percent of US ambassadors have been political appointees over the past fifty years.[14] They have often won their posts because of campaign contributions rather than as a result of their foreign policy expertise. This practice began to accelerate under Presidents Reagan and George H. W. Bush. Indeed, forty-seven of the first sixty names submitted by the first President Bush to the Senate Foreign Relations Committee for confirmation as ambassadors in 1989 were political appointees, including Della Newman, a real estate broker from Seattle and chairperson of Bush's Washington State presidential campaign. She told a reporter that she had no interest in foreign policy; and she was unable even to name the prime minister in her country of assignment, New Zealand.[15] More recently, President Obama's ambassador to Japan, John Roos, was a wealthy Silicon Valley attorney who gave substantial funds to the Obama election campaign but seemed to know little about his host country.[16]

At lower levels of the diplomatic rungs, however, members of the US Foreign Service are usually better qualified to carry out the nation's international agenda. There are exceptions to the rule. Some Presidents, including Franklin Roosevelt and John Kennedy, have found it frustrating to work with the professional diplomats in the State Department and preferred to rely on their own aides and personal envoys in the conduct of diplomacy abroad. Moreover, some non-professional diplomats have proven to be outstanding ambassadors, such as Senators Mike Mansfield (D-Montana) and Walter Mondale (D-Minnesota), both of whom served well in Japan. Obama's choice for US ambassador to Japan in 2013 was another non-professional diplomat and another outstanding pick: Caroline Kennedy, daughter of President Kennedy. Her intelligence, empathy, and popularity foreshadowed a period of exemplary service, even if she didn't speak Japanese.

Morgenthau recommended four "rules" to establish "a more effective diplomatic corps." These rules remain just as relevant today as when he first laid them out in his classic book, *Politics Among Nations*[17] (see Table 10.1 for a listing of the rules).

With these principles as a north star, Morgenthau believed that a nation's diplomatic initiatives had a chance to preserve peace and build an international community that might evolve into a peaceful world state, one led by a higher unifying authority to replace the current divisiveness of national sovereignty and the competition it

*Table 10.1*
*Morgenthau's Rules of Diplomacy*

1. Diplomacy must be divested of the crusading spirit.

2. The objectives of foreign policy must be defined in terms of the national interest and must be supported with adequate power.

3. Diplomacy must look at the political scene from the point of view of other nations.

4. Nations must be willing to compromise on all issues that are not vital to them.

engenders. Without the "accommodating processes of diplomacy, mitigating and minimizing conflicts," he wrote, the prospects for world peace were dim.[18]

International relations scholars have pointed to another feature of diplomacy that can be important: **coercive diplomacy**. This approach involves *signaling to other nations that a diplomatic settlement may be in their best interests because the alternative could mean the introduction of military force into the equation*. In this vein, Walter F. Mondale, vice president for Jimmy Carter and a former US Senator from Minnesota, wrote, "I've always been proud that our administration never started a war or dropped a bomb. But I've also believed that our ability to do both helped us change minds, tame rivals, and promote human rights—as well as prevent deadly attacks on Americans."[19] Similarly, CIA Director Leon Panetta of the Obama administration (later its Secretary of Defense) noted in 2010 that the Taliban extremists supporting Al Qaeda were unlikely to enter into negotiations with the governments of Afghanistan, Pakistan, or America "unless they're convinced that the United States is going to win and that they're going to be defeated."[20] The sword, or the threat of the sword, must sometimes prepare the way for the dove of peace—what was known as gunboat diplomacy in the nineteenth century.

## THE WIKILEAKS PAPERS: THE PRIVATE FACE OF DIPLOMACY

For the most part, diplomacy takes place behind closed doors. Rarely does the American public have an opportunity to read the reporting of US diplomats. In 2010, however, a massive leaking of classified State Department documents provided just such an opportunity. The papers came mainly from the Obama administration, transmitted by government leakers to an antisecrecy organization based in London called WikiLeaks: over 250,000 "secret" and "confidential" papers, including 2,700 diplomatic cables. By early 2011, WikiLeaks claimed it had only disclosed about 1 percent of this massive trove of government papers, but even this small amount captured the world's attention—and the wrath of Western governments.

WikiLeaks began its mission of exposing the inner workings of government in April of 2007. At that time, it released to the public a video from an Apache helicopter that displayed US fighters shooting down a group of men in Baghdad. Among the casualties, it turned out, were two Reuters journalists. Julian Assange, the WikiLeaks founder, became an instant household name. The merits of Assange's approach to journalism attracted wide debated, while government officials excoriated him for the unauthorized exposure of government secrets—including the names of CIA assets abroad, as well as delicate cable communications about the views and personalities of foreign leaders.

In 2010, WikiLeaks decided to establish an informal alliance with the mainstream media and began to distribute its leaks to the *New York Times*, the *Guardian* in England, and other media outlets. These newspapers handled the material more responsibly, removing the names of intelligence assets and the details of secret operations; plus, they checked with their respective governments to discuss what the repercussions might be if the leaks were published. In many instances, though, the newspapers decided to print classified documents over government objections. The WikiLeaks case began to move toward the courts in Britain and the United States for judicial review. In the meantime, America's worldwide diplomatic initiatives were on parade. The WikiLeaks cables lifted the veil on the inside frustrations of American foreign policy; and they imparted to the public a sense of US diplomacy that seemed to parallel the bargaining—the wheeling and dealing—usually associated with domestic politics in Washington.

The leaks revealed that, in most every case, the White House and the State Department attempted to achieve America's international objectives through a combination of two approaches: first, negotiations ("engagement") with other nations aimed at convincing them to do the right thing, that is, support US interests; and, second, when this method faltered, resorting to the use of economic carrots and sticks—or sometimes just military sticks—to win their allegiance. As one analysis of the WikiLeaks papers pointed out, the documents suggested that the United States would "engage, yes, but wield a club as well."[21] The approach was reminiscent of Teddy Roosevelt's "big stick" diplomacy. In 2010 and 2011, one could see the use of this twofold approach—a form of coercive diplomacy—during the war in Afghanistan. The US military pounded the Taliban with daily air strikes to bleed the insurgency and, at the same time, sought negotiations with its leaders to bring peace to the region. In the course of the Balkans wars during the Clinton administration, the United States similarly used force against the Serbian leader Milosevic, repeatedly bombing Belgrade, with the goal of bringing him to the negotiating table, as eventually happened with the Dayton Accords signed in Ohio.

The WikiLeaks documents underscored America's obsession with global terrorism since 9/11; they also revealed a belief in Washington that Russia was retreating from its short-lived experiment in democracy, and that China was rising even more rapidly than expected as a world power. Especially troubling to the Obama administration was how to know which leaders in Pakistan's government were trustworthy in the struggle against Al Qaeda and the Taliban, and which were secretly allied with the terrorists. The ultimate concern, noted one State Department cable from Islamabad, was that "someone working in GOP [government of Pakistan] could gradually smuggle enough [fissionable] material out to eventually make a [nuclear] weapon."

Here is a further sampling of topics disclosed in the WikiLeaks papers—snapshots of the preoccupations of US diplomats abroad in recent years:[22]

- To win Beijing's support for sanctions against Iran designed to block Tehran's WMD aspirations and thereby curtail a potential arms race in one of the most volatile regions of the globe, the Obama White House persuaded Saudi Arabia to promise a steady flow of oil to China in lieu of the Iranian oil;
- To gain Russia's support for the sanctions against Iran, the Obama administration agreed to replace the Bush II-era missile defense plan (which envisioned bases in Poland and the Czech Republic) with

a sea-based system that was just as effective but less threatening to the Kremlin;

• To winnow down the number of prisoners at Guantánamo Bay, the Obama administration offered a number of payoffs to nations willing to accept detainees. For example, Slovenia took a prisoner in return for a meeting with President Obama. The administration offered the island nation of Kiribati lucrative aid incentives to take in Chinese Muslim detainees, and told Belgium that it could gain "prominence in Europe" by accepting more prisoners;

• Worried about spent nuclear fuel from a reactor in Pakistan, the Obama administration leaned on officials in Islamabad to give up the potentially weapons-grade material to the United States; in response, Islamabad warned that if the local media caught wind of the deal "they certainly would portray it as the United States taking Pakistan's nuclear weapons";

• To prepare for future developments on the Korean Peninsula, the Obama State Department engaged in talks with South Korea about the potential collapse of North Korea and how China might react to such an event.

Further, the leaked documents showed that since 2008 American diplomats had been instructed to engage in activities abroad once reserved for the CIA and other intelligence agencies, namely, the clandestine collection of information abroad, not just overtly "keeping one's eyes open" in the usual diplomatic task of open information collection. For instance, diplomats were now expected to gather personal data on foreign leaders, such as their credit card and frequent flier numbers—a request unlikely to have been warmly greeted by Foreign Service Officers, who pride themselves on standing apart from the espionage activities of the CIA. In many countries, ambassadors are (in David Kahn's felicitous phrase) merely "legalized spies";[23] but throughout most of its modern history, the United States has tried to draw a bright line between diplomacy and espionage. Many Americans were disappointed to learn of the apparent return to seventeenth-century practices of US diplomats acting as spies. The WikiLeaks papers also revealed that Iran had obtained advanced missiles from North Korea, and that Syria was continuing to supply arms to the terrorist group Hezbollah in Lebanon. Moreover, the United States warned Germany in cables to be a good ally and think twice before deciding to prosecute CIA officers involved in a bungled rendition operation that took place on German soil in 2007.

The leaks disclosed, as well, private remarks uttered by foreign dignitaries meant for the ears of US diplomats and top American leaders alone—not for international public consumption. Their publication in the *New York Times* and other media sent Washington officials scurrying around the world to offer apologies. For example, the leaked cables reported the following:

- King Abdullah of Saudi Arabia urged Washington to "cut off the head of the snake"—a reference to destroying the Iranian regime before it could possess nuclear weapons;
- the King of Bahrain, who permits America's Fifth Fleet to moor in his nation's harbors, also cautioned that to let Iran's WMD program proceed was "greater than the danger of stopping it";
- Dhud Barak, Israel's Defense Minister, warned in May of 2009 that the world had less than eighteen months "in which stopping Iran from acquiring nuclear weapons might still be viable";
- the Italian Prime Minister is described in a cable as "feckless, vain, and ineffective," as well as "the mouthpiece of Putin" in Europe [referring to Vladimir V. Putin, Russia's prime minister at the time, and subsequently its president];
- Putin comes across as "a Mafia godfather," although frustrated by his inability to command the new Russian billionaires;
- Nicolas Sarkoszy, the President of France at the time, has a "thin-skinned and authoritarian personal style" with "monarchial tendencies";
- Angela Merkel, the German chancellor, is "rarely creative";
- Kim Jong II of North Korea (who has since died) is a "flabby old chap";
- Robert Mugabe of Zimbabwe is a "crazy old man"; and
- Ahmed Wali Karzai, the half-brother of the Afghan president, is a corrupt narcotics trafficker.

Advocates for government transparency were pleased by the WikiLeaks disclosures; but others in the government and elsewhere found the activities of the rogue journalist group highly detrimental to the conduct of quiet, behind-the-scenes, effective diplomacy. They argued that foreign leaders would be less willing to cooperate with the United States if these relationships were made public to potential terrorists. Even their own citizens might interpret cooperation with the United States as a form of international toadyism.[24]

## THE BREADTH OF DIPLOMACY

Leaks or no leaks, the responsibilities of diplomats move on—often in a dizzying rush of events. Officials in the George H. W. Bush administration, for example, immediately found their foreign policy agendas crowded with a host of perplexing international dilemmas inherited from previous administrations. Most of the problems defied quick resolution by way of secret agents or the dispatch of armed troops. Rather, they demanded the steady, patient attention of diplomats prepared to search tirelessly for those adjustments that might calm the conflicting interests of nations. The administration took little comfort from the advice of the British ambassador to the United Nations at the time. "I know it's a part of the American way of life to believe that you isolate a problem and solve it," the ambassador said, "but in international politics . . . you find arrangements, rather than final solutions. There is no final solution."[25]

When President Obama entered office in 2009, his foreign policy team similarly faced from day one a staggering number of complex Gordian knots in the international arena. What follows are some illustrations.

## Counterterrorism and the Islamic World

For the Obama administration, the first priority of American foreign policy continued to be (as with the prior administration of George W. Bush) tracking down members of Al Qaeda and putting them out of business before they were able to stage another 9/11 attack against the United States—this time perhaps with nuclear, biological, chemical, or radiological weapons. Most of President Obama's counterterrorism strategy was an extension of the plans put into place by his predecessor: capturing or killing as many members of Al Qaeda as possible, especially at the high echelons of the organization, along with their extremist allies among the Afghan-Pakistani Taliban tribes and other terrorist factions around the world.

The fight against terrorism requires the full range of foreign policy instruments. In the wake of the 9/11 attacks, America used military force against Al Qaeda and its allies, leading to two full-scale wars on Islamic soil: in Iraq and Afghanistan. Intelligence operations were a part of the response, with an increasing number of CIA drone attacks in northwestern Pakistan against suspected Qaeda sanctuaries, to augment small-scale US ground forces engaged in similar operations against these targets. These approaches were reinforced by diplomatic initiatives and economic statecraft. Both the George W. Bush and Obama administrations put into place trade sanctions against those who supported global terrorism and employed the inducements of aid and commercial opportunities for those who opposed global terrorism.[26] Further, the administrations used the soft power of **public diplomacy** to *project around the world an accurate picture of the United States through radio, television broadcasts, and other means of communications*, along with the truth about the barbaric acts perpetrated by Al Qaeda and the Taliban against Muslims throughout the Middle East and Southwest Asia—from beheadings and suicide bombings to throwing acid in the faces of schoolgirls to deter them from seeking an education. Moreover, the United States reached out to Pakistan through the Fulbright exchange program, with the number of students from that country (130) studying in American colleges second only to Germany (199) in 2010–11.[27]

In a high-profile speech delivered in Cairo, Egypt, early in his first term, President Obama eloquently signaled that he sought better relations with the world of Islam, with its over two billion people—most of whom are moderates and reject the violent agenda peddled by Qaeda and Taliban extremists. The President seemed prepared to work even with authoritarian regimes, such as Egypt, against the forces of terrorism. As the Arab Spring unfolded, thoughtful analysts in the West and in Arabic world pondered the role of Islam in democratic governments and considered reforms that would encourage pluralist societies to bloom in the Middle East and Southwest Asia, with tolerance, an ethos of inclusion, and respect for people of all faiths and ethnic origins.

In addition, the administration began to explore—again, behind the scenes—opportunities to negotiate with the more moderate elements of the Taliban leadership, such as the powerful Afghani warlord Mullah Omar. The administration attempted to entice more Taliban warriors over to the anti-Qaeda side through offers of jobs and financial aid for their tribes if they joined the struggle against global terrorism.[28] Here was US counterinsurgency at work in the Islamic world, just as the Marshall Plan had been a form of counterinsurgency directed toward keeping Europe free of communist influence in the early years of the Cold War.

Vital to America's success in Southwest Asia are good relations with Pakistan, the country where the Qaeda and Taliban leadership has taken refuge in the rugged mountains of the northwest, along the Afghan border, in a lightly governed region known as Northern Waziristan or the Federally Administered Tribal Areas (FATA). The relationship between the United States and Pakistan have been tangled. During the war to drive the Soviets out of Afghanistan in the 1980s, the CIA worked closely and secretly with Pakistani intelligence (ISI) and army officers, as well as the Taliban in Afghanistan. The United States departed the region immediately after victory, severing ties with these allies and soldiers (among them Osama bin Laden) without much thought about helping them deal with the grinding poverty and ignorance that plagues Southwest Asia. The United States continued to provide military aid, off and on, to Pakistan, as it did—in larger amounts—to India, a country that Pakistan views as a mortal enemy and with whom Pakistan has an ongoing conflict over the rightful ownership of the province situated between them known as Kashmir. Pakistan is far more concerned about the giant, India, on its border than about the Taliban or Al Qaeda; indeed, Pakistani intelligence and military officers have had close ties with the Taliban ever since they occupied the same foxholes in the war against the Soviets in the 1980s. Further, they view the Taliban as a much needed ally against India.

The Obama administration has found it difficult to woo the Pakistanis in the struggle against Al Qaeda and the Taliban, in large part because leaders in Islamabad are skeptical that the United States will sustain its interest in the region. They foresee America beating a hasty retreat again as soon as the terrorist problem is resolved, in a repeat of the abandonment experienced by Pakistanis after the US-aided defeat of the Soviets in Afghanistan during the 1980s. The administration has made some inroads with Pakistani officials through the enticements of foreign aid, military assistance (including Predator drones for use by the Pakistani military, though controlled by the United States), and promises to take a greater interest in the future economic development of this poor and largely illiterate nation. Almost two-thirds of the Pakistani population is under the age of twenty-five. Further, less than 40 percent of the nation's children are enrolled in school, significantly below the average of 56 percent throughout the rest of South Asia; and the schools that do exist are often run by the Taliban, which promotes an anti-America, anti-West curriculum.[29]

Every step forward, though, seemed to be offset by a slide backward. In 2010, the rude treatment of Pakistani government personnel traveling to United States, who were removed from airport waiting lines and forced by security guards to submit to scanners even though they were precleared official visitors invited to Washington, inflamed anti-Americanism even among moderate Pakistanis.[30] More significant still, the accidental killings of civilians by US-guided Predators and Reapers in strikes against villages in North Waziristan during hunts for Qaeda targets led to a pronounced turning of public opinion in Pakistan against the United States.

Pakistani anti-Americanism was fueled in 2011 by the Obama administration's night attack against Bin Laden in Abbottabad, without the knowledge (let alone the permission) of the Pakistani government, which claimed not to know about the presence of the Qaeda leader in this city near the nation's capital. Additional accidental killings of Pakistani soldiers and civilians by US airstrikes have occurred, including the death of twenty-four Pakistani troops on the Afghanistan border in November of 2011. This calamity led Islamabad to close its supply routes of US war materials bound for Afghanistan. The government of Pakistan renewed demands that America halt all drone activity in its country, as well as prohibit all intelligence activities and private security contractors (in 2011, a CIA contractor by the name of Raymond Allen Davis killed two Pakistanis in Lahore, he claimed in self-defense). Near the end of 2012, relations improved between the nations and the United States promised to reimburse Islamabad nearly $700 billion for the cost of stationing 140,000 troops on the border with Afghanistan.[31] Anti-Americanism has been a problem in Afghanistan as well, and for the same basic reasons: the death of innocents caught up in the fighting, and a belief that America will abandon its allies in the region before long.

### Russia and China

The Obama administration, like all other modern US presidencies, had to pay close attention to fellow behemoths in the international system: Russia and China. The centerpiece of efforts to reach out to Russia—and one of the most important foreign policy initiatives of the Obama administration—was a replacement of the Strategic Arms Reduction Treaty of 1991 (START) with a "New START" arms accord. The purpose was to resume mutual cuts in deployed strategic warheads and delivery systems by at least a quarter. The administration also sought to renew the Nunn–Lugar Cooperative Threat Reduction Program, which has aided the former Soviet Union in the cleanup of its WMD sites, dismantling thousands of nuclear weapons since the end of the Cold War. Financed by American taxpayer money and guided by US government expertise, the idea of the Threat Reduction Program has been to eliminate or secure vulnerable nuclear and chemical materials and sites.[32] Initially enacted by Congress in 1991, Nunn–Lugar was set to expire in 2013. In 2009 and 2010, Russian President Dmitri A. Medvedev slowed the renewal negotiations, in a fit of pique over Obama's intention to provide Romania and perhaps other Central European nations with an antimissile system. The system was supposedly important as a bulwark against a possible Iranian missile attack on the United States across the northern polar cap, but was perceived in Moscow as a belligerent act against Russia.

Some warming of the relationship occurred when the Kremlin allowed US war planes attacking Taliban extremists in Afghanistan to use Russian airspace for launching their missions. By the summer of 2010, Medvedev and Obama—surrounded by media—ate hamburgers together in a local Washington eatery, as if they were old college pals, during a visit to the United States by the Russian President. These were large steps away from the frosty days of the Cold War. In the middle of these more cordial relations, the US Senate finally approved the New START arms treaty with Russia in December of 2010. Under its provisions, for the next seven years neither country could deploy more than 1,550 strategic warheads (roughly a 30 percent reduction) or 700 launchers. Moreover, in both nations on-site armament inspections would resume, which had lapsed along with the original START Treaty in December of 2009. (The treaty did nothing to address the 11,000 total nuclear weapons that the two nations keep as backups.) Some key senators remained suspicious of this outreach to Russia. Sounding like a voice from the Cold War era, Senator John McCain (R-Arizona) asked, "How in the world are we going to trust them to adhere to a treaty?"[33]

By 2012, as this on-again, off-again relationship continued, the Obama administration began to have serious doubts about the intentions of Medvedev's successor, Vladimir V. Putin, who had again been elected president of Russia. Not only did Putin support the repressive Syrian regime against the pleas of the United States (starting in the early months of the civil war that had broken out there in 2011), but he increasingly adopted antidemocratic measures of his own at home—from night raids against opponents in their homes to heavy-handed responses to peaceful demonstrations in the streets of Moscow. America's ambassador to the UN at the time, Susan E. Rice, warned that the strife in Syrian threatened to become "a proxy conflict with arms flowing in from all sides," including from Russia.[34] Further, Putin reiterated the criticism about America's plans for a missile defense system based in Europe and flatly refused to renew Nunn–Lugar unless the plans for this system were abandoned. In 2013, the Obama administration canceled the final phase of this missile system, which Moscow leaders worried would focus on Russian ICBMs; the administration did not retreat, however, from its plan to pursue a land-based missile shield in Central Europe as a counter to the possible development by Iran of non-ICBM, shorter-range missiles.

One thing was certain: as Mary Elise Sarotte wrote in 2009, "Western attempts to manage everything from Iran's nuclear program to European energy supplies during the coming winter could be a great deal easier with Russia's cooperation."[35] The one bright sign in the midst of this US-Russia sparring was an invitation to Obama from Putin to visit Russia in September of 2013. American officials hoped this meant the two nations could eventually move forward with arms control measures to include renewal of Nunn–Lugar. Despite this invitation and America's abandonment of the European-based ICBM missile defense system, a chill seemed to hang in the air between the US and Russian presidents during the early summer of 2013. By late summer, the chill had turned to frost and in August the White House canceled a September summit conference long planned between the two leaders. The most immediate reason for the cancellation was Putin's granting of political asylum in Russia to Edward J. Snowden—a fugitive from the law wanted in the United States for his unauthorized disclosure of intelligence regarding NSA's data collection on the telephone calling patterns of all American citizens.[36]

As for China, the Obama administration could hardly ignore this rapidly rising world power, with its population of more than one billion and its massive exports to the United States, which outpaced American imports to China by a ratio of more than four-to-one.[37] The Chinese appetite for imports was formable, too. As a measure of its growing economic importance, China became the world's largest automobile market, with 14 million sales a year compared to 11 million in the United States; and was the second biggest market for American movies. China was now, as a historian noted in the *Wall Street Journal*, "the most dynamic new market for other people's stuff. And that wins friends."[38]

During a Strategic Economic Dialogue with Chinese leaders in Washington during July 2009, President Obama said, "The relationship between the United States and China will shape the 21st century." America's goal was to attract China into the ambit of Western consumer society, with its rule of law and democratic principles. Reaching out to Beijing proved at times, however, as prickly as overtures toward Moscow. Since the end of the Cold War, nothing in international diplomacy seemed to come easy. The trade imbalance between the China and the United States remains heavily lopsided in China's favor in large part because leaders in Beijing hold down the value of its currency, the renminbi, despite their promises to cease and desist in this practice.

Another point of friction between the two nations was the growing number of Chinese cyberattacks against private and government computers in the United States. In 2010, Secretary of State Hillary Rodham Clinton issued a warning to Beijing that the United States would vigorously defend itself against these attacks.[39] Later in the year, the administration took significant steps to protect the nation's computer infrastructure. A further dispute arose in 2010 over $6 billion in US arms sales to Taiwan, which enraged leaders in Beijing.[40] The United States and China bumped heads over humanitarian issues, too. For example, the awarding of the 2010 Nobel Peace Prize to the imprisoned Chinese dissident Liu Xiaobo led to acrimony between the two nations. Leaders in Beijing viewed the award as a direct affront to China, at the very time when Washington was applauding the choice. Beijing leaned on other governments to boycott the ceremony and managed to convince eighteen regimes to stay home (see Figure 10.1). The roster was an impressive display of China's clout in the world and underscored, as well, the fickle nature of America's "friendship" ties abroad.

Rather than demonizing the Chinese over the question of ongoing trade disputes, former national security adviser Zbigniew Brzezinski recommended in 2011 that the two major powers reconcile and, "guided by the moral imperatives of the 21st century's unprecedented global interdependence," together chart a unified course toward "defining

| | | |
|---|---|---|
| • Afghanistan | • Kazakhstan | • Serbia |
| • Colombia | • Morocco | • Sudan |
| • Cuba | • Pakistan | • Tunisia |
| • Egypt | • Philippines | • Ukraine |
| • Iran | • Russia | • Venezuela |
| • Iraq | • Saudi Arabia | • Vietnam |

*Figure 10.1*
Governments Boycotting the 2010 Nobel Peace Prize Ceremony

common political, economic and social goals."[41] Secretary of State Hilary Clinton was more guarded; she observed that the United States "must be pragmatic and agile" in its dealings with China.[42] The Secretary's hesitancy notwithstanding, the United States clearly planned to increase its attention toward Asia (especially in light of the increasing economic importance of the region). Still, as the Obama administration's national security adviser, Thomas E. Donilon, put it in 2012, the American–Chinese relationship would continue to have "elements of both co-operation and competition."[43]

## Europe

The democracies of Europe are among America's closest allies today. Officials in the Obama administration have leaned on European leaders, however, to contribute more robustly toward collective security measures undertaken by NATO. Robust participation was doubly important because, after the Cold War, NATO had expanded its focus beyond the boundaries of its member states in Europe and North America to include fighting in the Balkans during the 1990s and then in Afghanistan after the 9/11 attacks. The administration pointed out that only five of twenty-eight members were paying the established sum of 2 percent of gross domestic product (GDP) into NATO's coffers, compared to twice that amount contributed by the United States. This difference amounted to hundreds of millions of euros, depriving the Afghanistan mission of badly needed heavy-lift helicopters, cargo aircraft, aerial refueling tankers, and intelligence-gathering equipment. "The demilitarization of Europe has gone from a blessing in the 20th century," said Secretary of Defense Robert M. Gates, "to an impediment to achieving real security and lasting peace in the 21st."[44]

Paying their fair share to NATO became even more problematic for Europeans by 2012, when some members of the European Union—Greece, Spain, Italy—appeared on the verge of economic bankruptcy. A failure of these member states threatened to bring down the Union and its euro currency, with troubling rippling effects spreading across the Atlantic and exacerbating America's own teetering attempts to pull out of a recession. At the eleventh hour in 2012, the European Union decided—reluctantly— to loan more money to the Greeks in an effort to stabilize their economy; but the ability of this country, as well as Spain and Italy, to become financially viable members of the EU remained in question.

## Global Hot Spots

A daunting litany of other diplomatic challenges fell into the lap of the Obama administration. Among them were ongoing efforts to pressure North Korea and Iran into abandoning their nuclear weapons programs; halting Israel's construction of Jewish settlements on the West Bank, a major impediment to the rekindling of a Middle East peace initiative;[45] suppressing Qaeda influence in Yemen, Somalia, Nigeria, Mali, and across the Maghreb (a section of North Africa stretching from Mauritania to the Egyptian border that had become a prowling ground for AQIM—Al Qaeda in the Islamic Maghreb) and other locations around the world; keeping pressure on Sudan to maintain the fragile calm over the killing fields in its western province of Darfur, as well as in the newly independent nation of South Sudan; being a good neighbor to Canada and Mexico, major trading partners—with Mexico staggering from the threat of internal drug lords targeting soldiers and police for murder throughout the nation; and working to bring food and peace to the Horn of Africa, a site infested with Qaeda cells where (according to a Western official with years of experience in Somalia) diplomacy had not "really been tried."[46]

World events posed a number of other vexing challenges. For example, to what extent did the United States have a moral obligation to intervene in various African tribal disputes that threatened to result in mass murders, as was the prospect in Nigeria in 2010; to halt the expansion of a Qaeda-allied terrorist group in northern Mali that attacked a gas field in Algeria in 2013, murdering several workers and managers (including a number of Americans); or to deal with Boko Haram in Nigeria and ongoing piracy in the Gulf of Aden? What should be done about the ethnic strife inside Kyrgyzstan that boiled over into violence in 2010 and continued to plague that nation? Neither NATO nor CSTO (the Collective Security Treaty Organization, an alliance of seven former Soviet states, including Russia) appeared willing to step into the angry civil unrest that haunted Kyrgyzstan.

Then there were natural disasters that begged for a humanitarian response from the United States. An earthquake flattened Haiti in January 2010 and the United States reacted generously with over a billion dollars' worth of government assistance, plus millions more from private organizations. Further, the Obama administration sent 22,000 US soldiers and hundreds of aid workers to the island to help address the dire conditions and ensure stability.[47] A few months after the Haiti quake, a series of earthquakes struck Chile, bringing forth additional assistance (public and private) from the United States. Then in March 2011, Japan experienced a major earthquake and tsunami, leading to a nuclear power plant's partial meltdown. Again, America provided assistance.

At home, President Obama—like all of his predecessors—had to grapple as well with the question of the appropriate role for Congress in the crafting of major diplomatic initiatives. John Bricker was no longer in the Senate, but lawmakers still wanted their branch of government treated as a partner in the making of foreign policy, as the Constitution envisioned. This insistence on participation was especially strong on

Capitol Hill when it came to major agreements with other nations—a subject of controversy between the branches of government with deep roots.

## THE MAKING OF INTERNATIONAL AGREEMENTS

The United States uses three prominent forms of formal diplomatic agreements with other nations: the treaty; the statutory agreement; and, Senator Bricker's chief complaint, the executive agreement. Treaties, of which there have been about 1,500 since the writing of the Constitution, are required by Article II, Section 2, of the Constitution to have the approval (the "advice and consent") of two-thirds of those members of the Senate present and voting (see the discussion of the treaty power in Chapter 3). On any important treaty, quite likely all 100 members will be present, so the executive branch must muster at least sixty-seven votes—made all the more difficult by the possibility of filibuster or even a "silent hold" placed on the treaty proposal by one or more senators (allowed by the chamber's rules). As defined in Chapter 3, the statutory agreement involves legislative authority, too; however, instead of an extraordinary two-thirds approval in the Senate, which is difficult to achieve on contentious issues, this procedure requires an easier majority vote—but in both chambers of Congress, that is, 51 senators and 218 members of the House (if every member is present and voting). Easiest of all for a president—exactly Bricker's concern—is to bypass the Congress altogether by way of an executive agreement (also defined in Chapter 3), entered into by the executive branch with another country and bereft of advice and consent from the Senate or counsel from the House of Representatives.

The war in Vietnam awakened lawmakers in the modern era to the dangers of excessive presidential discretion in foreign policy. The decline of the Senate's treaty power became a focus for reformers concerned that the legislative branch had become a vestigial organ on the body politic, just like the appendix on the human body. Their critique centered, first, on the changes that had taken place in recent years in the **form of international agreements**: *treaties, statutory agreements, and executive agreements.* Increasingly, members of Congress believed that presidents and their aides were resorting to executive agreements, proclamations, and other unilateral actions as a way of circumventing their participation in the formulation of formal international commitments. Well in advance of the Vietnam War era, "diplomacy was conducted as often as possible to avoid formal congressional involvement," conceded a former US ambassador.[48]

Especially worrisome to lawmakers were the secret pacts with other nations signed by the White House or the bureaucracy and never revealed to Congress, including verbal "promises" and "understandings"—smile-and-wink deals that were seldom officially put in writing—along with a wide range of obligations sealed at lower levels of the executive branch without the knowledge of the White House or even the Department of State, let alone Capitol Hill (see Figure 10.2 for a continuum of approaches to international agreement making).

The overwhelming number—almost 87 percent—of all US agreements between 1946 and 1972 (the only period for which reliable, systematic data for the three

*Figure 10.2*
International Agreement-Making: A Continuum of Executive Discretion

More <-------------------------------Executive Discretion------------------------------> Less

| A    B | C  D | E | F    G |

Region of executive authority                    Region of institutional sharing

A. Secret verbal executive agreements ("understandings," "promises")
B. Secret written executive agreements (kept from Congress)
C. Secret verbal or written agreements (shared with select congressional committees)
D. Unclassified executive agreements
E. Statutory agreements
F. Agreements pursuant to treaties
G. Treaties

SOURCE: Loch K. Johnson, *The Making of International Agreements: Congress Confronts the Executive* (New York: New York University Press, 1984), p. 7. Reprinted by permission of New York University Press.

agreement forms are available) were statutory in form. They were based on legislative (indeed, bicameral) and executive branch approval (see Table 10.2), a method—essentially, the passage of a bill—permitted by Article I of the Constitution. (The treaty power is discussed in Article II.) In contrast, executive agreements and treaties accounted for only 7 percent and 6 percent of all the agreements, respectively. Although they never analyzed the frequency of statutory agreements (a laborious task that involves reading every international agreement to determine its specific legislative authority), researchers Krutz and Peake did find that in the years since 1972, treaties continued to account for only about 6 percent of the total.[49] The figures presented in Table 10.2 indicate that Congress has certainly been included in the agreement-making

*Table 10.2*
Form of US International Agreements by Administration, 1946–1972

| Form | ADMINISTRATION | | | | | |
|------|---------|------------|---------|---------|-------|---------|
|      | Truman | Eisenhower | Kennedy | Johnson | Nixon | Average |
| Executive agreements | 10.6% | 5.4% | 3.8% | 8.0% | 9.1% | 7.3% |
| Statutory agreements | 79.5 | 89.2 | 92.7 | 86.7 | 86.4 | 86.7 |
| Treaties | 9.8 | 5.4 | 3.4 | 5.2 | 4.5 | 6.0 |
| Total no. of agreements | 1,315 | 1,884 | 783 | 1,143 | 866 | (Total) 5,991 |

NOTE: Entries are percentages based on numbers shown at bottom of columns. Percentages have been rounded and therefore may not total 100%. Twenty-five agreements (1% of the total) are excluded from this table because I could not confidently classify them according to form.

process most of the time (executive agreements aside); indeed, lawmakers participated in the overwhelming percentage of international agreements by providing their authority through the statutory agreement process. These data confirm, too, that the treaty had been replaced by the statutory agreement as the primary method for the making of US commitments abroad.

Statutory agreements remain the dominant form of international commitment by the United States, regardless of the agreement's policy content.[50] The argument that *the executive branch has excluded the Congress from agreement making*—the so-called **evasion hypothesis**[51]—is not supported by the data from the Cold War. Nor is it supported by the findings of Krutz and Peake for later periods in American foreign policy.[52] Lawmakers in both chambers—not just the Senate, as the Constitution's treaty clause envisioned—have been active participants in formal diplomacy, even in the realm of military agreements. Still, there have been times when Congress has been shut out of deliberations over significant commitments abroad, as presidents and bureaucrats rely on executive agreements to carry out foreign policy on their own—the less visible dimension of American diplomacy that so agitated the Brickerites.

Secretary of State Hillary Clinton (left) shakes hands with US embassy staff and family during a meet and greet in Jakarta on September 4, 2012, on her way to China.

## The Hidden Side of Diplomacy

In a study released during the Cold War, members of the Senate Foreign Relations Committee reported, "As the committee has discovered, there have been numerous agreements contracted with foreign governments in recent years, particularly agreements of a military nature, which remain wholly unknown to Congress and to the people."[53] Although only 7 percent of all formal US commitments abroad from 1946 to 1972 were based on executive agreements, a central question remains: Were there—concealed within this modest percentage—obligations of sweeping significance? For an answer, one must turn to a more qualitative review of America's military commitments. These kinds of agreements have proven to be especially controversial and costly; the placement of US troops and weapons abroad, known as forward deployment, adds up to an expensive portion of the Pentagon's budget and can lead the United States into war.

The conventional wisdom, at least among some lawmakers, is that the executive branch has sought out the advice and consent of the Senate primarily for diplomatic initiatives of little substantive importance; for more important agreements, the evasion hypothesis rules. Senator Dick Clark (D-Iowa) lamented the denigration of the treaty process: "the treaty form has been used for a shrimp agreement with Brazil, an agreement on the conservation of polar bears, and an agreement regarding the uninhabited coral reefs in the Caribbean."[54] Other treaties have dealt with the recovery of lost archaeological objects in Mexico,[55] an increase in membership of the International Atomic Energy Board from twenty-five to thirty-five,[56] and the international classification of industrial designs.[57] "If an agreement involves a very minor matter on the allocation of radio waves with Mexico, it is presented as a treaty," observed the longest serving chairman of the Senate Foreign Relations Committee, J. William Fulbright, in 1971. "If it is a tax matter with Luxembourg involving equal treatment, it is a treaty. But if it involves circumstance likely to result in war, it is an executive agreement, kept a secret and then presented to Congress as a *fait accompli*."[58]

Despite the examples of treaties used for mundane negotiations, American's military treaties signed between 1946 and 1972 frequently did deal with significant commitments overseas. Of the forty-one military treaties signed in these years, thirty-two (or 78 percent) involved major defense obligations. Among them were security arrangements with Japan, the Republic of Korea, and the nations of Western Europe; major arms-control accords, including the nuclear test-ban treaty of 1963; and postwar peace treaties with former belligerents. Nine of the treaties (22 percent) did not rise to the level of "significant," but they nonetheless addressed the administrative details of major defense pacts, most notably NATO. This evidence fails to support the view that treaties have been altogether banished from their traditional role when it comes to important military obligations abroad. In more recent years, the treaty procedure has also been used for other major initiatives related to security affairs, such as the New START Treaty between the Russians and the United States approved by the Senate and ratified by President Obama in 2010.

Yet Senators Clark, Fulbright, and their colleagues did have some reason for concern. Although 43 of the 142 executive agreements dealing with military policy were routine and minor from 1946 to 1974, addressing such topics as the establishment of a practice bombing range in West Germany and reciprocal air rights with Canada for rescue operations, a striking number involved major obligations abroad. During the early Cold War, the United States entered into numerous commitments partly or completely through an assertion of executive authority, usually with the White House evoking the Constitution's commander-in-chief clause (see Table 10.3).

A total of 99 of 142 (70 percent) of the military agreements during this time period were important enough to have warranted closer scrutiny by the legislative branch. Several involved the establishment of overseas bases. This exclusion of a role for Congress in the making of such commitments has been a source of tension between the executive and legislative branches ever since these early Cold War years, as presidents have asserted authority under the commander-in-chief clause and Congress sometimes resisted what it perceived as unwise agreements entered into without the benefit of legislative review.

Krutz and Peake found that in later years of the Cold War, the executive agreement has still been used robustly by administrations—a pattern that continues today.

| Table 10.3 |
|---|
| Use of the Azores air bases by the United States (1947) |
| Placement of US troops in Guatemala (1947) |
| Placement of US troops in China (1948) |
| Military security in the Republic of Korea (1949) |
| US military mission in Honduras (1950) |
| Broad US military prerogatives in Ethiopia (1953) |
| US military mission in El Salvador (1957) |
| US military mission in Liberia (1958) |
| US base rights in Lebanon (1958) |
| Security pledges to Turkey, Iran, and Pakistan (1959) |
| Military use of the British island, Diego Garcia, in the Indian Ocean (1966) |
| Military use of Bahrain (1971) |
| Agreement terminating a military pact with Libya (1972) |

*Table 10.3*
Examples of
US Commitments via
Executive Agreement,
1947-1972

They look on this usage, though, as a healthy development in the implementation of foreign policy. "Rather than a usurpation of the balance of power," they write, "the modern executive agreement is a rational adaptation by modern presidents, in conjunction with Congress, to the complex foreign policy environment unforeseen by the framers of the Constitution."[59] It is true that many executive agreements are helpful administratively when used for accords regarding fairly routine matters, such as the safety of migratory birds passing from Canada to Mexico or the proper handling of archaeological artifacts; otherwise, the Senate would quickly be clogged up with treaties on minor subjects, leaving little time for other important work. Lawmakers and the public ought to be skeptical, however, about an overly rosy outlook on executive domination over America's vital commitments overseas. As the following examples illustrate, presidents have abused the executive agreement privilege in the past and there is no reason to believe they will refrain from doing so in the future. Indeed, the very philosophy that animated the creation of the Constitution would suggest that an abuse of executive power is quite likely, unless carefully watched by the legislative branch and the courts.

## Military Agreements

A number of case examples from the Cold War reveal how the misuse of executive agreements can have a pernicious effect on American foreign policy. These cases remain relevant because contemporary presidents may again attempt to bypass Congress by entering into far-reaching agreements with other nations. Thailand offers a telling illustration.

### Thailand

In 1962, Secretary of State Dean Rusk and the Foreign Minister of Thailand, Thanat Khoman, issued a joint statement in which Rusk expressed "the firm intention of the United States to aid Thailand, its ally and historic friend, in resisting Communist aggression and subversion."[60] This language went far beyond the wording of the SEATO treaty, which provided only that the member nations would "consult" in times of military peril and act to meet the common danger in accordance with their own "constitutional processes." The end result of the Rusk–Khoman joint communiqué was to convert the SEATO collective security arrangement into a bilateral US–Thai defense pact. Under the new relationship, the US Military Assistance Program for Thailand shot upward from $24 million in 1960 to $88 million in 1962.

Further, in 1966 the two nations entered into negotiations over a secret contingency agreement, which was signed in 1969. This arrangement promised joint action in the event of a conventional military attack against Thailand. The agreement also paid special bonuses to Thai combat troops in Vietnam—in essence the hiring of mercenaries to fight in this civil war on America's behalf. Through a communiqué and a secret executive agreement, the original intent of a solemn treaty approved by the Senate, SEATO, had been significantly altered.[61]

### Spain

The United States also entered into a series of executive agreements with Spain during the 1960s, which involved the use of Spanish soil for American military bases. Disclosure of these commitments led to a stormy debate in the Foreign Relations Committee. Senator Fulbright was not impressed by the argument of the Defense Department that the Senate Armed Services Committee had been kept informed of the negotiations. He rebuked the executive branch for its proclivity "to tell the Chairman of the Armed Services Committee, who usually is very sympathetic with these [executive] agreements, and the [Senate] Appropriations Committee," while leaving more critical lawmakers and the public in the dark.[62]

When the time came for the renewal of the Spanish bases agreement in 1975, the anti-executive agreement insurgency in the Senate was running at full tide. Prudently, the State Department submitted the new agreement for approval as a treaty. The Department also kept key senators and staff closely briefed on the progress of the negotiations as they proceeded in Madrid. According to a Senate staff aide, it was "a candid, open consultation."[63] These tactics of accommodation by the executive branch paid off with a Senate vote of 84-to-11 in favor of the treaty. Ironically, Spain itself had aggressively sought a treaty instead of an executive agreement; its government "yearned for the symbolic benediction that a solemn treaty approved by two-thirds of the Senate would provide."[64]

### Laos

During the 1960s, the executive branch launched a wide array of secret military and CIA paramilitary operations in Laos, without any written agreements whatsoever.

Everything was based on "oral understandings" that, according to a State Department official, were just as binding as written ones.[65] Among the commitments made in this manner were the placement of American spotters in combat zones. During hearings, a Senate Subcommittee sought to find out how all this had come to pass:

> Subcommittee counsel: Under what authority are the American personnel in Laos there?
> State Department official: They are there under the executive authority of the President.[66]

## THE DANGERS OF DIPLOMACY BY EXECUTIVE FIAT

These cases, and many similar examples, suggest a number of conclusions about the conduct of American diplomacy. First, US military commitments abroad have often been based on the most slender reeds of authority. Although the oral understandings with the government of Laos may represent an extreme example, the various other secret letters, communiqués, and agreements outlined previously also reflect a foreign policy dominated by anonymous bureaucrats, closed doors, and confidential covenants. Sometimes the "agreements" have been only tacit understandings susceptible to later misinterpretations. Further, the presence of American soldiers or bases overseas often seemed to mean more than the most elaborate and solemn treaty approved by the Senate.

"Whether or not we have such a treaty with a particular country," testified Secretary Rusk, "the presence there of a US base clearly [signifies] an interest and concern on our part with the security of that country."[67] The language of the NATO pact signed in 1949 provides an illustration. While the wording of this treaty is ambiguous, the fact that American troops were stationed in Western Europe during the Cold War—and are still there today—made it clear that a Soviet attack into Europe would inevitably draw in the United States. It is precisely this risk associated with the placement of US troops overseas that makes the initial commitment of military assurances such an important decision, one that—according to Senators Clark and Fulbright— begged for greater accountability by lawmakers.

Further, sometimes *America's diplomatic obligations are stretched far beyond the original intent of Congress, or even the White House*—a development known as **creeping commitments**.[68] This distortion occurs as executive branch officials seek to fill in the details once a broad agreement is reached. These "auxiliary arrangements" can assume a bewildering variety of forms, including memoranda of understanding, exchanges of notes, exchanges of letters, technical addendums, protocols, the *note verbale*, the *aide-mémoire*, agreed minutes, joint communiqués, joint military plans, military assistance programs, and the stationing of troops overseas.

These shell games, which often leave Congress, the media, and the public trying to guess about the true nature of US commitments abroad, also take place outside the domain of military affairs. Executive agreements have been used by the executive branch to conduct political negotiations and to carry out intelligence operations.

Chiding him for "obsessive secrecy," Senator Henry Jackson (D-Washington) accused Secretary of State Kissinger of withholding from Congress for two years several secret "understandings" reached with the Soviet Union during the initial SALT negotiations. In addition, Kissinger allegedly withheld "crucial communications" on the faltering US-Soviet trade talks in 1974.[69] The experienced diplomatic correspondent Tad Szulc concurred with Senator Jackson. "The fact is that virtually nobody—possibly not even [Presidents] Richard Nixon and Gerald Ford—knew precisely what promises and commitments Kissinger made to foreign leaders during his eight years in power: to Mao Tse-tung and Chou En-lai, Brezhnev and Dobrynin, Le Duc Tho, Sadat and King Faisal, Golda Meir or any number of other foreign presidents, foreign ministers and ambassadors."[70]

One of the controversial "understandings" reached by Kissinger was with Israel and Egypt in 1975 over the question of disengagement from the Sinai Peninsula. These negotiations included the stationing of US personnel on the peninsula to serve as monitors, in a region where military hostilities might have easily resumed with little warning. The State Department declared the "understanding" a proper exercise of executive authority, not a commitment that required a treaty. President Ford backpedaled, though, when congressional criticism mounted. He eventually sought legislative authority, via a statutory agreement, to implement the provisions of the Sinai "understanding."

All too often, charge critics, the executive branch has skipped past the Congress, making major foreign commitments with a simple signature by a bureaucrat across the dotted line on an executive agreement; or by merely writing a letter to a foreign dignitary—or even just by offering an oral assurance. Congress has long been aware of this practice, but it took some time before its efforts to place limits on this slippery form of diplomacy came to a head. At a Senate Foreign Relations Committee hearing in 1971, Chairman Fulbright declared, "We have discovered that the President does not always know best, and that, indeed, the country would be far better off today if the Congress had been more assertive in the exercise of its constitutional role, which consists as least as much in assertion and criticism as it does in subservience."[71]

## Constitutional Diplomacy

The underlying motive of the Bricker movement was "a retreat from the world," noted Fulbright in 1954.[72] A second uprising in Congress against presidential dominance over American diplomacy also displayed a jaded outlook toward unwarranted US involvement around the globe. This time following the leadership of Senator Fulbright, Capitol Hill insurgents during the Vietnam War era opposed an overextension of US obligations in far-flung corners of the globe that seemed of dubious relevance to the well-being of Americans. Despite their dramatically different views on most political topics, the Brickerites and the Fulbright insurgents were aligned in their belief in one bedrock principle: a distrust of excessive executive discretion in foreign policy. Resist executive "encroachment," declared Senator William F. Knowland of California, the Republican majority leader, in 1954; "Swing back the pendulum [of constitutional imbalance], urged Senator Frank Church of Idaho in 1970.[73] As Garrett has aptly noted, both movements were "substantially focused on the necessity of reasserting the prerogatives and status of the Congress as such if that institution is to maintain its vitality as a central component of the American Constitutional system."[74]

## Stirrings on the Fulbright Committee

President Johnson's misrepresentations over, and eventual invasion of, the Dominican Republic in 1965, followed by growing skepticism in the Senate about the wisdom of the Gulf of Tonkin Resolution, set the stage for a legislative reaction against excessive presidential discretion over US diplomacy. In 1968, Johnson hastily asked the Senate to approve a broadly worded resolution on foreign aid for Latin America. On the eve of a Western Hemisphere summit meeting in Punta del Este, Uruguay, the President sought congressional support for costly new agreements. The Foreign Relations Committee, with Fulbright at the helm, refused to write another blank check. Instead the Committee passed by unanimous vote a substitute resolution stating that all new foreign aid initiatives in Latin American would be given due consideration, but only in accordance with the Committee's normal legislative timetable. The panel's members would not be bullied by the president.

With this shot across the bow of the White House, the Fulbright Committee had gone beyond mere speech making in its search for an acceptable balance between Congress and the executive branch in diplomatic affairs. The mood of skepticism on Capitol Hill toward presidential power had turned into outright defiance. An institutional revolution was under way and, in June 1969, the Senate passed the landmark **National Commitments Resolution**:

> Be it resolved, that it is the sense of the Senate that a national commitment by the United States to a foreign power necessarily and exclusively results from affirmative action taken by the executive *and legislative* branches of the United States Government through means of a treaty, convention, or other *legislative* instrumentality specifically intended to give effect to such a commitment.[75]

Although this resolution was only an expression of opinion by the Senate, not a law, it sent a strong message to the White House: senators would no longer be ignored as players in America's diplomatic initiatives.

## The Case–Zablocki Act

By 1972, the Senate was ready to take a bigger step toward instituting tighter legislative controls over international agreements. So far, lawmakers had only passed resolutions—some toughly worded, to be sure, but still just statements of view without the force of law. Now the chamber turned its attention to statutory remedies. Out of a sense of despair over the inability of lawmakers even to find out what commitments the executive branch had been making overseas by executive agreement, especially in

Indochina, Senator Clifford Case (R-New Jersey) introduced legislation to remove this blind spot. He sought to guarantee that Congress—both the Senate and the House— had access to information on all of America's foreign commitments. To this end, the Senate passed the Case Act by an emphatic vote of 81-to-0. Representative Clement Zablocki (D-Wisconsin) introduced the same measure in the House; and, six months later, the proposal passed in that chamber, too, by a wide majority. On August 22, 1972, Richard M. Nixon—faced by a united Congress prepared to override a presidential veto—signed the **Case-Zablocki Act** into law. Henceforth, *the State Department would have to report to Congress on all international agreements being negotiated by the executive branch.*

Hesitant and cautious, in contrast to the bold attempt by the Brickerites to amend the Constitution, the Case-Zablocki Act nonetheless represented a significant move by Congress toward institutional sharing in the making of international agreements. As members of the Senate Foreign Relations Committee stated in a document issued during the debate:

> The principle of mandatory reporting of agreements with foreign countries to the Congress is more than desirable; it is, from a constitutional standpoint, crucial and indispensable. For the Congress to accept anything less would represent a resignation from responsibility and an alienation of an authority which is vested in the Congress by the Constitution. If Congress is to meet its responsibilities in the formulation of foreign policy, no information is more crucial than the fact and content of agreements with foreign nations.[76]

Whatever its virtues, the imperfections of the Case-Zablocki Act soon became evident. The sixty-day reporting provision in the law, for example, permitted the executive branch to *inform the Congress* fully *two months* after *a commitment had already been made to another country*—**ex post facto reporting**, in contrast to *in-advance* or **ante facto reporting**. With this late awareness of an agreement underway, lawmakers were faced with a *fait accompli*: they could either go along with the diplomatic initiative or wreck the arrangements by shutting off funds or otherwise barring implementation after the fact. "The reports come up here so late, we have to rely on contacts and leaks in the executive branch to find out when really important negotiations are under way," said a frustrated Senate aide.[77] More alarming still to members of Congress, the executive branch sometimes failed altogether to report to lawmakers on international agreements, despite the clearly stated requirements in the Case-Zablocki legislation. Inquiries by researcher David J. Kuchenbecker revealed in 1978 that "few major agencies could indicate even the number of international agreements they had entered into during the previous year."[78]

The most compelling evidence that something was amiss surfaced as part of an inquiry in 1976 by the General Accounting Office (now called the **Government Accountability Office,** *an investigative arm of the Congress*). The GAO report concluded that the transmission of executive agreements to the legislative branch under the provisions of the Case-Zablocki Act suffered from significant omissions. Limiting its examination of US agreements just to the Republic of Korea [commonly known as South Korea], the GAO documented more than thirty instances since the passage of Case-Zablocki in which agreements had never been sent to Congress. Several dealt with military matters, such as the joint use of Taegu Air Base and the transfer of $37.6 million worth of military equipment to South Korean troops. Not even the State Department was informed. As Nye has pointed out, "Nearly all the major executive departments have little foreign offices of their own. In 1973, for example, of 19,000 Americans abroad on diplomatic missions, only 3,400 were from the State Department and less than half of the government delegates accredited to international conferences came from the State Department."[79] How many of these "little foreign offices" were engaged in agreement making without the knowledge of the State Department, let alone the Congress? So wondered key lawmakers.

In 1978, Congress moved to tighten the Case-Zablocki reporting requirements. Lawmakers were insufficiently bold to demand advance notice of all international agreements—the powerful *ante facto* reporting requirement. They did add three new statutory stipulations, however, as amendments to the original Case-Zablocki law. First, any oral international agreements had to be reduced to writing and submitted to the Congress. Second, all late agreements (that is, beyond the sixty-day limit) required a written presidential explanation. And, third, the State Department's control over agency-to-agency agreements was increased by mandating consultation by the agency in question with the Department before an agreement could be signed. As one authority concluded, the patience of lawmakers was "clearly at an end."[80]

These reforms helped improve the State Department's control over agreement reporting procedures, and they focused accountability to allow more reliable monitoring by the legislative branch. Nevertheless, the number of late agreements reported to Congress persisted. According to a report prepared after the Case-Zablocki amendments, 132 agreements were still late in transmittal to lawmakers during 1979. The number dropped significantly the next year, after further congressional complaints, yet forty-six agreements still arrived late.[81] Additional progress has been made in more recent years toward compliance with Case-Zablocki; but, problems persist even with this simple reporting expectation, with late reports—and sometimes no reports.

## The Treaty Powers Resolution

In 1978, Senator Clark (D-Iowa) brought forth a much stronger proposal to ensure that the executive branch kept Congress in the loop on international agreements: the **Treaty Powers Resolution** (see *Perspectives on American Foreign Policy* 10.1). This initiative expressed *a sense of the Senate that any "significant" international agreement should be cast as a treaty and submitted to senators for their advice and consent.* Section 4 of the resolution bore sharp teeth: if the executive failed to submit an agreement that senators had decided (by a simple majority vote) should have been brought to their

---

## PERSPECTIVES ON AMERICAN FOREIGN POLICY 10.1

**SENATOR DICK CLARK on the Treaty Powers Resolution:**

Under the existing situation, there is no balance. The President of the United States alone decides what is to be sent up as a treaty. The Senate has no choice in that whatsoever. If the President of the United States decides to send the SALT agreement to this body as a treaty, we will consider it as a treaty. If the President of the United States decides that it an executive agreement, it will be an executive agreement. The Senate will not decide and will have no voice in that decision except insofar as the President may decide to consult with us.

The same is true of any other international agreement. It is really, under the existing situation, the President, and the President alone, who decides whether any agreement that is signed is going to be considered by this body at all. The President can dispense with Senate advice and consent merely by calling a treaty an executive agreement. I do not see that as a fair balance.

SOURCE: *Congressional Record* (June 28, 1978), p. S10010.

---

chamber as a treaty, then the Senate rules would declare it henceforth out of order "to consider any bill or joint resolution or any amendment thereto, or any report of a committee of conference, which authorizes or provides budget authority to implement such international agreement." The money spigots would be shut off for the disputed agreement until the Senate had an opportunity to consider the proposal.

A majority of the Senate proved unwilling, though, to endorse this intrepid challenge to executive agreements. In retrospect, an observer believes that the Clark proposal was chiefly a "finger-shaking" exercise by the Foreign Relations Committee aimed at the executive branch.[82] The initiative did have some effect, though, despite its defeat. It stimulated an exchange of letters between the chairman of the Committee, John Sparkman (D-Alabama) and the assistant secretary for congressional relations at the Department of State, Douglas J. Bennet Jr. The **Sparkman–Bennet letters** of 1978 led to *an understanding that, in the future, the Department of State would "inform the committee periodically, on a confidential basis, of significant international agreements which have been authorized for negotiation."*[83]

In turn, the Committee would advise the Department about any agreement that its members wanted to discuss further regarding its proper form: whether treaty, statutory agreement, or executive agreement. Sparkman made it clear that the arrangement "must cover all significant international agreements . . . regardless of the executive entity involved in the negotiation or approval process." He further emphasized that his Committee expected that "*consultation—not notification*—will occur at any time an option is opened or foreclosed to use the treaty or executive agreement form in the case of any international agreement of significance."[84] The message was plain: the less consultation from the executive branch, the more heat from the legislative branch. The problem with this well-intended exchange of letters, though, is that the understandings they expressed were not binding on subsequent administrations. Such understandings can become cobwebs, easily swept away by the next administration; only law demands that assurances are honored beyond the ebb and flow of government officials into and out of office.

Disputes between the branches have erupted, too, over whether Congress can insist on having lawmakers or their staff included as a part of US diplomatic delegations. Lawyers in the administration of George H. W. Bush declared that the president's powers "self-evidently" included the authority "to choose the individuals through whom the Nation's foreign affairs are conducted. That responsibility cannot be circumscribed by statute." In 2012, the Obama administration joined the fracas. Its Office of Legal Counsel in the Justice Department claimed "absolute discretion" for the president to choose "whomever he considers most suitable" to be his diplomatic agent.[85]

## Two Houses Do Not Make a Home

The two houses of Congress have sometimes been at one another's throats as well over the issue of international agreements. Secretary of State Dulles observed in 1953 that "an undefined and probably undefinable borderline [exists] between international agreements which require two-thirds Senate concurrence, but no House concurrence, as in the case of treaties, and [statutory] agreements which should have the majority concurrence of both chambers of Congress."[86] Leading members of the Senate, however, have been prepared to fight for what they view as their constitutional prerogatives with respect to the treaty power. "If they begin now to intrude on the treaty-making power of the Senate, we are going to find ourselves in a position where we can't do anything without the House's consent," fumed a senior member of the Foreign Relations Committee in 1977. "Their nibbles end up being big bites, and we are being bitten to death."[87]

The House of Representatives has both a constitutional and a logical case, though, for being included in the process of agreement making. As one of its senior aides put it, "Could the framers have intended otherwise than that the representatives of the taxpayers and citizens, who must fulfill these national commitments, have a voice in this approval?"[88] The statutory agreement with House involvement has been used for many important foreign policy initiatives, including NAFTA and WTO. Moreover, as some critics of the statutory agreement have incorrectly argued,[89] this approach has not been used only in the field of international trade. As Ackerman and Hathaway point out, "Both houses have acted under Article I to approve key national security accords, like the SALT agreement with the Russians or the recent United States-India nuclear agreement."[90]

Sometimes, for its own purposes, the executive branch takes advantage of the occasional divisiveness on the subject of the statutory agreement that arises between the House and the Senate. "The Clark resolution would constitute a very significant and unwise interference with the role of the House of Representatives," opined a State Department legal adviser for treaty affairs during the debate over the Treaty Powers Resolution, no doubt seeking support from the House to help block the resolution.[91] Usually the executive branch views the statutory agreement as somewhat easier to negotiate on Capitol Hill, because the required approval standard is a simple majority vote—albeit in both houses of Congress—rather than an extraordinary (two-thirds)

Senate majority. In 2002, for example, the George W. Bush administration preferred to submit the Treaty of Moscow (a nuclear arms reduction agreement) as a statutory agreement; the Senate complained vociferously, however, and on this occasion at least the administration consented to the treaty process (as the agreement's original name suggested should be the case).

## DIPLOMACY'S FAR REACH

Agreements with other countries have often been the precursor to overt or covert military or CIA intervention abroad by the United States. This is why, in the wake of the war in Vietnam, lawmakers have come to believe that Congress has a major stake in America's diplomatic initiatives. "If you've got children or grandchildren who might have to go [to war]," Robert C. Byrd (D-West Virginia), the Senate Majority Leader, once observed, "you'd feel much better with Congress being brought in, than leaving it to one man."[92] In this spirit of wider, democratic involvement and the rising sense of oversight responsibility that settled over the Congress during the 1970s, Senator Hubert H. Humphrey (D-Minnesota) warned Secretary of State Cyrus Vance as he prepared to depart on a trip to the Middle East: "Don't make any commitments until you've been back here [to Capitol Hill]—not even smiling ones."[93]

Most lawmakers and the public understand the need for privacy and secrecy during negotiations with other countries. They also understand, though, that democracy and the Constitution require broader participation than just the White House in the great decisions of diplomacy that can determine the fate of the American people.

## SUMMARY

Most international disputes are resolved not by force of arms or by secret intervention with the CIA, but through diplomacy—the art of negotiations between states leading to peaceful outcomes.

The United States has used three primary forms of international agreements in its formal negotiations with other nations: the treaty, the statutory agreement, and the executive agreement. They require, respectively, a two-thirds Senate vote, a majority vote in both chambers of Congress, and no legislative authority whatsoever. From 1946 through 1972, the United States used the treaty form in only 6 percent of its international agreements. Statutory agreements were the most prevalent form of formal negotiations, at 87 percent; and the executive agreement accounted for 7 percent. Recent research findings suggest a continuation of these earlier trends.

The executive agreement initially evolved to handle routine negotiations that would otherwise tie up the Senate to the point of paralysis. Yet executive agreements can be misused as a means for evading Congress on important diplomatic initiatives. Presidents have been drawn to the executive agreement especially for military commitments abroad.

Lawmakers have twice attempted to curb excessive executive discretion over American diplomacy: first, in a movement led by Senator John Bricker during the 1950s, and second, by anti-Vietnam War "doves" led by Senator J. William Fulbright during the 1970s. The Bricker movement failed by one vote in the Senate. Two decades later, the Fulbright insurgents had broader objectives and enjoyed more success with passage of the Case-Zablocki Act, which required the executive branch to report to Congress on the use of all executive agreements.

## KEY TERMS

*ante facto* reporting p. 328
Bricker Amendment (1954) p. 303
Case-Zablocki Act (1972, with amendments in 1978) p. 328
coercive diplomacy p. 308
creeping commitments p. 325
evasion hypothesis p. 321
*ex post facto* reporting p. 328

form of international agreements p. 319
George Amendment (1954) p. 304
Government Accountability Office (GAO) p. 328
National Commitments Resolution (1969) p. 327
public diplomacy p. 312
Sparkman–Bennet letters (1978) p. 330
Treaty Powers Resolution (1978) p. 329

---

## QUESTIONS FOR DISCUSSION

1. To what extent do you think the backing of military power is necessary for successful diplomatic negotiations? Why or why not?
2. Contrast the Brickerites movement with the rebellion stirred in Congress by Senator Fulbright two decades later.
3. What precipitated the passage of the Case-Zablocki Act?

4. Would you have voted for the Treaty Powers Resolution? Why or why not?
5. Would you support a reform in favor of *ante facto* reporting on executive agreements? How about the bicameral congressional approval of all non-treaty international agreements, as envisioned by the Brickerites and the George Amendment? Explain your position.

## ADDITIONAL READINGS

Glennon, Michael J. *Constitutional Diplomacy.* Princeton, NJ: Princeton University Press, 1990.
Johnson, Loch K. *The Making of International Agreements: Congress Confronts the Executive.* New York: New York University Press, 1984.

Kissinger, Henry A. *Diplomacy.* New York: Simon & Schuster, 1994.

---

For further readings, please visit the book's companion website.

### CHAPTER 11

# Military Force

## THE CAMBODIAN "INCURSION"

In April of 1970, under orders from President Richard M. Nixon, US troops crossed the South Vietnamese border and invaded Cambodia in pursuit of North Vietnamese and Vietcong enemy forces. When the President announced his new policy of a Cambodian "incursion" (a euphemism for invasion), college campuses across the nation erupted in protest. Marches were organized and demonstrators carried banners decrying "Nixon's gamble."

Even among the "silent majority" of Americans who were not protesting in the streets, many expressed profound dismay that the White House had expanded an already unpopular war. Previously, American armies fighting in Vietnam had stopped at the Cambodian border and allowed North Vietnamese and Vietcong soldiers to escape, rather than extend the Vietnam conflict into a neighboring country. Now, US troops continued after the enemy in hot pursuit—a presidential decision made without congressional consultation, let alone approval.

While a US tank blasts away with cannon and machine guns, a dismounted tank soldier aims his M-16 as an American tank patrol made enemy contact at a rubber plantation four miles inside in Cambodia on May 3, 1970.

Among the antiwar rallies was one held on Monday, May 4, at Kent State University in Ohio. When some Kent State students were accused of causing unrest in town over the weekend, Ohio governor Jim Rhodes sent the National Guard to campus to keep order. Among the thousands of students on campus that day, a few, like Jeffrey Miller, were activists strongly opposed to the war in Vietnam. They demonstrated peacefully on a campus quad. Most, though, like Allison Krause, Sandra Scheuer, and William Schroeder, were simply on their way to class or the library. After lobbing tear gas in an attempt to disperse the demonstrators, members of the National Guard suddenly panicked and opened fire. In a 13-second hail of bullets, they killed these four students and wounded nine others. Protests erupted as well at Jackson State University in Mississippi, where local law enforcement officers gunned down students.

The Kent State and Jackson State shootings shocked a nation already polarized by the war in Vietnam. Citizens who opposed the war—and now the incursion—reacted with outrage, whereas those who supported both also expressed approval for stopping the campus protests. In Washington, the White House viewed the antiwar

**LEARNING OBJECTIVES AND CONSTITUTIONAL ISSUES**

**By the end of this chapter, you will be able to:**

- *Describe the various uses of the war power.*
- *Identify the ways in which the sophisticated weapons of the nuclear age have changed the face of war.*
- *Discuss the principles of command and control with regard to nuclear and conventional weapons.*
- *Assess recent controversies surrounding the decision to use the war option, including whether resolutions passed by the United Nations or NATO should affect war-making authority in Washington.*

**THIS CHAPTER RAISES THE FOLLOWING CONSTITUTIONAL QUESTIONS:**

- The constitutional framers could not have imagined the power and the capability for swift delivery of modern WMDs. Does the nature of contemporary warfare and weaponry vitiate the role for Congress envisioned by the language of the Constitution?

- Is the War Powers Resolution a reasonable response by Congress to correct the erosion over the years of war-making authority on Capitol Hill? Would you amend—or perhaps repeal altogether—this 1973 law?

- Should the president be allowed to use nuclear weapons in a first strike without consultation with lawmakers? Perhaps only in a retaliatory (second) strike? What value, if any, can members of Congress bring to deliberations over sending US forces into combat? Over using WMDs?

- Is there merit in the arguments sometimes made by proponents of a strong presidency that this office has "inherent" and complete war-making authority? Should the president alone be able to order the firing of missiles from US ships in the Red Sea at airfields, runways, and aircraft on the ground in Syria or some other country without congressional authorization?

- To what extent should be president be allowed to rely on authority from UN or NATO resolutions to send American ground troops into combat? What about Air Force fighter pilots? Unpiloted drones?

protests as nothing less than "revolutionary terrorism" led by students who were out to "destroy their country."[1] Congressional doves responded to the national unrest with a legislative proposal to curb the war from spreading deeper into Cambodia. The initiative, known as the Cooper–Church Amendment, after its sponsors John Sherman Cooper (R-Kentucky) and Frank Church (D-Idaho), called for the Senate to cut off funding for the incursion. A top Nixon strategist recalled that the proposal was "the first restriction on presidential military action in wartime."[2]

Senator Church began the six-week debate on the amendment by explaining its importance: "If future developments were to lead the President to advocate a renewal of our attack upon Cambodian territory, or a more extensive occupation of that country, then he would be obliged to come to Congress, make his case before us, and ask the Congress to lift its prohibition against such an expanded war." He continued: "Are we going to permit our Government to slide relentlessly toward all power being concentrated in the hands of one chief executive? Are we going to permit our Government to become a Caesardom, or are we going to reassert the authority that the Constitution placed in Congress? That is the fundamental issue."[3] In contrast, Senator Robert Dole (R-Kansas) defended the President's decision. A president has "the power, under the Constitution," he said, "to go back into Cambodia or any country to protect American troops."

The Senate passed the Cooper–Church Amendment. Although it expired in conference committee in the House, President Nixon understood the magnitude of the opposition on campus, in the streets, and now in the US Senate. He withdrew the American troops from Cambodia. Lawmakers had come to realize anew that no topic addressed in the Constitution was more emotionally charged and significant than the war powers clause. Soon the Congress would engage in a major constitutional debate on this subject. ⁓

## THE LAST FULL MEASURE

President Abraham Lincoln addressed the fallen in the Civil War with these moving words at Gettysburg: "It is rather for us to be here dedicated to the great task remaining before us—that from these honored dead we take increased devotion to that cause for which they gave the last full measure of devotion."[4] Today, in Washington, DC, there are 58,156 names on the Vietnam War Memorial, Americans who gave the last full measure of devotion in another war. The death roster, carved in sleek, black marble, stirs a strong response in most visitors old enough to remember the war. The most visited site in the nation's capital, the Memorial stands above all as a reminder of the human costs that accompany warfare. The war power is the most extreme and hazardous means for the pursuit of foreign policy ends, especially in this age of WMDs. "The central fact of life in the nuclear age," wrote two authorities, "is the unquestioned and unambiguous ability of nations possessing nuclear weapons to destroy each other."[5] A primary concern of this book is the question of how well America's constitutional framework continues to fit the needs of contemporary foreign policy.

No topic reveals as emphatically as war making the ongoing disputes that accompany the Constitution's fundamental philosophy of power sharing.

## USES OF THE WAR POWER

The United States has periodically used overt military force for a wide range of purposes. General Andrew Jackson's bold military forays into Florida territory claimed by the Spanish were no doubt indispensable for persuading the government of Spain to negotiate a diplomatic settlement over the contested region. President Teddy Roosevelt's imperious show of force by sailing America's great battleships in convoy around the world made a memorable impression on observers, like the Japanese, who realized the United States was now a military force to be reckoned with. America's history has also been punctuated by the direct use of armed force abroad. Since 1798, the United States has been involved in more than 200 military actions overseas. Congress has formally declared war in only five of these instances: the war with Great Britain in 1812, with Mexico in 1846, with Spain in 1898, and the two world wars. In more than sixty other instances, lawmakers have given some other form of legislative approval, from the appropriation of monies to the passage of resolutions in support of war. In the two centuries between 1787 and 1987, however, fully 140 engagements—the overwhelming majority—were the result of decisions reached by the executive branch alone to employ the war power.[6] More recent presidents have also sometimes entered the United States into warfare without congressional debate or approval, as when President Obama provided air support and intelligence for the French-led effort to overthrow Col. Muammar el-Qaddafi of Libya in 2011.

The reasons for the overt use of force have varied: protecting America's trading opportunities abroad, as with Thomas Jefferson's operations against the Barbary pirates and, a century later, US intervention in the Boxer Rebellion in China; chasing European powers out of the Western Hemisphere; and Woodrow Wilson's promise, in his rousing war message to Congress, to defend "the rights and liberties of small nations." During the Cold War, US military strategy was based on the containment of communism, a policy backed up by an imposing arsenal of nuclear and conventional weapons, as well as by a ring of global military alliances that encircled the Soviet Union.

In the twenty-first century, the United States has taken up arms to fight terrorism in the Middle East (Iraq), Southwest Asia (Afghanistan and Pakistan), and elsewhere around the world. The **Authorization for Use of Military Force** (AUMF, in Pentagonese), enacted by Congress a few days after 9/11 to guard against further acts of terrorism, *gives the president authority to arrest or kill anyone who committed or assisted in the attacks, or who gave safe haven to the attackers.* This is the law that authorized the war in Afghanistan, the shooting of Osama bin Laden, and the ongoing drone attacks in Afghanistan, Pakistan, Yemen (where among the victims has been Anwar Al-Awlaki and his son, both American citizens), and elsewhere in pursuit of Qaeda affiliates. Although sympathetic to the need for fighting terrorism, critics have questioned the open-ended nature of this authority, which seems to give the president boundless rights to engage in military operations in every corner of the globe with little supervision.[7]

America's war power is meant *to persuade other nations or terrorist organizations not to use their own military forces in ways that might endanger the vital interests of the United States and its allies*. During the Cold War, this goal of **deterrence** was achieved by threatening—usually implicitly but, early in the Eisenhower administration, quite explicitly—a massive, retaliatory nuclear attack against the Soviet Union or China if their troops dared to invade Western Europe, South Korea, Japan, or other locations considered important to America's physical security and economic prosperity.

Deterrence is, in part, a psychological concept. In reality, the United States might not have been able immediately to halt a post-World War II Soviet invasion of West Germany; but the prospect of the subsequent triggering of US nuclear weapons against the Russian homeland was meant to give leaders in the Kremlin pause about streaming Red Army soldiers through the Fulda Gap. By 1957, a condition of credible mutual deterrence came into existence, as the Soviets had achieved their own capacity to strike the United States with long-range, nuclear-tipped missiles. Both superpowers were able to ward off the outbreak of a strike against their homelands, or their major allies, through this threat of mutual assured destruction (MAD). The prospect of mutual suicide stood as a potent psychological barrier against the outbreak of another global war. Political scientist Richard Smoke emphasized the importance of these twin foreign policy goals. "Containment and deterrence reigned supreme" in American strategic thinking during the early years of the nuclear age, he writes.[8]

When President Reagan took office in 1981, America's Vietnam debacle remained fresh in the nation's memory, leading some of the administration's top advisers to advocate caution with respect to the use of the war power. This new restraint was evident in Secretary of Defense Caspar W. *Weinberger's six commandments*. Drawing on what he said were lessons derived from Korea and especially Vietnam, the Secretary offered in 1984 these *guidelines for future US military engagement* that became known as the **Weinberger Doctrine**:

- The military action had to involve vital national interests.
- The United States must intend to win.
- The operation had to have clear-cut political-military objectives.
- These objectives had to be subjected to a continual reassessment.
- The American people had to be in support.
- All alternatives to the use of overt force had to have been tried first and found wanting.

Weinberger said that his intention was to "sound a note of caution" against the rash use of military force in dangerous situations. Secretary of Defense Robert M. Gates would sound a similar note in 2011 based on his observations of America's involvement in Iraq and Afghanistan. "I will always be an advocate in terms of wars of necessity," he said. "I am just much more cautious on wars of choice."[9] Many generals welcomed the Weinberger guidelines as an assurance against unpopular wars of attrition like the Vietnam conflict; but others raised questions about whether this so-called doctrine would in effect bind the US military from any action at all, short of a third world war.[10]

At the end of the George H. W. Bush administration, Chairman of the Joint Chiefs of Staff Colin L. Powell (later Secretary of State in the George W. Bush administration) argued that *if America were to go to war, the nation should use overwhelming force to win quickly.*[11] Although the **Powell Doctrine** made sense to some, others suggested that the approach was adventurous and could escalate a small war into a large one. A more recent Joint Chiefs Chairman, Admiral Mike Mullen of the George W. Bush and Obama administrations, backed away from the Powell Doctrine on grounds that it could lead to recklessness. The military, Mullen argued in 2010, "must not try to use force only in an overwhelming capacity, but in the proper capacity, and in a precise and principled manner"—and "only when the other instruments of national power are ready to engage, as well." The next Chairman of the JCS during the Obama administration, General Martin Dempsey, had an even more circumspect view on the use of the war power. "The use of military power must be part of a strategic solution that includes international partners and the whole of government," he said in 2013. "Simply the application of force rarely produces—and maybe never produces—the outcome we seek."[12]

## WEAPONS OF WAR IN THE NUCLEAR AGE

A nation's weaponry and other military capabilities are closely related to its foreign policy. As the French diplomat Jean-David Levitte said in 2013, "If you don't have the military means to act, you don't have a foreign policy."[13] Nothing has changed US foreign policy so much as the invention of WMDs. The No. 1 objective of foreign policy is to prevent a nuclear attack against the United States.

During the Cold War, Americans faced the possibility of annihilation by Soviet nuclear-tipped missiles. Today, experts warn that the nation's cities remain vulnerable to attack by terrorists armed with nuclear weapons—a calamity consider by some quite probable in the near future.[14] In this unsettling global environment (sometimes referred to as the Nuclear Age, beginning in 1945), the United States and other major powers have three broad forms of military response available to them: strategic nuclear, tactical nuclear, and conventional. The most fearsome are the strategic nuclear capabilities; that is, the use of weapons able to strike the enemy from afar with massive levels of destructive power caused by a release of nuclear energy. It is worth examining the nuclear threat, because these weapons hold out the prospect of unprecedented casualties if used by terrorists—and even mass extinction of the human species if the major world powers were to engage in a full-scale nuclear war.

## Backpacks and City Busters

The **strategic nuclear capability** includes *intercontinental ballistic missiles* (ICBMs, which were going to be called IBMs until the International Business Machines Corporation—an American business titan already widely known by that acronym—objected to the government); *submarine-launched ballistic missiles (SLBMs); and long-range bombers equipped with nuclear bombs or missiles.* The **tactical nuclear capability** encompasses *weapons that also rely on a nuclear reaction for their destructive force but are more limited in scope and designed for relatively small targets on the battlefield.* Some, though—so-called **theater nuclear weapons**—can deliver a greater punch ("yield") than the bombs dropped on Hiroshima and Nagasaki. During the Cold War, these weapons varied in size from *backpack warheads (for use by the infantry, say, to stop a tank) and howitzer shells* (with a range of twenty miles or so) to the *NATO Lance battlefield-support missile and its Warsaw Pact Frog-7* counterpart (with ranges of eighty and forty-three miles, respectively). This level of weaponry included, as well, *Intermediate-Range Nuclear Forces (INF): European-based cruise and Pershing IIs on the American side, along with SS-20s and similar missiles on the Soviet side*, with ranges varying from 180 to some 3,400 miles. America's INF missiles had the capacity to strike the USSR from West Germany within ten minutes; therefore, from the Soviet point of view, they were strategic weapons—a strong incentive for Moscow to negotiate their elimination in the INF Treaty of 1988.

In contrast, **conventional capabilities** include those *armaments that rely on non-nuclear technology: everything from M-16 rifles to the blast effect of chemical reactions like TNT.* This distinction can sometimes be artificial, however, because the power of selected high-yield conventional weapons are barely distinguishable in their heat and blast damage from low-yield tactical nuclear weapons.

## The Effects of Nuclear Weapons

"The survivors would envy the dead," said Soviet President Nikita S. Khrushchev, speaking about the possible outcome of a nuclear conflagration between the super-powers.[15] He was correct about the devastating power of nuclear weapons. When detonated, they have multiple effects, from the release of intense heat and high winds (the blast effect) to radiation and severe atmospheric disturbances.

### Blast and heat

The immediate consequences of a nuclear explosion are devastating. The figures in Table 11.1, based on the premise of a normal, clear day with twelve-mile visibility and 80 percent of the fireball dissipated, provide a sense of the relationship between bomb yield and the effects of heat, blast, and radiation. The energy distribution of a nuclear explosion consists of roughly 50 percent blast, 35 percent thermal energy (heat), and 15 percent ionized radiation. Viewed from the perspective of casualties inflicted, 50 percent of the deaths in the target area would come from the release of thermal energy, 35 percent from the blast wave, and 15 percent from the ionized radiation.[16] The larger the yield of the weapon, the more important the thermal effect becomes. As shown in the table, thermal radiation presents the greatest danger even at a substantial distance from the center of the explosion (ground zero).

| YIELD | RADIUS IN MILES OF THIRD-DEGREE BURNS | RADIUS IN MILES OF 165-MPH WINDS | RADIUS IN MILES OF 500 RADS OF RADIATION |
|---|---|---|---|
| 2 kT | 0.58 | 0.55 | 0.57 |
| 13 kT | 1.40 | 1.00 | 0.80 |
| 1 MT | 8.00 | 4.30 | 1.60 |
| 20 MT | 25.00 | 11.80 | 3.00 |

*Yield in kilotons (kT) and megatons (MT). 165-mph winds are equivalent to about 5 pounds per square inch (psi) pressure above normal atmospheric pressure. (An overpressure of 3 psi is sufficient to collapse a frame house.) SOURCE: Professor George Ralhjens, Harvard-MIT Summer Program on Nuclear Weapons and Arms Control, Cambridge, MA, June 17, 1985.*

At or near ground zero, the largest number of casualties resulting from the blast wave would stem from its indirect effects, such as collapsing buildings and flying shards of glass. Because *the primary enemy targets are usually military weapons* (a **counterforce** targeting strategy), or *cities with large populations and industrial and communications centers* (a **countervalue** targeting strategy), the blast effect is important. The destructive radius calculated from the blast wave is used as the key military criterion for targeting decisions, not a bomb's thermal effects.

### Radioactivity

In low-yield weapons (tactical nuclear warheads, for example), radiation can be the cause of more deaths than the heat or blast effects. The gamma rays emitted as particles in the radiation literally tear apart the molecules of human tissue as they pass through the body. They can produce genetic alterations in the next generation if they enter the testes or ovaries of individuals who survive and go on to produce offspring. The effects of radiation are often delayed. Some cancers caused by radiation appear five years after an explosion; others may lie dormant for as long as forty years. Sheltering can be an important protection against radiation attack; a sixteen-inch barrier of earth can reduce the radiation by a factor of 10.[17]

### Atmospheric alterations

The **electromagnetic pulse (EMP)** associated with nuclear explosions—that is, the *gamma rays emitted in a wave when a nuclear bomb explodes*—would also have profound consequences in the waging of modern warfare, especially if the nuclear warheads were detonated at a high altitude. According to a weapons specialist, "gamma rays will cause electrons to be ejected from atoms in the air, thus ionizing the atmosphere around the burst. This will result in disturbances of electromagnetic waves transmitted by radar and communications equipment."[18] These atmospheric disturbances could have disrupted or paralyzed all communications, radar operations, and early warning systems throughout NATO, for example, in the case of a first ("preemptive") strike by the Soviet Union during the Cold War.

Nor can one dismiss the possibility of a **nuclear winter**—*the freezing of the Earth following the detonation of large numbers of nuclear weapons in the aftermath of a major nuclear war, as a result of soot from burning buildings rising into the atmosphere and blocking out the sun's rays.* Using computer modeling, a group of American scientists during the Cold War predicted the atmospheric results of a nuclear exchange between the Soviet Union and the United States. Even a limited nuclear war could have catastrophic effects on climate if cities were targeted, the scientists concluded.[19]

Nuclear winter or not, the postattack conditions that followed a nuclear war would be decidedly grim. Radiation would linger, causing decreased sperm counts (among other pathologies); medical supplies, including antibodies, would be destroyed; and a sizable proportion of the total number of physicians and nurses would be killed or incapacitated. The flash from an exploding nuclear bomb would cause blindness in many of those driving automobiles at the time, leading to accidents and further complicating the job of first responders. (See *Perspectives on American Foreign Policy* 11.1.) Using the common baseline of a 6,500 megaton attack against the United States by the Soviet Union during the Cold War, about half of the US grain supply would have been destroyed immediately, and food distribution channels would have been enormously disrupted. In the filthy, garbage-strewn, postattack environment, a recrudescence of the rat population would have occurred. Preceding the possible nuclear winter-induced freezing of the Earth would have come, first, its scorching and sterilization with the initial impact of the nuclear warheads. From a psychological perspective, the populations of both superpowers—despite some acts of heroism—would have experienced profound and widespread depression. The United States and Soviet Union would have been thrown back into a "medieval setting."[20]

## Chemical, Biological, and Radiological Weapons

Experts on weaponry often speak of NBCR weapons: nuclear, biological, chemical, and radiological. Biological weapons might incorporate the use of smallpox virus or anthrax against targets. Chemical weapons could include the dissemination of the lethal nerve gas serin (dispersed by the Aum Shrinko terrorist group against the Tokyo subway system in 1995 and by Syrian authorities against rebels in 2013); and radiological weapons rely on the spewing of radioactive materials around a target, perhaps by detonating a canister of enriched uranium or plutonium with a TNT explosive.

A chemical, biological, or radiological attack against the United States by a rogue nation or terrorist group is an ever-present possibility. Soon after the end of the Cold War, government studies reported that three nations—Iraq, North Korea, and Russia—probably possessed hidden caches of the smallpox virus, with another fourteen nations "suspected of having or trying to acquire germ weapons."[21] No nuclear devices, smallpox virus and other biological materials, or nerve-gas weapons were ever found in Iraq when the United States invaded in 1990 and again in 2003. A Russian

## PERSPECTIVES ON AMERICAN FOREIGN POLICY 11.1

**PHYSICIANS FOR SOCIAL RESPONSIBILITY depict a nuclear detonation in a US city:**

A single one-megaton thermonuclear warhead explodes on a clear day over a major U.S. city. Within 1.5 miles of ground zero, blast overpressures as high as 200 pounds per square inch (psi) crush, collapse, or explode all buildings, however strongly constructed. 600 mile per hour winds blow debris at lethal velocities. The fireball, with temperatures exceeding 27 million degrees Fahrenheit, vaporizes everything.

All human beings within this zone immediately die. . . .

Between 1.5 and 2.9 miles from ground zero, blast overpressures range from 10 to 20 psi. All but the strongest buildings collapse. Winds reach 300 mph. The heat of the explosion evaporates aluminum siding, melts acrylic windows and causes spontaneous ignition of clothing.

50% of the population in this zone immediately dies. All exposed persons who do not die from the blast suffer third degree burns.

4.3 miles from ground zero, blast overpressures still reach 5 psi. Winds exceed 150 mph. Asphalt paving melts. Wood and fabric ignite.

8.5 miles from the center, winds continue to reach hurricane strength. Every fifth person outdoors suffers third degree burns. 70% of those outdoors suffer second degree burns.

All this within moments of detonation.

Death awaits many who survive these first few seconds. Radiation, stress, cold, hunger, and burns combine to undercut survivors' immunological systems, and in a world of spreading disease, thousands more die.

One bomb. One city. Tallahassee. Seattle. Chicago. Whatever the target, thousands, perhaps millions, die. Many others are critically injured with nowhere to turn. . . . In a major attack, most of the country's physicians and medical care personnel, concentrated in major urban areas, will be killed instantly. There will be no means to transport surviving physicians to the victims, nor the victims to the physicians. And with hospitals destroyed, there will be no equipment, beds, diagnostic and X-ray facilities, blood, plasma, or drugs with which to treat the millions who lie dying.

*SOURCE:* From a pamphlet distributed in 1985 by the Physicians for Social Responsibility, an organization established by American physicians as a means for educating people about the likely effects of nuclear warfare, which now has members from many countries throughout the world.

---

military scientist who defected to the United States reported, however, that Moscow had ordered the production of tons of smallpox virus during the Cold War, and had crafted special warheads to deliver the lethal scourge to the United States in long-range missiles, should a shooting war have erupted between the superpowers.[22]

After leaving office, former DCI R. James Woolsey referred to biological terrorism in 1999 as "the single most dangerous threat to our national security in the foreseeable future."[23] Biological terrorism remains a major threat—although the 9/11 attacks proved that terrorists can be inventive in their methods of warfare and don't have to use WMDs to wreak havoc. Some experts note that germs like smallpox are "far more deadly than a nuclear weapon . . . because most people are no longer vaccinated and hence have lost their immunity to the virus."[24] A study commissioned by the Congress in 1993 determined that a chemical or biological weapons attack on Washington, DC could be more lethal than a nuclear attack.[25] A small-scale 2001 attack in the nation's capital, using letters containing anthrax spores as a delivery device, demonstrated the lethality of this biological substance. The spores killed five letter recipients (the perpetrator has never been identified). Further, chemical and biological weapons are easier for adversaries to manufacture and to hide from the prying eyes of US intelligence agencies. They can be difficult to disseminate, however. When Aum Shrinko deployed sarin in the Tokyo subway, the gas pooled at the entrances rather than drifting throughout the underground tunnels as the perpetrators had planned.

## Star Wars

In 1983, the Reagan administration advanced an imaginative proposal that—despite the skepticism of scientific experts—sought to protect the United States against a nuclear attack by enemy missiles. The plan, which *envisioned shooting down enemy missiles in mid-flight with space-based laser technology*, was known as the **Strategic Defense Initiative** or **SDI**—labeled "Star Wars" by the media after a popular science fiction film loaded with laser guns and other electronic gadgetry. Today the more common term for such a system is a **ballistic missile defense (BMD).** Whether a BMD would actually work became a topic of intense debate during the end stages of the Cold War and remains a lively issue today.

Key American scientists remain doubtful about the science of an effective BMD shield, despite the $250 billion that has been spent on its research over the past thirty years. They calculate that it would be less expensive for a well-armed adversary to overwhelm a BMD system with hundreds of new missiles, along with thousands of cheap hollow decoys, than for the United States to strengthen its defenses against the bombardment.[26] In support of the Star Wars concept, Secretary of Defense Weinberger asked rhetorically in 1984, "We made it to the moon; why can't we do this?" The response of critics: "The moon didn't fight back!"[27]

As the debate continued, so did the government spending on BMD research and development (R&D), urged forward by some scientists with an interest in the physics—and the grant funding—associated with BMD studies and by some politicians who saw the project as a potentially good defense (and certainly good politics for those with defense contractors in their districts). By 2010, scientists were ready to test a limited BMD system, yet the results yielded a success rate of only 10 to 20 percent in the interception of incoming mock missiles—and that was under carefully controlled test conditions. Further testing has displayed somewhat more accuracy, but still the dummy targets have been hit just 50 percent of the time (eight successes out of sixteen tries). The latest failed test was in 2013, when an interceptor launched from Vandenberg Air Force Base in California missed its target over the Pacific Ocean—the third dud in a row. Nevertheless, the Obama administration announced in 2013 that the Pentagon will spend $1 billion to deploy additional BMD interceptors along the Pacific Coast, designed especially to counter the expanded reach of North Korean ICBMs. The Pentagon further anticipated the need eventually for an east coast site to guard against Iranian missiles (price tag: perhaps as much as $ 3.6 billion).[28]

In the now unlikely event that Russia and the United States were to have a nuclear war, and even if this country had a BMD system that worked at 90 percent efficiency, upward of 100 Russian warheads would still slip through the defensive shield—enough to make America's major cities look like so many spent campfires.[29] Since the end of the Cold War in 1990, the Kremlin has been concerned about the United States having a BMD system that would enable Washington to conduct a first strike against Russia, without fear of a successful retaliation—a highly destabilizing dynamic that silently accompanies the BMD proposal. In 2012, Russian leaders reported a successful test of a new type of ICBM designed to overpower an American BMD system and keep deterrence viable.[30] Even if US scientists could construct an impermeable laser-beam umbrella over the United States, it could prove useless because nuclear weapons are becoming increasingly smaller in size and easier to smuggle into America beneath a BMD shield—say, hidden inside a Conex container aboard a freighter entering a port in New Jersey or Los Angeles. The bomb dropped on Hiroshima weighed 10,000 pounds; its equivalent today weighs about 100 pounds and can fit into the trunk of an automobile or, before long, into a suitcase.[31]

In the second year of the Obama administration, the US Missile Defense Agency requested and received from Congress a budget increase of $700 million, for a total expenditure of $9.9 billion for BMD research—in the middle of a major recession and with little evidence to suggest such a system would work.[32] While the government and private scientists further explore the feasibility of a Star Wars defense, the protection of the United States against a nuclear attack continues to rest on deterrence and, at its core, a nuclear weapons triad.

## Deterrence and the Triad

The appeal of a BMD is understandable: Americans might well wish that the danger of nuclear war really could be eliminated with a "supershield," hermetically sealing off the United States from external danger like the tranquil Christmas scenes inside glass paperweights. This wish remained true during the Cold War against the prospect of Soviet missiles, and is alive and well today against the possibility of missiles coming from terrorists or a rogue nation. In early 2013, for example, the government in Pyongyang expressed its unhappiness about American-led UN sanctions against North Korea and warned Washington officials that it had missiles that could strike the United States.[33] The new BMD deployments on the Pacific Coast are meant to signal to the North Koreas that the United States takes its warnings seriously. But in place of wishes, at present the human race is forced to rely on the more fragile—if more realistic, according to critics of the BMD system—concept of MAD.

### Ground-launched missiles

The *strategic deterrent capability* of the United States takes the form of a **triad**, *based on its three types of weaponry: ground-based ICBMs, sea-based SLBMs, and airborne intercontinental bombers*. One of the great debates about this capability has surrounded the question of ICBM vulnerability. Soviet warheads became sufficiently powerful and accurate during the Cold War to raise concerns in Washington that a quick strike against America's ICBMs, which rest in underground silos located chiefly in Western and Midwestern states, might destroy them despite their "hardened" silo shells of thick concrete.

Various plans were proposed to protect this "leg" of the triad. President Nixon advocated an **antiballistic missile (ABM)** system, a precursor of SDI that relied *on nuclear-armed interceptors to destroy incoming warheads before they could strike American cities or ICBM silos.* Even though the Soviets also constructed a cluster of ABMs around Moscow, members of Congress rejected this approach to the protection of American cities as too costly and unlikely to work anyway—the same arguments now offered against the BMD proposals. By a margin of one vote, however, Congress did allow the development of a limited ABM system during the Nixon administration, to be built as a shield for a single ICBM silo in Minot, North Dakota. Local opposition to the shield, viewed by citizens more as a lightning rod attracting Soviet missiles than a shield, coupled with lingering doubts about its effectiveness, led to a prompt mothballing of the ABM site soon after its construction.

During the Ford and Carter administrations, the Pentagon conceived of a "racetrack" method for reducing the vulnerability of land-based US missiles to a Soviet first strike. According to this scheme, the United States would place its newest ICBMs—the Missile Experimental or MX—on railroad cars. The MX would shuttle along vast tracks in the Western states, providing each missile with twenty-three sequential hiding places so the Soviets would never know with certainty where to strike. To complicate Soviet targeting further, several additional railroad cars were to be left empty. Presumably, this shell game would *guarantee that some American missiles would always be available following an attack to strike back at Russia,* a **second-strike capability** that was meant to ensure the credibility of American deterrence.

Local opposition to this racetrack plan grew rapidly, however, as citizens of Utah, Nevada, and surrounding states refused to have their homeland turned into high-priority targets for the Soviet Union. The ecological problems were also daunting. Some engineers estimated that virtually all the water in the Western states would be required just to mix the concrete needed for the construction of the railway hiding places—amounting to the greatest engineering project since the building of the pyramids in Egypt.[34] Moreover, critics feared that the Soviet response would simply be to build more warheads, with even larger yields, to saturate the entire track configuration in time of war.

The Reagan administration eventually repudiated the racetrack concept and weapons designers turned to new possibilities, such as the placement of the MX off American shores, concealed beneath the waves on the continental shelf. The administration proved unable, though, to settle on a basing mode for the MX. Some members of Congress advocated a road-mobile missile with a single warhead, the "Midgetman." One wag suggested at the time, perhaps with as much credibility as the various official plans, that US missiles be placed in unmarked Volkswagens on the New Jersey Turnpike.

The debate over ICBM vulnerability continued, with the George H. W. Bush administration advocating a mix of MX and Midgetman missiles, a compromise designed to negotiate a settlement between the two weapons proponents. Regardless of this and similar land-basing debates, it was unlikely that the weaknesses of a single leg in the triad would have tempted the Soviets to attack during the Cold War; the United States could have still kicked back with its other two legs, from the air and the sea.

### Bombers

The bomber leg of the triad has some special advantages. During the Cold War, about 30 percent of this force was always on alert and would probably have survived a Soviet first strike. Several of the aircraft were aloft at all times, on a rotating basis—a costly procedure. Further, this is the only system that can be redirected, or even recalled after being set on its flight path. Critics, though, feel that bombers have become the dinosaurs of the nuclear age: large, slow-moving targets for enemy defensive missiles and fighter planes to knock out of the air with ease. The invention of the radar-elusive *Stealth* bomber was meant to add credibility to this portion of the deterrent structure, but many defense analysts are doubtful that even this expensive airplane could have made it through Soviet defenses.

### Submarines

Nuclear powered Polaris submarine.

The submarine leg is the least vulnerable component of the triad. Hidden deep beneath the ocean's surface, *each* of America's thirty-seven nuclear submarines during the Cold War carried more destructive power than the combined total released during every war fought since the dawn of humanity. Moreover, submarines are difficult for enemies to locate and, if found, they are hard to attack. As the Soviets improved their anti-submarine warfare (ASW) capabilities during the Cold War, the United States improved its deception measures to keep the submarines hidden. "Our subs look pretty invulnerable for a long time," concluded a weapons expert in 1985.[35] The major shortcoming in this leg of the triad is the difficulty of communicating to a submarine deeply submerged, although communications engineers are making significant strides toward solving this technical challenge.

## Command and Control

*The subject of disseminating information and orders from decision makers to their military commanders in the field*, called **command-control-communications-and-intelligence (C³I)**, presents some alarming scenarios. During the Cold War, computer chips were known to have failed in America's early warning system, giving false signals that a Soviet attack was underway. Once what seemed to be an attack of Soviet missiles that lit up US defense radar screens proved to be merely a flock of geese; on another occasion, a flock of swans was mistaken for a squadron of Soviet MIG aircraft. Moreover, not long after the Cuban missile crisis, a Finnish farmer accidentally plowed through the hot-line telephone link between the United States and the Soviet Union.[36] (Measures have been taken to improve the security of this communications line that connects Washington with the Kremlin.) Although none of these incidents produced or happened during a crisis, they underscore the fragility of the warning and communications systems on which peace might depend. Further, C³I systems are vulnerable to manipulation. Communications networks could become channels for disinformation, with America and its adversary trying to fool one another with false information to gain a military advantage. Moreover, the networks can be jammed, say, with heavy-metal rock music at 300 decibels.

Unfortunately, the United States today no longer enjoys much of a buffer of time and distance from its enemies. Some authorities believe that, in light of the growing number of nations with nuclear weapons and the increasing chances that a terrorist group might be able to buy or steal these devices, the chances of a nuclear exchange somewhere in the world are greater now than during the Cold War.[37] If a nuclear war were to start, the first half hour would streak by like a flash of lightning. Assume for a moment that America had been attacked by a Soviet first strike during the Cold War. Within a minute or two, US technical sensors (satellites and radar outposts) would have recorded and transmitted data homeward on the enemy's missile launch. Within ten to twelve minutes, the first SLBMs would have struck the United States from Soviet submarines in the Atlantic and Pacific Oceans, with salvos continuing over the next ten minutes. Some fifteen to twenty minutes later, the first wave of ICBMs would have arrived from Russia. The chaos under such conditions can be readily imagined.

A core C³I challenge is how to protect US command posts. According to an expert, this stands as "the most significant problem of modern strategic forces."[38] One can conceive of *a well-coordinated enemy strike against the White House, the Capitol, the Pentagon, and other command centers that would deprive the United States of its top leadership* in time of war—a swift military stroke referred to as **nuclear decapitation**. Headless, the body might have to surrender or face total annihilation.

As a protection against decapitation, this nation has fashioned various safeguards. One method has been the establishment of DUCs (deep underground centers) where the **National Command Authority (NCA),** the *nation's top political and military leaders,* can hide from the downpour of nuclear missiles. Caves have been constructed for this purpose in the mountains of Maryland, in the Virginia countryside, and in

Colorado at NORAD (North American Radar Defense) headquarters near Colorado Springs. In an alert condition indicating an imminent enemy attack or one already under way (Defense Condition One, or DefCon 1), the NCA is expected to rush to predesignated locations—the backyard of the White House is one—to be whisked away by helicopters to their mountain refuges. From within these underground caverns, however, communications with the outside world would be difficult. Moreover, likely as not during the Cold War, these locations could have been merely expensive cremation vaults, their steel doors targeted by Moscow with one-megaton warheads on SLBMs.

Another possibility is to go aloft. The president has a specially equipped airplane, officially known as the National Emergency Airborne Command Post or NEACAP (pronounced "kneecap"), designed to serve as a headquarters in time of nuclear war; but whether or not the president and top-level staff would have time to board the custom-built Boeing 747 stationed at Andrews Air Force Base in Maryland is problematic. Further, this airplane itself would be a top target for a surprise submarine-launched missile attack, were the enemy resorting to a decapitation strategy.

### The Arsenals

Although much has been done by the world's leading powers to reduce the risks of an accidental nuclear war, the weapons arsenals around the world remain enormous. The United States, Russia, United Kingdom, China, France, Israel, India, Pakistan, and North Korea all have nuclear weapons. Although Washington and Moscow have agreed to weapons cutbacks, the numbers of nuclear warheads in the world remains high, far more than necessary for a nation's deterrence. During the Cold War, just 300 American ICBM warheads, for example, would have been enough to kill 80 percent of the Russian population and destroy its industrial capacities.[39]

### *Strategic nuclear weapons*

Nuclear weapons designed for long-range attacks with high explosive yields are known as "strategic." Near the end of the Cold War, the United States possessed thirty Poseidon nuclear submarines and seven new Trident models. The Poseidons carry sixteen strategic missiles each. In eighteen of the Poseidons, the missiles are tipped with ten warheads or MIRVs (multiple, independently targetable reentry vehicles); in twelve, the number is eight warheads. The Tridents have twenty-four missiles, each with eight warheads. The aggregate sum is 5,760 warheads with a combined yield (at 100 kilotons per warhead) equivalent to some 576 megatons of TNT. Because about 60 percent of these submarines were at sea at any time, the fleet together always had some 3,456 warheads aimed toward the Soviet Union and other potential adversaries. Another 3,840 hydrogen bombs and missile warheads were ready in the cargo hatches of the American fleet of 324 strategic bombers. Finally, the United States had some 1,045 ICBMs with about 2,145 warheads.[40] In 2012, a former commander of US nuclear forces called for significant cuts in the number of nuclear warheads, down to 900. Further, a prestigious outside group, the Global Zero campaign (supported by former

| | UNITED STATES | RUSSIA |
|---|---|---|
| ICBMs | 500 | 1,087 |
| SLBMs | 1,152 | 528 |
| Bombers | 300 | 820 |
| Totals | 1,952 | 2,435 |

*Table 11.2*
Deployed Strategic
Warheads: A US and
Russian Comparison, 2012

SOURCES: *Robert S. Norris and Hans M. Kristensen, "Nuclear Notebook: U.S. and Russian Nuclear Forces, 2009," Bulletin of the Atomic Scientists (May/June 2012), pp.`84–91; Robert S. Norris and Hans M. Kristensen, "Nuclear Notebook: Russian Nuclear Forces, 2012," Bulletin of the Atomic Scientists (March/April 2012), pp. 7–97. The figures in this table exclude 15,000 stockpiled warheads kept as backup by the two nations, as well as thousands of short-range nuclear weapons.*

GOP Secretaries of State George Shultz, James Baker, and Henry Kissinger), advocated moving to 1,000 warheads as an interim step toward further reductions; and General James Cartwright, the retired vice chairman of the JCS, has also said that deterrence could be assured with 900 warheads, deploying half of them at any given time.[41]

During the Cold War, the Soviets had a similar capacity for destruction, although they placed their emphasis chiefly on ICBMs. Table 11.2 outlines the distribution of nuclear weapons across the triad for the United States and Russia more recently.

### Tactical nuclear weapons

Added to this mountain of strategic warheads are hordes of "tactical" nuclear weapons—that is, warheads with a shorter range and less yield (around the size of the bombs dropped on Japan in 1945 or less). About 20,000 of them exist in the US arsenal, of which some 6,000 are located in Europe. Russia has about 12,000 tactical warheads.

### Conventional weapons

Although the biggest bang remains in the nuclear arsenal, the biggest bucks are now spent on nonnuclear armaments, along with the soldiers, sailors, and pilots trained to use them—"conventional" weaponry. During the Cold War, former Secretary of Defense Robert S. McNamara explained why. "The fact that the Soviet Union and the United States can mutually destroy one another regardless of who strikes first narrows the range of Soviet aggression which our nuclear forces can effectively deter," he wrote. "We, and our allies as well, require substantial non-nuclear forces in order to cope with levels of aggression that massive strategic forces do not, in fact, deter."[42] This is why the United States stations almost 300,000 troops overseas, including 55,000 in Germany, 35,000 in Japan, 28,500 in South Korea, and 10,000 in Italy, armed mostly with conventional weapons—with "nukes" (chiefly tactical) on standby as a deterrent for use when conventional defenses fail.

The most well-known and controversial conventional weapon in recent years is the unmanned aerial vehicle (UAV) or drone. Today these robotic aircraft fly mainly around the Middle East and Southwest Asia, "piloted" by CIA and military personnel back in the United States. They are deployed for the purposes of both spying and killing. Some of the drones carry Hellfire missiles, which have been used since the George W. Bush administration to strike down suspected terrorists in these regions. Other robotic machines have been deployed to assist the American war fighter, such as bomb-sniffing devices. Moreover, the United States has a growing arsenal of "cyberweapons" designed to detect and knock out digital attacks from abroad, perhaps by injecting a destructive code into the enemy's computer systems. The extent to which Congress would be consulted on such operations in advance of their use remains unclear—a potential technical threat to the war making constitutional balance between the branches.

## How Much Is Enough?

In 2012, the United States spent nearly $700 billon on defense, equivalent to over 40 percent of the world's defense expenditures (for a nation that is about 4.6 percent of the world's population). In Afghanistan, the United States spent $300 million a day during 2011.[43] The Obama administration carried the security budget into new plateaus of record spending, asking Congress for $708.3 billion in defense funding for fiscal year 2011: $549 billion for the core defense budget, and another $159 billion for the wars in Iraq and Afghanistan. This represented a 6.1 percent increase over the budget during the George W. Bush administration. This defense expenditure figure surpasses what every other major nation spends on defense *combined*. As an example of the excess, the Navy seeks eleven aircraft carriers over the next three decades, at $11 billion per ship, while no other nation in the world has more than two—and that number is rare (Spain and Italy). America's battle fleet is larger than the next thirteen navies combined, according to Secretary of Defense Robert M. Gates.[44]

Much of the recent defense spending has been fueled by America's dual wars in Iraq and Afghanistan. (President Obama tripled the number of US troops in Afghanistan.) At a cost of $2 trillion by the end of 2014, these conflicts have been the most expensive in America's history, with the exception of the Second World War. Despite a recession, the strength of America's mighty economy allowed officials in Washington to fight wars with a smaller bite out of the nation's overall economy. In its peak year (1945), the Second World War consumed 35.8 percent of GDP, for example, while the recent Iraq and Afghanistan wars accounted for only 1.2 percent in 2008—the lowest percentage since World War II.[45] Nevertheless, for the first time in US history, neither the George W. Bush nor the Obama administrations raised taxes to fight the nation's wars and, as a result, Pentagon spending has contributed substantially to America's burgeoning $13 trillion debt. "The U.S. military enforces American foreign policy," observed Harvard University historian Jill Lepore in 2013, and the enforcement costs were substantial. No wonder another Harvard historian, Earnest R. May, once referred to Washington, DC, as more of a military headquarters than a national capital.[46] His observation remains as true today as when May offered this comment at the end of the Cold War.

Regardless of all the impressive hardware available in today's war inventory, no one is sure how much is necessary to deter real or potential enemies. "How much is enough?" has always been the central defense question.[47] The answer depends on one's perspective. The Pentagon is notorious for its "worst-case" analysis of the military threat. "The Army would need 54 divisions, instead of its 16, if all the [Pentagon's] worst-case analyses were followed," Kaufmann once concluded.[48] Professor Joseph S. Nye Jr. took this position in 2012: "We should learn from the prudence of Dwight Eisenhower. The number-one power does not have to man every boundary and be strong everywhere. The attempt to do so would violate Ike's prudence in resisting direction intervention on the side of the French in Vietnam in 1954."[49]

## Arms Control

In spite of the new emphasis on nonnuclear approaches to security, nuclear weapons remain a significant component of America's defense posture. Until a reliable BMD shield is constructed—and it seems unlikely that one can ever be built that would guarantee protection from a saturating storm of enemy missiles—the security of the United States will continue to rely ultimately on nuclear deterrence, what Winston Churchill called the 'balance of terror." Given this situation, the objective (in the view of many strategists) ought to be the careful maintenance of a military balance between the United States and its adversaries, so that no nation is tempted into a first strike. To be avoided *is a situation where one side seems too weak, which might invite an attack by the other side.* This is sometimes called the **Munich syndrome**, an allusion to the time when Hitler acted out of disdain for perceived weakness in the West. Risky as well *is a situation where one side seems too strong, which might provoke an attack by the weaker side in a paranoid, last-gasp attempt at self-defense*—the **Pearl Harbor syndrome**, as when Japan acted out of fear in 1941 and struck the United States in hopes of gaining a slight advantage for what Tokyo viewed as an inevitable war with the Americans.[50]

*Efforts to achieve a balance of arms, ideally at a lower inventory of weaponry, and to reduce the risks of war* are referred to as **arms control** measures. Advocates of arms control argue that it is better to negotiate than to fight and that, eventually, real progress can be achieved toward the goal of a world with fewer nuclear warheads and conventional weapons. In an attempt to make the world less dangerous, President Obama took a fresh look at nuclear strategy in 2010. He renounced the development of any new nuclear weapons; and he rejected the possibility of an American first strike with nuclear weapons against any nonnuclear nation that was in compliance with the Nuclear Non-Proliferation Treaty of 1970, which has been signed by 187 nations. "We are going to want to make sure that we can continue to move towards less emphasis on nuclear weapons," said the President, "to make sure that our conventional weapons capability is an effective deterrent in all but the most extreme circumstances."[51] The Obama administration planned to rely on a conventional Prompt Global Strike arsenal that could achieve the effects of nuclear weapons without resorting to that fearsome option.[52] This approach involves, for example, modernizing bombers, missiles, and submarines, as well as improving early warning surveillance satellites, reconnaissance planes, and human espionage services. Moreover, observers hoped that the administration would try to win Senate approval of the Comprehensive Test Ban Treaty, which has already been signed by 159 nations but was rejected by US senators in 1999.

The capacity that leaders now have for inflicting mass destruction in the world calls for even greater attention to the question of how decisions are made about foreign policy and the use of the war power. The War Powers Resolution states that the use of American troops abroad should rest on the "collective judgment of both the Congress and the President" (Section 2[a]). This principle, as constitutional scholar Louis Fisher observed in 1988, "is the dominant lesson of the past four decades."[53] In a similar vein, ten years earlier Professor Eugene Rostow, known for his support of a strong presidency, concluded nonetheless that "If the President and the executive branch cannot persuade Congress and the public that a policy is wise, it should not be pursued."[54]

## DECIDING TO USE THE WAR POWER

"When and where to go to war," observed Senator Thomas Eagleton (D-Missouri) in 1983, "is the most solemn and fateful decision a free nation can make."[55] Yet decisions to use overt military force are seldom made in the reflective manner envisioned by the nation's founders, nor is Congress typically involved in these decisions. That this country has declared war formally only five times in over 200 military actions (the last time, in 1941 as the United States entered World War II) led conservative commentator William F. Buckley Jr. to conclude in 1987, with measured understatement, that America has "some unfinished constitutional business."[56] The modern weaponry that has spread across the world makes decisions related to war making all the more poignant because small-scale conflicts often have the potential for drawing large powers into the vortex—along with their arsenals bristling with WMDs.

The struggle between the branches for control over the war power in the modern era reached a climax in 1973 with the passage of the **War Powers Resolution** (WPR). In earlier chapters in this volume I have alluded to the Resolution; in this chapter I take up the topic in more detail. The main thrust of the statute—arguable the most important law related to foreign policy in modern times—was *to place obstacles in the way of presidential authority to commit American forces abroad without congressional approval.*

The source of tension between the branches over the war power has its origins in two key passages of the Constitution: Article I, Section 8, and Article II, Section 2. A former staff director of the Foreign Relations Committee, Pat Holt, has written, "Where to draw the line between the power of Congress to declare war and the power of the president as commander in chief is one of the most controversial issues relating to the Constitution." The two articles established perfect conditions for an ongoing tug-of-war between the branches. When the war in Vietnam went badly and the presidency was weakened further by the Watergate scandal, Congress tightened its grip on the rope and yanked. "The War Powers Resolution, in essence," concluded Holt, "is an effort by Congress to give itself more leverage in the tug-of-war with the executive branch."[57]

## The War Powers Resolution

The War Powers Resolution, as it finally emerged for a vote in 1973 following draft after draft, was, in the words of one observer, "a complicated law in which a number of disparate strands of congressional thought were woven together."[58] The proposed statute required that the president "in every possible instance shall consult with Congress" before introducing armed forces "into hostilities or into situations where imminent involvement in hostilities is clearly indicated by the circumstances."

In addition, the proposal required the president to report to the Congress within forty-eight hours regarding the deployment of troops in three types of situations: when forces were sent into "hostilities" or into a region where hostilities were imminent; when forces "equipped for combat" were sent into any foreign nation; and when forces were deployed that "substantially enlarge" the number of combat-equipped US troops in a foreign nation. Only in the first instance of immediate or imminent hostilities, as stipulated in Section 4(a)(1), would the president's report start a sixty-day clock, after which the White House had to obtain congressional approval for continuation of the military involvement. Reporting by the executive branch to Congress under the other two provisions left the clock dormant. Except for President Gerald R. Ford on one occasion (examined below), every president has chosen to ignore Section 4(a)(1).

Further, the War Powers Resolution permitted Congress to force the withdrawal of US troops from a region at any time by a concurrent resolution, that is, by a simple majority vote in both chambers without the need for the president's signature or possible veto. This provision amounted to a legislative veto, critics maintained—a method of legislating that was invalidated by the Supreme Court in 1983 (the *Chadha* ruling), ten years after passage of the WPR. The resolution stipulated, moreover, that if Congress refused to endorse the president's use of force within sixty days of the initial report, the president *had to* withdraw the US troops. Congress could grant a thirty-day extension, though, if necessary to assure an orderly and safe exit. The constitutional authority of Congress to declare war, or to enact authorizations for specific combat operations according to normal legislative procedures, remained intact.

That the law took two years to pass indicates the difficulty that members of Congress faced in their attempts to modernize the war power. Those favoring the resolution argued for a return to a system of constitutional balance, rather than war making by the president alone. "Recent Presidents," said a report of the Senate Foreign Relations Committee, "have relied upon dubious historical precedents and expansive interpretations of the president's authority as Commander-in-Chief to justify both the initiation and perpetuation of foreign military activities without the consent—in some instances without even the knowledge—of Congress."[59] Added a senior Senator from Hawaii, "If we have learned but one lesson from the tragedy in Vietnam, I believe it is that we need definite, unmistakable procedures to prevent future undeclared wars. 'No more Vietnams' should be our objective in setting up such procedures."[60]

The proposed law had its detractors. Senator Barry Goldwater (R-Arizona), a leading conservative, thought it would undermine relations with US allies, who might perceive the statute as a restraint on a rapid response to threats against the collective security arrangements of the Western powers.[61] President Nixon argued (before the Watergate scandal broke) that the resolution "would seriously undermine this nation's ability to act decisively and convincingly in times of international crisis."[62] He warned that it "would give every future Congress the ability to handcuff every future president merely by doing nothing and sitting still." Especially odious to Nixon was the sixty-day limit on US troops abroad (absent congressional approval for a continuation), which he said would "work to intensify a crisis."[63] Nor did he look on the concurrent resolution as a proper instrument; indeed, he declared it unconstitutional because "the only way in which the constitutional powers of a branch of the government can be altered is by amending the Constitution—and any attempt to make such alterations by legislation alone is clearly without force."[64] A decade later, the Supreme Court would agree in the *Chadha* case.

Most worrisome to liberals was the possibility of a forty-eight-hour delay before the White House had to report on military interventions abroad. At first a leading advocate of war power legislation as a means for preventing future Vietnams by executive fiat, Senator Eagleton ultimately turned against the resolution because of this provision. The two-day leeway given to a president made the proposal, he was convinced, "a dangerous piece of legislation which, if enacted, would effectively eliminate Congress' constitutional power to authorize war"; the resolution had become "an undated declaration of war."[65] At the height of the congressional debate, Eagleton declared that "every president of the United States will have at least the color of legal authority, the advance blessing of Congress, given on an open, blank-check basis, to take us to war. It is a horrible mistake."[66]

The odd coalition of conservative and liberal opponents of the resolution stemmed from an examination by the two groups of different portions of the bill. Conservatives in Congress, as well as President Nixon, had no objection to the forty-eight-hour discretionary clause; but they recoiled from the limits on presidential power embodied in the sixty-day clock provision. Nor did they favor the congressional option of a concurrent resolution to force a troop withdrawal. For the liberals, the likes and dislikes were exactly reversed. Despite the left–right coalition of opponents, the proponents of the resolution were far more numerous—enough even for a rare override of Nixon's veto of the proposal in November 1973.

Senator Jacob Javits (R-New York), the resolution's chief architect, observed after the vote:

> With the war powers resolution's passage, after 200 years, at least
> something will have been done about codifying the implementation

of the most awesome power in the possession of any sovereignty and giving the broad representation of the people in Congress a voice in it. This is critically important, for we have just learned the hard lesson that wars cannot be successfully fought except with the consent of the people and with their support.

In his opinion, "At long last . . . Congress is determined to recapture the awesome power to make war."[67]

Since its passage, the War Powers Resolution has been dogged by controversy. Sam Nunn (D-Georgia), then chairman of the Senate Armed Services Committee, flatly declared in 1987 that the resolution "has not worked."[68] A former counsel to the Senate Foreign Relations Committee concluded that, because of *Chadha,* the concurrent resolution section of the law was now "clearly invalid."[69] Congress would now have to pass a joint resolution—susceptible to a presidential veto—if lawmakers wished to withdraw US troops from hostilities before the sixty-day time expiration. America's troops would still have to be withdrawn by the president when the sixty-day clock expired, however, unless Congress allowed a thirty-day extension or voted to continue the war.

The ambiguous language of the statute has led to other disputes, especially over the word "hostilities." As constitutional expert Louis Henkin noted: "Above all, the resolution suffers gravely from a lack of any definition of 'hostilities.'"[70] This flaw became a source of great consternation to some lawmakers in 1987 and 1988 when the Reagan administration placed American warships in the Persian Gulf without reporting under the provisions of the resolution. Officials in the executive branch claimed that no report was necessary, because the ships were merely on patrol to protect US-flagged Kuwaiti oil carriers. Yet, as members of Congress pointed out, American ships had been fired on and had fired back. Moreover, sailors on these ships were being paid dangerous-duty pay.[71] If this situation did not signify the presence of "hostilities," what did?

In 1987, in US District Court, 115 members of Congress filed suit to invoke the War Powers Resolution in this case. The court dismissed the suit, however, on grounds that it was a "by-product of political disputes within Congress" and, therefore, beyond the purview of the judiciary[72]—a position upheld by the Court of Appeals on February 29, 1988. When President George H. W. Bush contemplated sending US troops against the Iraqi army in Kuwait, members of Congress again brought action to require a declaration of war and were again rebuffed by the courts.

Events in the Persian Gulf in 1991 were hardly the first instance of controversy regarding the proper application of the War Powers Resolution. Its uneven acceptance by presidents had already become evident in a series of earlier US military operations abroad, summarized in Table 11.3. This inconsistency in the willingness of presidents to report automatically to the Congress when US troops had entered a region of hostilities—thereby starting the sixty-day time clock—rendered, in the view of one thoughtful legal authority, "largely pyrrhic the widely hailed victory of Congress in 'recapturing' its share of the war making power."[73]

### Wrestling over the Resolution

Following the passage of the War Powers Resolution, Congress and the executive branch engaged in a prolonged wrestling match over when its provisions should be honored, with presidents periodically going so far as to declare the statute unconstitutional and, therefore, null and void—even without a test in the courts. Among the incidents listed in Table 11.3, three of the most important—the *Mayaguez* rescue operation (1975), the peacekeeping in Lebanon (1982–1984), and US military support to NATO in Libya (2011)—are examined further to illustrate the nature of the struggle between the branches.

#### The Mayaguez rescue

In the unsuccessful attempt to rescue American merchant sailors abroad the vessel *Mayaguez,* captured by Khmer Rouge Cambodian forces in May 1975, President Ford reported to Congress under section 4(a)(1) of the War Powers Resolution (the "hostilities" section), thereby starting the sixty-day clock. This is the only time that a president has acted according to section 4(a)(1). Ford failed, however, to consult with a single member of Congress in advance of the decision. Leading lawmakers were simply "informed" beforehand through a brief presidential report. Representative Clement Zablocki (D-Wisconsin) stated at the time, "Clearly it was not the intention of the Congress [in the War Powers Resolution] to be merely informed of decisions made."[74] Further, Senator Eagleton complained with heavy sarcasm that "all the President has to do is make a telephone call . . . and say, 'The boys are on the way. I think you should know.' . . . Consultation!"[75]

Moreover, the official reports from President Ford and his successors in compliance with the War Powers Resolution have been skimpy at best. As one study concludes, "The reports . . . are one- to two-page letters that proffer less information than might be gleaned from reading newspaper coverage of the events. Indeed, the report on the *Mayaguez* operation made no mention of the number of casualties (forty-one lives lost in an attempt to rescue thirty-nine merchant marines), or the fact that bombing of a military airfield occurred after the ship and crew were already in US custody."[76]

#### Multinational peacekeeping force in Lebanon

Another contentious series of events related to the War Powers Resolution occurred in 1982 and 1983. In August of 1982, the government of civil-war-torn Lebanon asked for assistance in evacuating members of the Palestine Liberation Organization (PLO) from Lebanese territory. President Reagan responded by sending US military personnel to participate in a multinational operation. In this successful mission, 800 US Marines joined an equal number of French soldiers, plus 400 Italian troops. The President duly reported this use of American forces, under the provisions of the resolution, and withdrew the troops.

Table 11.3
Examples of Presidential
Reporting under the
Provisions of the War
Powers Resolution

| INCIDENT | APPLICATION OF RESOLUTION |
|---|---|
| Evacuation of US citizens from Cyprus, 1974 | No report |
| Evacuation from Danang, Vietnam, 1975 | Report filed, NC* |
| Evacuation from Phnom Penh, Vietnam, 1975 | Report filed, NC |
| Evacuation from Saigon, Vietnam, 1975 | Report filed, FC* |
| *Mayaguez* Rescue, 1975 | 4(a)(1) report filed, MC* (clock begun) |
| Evacuation of US citizens from Lebanon, 1976 | No report |
| Korean tree-trimming incident, 1976 | No report |
| Zaire airlift, 1978 | No report |
| Military advisers in El Salvador, 1978 | No report |
| Iranian rescue attempt, 1980 | Report filed, NC |
| Air combat over the Gulf of Sidra, 1981 | No report |
| Peacekeeping force in Sinai, 1982 | Report filed, MC |
| Peacekeeping force in Lebanon, 1982–1984 | A mixed report |
| Military assistance to Chad, 1983 | Report filed, MC |
| Grenada invasion, 1983 | Report filed, NC |
| Military aircraft for Saudi Arabia, 1984 | No report |
| Interception of *Achille Lauro* hijackers, 1985 | No report |
| US helicopters fired on in Honduras, 1986 | No report |
| Bombing of Libya, 1986 | Report filed, NC |
| US Navy in Persian Gulf, 1987–1989 | No report |
| US air sorties against Philippine rebels, 1990 | No report |
| Persian Gulf War, 1990–1991 | No report |
| Ongoing air sorties against Iraq, 1991–1993 | No report |
| Somalian humanitarian intervention, 1992–1993 | No report |
| Haiti intervention, 1995 | Report filed, MC |
| Bosnia, 1995 | Report filed, FC |
| Bombing campaign against Iraq, 1998 | No report |
| Combat in Afghanistan, 2001 | Report filed, FC |
| Antiterrorist operations, 2002 | Report filed, FC |
| War against Iraq, 2003 | Report filed, FC |
| Antiterrorist operations, 2009 | Report filed, FC |
| Air support for NATO against Libya, 2011 | Report filed, NC |

NOTE: *NC = no consultation with Congress; MC = minimal consultation; FC = full consultation.
For a more complete accounting, see Richard F. Grimmett, *The War Powers Resolution: After Thirty-Six Years*,
CRS Report for Congress, 7-5700, Congressional Research Service, Washington, DC (April 22, 2010).

A month later, however, the President sent the American soldiers back into Lebanon, this time with 1,200 Marines. Their assignment was much more ambiguous on this occasion: to help the prospects for peace by maintaining a physical presence in Lebanon. Since the Marines bivouacked in a supposedly secure location away from the direct fighting in the capital city of Beirut, the Reagan administration decided that the hostilities provision in the War Powers Resolution did not apply. No report—and, therefore, no time clock—was necessary. The killing of several Marines by sniper fire in 1983 strained the credibility of this argument and pressure mounted on Capitol Hill to invoke the War Powers Resolution. The administration steadfastly refused to send a report to Congress, though, because it wanted to avoid any possible infringement on the President's flexibility as commander in chief. "We want to cooperate with the President," responded the Senate Democratic leader Robert C. Byrd (West Virginia), "but this is the law, and the law cannot be winked at."[77]

Yet wink the Congress did. It decided in June 1983 to pass a resolution on Lebanon, the **Lebanon Emergency Assistance Act,** which *gave the president eighteen additional months to keep the troops where they were.* In signing this resolution, President Reagan said: "I do not and cannot cede any of the authority vested in me under the Constitution as President and as Commander-in-Chief of the United States Armed Forces. Nor should my signing be viewed as any acknowledgment that the President's constitutional authority can be impermissibly infringed by statute."[78] With passage of this act, Congress proclaimed that the war-powers clock had started, even though the War Powers Resolution required the *president* to start the clock with the issuance of a report, not the Congress. Then lawmakers stared down at their shoes as the commander in chief swept aside all restrictions on the use of troops in Lebanon.

"Congress drove a hard bargain," concluded a constitutional scholar sarcastically. "One wonders how its leaders emerged from the negotiations without agreeing to apologize for enacting the War Powers Resolution."[79] Senator Eagleton's appraisal of the Lebanese resolution was equally acidic: "We should face the fact that this language is a blank check to the President to do whatever he wants to do militarily in Lebanon. Cleverly worded, it is nonetheless the Lebanese Gulf of Tonkin Resolution."[80]

Then Reagan's "peacekeeping mission" in Lebanon unraveled. On October 23, 1983, a terrorist killed 241 US Marines in a suicidal truck bombing of their headquarters in Beirut. This tragedy, coupled with subsequent reports on the poor security arrangements for the American troops and a revelation that the Joint Chiefs of Staff had unanimously opposed sending the Marines to Lebanon in the first place, raised cries on Capitol Hill to tear up the blank check offered in the Lebanon Emergency Assistance Act. When the President ordered the battleship *New Jersey* to fire on enemy installations in Lebanon, the absence of hostilities claimed by the administration became more farcical still. Faced with rising criticism and, more tangibly, a congressional resolution calling for the "prompt and orderly withdrawal" of US forces in Lebanon, the President brought the Marines home on February 7, 1984.

## US air and intelligence support to NATO in Libya

More recently, the Obama administration argued that providing air support and intelligence for a NATO mission against the Qaddafi regime in Libya was not really a matter of being involved in hostilities, because the President never dispatched US *ground troops* into the fighting. According to this view, it was irrelevant to request congressional authority for the NATO operation under the War Powers Resolution. Yet US warplanes struck at Libyan air defenses about sixty times, and the administration used drones to fire missiles at Libyan forces about thirty times.[81] The President did report the action to Congress within forty-eight hours, as required by the WPR, which put the sixty-day clock in motion. The administration then ignored, however, the next and most significant provision of the law: obtaining approval from Congress to keep a military presence in the war zone. Since Obama failed to take that step within the sixty-day period, that left him with only thirty more days to maintain a US military presence in Libya. This was the section of the resolution the administration chose to disregard, based chiefly on the "no ground troops" argument. Further, the Justice Department issued a memorandum claiming that the president had inherent constitutional power to engage in an air campaign in Libya, because he could "reasonably determine that such use of force was in the national interest"—as open-ended an argument for war making by presidential fiat as one can imagine.[82]

Yale University law professor Bruce Ackerman accused the administration of setting a "troubling precedent that could allow future administrations to wage war at their convenience—free of legislative checks and balances." The administration was "undermining a key legal check on arbitrary presidential power," he concluded, and "allowing the trivialization of the War Powers Act."[83] Astounded by the administration's legal legerdemain, Louis Fisher pointed to the central constitutional principle that should have guided the Libya case: "Other than repelling sudden attack and protecting American lives overseas, presidents may not take the country from a state of peace to a state of war without seeking and obtaining congressional authority."[84] In June of 2011, the House of Representatives formally refused to authorize the US involvement in Libya, but at the same time representatives rebuffed the efforts of some members to limit financing to support the operations.

The Foreign Relations Committee also supported the President's actions, but the full Senate proved unable to approve or reject the support to NATO. Senator James Webb (D-Virginia) pointed out the absurdity of the administration's position that the "hostilities" provision of the War Powers Resolution was irrelevant in Libya. "When you have an operation that goes on for months," he said, "costs billions of dollars, where the United States is providing two-thirds of the troops, even under the NATO fig leaf, where they're dropping bombs that are killing people, where you're paying your troops offshore combat pay and there are areas of prospective escalation . . . I would say that's hostilities."[85] Speaker of the House John A. Boehner (R-Ohio) agreed: "It doesn't pass the straight-face test, in my view, that we are not in the midst of hostilities."[86]

## A House of Cards

As these and many other examples illustrate, attempts by Congress to play a stronger role in decisions regarding the use of the war power have met with erratic results. Since the passage of the War Powers Resolution, executive-branch consultation with Congress in advance of a military action has been sporadic at best. Concluded one authority, "In the absence of the executive's good faith adherence to the spirit of the resolution, which the sponsors also had mistakenly expected . . . the whole procedural edifice turned out to be a house of cards."[87] Senator Mark O. Hatfield (R-Oregon) placed the blame for the failure of the resolution on a lack of "political will" in the Congress to demand presidential adherence to the law.[88]

In 1988, Senators Robert Byrd and Sam Nunn declared the War Powers Resolution "broke" (meaning broken) and offered measures to fix it. They urged their colleagues to remember: "Under the Constitution the Founding Fathers gave Congress the power to declare war."[89] In this spirit, they offered *new legislation to improve the resolution.* The **Byrd–Nunn proposal** recommended *abandonment of the sixty-day clock, with reliance instead on executive consultation with a panel of congressional leaders to explain and defend the president's proposed use of overt force abroad.* The panel would include the majority and minority leaders of both houses, as well as the Speaker of the House and the president pro tempore of the Senate. If so requested by a majority of this panel, the president would have to consult in addition with an expanded group of lawmakers that included the chairs, along with the ranking majority and minority members, of the armed services, foreign affairs, and intelligence committees in both chambers. These congressional leaders could then recommend to Congress an appropriate response.

If members of Congress chose to limit or halt the use of force, a joint resolution—which requires a majority vote in both chambers, with a subsequent opportunity for a presidential veto—would be, according to the Byrd–Nunn prescription, the appropriate constitutional instrument. Thus, with the removal of the sixty-day clock and adoption of a joint-resolution procedure, the Byrd–Nunn proposal stood the original War Powers approach on its head: US troops would be permitted to remain at war unless Congress voted to the contrary. Critics were quick to denounce this retreat from a fixed time clock for troop removal. Further, some viewed the joint resolution procedure, with its opportunity for a presidential veto (in contrast to the concurrent resolution), as giving the executive branch too much control over war making—one of the very problems Byrd and Nunn had complained about when they introduced their reform proposal. Weighed down by too many criticisms, the Byrd–Nunn proposal soon collapsed.[90]

In 1995, the House defeated by a vote of 217-to-201 an amendment to repeal the central features of the War Powers Resolution. Since then, despite the law's imperfections, few in Congress have called for another try at repeal. As Robert A. Katzmann explained in 1990, repeal is "unlikely, if for no other reason than it would symbolize to many in Congress a surrender of its role in war-making decisions."[91] Moreover, the law seems to have had a subtle effect on both the George W. Bush and the Obama administrations. They have sought authorization from Congress for military interventions in Iraq and Afghanistan, rather than risk the controversy of appearing to be in violation of the War Powers Resolution—although Obama's freewheeling in Libya remains a sore spot for WPR defenders.

### The Use of Nuclear Weapons

As the debate continued over the status of the War Powers Resolution, a related issue attracted growing attention: whether to limit, by law, a possible presidential first use of nuclear weapons. The director of the Federation of American Scientists (FAS) argued in 1984 that the president alone should not be allowed to move "the nation into the line of fire, into the war zone."[92] Rather, Congress should establish a joint nuclear planning committee, which the president would be required to consult before ordering the first use of nuclear weapons. This proposal was not meant to undermine the authority of the president to defend the nation, should the United States be attacked. Under the proposal, the president would retain the right to order prompt retaliation (a second strike) if an adversary were to hit the United States with a nuclear first strike. To give the president full discretion over the momentous decision to initiate the use nuclear weapons in offensive circumstances, though, was, in the opinion of the FAS director, "unnecessary, unwise, unconstitutional and unlawful."[93]

The Department of Defense rejected the contention that the president should have to consult with the Congress prior to the first use of nuclear weapons. Deterrence, said the DOD's general counsel, "rests on the policy of flexible response, which would include the use, as required, of conventional weapons, non-strategic [tactical] nuclear weapons, and strategic nuclear weapons. To insure that the flexible response policy actually deters, a potential aggressor must be convinced that NATO is indeed ready to use any of the weapons it possesses, including, if necessary, nuclear weapons." Consultation with Congress, he continued, would just place "an additional procedural requirement" on first use, which would "tend to undermine NATO's deterrence policy."[94]

The nature of sophisticated weaponry in the nuclear age led Louis Henkin to wonder: "Have nuclear weapons effectively eliminated any meaningful role for Congress in decisions as to nuclear strategy? If so, our celebrated Constitution is no longer relevant for our most compelling concerns."[95]

## SUMMARY

With the invention of nuclear weapons, warfare reached a new level of potential violence. During the Cold War, the United States and the Soviet Union built enough nuclear warheads between them to reduce one another's societies to rubble. Yet these weapons may have helped to prevent a third world war. The condition of mutual deterrence, whereby each superpower maintained a capacity to annihilate the other, created a "balance of terror" that undergirded—paradoxically—a long period of global stability between the superpowers. This balance was precarious, however, with command-and-control facilities representing a major point of vulnerability. Arms control negotiations have tried to slow the nuclear and conventional arms race.

Given the heightened dangers of modern weaponry, the decision to use the war power has become ever more fateful. American foreign policy over the years, and dramatically so in recent decades, has witnessed a sometimes acrimonious struggle between the executive and legislative branches over the use of military force. In its efforts to reclaim lost authority over the war power, Congress fashioned in 1973 a rather clumsy new procedure in the War Powers Resolution. Designed to prevent future open-ended presidential discretion over the deployment of US troops into hostilities abroad (the Gulf of Tonkin scenario), the resolution has resulted in inconsistent results. Troubling ambiguities remain regarding its proper application. Further, whether and how presidential discretion should be limited with respect to the first use of nuclear weapons has become another bone of contention.

## KEY TERMS

antiballistic missile (ABM) p. 347

arms control p. 353

Authorization for Use of Military Force
    (AUMF, 2001) p. 338

ballistic missile defense (BMD) p. 345

Byrd-Nunn proposal (1988) p. 362

command-control-communications-and-intelligence
    ($C^3I$) p. 349

conventional capabilities p. 341

counterforce p. 342

countervalue p. 342

deterrence p. 339

electromagnetic pulse (EMP) p. 342

Lebanon Emergency Assistance Act (1983) p. 360

Munich syndrome p. 353

National Command Authority (NCA) p. 349

nuclear decapitation p. 349

nuclear winter p. 343

Pearl Harbor syndrome p. 353

Powell Doctrine p. 340

second-strike capability p. 347

Strategic Defense Initiative (SDI) p. 345

strategic nuclear capability p. 341

tactical nuclear capability p. 341

theater nuclear weapons p. 341

triad p. 346

War Powers Resolution (1973) p. 354

Weinberger Doctrine p. 339

## QUESTIONS FOR DISCUSSION

1. How would you evaluate the importance to US vital interests of the Iraq War that began in 2003? The war in Afghanistan that began in 2001?

2. Would you have voted for the War Powers Resolution? How would you amend the WPR—or would you repeal the law altogether?

3. Now that the Cold War is more than 20 years in the past, is the triad of US strategic weapons systems obsolete? Can the number of US nuclear warheads be reduced to zero? Do you think that the use of a nuclear weapon in warfare is more or less likely since the end of the Cold War?

4. Under what conditions should the United States intervene militarily overseas?

5. How much defense is enough? If you were president or a leading member of Congress, how would you have proposed spending the roughly $2 trillion that the United States invested in the Iraq and Afghanistan Wars? On those two wars? On foreign aid? On homeland security defenses? On health care? Education?

6. Should the president of the United States be the sole elected official to decide when a nuclear weapon should be used offensively? Who should decide when American troops should fight as part of a UN or NATO military force?

## ADDITIONAL READINGS

Betts, Richard K. *American Force: Dangers, Delusions, and Dilemmas in National Security*. New York: Columbia University Press, 2012.

Johnson, Chalmers. *Blowback: The Costs and Consequences of American Empire*. New York: Metropolitan Books, 2000.

Schell, Jonathan. *The Fate of the Earth*. New York: Knopf, 1982.

For further readings, please visit the book's companion website.

### CHAPTER 12

# Covert Action

## THE SPY AND THE SLEEPY WATCHDOG

Two young men stood on either side of an easel that supported oversized charts. One braced the charts, while the other occasionally moved a pointed marker up and down the slopes of red- and blue-colored trend lines.

Seated near them, a CIA officer in his mid-fifties read from a typed statement. He spoke precisely, seldom looking up from the pages, his words falling in dry monotone on the table before him. The officer and his deputy wore starched white shirts with buttoned-down collars and striped ties. Beyond the hearing room's spacious windows, draped in regal purple curtains, a fountain spewed a column of water high into the frigid morning air—a touch of Rome in the courtyard of the venerable Old Senate Office Building of the United States Senate.

Bay of Pigs invasion of Cuba by CIA-trained Cuban exiles, April of 1961.

A U-shaped bench dominated the room with its prongs facing the CIA men, as if they were trapped in a magnetic field. Within the concave space sat a stenotypist, her fingers dancing lightly on the keys of a machine. Two elderly lawmakers sat at the head of the bench, each a United States Senator and a member of the secretive Sub-committee on Intelligence. They listened as the intelligence officer droned through his prepared statement on CIA paramilitary operations. As the head of the Director-ate of Operations, he was expected to present a report to Congress from time to time. The older of the two senators rested his head in his arms and soon fell asleep. The other senator, the panel's chairman, stared blankly at the CIA briefer, nodded once in a while, discreetly stole a glance at his wristwatch, and then examined the newspaper folded in front of him on the bench.

This was not the first time the CIA officers had experienced the distant look in the eyes of a lawmaker, or even the first time they had seen one nod off. The briefer's job was to provide an update on Agency activities; how the briefing was received on the Hill was not his problem. He cleared his throat and raised his voice for a moment, more to relieve his own boredom than to stir his small audience. "*Paramilitary activities*," he emphasized, "have been an important part of our program since the early days of the Cold War."

The new inflection in the briefer's voice woke up the slumbering senator with a start. "*Parliamentary activities*? he bellowed. "You fellas can't go messin' round with parliaments. I won't have it!"

## LEARNING OBJECTIVES AND CONSTITUTIONAL ISSUES

**By the end of this chapter, you will be able to:**

- *Define the secret foreign policy instrument known as covert action*
- *Assess the value added by covert action to America's pursuit of objectives abroad*
- *Describe how covert action decisions are made*
- *Describe how Congress has sought to become a part of the covert action approval process*
- *Explain why covert action has become one of the most controversial instruments of US foreign policy*

---

**THIS CHAPTER RAISES THE FOLLOWING CONSTITUTIONAL QUESTIONS:**

- The Constitution is silent on the topic of covert action, but these secret operations have become a subject of dispute between Congress and the executive branch. Should Congress even have a role in covert actions, given the highly sensitive nature of these operations?

- What would the constitutional framers have likely thought about the idea of the doctrine of "plausible denial"?

- Should presidents determine foreign targets for assassination, or should Congress be consulted in advance? Does it matter if the potential target is an American citizen, as has been the case re-cently with CIA drone strikes in Yemen? Should there be a special court of jurists where the execu-tive branch would have to obtain a warrant before an assassination could be carried out, similar to the Foreign Intelligence Surveillance Act (FISA) Court that reviews warrants for national security wiretaps? Or should there be no US assassination operations at all, outside of an authorized war?

A silence fell over the room. The stenotypist's fingers stopped their dance. The briefer pursed his lips and looked ruefully at the subcommittee chairman, who said softly to his colleague, "Senator, this briefing is on paramilitary, not parliamentary, activity."

"Oh, well, uhruumph," replied the sleepy-eyed senator, clearing his throat and tugging at his ear. "Okay, but y'all stay away from parliaments, ya hear?" With that admonishment, he rose from his chair and shuffled out of the room. At a nod from the chairman, the briefer resumed his statement.[1] ∿

## COVERT ACTION: AMERICA'S SECRET FOREIGN POLICY

This tale from the 1950s continues to be told with glee at CIA Headquarters. The portrait is unfair to lawmakers; some of them at least made an attempt to monitor America's secret foreign policy after its creation in 1947.[2] Too few, though, pushed hard for details and asked follow-up questions during hearings. Whether the story of the sleeping octogenarian is factual or apocryphal remains unclear; but it is true that covert actions—and especially paramilitary activities—have often prompted concern and even alarm on Capitol Hill. The use of secret means to achieve foreign policy ends has been an attractive option to presidents and policy makers since the early years of the Republic. Of all the nation's intelligence missions, however, this is the one most likely to stir passions. Indeed, critics contend that covert action—nowhere mentioned in the Constitution—has done more to stain the reputation of the CIA, and thus the United States, than any other foreign policy activity.

In the modern world, how is the hidden hand of the CIA brought into play in the pursuit of US global objectives? And what is the role of Congress in America's secret foreign policy? Here are the central questions I address in this chapter. I also examine the four major forms of covert action and trace the decision path by which these operations are approved—yet another arena in which a struggle takes place between the executive and legislative branches over constitutional standing.

### Legal Underpinnings

In the United States, covert action (CA) is sometimes referred to as the "quiet option" by officials inside the CIA, the organization the White House relies on to plan and implement this instrument of foreign policy. The phrase is drawn from the debatable assumption that this approach to international affairs is less likely to be noisy and obtrusive than sending in a Marine brigade. Although sometimes this is true, there was nothing quiet about the Bay of Pigs fiasco in 1961; about the CIA's large-scale wars in such places as Laos (1962–1968) and Afghanistan (during the 1980s and again beginning in 2001); or about Hellfire missiles striking their targets in Pakistan or Yemen in recent years. Moreover, today's "covert" CIA drone attacks in the Middle East and Southwest Asia are routinely discussed in the media.

Another label for covert action is the "third option"—a choice for the president that lies between diplomacy, on the one hand, and overt warfare, on the other hand.

Henry Kissinger remarked in a 1978 news interview, "We need an intelligence community that, in certain complicated situations, can defend the American national interest in the gray areas where military operations are not suitable and diplomacy cannot operate."[3] Yet another favorite euphemism in Washington for covert action is the phrase "special activities."

To give this hidden approach to American foreign policy improved legal authority, in 1991 Congress belatedly crafted a formal statutory definition of **covert action** as "*an activity or activities of the United States Government to influence political, economic, or military conditions abroad, where it is intended that the role of the United States Government will not be apparent or acknowledged publicly.*"[4] Prior to this legislation, presidents relied initially on a boilerplate clause in the National Security Act of 1947 for legal justification to carry out covert actions. In a final section, the 1947 law provided authority for the DCI and the CIA to perform "such other functions and duties related to intelligence affecting the national security as the President or the National Security Council may direct."[5] Such are the slender legal reeds that supported covert action when the CIA was established.

## Policy Rationale

Although less so than the wording in the National Security Act of 1947, the language on covert action in the 1991 definition is still spongy. For example, the military—not just the CIA—engages in operations that could fit into this definition, yet the Pentagon denies that it is involved in covert actions and refers to its secret operations as "traditional military activities."[6] This practice blurs the line between legitimate CIA and military operations, and allows the Pentagon to bypass the formal procedures for approval and congressional notification that have evolved to supervise CIA covert actions (discussed later in this chapter).[7]

Behind the bland wording of the 1991 definition lies the reality that covert action is nothing less than an attempt to change the course of history through the use of secret operations against other countries, terrorist groups, or factions—"giving history a push," in the words of a senior CIA operative.[8] During the Cold War, the main concern of the CIA's Covert Action Staff within the Operations Directorate (the CAS is now known as the Special Activities or SA Division within the National Clandestine Service) was, according to one of its chiefs, "the global challenge of communism . . . to be confronted whenever and wherever it seemed to threaten our interests."[9] Today its foremost mission is to thwart global terrorism, with Al Qaeda at the top of the threat assessment list.[10]

Whether such targets as Iran (in 1953), Guatemala (1954), Angola (1975), Chile (1958–1973), or Somalia today qualified as truly threatening to the United States is a matter of debate. With respect to Angola during the Cold War, a CIA official maintained that "ultimately, the purpose was to throw the Soviets out, at which point we would leave, too."[11] Critics, though, find the arguments for some CIA interventions a stretch. With respect to Nicaragua, a prime target for US covert action during the

1980s, Nobel laureate Günter Grass asked plaintively, "How impoverished must a country be before it is not a threat to the US government?"[12] Frank Church (D-Idaho), who led a Senate inquiry into the subject of covert action in 1975, concluded that during the Cold War America's "targets were leaders of small, weak countries that could not possibly threaten the United States."[13]

## THE METHODS OF COVERT ACTION

The government initially established a CIA in the wake of World War II to improve the coordination of intelligence, as well as to defend the United States against the growing threat posed by the Soviet Union and to guard against future Pearl Harbors. Almost immediately, though, covert action became a central preoccupation of officials within the Agency and the White House. This aggressive secret approach to foreign policy has taken four major forms over the years: propaganda; political manipulation; economic disruption; and paramilitary (PM) operations or, in plain language, secret warfare.

The ebbs and flows of covert action since the creation of the CIA in 1947 are depicted in Figure 12.1. Use of this approach started off slowly in 1947, but accelerated dramatically with the outbreak of hostilities on the Korean Peninsula in 1950, as secret CIA operations augmented the overt military actions of the United States against the North Korean and Chinese armies. After this conflict ended in 1953, covert action declined in emphasis; but its expansion began again in 1965 with another large war in Asia, this time in Vietnam. For the United States, overt warfare and covert action go hand-in-hand. The souring of public and official opinion toward the Vietnam War led to another decline in the use of covert action. This approach was revived with great force in the 1980s, however, as the Reagan Doctrine turned to "the Agency" as its spearhead for global combat against communism. During this decade, covert action blossomed as a tool of American foreign policy, even though the nation had no major overt wars underway. The focus on covert action during the first several Reagan years, particularly in Nicaragua and Afghanistan, even surpassed the emphasis placed on this instrument during the Korea War. Another decline occurred, however, following the Iran-*contra* scandal in 1987, a cluster of illegal operations that stained the reputation of covert action as a legitimate policy option. The collapse of the Soviet Union in 1991 further reduced Washington's interest in the use of these hidden CIA operations because America's main target was no longer a mortal threat.

In reaction to the 9/11 attacks and the perception (false, as it turned out) that Iraq possessed WMDs, covert action attracted fresh support during the George W. Bush administration and has continued with even greater enthusiasm into the Obama years. The overt wars in Afghanistan and Iraq, along with PM operations ("ops") against global terrorists, brought "special activities" again back to the forefront of America's foreign policy instruments, surpassing the earlier high points of emphasis during the Korean War and the pursuit of the Reagan Doctrine in Nicaragua and Afghanistan during the 1980s.[14] The struggle against terrorism has also produced the CIA's most

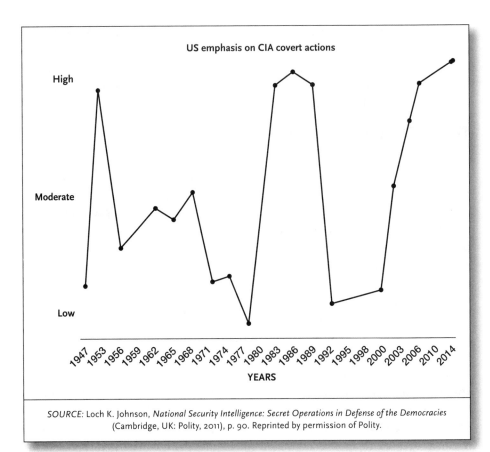

SOURCE: Loch K. Johnson, *National Security Intelligence: Secret Operations in Defense of the Democracies* (Cambridge, UK: Polity, 2011), p. 90. Reprinted by permission of Polity.

*Figure 12.1*
The Ebb and Flow of Covert Actions Carried Out by the United States, 1947–2014

lethal (and least covert) forms of PM activity: the use of Predator and Reaper drones armed with Hellfire missiles, thus far aimed at targets in the Middle East, Southwest Asia, North Africa, and Yemen.[15]

## Propaganda

No form of covert action is used more extensively than **secret propaganda** ("perception enhancement," in the CIA euphemism). To augment the flow of official information from Washington, DC and US embassies around the world during the Cold War, the Agency *released a flood of supportive material—some 70 to 80 items a day placed into foreign media outlets—distributed secretly by its vast underground network of "media assets."* These assets (agents) include reporters, newspaper and magazine editors, television producers, bloggers, social networkers—the whole range of media. Whatever themes the White House and the State Department may be communicating openly to the world at any given time, the CIA will likely be advancing at the same time through its covert channels, say, during the Carter administration the value of neutron bombs or Pershing missiles for Europe; during the Reagan administration, the pernicious influence of the KGB on the peace movement in Western

Europe; or, today, the dangers to democracy and world peace posed by Al Qaeda and other Islamic extremists.

In addition to support for the government's official propaganda themes, the CIA will use its media assets to promote or denigrate foreign political leaders or aspirants, depending on whether or not these individuals are likely to support the interests of the United States. A classic example is the CIA effort, under orders from Presidents Eisenhower, Johnson, and Nixon, to oppose left-wing activities in Chile and especially to discredit Chilean socialist leader Salvador Allende.[16] At first, the operations succeeded during the Eisenhower and Johnson years. During the Johnson administration, for instance, the CIA spent $3 million secretly in the 1964 Chilean election to blacken Allende's name. An expenditure of $3 million in that election would have been roughly equivalent, on a per capita basis, to an expenditure of $60 million in the American presidential election that year—an enormous amount of money at the time. Between 1963 and 1973, the CIA poured more than $12 million into Chile for use just on secret propaganda operations, along with additional funds devoted to more aggressive forms of covert action—such as the disruption of the Chilean economy through CIA-stimulated labor strikes and other methods. Subsequently, the Nixon White House escalated the use of the CIA to block Allende's ongoing attempts to win the presidency. Fearing that Allende might nationalize its business holdings in Chile, the International Telephone and Telegraph (ITT) corporation secretly offered $1 million to the Nixon White House for use by the Agency to derail Allende's campaign. Despite these efforts, Allende was elected President in 1970.

Over the years, the CIA's extensive propaganda capability has produced a great tide of information flowing unseen from Washington into hundreds of hidden channels around the world. Once released, the information cannot be bottled up or directed to only one spot on the globe, as one might apply an antiseptic to a sore. Rather, it is free to drift here and there, and even back to the United States. This can lead to **blowback**, or **replay**, *whereby false information directed toward enemies can find its way back home to deceive America's own citizens.*[17] This concern led the popular State Department official Bernard Kalb to resign over the often exaggerated anti-Qaddafi covert propaganda operations of the Reagan administration. A senior intelligence official during the Cold War conceded that it "use to worry me a lot" that false CIA propaganda about mainland China might fool China experts in the Department of State, skewing their analyses.[18]

## Political Manipulation

**Political covert action** takes the form of *secret financial aid to friendly politicians and bureaucrats abroad*: bribes, if one wishes to put a harsh light on the practice, or stipends to advance the cause of democracy if one prefers a rosier interpretation. Whatever one prefers to call this assistance ("King George's cavalry" is the expression favored by the British intelligence service, MI6),[19] the record is clear that through political covert action the United States has provided substantial sums of funding to various political parties, leaders, and would be leaders around the globe. A favored recipient during the Cold War was the Christian Democratic Party in Italy, which contested elections regularly with the Italian Communist Party (with its lavish clandestine funding from the KGB).

At times the SA Division at CIA headquarters has resembled nothing so much as a team of political consultants, producing campaign materials for favorable foreign candidates: brochures, bumper stickers, speech drafts, placards, even lapel buttons with slogans for use in remote regions of the world where they have never been seen before. During an African civil war, the CIA forwarded to the anticommunist faction over 50,000 political lapel buttons that proclaimed the partisan affiliation of the wearer: "I am a member of the _____ Party." Battlefield results—the waging of warfare between the communist and the CIA-led anticommunist factions in the jungles—proved more telling, however, than lapel buttons manufactured by the Covert Action Staff at CIA Headquarters and pinned to the fatigues of the soldiers on the Agency's side. The anticommunists found themselves outgunned and were forced to retreat into the hinterland.[20]

## Economic Disruption

With **economic covert action**, the Agency attempts when ordered by the White House to *disrupt the economies of America's enemies through secret means*. In one instance during the Kennedy years, although initially without the knowledge of the president, the CIA planned to damage Cuban-Soviet relations by lacing sugar bound from Havana to Moscow with an unpalatable, though harmless, chemical substance. A White House aide caught wind of the operation and informed the president, who rejected the idea immediately and had the 14,125 bags of sugar confiscated before they left for the Soviet Union. On ethical grounds, the United States was not going to tamper with food products from Cuba or anywhere else.[21]

During the efforts to undermine Allende once he became President of Chile (despite all the propaganda efforts to block his election), the Agency took up various covert measures to disrupt the Chilean economy. By heightening the level of unrest under the Allende regime, Washington hoped Chilean military forces would decide to oust the new president. Inciting massive labor strikes was one proposal considered by the CIA. Senior agency officials eventually abandoned this option; but the Agency continued to provide funding to groups in Chile directly involved in strike tactics, especially within the trucking industry, in an attempt to impede the flow of commerce inside the country.

Later in Latin America, as part of the Reagan administration's efforts to overthrow the Nicaraguan Sandinista regime in the 1980s, the CIA-supported *contras* carried out a range of secret attacks against the economy of Nicaragua, including the mining of piers in the nation's main harbors to discourage international shipping, as well as blowing up of power lines throughout the countryside. Other economic operations during the Cold War included counterfeiting foreign currencies to bring about inflation in certain communist regimes; depressing the world price of sugar to undermine the Cuban economy; mining harbors in North Vietnam; and preparing—but never using, again on moral grounds—parasites with the capacity to destroy foreign agricultural crops, such as Cuban sugarcane.[22]

## Paramilitary Operations

Even more severe is **paramilitary covert action,** which involves *the disguised use of military force overseas.* Some examples include the covert war waged by the CIA against communist guerrillas in Laos from 1962 to 1968; the unacknowledged sale of weapons abroad, as when the United States secretly sold arms to Iran in the 1980s in exchange for its influence over terrorists in Lebanon (part of the Iran-*contra* scandal); the training, advising, and supplying of foreign surrogate troops—mercenaries—to fight on behalf of America's foreign interests, such as the Nicaraguan *contras* and the Afghan *mujahedeen*; antiterrorist and security training for foreign intelligence services; and specific assassination plots, with Fidel Castro of Cuba only one of several CIA targets during the 1960s, along with Qaeda leaders in recent years.

In 2012, CIA paramilitary officers operating in Turkey helped funnel weapons (paid for by Turkey, Saudi Arabia, and Qatar) to insurgents in the Syrian uprising.[23] Further, using covert "cyberweapons," the CIA and NSA reportedly worked together in an operation codenamed "Olympic Games" to place a worm (known as "Stuxnet" and developed jointly by Israel and the United States) inside computers in Iran tied to its nuclear-enrichment facilities. The purpose was to disrupt the Iranian computer infrastructure and slow that nation's suspected development of nuclear bombs.[24]

However convenient for presidents as a means for avoiding the provisions of the War Powers Resolution and public debate about open warfare, the paramilitary approach has been fraught with controversy. Critics recoil from the CIA's murder plots and *coups d'état* against foreign governments, arguing that covert action represents the ultimate perversion of American ideals. Others view the option as a necessary instrument in the US foreign policy toolkit, should it be needed to protect and advance the interests of the United States abroad.

### Covert action authority

America's covert action authority operations are not subject to the provisions of War Powers Resolution, but to a different set of legislative checks designed by lawmakers to guard against the executive abuse of power in this hidden domain of government. These main "oversight" statutes include the Hughes–Ryan Act of 1974 and its strengthening successors: the Intelligence Oversight Acts of 1980 and 1991.[25] Before passage of these laws, the executive branch enjoyed a freedom of discretion over covert actions that makes the much maligned "blank check" of the Tonkin Gulf Resolution look like a finely embroidered contract.

According to the Pike Committee inquiry in 1975, all that was necessary to launch a covert action in previous decades was a telephone call over a secure line from the CIA to NSC members or their designated staff aides.[26] Rarely was Congress in the decision loop, other than a few trusted lawmakers on a couple of intelligence oversight subcommittees that existed in these early years; sometimes these meetings resembled the case study that opened this chapter. The Agency did not want to tell lawmakers about its sensitive operations; and, conveniently, the Congress did not want to know either. After all, lawmakers reasoned, the political risks might be too high for them if an operation went awry and became public. It was safer to remain in the dark; law-makers could then claim innocence and blame the CIA for its poor judgment, as in the case of the Bay of Pigs disaster.

Nor was the NSC consistently apprised of covert action operations. The Church Committee discovered that, out of the thousands of covert action projects from 1949 to 1968, only 600 went before the NSC for approval.[27] The tendency was for the CIA to ask the NSC for broad grants of authority that would then become the sire of sub-sidiary operations, many arguably warranting separate and specific approval. One member of the NSC, Dean Rusk, the Secretary of State for Presidents John Kennedy and Lyndon Johnson, apparently remained unaware of many CIA activities. "I never saw a budget of the CIA, for example," he recalled in 1977.[28] Nor did he or any other NSC official recollect any decisions or briefings on CIA assassination plots; all denied, under oath, knowledge of authority from Presidents Eisenhower, Kennedy, and John-son for these operations.[29]

Today, with the Hughes–Ryan legislation and the 1980 and 1991 Intelligence Oversight Acts, the decision pathway for covert action has become quite comprehen-sive. The "third option" has required formal authorization from the president; further, the law mandates reports to Congress on all approved covert actions. The failure of the Reagan administration to honor these reporting requirements during its Iran-*contra* operations led to scandal in 1986–87.

### Secret wars

No covert actions have held higher risk or been more subject to controversy than para-military activities. These operations have consumed a sizable percentage of the CIA's budget in any given year—indeed, over 50 percent of the Agency's annual funding during the historical peaks of covert action: the Korean War, the height of the Vietnam war, during the Reagan administration, and since 9/11 in the struggle against Al Qaeda and other global terrorists. Sometimes called **special operations** ("**special ops**") and *run by the Special Operations Group or SOG, part of the Agency's Special Activities Divi-sion, the paramilitary mission often entails nothing less than large-scale "secret" wars.* It is questionable, though, that any PM of that magnitude can remain secret for long.

From 1962 to 1968, for instance, the CIA backed the hill tribesmen of fog-shrouded northern Laos—the Hmong (pronounce with a silent H)—in a war against the North Vietnamese communist puppets known as the Pathet Lao, lowlanders in the southern region of Laos. The Ho Chi Minh Trail, along which the North Vietnamese sent supplies to its communist fighters in South Vietnam, ran chiefly through Laotian territory. The CIA-back Hmong played a significant role in slowing these supplies. Moreover, by keeping the Pathet Lao preoccupied in Laos, the CIA ensured that they were not fighting and killing US soldiers next door in Vietnam. About 35,000 Hmong died on the Laotian battlefields before the United States withdrew from the country in 1968 to focus more directly on the war in Vietnam. With the CIA's support gone, the eighteen clans of Hmong tribes still faced the Pathet Lao, which continued to receive a steady flow of arms and military guidance from China and the Soviet Union. The Hmong had been put "into this meat grinder, mostly to save US soldiers from fighting and dying there," recalls Lionel Rosenblatt, president emeritus of Refugees International.[30] Now they had to fend for themselves. They didn't fare well. Tens of thousands fled into Thailand. Those with the right connections sought refuge in the United States, settling mainly in Minnesota.

The Agency sponsored many other guerrilla wars during the Cold War, providing support for pro-Western insurgents in the Ukraine, Poland, Albania, Hungary, Indonesia, China, Oman, Malaysia, Iraq, the Dominican Republic, Venezuela, North Korea, Bolivia, Thailand, Haiti, Guatemala, Cuba, Chad, Mauritius, Lebanon, South Yemen, Cambodia, Suriname, Greece, Turkey, Vietnam, Afghanistan, Angola, and Nicaragua, to list some paramilitary targets that have made it into the public record.[31] Further, the Agency's paramilitary program has included assistance to the Defense Department in the development of its own unconventional warfare capability, known as Special Operations Forces (SOF, such as the Navy Seals mission that killed Osama bin Laden in 2011). America's use of the Stuxnet computer worm against Iranian nuclear centrifuges, in hopes of sabotaging Iran's WMD program, was the first known US act of pure cyberwarfare against another country, as well as "the most sophisticated cyberweapon ever deployed."[32]

## Assassination plots

The CIA's efforts to kill individual enemies of the United States in foreign countries are a special category of paramilitary activity.[33] Over the years, the Agency developed a storehouse of lethal chemicals and several inventive delivery systems for the purpose of assassination. The poisons, which included shellfish toxin ("saxitoxin"), curare, and cobra venom, were extensive and deadly enough to eliminate the entire population of a small city. One delivery system developed by intelligence scientists entailed first applying poison to a tiny dart the size of a sewing needle, labeled a "nondiscernible microbioinoculator" by an imaginative researcher. Then the needle was inserted into an electric dart gun (a "noise-free disseminator" resembling a .45 pistol with a telescopic sight), which could propel the dart silently toward the victim. The gun was accurate up to 250 feet—the ultimate murder weapon, able to kill without sound and with barely a trace. Initially, Army Intelligence intended to use the weapon to silence guard dogs overseas, if necessary; but the dart gun could have been used against human targets as well.[34]

*The Attempted Murder of Foreign Leaders.* The United States has resorted to assassination plots only infrequently and, at least with respect to foreign heads of state, never successfully—despite trying often in the instance of Fidel Castro.[35] In **Operation Mongoose**, the *Cuban President received during the Kennedy years (1961-1963) the full attention of the CIA's Covert Action Staff: propaganda, political and economic action, and paramilitary operations.* The Agency directed drugs and poisons his way through various ingenious, if unsuccessful, methods. Among the methods used were the placement of depilatory powder in his shoes, meant to enter Castro's bloodstream and make his charismatic beard fall off; LSD and botulinum toxin in his cigars, to disorient in the first instance and kill in the second; Madura-foot fungus in his underwater diving suit, causing a debilitating disease; and the deadly poison Blackleaf-40, readied for injection into his skin through the extraordinarily fine tip of a DS&T-crafted ballpoint pen.

These and similar efforts failed, for Castro was elusive and protected by a KGB-trained corps of bodyguards. So the Agency upped the ante. To eliminate the Cuban leader, the CAS hired organized crime figures who still had contacts in Cuba from pre-Castro days when Havana was a world gambling center. Mobster John Rosselli went to Florida on behalf of the Agency in 1961 and 1962. His task was to assemble assassination teams of Cuban exiles who would infiltrate their homeland and take Castro's life. Rosselli in turn called on two other crime figures: Chicago gangster Sam Giancana and Santos Trafficante, the Cosa Nostra chieftain for Cuba. Giancana's role was to find someone in Castro's entourage who could dissolve a poison pill into his soup; Trafficante was expected to enter the island and make arrangements for the murder. The mob sent several assassins to Cuba; none succeeded.

An earlier target for the CIA, during the final months of the Eisenhower administration, was the African leader Patrice Lumumba, a thirty-five-year-old charismatic leader and the first democratically elected president of mineral-rich Congo (now known as the Democratic Republic of Congo). When the United States refused to provide foreign aid to his struggling country, Lumumba turned in desperation to the Soviet Union, a move that in the eyes of Washington officials made him an enemy.

In the fall of 1960, the CIA's chief of station in Congo received from Agency Headquarters, via a State Department diplomatic pouch, an unusual assortment of items: rubber gloves, gauze masks, a hypodermic syringe, and lethal biological toxins. As one CIA officer assigned to the US embassy in Congo recollected, "I knew it wasn't for somebody to get his polio shot up to date."[36] The enclosed instructions explained how to inject the poison into Lumumba's food or toothpaste to bring about his quick death.

As an alternative to poisoning Lumumba, the CIA's chief of station in the Congo recommended the leader be shot. He cabled Agency Headquarters to request that a weapon be sent, again by way of a diplomatic pouch: RECOMMEND HQS POUCH SOONEST HIGH POWERED FOREIGN MAKE RIFLE WITH TELESCOPIC SCOPE AND SILENCER. The cable ended cryptically: WOULD KEEP RIFLE IN OFFICE PENDING OPENING OF HUNTING SEASON, which meant, according to congressional testimony by the CIA's African chief, Bronson Tweedy, that the weapon would not be used until final approval had been received from CIA Headquarters. Before the COS was able to carry out any of these operations, however, a rival

Congolese faction murdered Lumumba. Recent research suggests that the Agency's station chief may have helped arrange a rendition of the Congo leader into the arms of his assassins operating out of the Katanga region in the south of the country.[37]

In no instance was a CIA finger actually on the trigger of any weapon that killed a foreign leader—until the Obama administration's drone attacks against Qaeda leaders in Pakistan, Afghanistan, and Yemen. Technically, neither the CIA nor any other US government agency committed murder against a foreign head of state during the Cold War; but the government certainly tried. Whether the CIA acted as a **rogue elephant** in these operations, *off on a rampage of its own making without proper NSC and presidential supervision* (as a Senate critic once charged),[38] or just following White House orders, remains a matter of dispute. For many reasons, congressional investigators found it impossible in 1975 to pinpoint responsibility for the Agency's murder plots. The presidents who might have been involved in the plots—Eisenhower, Kennedy, and Johnson—and several of their top aides were no longer alive to give their testimony. Among the living, memories had faded, conveniently or otherwise; testimony conflicted; and some individuals seemed to yield to a sense of presidential loyalty and instincts of self-protection. High on the list of obstacles between the Committee and the truth was the system of decision making itself, particularly the doctrine of **plausible deniability**.

The purpose of plausible denial was to *erase any presidential ties to a covert operation*. The virtue of the nation had to be protected by shielding the reputation of its top leader; the president was to remain as pure as the proverbial Caesar's wife, far away from unsavory CIA activities that might be required in a hostile world. If the Agency found it necessary to discuss an "extralegal" or questionable operation with a president, euphemisms and doubletalk were the order of the day. This would leave the chief executive free to deny that the White House had granted specific authority for its conduct. It was decision making by a wink and a nod.

Richard Helms, DCI from 1966–1973, believed the CIA did have presidential authority for its plots against Castro, although the permission was heavily clothed in ambiguity and plausible denial. Senator Charles Mathias (R-Maryland) questioned Helms with a historical analogy:

> Senator Mathias: Let me draw an example from history. When Thomas Beckett was proving to be an annoyance, as Castro, the King said, "Who will rid me of this man?" He didn't say, go out and murder him. He said, who will rid me of this man, and let it go at that. . . . [Is] that typical of the kind of thing which might be said, which might be taken by the director or by anybody else as presidential authorization to go forward?

> Mr. Helms: That is right. But in answer to that, I realize that one sort of grows up in the tradition of the time and I think that any of us

would have found it very difficult to discuss assassinations with a president of the US. I just think we all had the feeling that we're hired out to keep those things out of the Oval Office.

Senator Mathias: Yet at the same time you felt that some spark had been transmitted, that that was within the permissible limits.

Mr. Helms: Yes, and if he had disappeared from the scene they would not have been unhappy.[39]

Helms, who was responsible for covert action at the CIA during the Kennedy years after the Bay of Pigs in 1961, conceded that he was never told directly by the President to kill Castro. Nevertheless, he remembered, "No member of the Kennedy Administration . . . ever told me that [assassination] was proscribed, [or] even referred to it in that fashion. . . . Nobody ever said that [assassination] was ruled out."[40]

Sometimes the evidence on assassination plots suggested nothing less than the CIA behaving as rogue elephant. Presidential adviser and noted historian Arthur M. Schlesinger Jr. wrote to President Kennedy in 1962: "One of the most shocking things which emerged after the last Cuban episode [the Bay of Pigs] was the weakness of top-level CIA control—the discrepancy between what high CIA officials thought their operatives were saying and doing in the field, and what these operatives were actually saying and doing."[41]

All the former presidential advisers who testified before the Church Committee denied under oath any knowledge of White House or cabinet-level orders to assassinate foreign leaders. At the Agency level, William Harvey, the paramilitary officer who worked with the mob to plan the assassination of Castro, admitted that he failed to tell incoming Director McCone about the murder plans. According to Richard Helms, Harvey kept the entire arrangement with the underworld figures "pretty much in his back pocket," that is, hidden out of view from his superiors in the White House and, apparently, within the CIA itself.[42] The CIA out of control, a wink and a nod, a misunderstanding—where was the truth? It was unlikely to be found in writing. "I can't imagine any cabinet officer wanting to sign off on something like that," Helms told Senate investigators. "I can't imagine anybody wanting something in writing saying 'I have just charged Mr. Jones to go out and shoot Mr. Smith.'"[43]

The controversy over assassination plots continues today, as the CIA uses drones—in this era, under the explicit orders from the second Bush and Obama administrations—to find and kill members of Al Qaeda, as well as extremist Taliban fighters in Afghanistan and Pakistan. The number of drone attacks has shot upward in recent years—more than 300 strikes in Pakistan alone since 2004.[44] The yearly rates in Pakistan during 2007, 2008, and 2009 were estimated to be, respectively, 5, 35, 53; then when President Obama took office, the number of drone strikes climbed to over 300 during his first term.[45] In 2009, the CIA's Hellfire missiles mounted on drones struck down 43 presumably innocent civilians; since then, the casualties among civilians has surpassed 3,000, according to one reputable estimate.[46] This "collateral damage" has had the effect of turning Pakistani public opinion against the United States. Nevertheless, in April of 2010, President Obama stepped up the drone attacks in Pakistan after Al Qaeda sneaked a suicide bomber into a CIA camp at Khost in Afghanistan, near the Pakistani border, and killed four Agency officers and three assets—a stunning blow to the CIA. The United States seemed to become more careful in its targeting in 2010. The rates of civilian deaths in Pakistan from drones from 2007 to 2010 were estimated to be 10, 50, 30, and 5 in each of these four years. In 2012, the Bureau of Investigative Journalism in Washington, DC, claimed that between 282 and 535 civilians had been killed by US drones since President Obama took office.[47]

Before CIA drones were armed with Hellfire missiles, the Clinton administration turned to cruise missiles fired by US Navy ships in the Red Sea to kill Qaeda terrorists. One attack barely missed the Al Qaeda leader, Osama bin Laden, who had decamped in Pakistan shortly before the missiles struck. On at least two other occasions, the CIA recommended further cruise missile attacks against Bin Laden, but President Clinton turned down these requests. In one instance, the Qaeda leader was surrounded by his wives and children; and, in another, he was with a party of United Arab Emirates princes during a bird-hunting expedition. Much to the dismay of the Agency officer in charge of hunting down Bin Laden,[48] the President's ethical and diplomatic reservations about killing women, children, or UAE royalty (the UAE is supposedly an ally of the United States in the Middle East) trumped a rare opportunity to eliminate the Qaeda chieftain before the 9/11 attacks. The President's decisions were made, it should be noted, before the United States understood the great danger Bin Laden and Al Qaeda held with respect to a direct attack on the American homeland.

*The Murder of Lower-Level Targets.* The most well-known operation to eliminate ("neutralize," in the Agency euphemism) large numbers of lower-level officials from the scene is the CIA's **Phoenix program**. The purpose of this program, carried out as part of the US war effort in Indochina, was to *subdue the influence of the communists in the South Vietnamese countryside, especially the Vietcong Infrastructure (VCI)*. According to former DCI William Colby, who for a time ran the program, some 20,000 VC leaders and sympathizers were killed as a result of its secret operations; but, Colby stresses, about 85 percent of those killed were engaged in military or paramilitary combat against South Vietnamese or American soldiers. Another 12 percent died at the hands of South Vietnamese security forces. None died through an authorized plan of "assassination." Critics find this argument a thin line, though, and even Colby conceded that assassinations might have taken place by overzealous South Vietnamese, or even American, participants in the Phoenix program.[49]

## Large-scale paramilitary operations

Beyond assassination plots and logistical support for friendly foreign intelligence services are covert actions of a much broader scope. These operations, referred to earlier, approach the same risk level as full-scale overt military interventions and they warrant a closer examination here. Secret wars are normally supported by the full panoply of covert action methods. Colby took special pride in two major successes: Western European resistance to communist political subversion and the victories of the Hmong in Laos from 1962 to 1968.[50] Among other conspicuous early successes, at least over the short term, were the operations waged in 1953 and 1954 that brought to power pro-American leaders in Iran and Guatemala, respectively. Hardly a shot was fired in either coup; the operations seemed to flow with the ease of a silk handkerchief from a magician's sleeve.

Coming as they did on top of earlier good fortune in Greece, Turkey, Italy, France, and Spain (as well as elsewhere on a smaller scale in Europe, Latin America, Asia, and Africa), the coups in Iran and Guatemala encouraged the view that the CIA could orchestrate events to remake countries across the latitudes more in America's likeness. Such quick and unobtrusive results gained through the use of the "quiet option" held strong appeal, compared to the frustrations of diplomacy and the risks—as well as the expense—of overt military conflict. In the global chess game with the Soviets, the United States now had a wonderful new instrument that—so it seemed—worked without a hitch. The national security establishment began to rely on paramilitary operations and other forms of covert action as a panacea to treat Marxist infections wherever they broke out. Similar pressure came from *the CIA's worldwide network of foreign agents (or assets),* known as the **infrastructure** or the "plumbing," used for both intelligence collection and covert actions. These individuals, admits a CIA insider, were not beyond fabricating various CA schemes "to make themselves appear busy and worth their keep."[51]

Yet the short list of early CIA covert action successes soon grew into a disheartening list of failures: the Bay of Pigs, Indonesia, Laos, and Vietnam, among others, as well as the bungled assassination plots. Some of the schemes appeared as if they had been written for the theater of the absurd. For example, the Agency planned to incite rebellion against Castro with fireworks shot from submarines off the coast of Havana late at night. Accompanying the fireworks display would be the dropping of leaflets over Cuba by CIA aircraft, announcing that Christ had come and Cubans should rise up against the anti-Christ, Fidel Castro. The Kennedy White House quickly scotched this madcap "Elimination by Illumination" proposal.

## LIMITS FOR COVERT ACTION

Some observers are enthusiastic about the quiet option, regardless of setbacks like the Bay of Pigs. They point to its early achievements in Western Europe, Latin America, and Laos; or to the Agency's support for the *mujahedeen* in driving the Soviets out of Afghanistan; the routing of the Taliban and Al Qaeda in Afghanistan soon after the 9/11 attacks; and the Obama administration's drone offensives against terrorists.

Others, though, have expressed serious reservations about the value of covert action. For critics, paramilitary operations and other CAs have amounted at best to the rather limited harassments of foes—modest help here and there for a few, chiefly Third World friends, and some efforts to curb terrorism and narcotics trafficking (with very limited outcomes against the drug lords). Overall, since 1947 covert actions have usually been modest in scope, as in Nicaragua where the *contras* proved to be little more than an annoyance to the Sandinista regime; or even trivial, such as the propaganda operations aimed at small nations.[52] Sometimes these operations have been wildly overdrawn, as with the Bay of Pigs invasion; or they have created a vacuum filled by heinous new leaders.

The US-backed coup to install the Shah (king) of Iran in 1953, for instance, led to the establishment of a cruel regime. In 1979, a revolution overthrew the Shah and produced a fundamentalist religious government—the world's first theocracy in the modern era—that is still at odds with the United States today. The Guatemalan coup of 1954 led to a series of repressive governments in the wake of the CIA intervention. As journalist Anthony Lewis writes, "The coup began a long national descent into savagery."[53] In the wake of Lumumba's death came a ruthless leader supported by the United States, Joseph Mobutu, who stripped the Congo of wealth for his own personal aggrandizement.[54] That the United States could have gotten by without the modest operations is plausible; that American foreign policy would have been better off without the overdrawn ones is persuasive. The latter have failed most of the time, opponents argue, at the cost of much money and—of greater importance—America's reputation as a nation more honorable than its communist or terrorist adversaries.[55]

Yet the temptation to resort to secret power in foreign affairs has remained strong. "As you look ahead to the next ten or twenty years, we don't know when another kind of political crisis might arise in the world," Colby once argued, "and I think it is better that we have the ability to help people in these countries where that will happen, quietly and secretly, and not wait until we are faced with a military threat that has to be met by armed force."[56] Quoting a conclusion reached by the Murphy Commission on Foreign Policy in 1974 (chaired by career diplomat, Ambassador Robert D. Murphy), Colby told Senate investigators in 1975 that "there are many risks and dangers associated with covert action. . . . But 'we must live in the world we find, not the world we might wish.' Our adversaries deny themselves no forms of action which might advance their interests or undercut ours. . . . In many parts of the world a prohibition on our use of covert action would put the U.S. and those who rely on it at a dangerous disadvantage . . . therefore . . . covert action cannot be abandoned."[57]

Other high-level witnesses appearing before the Congress have also acknowledged the necessity of maintaining a covert action capability; but they have emphasized that this approach should be adopted only in carefully restricted circumstances. "The guiding criterion," advised Clark Clifford, former Secretary of Defense and an author of the National Security Act of 1947 that created the CIA, "should be the test as to whether or not a certain covert project *truly affects* our national security."[58] Cyrus Vance, who would soon become Secretary of State in the Carter administration, emphasized to a congressional committee that he believed "it should be the policy of the

United States to engage in covert actions only when they are *absolutely essential* to the national security."[59]

## A LADDER OF ESCALATION FOR COVERT ACTION

In 1965, strategist Herman Kahn of the Hudson Institute published an influential volume in which he offered an "escalation-ladder metaphor" for understanding the coercive features involved in the overt use of force in international affairs. Kahn described the ladder as a "convenient list of the many options facing the strategist in a two-sided confrontation."[60] In a comparable ladder of escalation for covert actions (see Figure 12.2), the underlying analytic dimension traveling upward is the extent to which the options are increasingly harsh violations of international law and intrusions against national sovereignty. As the examples illustrate, covert actions can run the gamut from the routine to the extreme.

### Threshold One: Routine Covert Actions

At the lower end of the ladder for covert actions—Threshold One—are arrayed such relatively benign activities as support for the routine sharing of information (intelligence liaison, based on collection and analysis) between the CIA and friendly foreign intelligence services. These secret liaison conversations are usually about potential global "hot spots," or rogue nations and groups that may warrant some form of covert action in the future (Rung 1). Also at this threshold are attempts to recruit covert action assets from native populations, who are quite often the same individuals tapped for collection activities (Rung 2). At this threshold, as well, is the limited dissemination of truthful, noncontroversial propaganda themes (Rung 3) directed against closed, authoritarian societies (such as extolling to Iranians the benefits of better relations with the West that would occur if their leaders would abandon a nuclear-weapons program). These low-rung activities are commonplace in international affairs.

### Threshold Two: Modest Intrusions

With Threshold Two, the degree of intrusiveness against another country or group begins to escalate beyond the routine and the risks increase. This category would include the insertion of truthful, noncontroversial propaganda material into the media outlets of democratic regimes with a free press (Rung 4)—covert action against likeminded governments. Further, within this zone would be the payment of modest sums to political, labor, intellectual, and other organizations and individuals aboard who are favorably disposed toward, say, America's counterterrorist foreign policy objectives (Rung 5), and willing to quietly help.

### Threshold Three: High-Risk Operations

Threshold Three consists of controversial steps that could trigger within the target nation a response significantly damaging to international comity. At Rungs 6 and 7, propaganda operations remain truthful and compatible with overt policy statements; but now the themes are contentious and are disseminated into media channels within

*Threshold Four: Extreme Options*

29. Use of WMDs
28. Major secret wars
27. Assassination
26. Small-scale coups d'etat
25. Major economic dislocations; crop, livestock destruction
24. Environmental alterations
23. Pinpointed covert retaliations against non-combatants
22. Torture to gain compliance for a political deal
21. Extraordinary rendition for bartering
20. Major hostage-rescue attempts
19. Sophisticated arms supplies

*Threshold Three: High-Risk Options*

18. Massive increases of funding in democracies
17. Small-scale hostage rescue attempt
16. Training of foreign military forces for war
15. Limited arms supplies for offensive purposes
14. Limited arms supplies for balancing purposes
13. Economic disruption without loss of life
12. Modest funding in democracies
11. Massive increases of funding in autocracies
10. Large increases of funding in autocracies
 9. Disinformation against democratic regimes
 8. Disinformation against autocratic regimes
 7. Truthful but contentious propaganda in democracies
 6. Truthful but contentious propaganda in autocracies

*Threshold Two: Modest Intrusions*

 5. Low-level funding of friendly groups
 4. Truthful, benign propaganda in democracies

*Threshold One: Routine Operations*

 3. Truthful, benign propaganda in autocracies
 2. Recruitment of covert action assets
 1. Support for intelligence collection

SOURCE: the author's estimates, based on interviews with intelligence managers and officers over the years, along with a study of the literature cited in the notes of this chapter. Adapted from Loch K. Johnson, *Secret Agencies: U.S. Intelligence in a Hostile World* (New Haven, CT: Yale University Press, 1996), pp. 62–63.

*Figure 12.2*
A Partial Ladder of Escalation for Covert Actions

both (respectively) nondemocratic and democratic regimes—say, reporting that Taliban soldiers have sprayed acid into the faces of young girls on their way to school in Afghanistan or killed international aid workers in Pakistan (both true). At Rungs 8 and 9 (maintaining the distinction between nondemocratic and democratic regimes), propaganda activities take a nastier turn, employing deception and disinformation that run contrary to one's avowed public policies—say, falsely blaming an adversary for an assassination attempt or fabricating documents to damage an adversary's reputation.

Even propaganda operations against a nation without a free media are of concern here because of the blowback that can deceive citizens in the democratic regimes.

Rungs 10 and 11 reflect first a large, and then a massive, increase in secret funding for political purposes within an autocratic regime. Rung 12 stands for an escalation based on relatively modest levels of secret funding to affect elections, but this time within a democratic regime—a much more questionable step.

At Rung 13, the use of covert action involves attacks against economic entities within a target nation: a power line is destroyed here, an oil depot contaminated there; a virus or "worm" is inserted into the computer infrastructures of a foreign government; labor strikes are encouraged inside an adversary's major cities. The measures are carefully planned to remain at the level of harassment operations, with a low probability that lives will be lost; nonetheless, a nation at this rung on the covert-action ladder has entered into a realm of more forceful operations.

A nation resorts to paramilitary operations at Rung 14: the supply of arms to counter weapons previously introduced into the target nation by an adversary, perhaps accompanied by routine training. This is a major step upward, for now an intelligence service has brought guns into the equation. An intelligence agency might provide a modest arsenal of unsophisticated, but nonetheless deadly, arms to a favored rebel faction, as a means for balancing the correlation of forces in a civil war (as the CIA did in Syria during 2012–2013). At Rung 15, weapons are supplied to a friendly faction without the predicate of prior intervention by an outside adversary (Libya, 2011–2012). Rung 16 goes further still, with the training of foreign armies or factions for the express purpose of initiating combat. A hostage rescue attempt is envisioned at Rung 17, one that could well lead to the loss of life—although designed to be small in scale so as to limit the potential for fatalities.

At Rung 18, massive expenditures are dedicated to improve the political fortunes of parties friendly to the United States within a fellow democratic regime, say, $40 million in a small democracy and $100 million or more in a larger one. The objective is to bring the foreign faction into power that is likely to be most allied with one's own nation. For some critics, this amounts to a troubling attempt to tamper with electoral outcomes in free societies; for proponents, it is simply an effort to make the world a better place by aligning nations along a compatible democratic axis. Attempts at covert influence against truly democratic elections (say, Chile in the 1970s)—those in which the rights of political dissent and opposition are honored—represent a clear-cut violation of the noninterventionist norm (and related rules of international law) and have little claim of legitimacy, in contrast to lower-rung operations directed against self-interested autocratic regimes.

## Threshold Four: Extreme Options

With Threshold Four, a nation enters an especially dangerous and contentious domain of covert action: a secret foreign policy "hot zone." Here is where the lives of innocent people are apt to be placed in extreme jeopardy. At Rung 19, the types of weapons provided to a friendly faction are more potent than at earlier rungs, say, Stinger and Blowpipe antiaircraft missiles or UAVs armed with Hellfire missiles that enable the faction to take the offensive against a common adversary. At Rung 20, a nation might attempt an elaborate hostage rescue operation that could well entail extensive casualties, even if that was not the intention (Iran, 1980—the Argo Operation). Rung 21 involves an extraordinary rendition—the kidnapping of a hostage. In this case, force is intended, carefully planned, and directed against a specific individual. Depending on the intent, this approach might fall into the bailiwick of a collection or counterintelligence operation; but if the purpose is to use the hostage as pawn in secret negotiations toward some policy objective, then it becomes covert action.

Rising up another step, a hostage might be tortured in an attempt to coerce compliance in a hostage swap or some other secret deal (Rung 22). On the next rung (23), acts of brutality are directed against lower-level noncombatants in retaliation for a hostile intelligence operation—say, the rendering and torturing of a terrorist's relative in payback for a raid carried out by the terrorist cell (said to be a Russian specialty).

On the highest rungs, covert action escalates dramatically to include violence-laden environmental or economic operations, as well as paramilitary activities against targets of wider scope than is the case at lower levels on the ladder. Large numbers of noncombatants in the civilian population may become targets, whether planned or inadvertent. For example, the covert action may try to bring about major environmental alterations (Rung 24), from the defoliation or burning of forests to the contamination of lakes and rivers, the creation of floods through the destruction of dams, and operations designed to control weather conditions through cloud seeding in hopes of ruining crops and bringing about mass starvation. At Rung 25, the covert action aggressor attempts to wreak major economic dislocations within the target nation by engaging in the widespread counterfeiting of local currencies to fuel inflation and financial ruin, by sabotaging industrial facilities, or perhaps by destroying

An MQ-1 Predator unmanned aerial vehicle (UAV).

crops through the introduction of agricultural parasites like Bunga into the fields, or by spreading hoof-and-mouth disease or African swine fever among livestock.

Rung 26 has the covert action aggressor adopting even higher stake operations: overthrowing a foreign regime, though with minimal intended bloodshed (as in Iran in 1953 or Guatemala in 1954). The next step, Rung 27, arrives at the level of the assassination plot against specific foreign leaders or terrorists and includes, in recent years, the use of Predators and Reapers as the instruments of murder—with all the risks these

operations carry of incurring civilian casualties. At the top of the escalation ladder are two forms of secret warfare that inevitably affect large numbers of combatants and noncombatants: the launching of protracted, full-blown paramilitary warfare against an inimical regime. At Rung 28, the covert action perpetrator provides combat-ready intelligence officers to guide and arm indigenous rebel armies, comparable in scope to the CIA's covert war in Laos during the 1960s. Finally, at Rung 29, a nation introduces WMDs into the covert action calculus—nuclear, biological, chemical, or radiological arms meant to inflict widespread death in the population of the target nation (operations never carried out by the United States).

## AN EVALUATION OF COVERT ACTION

Some covert actions have been more useful than others. Perhaps the best case can be made for selected propaganda operations to spread the truth where America's adversaries would sow lies, and operations designed to combat genuine terrorism and the narcotics trade. The routing in Afghanistan of the Taliban regime and its Qaeda allies after the 9/11 attacks offers an illustration of an effective, well-run covert action. In this instance, the CIA operated in harness with local anti-Taliban warlords (the Northern Alliance) and were supported as well by military Special Operations Forces and overt bombing by the US Air Force. Moreover, even most critics of covert action agree that the United States must have a paramilitary capability for extreme circumstances, say, to thwart a terrorist nuclear attack against this nation.

The critics of America's secret power are persuasive, however, in their central theme: adoption of covert action whenever someone, somewhere, is a nuisance to this nation runs counter to America's democratic beliefs in fair play and usually ends in a waste of lives, money, and esteem. For example, former president Carter has been highly critical of US drone attacks. "Top intelligence and military officials," he writes, "as well as [human] rights defenders in targeted areas, affirm that the great escalation in drone attacks has turned aggrieved families toward terrorist organizations, aroused civilian populations against us and permitted repressive governments to cite such actions to justify their own despotic behavior."[61]

Covert action can also lead to the decline of constitutional government within the United States, as demonstrated by the attempts of the NSC staff and a few CIA officials in the Reagan administration to bypass Congress—and evidently even the president—in their conduct of the Iran-*contra* caper. In that controversial set of operations, the government violated US law, including an arms embargo against Iran and a statute that *banned covert action to support the contras in Nicaragua* (the **Boland Amendment**, sponsored by House Intelligence Committee Chairman Edward P. Boland, D-Massachusetts).[62] Despite the setback of the Iran-*contra* scandal in 1987, the intelligence oversight procedures put in place a decade earlier by the Church Committee and the Ford administration have led to dramatic improvements in the supervision of America's secret foreign policy. These new procedures warrant a closer look.

# COVERT ACTION DECISION MAKING

Since the passage of the **Hughes–Ryan Act** on December 31, 1974, *the president must approve all important covert actions and inform the Congress of these decisions.* Both requirements were radical departures from earlier practice and provide yet another example—this time in the domain of intelligence—of the ongoing, constitutionally based tug-of-war between the executive and legislative branches over the control of American foreign policy. The law's provisions required that

> No funds appropriated under the authority of this or another Act may be expended by or on behalf of the [CIA] for operations in foreign countries, other than activities intended solely for obtaining necessary intelligence, unless and *until the President finds* that each such operation is important to the national security of the United States *and reports*, in a timely fashion, a description and scope of such operations to the appropriate committees of the Congress (emphasis added).

From the verb "finds" in this act came the term **finding**, that is, *the president's formal approval for a covert action.* The "appropriate committees," to whom this finding was to be delivered "in a timely fashion" (within twenty-four hours was the understanding, based on the legislative colloquy that accompanied floor debate on the proposal), were initially three in the House of Representatives and three in the Senate: the committees on appropriations, armed services, and foreign affairs in both chambers. In 1976, lawmakers added a Senate intelligence committee to the list and, in 1977, a House intelligence committee. At this point, to make reporting more manageable, the Congress by its own internal rules trimmed back the list for covert action reporting to just the two new Intelligence Committees and, for funding purposes, a small subcommittee on each of the Appropriations Committees.

In 1980, the Intelligence Accountability Act, usually referred to simply as the **Intelligence Oversight Act of 1980,** made the change in reporting more explicit: findings would be reported to the Senate Select Committee on Intelligence (SSCI) and the House Permanent Select Committee on Intelligence (HPSCI). This 1980 statute, *the most important formal measure taken by Congress to strengthen its control over intelligence operations,* had the further effect of emphasizing that lawmakers on SSCI and HPSCI wanted to be informed of *all* important intelligence activities—not just covert actions sponsored by the CIA. This stipulation sought to close a loophole in the Hughes–Ryan Act that made it possible for a president to call on other agencies (presumably the military) for covert action and other sensitive intelligence operations, as a way of avoiding the Hughes–Ryan reporting requirements.

Moreover, with this statute the Congress took a firm stand in favor of prior (*ante facto*) notification of covert actions—not just after the fact (*ex post facto*), as the

Hughes–Ryan phrase "timely fashion" had allowed (these reporting time frames were discussed in Chapter 10). In emergency situations, the new law permitted a president to limit prior notice to eight leaders in Congress—the so-called Gang of Eight—with the expectation that the full intelligence committees would be briefed by the DCI or the Gang of Eight as soon as possible. The wording of the statute on the *ante facto* phase of reporting to lawmakers is quite clear on the point that this Gang of Eight approach would be used only in the rarest of circumstances:

> If the President determines it is essential to limit prior notice to meet extraordinary circumstances affecting the vital interests of the United States, such notice shall be limited to the chairmen and ranking minority members of the intelligence committees, the Speaker and minority leader of the House of Representatives, and the majority and minority leaders of the Senate.[63]

Yet during the Iran-*contra* scandal, President Reagan ordered the CIA not to report to Congress at all on his finding that approved a controversial sale of arms to Iran. Reagan also used just an oral authorization, rather than the written approval anticipated by (but never spelled out precisely) in the Hughes–Ryan Act. The question of when to report to SSCI and HPSCI remained a matter of dispute, which lawmakers attempted to resolve with passage of the **Intelligence Oversight Act of 1991**. This law *updated the Hughes–Ryan Act, defined covert action more exactly, required a presidential signature for authorization (no oral findings), and reinforced the 1980 oversight statute by again requiring the president to report in advance on covert actions whenever possible— although continuing to allow the White House a Gang-of-Eight escape hatch in "extraordinary circumstances."* In times of emergency, the understanding was that the reporting on a covert action finding would be delivered to the full congressional intelligence committees "within a few days." For some critics, this new law seemed a troublesome retreat from the principle of prior notice, but the language was generally considered to mean that the full committees would be informed within forty-eight hours, and that in all but the most unusual circumstances *ante facto* reporting would remain the rule.[64]

Still, controversy persists. The George W. Bush and the Obama administrations have both balked at reporting on some intelligence operations, including covert actions, to the full Intelligence Committees, preferring instead to deal just with the Gang of Eight—or fewer lawmakers, perhaps a Gang of Four or even just whispering secrets into the ears of the SSCI and HPSCI chairs. Often, the executive branch has demanded that SSCI and HPSCI staff leave the room during covert action and other sensitive briefings, leaving lawmakers who may have limited intelligence expertise faring for themselves. The whole purpose of staff is to provide members with expertise so members of Congress can more fully and accurately appraise a proposal from the executive branch. In response to these efforts to constrict briefings to only a few, some lawmakers vowed to insist on full reporting to SSCI and HPSCI, including the presence of some staff.[65] In 2010, the Intelligence Authorization Act passed by Congress required the president to report covert action findings to the full membership of SSCI and HPSCI—a reemphasis of the provisions in the 1991 Intelligence Oversight Act. Additional questions have arisen about whether the Pentagon has crept into the covert action business, taking advantage of the cloudy language of the 1991 Oversight Act that defines the boundaries of covert action and evading the expected decision and reporting procedures that had been set up for the CIA with passage of the Hughes–Ryan Act in 1974.[66]

## Executive Branch Decision Procedures

Most covert action proposals originate in CIA stations overseas, as well as from within the Special Activities Division and the Special Operations Group at Agency Headquarters in Langley, Virginia. Occasionally important proposals, such as the improper Iran-*contra* operations, germinate from within the NSC itself. The typical covert action recommendation advances through the Agency hierarchy as depicted in Figure 12.3. Prior to gaining final approval within the CIA, covert action proposals are reviewed by a variety of offices at the Agency, including the Office of the D/CIA, the Comptroller, the Office of General Counsel, the Legislative Counsel, and the Intelligence Directorate. Moreover, covert propaganda is coordinated with the State Department's overt information programs. Covert action proposals are also reviewed by the DNI, as well as a panel of NSC staff experts, before going to the back to the D/CIA for a final scrub and advancement to the Oval Office for the president's consideration.

The NSC staff panel, known as the "covert action working group," is responsible for subjecting each covert action proposal to an acid bath of criticism. In this forum, a high percentage of the proposals are rejected outright, or, in most cases, at least sent back to the CIA for clarifications or modifications. In preparation for this review by the working group, the Agency has to make sure that its proposals address several points: justification for the project; expense; alternatives; risks; prior coordination with other relevant government agencies, such as DOD; past related activities; and whether the proposal is important enough to require presidential review and congressional reporting. During these reviews, the questions of risk, compatibility with American foreign policy goals, likelihood of success, value of outcome, cost, and the prevailing political climate all weigh in the balance.

The NSC working group is not a decision committee; within the executive branch, only the president has the authority to approve important covert actions. Rather, it acts as a staff advisory panel. If a covert action is supported at this level (typically following one or more revisions) as well as by the DNI and the D/CIA, it goes to the deputy secretaries who serve the four NSC principals. These deputies examine the merits of the covert action and submit a policy recommendation, along with their comments and dissents (if any) to the president, the vice president, the secretary of State, and the secretary of Defense. An approval by the president—a finding—is then reported to the Congress, or, more exactly, to SSCI and HPSCI. This reporting

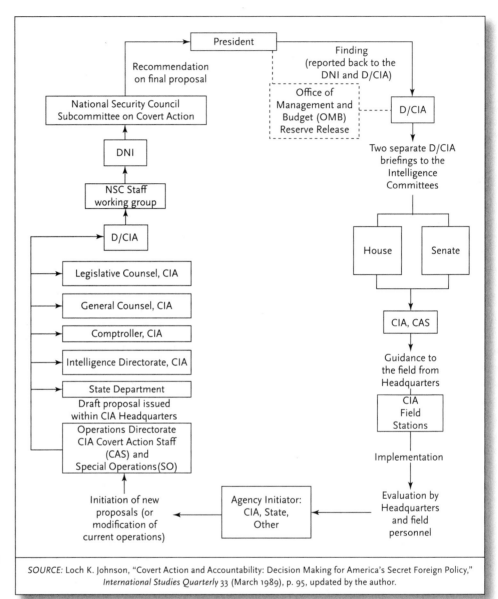

*Figure 12.3*
The Decision Pathway
for Covert Action
Since 1974

SOURCE: Loch K. Johnson, "Covert Action and Accountability: Decision Making for America's Secret Foreign Policy," *International Studies Quarterly* 33 (March 1989), p. 95, updated by the author.

provision applied only to the CIA until passage of the 1980 Intelligence Oversight Act, at which time it applied to all government "entities" engaged in significant intelligence activities, including the Pentagon if it were to contemplate involvement in a covert action, and to the NSC staff that improperly skirted these provisions during the Iran-*contra* affair.

## Reporting to Congress

The DNI or, more commonly, the DNI's designee (typically the D/CIA) is responsible for reporting to members of SSCI and HPSCI about all new findings. The reporting takes place before both of the Intelligence Committees, which are briefed separately. The finding document itself is usually short and often ambiguous. If individual law-makers on the oversight committees wish to receive further details, they must pose questions at the briefing. The quality of these briefings has varied, usually depending on how interested SSCI and HPSCI members are in asking questions (recall the deter-mination of Representatives Aspin and Mazzoli related in the introduction to Chapter 8), and how astute these questions and follow-ups prove to be.

The most well-known example of a poor briefing—and poor questioning by com-mittee members, too—occurred in1984. In his report to SSCI on Agency covert ac-tions in Nicaragua, DCI William J. Casey slid over the fact—all too quickly and in an obscure mumble for which he was notorious—that the CIA had escalated its operations to include the mining of Nicaraguan harbors. President Reagan had approved this find-ing earlier in the year, but at least some members of the Senate committee remained unaware of the risky operation, which endangered not only Nicaraguan vessels but also international shipping. Apparently, the Agency had briefed HPSCI reasonably well, thanks to persistent questioning by a few members of that panel. When the full Senate Committee met, however, only one sentence in a briefing that lasted over an hour dealt with the mining. In the days that followed, DCI Casey tried to deflect questions on the subject by flatly denying that Nicaraguan *harbors* had been mined. Only later did sena-tors discover this was merely a semantic subterfuge; Casey had relied on a technical distinction that the CIA had mined *piers* within the harbors.[67]

Not even the SSCI chairman, Barry Goldwater—usually an unerring supporter of CIA operations—had heard and understood the reference to the mining. Later, when he learned of the subterfuge from a member of his Committee who had looked into the matter further, Goldwater was furious. He sent a letter to Casey, which said, in part, "It gets down to one little, simple phrase: I am pissed off!"[68] It may be true that Casey, with his succinct reference to mining, had honored the letter of the law; but, as a former DCI, Stansfield Turner, concluded, "hardly the intent. . . . The CIA did go through the motions of informing, but it wasn't speaking very loudly."[69]

## Legislative Prerogatives

Briefings on findings are supposed to be provided, by law, whenever a covert action is approved and, by custom, whenever a "significant change" to an existing covert action is made. Following a briefing on a finding, SSCI and HPSCI members face a decision about how to react to a covert action already approved by the president and on the brink of implementation, if not already under way. Under current law, the Intelligence Committees are not authorized to formally approve or disapprove a finding; the DNI is required only to report the finding to SSCI and HPSCI and, by tradition, then report back to the White House on any dissent. The failure of lawmakers to dissent is widely regarded within the executive branch as tacit approval of the finding by the Congress. This kind of briefing, therefore, takes on a greater significance than other CIA appearances on Capitol Hill; SSCI and HPSCI, which meet in their respective chambers, must decide whether to place their tacit approvals and their reputation behind each covert action finding.

If SSCI and HPSCI members are unhappy with a covert action, they have a number of options available to them. One or more members may voice reservations during the briefing and ask the DNI to make these objections known to the president. Obviously the larger the number of those objecting, the more serious the negative response is taken by the White House. Exactly who is objecting is important, too; if the dissenters include the chair of the committee, or worse yet for the executive branch, the chair *and* the ranking minority member, this amounts to serious opposition. To emphasize their seriousness, one or more members of the Intelligence Committees might formally write—or even pay a visit—to the president or the national security adviser, underscoring why they believe the operation is ill-advised. Further, one of the Committees, or both, may decide to take a formal vote on a finding, as a way of registering clearly the opinion of members. Lawmakers on SSCI and HPSCI have done this on a few occasions, and at least twice a negative formal vote by SSCI caused a president to rescind his approval of a covert action. One instance reportedly involved the renewal of funding for the Christian Democratic Party in Italy.[70]

So even though the Congress has no legal role in the formal approval of covert actions, it has a tacit opportunity to oppose a finding. This latent "veto" power may be ignored by a president, but the White House may then have to pay a political price. The president must work with the Intelligence Committees in the future; and the CIA must come to them many times each year for budgetary requests, as well as for other items of business—at least since 1975, when Congress began to insist on greater involvement in the shaping of intelligence initiatives. The members of SSCI and HPSCI, especially the senior leadership on these panels, are not good enemies for the White House, the DNI, or the D/CIA to make. As designed by the Constitution, the power of the purse held by Congress remains a potent corrective to uncooperative behavior in the executive branch. In 1978, the Senate Intelligence Committee terminated one covert action during the panel's review of the CIA's annual budget request simply by striking the monies designated for it.[71]

The Intelligence Committees may also take their opposition to their parent chambers, which by the rules of Congress can meet in secret session to hear such matters—although such meetings are rare because it is unlikely that an operation would remain "covert" for long with so many people knowing about it (535 members of Congress). Nevertheless, as illustrated by the Boland Amendment to limit covert action in Nicaragua in the 1980s, Congress occasionally reaches a point of sufficient frustration over some intelligence operations that a majority of its members are prepared to hold a debate in the full Congress. Here is a chance for the entire legislative membership to vote up or down on a "covert" action—*an erstwhile secret operation* that, at this point, is likely to become an **overt-covert action**. This is exactly what happened in the case of the Boland Amendment, which was supported by a majority in the Congress during a secret session, resulting in the termination of covert actions in Nicaragua—and sending the Reagan administration secretly underground in its illegal creation and financing of a covert action capability outside the framework of government and the Constitution's appropriations process.

Then, too, a lawmaker could privately tip off the media about a proposed covert action briefed to SSCI and HPSCI—an improper "leak item veto" that could stop the operation dead in its tracks by revealing operational details on the front page of the *New York Times*. Members of Congress have rarely stooped to this level of an unauthorized release of classified information. A HPSCI member, Robert G. Torricelli (D-New Jersey), however, did reveal classified information to the media in 1995 about CIA intelligence-collection operations in Guatemala, which he opposed on moral grounds because one of the Agency's assets was a suspected murderer.[72] His fellow HPSCI members strongly criticized Torricelli's behavior and he was ostracized by most House members for this inappropriate action. He nevertheless managed to win a US Senate seat from New Jersey; but, during his first term, Torricelli was convicted of campaign fraud and sent to prison.

## Accountability versus Micromanagement

The decision-making process for covert action has matured since 1975 into a complex matrix of checkpoints and overseers—too much so from the perspective of some intelligence professionals. "What we have is covert action by national consensus!" complained a deputy director for operations (DDO) in the CIA in 1984.[73]

Covert action decisions can be time consuming, exhausting, and agonizing. In one instance involving a terrorist hijacking of an airplane in the 1970s, a counterterrorist team in a NATO country requested help from the CIA. The team sought expert advice from the United States on how to blow open the door of the airliner without harming passengers inside, a skill the CIA and only one other Western intelligence agency had developed to a high degree. A CIA station in the NATO country cabled headquarters for permission to help with this covert action. Hours passed. Finally, over two days later, with still no decision from the United States, the NATO nation turned to the other Western intelligence agency, which responded affirmatively over the telephone on the first call. Within a few hours, paramilitary commandos from that country were en route to the hijacked plane and soon blew off the door and rescued the passengers and crew in a remarkably successful counterterrorist operation.[74]

For some intelligence professionals, the conclusion to be drawn is self-evident: US intelligence has been paralyzed, or at least maimed, by the oppressive layers of decision makers and overseers brought on by congressional inquiries and investigative journalism run wild in the 1970s. These intelligence bureaucrats lament what they refer to as **micromanagement**—*too many executive and legislative policy makers with their clumsy* *fingers in the fine wheels of covert action and other delicate intelligence operations best left to the pros.*

A strong case can be made, though, that too much discretion has existed in some parts of the intelligence chain of command—Senator Church's concern in 1975 that the CIA had become a rogue elephant. In 1983, Representative Boland similarly observed, after chairing HPSCI for six years, that the Agency was "almost like a rogue elephant, doing what it wanted to do."[75] These harsh judgments came from a deep sense of dissatisfaction over what senior lawmakers found to be dangerous Agency excesses: in the instance of Church, the assassination plots with underworld connections; the use of covert action against a democratic regime (Chile); domestic spying (Operation Chaos); and the Agency's sequestering of shellfish toxins despite a presidential order to destroy them.  In the instance of Boland, which occurred before the revelation about the Iran-*contra* operations, the HPSCI Chairman discovered that the CIA was attempting to circumvent his amendment to limit paramilitary operations in Nicaragua. Further, supporters of the higher level of intelligence accountability on Capitol Hill (instituted with the creation of SSCI and HPSCI in 1976 and 1977, respectively) note that the procedures of Hughes–Ryan and subsequent oversight statutes do not prevent the president, the bureaucracy, and the Congress from responding to threats quickly in a crisis. For example, all the approval points outlined in Figure 12.2 can be addressed over secure telephone connections and completed within hours.

DCIs William H. Webster (1987–1991) and Robert M. Gates (1991–1993) succeeded in improving the CIA's relations with SSCI and HPSCI after they were badly torn asunder by the Iran-*contra* scandal. Webster's reputation for integrity and experience—he had also directed the FBI—helped restore trust between Congress and the Hill; and Gates received high marks for sharing intelligence with lawmakers. During Gates's tenure, the Agency provided Capitol Hill with more than 1,000 briefings and over 7,000 intelligence reports each year. Nevertheless, conscientious members of Congress continue to wonder whether "rogue elephants" still might be roaming around CIA Headquarters, or perhaps inside other US intelligence agencies or out in the field. Certainly the 2005 scandal about NSA warrantless wiretaps, along with the controversies over secret CIA prisons, extraordinary rendition, and the use of torture, has raised serious questions about how properly the secret agencies are behaving—and how well they are being supervised by members of Congress and the NSC.

Again, in 2013, the disclosures by Edward J. Snowden about the wide scope of NSA's intelligence collection of US telephone and social media records has led lawmakers to question this data dragnet approach, in contrast to the legitimate intelligence targeting of specific terrorist suspects. Pressure began to mount on Capitol Hill, even among loyal supporters of the Intelligence Community, to draw back the NSA into a more acceptable range of data collection related narrowly just to targets of a federal terrorism investigation.

On its side, the Intelligence Community continues to have concerns about congressional oversight. For example, former DCIs Gates and Turner raised questions about the quality of supervision provided by the two oversight committees. "Very few members appear to devote much time to their intelligence oversight responsibilities," Gates once observed, chastising lawmakers for rarely visiting the CIA and for delegating their duties to staff aides. He was appalled, too, that the SSCI devoted only a single meeting to approve the annual intelligence budget for 1993–1994, with only one member of the Senate—the Committee Chairman David L. Boren (D-Oklahoma)—even bothering to stay for the whole meeting. Similarly, Turner gave legislative overseers a B grade "at best," and he declared that there is "no greater need than to sort out the problems of oversight."[76] Other officials in the IC have complained that the Congress is too involved in intelligence review—the micromanagement argument. Moreover, DNI James R. Clapper, Jr. argued in 2013 that the wide scope of NSA collection against American telephone and social media accounts was necessary to fight global terrorism.

Addressing the anemic state of intelligence oversight as perceived by Gates and Turner, a subsequent DCI, William H.Webster, undertook a campaign to ensure that intelligence officers briefed their legislative overseers regularly and fully, in the spirit of power sharing advocated in the language of the Constitution. The CIA's Office of Congressional Affairs prepared an internal document, entitled "Briefing Congress," which included the requirement that Agency officers follow "the four C's" in their relations with lawmakers: candor, completeness, consistency, and correctness. Gates also repeatedly emphasized the necessity for dealing openly with the SSCI and HPSCI. "We have learned that law and oversight are totally compatible with our responsibilities to protect our sources and methods," he told the American Law Institute in the spring of 1992, for example. In *Perspectives on American Foreign Policy* 12.1, Gates comments further on intelligence oversight as a valid method for controlling possible future abuses of power by America's espionage agencies—although he continued to wish that SSCI and HPSCI members would be more involved in their review of intelligence activities.

Congress has no direct authority to approve covert actions and other sensitive intelligence operations; nevertheless, the very requirement of reporting to lawmakers on these activities serves as a deterrent against the kind of zany proposals that surfaced within the intelligence bureaucracy more easily in the past (recall "Elimination by

---

## PERSPECTIVES ON AMERICAN FOREIGN POLICY 12.1

**ROBERT M. GATES on intelligence accountability:**

Some awfully crazy schemes might well have been approved had everyone present not known and expected hard questions, debate, and criticism from the Hill. And when, on a few occasions, Congress was kept in the dark, and such schemes did proceed, it was nearly always to the lasting regret of the Presidents involved.

*SOURCE:* Reprinted with the permission of Simon & Schuster Publishing Group from *From the Shadows: The Ultimate Insider's Story of Fire Presidents and How They Won the Cold War* by Robert M. Gates. Copyright © 1996 by Robert M. Gates. All rights reserved.

Illumination"). A major source of congressional influence over covert action is the **law of anticipated reactions** that political scientist Carl Friedrich knew to be so vital in all executive–legislative relations. *The potential for a negative legislative reaction to a proposal from the executive branch can have a sobering effect on bureaucrats who must obtain annual funding from the Congress, thereby by causing them to bring their requests more in line with likely legislative expectations.* If a sufficient number of lawmakers on SSCI or HPSCI—presumably a majority, or at least an intense minority—object to a particular operation, a prudent chief executive will have second thoughts about moving forward with the plan.

Still, even with the then-new statutes in place (Hughes–Ryan in 1974, followed by the 1980 and 1991 Intelligence Oversight Acts), the Reagan administration managed to evade these safeguards and draw parts of the intelligence community into the Iran-*contra* scandal, the low point in President Reagan's otherwise remarkable tenure. This scandal underlines a lesson as old as Greek civilization and the writings of Plato and Aristotle: government is only as good as the individuals who control it. This places a heavy burden on citizens to vote for men and women of high integrity, in hopes that they—and the bureaucrats and staff they hire—will honor constitutional principles and the rule of law.

## INTELLIGENCE AND PROPRIETY

In the aftermath of the Iran-*contra* scandal, Congress crafted new oversight legislation to further tighten its supervision over the nation's secret agencies. For example, in 1989 lawmakers enacted an Inspector General Act, which strengthened the authority of the CIA inspector general and made that office accountable to the Senate through confirmation hearings and mandatory biannual reports. Then the Congress passed the Intelligence Oversight Act of 1991, bringing at least some improved understanding of the boundaries for covert action and emphasizing that lawmakers expected prior notice on all covert actions, except in times of emergencies when a two-day delay in reporting to the full Intelligence Committees would be tolerated.

Debate continues, just as during the Cold War, over whether "bright lines" (limitations) ought to exist when presidents turn to America's secret agencies to achieve America's foreign policy goals. Realists and idealists squared off on this subject during the 1980s and their respective arguments are still heard in Washington, DC. Dr. Ray Cline, a former high-ranking CIA official, represented the realist school. "We are already engaged in a protracted secret war against the Soviet Union," he declared. As a result, America needed to get on with the business of winning the war, using covet action wherever and whenever it might aid this objective. "The United States is faced with a situation in which the major power opposing our system of government is trying to expand its power by using covert methods of warfare," Cline continued, asking rhetorically, "Must the United States respond like a man in a barroom brawl who will fight only according to Marquess of Queensberry rules?"[77]

In contrast, an idealist, George W. Ball, undersecretary of state during the Kennedy and Johnson administrations, underscored the importance of world public opinion,

---

### PERSPECTIVES ON AMERICAN FOREIGN POLICY 12.2

**DCI WILLIAM H. WEBSTER'S** guidelines for evaluating the merits of a proposed covert action:

- Is it legal [according to U.S. law]?
- Is it consistent with American foreign policy and, if not, why not?
- Is it consistent with American values?

- If it becomes public, will it make sense to the American people?

*SOURCE:* Remarks, Aspin–Brown Commission staff interview (1996); see Loch K. Johnson, *The Threat on the Horizon: An Inside Account of Intelligence Reform Between the End of the Cold War and 9/11* (New York: Oxford University Press, 2010), p. 281.

---

image, and morality in foreign policy. "In principle I think we ought to discourage the idea of fighting secret wars or even initiating most covert operations," he argued. "When the United States violates those principles—when we mine harbors in Nicaragua—we fuzz the difference between ourselves and the Soviet Union. We act out of character, which no great power can do without diminishing itself. . . . When we yield to what is, in my judgment, a childish temptation to fight the Russians on their own terms and in their own gutter, we make a major mistake and throw away one of our great assets."[78] Toward the idea of honoring some limits on covert action, DCI Webster held the CIA to the set of guidelines presented in *Perspectives on American Foreign Policy* 12.2.

An important current debate concerns the use of drones for CIA paramilitary operations. Sometimes suspected terrorists have been blown to pieces by Hellfire missiles fired from Agency drones without knowing exactly who the targets are or establishing their guilt beyond a reasonable doubt—the glory of American judicial philosophy. For example, in 2002 a Predator killed six men in an automobile that was racing across a desert in Yemen; only later did US authorities learn that one of the passengers was an American citizen. In 2011 and 2012, President Obama himself specifically ordered the killing of Qaeda leaders in Yemen, at least two of whom were American citizens.[79] As the constitutional framers would have advocated, foreign policy decisions—even in the hidden domain of America's secret agencies—should be subject to the judgment of more than one branch of government.

## SUMMARY

In addition to the gathering, analysis, and coordination of information, national security intelligence involves the use of covert action. This approach to American foreign policy objectives entails the secret interference in the affairs of other countries or factions by the CIA, usually at the order of the White House. Covert action may take the form of secret propaganda, political manipulation, economic disruption, and paramilitary operations (including assassinations).

The paramilitary operations of the CIA illustrate the widespread attraction that America's secret power has had over presidents throughout the years. The United States has carried out these warlike activities around the globe, including murder plots against Fidel Castro of Cuba and Patrice Lumumba of Congo; arms shipments to a host of insurgents; training to foreign intelligence services; large-scale secret wars, like the one against communist guerrillas in Laos during the 1960s; and, today's most prominent and lethal form of paramilitary covert action, drone attacks against terrorists. In combination with other forms of covert action, the United States has also used the paramilitary option in an attempt to topple unfriendly regimes. The most widely documented case is Chile, where from 1958 to 1973 the CIA carried out extensive secret operations designed to undermine the presidential candidacy of Salvador Allende and then, once he was elected anyway, the viability of his regime.

In the years since 1974, the decision process for covert action has grown complex, with new checks and balances and a vigorous role for lawmakers as intelligence over-seers. Criticism has arisen within the intelligence agencies over whether these proce-dures have become too intricate ("micromanagement"), thereby crippling the ability of America's secret agencies to act with speed and effectiveness against ruthless adver-saries abroad. In the spirit of James Madison, reformers maintain, however, that the checks and balances are necessary to keep the CIA and the other secret agencies within the Constitution and the rule of law, and that the new system can still move quickly and effectively when necessary.

The Iran-*contra* affair during the 1980s revealed anew the risk of secret opera-tions for constitutional government. Officials on the NSC staff and at the top reaches of the CIA secretly diverted funds from a covert arms sale agreement with Iran to finance legally banned paramilitary operations in Nicaragua. Contrary to established reporting requirements, neither the arms sale nor the diversion of funds to Central America—both covert actions—were reported to Congress. Apparently, even Presi-dent Reagan was excluded from an awareness of the diversion of funds, so he could plausibly deny knowledge of the operation if it came to light. Moreover, the NSC staff sought funding for the Nicaraguan counterrevolutionaries (the *contras*) from private sources, including wealthy conservative Americans and friendly foreign gov-ernments. This privatization of American foreign policy raised serious questions of propriety in the minds of critics who viewed this approach as tantamount to an attack against the constitutional underpinnings of American government, especially Congress's power of the purse.

The debate over how to balance the effectiveness of the nation's secret agencies with the need to ensure their accountability continues today, with scandals erupting in 2005 over warrantless national-security wiretaps conducted by the George W. Bush administration (in violation of the Foreign Intelligence Surveillance Act of 1978) and, in more recent years, over the use of torture and other questionable prac-tices by the CIA and military intelligence agencies against suspected terrorists. In 2013, fresh concerns arose over a NSA program disclosed by computer specialist Edward Snowden, which entailed the gathering of all the telephone and social media records of American citizens.

## KEY TERMS

blowback (replay) p. 373
Boland Amendment (1983) p. 388
covert action p. 370
economic covert action p. 374
finding p. 389
Hughes–Ryan Act (1974) p. 389
infrastructure p. 382
Intelligence Oversight Act of 1980 p. 389
Intelligence Oversight Act of 1991 p. 390
law of anticipated reactions p. 398

micromanagement p. 395
Operation Mongoose (1961–1963) p. 378
overt-covert action p. 395
Phoenix program (Vietnam War) p. 381
plausible deniability p. 379
rogue elephant p. 379
paramilitary covert action p. 375
political covert action p. 373
secret propaganda (perception enhancement) p. 372
special operations (special ops) p. 376

## QUESTIONS FOR DISCUSSION

1. How could the Iran-*contra* affair have occurred, in light of the many new intelligence oversight rules that were in place at the time?
2. Where is your own personal "bright line" for impermissible covert actions on the ladder of escalation presented in this chapter?
3. To what extent does the doctrine of plausible deniability have merit as a policy position today?
4. Compare the reporting requirements in the major intelligence oversight laws. Is the Gang of Eight a sufficient forum for reporting? Or should the full memberships of the SSCI and HPSCI be included,

as required by the Intelligence Oversight Acts of 1980 and 1991?
5. How could the United States guard against the negative effects of blowback?
6. What can be done to restrain "rogue elephants" in the Intelligence Community?
7. Has the decision process for covert action become too democratic, thus undermining necessary secrecy and speed of action required for effective intelligence operations?
8. Should the United States use drone attacks against its enemies? Against American citizens overseas who may be critical of US foreign policy? Who should authorize such attacks?

## ADDITIONAL READINGS

Coll, Steve. *Ghost Wars*. New York: Penguin, 2004.
Cohen, William S. and George J. Mitchell. *Men of Zeal: A Candid Inside Story of the Iran-Contra Hearings*. New York: Penguin, 1988.

Johnson, Loch K. *America's Secret Power*. New York: Oxford University Press, 1989.

For further readings, please visit the book's companion website.

### CHAPTER 13

# Economic Statecraft

**A KING BUYS A SPECIAL AIRPLANE**

King Abdullah of Saudi Arabia opened the personal letter brought to his Jeddah office in 2006 by a high-ranking official in the US Department of Commerce. Signed by President George W. Bush, the letter came straight to the point: the King should consider modernizing the Saudi Arabian Airlines (SAA) fleet, as well as the royal family's own private planes. The President suggested the purchase of 43 Boeing jets for SAA and thirteen jets for the family. The King laid down the letter. "I am instructing you to tell the President and all concerned authorities," His Royal Highness said politely to the American envoy, "that I would like to have all the technology that my friend, President Bush, has on Air Force One." Should the

A Boeing 747 belonging to Saudi Arabian
King Abdullah.

**CHAPTER OUTLINE**

United States consent to provide the King with the same advanced telecommunications and security equipment for his jet as enjoyed by the President of the United States, then, continued His Royal Highness, "God willing, I will make a decision that will please you very much."

The King's response sent US diplomats scurrying to see if his wishes could be met. The deal with Saudi Arabia held out the promise of billions in profits for Boeing, a Washington State manufacturer that earns some 70 percent of its commercial airplane profits from foreign sales. The fact was not lost on officials in Washington, DC that every $1 billion in sales abroad translates into an estimated 11,000 jobs in America. The proposal urged by President Bush could amount to sales of over $3 billion. Yet, in the era of globalization, US manufacturers confront stiff competition. Boeing knew its chief rival, Airbus of France, was also attempting to woo the Saudi King into buying jetliners. It was up to President Bush and his diplomatic corps—the US government's sales force—to close the deal with King Abdullah.

At least the King's request might be easier to satisfy than a demand from Bangladesh's Prime Minister, Sheik Hasina Wazed. In exchange for purchasing Boeing airplanes, Ms. Hasina wanted guaranteed landing rights for Biman Bangladesh Airlines at Kennedy Airport, a facility already overcrowded. "If there is no New York route, what is the point of buying Boeing?" she reasoned, according to State Department officials. Or there was the Turkish government, which insisted that one of its

**LEARNING OBJECTIVES AND CONSTITUTIONAL ISSUES**

**By the end of this chapter, you will be able to:**

- *Describe the setting in which economic policy is decided, one characterized by institutional fragmentation at home and a relative decline of America's influence abroad.*

- *Identify the specific instruments of economic power, including negative economic sanctions as well as positive economic inducements.*

- *Assess the role of foreign aid as an instrument of economic influence in America's relations with other countries.*

**THIS CHAPTER RAISES THE FOLLOWING CONSTITUTIONAL QUESTIONS:**

- Modern international trade can be highly technical and legalistic. Does the expertise of bureaucrats in the departments of State, Treasury, and Commerce trump participation by generalists in Congress when it comes to international statecraft?

- Was it a mistake for lawmakers to place limits on their role in international trade agreements—and their constitutional prerogatives—by introducing "fast-track" procedures in Congress for this policy domain?

- What is the relationship between multinational corporations based in the United States and the US Constitution? Do MNCs operate outside of the constitutional framework? Should they?

- Has international economic policy making become too fragmented inside the United States, carrying power sharing to an unworkable extreme?

astronauts be allowed to join a NASA space flight in the near future—or maybe no Boeing jet sales.

King Abdullah got his request for an aircraft "upgrade." Now there would be a Saudi Air Force One in the royal hanger. In return, President Bush received a pleasant letter back from the King: Saudi Arabia would buy twelve 777-300ER airliners immediately, with options for ten more. Make that $3.3 billion on the Boeing cash register, and counting. Bangladesh and Turkey brought Boeing planes, too, even though their specific requests went unfulfilled. They were provided with other inducements, however, such as technical help with the Turkish astronaut program. "That is the reality of the 21st century," said the undersecretary of economic affairs at the State Department, Robert D. Hormats, looking back at the Saudi transaction. He added, "Governments are playing a greater role in supporting their companies, and we need to do the same thing."[1] ⌇

## TRADE AS AN INSTRUMENT OF AMERICAN FOREIGN POLICY

An examination of trade as an instrument of America's foreign relations must begin with a description of the setting in which international commerce takes place. This setting has evolved in recent decades into a much more complex array of market relationships than was true immediately after World War II—an important aspect of globalization, defined earlier in this book as economic and other forms of growing interdependence among nations. In the words of an economic analyst, "A debt crisis in Greece can lead to a sudden panic on Wall Street."[2] The US-based Xerox Corporation gave substance to this warning in 2012 when its shares fell dramatically after reports of an economic meltdown in some countries of the European Union, where it has business relationships. Unemployment rates soared in Greece to 20 percent and in Spain to 25 percent, as both nations (and Italy close behind) confronted an economic crisis.

With globalization has come intense competition for the United States in the international marketplace. Whether Americans are able to respond effectively to this rivalry has become one of the great issues of American foreign policy. In the final cabinet meeting of the Carter administration, the President asked the departmental secretaries to reflect back on what each had learned during his or her time in office. The Secretary of Defense, Harold Brown, replied: "I learned that if you don't have sustainable economics, you will not have a good defense. They go together. If we want to be strong, it begins with a good economy."[3] Few, if any, cabinet members since then would disagree with this assessment.

The United States faces a harsh economic reality in world affairs. America's trade deficits oscillated between $130 billion and $150 billion as the Cold War ended, dropping to $81 billion in 1993. By 2008, however, the figure had risen again dramatically to $865 billion. According to one report, about nine out of ten Christmas presents opened around the tree in America during the 1950s were made in the United States; today that number is less than half.[4] This trade imbalance was made all the more worrisome by the cloud of economic distress that has come to be referred to as the Great Recession, beginning in 2008 and still ongoing.

The balance of international trade, as always, proved highly sensitive to the price of oil in the world, which climbed in 2009 and further set back American efforts to tame its trade deficit. Urged by the US Chamber of Commerce to take quick action, the Obama administration vowed to double this nation's exports by 2015 and thereby create two million new jobs at home, a goal easier to announce than to achieve—although by 2014 this goal was well on its way to being met. The administration made impressive strides on the oil front, with the United States becoming an oil exporter for the first time ever in 2012, thanks to new oil-drilling technologies used to tap America's own oil deposits. The International Energy Agency (IEA, an energy alliance of wealthy nations) predicted that the United States would become the world's largest oil producer by 2020, surpassing Saudi Arabia and Russia.[5]

## A Portrait of US Trading Practices

A look at overall world trade patterns in the mid-1980s reveals that most of the globe's commercial activities resided within the Western industrialized nations. Some 42 percent of the total world exports and imports took place within the circle of these market economies, as did over 50 percent of US trade. These twenty-three nations also had a combined percentage of total exports and imports tallying about 9 percent with the 113 developing nations outside **OPEC** (the *Organization of Petroleum Exporting Countries, a global oil cartel*), 6 percent with OPEC (13 countries), and only 3 percent with the struggling economies of the former Soviet bloc (12 countries).[6] For the United States, though, the non-OPEC developing world—home for three-quarters of the world's population—was a more significant trading region than these overall figures suggest. These nations supplied the United States with such essential resources as tin, rubber, bauxite, and oil. They were also the fastest growing markets for US exports, accounting for more than Japan and the European Economic Community (EEC) combined.

Despite a relative decline in the past two decades, the United States remains by far the single largest international trader, engaging in commercial transactions with all the countries of the world. Imports into the United States have consisted primarily of consumer goods, automobiles, and fuels. Looking back at the evolution of the US trade profile, petroleum imports alone accounted for 30 percent of total imports into the United States in 1977. In 1984, though, oil imports dropped to 17 percent of the total, as a global recession forced down OPEC oil prices. Moreover, OPEC members proved unable to hold prices high as a disciplined cartel; and other sources of oil, the North Sea among them, became available.[7] In 1981, Saudi Arabia, the leading OPEC producer, earned almost $100 billion in oil revenues; in 1986, just $18 billion.[8] By 2008, however, the value of Saudi petroleum exports had spiraled upward again to $283 billion, and the United States had increased its dependence on imported petroleum to the tune of 57 percent of the annual total world consumption. These outlays represented a hemorrhaging of US wealth to the Middle East, until recent advances in drilling at home led America toward greater oil self-sufficiency.

The United States relies on imports most notably when it comes to the following products: passenger motor vehicles; wearing apparel; iron and steel; consumer electronics; nonferrous metals; footwear; trucks and buses; coffee, tea, and spices; natural gas; paper; telecommunications equipment; alcoholic beverages; toys and sporting goods; and fish. For some imports, the US domestic economy provides no alternative products, as is the case for nonsynthetic diamonds and coffee (with the exception of a small amount of coffee beans grown in Hawaii). In the opposite direction, American exports consist primarily of food products, chemicals, and machinery. The United States enjoys significant trade surpluses in some goods, including cereals and grains, aircraft equipment and spacecraft, oilseeds, computers, coal, scientific and engineering equipment, military arms and vehicles, construction equipment, plastic and rubber, cotton, animal feed, tobacco, power generating equipment, organic chemicals, and pharmaceutical products.[9]

## North and South of the Border

Among the various economic ties between the United States and the rest of the world, the most significant relationships are with Canada and Mexico within the Western Hemisphere, and with China, Japan, and Germany outside the Western Hemisphere.

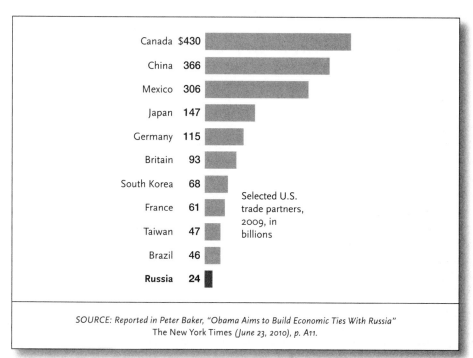

*Figure 13.1*
Examples of U.S. Trade Balances, 2009 (in billions of U.S. dollars)

SOURCE: Reported in Peter Baker, "Obama Aims to Build Economic Ties With Russia" The New York Times (June 23, 2010), p. A11.

Canada exports more to the United States than to any other country and, in return, takes in 20 percent of all US exports. The merchandise trade (exports plus imports) between the two nations totaled $430 billion in 2009. In contrast, US-Japanese merchandise trade summed to only $147 billion that year, and US merchandise trade with the leading European economies of Germany, Britain, and France added up to just $169 billion.

A look at US trade balances with selective countries from 1985 to 2009 is provided in Figure 13.1 and Table 13.1. The data in Figure 13.1 indicate a wide range of trading relations in 2009, from the robust in the case of Canada to the more limited transactions with Russia; and Table 13.1 illustrates the evolution of trading patterns over more than two decades (1985–2008), with US trade imbalances increasing with almost every nation and trading alliance—and especially with Europeans and OPEC traders. The exception is US trade with the Newly Industrialized Countries (NICs), which include Brazil, China, India, Malaysia, Mexico, Philippines, Thailand, and Turkey.

Trading relations between Russia and the United States took a step backward in 2012. The Congress finally repealed a thirty-eight-year ban that had punished the Soviet Union because of its restrictive emigration rules. This action appeared to be a conciliatory measure; however, lawmakers subsequently approved new legislation that chastised the Russian human rights record and barred any Russian citizens designated as violators of human rights from traveling to the United States. Furthermore, the financial assets in the United States of violators would be frozen. In response, Russian President Putin signed a law prohibiting the adoption of Russian children by American citizens. Here were additional bumps in the road of US-Russian relationships (see Chapter 10). Advised a former State Department official, "Russia behaves like Russia.

*Table 13.1*
Examples of US Trade Balances, 1985–2008 (in Billions of US Dollars)

| | Time Period | | | | | | |
|---|---|---|---|---|---|---|---|
| **PARTNER** | **1985** | **1986** | **1987** | **1992** | **1998** | **2003** | **2008** |
| Canada | −17.8 | −14.9 | −13.8 | −15.0 | −16.6 | −51.7 | −78.3 |
| EC/EU | −20.9 | −25.2 | −22.9 | 5.5 | −27.3 | −93.1 | −110.2 |
| Japan | −46.6 | −59.0 | −57.1 | −48.9 | −64.0 | −66.0 | −74.1 |
| NICs | −33.3 | −37.2 | −44.8 | −12.3 | −22.7 | −21.2 | 2.2 |
| OPEC | −11.2 | −9.1 | −13.1 | −10.9 | −8.7 | −51.1 | −177.7 |
| Other | −0.5 | −6.4 | −6.3 | −7.7 | −107.6 | −264.4 | −402.1 |
| Worldwide | −130.5 | −158.2 | −158.2 | −99.4 | −246.9 | −547.5 | −840.2 |

*SOURCES: Years 1985–1992: Adapted from US Department of Commerce figures compiled in "Composition of the U.S. Merchandise Trade Deficit,"* International Economic Review, *Office of Economics. US International Trade Commission, March 1988, p. 23, and March 1993. Years 1998–2008, Report FT900, 1998, 2003, and 2008. Bureau of the Census, Foreign Trade Division, Final.*

Russia pursues its own hard-core national interests, That is realpolitik. We should desentimentalize our relations."[10]

Although the US-Canadian trade volume has declined relative to the entire portfolio of US global trading transactions in recent years, this commercial partnership

| YEAR | CHINESE EXPORTS TO U.S. | CHINESE IMPORTS FROM UNITED STATES |
|------|------|------|
| 1980 | 982 | 3,755 |
| 1981 | 1,505 | 3,602 |
| 1982 | 1,764 | 2,912 |
| 1983 | 1,713 | 2,173 |
| 1984 | 2,312 | 3,004 |
| 1985 | 2,336 | 3,855 |
| 1986 | 2,632 | 3,106 |
| 1987 | 3,030 | 3,497 |
| 1988 | 3,398 | 5,016 |
| 1989 | 4,413 | 5,807 |
| 1990 | 5,313 | 4,807 |
| 1991 | 6,197 | 6,287 |
| 1992 | 8,598 | 7,469 |
| 1993 | 16,976 | 8,767 |
| 1994 | 21,421 | 9,286 |
| 1995 | 24,743 | 11,748 |
| 1996 | 26,730 | 11,977 |
| 1997 | 32,743 | 12,805 |
| 1998 | 38,000 | 14,258 |
| 1999 | 42,003 | 12,943 |
| 2000 | 52,161 | 15,963 |
| 2001 | 54,395 | 19,234 |
| 2002 | 70,063 | 22,052 |
| 2003 | 92,633 | 28,418 |
| 2004 | 125,155 | 34,721 |
| 2005 | 163,348 | 41,836 |
| 2006 | 203,898 | 55,224 |
| 2007 | 233,181 | 65,238 |
| 2008 | 252,786 | 71,457 |

*SOURCES: International Monetary Fund, Department of Trade Statistics.*

*Table 13.2*
US-China Trade, 1980–2008 (in Millions of US Dollars)

*Table 13.3*
A Profile of US Trading
Partners, November 2012

| Total Trade (Goods) | | |
| --- | --- | --- |
| RANK | COUNTRY | PERCENT OF TOTAL TRADE |
| 1 | Canada | 16.2% |
| 2 | China | 14.0% |
| 3 | Mexico | 13.0% |
| 4 | Japan | 5.7% |
| 5 | Germany | 4.1% |
| 6 | United Kingdom | 2.9% |
| 7 | Korea, South | 2.7% |
| 8 | Brazil | 2.0% |
| 9 | Saudi Arabia | 1.9% |
| 10 | France | 1.9% |
| 11 | Taiwan | 1.6% |
| 12 | India | 1.6% |
| 13 | Netherlands | 1.6% |
| 14 | Venezuela | 1.5% |
| 15 | Italy | 1.4% |

SOURCE: Top Trading Partners, *US Census Bureau, Department of Commerce (Washington, DC: November 2012).*

remains of great importance to both nations. South of the border, Mexico's prominence is reflected in its standing as the fourth largest export market for the United States, strengthened by the passage of the NAFTA. The most noteworthy change in US trading partners is the increasingly high profile of China, as displayed in Table 13.2. A profile of the chief trading partners for the United States in 2012 is offered in Table 13.3.

## Mosel Wine and BMWs

Although China, Germany, and Japan are among the most valued trading partners of the United States, they have also loomed since the end of the Cold War as economic competitors. With over 30 percent of their GNP generated by international trade, China and Germany depend heavily on an open world economy. At its foundation, the US-West German trading relationship during the Cold War rested on the exchange of American military protection against possible Soviet aggression in return for West German guarantees of US access to the lucrative EEC markets for goods and investment. Today, Germans and other Europeans no longer have to fear a Soviet invasion; and many of their economies—Greece, Spain, and Italy to the contrary—have flourished since the establishment of the single EEC market made "Western Europe the most populous, most productive, and richest industrial community on earth"—which it remains today.[11]

## China Rising

China, the world's most populous nation, surpassed Japan in 2010 to become the world's second-largest economy. Some forecasters warn of an inevitable clash between the United States with its democratic principles but slow economic growth rate, on one hand, and China, with its illiberal political system and vibrant economy, on the other hand. A once comfortable argument that liberal democracy will trump authoritarian regimes on the march into modernity has been questioned by many observers around the world who are impressed by the powerful Chinese economic model. Indeed, many small and middle-sized developing nations—such as Cambodia, Kenya, and Vietnam—have been drawn more toward the Chinese than the American model in recent years.[12]

Beyond these profound philosophical differences about the proper form of governance, several issues have troubled the US-Chinese trade relationship, including fierce competition over the worldwide sale of automobiles, automobile parts, solar panels, and a host of other commodities.[13] China has also been uncooperative in meeting US requests for access to rare minerals mined in China—substances that are indispensable to modern technologies. Nevertheless, the United States and China are not necessarily on a collision course. Many observers see the possibilities for vigorous trade between the two that could benefit both sides. Currently, the trade deficit balance greatly favors China, but this imbalance is adjusting toward more of an equilibrium. Buick, for example, is now the top selling automobile in China and Kentucky Fried Chicken is the most popular restaurant.[14] American exports to China ran at about $180 billion a month in 2012, up from $140 billion a month in 2010.[15]

America's trade with China has been complicated by Beijing's policy of holding down the value of its currency, the renminbi. As the *New York Times* reported in 2010: "China buys dollars and other foreign currencies—worth several hundred billion dollars a year—by selling more of its own currency, which then depresses its value. That intervention helped Chinese exports to surge 46 percent in February compared with a year earlier."[16] The renminbi's fixed and artificially cheap exchange rate has a ripple effect on the rest of the world's economic development, as the cheapness of China's currency undercuts the exports of other countries and thereby accelerates global trade and financial imbalances. Exports from China to the United States continue to outpace imports by more than four to one (Table 13.2). As 2010 came to an end, the US trade deficit with China was $66.2 billion.[17] Economist Joseph E. Stiglitz noted ironically that the United States is the world's largest recipient of foreign aid because this nation borrows money from its own treasury by printing dollars, then selling these dollars to China and using the "profits" to buy foreign goods from China.[18] In response to such criticisms, Chinese officials have agreed to readjust the renminbi–although that assurance has been heard many times before.[19]

Xi Jinping, Vice President of China, visits the China Shipping Terminal at the Port of Los Angeles in 2012.

Despite its stunning economic growth rates that have pulled millions of Chinese from the depths of poverty and into middle-class status, China is (in the words of *New Yorker* writer John Cassidy) still a pretty poor place, with a per-capita GDP of about three thousand dollars in 2008. By 2050, according to a recent study from the Carnegie Endowment, this figure will rise to about thirty-three thousand dollars, which would place China roughly where Spain is today.[20] Moreover, writes a London *Times* correspondent who covers China, everyday life in the world's most populous nation is characterized by turmoil: "the mélange of cultures in its cities, the violent uprisings of its peasants, the factional struggles in its leadership, the pollution in the air, the gridlock on the streets, the bubbly economy and the corrupt bureaucracy."[21] The remarkable economic growth in China since the end of the Cold War could well be slowed, or even reversed, by these internal strains in the coming years.

## PROTECTIONISM VERSUS FREE TRADE

Negative trade statistics, plus the loss of sales to US manufacturers and the loss of jobs, traditionally cause a tide of **protectionism** to swell in company towns across America; that is, support for *the use of government tariffs and quotas against imports as a means of protecting US industries from foreign competition*. In the 1980s, President Reagan steadfastly defended a policy of **free trade**, that is, *the removal of government tariffs or other restrictions on international commercial transactions*. Like his successors, though, he applied behind-the-scenes pressure on the Japanese and other nations to buy more US products.

In contrast, one of 1988's leading presidential contenders, Representative Richard Gephardt (D-Missouri), ran chiefly on a protectionist platform. More recently, in 2008, presidential candidate Barack Obama successfully used protectionist appeals in Ohio and other primary states to garner votes from workers in anguish over the decline of jobs and earning power. With a sense of frustration toward Beijing's trade policies, President Obama placed a tariff of up to 35 percent on automobile tires imported from China in 2010. The World Trade Organization upheld the tariff, on grounds that competition from China threatened to seriously harm the US tire industry.[22]

## GATT

The George H. W. Bush and the Clinton administrations found themselves in the thick of a protectionist versus free trade crossfire. The Uruguay session of **GATT** (the **General Agreement on Tariffs and Trade,** commonly referred to as *a trade "round" where over one hundred nations have participated in talks about international commerce between 1947 and 1994,* revealed sharp disagreements over international trade in 1992 and 1993, even among allies. Agricultural subsidies presented a major headache for negotiators. French farmers, a well-organized group with no qualms against using violent protests at home to underscore its demands, steadfastly rejected GATT-imposed reductions in agricultural subsidies from the French government; and American negotiators balked at a GATT proposal that the United States cut its highest tariffs, such as those on textile goods, by over 30 percent. The debates seemed to carry on endlessly about the proper production levels for everything from oilseeds to bananas and rice, not to mention industrial goods. As always, the GATT talks were haunted, on one hand, by the specter of electoral defeat at home if major interest groups were angered, and, on the other hand, by the even more unsettling possibility of a global trade war if the diplomats failed to reach a workable compromise.

One reason the Uruguay round was more contentious than earlier GATT negotiations had to do with the session's swollen membership: 117 nations, up almost fivefold since the first GATT round in Geneva in 1947. Further, the Uruguay round may have been too ambitious, involving tariff discussions on such topics as services, textiles, intellectual property, and—the major sticking point—agriculture, all of which had been left out of earlier GATT talks. Additional points of friction included the uncertainty of the American presidential elections (coming near the end of the round), along with a shadow of concern about a worldwide recession. Despite these difficulties, the Uruguay round came to a reasonably successful conclusion in the waning days of 1993. After seven years of tortuous negotiations, the GATT membership struck an agreement in favor of an onward march toward liberalized trade. In an unprecedented move, the negotiators endorsed the inclusion of agriculture, services, textiles, and investments under the international rules of fair trade. Japan even agreed to import rice, over the strenuous objections of its own rice growers.

## NAFTA

In the Western Hemisphere, President George H. W. Bush's North American Free Trade Agreement, a 1,100-page proposal to improve trading relations among the United States, Canada, and Mexico, also became a source of controversy. Bush argued in favor of the pact in 1991 on grounds that "a NAFTA offers an historic opportunity to bring together the energies and talents of three great nations . . . [and to] create jobs and promote growth in the United States." Yet many people in the United States, labor unions not the least, feared that US companies—jobs—might move south of the border in search of cheap labor. Others warned that Mexico would fail to uphold the strong environmental standards of the United States, or its laws regulating labor standards and worker rights.

Throughout 1993, the NAFTA debate brought trade policy to center stage in Mexican, Canadian, and US political discourse. When he followed the first Bush into the presidency, Bill Clinton took up the NAFTA cause and energetically worked to win over Republicans into a supportive coalition with Democrats on Capitol Hill. Finally, in 1993, the Congress approved the statutory agreement, which promised an opening up of markets in North America among the three NAFTA countries that together account for $6.6 trillion in exports and imports. So far the judgment on NAFTA is mixed, but tipping toward "favorable."

The Bush and Obama administrations pursued additional Free Trade Agreements (FTAs) in Latin America, such as the Central American Free Trade Agreement (CAFTA), signed as a statutory agreement by President Bush in 2002. It established better trade relations among Costa Rica, El Salvador, Guatemala, Honduras, Nicaragua, and the United States (and added the Dominican Republic in 2004). Similar free-trade agreements are envisioned between the NAFTA nations and Europe. In 2013, Mexico has already entered into such an agreement; Canada was close to signing on; and the United States is engaged in negotiations to this end.

Southwest Asia has been another thorny domain on trade questions. One of most important allies for the United States in the struggle against Al Qaeda is Pakistan, as the leading figures of this terrorist organization are reportedly burrowed into its northwest mountains. Yet protectionism has gotten in the way of this relationship. Textiles are Pakistan's major industry and the United States is its most important trading partner. Washington refused to grant duty-free access for Pakistani imports, however, at the same time America's leaders asked the Pakistani military to die in battles against Al Qaeda and radical Taliban warriors.[23] This sticking point, along with CIA drone raids that violate Pakistani airspace and sometimes kill local noncombatants, have contributed significantly to the 82 percent anti-American opinion in Pakistan reported in a recent survey.[24]

## THE UNITED STATES: NO LONGER THE SOLITARY ECONOMIC BEHEMOTH

A relative decline in America's share of the international market was to be expected, as the Germans, the Japanese, and the Chinese (among others) began to rebuild their economies after World War II. Several additional influences have contributed, though, to America's declining global economic prowess in recent decades.

Among the reasons for America's relative decline in world trade has been the drain on US trade balances stemming from, first, the domestic consumption of foreign oil and, second, various overseas market barriers faced by American exporters. Sometimes these barriers take the form of formal import tariffs and quotas; more often, they are less visible and, therefore, more insidious. These hidden **nontariff barriers (NTBs)** include *local "buy national" campaigns; inspection requirements; customs valuation procedures; industrial and environmental standards; domestic content stipulations; and* *distribution intricacies, along with legal and language idiosyncrasies.* Japan's distribution system is particularly complex and antiquated. Several of these barriers are imposed by foreign nations in an attempt to block free trade with the United States. Japan appears guilty of this charge with such commodities as tobacco and citrus fruits, although negotiations since the end of the Cold War have led to some Japanese NTB reductions. Moreover, Japan's production of some of its automobiles in the United States, along with the making (under license) of more US products in Japan—Budweiser beer for one—has eased the bilateral trade tensions and Japan is now America's fourth largest trading partner. This evolution in Japanese trading relations is hardly unique; for example, several other countries now assemble their automobiles in the United States, including German BMWs and Mercedes and South Korean Hyundais and Kias.

American businesspeople could mitigate some trade barriers with additional effort, such as greater devotion to the study of the distribution system in China and Japan, along with a determination to learn the languages of these two important nations. In Manhattan, hundreds of Chinese and Japanese businesspeople can be found negotiating deals in perfectly acceptable English, while probably less than a hundred of their American counterparts are similarly engaged in Beijing speaking Chinese or in Tokyo speaking Japanese.[25]

The competitive edge of the United States for high-technology products is also eroding. Whereas this nation remains the chief exporter of high-tech products, the advanced industrialized nations are closing rapidly. "Forty percent of the college graduates in Japan and West Germany are in engineering and the sciences, compared with 16 percent here," cautioned one observer in 1989, adding, "In the 1970s, we generated 75 percent of new science and technology; in the 1990s, we will generate only about one third, and a majority of our effort goes into the military."[26] This trend of falling behind other countries in the sciences seems to be continuing, as suggested by an international comparison of educational standards. The United States came in twenty-third or twenty-fourth in most subjects during a worldwide test in 2010, including average math scores that put this nation's students below thirty other countries.[27]

## ECONOMIC FRAGMENTATION AT HOME AND ABROAD

The world economic scene in the twenty-first century is characterized by a plethora of organizations trying to provide leadership in a fragmented international setting. What follows is a list of institutions and movements—some old, some new—that have garnered increased importance:

- *International Monetary Fund (IMF).* Created by the Bretton Woods agreement in 1944 (at a meeting of nations at the retreat in New Hampshire bearing this name), the **International Monetary**

**Fund**'s *chief responsibility has been to maintain international monetary stability.* The resources of the IMF, contributed by members as an initiation fee, are used as a revolving fund. Its significance has been magnified in recent years as a primary hope of financial support for the developing nations. Among a wide range of activities, the IMF makes short-term loans to aid countries with balance of payment deficits. In 2010, for example, the IMF provided Greece with a 120 billion euro loan over three years to ease a growing European debt crisis (to little avail). The Fund's charter requires borrowing nations to adopt economic discipline at home in return for loan support.

• *General Agreement on Tariffs and Trade (GATT).* As discussed earlier in this chapter, GATT is a multilateral trade treaty entered into by twenty-three nations in 1947. It soon became the main code of conduct for international trade accepted by most nations in the world.

• *World Trade Organization (WTO).* One of the most important global economic organizations, the WTO was founded in 1995 for the purpose of absorbing and expanding on the GATT. It has three major responsibilities in today's multilateral trading system: to serve as a center where rules guiding commercial transactions are kept; as a forum to seek ongoing reductions in trade barriers; and as neutral judge to arbitrate trade disputes between nations. American critics of the WTO worry that it might seek to undermine national sovereignty by deciding trade disputes against the interests of the United States. So far, however, WTOs decisions have been widely viewed as impartial and legitimate. Sometimes the United States has won disputes before WTO judges, and sometimes it has lost. In 2011, the Obama administration began an investigation into whether China had violated the WTO's free trade rules with its extensive subsidies to the manufacturers of solar panels. The subsidies had successfully tempted a major US company, Ever Green Solar, to move its production facilities from Massachusetts to China, resulting in a loss of 800 jobs in the United States.[28]

• *International Bank for Reconstruction and Development (IBRD, or World Bank).* Another Bretton Woods institution that remains important as a loan bank and source of technical assistance for developing nations, the World Bank is a key source for economic statistics from countries around the world.

• *Organization for Economic Cooperation and Development (OECD).* Established in 1961, the OECD has a membership of twenty-two industrialized market economies of North America, Europe, and the Far East. Among its objectives are the economic development of its member states, assistance to the Third World and the Fourth World (the very poorest nations with per capita income below $200), and increased world trade.

- *European Union (EU)*. An organization of twelve European nations dedicated to economic integration based on the euro currency, the EU has a combined economy larger than that of the United States (as measured by national output using current exchange rates).

- *Asian Pacific Economic Cooperation (APEC)*. This organization of twenty-one member nations was formed in 1989 with an eye toward creating a Pacific economic infrastructure, with improved transportation and environmental protection high on the agenda. The membership of APEC includes Canada, the United States, Chile, Mexico, Peru, Russia, and many Asian Pacific nations from China and Japan to Australia and New Zealand.

- *G-8*. This group is made up of the economically strongest democracies in the world—Britain, Canada, France, Germany, Italy, Japan, the United States, and (the most recent member) Russia—who gather for influential annual economic discussions and planning.

- *G-20*. Founded in 1999, this group of twenty finance ministers and central bank governors from the world's leading nations and the European Union—accounting for 80 percent of international trade—meets regularly to promote global financial stability. Since 2009, the group has permanently replaced the G-8 as the world's foremost economic forum.[29] Its 2010 session in Toronto focused on accelerating the economic recovery from the worldwide recession that began in 2008. The members endorsed a goal of a 50 percent reduction in government deficits by 2013, as well as a stabilization of the ratio of public debt to GDP by 2016.[30] In 2012, the G-20 met in Mexico with the problems of EU economic instability high on the agenda. The results were modest, with German Chancellor Angela Merkel balking at the suggestion that her government should engage in more spending to alleviate Europe's debt crisis.[31]

This is only a partial listing of organizations. In addition, various nations have established (among other examples) an African Development Bank; an Asian Development Fund; the Inter-American Development Bank; a UN Industrial Development Organization; a Food and Agriculture Organization (FAO); and, within the government of the United States, an Agency for International Development (USAID) and an Overseas Private Investment Corporation (OPIC, which provides risk insurance for American development projects in poorer nations).

A McDonalds in Xuchang City, located in central China's Henan province.

The challenge for these organizations and initiatives is to maintain the prosperity of the industrialized nations while, at the same time, bringing the fruits of modern affluence to the developing nations. This will require an economic tide able to lift all the boats of the world, a Herculean task that presently is guided more by the dreams of idealists than a carefully designed plan.

## The Multinationals

The international economic system is made all the more complicated by the existence of **multinational corporations (MNCs)**, companies *"with foreign subsidiaries which extend the production and marketing of the firm beyond the boundaries of any one country."*[32] The MNCs grew up in the postwar era as a product, in part, of the global revolution in transportation and communications; it became technically possible for businesses to have ties that stretched around the globe. A car sold in the United States can have component parts from a dozen other nations.

The effects of the MNCs have been much debated. Some observers view them positively as benign contributors to world trade; others see them as the spearhead of imperialism. Most political economists, though, look on the MNC as an inevitable outcome of globalization, with some good and some bad effects. In market economies like Canada, France, and Great Britain, for instance, American-owned MNCs seem to have produced positive results in the host economy, especially in capital formation and improved access to advanced technology and management skills.[33]

The MNCs, however, have also cast a long shadow. Some have displayed alarming predatory behavior, exemplified by the efforts of ITT to undermine the freely elected government of Chile under President Allende in the 1970s.[34] In China today, the US-based Apple company reportedly subjects its local employees to harsh—and some-times deadly—working conditions, including the use of a poisonous chemical to clean iPhone screens. Explosions at iPad factories have killed four people and injured 77.[35] Further, journalist Steve Coll reports that giant oil company ExxonMobil has its own foreign policy that may or may not coincide with that of the United States. Whether Americans buy its products, or they are sold to Japan, China, or any other high bidder, is largely immaterial to the corporation's chief goal of making a profit.[36]

Some analysts maintain that the MNC is rapidly replacing the nation as the key entity in the shaping of international economic policies, as was implied as long ago as 1971 by the title of Raymond Vernon's influential book *Sovereignty at Bay*.[37] Whereas this outcome seems unlikely (although ExxonMobil does have its own army), no one can deny that MNCs have further complicated an already fragmented international economic setting. This fact was illustrated during the Angolan civil war, which began in 1975 and continued until 2002. In this African nation, an American-owned MNC—Gulf Oil Company—allied itself with a Marxist regime based in northern Angola, the site of rich oil fields. The Marxists were locked in an on-again, off-again battle against a rebel faction operating out of the southern hinterland. At the same time that the US government purchased 75 percent of the Gulf oil produced in the Marxist regime (making the United States the chief trading partner of Angola), the CIA continued to train and finance the anti-Marxist counterrevolutionaries in the countryside.[38]

## Fragmentation of Economic Power at Home

Just as the international economic setting is characterized by a fragmentation of power, so are the US domestic institutions that deal with international economic policy. Prior to World War II, the Department of State was the exclusive "club" for addressing most problems of international commerce. Diplomats like Cordell Hull, Sumner Wells, and Breckenridge Long, all experts in trade strategy, made the key decisions. Today, this policy-making role has become markedly diffused; and, as a former senior State Department official remarked in 1983, "diffusion has led to confusion."[39]

### *Divisions within the executive branch*

Consider, first, the multiplicity of organizations in the executive branch involved directly in some aspect of international economic policy. Here is just a sampling:

*Presidential Advisory Bodies*
National Security Council
Council of Economic Advisers
Office of Management and Budget
Office of the Special Representative for Trade Negotiations (SRT)

*Department of State*
Office of the Under Secretary for Economic Affairs
Agency for International Development
United States mission to the United Nations

*Department of Defense*
Office of the Assistant Secretary for International Security Affairs

*Department of the Treasury*
Office of Trade and Commodity Research
Assistant Secretary of International Economic Policy
Economic Policy Group

*Department of Commerce*
Office of the Assistant Secretary for Industry and Trade Administration

As a knowledgeable Washington observer noted in 1988, "the machinery of American foreign policy has become so sprawling and cumbersome that no one has exclusive domain over foreign and national security policy."[40] That fragmentation has remained a fixture of international economic policy making since the end of the Cold War.

I. M. Destler, a leading authority on US trade policy, suggested in 1980 that some degree of decentralization is inevitable, but which agencies should take the lead on certain issues needs to be clarified. He recommended that the **United States Trade Representative (USTR)**, *America's chief trade negotiator*, be given responsibility for trade; the Department of Agriculture for food; the Department of Energy for energy issues; Treasury for monetary matters; and State for foreign aid. This division of labor has turned out to be the case. The USTR has the primary responsibility for the formulation and administration of America's trade policy and serves as the chief negotiator for all trade agreements. The individual who holds this office is expected to coordinate policy initiatives with the Departments of Agriculture, Commerce, Labor, State, and Treasury. Since 1995, there has also been a **National Economic Council (NEC)** in the White House, which is *analogous to the National Security Council and was created to make sure that the presidential view is brought to the table in domestic debates over US trade policy.*

The success of the USTR depends on his or her access to the president, the stature of the person holding the office, and whether other nations are willing to negotiate trade deals. The Trade Representative is only one of several important players in the trade domain and sometimes the various cabinet departments demand a leading role in international commercial negotiations. Given this institutional pluralism, Destler concludes that it is hard to assure that the various components of the trade apparatus "will keep their parochialism in check. And no single department or cabinet member can exercise effective oversight of overall foreign economic policy."[41]

### Fission on Capitol Hill

Congress has grown increasingly interested in international economic issues, too, and has experienced a proliferation of committees and subcommittees competing for authority over this jurisdiction—an energetic involvement of lawmakers, as encouraged by the Constitution. The partial listing that follows illustrates that the decentralization of authority for US foreign economic policy has been just as rampant on Capitol Hill as it has been "downtown" in the executive branch. On top of this structural fission comes the additional fragmentation that results from the attempts of 535 lawmakers in Congress to protect the interests of their own constituents and trade groups at home.

> *The Senate*
> Subcommittee on Foreign Agricultural Policy (Committee on Agriculture)
> Subcommittee on Foreign Operations (Committee on Appropriations)

Subcommittee on International Finance (Committee on Banking, Housing and Urban Affairs)

Subcommittee on International Trade (Committee on Finance)

Subcommittee on Foreign Assistance (Committee on Foreign Relations)

Subcommittee on Foreign Economic Policy (Committee on Foreign Relations)

*The House of Representatives*

Subcommittee on Foreign Operations (Committee on Appropriations)

Subcommittee on International Development Institutions and Finance (Committee on Banking, Finance and Urban Affairs)

Subcommittee on International Trade, Investment, and Monetary Policy (Committee on Banking, Finance, and Urban Affairs)

Subcommittee on International Development (Committee on Foreign Affairs)

Subcommittee on International Economic Policy and Trade (Committee on Foreign Affairs)

Regional Subcommittees (Committee on Foreign Affairs)

Committee on Interstate and Foreign Commerce

Committee on Merchant Marine and Fisheries Subcommittee on Trade (Committee on Ways and Means)

Ad Hoc Committee on Energy

Subcommittee on International Economics (Joint Committee on Economics)

Congressional Budget Office

A comprehensive trade pact signed with Canada in 1988 suggests how different segments of the legislative branch can slow, or even stop, a major international commercial agreement. "The Congressional hurdle is the major hurdle full of potential pitfalls," worried a Canadian official.[42] The causes of his frustration were evident. Among them, senators from Wyoming balked because of the pact's potential effect on uranium miners in their state; representatives from Ohio and Pennsylvania worried about provisions related to the steel industry in their states; lawmakers from South Carolina fussed over subsidies given to Canada's textile companies; additional lawmakers from America's farm states expressed concern over Canada's subsidized beef, wheat, potatoes, and hogs; and representatives from Maine gave long speeches about subsidized fish. Both Canadian and American officials valued their close alliance too much to see these negotiations fail; but before final passage, a host of lawmakers added changes here and there on everything from cattle and wheat to lead and zinc, in an effort to protect the interests of constituents.

During President Obama's first term, another Canadian controversy arose involving the Keystone XL Pipeline, designed to carry synthetic crude oil and diluted bitumen from Alberta to various destinations in the United States (including Illinois, Oklahoma, Nebraska, Louisiana, and Texas). Many of the same arguments heard in

1988 echoed again in Washington, DC. This time, though, the White House blocked the proposal in early 2012 on environmental grounds—especially the protection of the vulnerable Sand Hills region in Nebraska. Subsequently, the President authorized partial construction of the pipeline in less environmentally sensitive locations south of Oklahoma. Republicans in Congress were able to pass legislation requiring a decision on further pipeline construction within sixty days; Obama balked, however, and said that this deadline did not give the White House enough time to have "a full assessment of the pipeline's impact."[43] He promised to resolve the controversy during his second term, after finding a way to protect the environment while at the same time finishing construction of the pipeline.

Congress has shown through the passage of tough legislation that it intends to be a major player in the formulation of US policy on trade and aid. Clearly, the Constitution is alive and well within the domain of international economic policy. Further, lawmakers routinely slash the foreign aid budget proposed by the executive branch; and, for the purposes of national security interests, Congress has placed strict prohibitions on some forms of trade policy, such as the sale of advanced computers to the Chinese.

If carried to an extreme, though, congressional intervention can lead to *a protectionist stampede detrimental to world trade.* In an example from the early twentieth century, the **Smoot-Hawley Act** of 1930 exacerbated global trade relations, contributing significantly to the Great Depression and to the outbreak of the World War II. This fiasco serves as a painful reminder of the harmful consequences that can accompany extreme tariff rates. At the time, the executive branch meant only to raise duties chiefly on agricultural products, but pressure groups soon turned to Smoot-Hawley in search of protection for each of their own narrow interests. When the law finally passed, it had elevated the average rate on dutiable goods by more than 50 percent—a record high—and included more commodities than ever before under the new tariff umbrella. Nations throughout the world retaliated by raising their own tariffs against US exports. A trade war was on.

Short of this extreme, however, someone (as James Madison might put it) must remind the drafters of econometric charts in the bowels of the bureaucracy that behind their sweeping parabolas lie real human costs for American citizens. Lawmakers, constantly in touch with constituents, are well positioned for the task of defending the interests of auto workers and citrus farmers, textile machinists and semiconductor technicians, and all the other Americans who struggle against the sometimes unfair trade practices of China, Japan, and other nations. This is an important part of a representative's role in a democracy and a central tenet of the Constitution.

Mindful, though, that Congress can be a cumbersome institution, lawmakers decided in the Trade Reform Act of 1974 to grant President Gerald R. Ford so-called "fast-track authority" on trade legislation—a practice that has continued and is now known as **trade promotion authority**.[44] Under this rule, *congressional committees can hold up trade agreements with other countries no longer than forty-five days once* *the White House submits them for congressional review. The two chambers of Congress then must either approve or reject the deals—without amendments—within fifteen days.* This law has stepped up the progress of American economic negotiations abroad and has limited the opportunities for individual lawmakers to add legislative "riders" on impending trade bills to benefit individual constituents or pressure groups. Republicans in Congress and the Obama administration showed in 2011 that they could overcome their deep-seated political differences to support important international trade measures. For example, they joined forces to approve commercial agreements with South Korea, Colombia, and Panama—the first trade pacts to pass Congress since 2007.[45]

## THE USE OF TRADE SANCTIONS

Despite experiencing a relative decline, the United States remains the leading economic power in the world and various trade sanctions at its disposal can be significant tools of foreign policy. In a desperate hope to stop Iran's production of nuclear weapons, for example, in 2010 Washington officials ratcheted up their efforts to use trade sanctions against the government in Tehran. Success, though, required the cooperation of China and Russia, whose positions remained unclear. The Russian Foreign Minister hinted at his nation's likely stance, though. "Iran is a partner that has never harmed Russia in any way," he said in 2009.[46] By mid-2010, Russia and China seemed more willing to join the United States, at least with limited sanctions against Iran. Then, in autumn, Moscow reversed course again and announced a program of cooperation with Tehran that seemed to encourage Russian companies to circumvent the sanctions adopted by President Obama.[47] (Sanction busters are sometimes called "Black Knights" by critics.) Nonetheless, the Obama administration claimed in 2011 that US sanctions had left the Iranian regime economically strained, diplomatically isolated, and torn by internal divisions.[48]

Although willing to permit trade promotion authority to the executive branch, lawmakers were not prepared to relinquish the international economic field altogether. Congress reentered the thicket of Iranian sanctions in 2012 with a proposal to toughen the resolve of the Obama administration. The legislation under debate would have required President Obama to cut off access to the United States, within 180 days, for any public or private institution that bought oil through the Central Bank of Iran. The (rare) bipartisan goal on Capitol Hill was to shut down the Iranian Central Bank, if necessary, as a means of depriving financing for Iran's WMD program.[49]

Elsewhere in the Middle East, the United States led efforts in 2012 and 2013 to impose sanctions against the Syrian regime, responsible for the deaths of thousands of insurgents in revolt as part of the Arab uprising in the region. Again the chances for success of the sanctions depended on Russian and Chinese cooperation, which was not forthcoming. A chief US goal with respect to Syria and other belligerent nations is to use **smart sanctions**, that is, *economic inducements that punish the elites in a target country, not the average person on the street.* The United States drew back from its talk of cutting off refined gasoline products to Iran in 2010, for instance, out of concern that this approach would hurt the masses more than the government in Tehran.[50]

## Economic Carrots and Sticks

The policy of **"most-favored-nation" (MFN)** *is a form of economic inducement in which one nation bestows on another nation the best available trading relationship for its imports.* This amounts to a form of economic reward for those regimes overseas considered important to America's foreign policy interests and who are prepared to allow the United States reciprocal trade opportunities. When leaders in Beijing used force against pro-democracy demonstrators in the 1989 Tiananmen Square protests, infamously crushing one demonstrator with a tank and subsequently executing several in hastily staged trials, some members of Congress called for the termination of MFN privileges for China. President George H. W. Bush, a former US envoy to Beijing, was unwilling to go that far, however, and instead cut off the sale of all American military equipment to China.

**Embargoes**—*prohibition on exports*—are another instrument of economic statecraft, as are **boycotts**: *prohibitions against imports or other forms of business cooperation with another country.* Both represent methods of economic punishment. The United States instituted a boycott against Cuban sugar when its communist leader, Fidel Castro, came to power in 1959 and has maintained the boycott ever since—a position strongly backed by the American sugar beet industry as a way of eliminating competition from the island nation; and the United States also boycotted the Soviet-sponsored Olympics in 1980 in response to its invasion of Afghanistan the year before. Iraq's invasion of Kuwait in 1991 provoked a worldwide boycott of Iraqi oil sales, depriving the Saddam Hussein regime of an estimated $17 billion a year in revenues. This action was part of a general trade embargo against Iraq, one that was only partially successful because a neighboring country, Jordan (an American ally), refused to take steps to curb illegal goods traveling across its borders. The UN also instituted a trade embargo against the Serbs in Yugoslavia as a punishment for starting a civil war in 1991, again with limited effectiveness. David Baldwin has divided these and other economic actions into a catalog of positive and negative inducements, as outlined in Table 13.4.

## The Limits of Economic Sanctions and Inducements

The list in Table 13.4 may seem potent; however, these tools have proven to have only modest value as a means of forcing other nations to cooperate with the United States. Embargoes and boycotts, for example, often fail against a target nation because other nations refused to honor them. When the United States sought to deprive the Soviet Union of grain during the Cold War, for instance, Canada and Argentina were pleased to fill the demand; and recall from Chapter 8, American farmers—reluctant to lose these sales—clamored to have the sanctions removed. As foreign policy expert Richard N. Haass has noted, "In a global economy, unilateral sanctions tend to impose greater

*Table 13.4*
Tools of US Economic
Power in World Affairs

**POSITIVE INDUCEMENTS**

**Trade**

Favorable tariffs

Most-favored-nation (MFN) rights

Tariff reduction

Direct purchase

Subsidies to exports or imports

Granting of export and import licenses

**Capital**

Providing of aid

Investment guarantees

Encouragement of private capital

Favorable tax measures

**NEGATIVE SANCTIONS**

**Trade**

Embargo

Boycott

Tariff discrimination

Withdrawal of MFN rights

Blacklist quotas

License denial

Dumping

Preclusive buying

**Capital**

Freezing assets

Import and export controls

Suspension of aid

Expropriation

Unfavorable taxation

Withholding of dues to IMF and similar agencies

SOURCE: *Adapted from David A. Baldwin,* Economic Statecraft *(Princeton, NJ: Princeton University Press, 1985),*
*pp. 41–42.*

---

### PERSPECTIVES ON AMERICAN FOREIGN POLICY 13.1

**BENJAMIN CONSTANT, writing at the end of World War II, contrasted the war power and the economic power:**

War and commerce are but two different means of arriving at the same aim which is to possess what is desired. Trade is nothing but a homage paid to the strength of the possessor by him who aspires to the possession; it is an attempt to obtain by mutual agreement that which one does not hope any longer to obtain by violence. The idea of commerce would never occur to a man who would

always be the strongest. It is experience, proving to him that war, i.e., the use of his force against the force of others, is exposed to various resistances and various failures, which makes him have recourse to commerce, that is, to a means more subtle and better fitted to induce the interest of others to consent to what is his own interest.

*SOURCE:* National power and the structure of foreign trade by HIRSCHMAN, ALBERT O. Reproduced with permission of UNIVERSITY OF CALIFORNIA PRESS in the format Republish in a book via Copyright Clearance Center.

---

costs on American firms than on the target, which can usually find substitute sources of supply and financing."[51] Moreover, some countries are able to resist outside pressures regardless of the resulting internal economic deprivations. Chinese leaders, for instance, remained adamant about snuffing out all vestiges of revolutionary fervor among their young people in 1989, despite a sharp international reaction that included threats of economic reprisal against the regime's brutality.

Economic power is by no means useless, as the discussion of foreign aid emphasizes later in this chapter; but its instruments have definite limitations. One authoritative study on embargoes concluded that they have "not been notably successful except as a direct adjunct of war."[52] Despite a history of uneven results, the United States will no doubt continue to turn at times to economic measures—positive and negative—in pursuit of foreign policy goals. This approach provides a less far-reaching and irrevocable use of power than overt military force and, for that reason alone, it will remain attractive to many policy makers. (See *Perspectives on American Foreign Policy* 13.1.)

## FOREIGN AID

**Foreign aid** may be defined as *"economic and military assistance on a government-to-government level, or through government-supported agencies or programs."*[53] **Economic (or development) assistance**, referred to by one authority as "an obvious weapon in the contest for global influence,"[54] *includes direct grants, technical cooperation, and loans that are either "hard" (that is, offered at commercial bank interest rates) or "soft" (which are concessional, that is, provided at low interest rates).* Most US economic aid to the developing world has been in the form of soft loans.

**Military assistance**, often called **security assistance**, includes *the use of military advisory groups, equipment, and defense-oriented economic support,* such as funding for the construction of dock facilities and railroads. It comes in five categories: the military assistance program (MAP), which provides friendly nations with military hardware and services on a grant basis; foreign military sales, which offers the same benefits on a credit and loan basis; security support assistance—the most expensive category—designed to foster economic and political stability in regions where the United States has military bases or other security interests; military training, which provides instruction in military science to foreign soldiers studying within the United States; and peacekeeping missions, which help fund UN forces in troubled zones like the Sinai Peninsula and Cyprus, and more recently, Somalia, Cambodia, the Balkans, North Africa, and Syria.

## A Portrait of US Foreign Aid

During the early years of the Carter administration, the various forms of economic and military assistance cost about $6.8 billion a year. Then, as a result of the Camp David Accords signed by President Carter, this figure rose by several billion a year when Egypt and Israel became the recipients of the largest amounts of US foreign aid ever: about $5 billion annually to each of the two countries. By fiscal year 1988, the overall spending figure for economic (development) assistance had reached almost $20 billion; and President Reagan authorized large increases in the military assistance program as well. In 2005, the figure for economic assistance rose to a record $27.6 billion—more than double the amount provided by Japan, the second largest donor to poor nations. The total in 2008 climbed slightly to $27.9 billion; and, in 2010, the budget broke through the $30 billion ceiling.

With wars underway in Iraq and Afghanistan, coupled with military strikes into Pakistan against Al Qaeda and its Taliban allies, foreign aid mushroomed in these particular countries. For example, Pakistan alone has received more than $20 billion in foreign aid since the 9/11 attacks, following a decade of virtually no assistance from the United States. In fiscal 2010, US aid to Pakistan totaled nearly $4.5 billion, up substantially from the previous year (as discussed later in this chapter).[55] Israel and Egypt also continued to attract sizable amounts of US foreign assistance. Israel is the largest cumulative beneficiary of America's foreign assistance program since World War II—some $115 billion in bilateral aid.[56]

As shown by data in Table 13.5 on the top recipients of American foreign assistance in 2008 and in 2012, some US aid priorities have maintained a relatively steady state (as in the cases of Israel and Pakistan) and some have shifted (such as Afghanistan). Almost all of the aid for Israel goes toward the purchase of weapons, 75 percent of which are manufactured in the United States.[57]

In overall (aggregate) dollar terms, the United States is the leading provider of foreign aid in the world—without even counting large amounts of private donations and private investment. It also provides over half of the world's food aid. Yet America's levels of development assistance have been modest when looked at from the vantage point of the nation's enormous economic output. From this perspective, foreign aid

Table 13.5
The Top Recipients of
American Foreign Aid,
2008 and 2012

| | 2008 | 2012 |
|---|---|---|
| No. 1 | Israel: $2.4 billion | Israel: $3.0 billion |
| No. 2 | Egypt: $1.7 billion | Afghanistan: $2.3 billion |
| No. 3 | Pakistan: $798 million | Pakistan: $2.1 billion |
| No. 4 | Jordan: $ 688 million | Iraq: $1.7 billion |
| No. 5 | Kenya: $586 million | Egypt: $1.6 billion |
| No. 6 | South Africa: $574 million | Jordan: $676 million |
| No. 7 | Mexico: $551 million | Kenya: $652 million |
| No. 8 | Colombia: $541 million | Nigeria: $625 million |
| No. 9 | Nigeria: $491 million | Ethiopia: $580 million |
| No. 10 | Sudan: $479 million | Tanzania: $531 million |

has accounted for only about 1 percent of the US budget in recent years. "The total cost in tax dollars for all our security and economic assistance programs in the developing countries is $43.91 per person," reported Secretary of State George P. Schultz in 1983. "In contrast," he continued, "we Americans spend $104 per person a year for TV and radio sets, $35 per person per year for barbershop and beauty parlors, $97 per person per year for soap and cleaning supplies, and $21 per person per year for flowers and potted plants." More recently, commentators have used similar comparisons to chide Americans on their lack of support (on a per capita basis) for foreign assistance, noting that citizens spend more on their pets, and almost as much on candy and lawn maintenance, as the US government does helping others abroad through aid programs.[58]

The United States remains near the bottom of industrialized nations in its per capita expenditures on foreign aid; consequently, as foreign aid expert Steven W. Hook observes, "the world's most prolific aid donor [in aggregate expenditures] is also widely considered its biggest miser."[59] While the United States is the richest nation in the world, the United States ranks last among the twenty-two Western industrialized nations with serious aid programs, as measured by the percentage of gross national income (GNI) expended. In the 1970s, the Paris-based Organization for Economic Cooperation and Development (OECD) proposed a foreign aid standard for the wealthy nations: at least 0.7 percent of their GNI.[60] In 2002, world leaders renewed their commitment to this standard. Using this index, the United States ranked next to last among the industrialized nations as an aid giver in 1987 (at 0.2 percent, above only Austria's 0.17 percent).[61] By 2012, Austria had improved its standing slightly, whereas the United States remained at a 0.2 percentage score—just ahead of Italy, Japan, South Korea, and Greece (see Figure 13.2). Only Denmark, Luxembourg, Netherlands, Norway, and Sweden met the OECD target.[62]

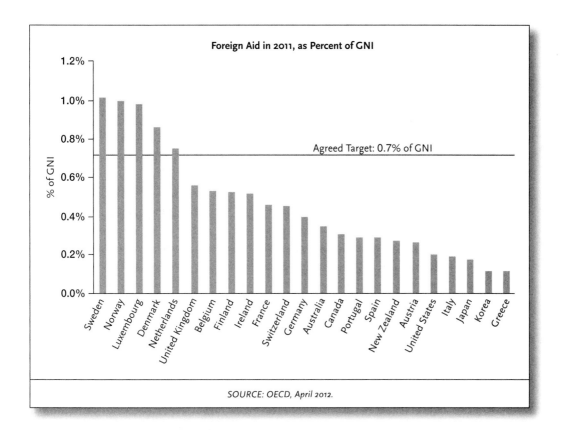

Such comparisons, though, fail to take into account the generous outpouring of private monies from US citizens and groups sent abroad for humanitarian purposes. Alex Perry, a journalist with *Time*, estimates that private foreign aid from Americans reached $37.3 billion in 2008—more than $10 billion over US government aid programs that year.[63]

In the 2008 presidential campaign, Barack Obama promised to "double our foreign assistance to $50 billion by 2012," but his aid figures have remained at the same level as those of his predecessor, George W. Bush. President Bush set a good example by establishing the **Millennium Challenge Corporation (MCC)** to *provide aid to nations that have displayed a capacity for economic reform.* Moreover, the Bush administration increased the amount of funding for development assistance over what the Clinton administration had authorized. Although both the Bush and Obama administrations fell behind in promised payments to the MCC, their new emphasis on foreign aid—especially toward combating disease in Africa—significantly assisted many poor countries.

*Figure 13.2*
Development Assistance Provided by the Industrialized Nations as a Percentage of Gross National Income (GNI), 2012

## A Pound of Containment and a Dash of Altruism

The disparity in lifestyles between rich and poor has created deep-seated resentments among those living on $1 to $2 a day in developing nations. (In sub-Saharan Africa, half the population lives below $1 dollar per day.)[64] In 1975, economist Robert L.

Heilbroner compared the world to "an immense train, in which a few passengers, mainly in the advanced capitalist world, ride in first-class coaches, in conditions of comfort unimaginable to the enormously greater numbers jammed into the cattle cars that make up the bulk of the train's carriages."[65] This metaphor remains valid today. In sub-Saharan Africa, infectious diseases, childhood illnesses, and maternity-related causes of death have persistently accounted for about 70 percent of the region's disease burden, and this area lagged dramatically behind the industrialized nations in mortality gains as well.[66] A 1984 public health study found that—all too typically—villagers in remote parts of the world had access only to filthy, unfiltered water from a mud hole.[67] Since then, however, progress has been made toward the goal of safe drinking water around the world. In 2012, 89 percent of the world's population enjoyed access to safe water, up from 76 percent in 1990.[68]

Over the years, private Americans have given generously to less fortunate people abroad. For example, they responded with significant donations to assist with the earthquake-spawned tsunamis in South Asia that killed 60,000 people in 2004; and with the earthquake disaster in Haiti in 2010, where US citizens provided over $1 billion in aid. The government in Washington has responded as well to these and other natural calamities, such as the flood disaster from monsoon rains that struck Pakistan in 2010 and submerged a fifth of the country. Officials sent helicopters for rescue and supply missions, along with prefabricated bridges and more than $70 million in relief and resettlement funds. Also in 2010, the United States pledged $4 billion over three years to the Global Fund to Fight AIDS, Tuberculosis and Malaria, a 38 percent increase over the preceding three years and far ahead of any other donor nation.

Self-interest has played a role in the willingness of the United States to aid countries·in distress. Diplomatic historian Dana G. Monro observed, with reference to Central America during the early days of the Cold War: "We were interested in economic development in the Caribbean because the poorer countries were not likely to have better governments [that is, pro-Western democracies] so long as the masses of the people lived in ignorance and poverty."[69] Along these lines, President Lyndon Johnson once declared that foreign aid was "the best weapon we have to ensure that our own men in uniform need not go into combat."[70] Coupled with the core objective of immunizing poor countries against communism during the Cold War was the additional goal of gaining access to overseas markets through the admission ticket of foreign assistance. More recently, Eric V. Larson noted that humanitarian assistance and disaster relief in places like Indonesia and Pakistan can help the United States "soften its image abroad, build goodwill in Muslim nations, and help to inoculate their populations against al Qaeda propaganda and rhetoric promoting violence against America."[71]

In a history of the US foreign aid program, Bickerton wrote that by 1960 soft loans had become "the single most important tool employed in the U.S. foreign aid program."[72] Among the landmarks of this period were the establishment of the Agency for International Development (AID) in 1961, which instituted a better organizational

---

## PERSPECTIVES ON AMERICAN FOREIGN POLICY 13.2

**The American diplomat DAVID D. NEWSOM on the Peace Corps:**

Although not officially part of our assistance programs, the Peace Corps has done wonders around the world in showing people that, with the right kind of effort, things can be done. Some years ago, I was at the opening of a six-kilometer road from a village in a West African country to a main road. Before the road was built, all the products of the village had to be portaged over a narrow path fording two streams. The road was made possible

because an American technician, in this case a 61-year-old former telephone lineman from Chicago, had discovered a field of castaway truck chassis and had shown how, by welding the chassis together, small bridges could be built. His was the ingenuity and the motivation. The work was that of the villagers.

*SOURCE:* David D. Newsom, *Diplomacy and the American Democracy* (Bloomington: Indiana University Press, 1988), p. 178. Reprinted Courtesy of Indiana University Press. All rights reserved.

---

focus within the State Department for America's foreign assistance program; and, in the same year, the creation of two complementary programs: the Peace Corps (see *Perspectives on American Foreign Policy* 13.2) and the Alliance for Progress, designed to strengthen the US economic aid package for Latin America. Today, the Peace Corps has 7,671 volunteers serving around the world, with 37 percent in Africa and 24 percent in Latin America—the two largest contingents.

## Souring on Aid

By the mid-1970s, however, pessimism about the usefulness of foreign aid had spread throughout Washington, DC, even though lawmakers were willing to go along with huge increases in assistance to Israel and Egypt in return for peace in the Middle East (temporarily at least) through the Camp David Accords. Pessimism over the aid program is nothing new; it has long had critics. "The greatest give-away in history," perennially groused Representative Otto Passman (D-Louisiana), the powerful chairman of the House Appropriations Subcommittee on Foreign Assistance in the 1960s and early 1970s. Passman said that US foreign aid was merely an exercise in "taking money from poor people in rich countries and giving it to rich people in poor countries."[73] Opposition on Capitol Hill toward foreign assistance became more extensive in the 1970s and beyond. Despite the billions of dollars in foreign aid pumped into Vietnam, the failure to achieve success there cast a pall over the economic program soon after the US troop withdrawal in 1973. Further, with the coming of détente with the Soviets that same year, the need to shore up the developing world against communism seemed less pressing.

Moreover, liberals on Capitol Hill decided to put a halt to a certain kind of aid: funding sent to unsavory regimes that tortured dissidents and otherwise violated human rights. The **Harkin Amendment**, sponsored by Thomas Harkin (D-Iowa) and narrowly passed in 1974, *placed a ban on aid to "any country which engages in a* *consistent pattern of gross violations of internationally recognized human rights" unless the president "determines that such assistance will directly benefit the needy people in such country and reports such determination to the Congress."* This law also gave either chamber of Congress the right to override the presidential judgment and, therefore, to stop the aid by a majority vote in just one chamber—a legislative-veto provision nullified by the *Chadha* decision in 1983.

According to critics, all too often aid seemed merely to prop up dictators who siphoned off funds for their own aggrandizement. They pointed to the large foreign bank accounts held by Somoza of Nicaragua and other US cronies in the Third World during the 1980s. In 1986, photographs of the 3,000 pairs of shoes purchased by Imelda Marcos, the wife of the deposed Philippine dictator, Ferdinand Marcos, a recipient of enormous sums of US assistance, disgusted aid critics. "Compared to Imelda, Marie Antoinette was a bag-lady," scoffed a leading member of Congress.[74] Today, Yemen offers another of many examples. "Corruption has taken a good part of our [foreign aid] funding," conceded a security expert from that nation, which has become a nest of Qaeda operatives. Further, a 2012 review of US economic aid programs toward Afghanistan documented that "gushers of cash have been pumped into one of the world's poorest economies, creating Potemkin progress and a tidal wave of corruption."[75] A UN Security Council report disclosed that in Somalia half the food aid in the past few years had been diverted from the mouths of the hungry to a network of local thugs and terrorists, as well as to corrupt UN staff members.[76]

Even more important in the demise of support for America's foreign aid program was the lingering doubt about whether aid had much of an effect on a poor nation's development. "We don't know how to use aid to reduce poverty," wrote the prominent journalist David Brooks.[77] He pointed to China, which has received little foreign aid but has experienced significant declines in poverty, whereas just the opposite has been true for Haiti. Indeed, some critics argue that US assistance might actually retard a nation's progress by establishing an unhealthy relationship of dependency. For example, Professor William Easterly of New York University argued for a more modest, homegrown approach to aid for Haitian earthquake victims. "I think the whole idea of the earthquake being an opportunity for foreigners to do more aggressive interventions is really problematic and objectionable," he wrote. "We have tried basically everything in the book already in Haiti as far as grandiose plans, and those haven't worked."[78] Aid to Pakistan raises another concern. Some Washington officials claim that the Pakistani government has diverted US aid, meant to shore up internal support against Al Qaeda and the radical Taliban insurgents, toward strengthening defenses against the nation's archenemy, India.

Critics note in addition that many countries to which the United States has provided aid seem to have no compunction against voting in opposition to America's objectives in the UN and other international forums. Was foreign aid worth the cost? critics asked—especially when the United States has underdeveloped regions of its own where the limited resources of the taxpayer might be better spent? An example is Appalachia, or the ghettos of America's cities. "I go home and see farmers' wives cry in front of me," a Midwest lawmaker once observed (who also happened to be chairman of the Appropriations Subcommittee on Foreign Operations, the key House panel on foreign assistance). "Don't tell me about the Philippines."[79]

What have been the results of America's expensive investment in foreign aid over the years? One scholarly review of the US aid program during the Cold War could only answer: "The impact of foreign aid remains obscure and perplexing."[80] More recent studies have reached a similar conclusion.[81]

During the 1980s, Congress began to slash aid routinely for some nations by over 50 percent. Only those countries with effective lobbies in Washington—most notably, Israel—managed to avoid the ax. As Figure 13.3 illustrates, the decline in US foreign aid continued through 2002, as a percentage of GDP. In a reversal, the George W. Bush administration increased foreign aid spending in 2003 and the expenditures rose steadily upward in a low trajectory. They continued to climb more steeply during the Obama administration's first term, from $17 billion in 2003 to $55 billion in 2010. Then, in 2011, the ax fell again, as spending on foreign aid and the State Department's

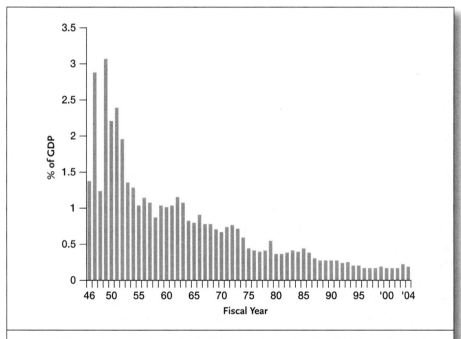

*Figure 13.3*
Foreign Aid as a Percentage of GDP, 1946–2004

SOURCE: Curt *Tamoff and Larry Nowels*, Foreign Aid: An Introductory Overview of U.S. Programs and Policy, *Congressional Research Service Report for Congress, Library of Congress (April 15, 2004). See also, Curt Tamoff and Marian Leonardo Lawson,* Foreign Aid: An Introduction to U.S. Programs and Policy, *Congressional Research Service Report for Congress, Library of Congress (February 10, 2011).*

operational budget dropped to $49 billion. The deepest cuts came in food and medicine for Africa; in disaster relief for Pakistan and Japan; in political and economic assistance for the new democracies of the Middle East; and in support for the Peace Corps.

Republicans also insisted that aid be halted for any organizations that perform abortions or provide needle exchanges for drug treatment. Only Israel escaped the cuts, with a continuation of its $3 billion a year. In 2012, the aid budget crept upward again to $54.9 billion; nevertheless, US foreign assistance programs remain persistently unpopular among many Americans who would prefer to see that money spent at home. This anti-aid perspective overlooks the fact that foreign assistance helps the United States win friends around the world—and allies in the important struggle against global terrorism.[82]

Given America's financial stresses at home, some budget cutting was to be expected in the aid program. Yet to what extent can the United States afford to turn a cold shoulder to the needs of developing nations? "We need officials who care about these poor, weak nations and their peoples, officials who will show up occasionally to ask, 'What are your special problems? What can we buy from you, and what can we sell? What is it in medicine, food, education, technology that we can provide?'" advocated Carl Rowan, a former US ambassador, in 1979. He continued: "When the automatic rifles are being fired, and artillery shells are exploding, as in El Salvador and Nicaragua, it is a bit late for the U.S. to fashion a policy."[83] This insightful statement stands as a guiding light for America's foreign economic assistance programs today.

## Foreign Aid Successes

Despite the ups and downs for spending on foreign aid and the controversies over its effectiveness, some programs have clearly produced results—sometimes even dramatic successes. For instance, in Sauri, Kenya, one of more than eighty "Millennium Villages" established by the United States in Africa, an American government project spearheaded by Columbia University economist Jeffrey D. Sachs has led to the doubling of agricultural yields; a drop in child mortality rates by 30 percent; soaring school attendance; an increase in the use of bed nets against mosquito-borne malaria; and widespread cell phone ownership (a sign of prosperity in rural Africa).[84] Professor Sachs places an emphasis on tightly focused, technology-based programs that proceed across a broad front simultaneously, including health care, education, and job training. The challenge is how to move from his focus on small villages to apply these methods successfully to larger areas and denser population tracts in Africa and elsewhere.

Important, too, is a more scientific approach to measuring the effects of various foreign aid programs. Economist Esther Duflo and her colleagues at MIT are engaged in research on these effects by using laboratory methods, such as control groups and evidence-based experiments, to test the value of various aid initiatives. In one experiment, for example, researchers found that the usage rates of malaria-fighting mosquito bed nets are the same, whether African villagers pay for them or get them for free; but that the villagers are more likely to buy them in the future if they are given them for free or pay only a little at first. Hard data of this kind hold promise for improvements in the effective delivery of aid programs.[85]

## SUMMARY

International economic objectives have always been a part of America's foreign policy agenda. In the first few decades following World War II, the United States enjoyed an enviable position in the world; but as the Germans and Japanese rebuilt their economies (with substantial American assistance), the United States soon found itself just one strong trading nation among many others, including a dramatically rising China.

Canada and Mexico are among the most important and reliable US trading partners, a partnership strengthened significantly by the North American Free Trade Agreement (NAFTA) adopted in 1993. Other key trading partners have been two new giants, Germany and Japan, and, soon thereafter, China.

A proliferation of new international organizations and arrangements—the IMF and the GATT, among a host of others—provide, however imperfectly, some order in the present environment of global economic fragmentation. Offering a degree of overarching cohesion, too, are multinational corporations. These new structures have been the subjects of criticism: the international organizations for, among other things, failing to accommodate the needs of the poorer nations; and the multinationals for, among other things, undermining the sovereign authority of nations.

At home, too, centers of economic authority have proliferated. Within the executive branch, an increasing number of agencies claim a role in the making of international economic policy. Similarly, Congress has experienced a fragmentation into a host of subcommittees dealing with foreign economic policy. The end result is a federal government often unable to deal coherently and consistently with intricate trade issues.

America's efforts to use economic power as an inducement to change the behavior of other nations have met with mixed results. For the most part, the use of trade incentives, both positive and negative, has proved unsatisfactory. Other nations are simply less vulnerable to US economic pressure than some policy makers anticipated.

Foreign aid has been an additional instrument of US economic statecraft. This approach has come mainly in two packages: economic (development) assistance and military (security) assistance, with an emphasis on the latter. Although sometimes motivated by humanitarian concerns, America's foreign aid program was viewed by most policy makers during the Cold War primarily as a way to implement the containment doctrine. Since then, criticism of America's aid program from scholars and government officials alike has increased, chiefly on grounds of its ineffectiveness. The new challenges to US commercial supremacy in the world have brought forth calls for closer attention to the use of economic power as an instrument of American foreign policy.

## KEY TERMS

boycotts p. 424
economic (development) assistance p. 426
embargoes p. 424
foreign aid p. 426
free trade p. 412
GATT (General Agreement on Tariffs and Trade, 1947–1994) p. 413
Harkin Amendment (1974) p. 431
International Monetary Fund (IMF) p. 415
military assistance (security assistance) p. 426
Millennium Challenge Corporation (MCC) p. 429

most-favored-nation (MFN) p. 424
multinational corporations (MNCs) p. 417
National Economic Council (NEC) p. 420
nontariff barriers (NTBs) p. 414
OPEC (Organization of Petroleum Exporting Countries) p. 406
protectionism p. 412
smart sanctions p. 423
Smoot-Hawley act (1930) p. 422
trade promotion authority p. 422
United States Trade Representative (USTR) p. 420

## QUESTIONS FOR DISCUSSION

1. The United States is widely considered the world's only superpower, but is this an apt description when it comes to foreign economic policy?

2. Debate the merits of free trade versus protectionism. How would you characterize current US trade practices? What would be your stance as a member of the House representing the district where your university or college is located?

3. Can the United States manage to maintain a robust economy at home and, at the same time, help the poor people of the developing world seek a better standard of living?

4. Do you think sanctions will eventually work to persuade Iran to abandon its nuclear weapons aspirations? Is it realistic to support only "smart" sanctions?

5. Do you support a lower or higher level of US foreign economic assistance? How about military assistance?

6. Would you have voted for the Harkin Amendment? Why or why not?

## ADDITIONAL READINGS

Destler, I. M. *American Trade Politics: System Under Stress*, 3rd ed. Washington, DC: Institute for International Economics, 1995.

Kennedy, Paul. *The Rise and Fall of the Great Powers: Economic Change and Military Conflict from 1500 to 2000.* New York: Random House, 1987.

Stiglitz, Joseph E. and Andrew Charlton. *Fair Trade for All: How Trade Can Promote Development.* New York: Oxford University Press, 2005.

For further readings, please visit the book's companion website.

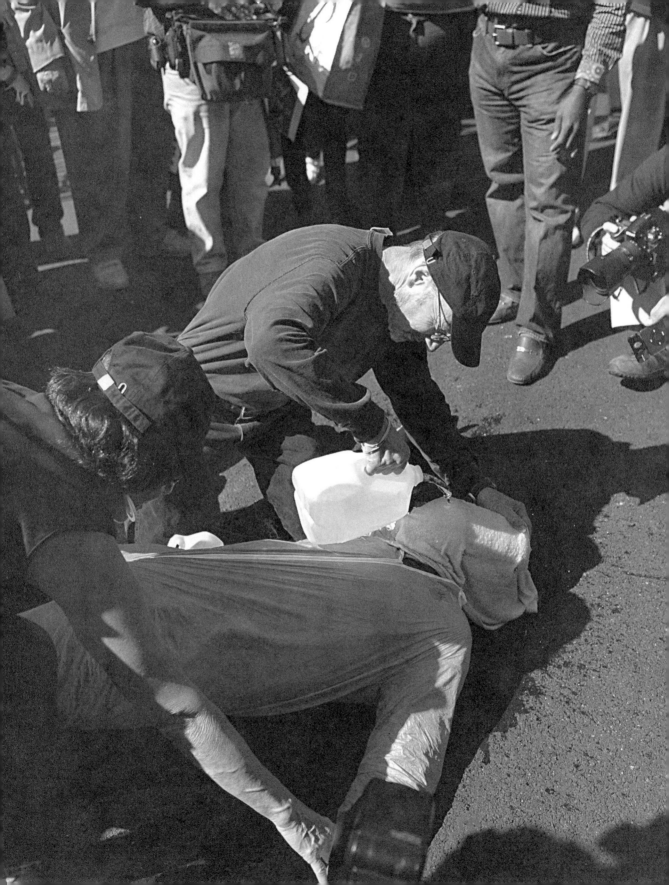

# Cultural and Moral Suasion

## AMERICA VEERS OFF COURSE

For sixteen days the interrogators kept their victims blindfolded. At first the questions came gently, then the interrogators put electrodes on sensitive parts of the victims's bodies. Every night they had to sleep standing up. During the day, the routine consisted of beatings and soon their muscles deteriorated into a permanent state of spasm and shivering. On the eighth day, the chief interrogator, a military captain, fired four shots from a revolver in the concrete bunker where the victims were being held. He informed them that there were two bullets left in the chamber of the pistol. The captain forced one of the victims to take the weapon and place the barrel end against his temple, then squeezing the trigger every time he answered a question negatively. The "crime" of these Chilean citizens? They were said to have criticized their government. The destiny of many other dissenters proved to be even

Antiwar activists demonstrate the torture technique of waterboarding during a protest in front of the White House in Washington, DC, held on October 5, 2009.

less fortunate. Thousands were killed or imprisoned during the 1970s and 1980s in Chile. Hundreds more simply "disappeared."[1]

Scenes like these are familiar to those who track the state of human rights in dictatorships around the world. During the Cold War, the United States often ignored such brutal activities, as long as the regime was anticommunist. Sometimes, though, Washington officials spoke out against human rights abuses, most adamantly during the Carter administration. Many people around the world admired President Carter's advocacy of human rights and the willingness of the United States to take a stand against dictators.

From these lofty heights of idealism, the fall was long and hard when photographs surfaced in 2004 that revealed US military intelligence personnel engaged in harsh interrogation techniques against prisoners in Iraq. The photographs could just as well have come from a Chilean prison during the height of the Cold War. The victims were men of all ages, captured after America's invasion of Iraq in 2003 and held in a Baghdad prison known as Abu Ghraib (pronounced "áboo gráb"). Several of the prisoners—all men, of various ages—were blindfolded and stripped, even those whose identities and loyalties were unclear. They were forced to stand exposed before snarling police dogs and women interrogators. Some had to stand, hooded, on boxes with electrical wires running to sensitive body parts. Some died from the rough handling.

Other reports surfaced in the American media about US intelligence officers using waterboarding techniques against Iraqi detainees and suspected Al Qaeda terrorists. In waterboarding, a victim is tied down on his back, then his face is covered with a

---

**LEARNING OBJECTIVES AND CONSTITUTIONAL ISSUES**

**By the end of this chapter, you will be able to:**

- *Assess the importance of ethical considerations in the making of American foreign policy decisions*
- *Describe several cases in which America's leaders have had to weigh the morality of their*

*actions in the pursuit of US objectives overseas and at home*

- *Evaluate a range of proposals for raising the profile of the ethical component in America's relations with the rest of the world*

---

**THIS CHAPTER RAISES THE FOLLOWING CONSTITUTIONAL QUESTIONS:**

- The Constitution is a legal document—the most important one in the history of the United States—but is it also a statement on morality? In what sense can the Constitution be viewed as a set of ethical principles?

- Are any of the three branches of government likely to have a monopoly on moral judgment? If not a monopoly, can one at least make a convincing argument that one branch—say, the judiciary—is more likely than others to display ethical wisdom?

- Have American values changed since 1787 to such an extent that the Constitution can no longer be viewed as a reliable guide to what citizens in the United States today embrace as legitimate principles for democratic governance?

cloth and a steady stream of water is poured on his face, producing a sensation of drowning. Several high-level officials in the second Bush administration, including Vice President Dick Cheney, publicly denied this method was torture, even though at the end of World War II the United States prosecuted Japanese soldiers as war criminals for waterboarding GIs.

Eventually, the Bush White House abandoned the technique; and the Obama administration publicly acknowledged this method of interrogation as torture and banned its use. The GOP presidential nominee in 2012, Mitt Romney, refused to renounce waterboarding, however, even though his party's nominee four years earlier, Senator John McCain (who had been tortured as a pilot captured by the North Vietnamese during the Vietnam War), adamantly rejected this approach to counterterrorism interrogations. ⌒

## CULTURAL VALUES AND ETHICS IN FOREIGN POLICY

The nightmares that emerged from Abu Ghraib were soon joined by other disturbing revelations. In Guantánamo, Cuba, other detainees from the war in Iraq were held indefinitely, as were men captured in Afghanistan as the CIA swept across that country in 2001 in search of Qaeda members. Charges were never brought against these prisoners and they remained without legal counsel. News reports surfaced, too, about secret CIA prisons in Eastern Europe—"black sites"— where yet more detainees were being held. Moreover, documented reports came to light about the CIA's involvement in **extraordinary rendition**, whereby *Agency personnel would kidnap suspected terrorists off the streets of Stockholm or some other European or Middle Eastern location, then fly them for purposes of interrogation to Egypt or some other nation less squeamish than the United States about human rights abuses.*[2] At these interrogation sites, foreign intelligence officers would torture the suspects and later forward the information to the CIA or US military intelligence agencies. This arrangement supposedly left Washington officials with an opportunity to claim plausible deniability—as if it were so easy for them to deny culpability in the harsh interrogation methods of secret allies abroad.

As legal scholars Cole and Dempsey have noted with respect to Abu Ghraib, this departure from America's long-standing principles against torture and other mistreatments of prisoners was "not only wrong but actually harms national security by fueling anti-American sentiment."[3] The United States was entitled to hunt down the 9/11 attackers, of course, using the full array of overt and covert force in Afghanistan (where Al Qaeda maintained a haven). In retaliation against the attacks, however, critics maintain that the second Bush Administration adopted excessive measures and tarnished America's most important attribute: the nation's good name and high moral standing in the world.

Moral considerations have often influenced world public opinion. One tragic illustration comes from the era of eighteenth-century colonialism. King Leopold II of Belgium employed barbarous means to extract ever larger quotas of rubber from

Congo, an African nation he had acquired as a private estate for business purposes. Africans who failed to meet the King's quotas became victims of atrocities. Finally, a newspaper photographer returned to Europe from Congo with a gruesome picture of a father sitting next to the hand and foot of his little girl. King Leopold's sentries had severed them as a punishment for the failure of the father's village to meet the King's rubber production quotas. This photograph and other press reports of brutalities in the Congo shocked Europeans and eventually forced the Belgian King to transfer the administration of Congolese affairs in 1908 over to more humane Belgian government authorities.[4]

The twentieth century witnessed worldwide moral outrage over Hitler's unspeakable ethnic atrocities during the Holocaust, as well as the mass murders authorized by Mao Tse-tung of China, Joseph Stalin of the Soviet Union, and Pol Pot of Cambodia. This gruesome set of dictators was responsible for the deaths of millions of political opponents and members of ethnic groups whom they opposed.

Some ethicists would argue that even the unjust targeting of an individual for death is reprehensible, as when Iran's religious leader, Ayatollah Khomeini, issued a decree (a *fatwa*) in 1989 to kill a London-based Indian novelist, Salman Rushdie. The novelist's offense was to have written a book with passages thought by Islamic fundamentalists to have blasphemed the Muslim faith. The *fatwa* stirred a global backlash of criticism. "We do not believe people should be killed for writing books," declared an official in the Clinton administration when the decree was reinstated in 1993, adding: "We regard the *fatwa* as a violation of Mr. Rushdie's basic human rights, and therefore a violation of international law." The administration rejected Iran's bid for normalized trade relations with the West until the death decree was rescinded. Principle would come before commercial profit.

Moral considerations have long been a part of US foreign policy, as in the cases of the missionary zeal at the end of the nineteenth century that sent thousands of Americans overseas to disseminate religious ethical teachings; Woodrow Wilson's call for transparency in global diplomacy ("open covenants openly arrived at"); the Harkin Amendment of 1974 on human rights; the revulsion over CIA assassination plots that led to an executive order in 1976 banning this approach to foreign policy except in times of authorized war; and the widespread criticism of moral expediency displacing principle in foreign policy (see *Perspectives on American Foreign Policy* 14.1). Bob Woodward, the *Washington Post* journalist famous for helping to uncover the Watergate scandal in 1973, expressed a view held by many Americans regarding the moral blindfolds worn by the DCI Casey of the Reagan administration, who was a leading conspirator in what became the Iran-*contra* scandal. In Woodward's words:

> If there's a tragic part of Casey, and I guess there is, it is that he ultimately didn't realize what this country is about. That we are different; that, yes, we will have an intelligence agency; yes, we will do things in

---

**PERSPECTIVES ON AMERICAN FOREIGN POLICY 14.1**

**GARY HART, former US Senator from Colorado (D), comments on the power of constitutional principles:**

. . . . the power of principles upon which our Constitution and system of government are based . . . attracts the peoples of the world. When we pursue policies based on these principles, we are most successful and when we neglect or violate these principles out of short-term expediency, we weaken ourselves. . . .

Expediency is the enemy of principle. To be a nation of laws not of men is to be committed to open and honest government, accountability of leadership, and the ability of the people to know what is right and what is wrong. There was a time when I heard chanted like a mantra, "Unless you want it on the front page of the *Washington Post*,

don't do it," regarding one's personal life. Curiously, many of those doing the chanting were up to conduct regard the public's business that they most certainly did not want on the front page of the *Washington Post*.

The first principle underlying a national security strategy, then, should be *the willingness and ability of government to justify its activities and conduct in pursuit of security before the American people in the court of public opinion*. Hard-liners and pragmatists will find this notion amusing and possibly even quaint. It's a dirty world out there, is their premise, and sometimes we have to do dirty things to protect ourselves. . . .

*SOURCE: Gary Hart, The Shield and the Cloak: The Security of the Commons* (New York: Oxford University Press, 2006), pp. 105–108.

---

secret—but those nation-defining activities, like war, can't be done in secret. That we can't go out and try to get the Saudi intelligence service to kill people we don't like, because in America we don't do that in secret, because that tells the world who we are. It tells *us* who we are.[5]

The choices faced by foreign policy officials are rarely ones of a simple dichotomy: morality versus pragmatism, or idealism versus realism. As Henry Kissinger, well known for his realism, remarked in a 1976 interview: "Our cause must be just, but it must prosper in a world of sovereign nations and competing wills." Arguing that sound policy must "relate ends to means," Kissinger reasoned that "neither moralistic rhetoric nor obsession with pure power politics will produce a foreign policy worthy of our opportunity—or adequate for our survival."[6] In this chapter I explore the ongoing balancing act between ethical values and power politics in US relations with the rest of the world.

## ETHICAL DILEMMAS OF THE TWENTIETH CENTURY

Two decisions during World War II—appeasement and dropping atomic bombs on Japan—caused considerable moral anguish in the high councils of government in Britain and the United States, respectively.[7] The advent of atomic weapons also led to the vexing question of nuclear deterrence, a dilemma that preoccupied many ethicists during the Cold War and that continues to this day.

## The Munich Pact

If the League of Nations represents the most conspicuous early failure of idealism in the twentieth century, second in line for this dubious honor is British prime minister Neville Chamberlain's policy of appeasement toward Adolf Hitler and the Nazi government—a decision that would have a strong influence on American foreign policy after World War II, as explored in Chapter 5. One motivation above all others seems to have impelled Chamberlain toward his Faustian bargain of "peace in our time" in exchange for Nazi control over Czechoslovakia: a desperate hope that war in Europe could be averted. The Prime Minister seemed to signal, in Hitler's interpretation at least, that the United Kingdom longed for peace at virtually any cost. To Hitler, this evidently led to only one conclusion: Chamberlain was a coward who could be bullied as the Third Reich fulfilled its territorial ambitions in Czechoslovakia, Poland, and beyond. Hitler, however, misjudged how far Britain would allow the Nazis to proceed down this pathway of aggression—an error of stupendous cost for the British and the Germans, not to mention the other nations that would soon be caught up in the global conflagration caused by the Nazis.

Of interest here is the ethical dimension of Chamberlain's decision to trust Hitler's promises. If Chamberlain's intuition had been correct that Hitler's appetite could be satiated by the Czech morsel, a great many lives would have been saved in the avoidance of war—although certainly the freedoms of Czech citizens (another moral good) would have been sacrificed on this alter of a broader peace. Chamberlain's idealism and longing for peace blinded him to Hitler's diabolical intentions. "It is possible to make the historical judgement," concluded a 1989 study, "that Chamberlain, by allowing this hatred [of war] to dominate his political action, encouraged Hitler's misjudgement, and thus contributed to the outbreak of the very war he so desperately hoped to avoid."[8] In the balancing of competing moral claims, the Prime Minister had badly miscalculated and thus entered the ranks of historical ignominy.

## Hiroshima and Nagasaki

Whether to use a nuclear weapon against the Japanese in 1945 was a decision laden with obvious and painful ethical implications. The atomic bomb had the destructive power to level cities in seconds, sending civilian populations—noncombatant women, children, and the aged among them—to a fiery death. Even those who survived might wish they had been at ground zero, considering the long-range illnesses and even genetic alterations that were known to result from exposure to radioactive emissions from a nuclear bomb.

Still, as in so many foreign policy decisions, a failure to use the bomb would have had ethical implications, too. Hundreds of American lives were lost every week that the war in the Pacific continued to rage. The United States saw 75,000 of its soldiers perish on the island of Okinawa alone. By April 1945, kamikaze raids had sent to the bottom of the Pacific Ocean thirty-four US ships, including three aircraft carriers. An invasion of Japan would probably have incurred several hundred thousand American casualties (according to estimates by the Joint Chiefs of Staff at the time), as well as an even larger number of Japanese deaths—far more loss of life than what one atomic bomb, or even two, would produce. Primarily to save as many American lives as possible, President Truman made the decision to use this ultimate weapon against Japan.

The decision was not made lightly. Truman's Secretary of War, Henry L. Stimson, and others high in the administration agonized over the dreadful power of the new weapon. Even after Truman arrived at the decision to drop the atomic bomb, Stimson argued on moral grounds against hitting certain targets. The government's target selection committee had identified Kyoto, the former capital of Japan and a city of great beauty and cultural significance, as one potential target. That city was spared, however, after Stimson informed Truman—in a revealing mixture of realism and idealism—that "Japan's help against Russia might be needed in the future but that if Americans destroyed this cultural shrine they would never be forgiven."[9]

Some critics have questioned whether the use of an atomic bomb against any Japanese city was necessary. They suggest that US authorities could have told their Japanese counterparts about the weapon, then demonstrated its effects on an uninhabited Pacific atoll near Japan, or perhaps dropped the bomb on a flotilla of Japanese naval ships at sea. The rebuttal to these arguments is twofold. First, the United States only had three atomic bombs and could ill afford to squander one in a demonstration that might have been a dud—and a windfall for Japanese scientists to capture and dissect. Second, the Japanese were so resolute in their determination to fight down to the last soldier, in fidelity to the ancient samurai code of the Japanese warrior class, that the Truman administration estimated it would take something as profoundly shocking as the nuclear bombing of a major city to convince them that further resistance was futile.

Critics of the bombing maintain, also, that the United States should have at least provided a clear warning to the Japanese about which city was targeted, so noncombatants could have been evacuated. Yet a warning might have caused the Japanese to gather American prisoners of war into the target city as a means for deterring the bombing. Further, the Japanese might have concentrated their meager air defenses around the proposed target in an effort to shoot down the US bomber carrying the superweapon.

Even more controversial than the bombing of Hiroshima was the attack only three days later against a second key city, Nagasaki. This brief interlude left little time for the Japanese war cabinet to assemble, consider the dangers of further delay, and arrive at a declaration of surrender. The US military advanced the timetable for the bombing of Nagasaki because of approaching bad weather—hardly a satisfactory reason for extinguishing the lives of 40,000 people when a second bomb might have proved unnecessary. Critics argue that the use of an atomic weapon against Nagasaki was a tragic moment in American foreign policy, when a heightened moral sensitivity might have saved a city bustling with human beings—few, if any, of whom were military combatants.

## Nuclear Deterrence

Nothing so defines the post-World War II era as the existence of nuclear weapons. The proliferation and stockpiling of these armaments produced not only a widespread sense of anxiety about the risk of them being used again but also subtle, yet profound, ethical questions about nuclear warfare and how to guard against it. In 1982, the largest public demonstration in American history took place as over a million advocates of a nuclear freeze—the simultaneous cessation of nuclear warhead production in both the United States and the Soviet Union—rallied in the streets of New York City.[10]

The freeze movement failed to achieve its larger objective of nuclear disarmament, but it did succeed in drawing large numbers of American citizens into the debate about WMDs. Across the land, in cities and even small towns, people convened to discuss the freeze and related proposals, and often passed nuclear-freeze resolutions in their city and town councils—a rare excursion of local government into the realm of foreign policy. Behind these discussions and debates lay the issue of **nuclear ethics**, with its fundamental moral question: *can the possession of nuclear weapons, poised in their launch silos ready to annihilate millions of people—perhaps destroy all humanity in an all-out war between nuclear powers—be justified?*

### Kant and the consequentialists

One school of thought on this question argues that America's reliance on nuclear weapons during the Cold War to keep the superpowers at bay (the theory of deterrence) must be rejected, for it is patently wrong to place in jeopardy the lives of millions of noncombatant civilians.[11] This argument represents a radical critique of existing policy. In its stress on the wrongness of even the *threat* to kill—the very core of deterrence—this critique finds itself in harmony with the beliefs of the German philosopher Immanuel Kant. "Do what is right though the world should perish," Kant admonished. Above all else, he cherished the *moral purity of the individual*.[12] Applying the logic of this moral stance to nuclear deterrence, modern-day **Kantians** insist that what one ethically cannot do—murder millions of innocent men, women, and children—one cannot *intend* to do either, with nuclear missiles ready for firing at a moment's notice. Therefore, the nuclear option must be discarded. In this spirit, the theologian Paul Ramsey famously drew an analogy between nuclear deterrence and the tying of babies to the bumpers of automobiles during the holiday season. Under these conditions, people would presumably drive more carefully and lives would be saved—a moral good. The method used, however, would be so repugnant as to be clearly wrong and unacceptable.[13]

A second school in Western moral tradition, the **consequentialists**, offers a different perspective—one that *highlights the outcome of an act, not the goal of maintaining the goodness of the individual involved.* From this vantage point, nuclear deterrence serves a useful purpose, despite the sword of Damocles that it suspends above humanity. Since the bombing of Nagasaki, no nuclear weapon has been fired in anger; the world has escaped the outbreak of global conflict between major powers—a Third

World War—perhaps in part as a consequence of the deterrent effect provided by these weapons. The existence of nuclear weapons aimed at one another has become a part of the human condition ("existential deterrence"[14]), to be accepted as the price one must pay to keep a balance of power and, thereby, thwart aggression by the major nations. For the consequentialists, the *effect* of one's decision is of overriding importance, not the moral purity of the individual decision maker.

Joseph S. Nye Jr. suggested in 1986 that both the Kantian and the consequentialist traditions "express important truths."[15] By employing a vivid hypothetical situation (see *Perspectives on American Foreign Policy* 14.2), he illustrated just how difficult choices can be, however, for proponents of both traditions. In the setting presented by Nye, would you join the ranks of the Kantians or the consequentialists? What if the stakes were raised—say, the possibility of saving a hundred or a thousand peasants rather than one? Or, in another scenario, what if a terrorist clutched a child—perhaps a member of your own family—in one arm to protect himself, while with his free hand he gripped a plunger on an explosive device that could detonate a nuclear bomb in the heart of a metropolis if his demands went unmet? Should one shoot through the body of the child to kill the terrorist and save the million-plus inhabitants of the city? Would Kant himself refuse? "At some point does not integrity become the ultimate egoism of fastidious self-righteousness," Nye has asked, "in which the purity of the self is more important than the lives of countless others?" He noted further that, in the conduct of foreign policy, the absolutist ethics of Immanuel Kant "bears a heavier burden of proof in the nuclear age than ever before."[16]

### The pastoral letter

In 1983, the National Conference of Catholic Bishops on War and Peace (an ongoing organization) published one of the most thoughtful attempts to go beyond theory and

---

### PERSPECTIVES ON AMERICAN FOREIGN POLICY 14.2

**The KANTIAN AND CONSEQUENTIALIST SCHOOLS of ethics explored through a hypothetical case:**

Imagine that you are visiting a Central American country and you happen upon a village square where an army captain is about to order his men to shoot two peasants lined up against a wall. When you ask the reason, you are told someone in this village shot at the captain's men last night. When you object to the killing of possibly innocent people, you are told that civil wars do not permit moral niceties. Just to prove the point that we all have dirty hands in such situations, the captain hands you a rifle and tells you that if you will shoot one peasant, he will free the other. Otherwise both die. He warns you not to try any tricks because his men have their guns trained on you. Will you shoot one person with the consequences of saving one, or will you allow both to die but preserve your moral integrity by refusing to play his dirty game?

*SOURCE:* Reprinted with the permission of Simon & Schuster Publishing Group from the Free Press edition of NUCLEAR ETHICS by Joseph S. Nye, Jr. Copyright © 1986 by Joseph S. Nye, Jr. All rights reserved.

hypothetical cases about nuclear war to examine practical aspects of a world with nuclear weaponry. Following the conference, the *bishops issued a document, known as a pastoral letter, that summed up their deliberations on the real-world moral implications of nuclear deterrence.*

The **American bishops' letter** was filled with tension, mirroring the ambivalence felt by the broader public, and Washington leaders as well, toward the existence of nuclear weapons and the doctrine of deterrence.[17] At first look, the bishops seemed to break radically with the "balance of terror," Churchill's description of deterrence in the nuclear age. In Kantian terms, they rejected the first use by the United States of any nuclear weapon. Further, drawing on the moral **principle of noncombatant immunity**, they *shunned the use or even the targeting of nuclear weapons at any time against "population centers or other predominantly civilian targets"* (countervalue targeting). "The moral demands of Catholic teaching require resolute willingness not to intend or to do moral evil, even to save our own lives or the lives of those we love," they wrote in a Kantian spirit.

Yet the bishops pulled back from a complete condemnation of nuclear deterrence. In their view, "in current conditions 'deterrence' based on balance, certainly not as an end in itself but as a step on the way toward a progressive disarmament, may still be judged morally acceptable." In this brief statement, the bishops obliquely acknowledged that deterrence might have some redeeming value as a source of restraint against belligerent acts between the major powers—at least until the human race had passed beyond the threat of nuclear warfare in its search for greater wisdom and maturity. The bishops were, therefore, unwilling to exclude from US strategic considerations the possible moral necessity of preparedness for a second-strike use of nuclear weapons against military (counterforce) targets. "The nature of that use is never spelled out," recalled one of the conference participants, "but the criteria point toward a limited second-strike force target on military objectives."[18] So the circle the bishops had begun to draw against the evils of deterrence was never fully closed; left open was "a centimeter of ambiguity."[19]

The bishops arrived at this partial endorsement of deterrence out of a commitment to an overriding moral imperative: the prevention of nuclear war. If, as seemed possible, a second-strike, counterforce strategy had helped to keep the superpowers at bay during the Cold War, then—as the bishops shifted from a Kantian to a consequentialist stance—a conditional (no first use, no countervalue) moral acceptance of deterrence might be justifiable: barely.

The position on deterrence taken by the bishops grew out of the **just war tradition**, a compromise between pacifism and militarism. According to this *venerable philosophy of war, a nation (like a person) has the right to defend itself against the unjust use of force.* "Governments threatened by armed unjust aggression *must* defend their people," emphasized the bishops. In its use of self-defense, however, the moral nation would be expected to follow certain limitations on its use of force. Chief among them is the **principle of discrimination**; that is, *the avoidance of the use of force against noncombatants—another way of expressing the idea of "noncombatant immunity."*

Important, too, was the **principle of proportionality**, which requires that *one's use of force be roughly equivalent in scope and magnitude to that employed by the belligerent.* If in the (currently unlikely) event that Russia or China were to launch a military strike against a single American nuclear submarine, retaliation by the United States against the city of Moscow or Beijing would be out of proportion; the appropriate response, according to this principle, would be a counterstrike against a Russian or Chinese nuclear submarine.

Thus the bishops came to rest on a counterforce, but not a first-strike, posture. They recognized, however, how problematic an attempt might be to impose limits on nuclear war in the heat of battle. For the time being, though, until a more enlightened world order arrived, a centimeter of acceptability for nuclear weapons had to be granted. The bishops' letter also reflected political realities inside the Catholic Church. The Church consists of a mix of Kantian and consequentialist moral traditions. For the American bishops to have rejected the Church's consequentialist heritage would have been to venture beyond the scope of Vatican permissibility. Moreover, papal doctrine aside, most members of the conference had reached the conclusion that a full closing of the anti-deterrence circle would have seriously undermined the credibility of the nuclear standoff, a result that might in itself prove to be a dangerous moral error. Finally, the release of a pastoral letter requires a two-thirds vote of conference participants; and, to enhance legitimacy, tradition expects the support of some 85 percent of the membership. This meant broad support had to be achieved through compromises reached between the Kantians and the consequentialists among the bishops. In this sense, the preparation of the letter was "something of a political high-wire act," in Nye's summation.[20]

The conclusions reached by the Catholic Conference on War and Peace stirred public criticism from various quarters, including within the Church itself. An American archbishop disagreed sharply with the pastoral letter, insisting that no Catholic commander of a nuclear submarine or missile silo could morally turn the key for weapons launch under *any* circumstances.[21] French bishops argued that the actual use of nuclear weapons would indeed be immoral; but, rejecting the Kantian perspective, they believed that the mere threat to use these weapons (deterrence) did not constitute their use. So, according to this wing of the Catholic Church, one could evidently bluff so long as one did not follow through. This seemed an odd prescription since the act of bluffing would seem to have no credibility if it were clear in advance that one would never go beyond the bluff itself.

Other critics pointed to the practical difficulty of distinguishing countervalue from counterforce. As Susan Okum has noted, to think of targeting simply in terms of countervalue and countersilo (counterforce) is a mistake. The United States, like the Soviet Union, had a whole range and mix of targeting priorities during the Cold War, many of which overlapped.[22] For example, some sixty US counterforce targets were reputedly within the heavily populated city limits of Moscow.[23]

Some observers further chastised the American bishops for failing to address the potential virtues of the Strategic Defense Initiative (SDI). In this view, strongly supported by President Reagan, a Star Wars-like shield represented the best moral position because eventually (if it worked) this defense would make nuclear weapons obsolete—at least those fired through the air, as opposed to a nuclear bomb in the trunk of a car parked near Times Square. The SDI—or, in today's parlance, BMD—would at last remove the constant threat of Armageddon brought on by a downpour of enemy missiles.[24] From still another perspective, some remained convinced that MAD—the essence of deterrence—was a condition here to stay. In the cliché, the atomic genie could not be stuffed back into the bottle, so it had to be dealt with in realistic terms; that is, through reliance on deterrence, which (so far at least) had worked. Although immoral in the Kantian sense, MAD had the highly moral consequence during the Cold War of fending off a Third World War pitting the United States against the Soviet Union. Whether deterrence would work against a fiery, hate-filled terrorist group like Al Qaeda, or an unpredictable and dogmatic regime like the theocracy in Iran, were other matters.

The debate over nuclear ethics continues to be as lively as it is inconclusive. So, too, is the debate over another controversial component of American foreign policy: the use of secret intelligence operations. Despite the cynical joke that **intelligence ethics** is an oxymoron (some would say just moron), *spying has an ethical dimension*, too.[25]

## ESPIONAGE

Today espionage is practiced around the globe by every nation, with one degree of sophistication or another that often depends on how much wealth the nation has to purchase expensive listening and photographic "platforms," such as elaborate ground-based antennae and surveillance satellites in space.[26] In the 1920s, though, Secretary of State Henry Stimson (who, as mentioned earlier in this chapter, went on to serve as Secretary of War during World War II) found the practice of espionage morally objectionable and ordered the Department of State to halt its cloak-and-dagger operations. "Gentlemen don't read other people's mail," he supposedly sniffed.[27] As Stimson became increasingly wary of the dangers to the United States posed by totalitarian regimes, however, he abandoned his moral stance against espionage and encouraged the US intelligence services to acquire the best information it could about threats from abroad, using whatever clandestine methods worked.

Despite its widespread practice, and the improbability that any major nation will adopt the puritan attitudes displayed by Stimson early in his career, much thought has been given to the question of whether—even in this dangerous world—some restraint ought to govern the use of the "dark arts" in foreign policy. This question came to the forefront in the Church Committee investigations into intelligence in 1975. At that time and on many occasions since, critics have expressed strong reservations about what they perceive to be excesses in the practice of covert action and counterintelligence, and some aspects of espionage have raised doubts as well.

On one conclusion most Americans agree: the government of the United States has a moral obligation to protect its citizens against attacks from abroad. No more

Pearl Harbors and no more 9/11s—or worse. To honor this obligation, the government spends far more money than any other nation on various intelligence activities (some $80 billion in recent years).[28] Regardless of this broad consensus in favor of gathering global intelligence, a key ethical question arises: should any limits be placed on the secret agencies in their quest for information to protect and advance the interests of the United States? Whereas the response of some experts, particularly inside the intelligence agencies, is a resounding no, observers with a concern for the protection of America's civil liberties, as well as the nation's reputation abroad, argue on behalf of some restraint. The argument has both a domestic and a foreign dimension.

## Domestic Intelligence Restraints

On the domestic side, critics argue that certain American groups and institutions ought not to be used by the CIA or its companion agencies for purposes of intelligence gathering. High on this "off-limits" list is the media, accorded special status by the Constitution's First Amendment, with its bow toward freedom of the press. America's secret agencies have long been attracted to the secret employment of US and foreign media personnel abroad, chiefly because correspondents have excellent access to foreign leaders. During the 1950s, several US journalists worked secretly for the CIA, some for pay and some purely out of a sense of patriotism.[29] This relationship came under fire in the 1970s, however, in light of ethical reconsiderations about government activities in the wake of the Watergate scandal.

Critics of the CIA-media relationship argue that it is unethical for intelligence officials to recruit American media personnel for espionage operations. A newsperson on the payroll of a secret agency might no longer be able to report objectively, especially on an intelligence-related story. Moreover, if a reporter with media credentials were caught spying overseas, the credibility of all US journalists abroad would be eroded, regardless of whether they were or were not intelligence "assets." The end result of a CIA-media bond would be the undermining of a free press within the United States, as well as the endangerment of legitimate American reporters abroad. In response to the ethical denunciation of reporters-as-spies by various US media associations and by lawmakers, the CIA has backed away from the relationship. Internal CIA regulations now prohibit the recruitment of *accredited US* media personnel by the nation's intelligence agencies for the purpose of espionage. This leaves open the possible recruitment of freelancers and all foreign journalists.[30] An amendment to the Intelligence Authorization Act of 1996 requires a timely report to the congressional intelligence committees if the DNI or the D/CIA override the non-recruitment rules in special circumstances.

Other domestic institutions attractive to the CIA are the nation's universities and colleges. Since its creation in 1947, the Agency has established a wide array of connections with America's institutions of higher learning.[31] Initially, the attraction stemmed from the rich reservoir that campuses represent for the hiring of intelligence officers. Many of today's senior CIA officers were recruited by professors with ties to the Agency who passed along the names of promising students. As more and more foreign students came to study in the United States after World War II, the universities and colleges took on an added allure for US intelligence managers. Here was an opportunity to recruit a potential foreign spy in the secure environment of an American campus, rather than overseas in the often dangerous setting of the student's homeland. Some of the foreign students might even turn out to be leaders of their native lands one day. The universities and colleges held still another appeal to intelligence professionals: the foreign travel of professors and students. As with the media, why not have selected professors and students—archeologists are a favorite for Britain's MI6—carry out espionage operations while engaged in their own research abroad?

Critics object strongly to CIA-campus relations. America's universities and colleges ought to be free and open places, they insist, not locales for secret operations where professors observe and screen American students for intelligence jobs; where foreign students become subjects of intensive surveillance and recruitment efforts designed to turn them into traitors against their own countries; where professors are not so much objective scholars in search of truth but paid agents of the government—a place where cloaks replace gowns.[32] Further, just as the arrest (or worse) of US correspondents caught spying abroad endangers other correspondents, so does the discovery of a single professor engaged in espionage overseas harm the reputation of all other scholars, most of whom have no ties whatsoever to any intelligence agency.

Other domestic groups have clamored for protection from use by the CIA: missionaries abroad, for instance, as well as Peace Corps volunteers and Fulbright scholars (two programs the CIA has been prohibited from using since their inception), and a long list of others who travel overseas and worry that suspicions about them being connected to the Agency will curb their freedom of movement and possibly even make them targets of terrorist groups. Intelligence managers began in 1967 and then more extensively in 1976—in both instances, responding (respectively) to executive and legislative investigations—to move away from the broad use of American groups for intelligence purposes.[33] Though many groups continue to be "fair game" from the CIA's point of view (such as business organizations), the Agency has circumscribed its role on campuses. Professors are less likely to be asked by Agency personnel to turn over the names of American students for recruitment purposes without the knowledge and permission of the students. It remains "open season," though, when it comes to the recruitment of foreign students on US campuses.[34]

## Intelligence Restraints Abroad

As for ethics and espionage abroad, a related set of issues concern some observers. For example, should the United States suborn foreign media personnel? Soviet government-controlled reporters working for *Pravda*, yes, of course, during the Cold War; but what about the media in fellow democracies, such as correspondents for the *Frankfurter Allegemeine Zeitung* or *Die Zeit* in Germany, or *Le Monde* in France? A realist might argue that if the CIA is clever enough to recruit journalists from these news organizations, and if the foreign journalists can carry out espionage or propaganda operations that help protect the United States, then all to the good. The idealist might object: if Americans are unwilling to see their reporters recruited as spies by foreign powers, shouldn't that rule apply to the CIA's recruitment of reporters in other democracies? On this point of foreign recruitments, the cries for reform have been considerably softer within the United States than on the matter of CIA "interference" with strictly American groups; no prohibitions regarding foreign media personnel have been adopted by the CIA or lawmakers.

Worrisome also for those who are sensitive about the ethical dimensions of American foreign policy has been the way in which the United States trains its intelligence officers and how they acquire assets abroad. During World War II, for example, young recruits stationed overseas were taught a code that seemed to reject moral considerations, advancing instead a doctrine of dishonesty that became a part of the officer's tradecraft. "A man should not have too many ideals," advised a US intelligence manual written for the Office of Strategic Services (the CIA's precursor), and this norm had an influence on America's subsequent intelligence agencies.[35]

The primary job of an American intelligence officer overseas is to persuade local nationals to spy against their own nations on behalf of the United States. This in itself is an activity that stirs qualms in the minds of some ethicists. They find it appalling that the CIA teaches its spy handlers how to undermine the moral fiber of other human beings, transforming foreign nationals—even within democracies—into traitors. The Agency's response to this criticism rests on the premise that it honors a higher moral good: the protection of the United States and its citizens through a wide network of "watchers" (spies) in other lands. Moreover, no one holds a gun to the head of a foreign recruit. For money, sex, or some other reason (quite often, an ideological loathing of, or at least disenchantment with, the regime in which they live), potential foreign spies enter into arrangements with the CIA usually under their own free will. Occasionally, though, the Agency may attempt to blackmail a foreign asset into an espionage role.

### Deutch rules

Sometimes the US intelligence agencies have recruited individuals of notably unsavory character, including former Nazis after World War II, to spy on behalf of the United States. In 1995, DCI John Deutch, a former MIT chemistry professor and provost, issued new *regulations to prevent the recruitment of particularly despicable agents abroad.* These regulations became known as the **Deutch rules**. The stimulus was the case of a Colonel Alpirez in Guatemala, a military man accused of complicity in the murder of a US citizen at the same time he was also on the CIA payroll. Deutch expressed concern that the Agency had failed to keep Congress and the Justice Department properly informed about developments in the case, as required by law (the 1991 Intelligence Oversight Act). Deutch took steps to make sure Agency personnel stationed in Latin America were more fully aware of their obligation to support democracy and human rights throughout the Western Hemisphere. In the light of the Alpirez controversy, Deutch informed lawmakers that he intended to issue additional guidelines to CIA field officers that would "offer clear guidance on this subject beyond previous directives." It would take time to change the "culture or mind-set" at CIA headquarters, he cautioned senators—perhaps requiring years, "not weeks or months."[36]

Deutch informed *New York Times* reporters that his guidelines would require CIA officers to become more discriminating in their recruitment of spies. He was aware, he said, that "you are not going to be able to do the clandestine collection of intelligence with all wonderful and nice people." Nevertheless, the Agency would have to "balance here the character of the individual with respect to the intelligence you are gathering."[37] These rules would stamp John Deutch, at least in the eyes of some critics (especially inside the Directorate of Operations or today's NCS), as hopelessly naive about the sordid reality of what it takes to gather human intelligence. Before the regulations were released in 1995, a senior intelligence officer told a commission of inquiry, "It may be necessary to recruit criminals and crooks; you can't rely on the local minister for espionage."[38] He suggested that "Joe Sixpack"—the American public—"was much more troubled by the Ames case than by the fact that the DO had a relationship with unsavory types in Guatemala." (Aldrich Ames was a CIA traitor working for Russia, uncovered by the CIA and the FBI in 1994 and sentenced to life in prison.) Another senior intelligence officer ridiculed the "motherhood and apple pie intelligence" advocated by Deutch.[39]

With respect to the Deutch rules, a CIA general counsel has written, "In my experience the guidelines did not prove an unnecessary burden in recruiting human assets . . . we must know whom we're dealing with and case officers must have the knowledge that they will be backed up by headquarters in their dealings with these people. That can only be assured by a system in which headquarters knows what is going on and approves. That is what these guidelines provide and I believe they will prove in the long run to be a great benefit to CIA and its officers."[40] Deutch assured the Agency and the public that his new rules would in no way prohibit case officers from aggressively recruiting terrorists or those close to terrorist organizations; in these instances, the rules would be lifted. As a savvy CIA operative confirms, "There is simply no such thing as a case officer who didn't try to recruit a Middle Eastern terrorist because of concerns about the possible legal blow back from associating with someone who may have engaged in criminal behavior."[41]

Nevertheless, Smith later concluded that the Deutch rules were a mistake, in part because "many in the field resented the guidelines and some may have used them as an excuse when they were not able to recruit sources in terrorist groups . . . it became a kind of mantra that the guidelines were a tremendous hindrance to recruiting."[42] In 2002, DCI George Tenet rescinded the Deutch rules, concluding they had become politically unpalatable. Among those in favor of scrapping them was Representative Porter Goss (R-Florida, who would later serve as DCI). He observed in a speech in 1996 that some think "we should only deal with clean assets, that we should only work with reputable and morally responsible individuals. Well, you don't get the penetrations and you don't get the asset you need [with that approach]."[43]

Goss's comment was reminiscent of Secretary of State Henry Kissinger's realpolitik perspective on the State Department. In a meeting that took place in 1973 with staff from the Department's Latin American division, Kissinger said that the briefing papers produced by the staff were too moralistic and oriented toward questions of human rights. He complained: "The State Department is made up of people who have a vocation for the ministry. Because there were not enough churches for them, they went into the Department of State."[44]

Some US government documents support the spy novelist John Le Carré's image of the foreign intelligence agent as someone less than human, to be used and discarded without sentimentality. "No agent should be recruited without serious thought being given to the means of disposing of him after his usefulness has ended," stated an OSS manual in a matter-of-fact manner.[45] When the United States evacuated US personnel from Saigon in 1975, the CIA left behind scores of local spies who had worked secretly for the United States during the Vietnam War, along with the files that revealed their identities. Once in the hands of the invading North Vietnamese army, the documents in these files became death warrants for the US agents.[46]

### Covert action

Far more controversial than the ethics of espionage has been the debate over limits for covert action. Obviously, policies involving the secret bribing of politicians, planting propaganda in foreign news media, toppling foreign regimes, dynamiting oil storage facilities, and mining harbors—not to mention assassination plots against foreign leaders—raise serious moral questions.[47]

Assassination is the most extreme case. During the Eisenhower and Kennedy administrations, the CIA carried out several assassination plots against foreign leaders (though none were successful, as discussed in Chapter 12). More recently, on May 1, 2011, a US Navy Seals team raided Al Qaeda terrorist leader Osama bin Laden's compound after dark in Abbottabad, Pakistan. The team killed him and several others at the fortified house, located some fifty miles from the nation's capital of Islamabad. Later, in the fall of 2011, a CIA drone struck down a religious leader, Anwar Al-Awlaki and his son, both American citizens (born in New Mexico and Colorado, respectively). They were living in Yemen and had been critical of the United States. A naturalized US citizen, Samir Khan, was killed alongside Awlaki. Another US drone attack in the fall of 2011, this time in Libya and accompanied by a French warplane, brought a fleeing caravan of Libyan leaders—including the dictator Muammar Qaddafi—to a halt by blasting their vehicles at a traffic circle near Surt, Qaddafi's hometown. The hunted dictator managed to escape and hid in a pipeline, but was soon found and executed by Libyan rebels.[48] In addition, US drones attacks in Afghanistan, Pakistan, and Yemen have killed some 3,500 people in 420 strikes (as of February 2013)—including several hundred civilians accidentally caught in the bombings.[49] (Military-age males in these target zones were not considered civilian casualties.[50])

Outside the bounds of overt warfare, should the government of the United States order its secret agencies or the military special forces to kill someone abroad who has become a danger—or perhaps just a nuisance—to this nation? Does it matter whether or not the "kill target" is an American citizen, never tried for his or her alleged offenses in a court of law? Should such decisions be made by the president, by the Congress, by the judiciary—or perhaps some combination of these three institutions? As *New York Times* reporter Scott Shane observed in January of 2013, "There has never been a serious public congressional debate about whether it's a good idea for the president to be able to order the killing of American citizens."[51]

In 2013, the debate in Washington and around the country on this topic began to heat up. Some members of Congress insisted that the Senate and House Intelligence Committees be given access to a Department of Justice memorandum that provided the legal justification for the assassination of Awlaki. A DOJ "white paper" (that is, a policy background brief) on this matter leaked to the media (NBC News) in early 2013; but the underlying legal memo remained bottled up in the executive branch, despite criticism from leading lawmakers who demanded access to the document.[52] How, they asked, were they supposed to make informed judgments about foreign policy as a separate branch of government if they remained in the dark about the President's fundamental goals with the use of drones? A senior member of the Senate Select Committee on Intelligence, Ron Wyden (D-Oregon), noted that lawmakers and the public had not even learned if the president's authority for targeted killing extended to territory inside the United States.[53]

Former DCI John McCone argued during the 1960s that assassination plots against Fidel Castro of Cuba were a reasonable policy in light of the times. "Here was a man," he said, "that turned over the sacred soil of Cuba in 1962 to the Soviets to plant nuclear warhead short-range missiles, which could destroy every city east of the Mississippi."[54] A veteran intelligence officer speculated further that "if Congress had been asked to vote on the assassination of Fidel Castro in the early 1960s, the measure would have passed by at least a two-to-one majority, and the person who introduced the bill would have been given a medal."[55]

Whatever the merits of these viewpoints with respect to Castro, the Ford administration decided in 1976 that assassination in peacetime went beyond the pale of moral acceptability for the United States. Beginning with an executive order on intelligence signed by President Ford, each president has officially prohibited assassination as a US policy, unless authorized by a presidential finding in the context of a war formally authorized by Congress. In the case of Bin Laden and other Al Qaeda terrorists, the assassination ban was lifted by virtue of a law passed in the immediate aftermath of the 9/11 attacks against the United States: AUMF. This statute, recall, granted the president authority to use all "necessary and appropriate force" against those whom he determined had "planned, authorized, committed or aided" the 9/11 attacks or who provided safe haven for the attackers. President George W. Bush signed the AUMF law on September 18, 2001, and it remains in effect.

The existence of President Ford's executive order failed to deter the Reagan administration from bombing the home of Libyan leader Qaddafi in the mid-1980s. Except for Qaddafi's good luck, the bombs might have killed him. He was away from home at the time, but the attacks did result in the death of his adopted infant daughter and the severe injury of his two sons. The bombs accidentally hit a nearby French hospital, as well, harming patients and other civilians.[56]

Some realists argue that a man widely reputed to be a terrorist leader, like Qaddafi, ought to be assassinated before he is able to inflict damage against the American homeland—just as some think that, in retrospect, the murder of Hitler before he achieved power in Germany would have been a good idea. (Reputedly, British intelligence reasoned at the time, however, that it made sense to allow Hitler's rise to power, under the assumption that someone that insane would surely lead Germany to ruin.[57]) In the 1980s, the Reagan administration reached the conclusion that Qaddafi was trying to purchase nuclear weapons from China and needed to be stopped in his tracks. Ironically, he developed friendly terms with the United States during the 1990s and, at the request of officials in Washington, he abandoned a Libyan nuclear weapons program in return for US development assistance. In 2011, the Obama administration turned against him in support of the Arab uprising that drove Qaddafi from power and resulted in his murder by insurgents.

The Bin Laden, Awlaki, and Qaddafi cases, as well as the CIA murder plots against Castro and Lumumba of Congo during the Cold War, raise the question of whether the United States wishes to become a kind of international "Godfather," in the mob sense of the word, putting out contracts on the lives of foreign leaders, terrorists, and suspected terrorists. Should rubber gloves, gauze masks, hypodermic syringes, and lethal biological materials be instruments of American foreign policy? Should the CIA have on the ready electric dart guns and poison darts laced with curare? During the late 1950s and early 1960s, these "shoulds" were answered with a secret and decidedly unKantian "yes" by White House officials and CIA managers (Chapter 12). Today's comparable questions are: should CIA and military drones eliminate US adversaries abroad and, if so, based on what evidence, with what form of due process (if any), and reviewed by whom? So far the answers are again, an unKantian "yes" to large-scale drone attacks, with no due process, and sometimes based on skimpy evidence reviewed only by officials within the executive branch.

Morals aside, even from a practical perspective some observers wonder how useful a policy of assassination is. If Castro had been killed decades ago, he would have been replaced by his brother, Raúl Castro, who is Cuba's leader today. This would have amounted to no improvement at all; indeed, Raúl Castro seemed (in the 1960s, at least) to be an individual even more truculent toward the United States than Fidel. As former DCI William Colby once remarked, even the murder of Hitler would have provided no guarantee that the evils of the Third Reich could have been avoided because next in line was Hermann Goering, who was just as criminal in his war aims.[58] In more recent times, America has proven itself efficient in killing members of Al Qaeda, but new recruits to the terrorist organization continue to pop up to fill the emptied leadership spaces. Furthermore, in a dangerous cascading effect, to kill others abroad is to invite the murder of America's own leaders, who are officeholders much more easily targeted in this nation's open society. Assassinations raise the lid on a Pandora's box of retaliations and counterretaliations, as the leaders of Israel and Palestine have demonstrated in their running gun battles over the years, with no end in sight and no lasting benefits accrued to either side.

When the United States resorted to assassination plots against Castro, it hired disreputable characters: mobsters like John Rosselli, Sam Giancana, and Santos Trafficante. These individuals were hardly the sort of companions George Washington, John Adams, Thomas Jefferson, and James Madison would have advocated. In a 1975 document, declassified as part of the Church Committee's investigation into the CIA assassination schemes, an Agency official described an agent selected for covert operations in Africa. "He is indeed aware of the precepts of right and wrong," said the document, "but if he is given an assignment which may be morally wrong in the eyes of the world, but necessary because his case officer ordered him to carry it out, then it is right, and he will dutifully undertake appropriate action for its execution without pangs of conscience. In a word, he rationalizes all actions."[59]

Idealists also question the practice of bribing foreign officials in democratic regimes and planting stories in their media—other forms of CIA covert action. Such operations outrage Americans when carried out by foreign governments against the United States. After investigative journalists discovered that South Korean intelligence operatives were bribing US lawmakers in the 1970s, the public outcry from Americans led to a government investigation and indictments. Yet such practices are commonly implemented by the CIA overseas—even against fellow democracies—in operations approved by the NSC. Perhaps most questionable of all in the minds of critics are the moral implications of large-scale paramilitary operations, for in these instances thousands of individuals can be affected and often in the most brutal manner. Especially controversial today are CIA Predator and Reaper drone attacks against Qaeda and extremist Taliban targets in Pakistan (a country with which the United States was not at war), chiefly because of the civilians inadvertently killed when the Hellfire missiles strike targets in the mountain villages and redoubts of the North Waziristan province.

Realists swallow twice and accept the necessity of dealing with witches as the price Americans must pay to protect their global interests. ("Fair is foul, and foul is fair/Hover through the fog and filthy air," the witches chant in *Macbeth*.) The CIA should not be confused with the Boy Scouts of America, former DCI Richard Helms often pointed out; and Secretary of State Kissinger was fond of observing, too, that the CIA is not engaged in missionary work.[60] Yet others, including members of the

---

### PERSPECTIVES ON AMERICAN FOREIGN POLICY 14.3

**THE CHURCH COMMITTEE on the inappropriateness of involving US crime figures in CIA assassination plot against foreign leaders:**

We conclude that agencies of the United States must not use underworld figures for their criminal talents in carrying out Agency [CIA] operations. In addition to the corrosive effect upon our government, the use of underworld figures involves the following dangers:

- The use of underworld figures for "dirty business" gives them the power to blackmail the government and to avoid prosecution, for past or future crimes.
- The use of person experienced in criminal techniques and prone to criminal behavior increases the likelihood that criminal acts will occur . . .
- There is the danger that the United States Government will become an unwitting accomplice to criminal acts . . .

- There is a fundamental impropriety in selecting persons because they are skilled at performing deeds which the laws of our society forbid.

The use of underworld figures . . . raises moral problems comparable to those recognized by Justice Brandeis in a different context five decades ago: "If the Government becomes a law-breaker, it breeds contempt for law; it invites every man to become a law unto himself [*Olmstead* v. *U.S.* 277 U.S. 439, 485 (1927)]. . . ."

The spectacle of the Government consorting with criminal elements destroys respect for government and law and undermines the viability of democratic institutions.

*SOURCE:* "Alleged Assassination Plots Involving Foreign Leaders," *An Interim Report*, Select Committee to Study Governmental Operations with respect to Intelligence Activities, chaired by Frank Church, US Senate, Washington, DC, US Government Printing Office (November 1975), pp. 259–60.

---

Church Committee that investigated CIA assassination plots, refuse to dismiss the worthy principles extolled in the nation's founding documents and in the speeches of its best leaders. Church Committee members shook their heads at the hypocrisy that a CIA partnership with US crime figures made of these principles (see *Perspectives on American Foreign Policy* 14.3).

### Counterintelligence

Counterintelligence is an important and respectable defensive arm of American foreign policy. Washington officials must know about, and protect the nation from, clandestine operations conducted against the homeland and US troops overseas by hostile nations and terrorist organizations. Further, traitors like Ames and Hanssen can rob the United States of its legitimate secrets (such as the names of its foreign agents and the blueprints of its advanced weaponry), leaving the nation vulnerable. Yet as importance as counterintelligence is, the Huston Plan of 1970 and the events at Abu Ghraib in 2004 are reminders that these protective activities can result in a fundamental moral perversion. In the case of the Huston Plan, America's secret agencies turned against the very citizens they were established to protect; and in Abu Ghraib, torture tarnished America's worldwide reputation for high principle and fair play.

The Huston Plan arose in the context of war in Vietnam. Both Presidents Johnson and Nixon remained convinced that leaders of the antiwar protest movement had to be agents of the Soviet Union, receiving funds from the KGB. During the Johnson presidency, the intelligence agencies reported that no evidence could be found to support this allegation; rather, the student demonstrators genuinely opposed the war in Indochina and were prepared to say so without the help of any foreign powers.

When President Nixon entered the White House, he refused to accept this conclusion. In 1970 he gave one of his young aides, Tom Charles Huston, authority to prepare a master counterintelligence plan that directed the intelligence agencies to reexamine the suspected Soviet connection to antiwar protesters. As authorized by the President, the Huston Plan permitted the CIA and its companion services to carry out espionage operations inside the United States against Vietnam War dissenters as well as civil rights organizations. This master spy document violated several laws, including the National Security Act of 1947, which prohibits CIA involvement in domestic operations. President Nixon withdrew his support for the plan when FBI Director J. Edgar Hoover, who initially signed onto the operation (along with three other top intelligence officials, including DCI Helms), became nervous about the prospect that it might be discovered by the media. Despite the President's rescission of the spy plan, however, the CIA and other agencies continued their domestic surveillance operations. More astonishing still, Senate investigators learned in 1975 that the intelligence services had been involved in similar operations even before the presidential authorization of the Huston Plan, a fact they never bothered to tell President Nixon or his aide, Tom Huston.

The intelligence agencies turned to these illegal methods of counterintelligence not out of any fear that the KGB was influencing antiwar protestors or civil rights groups, but because counterintelligence officers sought to expand their coverage of suspected foreign intelligence officers inside the United States. As an FBI counterintelligence officer told a congressional investigator in 1975, "I was a Soviet specialist. I felt—and still feel—that we need technical coverage [that is, electronic eavesdropping] on every Soviet in the country. I didn't give a damn about the Black Panthers [a radical civil rights group in the United States during the 1960s] myself, but I did about the Russians."[61] As would occur during the Iran-*contra* scandal a decade later, overzealous intelligence officers went from their rightful concern about the Soviet threat to an illegal expansion of their operations—in this case, against American citizens across the land who were simply exercising their constitutional rights to protest against an unpopular war or to join the civil rights movement.

Few, if any, Westerners would volunteer to live in North Korea, a paranoid nation saturated with surveillance cameras, listening devises, and informants. It is a place without freedom: the perfect counterintelligence regime, where dissent can mean death, where security and obedience are the be-all and end-all. For a time during the experience with the Huston Plan, the United States slid down this slope toward an

Orwellian state, stopped by J. Edgar Hoover's second thoughts (though he had displayed no reservations against such activities earlier in his long career).[62] In 1974, a leak to the *New York Times* about the illegal domestic surveillance led to the establishment of the Church Committee and the other intelligence investigations of 1975 and a new era of accountability for the dark side of government.

# HUMAN RIGHTS

A display at the Carter Presidential Library in Atlanta proudly proclaims that "no issue was closer to Jimmy Carter than human rights." A strongly religious, born-again Christian, President Carter blended his foreign policy with a larger measure of moralism than any other president since Woodrow Wilson. Carter's dedication to **human rights** focused on *the dignity of human beings around the world, including the fundamental right to freedom from repression.* The remarks of his national security adviser, Zbigniew Brzezinski, near the end of Carter's time in office, revealed this emphasis on ethics. As Brzezinski explained, the purpose of the Carter administration had been to be both "compassionately and morally concerned" while at the same time "preserving a stable balance of power."[63]

## Freedom and Human Dignity

In Brzezinski's view, the United States should be guided by both the power of principle and the power of military strength, although his critics maintain that in practice he tilted too far toward the latter.[64] In his writings at least, Brzezinski rejected the notion that the two objectives were in conflict. He chastised Nixon and Kissinger for a "tendency to dismiss moral concerns in foreign policy as somehow equivalent to sentimentality." Nor did he spare the Democratic party for its "tendency to dismiss the importance of [military] power as somehow historically irrelevant." The Carter administration, he said, had

> tried as best we could on the one hand to make the United States relevant to the moral concerns of our times, to the aspirations of peoples who previously have not participated in the global political process, while at the same time revitalizing and making credible the presence of American power in a world very turbulent, a world which without such American power could easily slide into anarchy and growing conflict.[65]

The moral concerns of the Carter presidency were concentrated mainly on the plight of developing nations. More than ever before, officials in Washington shifted their attention toward relations with the poorer nations (the north–south global axis), instead of their usual fixation with the wealthy industrial nations (east–west). The President and his foreign policy advisers often spoke of the dignity that should be accorded the former colonial powers. They stressed the rightness of majority rule for South Africa, a relationship of greater political equality between large and small nations, and a more equitable sharing of the world's economic wealth. "Human rights has been a special concern of this administration," said Carter's second Secretary of

State, former senator Edmund S. Muskie (D-Maine), who succeeded Cyrus Vance in 1980. "We stand for the right of people to be free of torture and repression, to choose their leaders, to participate in the decisions that affect their daily lives, to speak and write and travel freely." In Muskie's view, military arms were insufficient to defend America's vital interests: "We must also arm ourselves with the conviction that our values have increasing power in today's world."[66]

Muskie acknowledged, though, that "there are limits on our capacity to influence affairs in other countries." During the Cold War, the violations of human rights by powerful nations like the Soviet Union were difficult to remedy, for the United States had little leverage. In a review of US-Soviet relations, diplomatic historian Gaddis concluded that America had minimal opportunities to force change in internal Soviet policies through trade or other inducements and sanctions. The USSR was self-sufficient enough to endure penalties imposed by the West.[67] In 1989, the George H. W. Bush administration reached a similar conclusion with respect to mainland China.

Moreover, the resources of the United States are finite and this nation can ill afford to fight freedom wars for every oppressed country. Surely that is a central lesson from America's experience in Vietnam. Even the dictators of small nations can be fiercely resistant to US pressures for democracy. For example, the efforts of the George H. W. Bush administration to use economic and political sanctions to oust Panama's dictator, General Manuel Antonio Noriega, collapsed, forcing the President to engage in a military invasion of Panama to achieve this objective. Understanding the limitations of pursuing human rights as a foreign policy objective, the Carter administration adopted for what Muskie referred to as a "practical approach"—doing what it could, where it could, "holding up the banner of human rights."[68] This was essentially the same modus operandi adopted toward the ethnic cleansing that occurred in the Balkans during the George H. W. Bush and Clinton administrations, and the same approach used by President Obama in dealing with the "Arab Spring" uprisings that began in 2010. To assist in the guidance of his administration toward ways in which global human rights might be protected, Obama established an Atrocities Prevention Board in 2012 that would be run directly out of the White House.

## Quality of Life

Just as disconcerting to observers as political repression throughout the world are the staggeringly bad economic conditions under which citizens of poor countries must live. In Haiti, the average income per person is less than $1 a day; one of every five children dies before age five; and only 20 percent of the people have access to clean drinking water—conditions sharply aggravated by a devastating earthquake in 2009.[69] Such statistics are all too common around the globe. Alarming, too, and raising additional ethical issues, is the damage being done to the world's environment by the growth-oriented industrialized societies. Noting the stress evident already in each of the Earth's major biological systems—oceanic fisheries, grasslands, forests, and crop lands—an authority on global ecology argued as long ago as 1978 that "if civilization as we know it is to survive, [an] ethic of accommodation must replace the prevailing growth ethic."[70]

Today the need for accommodation grows ever more urgent, as President Obama underscored in his State of the Union Address on February 12, 2013, in reference to the perils of global climate change in the twenty-first century. A few months later at Georgetown University, the President vowed: "I refuse to condemn your generation and future generations to a planet that's beyond fixing."

Standing next to the basic human rights of freedom and dignity, of basic nourishment and shelter, is an **ethics of ecology—** *a concern for the moral requirement of keeping the planet habitable for the human race now and in the future.* The 1986 accident at the Chernobyl nuclear plant in Ukraine, a Soviet

Global warming results in a decline of sea ice, where polar bears breed as well as capture their prey.

satellite at the time, served as a deadly reminder of how vulnerable modern society is to the dangers of technology. In the years after the meltdown, cancer cases doubled in the region near the stricken plant. The animal population was even more adversely affected. Calves, for example, were routinely born without heads and limbs. "My daughter recently got married," said a mother who cared for pigs at a nearby tainted farm. "What kind of grandson will I have?"[71] With concern about widespread safety deficiencies in other nuclear reactors, a high ranking UN official estimated at the time that "up to 40 potential Chernobyls are waiting to happen in the former Soviet Union and Central Europe."[72]

The quality of life for Americans and everyone else on this globe is of utmost importance to US foreign policy. When people are deprived of food, shelter, access to adequate health care, and a safe environment with clean air and pure water, they rebel. The result is anger and unrest in the world—even violence—that can draw in outside powers, or be directed at them. The United States has attempted to address such matters through diplomatic initiatives, trading opportunities, and development assistance. No nation by itself, though, can bring about the decent quality of life deserved by every citizen on this planet; all nations must be partners in this quest. Nevertheless, Americans by themselves can provide leadership through their own approaches to conserving energy, protecting the environment, and leaving a lighter global footprint. "If America has a service to perform in the world—and I believe it has—," said J. William Fulbright (D-Arkansas), one of the giants of the Senate during the Cold War years, "it is in large part the service of its own example."[73] This form of leadership applies not only to quality-of-life issues but also to how well Americans are able to conduct themselves in fighting terrorism without losing sight of the nation's traditional values, constitutional principles, and high ethical standards.

## CHARTING A MORAL COURSE

Moral questions are very much a part of American foreign policy. They are, in fact, "inescapable."[74] Because the world continues to be dominated by calculations of military strength, the perspective of the realist with its emphasis on the balancing of military power will no doubt remain the core consideration in the minds of policy makers, at least for the foreseeable future. After all, the failure of military balance can produce decidedly immoral results, as humanity has learned from two world wars. Yet ethical issues cannot be ignored. In the weighing of moral considerations, Nye points out that a reliance on one-dimensional rationalizations—be they pure Kantian, pure consequentialist, or pure anything else—would be an error.[75]

## Three-Dimensional Ethics

The ethical strands interwoven into the choices that leaders must make are complex. Policy makers and policy analysts must be aware of the *interplay between the motives of decision makers, the means they propose, and the likely consequences of their choices*: a **three-dimensional ethics**.

Are the intentions of policy makers worthy? Have they given careful attention to the appropriateness of their methods? Are the results acceptable? Here are key questions regarding motives, means, and consequences that must be addressed for a more reliable judgment about the moral goodness of a foreign policy decision. As Nye remarks, if a child were to be killed in an automobile accident on an icy road as a well-meaning driver attempted to bring her home, the driver's inadequate consideration of the road conditions (facts about the means), along with the tragic consequences for the child, would warrant a negative moral judgment about the driver's decision, mitigated only slightly by his worthy desire to see the child safely home to her parents on a cold winter night.[76]

When Nye applies his threefold categories to the ethical problem presented by the existence of nuclear weapons, he derives the following rules of conduct:

*Motives*
1. Self-defense is a just but limited cause.

*Means*
2. Never treat nuclear weapons as normal weapons.
3. Minimize harm to innocent people.

*Consequences*
4. Reduce risks of nuclear war in the near term.
5. Reduce reliance on nuclear weapons over time.[77]

Nye concedes that these maxims fall short of a solution for every ethical dilemma posed by nuclear weapons; but they do provide, like the Catholic bishops' letter they closely parallel, both policy makers and citizens with some further guidance through this difficult age. Moreover, Nye's insistence on a three-dimensional ethics helps the decision maker steer away from overly simplified, and therefore misleading, judgments about the appropriate moral stance to take on a wide range of international issues. Few of the ethical issues confronted by foreign policy officials in Washington are likely to

---

### PERSPECTIVES ON AMERICAN FOREIGN POLICY 14.4

**The historian ARTHUR M. SCHLESINGER Jr. on international morality:**

The assumption that other nations have legitimate traditions, interests, values, and rights of their own is the beginning of a true morality of states. The quest for values common to all states and the embodiment of these values in international covenants and institutions is the way to establish a moral basis for international politics.

This will not happen for a long, long time. The issues sundering our world are too deep for quick resolution. But national interest, informed by prudence, by law, by scrupulous respect for the equal interests of other nations, and above all by rigorous decency, seems more likely than the trumpeting of moral absolutes to bring about restraint, justice and peace among nations.

*SOURCE:* Excerpt from THE CYCLES OF AMERICAN HISTORY by Arthur M. Schlesinger, Jr. Copyright © 1986 by Arthur M. Schlesinger, Jr. Reprinted by permission of Houghton Mifflin Harcourt Publishing Company. All rights reserved.

---

be easy, and judgments are apt to remain clouded by uncertainty; nevertheless, an understanding of ethics and international affairs has improved in recent years. One can hope, along with historian Arthur M. Schlesinger Jr., in *Perspectives on American Foreign Policy* 14.4, that with this growing sophistication will come greater wisdom.

## Muscle and Morality

Few students of foreign policy would question Stanley Hoffman's observation, cited early in this book, that realism "remains the dominant paradigm in the study of international affairs."[78] The failure of the League of Nations and the naiveté of Neville Chamberlain eroded the world's faith in idealism as an approach to foreign policy. Yet who would be so bold as to deny that the power of principle—the pursuit of high ideals—can hold strong sway over the opinions of human beings around the world? Clearly the speeches and often the actions of American leaders are drawn in this direction, with the food and other relief for Haiti after its earthquake in 2009 only one of many recent examples. "Should we use military power to intimidate smaller nations? Should we no longer stand up for the ideals we believe and that we share with all humanity?" asked Vice President Walter Mondale in 1980. "I reject that view as naive and dangerous," he answered, adding that "strength without principle is weakness."[79] At Texas A&M University on the eve of his retirement in December of 1992, President George H. W. Bush reminded his audience that "our country's tradition of idealism [has made us] unique among nations."

The influences of America's culture and moral standing, what Nye has referred to as soft power, are a vital part of US policy. This nation's grand strategy for foreign policy will continue the search for a proper blend of hard power (the instruments of the military and economic statecraft) and soft power (attraction to American values, from the freedoms safeguarded in the Constitution to contemporary fashion and arts). Or in Nye's phrase for this blend: smart power.[80] A contemporary Chinese scholar, Yan Xuetong, predicts that his country will win the race with the United States for world leadership. "It is the battle for people's hearts and minds that will determine who eventually prevails," he writes. "And, as China's ancient philosophers predicted, the country that displays more humane authority will win."[81] One cannot quarrel with his measure for success. The world will be watching to see whether the United States or China is better at displaying "humane authority." In his 2013 State of the Union Address, President Obama made a reference to a man in the street in Rangoon, Burma, waving an American flag along with thousands of others when the President visited Burma. Obama proudly recalled the man saying, "There is justice and law in the United States. I want our country to be like that."

## SUMMARY

Ethical considerations can play a key role in foreign policy decisions. With a misguided faith in the promises of Adolf Hitler, British Prime Minister Neville Chamberlain signed a worthless peace pact with the Nazis, thereby emboldening Germany to discount the British as spineless moralists who preferred peace at all costs. The United States selected its targets in Japan for atomic bombs based, in part, on moral considerations, although critics maintain that Washington officials were insufficiently sensitive to ethics in their hasty use of this weapon against Nagasaki. Ethical questions have swayed America's appraisal of nuclear weaponry throughout the Cold War and afterward. The American Catholic bishops' influential pastoral letter provides an example of an attempt to reconcile Kantian and consequentialist moral strains with regard to nuclear deterrence.

National security intelligence and human rights policies have also attracted moral debate. Espionage, covert action, and counterintelligence all raise serious ethical questions about what boundaries, if any, should be placed on the operations of America's secret agencies. After the 9/11 attacks against the United States, the use of extraordinary rendition and harsh interrogation methods by the second Bush administration became controversial moral issues.

The relationship between ethics and international affairs is a complex topic and no one has a guaranteed set of rules to guide policy makers with certitude toward the best mix of morality and pragmatism in foreign affairs. Nevertheless, analysts have become more sophisticated in their study of this elusive subject. They emphasize the importance of three key dimensions that constitute most decisions: the motives of the decision makers, their attention to means, and the consequences of their choices. Military power continues to dominate world politics; yet ethical questions are inescapable in the affairs of nations and sometimes principle prevails over the use of force.

## KEY TERMS

American bishops' letter (1983) p. 448
consequentialists p. 446
Deutch rules (1995) p. 453

ethics of ecology p. 463
extraordinary rendition p. 441
human rights p. 461

---

## QUESTIONS FOR DISCUSSION

1. Using a Kantian-consequentialist dialogue, how would you appraise the decision to bomb Hiroshima in 1945? Would your analysis apply equally well to the bombing of Nagasaki?

2. Are there circumstances you can envision in which it would be proper for the United States to engage in an assassination plot against a foreign leader? The leader of a terrorist organization overseas? How about inside the United States? An American citizen abroad who is critical of the United States and makes speeches worldwide to discredit its foreign policy? An American citizen inside the United States?

3. Which branch (or branches) of government should be involved in the selection of targets (so-called high-value individuals or HVIs) for killing by US drones?

4. Do you accept the arguments made in the Catholic bishops' letter on nuclear deterrence? What changes, if any, would you make in applying its argument to America's posture of nuclear deterrence today?

5. Why do you think President Nixon and the nation's top intelligence chiefs so readily signed onto the Huston Plan?

6. Are there circumstances when extraordinary renditions and harsh interrogations might be necessary activities for the United States— say, when intelligence suggests that a nuclear device has been sneaked into the nation (a "ticking bomb scenario")? How likely is this scenario? Should laws be based on unlikely events, or is it understood that in times of great danger America's leaders may have to take extra-constitutional and extralegal steps, just as Abraham Lincoln did in 1861?

7. Can you apply the idea of three-dimensional ethics to an argument for or against US intervention Afghanistan in 2001? The Syrian civil war?

## ADDITIONAL READINGS

Pfiffner, James P. *Torture as Public Policy: Restoring US Credibility on the World Stage*. Boulder, CO: Paradigm, 2010.

Power, Samantha. *"A Problem From Hell": America and the Age of Genocide*. New York: Basic Books, 2002.

Sandel, Michael J. *Justice: What's the Right Thing to Do?* New York: Farrar, Straus & Giroux, 2009.

---

For further readings, please visit the book's companion website.

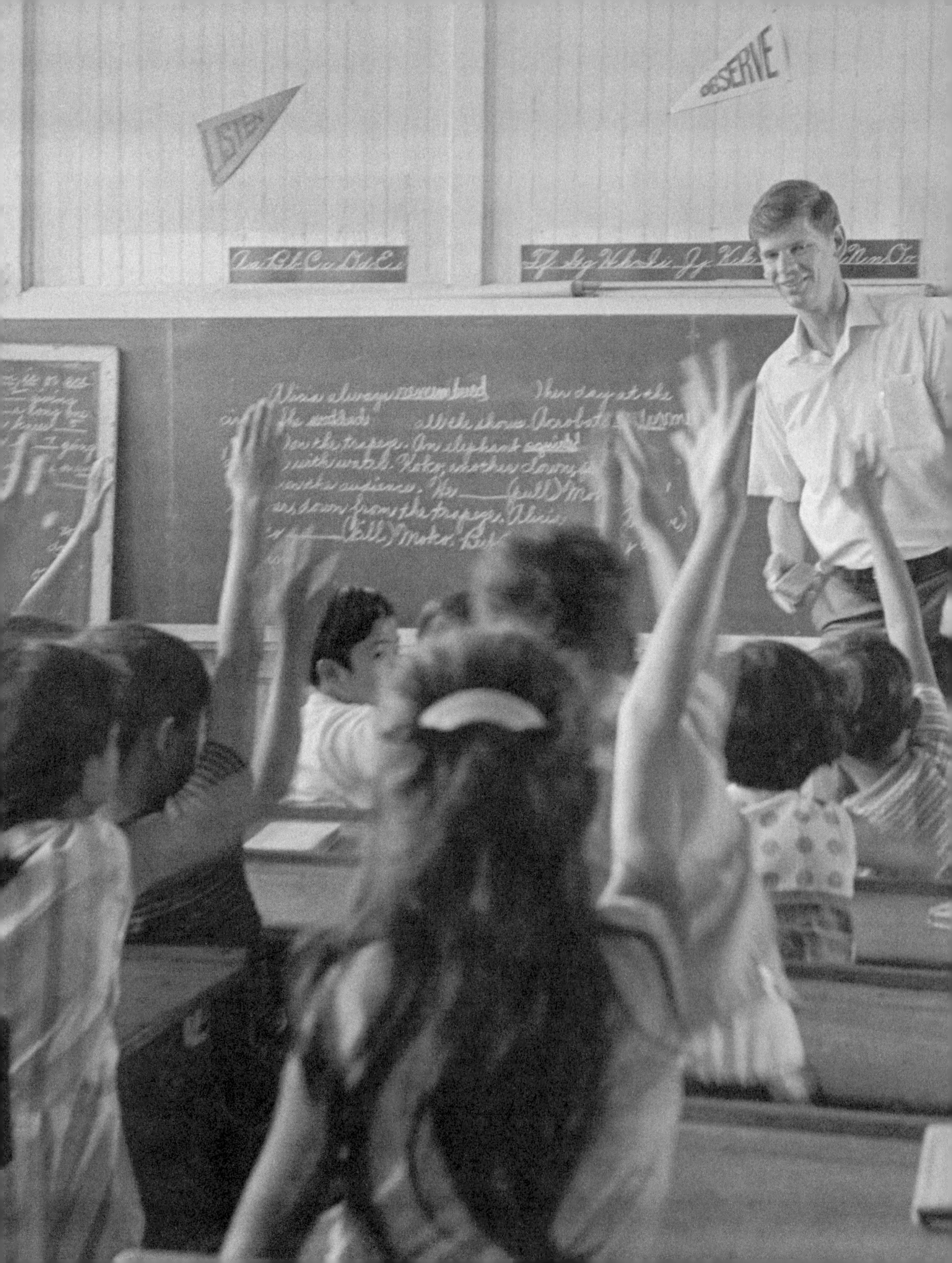
LISTEN
OBSERVE

# New Directions for American Foreign Policy

## CONSTITUTIONAL GOVERNMENT AND TRUTH TELLING

America's form of constitutional government requires cooperation and honesty among the branches—the *sine qua non* for effective foreign policy in a system of separated powers and institutions. Yet executive branch officials have often been less than forthcoming with lawmakers, making it difficult for them to perform their roles as overseers and undermining the balance between the executive and legislative branches established by the Constitution.

During hearings into the Iran-*contra* scandal in the 1980s, for example, the chief of the CIA's Central American Task Force (C/CATF) attempted to sidestep efforts by Congress to investigate the illegal arms sales to Iran and

Stephen C. Rye, of Farmersville, California, a Peace Corps volunteer, teaches English at the Central Elementary School in the Philippines.

the use of those funds (and other monies raised secretly) to sponsor covert actions in Nicaragua expressly prohibited by Congress. Investigators soon discovered the C/CATF had misled them. They placed him under oath in a hearing and asked him to explain himself. He replied that he had been "technically correct, [if] specifically evasive"—a form of CIA gobbledygook that lawmakers too frequently encountered during their inquiry into the scandal and in other efforts to monitor foreign policy activities. In response, Senator George J. Mitchell (D-Maine) offered the intelligence bureaucrat a pertinent civics lesson. "Every executive branch official has an obligation," Mitchell said, "to obey and uphold the law, and not to select which laws will be obeyed or not."[1]

The Reagan years were hardly the only time the executive and legislative branches were at loggerheads over information. Earlier, both the Johnson and Nixon administrations were notorious for failing to keep the American people—or even their representatives in Congress—well informed about the war fighting in Vietnam.[2] In more recent years, the second Bush administration kept all but a few lawmakers ignorant about its decision in 2001 to bypass the Foreign Intelligence Surveillance Act of 1978 that required presidents to obtain a warrant from special court (the FIS Court in Washington, DC) before conducting a national security wiretap. The handful of members of Congress who were

**LEARNING OBJECTIVES AND CONSTITUTIONAL ISSUES**

**By the end of this chapter, you will be able to:**

- *Identify four major foreign policy vulnerabilities that must be addressed if the United States wishes to remain a leading world power.*
- *Suggest ways to expand the knowledge base of US citizens about foreign affairs.*
- *Describe how the fragmentation of foreign policy institutions might be overcome.*

- *Explain why a greater empathy among Americans for the plight of foreign nations could help the standing of the United States in the world.*
- *Assess whether the United States has been too quick to intervene overseas with armed force or with the CIA.*

**THIS CHAPTER RAISES THE FOLLOWING CONSTITUTIONAL QUESTIONS:**

- At the foundation of the Constitution is the belief in the importance of democracy—government by the people. Is this theory fatally undermined by the low level of information Americans seem to have about international affairs?

- A theme running through this book, and through the Constitution as well, is that multiple centers of power in a government guard against the danger of the too strong a president. Yet are there now too many power centers, preventing the efficient conduct of foreign policy?

- If presidents find that Congress will not pass their proposed legislation, leading to a policy stalemate—a situation that President Obama has often confronted—does that suggest America's constitutional form of government has failed?

- Which branch of government do you think is responsible for America's frequent use of military force abroad? Does the Constitution have a bias toward the war power over diplomacy? Or are such decisions more a result of broader political considerations involving interest groups and public opinion?

informed about this evasion of the law were prohibited from discussing the operation with staff or other members of the two congressional Intelligence Committees, effectively neutralizing any opportunity for meaningful legislative review or response.[3] President Bush also hid from lawmakers the extent to which torture and extraordinary renditions were used in CIA and military counterterrorism operations.[4]

During the Obama administration, the executive branch again played shell games with Congress, refusing, for example, to share with members of the Intelligence Committees the legal reasoning behind its authorization of drone kill lists—which included the names of American citizens—in the Middle East, Northern Africa, and Southwest Asia. When a white paper on the legal authorization leaked to NBC News, the chair of the Senate Select Committee on Intelligence, Dianne Feinstein (D-California) said that she had been "calling for the public release of the administration's legal analysis on the use of lethal force—particularly against US citizens—for more than a year."[5] Further, the administration refused to share with lawmakers Presidential Policy Directive 11 (PPD 11), which set the terms for the future size and configuration of America's nuclear arsenal. Senator Richard Lugar (R-Indiana) reminded the adminis-tration, to no avail in this instance, that "our country is strongest and our diplomacy is most effective when nuclear policy is made by deliberate decisions in which both the legislative and executive branches fully participate."[6]

In the absence of access to information about executive branch activities overseas, the Congress becomes little more than a foreign policy eunuch. The Madison system of governance embedded in the language of the Constitution only works when the separate institutions of American government share power. In what is often referred to today as the Information Age, information is power. When the executive branch monopolizes this power, the other branches wither. President John F. Kennedy expressed the necessary spirit of institutional comity during his State of the Union Address in 1962, noting that the Congress and the presidency were "not rivals for power, but partners for peace."[7] ∼

## A FRESH AGENDA FOR THE UNITED STATES ABROAD

In previous chapters in this book, I have presented key analytic concepts; historical background; a look at how Washington, DC, operates; and an examination of the main instruments employed by the United States in its relations with other countries. In this final chapter, I shift gears from an empirical (fact-based) perspective to a more normative (value-oriented) look at the future of American foreign policy, including the question of how this nation might nurture improved institutional relations in Washington, DC as a guard against the kind of information legerdemain engaged in by several administrations over the years.

In 2010, Secretary of State Hillary Rodham Clinton declared, "The United States can, must, and will lead in this new century."[8] Yet the question remains: lead in what manner and in what direction? In this chapter I encourage students of foreign policy to think about how they would like this nation to move forward in the world. A set of proposals are offered here, not for the purpose of proselytizing any specific approach to US relations overseas, but rather to stir discussion about how Americans might best achieve the nation's objectives abroad, without compromising its reputation for integrity and fair play. The world is constantly changing and American foreign policy must adapt with new times. Given recent events in the world, what course corrections would you recommend to the president and lawmakers?

The prominence of the United States as a global power is a relatively new phenomenon. As statesman George F. Kennan recalled in 1951, at the beginning of the twentieth century US foreign policy was guided by "the concepts and methods of a small neutral nation." When he began his distinguished diplomatic career in the 1920s, the Department of State was "a quaint old place, with its law-office atmosphere, its cool dark corridors, its swinging doors, its brass cuspidors, its black leather rocking chairs, and the grandfather's clock in the Secretary of State's office."[9] Those simple days are gone. Today, the Department of State is a sprawling edifice (now named the Harry S. Truman Building, located in the Foggy Bottom region of Washington, DC), with seemingly endless hallways, government-gray desks, intricate operating procedures, and thousands of busy officials—in short, a modern bureaucracy.

The life of the Foreign Service officer overseas has changed dramatically, too. Seldom in earlier times were the lives of American diplomats at risk. The seventy-three who died in the first 189 years of the nation's history were, in almost all cases, the victims of shipwrecks, natural disasters, or tropical diseases. Since 1965, in contrast, more than eighty have died at the hands of terrorists, including seven ambassadors in the past eighteen years. The most recent was Ambassador J. Christopher Stevens in 2012, attacked by terrorists in Benghazi during the unrest in Libya that followed the Arab Spring uprisings across northern Africa in 2010. In place of the once attractive prospect of living abroad, with low-cost housing and affordable servants, villas with tennis courts and swimming pools, frond-trimmed verandas with lazy fans and trays of tax-free Scotch, today's diplomat lives more frugally and faces the constant threat of harassment and terror.

Just as distant countries have grown more dangerous to Americans, so have they become more important. As Americans learned tragically in 2001, the world is increasingly difficult to ignore with its potential for terrorist attacks; the spread of sophisticated weaponry; trading competition—and barriers—that affect the vitality of America's domestic economy; the need for access to mineral resources overseas critical for industrial manufacturing; the vanishing rain forests with their precious flora and fauna; and the human rights abuses wrought by corrupt dictators. The early American colonists also faced enormous challenges, surrounded as they were on one side by an ocean dominated by powerful, hostile navies and on the other side by a vast wilderness. Nonetheless, the contemporary perils of terrorism and WMDs, as well as the intricate patterns of trade interdependence and a rising level of environmental pollution, have made this age one of even greater complexity and danger.

At the same time, advances in knowledge—from medicine and astrophysics to communications and the art of governing—encourage the hope that with every passing year human beings are becoming better equipped to cope with global challenges. Shadows darken this optimistic forecast, however. As the twenty-first century unfolds, Americans face four major foreign policy vulnerabilities that must be addressed if the United States wishes to remain a leading world power. First is the parochialism of US citizens; second, disarray within America's institutions of governance that plan and implement foreign policy; third, the nation's habit of turning first to the foreign policy instruments of military force and covert action, rather than diplomacy, economic statecraft, and soft power; and, fourth, a proclivity to intervene too readily in the affairs of other countries.

## Improved Citizen Awareness of Global Affairs

One shortcoming in America's preparation for global leadership, and a weakness each citizen can do something about, is the nation's inadequate knowledge base about foreign affairs. This ignorance shrinks the pool of citizens able to assume positions of foreign policy responsibility in the government and, as well, limits the ability of voters to evaluate the foreign policy proposals advanced by candidates for high office. Consider the following results from a survey on **citizen awareness** in the United States about world geography—one telling index of a citizen's *interest in, and understanding of, international relations.* A few months before the United States led a multinational invasion force into Iraq in 2003, a National Geographic Society survey found that only about one in seven (13 percent) of Americans between the ages of 18 and 24 could find Iraq on a world map. Or Iran and Israel. Only 17 percent could locate Afghanistan, where the United States was already at war; and just 24 percent could point to Saudi Arabia, a prime source of oil to fuel the West's industry and transportation.

The Americans polled in the survey could find only seven of sixteen prominent nations on the map. Thirty percent could not locate the Pacific Ocean, the world's largest body of water; and 56 percent did not know where India was, home to 17 percent of the world's population. Only 19 percent could name at least four countries that officially acknowledge their possession of nuclear weapons. Overall, Americans came in next to last in the quiz with a "D" grade, beating out only Mexico. The youth of Sweden came out on top, followed by respondents in Germany and Italy. In a report on the survey, the president of the National Geographic Society observed that "more students can tell you where an island is located that the *Survivor* TV series came from [the Marquesas Islands in the eastern South Pacific] than can identify Afghanistan or Iraq. Ironically, a TV show seems more real or at least more meaningful and interesting or relevant than reality."[10]

This parochialism is not isolated to young Americans. In 1997, for example, only 10 percent of a broad sampling of Americans could name any of the three nations invited to join NATO that year, even though the invitation to Hungary, Poland, and the Czech Republic had been widely discussed in the media. Even though the media widely reported the absence of WMDs in Iraq following America's invasion in 2003 to destroy these suspected weapons, over 70 percent of Republicans, 50 percent of Independents, and 30 percent of Democrats continued to believe that Saddam Hussein possessed WMDs.[11]

In 2006, another National Geographic Society survey found that almost half of the US public thought that India was the world's largest Islamic nation, when in fact

India's population of over 1 billion is predominantly Hindu (although it does have a sizable Muslim population as well). Indonesia has the largest Muslim population. Three months after a devastating earthquake struck Pakistan in October of 2005, claiming 70,000 lives, two-thirds of Americans could not recall where the catastrophe had taken place. Further, three-quarters of the respondents checked the box next to "English" as the most widely spoken language in the world, when the correct answer is "Mandarin Chinese."[12] Another survey taken in 2006 revealed that almost 60 percent of the public had little or no knowledge about Islam.[13] America's citizens will remain unable to appraise the foreign policy decisions of Washington officials unless and until they learn more about the geography, culture, languages, history, and politics of other lands. Nor can the United States comfortably wear the mantle of world leadership if its citizens express ignorance of, and little interest in, global affairs.

In the 1980s, a study issued by the Southern Governors Association reported that only 1 percent of Americans have ever studied a foreign language, even though three-fourths of the people of the world speak a language other than English. Moreover, ten thousand Japanese, fluent in English, were conducting business within the United States, while only about 900 American businesspeople—few of whom knew Japanese—were engaged in commercial activities in Japan.[14] These figures have improved somewhat, yet the overall number of native-born Americans able to converse in any language other than English currently remains less than 10 percent. (The inclusion of recent immigrants raises the figure to 20.1 percent.) In contrast, 56 percent of citizens in the European Union speak a language other than their native tongue, and 28 percent had mastered two foreign languages. Further, the number of Chinese studying English exceeds the number of Americans studying Mandarin by a ratio of 600-to-1; and Japanese businesspeople at work in the United States and fluent in English continue to outnumber their American counterparts in Tokyo.[15]

The United States was, and still is, the only place in the world where scholars can earn a doctorate without any foreign language study whatsoever; and the US Foreign Service remains the only diplomatic corps that does not require its officers to achieve full fluency in another language. In several American universities, it is possible to earn a degree in international business without having to take a single foreign language course or without ever traveling abroad.[16]

Moreover, scholars have seen their opportunities for studying abroad dwindle. The founder of the Fulbright International Educational Exchange program in 1946, J. William Fulbright, who later served a record thirteen years as chairman of the Senate Foreign Relations Committee, lamented near the end of the Cold War that "there are fewer fellowships now than there were 25 years ago. It is evident that some important political leaders in Washington have failed to recognize that the exchange program is more than just a laudable experiment, that it is also an important instrument of foreign policy, designed to mobilize human resources of intellect and judgment, just as military and economic programs mobilize physical resources."[17] The number of

Fulbright fellows fluctuated during the Cold War, although remained consistently at a lower level than during the heydays referred to by Senator Fulbright. Since 1991, however, the program has enjoyed a renaissance. The total number of fellows (American and foreign) rose from 3,211 in 2004–2005 to 5,550 in 2010–2011.[18] This is one trend pointing in the right direction; but the ongoing deficiencies of Americans in the study of foreign languages, along with their limited knowledge of the history, customs, and geography of other nations, remain a barrier to effective global leadership.

## Overcoming Institutional Fragmentation

For those who do possess the education and qualifications to become officials in Washington's foreign policy bureaucracy, there is another challenge alluded to in every chapter of this book: to work with one another more effectively, in a spirit of mutual respect for the involvement of each branch of government in the making of foreign policy. Intolerable in a constitutional democracy are executive subterfuges epitomized by Lyndon Johnson's hidden escalation of the war in Vietnam and Richard Nixon's secret invasion of Cambodia. Disturbing, too, has been the misuse of the intelligence agencies at home and abroad, from domestic spying and an alliance with the underworld for carrying out murder plots against Fidel Castro during the 1960s; the Iran-*contra* affair in the 1980s; and the warrantless wiretaps and use of torture during the second Bush administration. The second Bush administration also ignored doubts in the Intelligence Community about the presence of WMDs in Iraq in 2002 while taking the nation to war on that shaky premise. And the Obama presidency has often been unwilling to share information with authorized members of Congress about its foreign policy activities—most conspicuously, with respect to its legal justification and standard of targeting evidence for the killings of US citizens abroad suspected of terrorist collusion, but also about the wide scope of NSA data collection on telephone and social media use by Americans revealed in 2013.

When this nation strays from its founding values and sense of moral purpose, Americans begin to look like hypocrites. The world is left wondering, as former Vice President Walter F. Mondale put it, "who stands for the rule of law and respect for civil liberties?" Mondale quoted General David H. Petraeus, America's top military commander for a time during the recent wars in Iraq and Afghanistan, who said "Abu Ghraib and other situations like that are nonbiodegradable. They don't go away. The enemy continues to beat you with them like a stick."[19] All of these experiences point to a central conclusion: the greatest challenge for foreign policy is to remain faithful to America's constitutional principles and democratic ideals.

Political scientist Aaron Wildavsky, long an astute observer of American government, had this to say about the final decades of the Cold War: "Three Presidents [Johnson, Nixon, and Reagan] have now brought an arrogance to power and a conviction of righteousness that allowed them to act as if they, not the American people, were sovereign."[20] His list could be expanded to include George W. Bush's warrantless wiretaps and the issuing of vague Justice Department legal judgments that permitted torture, rendition, and the controversial handling of war detainees in secret prisons abroad; or Barack Obama's escalation of drone killings abroad and massive NSA data collection at home, without full hearings on Capitol Hill (in executive or closed session, if necessary) and clear authority from lawmakers—not just a whisper in the ears of a few members of the Intelligence Committees.[21]

According to the Constitution, lawmakers have the right to participate in the great decisions of war and peace, the making of international agreements, the use of trade sanctions and inducements, and the direction and control of the nation's secret intelligence agencies—not just the president. "Contrary to popular belief, the powers are not separated in the foreign policy-national security area," advised the constitutional lawyer Lloyd N. Cutler in 1987. "They are shared for the most part, and neither Congress nor the President can do much without the other."[22] Humility would be a refreshing trait for occupants of the White House—of both parties—to display.

Congress, too, must be willing to stay within its constitutional boundaries. The spectacle of individual lawmakers playing the role of secretary of state, off in some distant capital negotiating for this or that policy objective, is unhelpful to the well-established procedures of US diplomacy. Neither are too many hearings on Capitol Hill that focus on the same subject fair to busy program managers in the executive branch, nor multiple subcommittees and committees engaged in supervision of the same agency. These redundancies pose an unreasonable surcharge on the time and energy of bureaucrats, in addition to sowing confusion as to which lawmakers are responsible for foreign policy oversight. The 9/11 Commission concluded, for example, that present-day intelligence accountability on Capitol Hill is "dysfunctional," with too many other committees involved in the review of the nation's secret agencies when SSCI and HPSCI should manage this task.[23]

One useful step would be for Senate members to reject the notion that statutes must be routinely pass by an extraordinary majority of sixty votes or else face the prospects of a filibuster.[24] The opportunity for a filibuster on foreign (or domestic) policy, whereby a small group of lawmakers can slow down the movement of controversial bills through the legislative process by demanding to examine their implications through more thorough debate, can be a valuable constitutional safeguard and should be retained. This method ought to be permitted, however, only in the case of major policy initiatives that warrant a full airing, not as a handy tool to stymie—through the technique of endless speechifying—most every legislative initiative proposed by the opposition party. The expectation laid out in Constitution is that laws will be enacted by a simple majority in most instances, without requiring a paralyzing extraordinary majority to bring debate to a close on routine roll-call votes.

A related matter is the use of the "hold" to stall presidential nominations. A hold is an informal method by which any senator may slow or prevent a vote, without providing a reason or even identifying himself or herself. It takes a vote of sixty senators to override a hold, just like the filibuster. In 2005, Democratic senators adopted this approach to delay confirmation of President Bush's nominee to be the US ambassador to the UN, John R. Bolton; and, in 2013, Senator Lindsey Graham (R-South Carolina) threatened to stop the nominations of Chuck Hagel as secretary of defense and John O. Brennan as CIA director, by way of a hold, until the Obama administration provided him with additional information about the President's response to the death of America's ambassador in Libya, J. Christopher Stevens.[25]

Both the legislative and the executive branches must also continue to search for a proper balance between the extremes of micromanagement by lawmakers, on one hand, and the perils of excessive executive discretion over foreign affairs, on the other hand. "The institutional lesson to be learned . . . is not that the presidency should be diminished, but that other institutions should grow in stature," wisely counseled Wildavsky in 1975. "The people need the vigor of all their institutions."[26]

*A vigorous Congress and presidency working together, both vital pistons in the engine of democratic government that complement one another through constructive criticism and mutual respect*—here's the proper form of **institutional comity** envisioned by the constitutional framers. Recall that in 1988, Senators Robert Byrd (D-West Virginia) and Sam Nunn (D-Georgia) began in this spirit to revise the War Powers Resolution, advocating the establishment of a panel of eighteen congressional leaders and key committee chairs to consult with the president before US troops were sent into hostile regions. In addition, their proposal envisioned the establishment of a "permanent consultative body" of six individuals—the Speaker of the House, the president pro tempore of the Senate, and the majority and minority leaders of both chambers—with whom the president would be required to discuss the use of all military force abroad.[27] Although this proposal never came to a vote in Congress, its suggestions for improved consultation between the branches merit revival and adoption, especially for use during times of potential warfare abroad.

Partisan differences and institutional tensions will continue to interrupt the smooth functioning of America's government from time to time, even under the best of circumstances when the executive and legislative branches are trying to cooperate with one another in good faith. After all, the nation's founders explicitly sought to build into the Constitution checks on the use of power and this arrangement is bound to lead to institutional friction. The appropriate, constitutional remedy when America's governing institutions are at loggerheads over major policy initiatives is clear: open debate before the court of public opinion, followed by a majority vote up or down in Congress on a proposed law, with a possible presidential veto as well as a chance for lawmakers to override the veto if feelings are strong enough to muster a special two-thirds vote in both chambers. Sometimes this system leads to stalemate—exactly what the founders had in mind if the representatives of the people disagree for the time being on how to proceed. Commentator George Will notes that the logjam faced by President Obama on Capitol Hill is "not a defect. It is an American achievement to slow things down" (ABC Television, June 17, 2012).

Senate Majority Leader
Lyndon B. Johnson
(D-Texas), left, and
Minority Leader Everett M.
Dirksen (R-Illinois) in
1960, when partisanship
on Capitol Hill was more
muted than today.

George Will is correct: this is the framework laid out by the Constitution, not the practices too often seen in recent decades of executive branch officials who have attempted to bypass the legislative branch—even lying to congressional committees and ignoring statutory reporting requirements—and of senators threatening or engaging in filibusters and private holds on practically every bill. Or the "gotcha" politics that concentrate more on scoring rhetorical points against the opposition party than working together toward bipartisan solutions to solve the nation's problems. Or bureaucrats dismissing legal restrictions on foreign operations, as when the NSC staff thumbed its nose at the Boland Amendment in the 1980s. Or, as also occurred during the Iran-*contra* episode, NSC staff privatizing foreign policy through secret fundraising outside the established appropriations process mandated by the Constitution. Or, more recently, intelligence bureaucrats in the George W. Bush administration adopting methods of torture and rendition against suspected terrorists without proper legislative authority, as well as simply ignoring the FISA law and engaging in warrantless wiretapping.

A further challenge is the partisan acrimony that cropped up between the branches during the late 1980s and early 1990s and continues to plague America's government. This bickering has "confused our allies and emboldened our enemies," said Senator David Boren (D-Oklahoma), the SSCI chairman, in 1989.[28] In the decades since Boren's observation, partisan vitriol has further intensified in Washington and today threatens to paralyze the ability to govern the United States. The ultimate solution to this extraconstitutional mud wrestling is for voters to send to Capitol Hill and the White House men and women willing to shed extreme partisanship and who understand that democracy requires bargaining and compromise to succeed. Most voters tend to like their own representative while at the same time criticizing Congress as a whole. In a vibrant democracy, however, citizens must take the time to examine more carefully the individual voting records of their own representatives. Only in this manner can they tell if the lawmaker they sent to Washington has become excessively partisan and unwilling to compromise. This essential citizen responsibility could be substantially aided by more extensive reporting by the nation's journalists, scholars, and pundits on the specific voting records of lawmakers, as well as on the media posturing of extreme partisan obstructionists who create a logjam in Washington as they pursue their own narrow, ideological objectives.

## Toward Greater International Empathy

During the period of Soviet decline that led to the fall of the Berlin wall in 1989, the United States urgently needed to shift its attention away from an abiding concern about global communism and toward other international issues vital to the prosperity of Americans, such as international trade, world health, global ecology, refugee migrations, international food supplies, and population control. "The struggle between the Soviet Union and the West may become less central," diplomat David D. Newsom accurately observed before the Soviet breakup, "as both camps look over their shoulders at circumstances outside their experience."[29] The erosion of the ozone layer that protects humans from dangerous ultraviolet solar rays, along with pressures that accompany a bursting world population (now rapidly approaching 7 billion people), hold greater potential calamity for citizens of both the United States and the former Soviet republics than the relatively limited number of disagreements that separated Washington and Moscow during the Cold War.

Virtually every student of international affairs agrees that a slowing down of the global population explosion is critical to the future of the planet. Currently, the world's population is growing at a rate of 1 billion people every eleven years. The poorest nations, precisely those that are in the worst shape to deal with burgeoning growth, will see the most alarming increases in birth rates. Within twenty-five years, for example, it is estimated that Nigeria will undergo a population spurt to reach the level of 300 million people, or about the same number of people in the United States in 2012—but Nigeria is only the size of Arizona and New Mexico.[30] Sub-Saharan Africa's population has more than tripled over the past fifty years, to 875 million people. As Yale University historian Paul Kennedy accurately forecast in 1993, 95 percent of the projected doubling of the world's total population by the middle of the twenty-first century "will take place in developing lands"—a projection confirmed by the *CIA World Factbook* in 2012.[31] Professor Jack A. Goldstone notes further that this growth will be increasingly concentrated in the "poorest, youngest, and most heavily Muslim countries."[32]

The largest urban centers will sprout up within the poorest nations. Feeding this expanding world population will be a daunting task, as farm output has slowed to the point where it is no longer keeping up with the global demand for food driven by these population increases. Population growth will put a heavy strain on global water resources as well; and the loss of tropical rain forests is apt to decrease the energy output of hydroelectric projects in Brazil and elsewhere, which are vital to support the economic growth needed to sustain a larger world population.[33] As the Cold War came to end, foreign policy challenges would go far beyond the threats of terrorism and the spread of WMDs, making executive-legislative consultation all the more important (see *Perspectives on American Foreign Policy* 15.1).

---

## PERSPECTIVES ON AMERICAN FOREIGN POLICY 15.1

**THE HOUSE FOREIGN AFFAIRS COMMITTEE on the virtues of consultation between the executive and legislative branches in the conduct of American foreign policy:**

Consultation offers a way for the two branches to work together in formulating foreign policy within the constitutional separation of powers . . . It indicates that enough time has been taken in shaping a policy to seek the views of those whose support is required for the policy to be successful. It also indicates a willingness to have the policy exposed to criticism, debate, and suggestions for improvement. . . .

Consultation could be a valuable tool for both the legislative and executive branches. It could be useful to the executive branch as a consensus-building device to increase the likelihood of having the congressional and public support necessary to carry out a policy or program. It could be useful to the Congress as a channel for constructively influencing foreign policy. These potential benefits appear fairly clear, yet good consultation is and has always been quite rare.

*SOURCE:* "Strengthening Executive-Legislative Consultation on Foreign Policy," *Congress and Foreign Policy Series*, No. 8 (October), Committee on Foreign Affairs, House of Representatives, Washington, DC, US Government Printing Office, 1983, p. 2.

---

One of the major problems faced by nations during the Cold War and today is, as former president Jimmy Carter wrote in 1988, "the increasing disharmony and lack of understanding between rich and poor nations."[34] According to a report on the developing world issued by the United Nations in 2010

- 1 billion children are deprived of services essential to survival and development
- 148 million children under five years old in developing regions are underweight for their age
- 101 million children are not attending primary school—especially girls
- 22 million infants lack protection from diseases by way of routine immunization
- 7.6 million children worldwide died before their 5th birthday in 2010
- 4 million newborns worldwide are dying in the first month of life
- 2 million children under 15 are living with HIV
- More than 500,000 women die each year from causes related to pregnancy and childbirth[35]

In Hwange, Zimbabwe, in 2010, the principal of a local school told a reporter, "We don't have desks. We don't have chairs. We don't have books."[36] Nor did the school have electricity or water, and the first-grade "classroom" consisted of students sitting beneath a nearby tree. In the next village over, a school had so few pens that one student would finish his work, then pass the pen along to the next student. "We can't realistically hope to achieve security and stability in a world where more than half a billion people exist in poverty and hunger," stressed Representative Mickey Leland (D-Texas) when he chaired the House Select Committee on Hunger in 1986.[37] Africa has experienced a remarkably good 5 to 6 percent economic growth rate in 2012, despite a world recession—thanks to oil exports, basic infrastructure improvements, and expanding ties with China and other Asia economies. Nevertheless, Robert Vos, director of the Development Policy and Analysis Division of the United Nations Department of Economic and Social Affairs, observed that even this strong growth will not hasten the end of the continent's poverty.[38] As the statistics on global health conditions in Figure 15.1 underscore, disease remains one of the greatest challenges.

People in poor nations remain locked in a vise of poverty and inadequate health care, while the media transmit stories around the globe about the life of luxury enjoyed by Western elites. In the 1980s, hotels in New York City and East Hampton charged $500 or more a night; galas in Washington, DC, boasted maids who filled toilet bowls with freshly chopped carnations after every flush.[39] Now, three decades later, lifestyles for the rich in the United States continued to grow more extravagant, as the gap between the well-to-do (the "1 percenters") and the rest of America (the "99 percenters") further widened during the administrations of George W. Bush and Barack Obama. The top 1 percent of households in the United States had a minimum income of $516,633 in 2010, according to calculations by the Tax Policy Center in Washington, DC. In contrast, the bottom 60 percent earned a maximum of $59,154 in 2010; the bottom 40 percent, a maximum of $33,870; and the bottom 20 percent, a maximum of just $16,961. In New York City, the imbalances are even more skewed: in 2012, the top 1 percent enjoyed an annual average of $3.7 million in income; and, in 2009, the earnings of the top twenty-five hedge fund managers in the United States (most of whom practice in New York City) averaged $1 billion.[40] Protests known as "Occupy Wall Street," spawned by the financial chasm between the 1 percent and the 99 percent, sprang up across the United States in 2011.

This chasm between the rich and the poor in the United States carried implications for foreign policy. The growing inequities were apt to make this nation less of an admired model for other nations. Drawn to America's constitutional principles of fairness and equality, the world's poor may well be repelled by the apparent failure of the United States to live up to these principles. The wealth disparities within America

*Figure 15.1*
The Toll Taken by Global Disease

Twenty-five thousand children around the world die of preventable causes every day. As economist Esther Duflo observes, "Nine million children under the age of five die every year in the world, which is the equivalent of a Haiti earthquake every eight days" ("Marshaling the Evidence," *RAND Review*, Spring 2010, p. 8). HIV/AIDs is the leading killer among communicable diseases in the world, followed by tuberculosis and malaria. In developing countries, *every year*:

- 800,000 children die from tetanus.
- 600,000 children die from whooping cough.
- 2 million children die from measles.
- 5 million children face handicaps as a result of preventable diseases.
- More than one-fourth of the children suffer from undetected malnutrition.
- Children suffer from 1 billion episodes of diarrhea.

raised serious questions, too, about whether US citizens, struggling to make ends meet, could find the time to act as thoughtful, informed voters able to appraise the nation's foreign policy initiatives and the quality of electoral candidates who seek their votes. Further, declining morale among the working class is a weak prescription for US competiveness in the world marketplace. The widening wealth gap suggested that the United States was at risk of sliding from a constitutional democracy into a plutocracy—rule by the wealthy, whereby decisions of war and peace, trade and aid, overt and covert action, would be made less on behalf of the public than for a self-interested governing oligarchy of corporate executives and hedge-fund managers, along with (their handmaidens) politicians and military officers.[41]

In addition to rebalancing the alarming income divide in the United States, a fresh approach to American foreign policy could place a greater emphasis on improving relations with the poorest nations, as well as with other countries the United States has long ignored. Through patient diplomacy, the leading nations of the world may be able to join together more effectively in fighting against what George C. Marshall understood to be the real enemies of international peace. In preparation for his Harvard commencement speech of 1947 announcing the European Recovery Program (later known as the Marshall Plan), Secretary of State Marshall crossed out a reference in an early draft to "the Communist threat." The enemies he chose to list were global "hunger, poverty, desperation and chaos."[42]

The painstaking application of diplomacy to these difficult challenges, coupled with increased attention to international economic cooperation through trade and development assistance, hold out greater hope for managing—even, in many cases, resolving—the world's problems than does the use of military might. Americans must always remember, though, from the experiences of Hitler, Stalin, and Bin Laden, that sometimes diplomacy simply will not work and arms must be taken up. Fortunately, the United States and the Soviet Union were able to settle their differences without a global war. Today the United States has a close trading relationship with the Socialist Republic of Vietnam—its bitter enemy only four decades ago. Surely the United States has learned from these experiences and can resolve current disputes peaceably with other nations.

The first step is for officials in Washington to slough off the siege mentalitythat characterized the Cold War and, now, the struggle against terrorists. Foreign policy driven by fear has prevented the consideration of fresh approaches to global challenges. Fear and ignorance have also interfered with America's ability to empathize with the historical experiences of other peoples.

Certainly empathy was in short supply during the Cold War, a major reason why it stretched out for so long. Had Americans considered with greater compassion the staggering loss of life endured by Russians during World War II—more than 20 million fatalities—the United States might have understood their concern about the defense of Russia's national borders. If one minute of silence were observed for each Russian killed in that war, the silence would last for thirty-seven years. Americans might have been more sensitive as well about the effect of the harsh anti-Soviet ("evil empire") rhetoric that so often came out of Washington during the early Cold War years and again in the 1980s; or the threat that SDI might appear to hold from the Soviet point of view. Seen from Russian soil, SDI and BMD systems look like the early stages of a potential US first-strike capability against a Russia that would lose its second-strike deterrent capacity because of America's missile shield.

Conversely, Soviet citizens and their leaders might have weighed more carefully the likely effects on Americans during the Cold War of Moscow's own hostile rhetoric; the vigorous Soviet arms buildup, including highly sophisticated conventional weapons; the billions of rubles worth of military weaponry provided to Cuba and Nicaragua, among other nations; the rashness of the Cuban missile adventure in 1962; a Soviet ballistic missile defense system that violated the Antiballistic Missile Treaty of 1972; and an extensive system of suspicious civil defense facilities in Moscow and other Russian cities that had the alarming hallmarks of a Soviet nuclear first-strike plan.

More recently, the harshness of the foreign policy pronouncements in the State of the Union Address offered by George W. Bush on January 29, 2002, also had untoward repercussions. In this speech, the President named Iraq, Iran, and North Korea as implacable enemies of the United States—indeed, an "axis of evil." This drove North Korea and Iran toward the development of nuclear weapons programs to defend themselves against a feared US invasion, like the one carried out against Iraq in 2003.

Today, Americans should ask how the United States might again be unnecessarily **demonizing adversaries**, *converting potential allies into enemies through hostile rhetoric and behavior*. What are the commonalities that Americans, along with European and Japanese allies, share with the governments of Russia and China? On this list of shared interests would be a mutual disdain for international drug lords and terrorists, along with a common concern about global pollution and potential pandemics.

Further, how well do Americans really understand the Islamic world, whose vast majority find the extreme measures of Al Qaeda just as appalling as does the rest of the world? Have Washington officials seriously considered the possibilities of negotiations with nonextreme elements among the Taliban? Has Washington tried hard to see the world through the eyes of Arabs and others with whom the United States has had disagreements recently? To what degree did the George H. W. Bush administration try—really try—to seek diplomatic negotiations between Kuwait and Iraq before the Persian Gulf War? What if a UN peacekeeping force had encamped along the Kuwaiti border before the war? Would Iraq still have attacked? It seems unlikely. To what extent did the second Bush administration try hard to confirm the presence of WMDs in Iraq, as two of America's leading allies—Germany and France—urged in 2002, before the US attacked the Saddam Hussein regime a second time in 2003? What significant measures have Washington officials taken to reach out with **empathetic diplomacy**—*genuine gestures of friendship and peace, backed by fair economic agreements*—to the leaders of North Korea, Iran, and Cuba, just as America did with Vietnam in the 1980s?

Empathetic diplomacy, not saber rattling, should be an important guiding principle for American foreign policy. In solidarity against the thugs affiliated with Al Qaeda and other terrorist organizations, the United States must seek out new friends in the world. The handshake of the economic deal and the cultural exchange can replace the mailed fist, as all the civilized nations join against Al Qaeda and the extremist Taliban agenda of death and chaos. Some violence-prone factions will understand only force. For these despoilers of the international community of nations, the civilized world must respond bravely, promptly, and with whatever legal means necessary to restore order—including an overpowering multinational military force. A starting point should be strong economic sanctions backed by the United Nations and designed to isolate renegade nations and groups, as befits international pariahs—with the same treatment applied against nations that violate the sanctions.

If these economic measures fail, the civilized world must work together through collective security arrangements, under the auspices of a strengthened UN, NATO, and other regional pacts, to adopt a prudent, carefully measured escalation of covert intervention and military force, until the outlaw nations or terrorist cells are brought into an alignment with international norms of justice and the rule of law. Either the democracies will adopt this approach or the world will return to the state of anarchy that has plagued humanity throughout history. In most cases, the best approach will be diplomacy: the signing of mutually beneficial economic, cultural, and technical agreements with other nations. Moreover, through the use of worldwide communications channels—public diplomacy—Western democracies can do a better job of informing people around the globe about opportunities for a good life that accompany open societies, a system of free enterprise, and the rule of law, in marked contrast to the doctrine of violence (85 percent of Qaeda victims have been Muslims)[43] and the dismal, barbaric, fourteenth-century life advocated by Islamic extremists.

## An End To Compulsive Interventionism

Another troubling weakness of America's foreign policy has been the tendency to exaggerate military threats abroad, then to respond with a military buildup or even the use of military force. You "cannot relax for a minute," the Reagan administration's Secretary of Defense, Caspar W. Weinberger, warned about possible Soviet aggression. The United States had to hold on tightly to every acre of the world, he argued. "If you don't deal with it, they [the Soviets] get a foothold."[44] A deputy assistant secretary of the Air Force during the Reagan years similarly advised a forum at the National Defense University: "The most critical special operations mission we have . . . today is to persuade the American people that the communists are out to get us."[45] Troops to Lebanon, the Grenada operation, the "secret" and illegal war in Nicaragua, an American armada in the Persian Gulf without strategy or timetable—during the Reagan years practically every US intervention abroad became justified as part of an anti-Soviet crusade.

Similarly, since the 9/11 attacks, Washington has allowed the fear of Al Qaeda and terrorism to draw the United States into two major wars in the highly inhospitable locations of Iraq and Afghanistan. The United States has poured over two trillion dollars into these wars (some say as much as three trillion)[46] and has lost over four thousand American lives in combat. Meanwhile, the Qaeda leadership has carved out a refuge in the mountains of Pakistan—although sans its top leader, Osama bin Laden, killed in Pakistan by a Navy Seals team in 2011. The number of these hard-core terrorists is often exaggerated. In fact, Al Qaeda has relatively few operatives—in 2010, an estimated 50 in Afghanistan and some 300 in Pakistan, for instance. Nonetheless, some offshoots of "Al Qaeda Central"—the remaining original Qaeda leadership cadre suspected of hiding out in northwest Pakistan—have displayed growth in their number of adherents, such as the AQAP faction in Yemen.[47] Many security experts believe that Qaeda disciples wherever they are may be best captured or killed by small-unit interventions, using CIA paramilitary operatives, Special Operations Forces operating in tandem with the Pakistani Army, and pinpointed drone attacks (also run jointly with the Pakistanis), rather than large standing US armies in the Middle East and Southwest Asia—a provocation to Muslims that is likely to swell the ranks of the Taliban and Al Qaeda.

In uneasy cooperation with the government of Pakistan, President Obama has authorized attacks against the Qaeda leadership and the Taliban, using drones as well as elite US troops; but the United States remains bogged down in a wider war against the Afghani Taliban, the loose band of warlords that gave Al Qaeda a safe haven in the lead-up to the 9/11 assaults against the United States. Americans are inclined to lump all of the Taliban together, as if they were a cohesive and implacable enemy. Some of its warriors are, in fact, so extremist and tightly aligned with Al Qaeda that they warrant their status as prime US military targets. Many, though, are less wedded to a global terrorist agenda; they are local warlords interested in their own economic well-being and the improvement of life for those who belong to their tribes.

One leading Taliban warlord south of Kabul, for instance, has a tribal marble business. Unskilled in the craft, he and his men use dynamite to extract the marble out of nearby mountains by using TNT explosives. In this crude manner, they lose about 90 percent of the high-grade ore. American specialists understand how to mine marble much more efficiently, with an ability to salvage most of the valuable ore for profit. By assisting the warlord with his marble business, which is apt to accrue large profits if carried out with modern techniques, and by helping him with what all tribes of Afghanistan seek—clean water, health clinics, schools, the development of an economic infrastructure—his allegiance may be shifted to the West and away from Al Qaeda and extremists within the Taliban camp.[48]

Small bands of well-armed US troops will be necessary in the region to protect American construction workers, doctors and nurses, teachers, and entrepreneurs working with their Afghan and Pakistani counterparts. They will have to be backstopped by special forces from the other democracies, as well as by carefully targeted Predator and Reaper drones strikes against local extremists when necessary. This formula offers a better chance of success in Southwest Asia and the Middle East than a major Western military presence.

An obsession with Al Qaeda has constricted the agenda for US global priorities. During the Cold War, Americans were slow to reject the overheated rhetoric about the domino theory and the rising tide of global communism. In reality, communism had become far less of a threat to the United States by the 1970s than it had been in earlier decades. Even President Reagan eventually understood this change. In 1988, he retracted his characterization of the USSR as an "evil empire"[49] and sought better relations with Kremlin leaders, beginning with an agreement to eliminate intermediate-range nuclear weapons (the INF treaty) in Europe. One of the Democratic candidates for president in the last presidential election of the Cold War (1988), former Arizona governor Bruce Babbitt accurately emphasized in his campaign speeches a significant new reality of global politics. "Marxism as an economic theory," he said, "has been a total, unqualified flop everywhere."[50]

Nations around the world understood that the "Soviet model" had failed. Nor, for that matter, was the "American model" foremost in the minds of leaders in developing nations as the Cold War ended. Japan, South Korea, and Taiwan—new commercial powerhouses—had become economic showcases with broad appeal throughout the Third World, and they would soon be surpassed by China and Singapore as attractive models to poor countries.

Moreover, despite the overheated rhetoric of the Reagan administration, Soviet troops had experienced only limited success abroad. The Red Army underwent a meltdown in Afghanistan, where a Kremlin-devised "pacification campaign"—the most costly Soviet military operation since World War II—had to be abandoned in 1989 after extensive losses in the field against the *mujahedeen* (the Afghan guerrilla forces).[51] The Soviets had met their own Vietnam. The defeat was aided by the supply of US weapons, especially the CIA's secret funneling of sophisticated Stinger and Blowpipe antiaircraft missiles to the *mujahedeen*. Even before these modern weapons came into the hands of Afghan warriors, however, the war had become a quagmire for the Soviet military, holding little prospect for victory.

In the four-and-a-half decades of Cold War that followed the end of World War II, the Soviet "empire" remained relatively static. Its firm domination was limited to the Eastern European bloc and Mongolia. Within this domain, nations such as Poland and Yugoslavia, and even the small states of Estonia, Latvia, and Lithuania inside the Soviet Union, sorely tested the Kremlin's ability to hold together its existing territories, let alone consolidate other foreign ventures. Once-obedient Cuba drifted away from Soviet bondage during the 1980s. The Soviet leadership faced a bleak reality during the Cold War: the USSR was bound not by a Canada or a Mexico, but by thirteen hostile nations, not to mention the several antagonistic "republics" and ethnic groups within its own borders.

Obsessed by the Soviet Union during the Cold War, the United States *abandoned its traditional instincts of caution in foreign affairs* and embraced instead a posture of **compulsive interventionism**. Yet if anything is clear from US foreign policy over the past hundred years, it is that this country cannot shape the world to its liking. As a grand strategy, that approach is a nonstarter. The United States has neither the wealth nor the will for such a mission—or the right.

Henry Kissinger, Secretary of State for Presidents Nixon and Ford, outlined three questions that ought to guide rational planning for America's grand strategy: What global changes is the United States prepared to resist? What are this nation's goals? What resources does the nation have to pursue these goals?[52] Failing to consider the resources side of the equation well enough, some policy makers during the Cold War believed that America had to take a stand against the Soviet Union virtually everywhere around the globe. They believed in "zero-sum" outcomes in world politics, like John Foster Dulles, who saw the world in black-and-white terms—as if the planet were merely an arena for combat between the United States and the Soviet Union. Recall the declaration of the House Armed Services Committee chairman in 1970 that America was joined in a battle "between Jesus Christ and the hammer-and-sickle" (Chapter 2). For those who shared this stark view of the world, every tremor of revolution in Chad, Grenada, or Nicaragua required a US response, regardless of how small the nation, how large the potential loss of American lives, or how extensive the drain on the federal treasury.

And all the while the needs of the American people at home begged for greater attention. The consequences of pouring the contents of the federal treasury into foreign adventures are now being felt. Today, 12.7 percent of the US population lives in poverty, including a quarter of all preschool children; 14 percent of these preschoolers suffer from nutritional deficiencies.[53] America's population centers face traffic gridlock; teenage pregnancies are on the rise; suicide rates have climbed to 33,000 a year, or one about every sixteen minutes; gender-based violence is epidemic; and the nation's cities and towns are plagued by cocaine, heroin, and methamphetamine distribution.[54]

Consider these further statistics about contemporary life in the United States:

### Economic Woes

- More than fifteen million Americans found themselves jobless in 2012, and in recent years job training and employment programs have been cut by almost 70 percent, with an annual budget for this purpose equivalent to about half of what the United States spent in one month of fighting in Iraq in 2009;[55]
- The number of Americans living below the poverty line is 46.2 million—the highest level in the fifty-two years the Census Bureau has kept this tabulation;[56]
- An international survey of "social justice" that looked at such matters as poverty rates among children and senior citizens, as well as income inequality and healthiness, placed the United States among the bottom of the industrial nations;[57]
- Nearly 35 percent of African American children live in poverty, as do one in five children among the wider population;[58]
- The number of people living in neighborhoods of extreme poverty grew by a third over the decade from 2000 to 2010;[59]
- The federal debt reached $16.4 trillion in 2012 (much of this sum the result of spending in wars overseas) and accruing annual interest payments that are an enormous drain on American taxpayers and their progeny.

### Incarceration

- 2 million Americans are in prison—the highest percentage of any nation, and the money spent on prisons has risen at six times the rate of spending on higher education;[60]
- The US prison population has doubled in the past two decades.[61]

### Health, Disease, and Mortality

- Americans experience higher rates of disease and injury, and die sooner, than people in other high-income countries;[62]
- US men ranked last in life expectancy among seventeen affluent countries, and US women ranked next to last;[63]
- 49 percent of America's school children arrive at school hungry;[64]
- Every three hours, a child is killed by a gun; and 85 percent of the children in the world who perish in this manner are in the United States;[65]
- More Americans have been killed in the United States by guns since June 4, 1968, when Democratic presidential candidate Bobby Kennedy (former Attorney General in the Kennedy administration) was assassinated, than in all the wars fought by the United States;[66]
- As Professor Nye has stressed, among the nations of the world, America is not at the top in life expectancy, primary education, job security, access to health care, or income equality.[67]

Recall, as well, the alarming educational statistics from earlier in this book that show the youth of America lagging behind students around the world in math, science, and reading. In 2010, a keen observer of the United States, George Packer of *The New Yorker*, wrote: "In America, the gap between the rich few and the vast majority widened dramatically, contributing to a historic financial crisis and an ongoing recession; the poisoning of the atmosphere continued unabated; and the Constitution had less and less say over the exercise of executive power."[68]

At the end of the Cold War, former president Jimmy Carter highlighted the fact that 45 percent of African Americans and other minorities in this country live in poverty. He added, "Forty percent of black males are functionally illiterate, and among younger adults, one-fourth are now in prison or on probation. Their chance of being killed by violence is greater than it was for the average soldier who went to Vietnam." The former President reported further that "twenty percent of the babies born at Grady Hospital in Atlanta, Georgia, are already addicted to crack cocaine."[69] The $100 million proposed by the Reagan administration for the *contras* in 1985 could have been spent in the United States to address such problems, enabling 150,000 students to attend college or providing 540,000 poor children with meals for a year. The trillions spent in Iraq and Afghanistan from 2003–2010 could have set the tilting US economy aright and bolstered America's homeland defenses.

"So where's the best place to spend $100 billion a year?" asks journalist Nicholas D. Kristof. "Is it on patrols in Helmand [a province in Iraq]? Or is it to refurbish our health care system."[70] For Kristof, the answer was clear enough: spend the money at home, where tangible results could be realized. Another thoughtful observer of American foreign policy, Thomas L. Friedman, agreed. He understood the importance of defeating Bin Laden and Al Qaeda, but not the expenditure of US taxpayer money in a futile effort to "make Afghanistan into Norway." That goal was simply too expensive "when balancing our needs for nation-building in America."[71]

Aaron B. O'Connell, a professor of history at the US Naval Academy and a Marine reserve officer, reminds Americans of an important warning from President Eisenhower early in his presidency. In 1953, the President said

> Every gun that is made, every warship launched, every rocket fired, signifies, in the final sense, a theft from those who hunger and are not fed, those who are cold and are not clothed. The cost of one modern heavy bomber is this: a modern brick school in more than 30 cities. It is two electric power plants, each serving a town of 60,000 population. It is two fine, fully equipped hospitals. It is some 50 miles of concrete highway. We pay for a single fighter plane with a half million bushels of wheat. We pay for a single destroyer with new homes that could have housed more than 8,000 people.[72]

Today, heavy bombers, fighter planes, and destroyers with their elaborate electronic equipment are dramatically more costly and add up to an even deeper erosion of potential spending for nonmilitary needs.

The regrettable state of homeland security almost a full decade after the 9/11 attacks is a good illustration of how America's resources can be tragically misspent on unnecessary adventurers abroad, at the expense of urgencies at home. While draining the American treasury to maintain armies in Iraq and Afghanistan, the George W. Bush administration only budgeted $600,000 to safeguard the nation's seaports, railways, bridges, tunnels, mass transit systems, and energy facilities—an amount equivalent to what the nation spent in a day on the wars in Iraq and Afghanistan during 2010.[73] Frank Church, a member of the Senate Foreign Relations Committee, had it right several decades ago when he declared: "The sooner we learn to impose some reasonable restraint on our own tendency to intervene too much in other people's affairs the happier land we will have, and the less burden we will place upon our own people to undertake sacrifices that are not really related to their own good or the good of their country."[74] A contemporary US Senator, Rand Paul (R-Kentucky)—a champion of greater legislative involvement in decisions of war and peace—has put it this way: "We need a foreign policy that works within the constraints of the Constitution and the realties of our fiscal crisis."[75]

Beyond the financial costs of excessive intervention abroad lies the growing realization that Americans can exercise only a limited influence on the affairs of other nations. Vietnam provides an example seared into the nation's memory. Consider the sacrifices made by the United States in the jungles of Southeast Asia during the 1960s and 1970s: over 58,000 GIs killed and 153,300 injured, along with the untold numbers who continue to suffer from the effects of Agent Orange and other chemical defoliants used during the war, as well as from lingering psychiatric and drug disturbances. Yet the wide range of overt and covert force used by the United States proved unable to curb the internal corruption of the South Vietnamese government, unite its army into an effective fighting force, or defeat the North Vietnamese.[76]

## EMBRACING A MORE DISCRIMINATING FOREIGN POLICY

Even given the importance of the needs inside the United States, a return to isolationism would be ill-advised. Two world wars have taught Americans the impossibility of escaping from the world, however tempting that may be; like it or not, the United States is inextricably bound to the other nations of this planet. Instead of isolation or excessive intervention abroad, Americans can demand a more prudent and **discriminating foreign policy,** one with a *more refined balance between realistic national goals and the availability of resources to achieve them.* The United States could "intervene" overseas with brigades of school and home builders; with nurses and physicians; with teachers, farmers, and economists; with the diplomats of the Foreign Service; and with the Peace Corps—and only in the most dire situations with the CIA or military force. America could exhibit the kind of benevolent and admired global leadership envisioned by Louis J. Halle in *Perspectives on American Foreign Policy* 15.2.

Professor Paul Kennedy of Yale University has suggested some specific ways in which the United States could be a helpful neighbor in the world, particularly in relationships with the developing nations. His worthy list of foreign policy initiatives includes "environmental pacts, increases in overseas aid from today's pitifully low percentages, the maintenance of open access to the third world's exports, and reduction of fuel use and greenhouse emission."[77] Much of what the United States can achieve abroad does not demand great expense. An example is the prospect of assisting poor nations in the construction of fertilizer plants, whose product can greatly help farm productivity. For example, the red acidic soil of Africa badly needs fertilizer; however, in all of sub-Saharan Africa there were only two major fertilizer plants in 1992, both in Nigeria.[78] This number increased over the next two decades—but

---

### PERSPECTIVES ON AMERICAN FOREIGN POLICY 15.2

**LOUIS J. HALLE on medieval knighthood as a model for U.S. global leadership:**

The national ideal of a supremely great power like the United States should be that of the gentle knight—exemplified in medieval literature by Lancelot, by Percival, by King Arthur. The gentle knight was strong, but his strength aroused neither fear nor resentment among the people because they knew it to be under the governance of moral responsibility and in the service of the general welfare. Precisely because he was strong, the gentle knight could afford to be modest, considerate, and courteous. His strength threatened only such outlaws as themselves constituted a threat to society. Consequently, his strength was not only in his arm *but in the regard of humankind.* Wherever he went, his quiet voice represented legitimacy, speaking with its authority.

SOURCE: Louis J. Halle, *The Elements of International Strategy: A Primer for the Nuclear Age* (Lanham, MD: University Press of America, 1984), p. 120, emphasis added. Reprinted by permission of The Rowman & Littlefield Publishing Group.

thanks chiefly to foreign assistance from the Chinese, not the United States. In 2012, however, the US Overseas Private Investment Corporation approved a $250 million loan to fund a nitrogen fertilizer facility in this important African nation.[79] America's technical know-how and experience with market economics are valuable assets that can be shared with others while winning new friends in the developing world.

Jimmy Carter reported when he visited the city of Janeiro, Zambia, in 1990, that "twenty-three percent of the babies are born with the HIV/AIDS virus."[80] This disease has already claimed some 25 million deaths over the years.[81] The United States can help educate people about sexually transmitted diseases and how to guard against them, and can make vaccines more available. Currently only two million of the world's 14.2 million AIDS victims have access to treatment medications. Progress in the fight against AIDS has been made, though; the number of people dying from this disease has fallen from 2.2 million in 2008 to 1.8 million in 2011. Nevertheless, according to a recent report, "the disease is still infecting people faster than they can be tested and treated."[82] In South Africa, for instance, youngsters about to turn fifteen have a 50 percent risk of becoming infected with the virus.[83] Even though the epidemic is believed to have peaked, HIV/AIDS still accounts for 1.5 million deaths worldwide each year.[84]

The work of the Carter Center in Atlanta to eradicate the Guinea worm in Nigeria and Ghana offers another illustration of what can be achieved overseas without exorbitant costs (see *Perspectives on American Foreign Policy* 15.3). By 2013, the eradication of the Guinea worm was in reach. When this happens, it will join smallpox among the only infectious diseases ever eliminated. As Kristof notes, "The Guinea worm campaign underscores that a determined effort, with local people playing a central role, can overcome a scourge that has plagued humanity for thousands of years."[85] The Gates Foundation is another organization that has achieved considerable success in battling global disease.[86]

A further illustration comes from an American organization called "Room to Read," which helps pay for the education of children overseas and builds libraries in their local schools. The cost per girl for a program in Vietnam, for example, is $250 annually. Journalist Kristof has visited one of the schools and came away with this conclusion: "We launch missiles, dispatch troops, rent foreign puppets and spend billions without accomplishing much. In contrast, schooling is cheap and revolutionary. The more money we spend on schools today, the less we'll have to spend on missiles tomorrow."[87]

The United States, working through both government and private programs abroad, may not always succeed in its efforts to help others, and this nation's own economic ups and downs preclude the sponsorship of modern-day Marshall Plans around the world. Yet within the bounds of what Americans can afford, as the nation extricates itself from expensive wars in the Middle East and Southwest Asia, the United States can help more than has been the case in the past, and Americans will know that what they have done is right.

High on a new foreign policy agenda will also be a determination to stop **global warming**, *the gradual increase in the earth's temperature that is caused by the entrapment*

---

### PERSPECTIVES ON AMERICAN FOREIGN POLICY 15.3

**The CARTER CENTER Guinea Worm Eradication Program:**

. . . . the international Guinea worm eradication campaign spearheaded by The Carter Center has reached its final stages with only 542 cases reported worldwide in 2012 . . . . "Having only 542 Guinea worm cases worldwide in 2012 is a testament to the hard work of the endemic and formerly endemic communities, supported by The Carter Center and our partners," said President Carter, who has been personally committed to the campaign for nearly three decades. "The collateral impact of this campaign is immense; it empowers people in some of the world's most neglected communities to protect themselves from a terrible disease and to believe in the possibility of a brighter future."

There were 3.5 million cases of Guinea worm in 21 countries in Africa and Asia when The Carter Center began leading the international campaign in 1986. Today, cases have been reduced by more than 99.999 percent. In 2012, South Sudan reported the majority of cases (521) from a handful of isolated locations. The remaining cases in 2012 were reported by Chad (10), Mali (7), and Ethiopia (4) . . . . The Center's success in leading the battle against Guinea worm disease is in the vanguard of a new worldwide push to combat neglected tropical diseases (NTDs) . . . .

Guinea worm disease afflicts the world's poorest and most isolated communities. Also known as dracunculiasis, Guinea worm disease is contracted when people consume water contaminated with Guinea worm larvae. After a year, a meter-long worm slowly emerges from the body through a painful blister in the skin. The ancient disease is being wiped out through health education and behavior change, such as teaching people to filter all drinking water and keeping anyone with an emerging worm from entering water sources. There are no vaccines or medicines to prevent or treat the disease, but thanks to the tenacity of thousands of health workers involved in the international campaign, Guinea worm is poised to be the second human disease eradicated after smallpox.

"We are so close and I look forward to personally announcing that we have stopped transmission of Guinea worm disease worldwide," said President Carter.

*SOURCE:* The Carter Center, January 17, 2013. Reprinted by permission of The Carter Center.

---

*of gases inside the upper atmosphere instead of their escape into space.* Recall, the major culprit in creating this "greenhouse effect" is the gas carbon dioxide ($CO_2$), which is emitted into the air by burning coal, oil, and other fossil fuels. In the past two decades, this planet experienced the hottest period since modern records have been kept—a dominant theme in President Obama's State of the Union Address in 2013.[88] The Intergovernmental Panel on Climate Change (IPCC), founded in 1988 under the sponsorship of the United Nations, concluded in 1995 that this warming went beyond any natural cycle and reflected "a discernible human influence."[89] In 2010, carbon dioxide in the atmosphere bumped up 5.9 percent—the largest absolute jump since the beginning of the Industrial Revolution.[90] In just one measure of global warming, specialists predicted in 2009 that by 2029 most of the Earth's glaciers will have disappeared.[91] A remedy is to provide better stewardship over the world's forests, which are disappearing at a disquieting rate. Trees act as sponges to absorb carbon dioxide, thereby slowing global warming—an ecological process crucial to the survival of life on Earth. Destruction of tropical forests around the world is estimated to account for about 20 percent of greenhouse gas emissions.[92]

Before he became vice president and a world leader for environmental reform, Senator Al Gore forcefully expressed on the Senate floor his concern about the risks posed by vanishing forests. "Around the world we lose between 1 and 1.5 acres of forest every second," he said. "With this loss, plant and animal species are disappearing from the face of the Earth at a rate that is 1,000 times faster than at any point in the previous 65 million years." His conclusion: "The effort to save the global environment must become the central organizing principle in the post-cold war world."[93] More recently, Gore has stressed that "we are continuing to dump 90 million tons of global-warming pollution every 24 hours into the atmosphere—as if it were an open sewer."[94] In *Perspectives on American Foreign Policy* 15.4, Gore outlines some of the consequences should the world fail to act on this reckless despoiling of the only home human beings have.

On the eve of a G20 summit held in Pittsburgh, Pennsylvania, in 2009, a group of protesters rappel from the West End Bridge with a banner denouncing global warming, which they blamed on the unbridled economic growth promoted by the G20 members.

Among the lost flora in the disappearing rain forests may be yet undiscovered plants that can offer wondrous cures for disease. Take, for example, the forests in the African nation of Madagascar. This fourth-largest island in the world boasts 14,000 species of plants, most of which exist nowhere else. The Madagascar periwinkle, discovered by botanists in these forests, contains a substance that has been successful in treating leukemia in young children. Yet some 90 percent of Madagascar's forests have been sacrificed to slash-and-burn agriculture, with unknown losses in potentially valuable plant-based drugs.[95] Similarly, the Pacific yew in Oregon contains a substance

---

## PERSPECTIVES ON AMERICAN FOREIGN POLICY 15.4

**FORMER VICE PRESIDENT AL GORE on the dangers of global warming:**

Here is what scientists have found is happening to our climate: man-made global-warming pollution traps heat from the sun and increases atmospheric temperatures. These pollutants—especially carbon dioxide—have been increasing rapidly with the growth in the burning of coal, oil, natural gas and forests, and temperatures have increased over the same period. Almost all of the ice-covered regions of the Earth are melting—and seas are rising. Hurricanes are predicted to grow stronger and more destructive, though their number is expected to

decrease. Droughts are getting longer and deeper in many mid-continent regions, even as the severity of flooding increases. The seasonal predictability of rainfall and temperatures is being disrupted, posing serious threats to agriculture. The rate of species extinction is accelerating to dangerous levels.

called taxol, shown to be effective in the treatment of ovarian cancer. Only some 30 percent of the world's flora have been studied by botanists and other scientists. How many other plants hold such gifts? How many will be destroyed at the hands of loggers who wantonly strip the world's forests for their corporate masters, before scientists have studied the possibilities of more miracle cures? "We've been saying for some time that the ancient forest may hold answers to questions that nobody has yet to ask," emphasized an American ecologist in 1992.[96]

Disconcerting, too, is the accelerated disappearance of the world's animal species. From 1987 through 1992, the endangered species list in the United States alone leaped from 451 species to 617—a 37 percent increase. And in Africa, in 2012, ruthless poachers—motivated by the $1,000 a pound that ivory can fetch on the global black market—killed 350 elephants in Kenya. Further, in Chad, in 2002, 4,350 elephants roamed the Zakouma National Park; now, as a result of poaching, only about 450 had survived at the end of 2012.[97] The African lion population has declined from some 450,000 forty years ago to just 20,000 in 2012.[98] As with flora, so with fauna: they are essential to the global ecological balance that supports human life everywhere.

Recent research indicates that the world has experienced a decline in all kinds of warfare, including civil wars, genocides, and terrorism. This is good news. Other research shows, however, that civil conflict has been more likely to break out in nations suffering from especially high annual temperatures. These results lead philosopher Peter Singer to conclude that "a warming world could mean the end of the relatively peaceful era in which we are now living."[99]

Even though the world may be livable at the moment, how long will it be before Earth's climate becomes intolerable, and before it is too late to reverse the greenhouse effect caused by accumulating carbon dioxide? The atmosphere will not wait patiently for the world's biggest polluters to finally reach a grand bargain to do something about gas emissions, so what year is the tipping point? America's diplomats at the Earth summit meeting in 1992, formally known as the UN Conference on Environment and Development, held in Rio de Janeiro, displayed a less than inspiring effort to confront global warming. Every other major industrial country expressed support for targets and timetables to limit greenhouse gas emissions, except the United States. Remarked a Japanese diplomat: "If the US cannot commit itself to stabilize $CO_2$ emissions, then developing countries like China, India, Brazil, and Mexico won't make commitments, either. We need a strong $CO_2$ convention—one with teeth in it."[100]

At subsequent international environmental conferences, the position of the United States, which after China is the world's second greatest greenhouse gas polluter (at 20 percent of the total), has been largely a defense of the status quo. President George W. Bush rejected the Kyoto climate change treaty out of hand, without even an assurance that his administration would seek alternative proposals. His own Secretary of State, Condoleezza Rice, referred to this behavior in her memoir as a "self-inflicted wound."[101] In the UN climate change conference held in Copenhagen in 2009,

President Obama and China's leaders sidestepped calls for a binding treaty to lower greenhouse gas emissions. At least, though, Obama pledged to lower these gases over the next decade to about 17 percent below 2005 levels. He also helped negotiate an offer of $100 billion from the industrialized nations to poorer countries as a means for assisting their move in the direction of less-polluting sources of energy, as well as to ameliorate droughts caused by warming. China also provided some hope for the future by promising to submit to a pollution verification system, an important step toward transparency in determining global sources of warming.

At the Durban, South Africa, meeting for climate talks in 2011, however, "the world's negotiators kicked the can down the road," an observer concluded, as the large nations once again stalled on measures to cut back greenhouse gas emissions.[102] A *New York Times* correspondent referred to Obama's journalist Thomas L. Friedman referred to Obama's go-slow response to the emission dangers as "an invisible embarrassment."[103] The annual meeting of the UN climate change negotiations in 2012, held in Doha, Qatar, witnessed the industrial nations pledge to secure $200 billion a year by 2020 in public and private financing to help poor countries cope with climate change; but the *New York Times* reported that these nations "have been vague about what they plan to do before then."[104]

President Obama supported the idea of **cap-and-trade measures** to reduce greenhouse emissions. This approach rests on *market-driven incentives to set a ceiling on pollution, while permitting companies to trade permits to meet the ceiling by using a carbon-credits bartering system that puts a price on greenhouse gas emissions.* The House of Representatives passed a bill along these lines in 2009; but during the next year the idea became widely discredited—a victim, according to the *New York Times,* of "the weak economy, the Wall Street meltdown, determined industry opposition, and its own complexity."[105] Critics of this approach voiced concern that it would raise electricity and fuel prices to unacceptable levels. In rebuttal, advocates claimed that the cap-and-trade remedy would cost no more than $150 a year per American household—worth it, in their view, to halt climate change.[106] Lawmakers and the administration scrambled to come up with more palatable, business-friendly proposals. Corporations, the US Chamber of Commerce, and other business interests resisted the environmental initiatives, though, for fear that this approach would cost millions of jobs in a time of recession and high unemployment rates.[107]

In 2010, the massive oil spill from the British Petroleum (BP) Deepwater Horizon rig in the Gulf of Mexico, which led to newspaper and television images of pelicans wallowing in black crude and choking to death in the surf along the Louisiana coastline, underscored the need for alternative, less ecologically disastrous energy sources. The oil spill led President Obama to call for a "national mission" to reduce America's fossil fuel dependency. Yet controversy arose over the use of "fracking" technology to extract oil from the ground inside the United States. Critics feared the risk of ground water pollution, as well as the threat of sucking America's aquifers dry faster than they could be replenished.[108]

## MAXIMS FOR AMERICAN FOREIGN POLICY

A shift in the focus of US foreign policy toward environmental and economic issues could be accompanied by less emphasis on military armaments and foreign invasions to solve global problems. This would require a more patient and tolerant America, one that refuses to rush into foreign conflicts without serious debate and formal approval by both the Congress and the president. The current war in Afghanistan is an example of past ways. That war began in 2001, but was never debated on the floor of the House until March of 2010.[109]

In addition, America will have to understand that the world will continue to have civil wars, tumult, and unrest that must be resolved by the people involved and seldom by interlopers. A passage from John Quincy Adams's Inaugural Address is as sensible today as when it was pronounced in 1825. The sixth President said that America should be "the friend of all the liberties in the world, [but] the guardian of only her own." With this in mind, the United States could vow to use—arm in arm with the other democracies—intelligence collection, diplomacy, economic statecraft, and cultural and moral suasion as the most important instruments in its relations with other countries, rather than a precipitous dispatch of Marines or paramilitary operatives into foreign lands. What follows are a set of concluding **American foreign policy maxims**, simple but far reaching, that encompass the spirit of a new approach to foreign policy. They apply to relations between the executive and legislative branches at home, as well to America's relations with other nations overseas:

**Maxims for American Foreign Policy, at Home and Abroad**

1. *Listen*
2. *Help*
3. *Set a good example*
4. *Seek consensual solutions*

## SUMMARY

This book concludes with a look at some weaknesses in existing American foreign policy. A promising new direction would include greater global awareness among US citizens; improved institutional comity and allegiance to constitutional procedures; an increased sense of empathy toward other nations; and a more discriminating exercise of power abroad that gives ascendency to the foreign policy instruments of intelligence collection, diplomacy, and economic statecraft, as well as cultural and moral suasion, over the use of military force and covert action.

## KEY TERMS

American foreign policy maxims p. 496
cap-and-trade measures p. 495
citizen awareness p. 473
compulsive interventionism p. 486
demonizing adversaries p. 483

discriminating foreign policy p. 490
empathetic diplomacy p. 483
global warming p. 491
institutional comity p. 477

---

## QUESTIONS FOR DISCUSSION

1. What can be done to improve the awareness of Americans about the world and international affairs?

2. How can cooperation be increased between Congress and the executive branch in the conduct of foreign policy?

3. What can be done to heighten the degree of empathy among Americans toward the world's poor nations?

4. Where would you draw the line on US involvement in the affairs of other nations? Should America have intervened in Somalia in 1993? In the civil war in the Balkans during the 1990s? In Iraq in 1990 and again in 2003? In Afghanistan after the 9/11 attacks? In the Syrian civil war? Should the United States intervene militarily in Iran to halt its suspected nuclear-weapons program?

5. Can you envision your university or college starting up a service project in a developing country, similar to the Carter Center's guinea worm eradication program in Africa or the "Room to Read" program?

6. If you were inaugurated president of the United States, what would be your most important foreign policy initiatives? Would you try to involve lawmakers in their pursuit? Would ethical considerations enter into your decisions?

## ADDITIONAL READINGS

Gore, Al. *The Future*. New York: Random House, 2013.
Jervis, Robert. *American Foreign Policy in a New Era*. New York: Routledge, 2005.

Zakaria, Fareed. *The Post American World*. New York: Norton, 2009.

---

For further readings, please visit the book's companion website.

# NOTES

## Preface

1. On the three levels of analysis, see Kenneth N. Waltz, *Man, the State, and War* (New York: Cambridge University Press, 1959).

2. See Jane Mayer, *The Dark Side: The Inside Story of How the War on Terror Turned into a War on American Ideals* (New York: Doubleday, 2008); and Jack Goldsmith, *The Terror Presidency: Law and Judgment Inside the Bush Administration* (New York: Norton, 2007). The legal writings of a former Justice Department attorney in the second Bush administration, John Yoo, are often cited as the leading scholarly argument in favor of the unitary presidency; see, for example, his *The Powers of War and Peace: The Constitution and Foreign Affairs after 9/11* (Chicago: University of Chicago Press, 2005); and *Crisis and Command: A History of Executive Power from George Washington to George W. Bush* (New York: Kaplan, 2010). For a contrary point of view, see Louis Fisher, *The Constitution and 9/11: Recurring Threats to America's Freedoms* (Lawrence: University Press of Kansas, 2008).

3. See, for example, Gary Hart, *The Shield & the Cloak: The Security of the Commons* (New York: Oxford University Press, 2006); Chalmers Johnson, *The Sorrows of Empire: Militarism, Secrecy, and the End of the Republic* (New York: Henry Holt, 2004); Loch K. Johnson, *Seven Sins of American Foreign Policy* (New York: Pearson/Longman, 2007); and Joseph S. Nye Jr., *The Paradox of American Power* (New York: Oxford University Press, 2002).

## Chapter 1

1. Drawn from Loch K. Johnson, *National Security Intelligence* (Cambridge, UK: Polity, 2011), based on the findings of *The 9/11 Commission Report: Final Report of the National Commission on Terrorist Attacks Upon the United States* (New York: Norton, 2004)—the Kean Commission, led by Thomas H. Kean, Chair, and Lee H. Hamilton, Vice Chair.

2. Richard J. Barnet, "Reflections: National Security," *The New Yorker* (March 21, 1988), p. 104.

3. Joseph S. Nye Jr., *The Paradox of American Power* (New York: Oxford University Press, 2002), p. 78, emphasis added. In Jan Aart Scholte's conception of globalization, the world is experiencing a "growth of transplanetary and more particularly supraterritorial social relations" [*Globalization: A Critical Introduction*, 2nd ed. (Basingstoke, UK: Palgrave, 2005), p. 20].

4. Sam Dillon, "Top Test Scores From Shanghai Stun Educators," *New York Times* (December 7, 2010), p. A1, with score results and the presidential statement at p. A20. In results from a battery of tests given in over fifty nations during 2012, the United States ranked 11th in fourth-grade math, 9th in eighth-grade math, 7th in fourth-grade science, and 10th in eighth-grade science [Motoko Rich, "U.S. Students Still Lag globally in Math and Science, Tests Show," *New York Times* (December 11, 2012), p. A13].

5. See, respectively, Anthony Lake, *Managing Complexity in U.S. Foreign Policy*, US Department of States, Bureau of Public Affairs (March 14, 1978), p. 1; and *Fundamentals of U.S. Foreign Policy*, US Department of State, Bureau of Public Affairs (March 1988), p. 1. In National Security Directive 238, President Reagan wrote that the primary objective is "to preserve the political identity, framework and institutions of the United States as embodied in the Declaration of Independence and the Constitution" [reported by Steven Aftergood, *Secrecy News*, Federation of American Scientists (October 17, 2012), p. 1].

6. Barack Obama, Speech, West Point, New York (December 1, 2009).

7. Rick Atkinson, *Crusade* (Boston: Houghton Mifflin, 1993), p. 477. The United States suffered 148 combat fatalities in the war.

8. Jo Becker and Scott Shane, "Secret 'Kill List' Proves a Test of Obama's Principles and Will," *New York Times* (May 29, 2012), p. A1.

9. These figures are from the Stockholm International Peace Research Institute, cited by Joseph S. Nye Jr., "International Security Studies," in Joseph Kruzel, ed., *American Defense Annual, 1988–1989* (Lexington, MA: Lexington Books, 1988), p. 242; also, Samuel W. Lewis, president of the US Institute of Peace, remarks, Atlanta, Georgia (May 9, 1989).

10. Bernard Lown, public address, "Beyond War" Convocation, San Francisco (September 12, 1985); MacArthur, speech, West Point, New York (May 12, 1962). During the US Civil War, more than twice the number of soldiers died from disease as from combat; by the time of the Second World War, less than one percent of American soldiers died from disease [Rivka Galchen, "Every Disease on Earth," *The New Yorker* (May 13, 2013), p. 54].

11. Warren M. Christopher, US Secretary of State nominee, *Confirmation Hearings*, Committee on Foreign Relations, US Senate (January 14, 1993), p. 5.

12. Carnegie Endowment for International Peace, National Commission on America and the New World, *Changing Our Ways: America and the New World* (Washington, DC: Brookings Institution, 1992), p. 2.

13. Stephen R. Kelly, "Oil Under Our Noses," *New York Times* (March 20, 2012), p. A27.

14. "Burden of Disease and Cost-Effectiveness Estimates," *Water Sanitation Health*, World Health Organization (WHO), 2004; Ashley Seager, "Dirty Water Kills 5,000 Children a Day," *The Guardian* (November 11, 2006), p. A6.

15. Camille Saadé, Massee Bateman, and Diane B. Bendahmane, *The Story of a Successful Public-Private Partnership in Central America: Handwashing for Diarrheal Disease Prevention*, Basic Support for Child Survival Project (BASICS II), the Environmental Health Project, the United Nations Children's Fund, the United States Agency for International Development, and The World Bank, Arlington, Virginia (September 2001), p. 10.

16. Lester R. Brown, et al. *State of the World*, 1992 (New York: Norton, 1992), p. 22.

17. Senator Al Gore, remarks, *Congressional Record* (April 7, 1992), pp. S4872, S4874; Alok Jha, "Amazon Rainforest Vanishing at Twice Rate of Previous Estimate," *The Guardian* (October 20, 2005), p. A4.

18. Simon Romero, "Swallowing Rain Forest, Cities Surge in Amazon," *New York Times* (November 25, 2012), p. Wk. 5.

19. Al Gore, *Congressional Record,* p. S4872. See, also, Al Gore, *Earth in the Balance: Ecology and the Human Spirit* (New York: Penguin-Plume, 1993).

20. See, for example, the results in West Africa: Michael Mortimore, *Adapting to Draught: Farmers, Famines, and Desertification in West Africa* (Cambridge, UK: Cambridge University Press, 1989).

21. Justin Gillis and John Broder, "With Carbon Dioxide Emissions at Record High, Worries on How to Slow Warming," *New York Times* (December 3, 2012), p. A6.

22. J. R. Beddington et al., "What Next for Agriculture After Durban?" *Science* 335 (June 20, 2012), p. 289.

23. "Comment: Global Gunslinger, Global Copes," *The New Yorker* (January 11, 1993), p. 5. See also Robert Patman, *Strategic Shortfall: The Somalia Syndrome and the March to 9/11* (Westport, CT: Praeger Security International, 2010).

24. *Fundamentals of U.S. Foreign Policy*, US Department of State, Bureau of Public Affairs (March 1988). One important human right is a person's safety from physical harm, yet the World Bank reports that more women between the ages of fifteen and forty-four are at risk from rape and domestic violence than from cancer, car wrecks, war, and malaria combined [unsigned editorial, "Unholy Alliance," *New York Times* (March 12, 2013), p. A18].

25. Based on the on the notes of Dr. James McHenry, a Maryland delegate to the Constitutional Convention, *The Records of the Federal Convention of 1787*, ed., Max Farrand, Vol. 3, Appendix A (New Haven, CT: Yale University Press, 1911), p. 85; see also Charles C. Tansill, ed., "Debates in the Federal Convention in 1787 as reported by James Madison," *Documents Illustrative of the Foundation of the Union of the American States* (Washington, DC: US Government Printing Office), 1927, p. 128. Author Jared Cohen estimates that "57 percent of the world's population is under an autocracy" [interview, *News Hour,* Public Television (May 2, 2013)].

26. Lake, *Managing Complexity in U.S. Foreign Policy,* p. 6.

27. George W. Bush, Remark, third presidential debate, Arizona State University, Tempe (October 13, 2004), moderated by Bob Schieffer.

28. Rania Abouzeid, "Bouazizi: The Man Who Set Himself and Tunisia on Fire," *Time* (January 21, 2011), pp. 16–19.

29. Thom Shanker and Eric Schmitt, "Seeing Limits of 'New' War," *New York Times* (October 22, 2011), p. A7.

30. Zainab al-Khawaja, "Bahrain, a Brutal Ally," *New York Times* (December 26, 2012), p. A19; see also Thom Shanker and J. David Goodman, "Pentagon Watches Unrest in Bahrain," *New York Times* (February 17, 2011), p. A1.

31. Seth G. Jones, "The Mirage of the Arab Spring," *Foreign Affairs* (January/February 2013), p. 63. On the revolution in Syria, see Dmitri Trenin, "Syria Could Unite Russia and China Against the U.S.," Bloomberg.com (June 7, 2012).

32. Thomas L. Friedman, "Thinking About Iraq," *New York Times* (January 22, 2003), p. A23.

33. "Survey of Young Americans Attitudes Toward Politics and Public Service: 21 Edition," Institute of Politics, Harvard University (April 24, 2012).

34. See Loch K. Johnson, ed., *The Oxford Handbook of National Security Intelligence* (New York: Oxford University Press, 2010), and *National Security Intelligence* (Cambridge, UK: Polity, 2011).

35. Graham Allison, "How It Went Down: The Inside Story of Osama bin Laden's Last Days," *Time* (May 7, 2012), pp. 35–41. The extent to which "harsh interrogations"—the torture of captured Qaeda members—led to the desired information about Bin Laden's whereabouts remains a matter of debate; according to the head of the CIA, however, the preponderance of evidence supports the conclusion that traditional intelligence-gathering procedures (such a telephone taps and HUMINT) were more effective and reliable [remarks by acting CIA Director Michael J. Morell, cited by Scott Shane, "Acting C.I.A. Chief Critical of Film 'Zero Dark Thirty,'" *New York Times* (December 23, 2012), p. A23].

36. Michael Warner, "Central Intelligence: Origin and Evolution," in Roger Z. George and Robert D. Kline, eds., *Intelligence and the National Security Strategist: Enduring Issues and Challenges* (Washington, DC: National Defense University Press, 2004), p. 43.

37. Jane Mayer, *The Dark Side: The Inside Story of How the War on Terror Turned into a War on American Ideals* (New York: Doubleday, 2008), p. 23.

38. See M. M. Kostecki, "Marketing Strategies and Voluntary Export Restraints," *Journal of World Trade* 25 (1991), pp. 87–100; and *A Review of Recent Developments in the U.S. Automobile Industry, Including an Assessment of the Japanese Voluntary Restraint Agreements*, United States International Trade Commission (February 1985).

39. Elisabeth Bumiller, "The War: A Trillion Can Be Cheap," *New York Times* (July 25, 2010), p. Wk. 3.

40. Dean Rusk, with Richard Rusk and Daniel S. Papp, *As I Saw It* (New York: Norton, 1990), p. 237.

41. Admiral Stansfield Turner, *Burn Before Reading: Presidents, CIA Directors, and Secret Intelligence* (New York: Hyperion, 2005), p. 98.

42. Stephen R. Weissman, "An Extraordinary Rendition," *Intelligence and National Security* 25 (April 2010), pp. 198–222.

43. On this and the other CIA assassination plots, as well as the use of additional covert actions related to propaganda, political, and economic operations, see Select Committee to Study Governmental Operations with Respect to Intelligence Activities (the Church Committee), "Alleged Assassinate Plots Involving Foreign Leaders," *Interim Report S. Rep. No. 94–465,* Government Printing Office (November 20, 1975).

44. See Loch K. Johnson, *America's Secret Power* (New York: Oxford University Press, 1989).

45. William J. Broad, "Iran is Shielding Nuclear Efforts in Tunnel Mazes," *New York Times* (January 6, 2010), p. A1.

46. On CIA economic covert actions against Iran using computer viruses, see David E. Sanger, *Confront and Conceal: Obama's Secret Wars and Surprising Use of American Power* (New York: Crown, 2012).

47. Eric Sevareid, interview with William O. Douglas, *CBS Evening News* (January 19, 1980).

48. Joseph S. Nye Jr., *Soft Power: The Means to Success in World Politics* (New York: Public Affairs, 2004), p. 17.

49. See, for example, Louis Fisher, *The Constitution and 9/11: Recurring Threats to American's Freedom* (Lawrence: University Press of Kansas, 2009); Mayer, *The Dark Side*; and Frederick A. O. Schwarz Jr. and Aziz Z. Huq, *Unchecked and Unbalanced: President Power in a Time of Terror* (New York: The New Press, 2007).

50. Richard Jackson, *An Historical Review of the Constitution and Government of Pennsylvania* (published by Benjamin Franklin, Philadelphia, in 1759), p. 8.

51. Thomas L. Friedman, "Father Knows Best," *New York Times* (January 6, 2010), p. A19.

52. Jennifer Sterling-Folker, "Liberal Approaches," in Jennifer Sterling-Folker, ed., *Making Sense of International Relations Theory* (Boulder, CO: Lynne Rienner), pp. 55–62. Gelb and Rosenthal note that "morality, values, ethics, universal principles— the whole panoply of ideals in international affairs that were once almost the exclusive domain of preachers and scholars—have taken root in the hearts, or at least the minds, of the American foreign policy community" [Leslie H. Gelb and Justine A. Rosenthal, "The Rise of Ethics in Foreign Policy: Reaching a Values Consensus," *Foreign Affairs* 82 (2003), pp. 2–7].

53. See Oliver Daddow, *International Relations Theory* (London: Sage, 2009), pp. 69–76; R. Jackson and G. Sørensen, *Introduction to International Relations: Theories and Approaches* (New York: Oxford University Press, 2007); and Martin Høllis and Steve Smith, *Explaining and Understanding International Relations* (London: Clarendon Press, 1990), p. 110. For essays that examine a range of foreign policy and international relations philosophies, see Jennifer Sterling-Folker, ed., *Making Sense of International Relations Theory* (Boulder, CO: Lynne Rienner, 2006); Sterling-Folker, ed., Making Sense of International Relations theory; and Steven W. Hook and Christopher M. Jones, eds., *Routledge Handbook of American Foreign Policy* (New York: Routledge, 2012).

54. Alynna J. Lyon, "Liberalism," in Steven W. Hook and Christopher M. Jones, eds., *Routledge Handbook of American Foreign Policy* (New York: Routledge, 2012), pp. 75–92, quote at p. 86.

55. See Robert O. Keohane, "The Demand for International Regimes," *International Organization* 36 (1982), pp. 325–355; and Steven D. Krasner, ed., *International Regimes* (Ithaca, NY: Cornell University Press, 1983).

56. See, for example, Andrew Moravcsik, "Taking Preferences Seriously: A Liberal Theory of International Politics," *International Organization* 51 (1997), pp. 513–553.

57. Jennifer Sterling-Folker and Dina Badi, "Constructivism," in Steven W. Hook and Christopher M. Jones, eds., *Routledge Handbook of American Foreign Policy* (New York: Routledge, 2012), pp. 104–117; see as well Vendulka Kubalkova, "A Constructivist Primer," in Vadnulka Kubalkova, ed., *Foreign Policy in a Constructed World* (New York: M.E. Sharpe, 2001); and Paul Kowert, "Towards a Constructivist Theory of Foreign Policy," also in Vadnulka Kubalkova, ed., *Foreign Policy in a Constructed World* (New York: M.E. Sharpe, 2001).

58. Alexander Wendt, *Social Theory of International Politics* (Cambridge, UK: Cambridge University Press, 1999).

59. Senator Frank Church, "Covert Action: Swampland of American Foreign Policy," *Bulletin of the Atomic Scientists* 32 (February 1976), p. 11.

60. Stephen J. Solarz, remarks, C-Span Television (May 22, 1988).

61. E. H. Carr, *The Twenty Years' Crisis, 1919–1939* (Basingstoke, UK: Palgrave, 2001; originally published by Macmillan, London, 1939).

62. Henry R. Nau, "Realism," in Hook and Jones, eds., Routledge Handbook of American Foreign Policy, pp. 61–74.

63. Daddow, International Relations Theory, p. 81.

64. Stanley Hoffmann, "Reconsiderations: A New World and Its Troubles," in Nicholas X. Rizopulos, ed., *Sea-Changes: American Foreign Policy in a World Transformed* (New York: Council on Foreign Relations Press, 1990), p. 277.

65. Hans J. Morgenthau, *Politics among States: The Struggle for Power and Peace* (New York: Knopf, 1948).

66. Joseph S. Nye Jr., "Ethics and Foreign Policy," *An Occasional Paper* (Queenstown, MD: Aspen Institute, 1985), p. vii.

67. Kenneth N. Waltz, *Man, the State, and War* (New York: Cambridge University Press, 1959), and *Theory of International Politics* (Boston: McGraw Hill, 1979).

68. See Steven E. Lobell, Norrin M. Ripsman, and Jeffrey W. Taliaferro, *Neoclassical Realism, the State, and Foreign Policy* (New York: Cambridge University Press, 2009); and Gideon Rose, "Neoclassical Realism and Theories of Foreign Policy," *World Politics* 51 (1998), pp. 144–172.

69. Robert Jervis, "Cooperation under the Security Dilemma," *World Politics* 30 (1978), pp. 167–214.

70. "Roundtable on American Foreign Policy," University of Nebraska, Lincoln (April 8, 2005); see also Chalmers Johnson, *The Sorrows of Empire: Militarism, Secrecy, and the End of the Republic* (New York: Henry Holt, 2004), pp. 70–71.

71. Francis Fukuyama, *America at the Crossroads: Democracy, Power, and the Neoconservative Legacy* (New Haven, CT: Yale University Press, 2006).

72. G. John Ikenberry, Thomas J. Knock, Anne-Marie Slaughter, and Tony Smith, *The Crisis of American Foreign Policy: Wilsonianism in*

the Twenty-First Century (Princeton, NJ: Princeton University Press, 2008), p. 108.

73. See Colin Elman and Mariam Fendius Elman, *Progress in International Relations Theory: Appraising the Appraising the Field* (Cambridge, MA: MIT Press, 2003), as well as Daddow, *International Relations Theory;* Martin Hollis and Steve Smith, *Explaining and Understanding International Relations* (London: Clarendon Press, 1990); Valerie M. Hudson, "Foreign Policy Analysis: Actor-Specific Theory and the Ground of International Relations," *Foreign Policy Analysis* 1 (2005), pp. 1–30; and Sterling-Folker, ed., *Making Sense of International Relations Theory.*

74. Joseph S. Nye Jr., *The Powers to Lead* (New York: Oxford University Press, 2008), p. 43.

**Chapter 2**

1. Based on Martin J. Sherwin, "Hiroshima and Nagasaki Bombings of 1945," in Bruce W. Jentleson and Thomas G. Paterson, eds., *Encyclopedia of U.S. Foreign Relations*, Vol. 2 (New York: Oxford University Press, 1997), pp. 296–297; and "*Truman and the Atomic Bomb*", Film (New York: Learning Corporation, 1969).

2. Harry S. Truman, interviewed in "Truman and the Atomic Bomb," a Learning Corporation film (1969) Atomic Bomb. The desire of some scientists to see the effects of two bombs is an aspect of this history described to me in an interview with a former Manhattan Project physicist at the Harvard University-MIT Program on Nuclear Weapons, Cambridge, Massachusetts (June 25, 1985).

3. For additional reading on the concept of grand strategy—a comprehensive foreign policy plan of action that balances a nation's ends and means—see Williamson Murray and Mark Grimsley, "Introduction: On Strategy," in Williamson Murray, MacGregor Knox, and Alvin Bernstein, eds., *The Making of Strategy: Rulers, States, and War* (New York: Cambridge University Press, 1994), pp. 1–23; as well as B. H. Liddell Hart, "Fundamentals of Strategy and Grand Strategy," in *Strategy*, 2nd ed. (New York: Faber & Faber, 1967), pp. 319–370.

4. This construct, although considerably modified, draws on M. Brewster Smith's suggestive "scanning devise" presented in his "A Map for the Analysis of Personality and Politics,"*Journal of Social Issues* 24 (July 1968), pp. 15–28; and his "Political Attitudes," in Jeanne N. Knutson, ed., *Handbook of Political Psychology* (San Francisco: Jossey-Bass, 1973), pp. 57–82. For a classic statement on the three levels of analysis, see Kenneth N. Waltz, *Man, the State, and War* (New York: Columbia University Press, 1954).

5. Fred I. Greenstein, "The Study of Personality and Politics: Over-all Considerations," in Fred I. Greenstein and Michael Lerner, eds., *A Source Book for the Study of Personality and Politics* (Chicago: Markham, 1971), p. 14.

6. Jonathan Bendor and Thomas H. Hammond, "Rethinking Allison's Models," *American Political Science Review* 86 (June 1992), pp. 301–322.

7. Yale H. Ferguson and Richard W. Mansbach, *The Elusive Question: Theory and International Politics* (Columbia: University of South Carolina Press, 1988), p. 187; see also their *A World of Politics: Essays on Global Politics* (London: Routledge, 2008).

8. Edward A. Kolodziej, "Renaissance in Security Studies? Caveat Lector!" *International Studies Quarterly* 36 (December 1992), p. 424.

9. In the scholarly literature, a distinction is often made between the terms "nation" and "state," based on the degree of cohesion among the populations of these entities. Some countries have poorly integrated ethnic groups, such as the Kurds in Iraq (who often refer to themselves as "the Kurdish nation" even though they remain a part of Iraq); thus, the use of the term *nation* could be considered misleading because the ethnic group's allegiance to national symbols may be weak or even nonexistent. In this book, I opt, nevertheless, for a more conventional usage: here a nation is the same thing as a country (say, the United States or Germany), whereas a state (California or Bavaria) is a subset of a nation. The student delving into the scholarly literature should be aware, though, that for many academics "state" is the pre-ferred designation for a collection of people with a common territorial boundary, and "nation" is a reference to how people may identify themselves (the Kurds, for example). Further, a nation-state may be considered a combination of the two, as illustrated by the loose association of the Kurds, the Sunnis, and the Shiites in contemporary Iraq. On these distinctions, see Hedley Bull, "The State's Positive Role in World Affairs," *Daedalus* 108 (Fall 1979), pp. 111–122; and Seyom Brown, *New Forces, Old Forces, and the Future of World Politics* (Boston: Scott Foresman, 1988), pp. 3–4.

10. Hollis W. Barber, *Foreign Policies of the United States* (New York: Dryden, 1953), p. 9.

11. John Lewis Gaddis, *Strategies of Containment: A Critical Appraisal of Postwar American National Security Policy* (New York: Oxford University Press, 1982), p. viii. For a classic statement on balance of power, see Arnold Wolfers, "The Balance of Power in Theory and Practice," *Naval War College Review* 11 (January 1959), pp. 1–19.

12. H. Mackinder, *Democratic Ideals and Reality* (New York: Henry Holt, 1919), p. 105.

13. N. J. Spykman, *The Geography of the Peace* (New York: Harcourt, Brace, 1944), p. 98.

14. Thomas P. M. Barnett, *The Pentagon's New Map* (New York: Putnam, 2004).

15. See, for example, Rick Atkinson, *Crusader* (Boston: Houghton Mifflin, 1993), p. 492.

16. Zbigniew Brzezinski, *Between Two Ages: America's Role in the Technotronic Era* (New York: Viking, 1970), p. 275.

17. Quoted in *U.S. News & World Report* (July 15, 1985), p. 24.

18. Steven W. Hook, *U.S. Foreign Policy: The Paradox of World Power*, 3rd ed. (Washington, DC: CQ Press, 2011), pp. 244–245.

19. For the survey, see Norm Ornstein, Andrew Kohut, and Larry McCarthy, *The People, the Press, and Politics* (Reading, MA: Addison-Wesley, 1988); the quote is from Doris Graber, *Mass Media and American Politics*, 5th ed. (Washington, DC: CQ Press, 1997), p. 145.

20. Remark, "The 2012 Presidential Election," *Time* Roundtable, New York City (May 17, 2012), my notes.

21. McLuhan, an icon of the 1960s, was not always optimistic about this idea of global integration. He once warned that "when people get close together, they get more and more savage, impatient with each other. The global village is a place of very arduous interfaces and very abrasive situations" [quoted by David Carr, "Media Savant," *New York Times Book Review* (January 9, 2010), p. 10].

22. Joseph S. Nye Jr., *The Paradox of American Power* (New York: Oxford University Press, 2002).

23. Professor Larry Pintak, remarks, PBS *NewsHour*, PBS Television (September 21, 2012)].

24. On the polling about war in Afghanistan, see *New York Times/ CBS* poll, March 2012, http://www.nytimes.com/2012/03/27/world/asia/support-for-afghan-war-falls-in-us-pollfinds.html; and on the polling related to Syria and to US world leadership, see *New York Times* (June 7, 2013), p. A14.

25. See Daniel S. Papp, Loch K. Johnson, and John E. Endicott, *American Foreign Policy: History, Politics, and Policy* (New York: Longman, 2005).

26. Attributed to Mr. Burlingham, in *The Diplomatic Review* 19 (1881), p. 177.

27. Quoted by Stanley Karnow, *Vietnam: A History* (New York: Viking, 1983), p. 479.

28. Quoted by Charles McCarry, "Ol' Man Rivers," *Esquire* (October 1970), p. 171.

29. Address to the nation (October 7, 2001).

30. See, generally, Richard E. Neustadt, *Presidential Power* (New York: Wiley, 1960); and, specifically on the relationship between power and authority, Robert A. Dahl, *Modern Political Analysis* (Englewood, NJ: Prentice-Hall, 1963). For the Lewis quote, see Robert B. Semple, Jr., "Anthony Lewis, Champion of the Law," *New York Times* (March 26, 2013), p. A22.

31. See the Senate Select Committee on Secret Military Assistance to Iran and the Nicaraguan Opposition and House Select Committee to Investigate Covert Arms Transactions with Iran, *Hearings and Final Report* (Washington, DC: Government Printing Office, 1987).

32. Press conference, Washington, DC (May 7, 1987), quoted in William S. Cohen and George J. Mitchell, *Men of Zeal: A Candid Inside Story of the Iran-Contra Hearings* (New York: Viking, 1988), p. 76.

33. See Jane Mayer, *The Dark Side* (New York: Doubleday, 2008).

34. George F. Kennan, *American Diplomacy: 1900–1950* (Chicago: University of Chicago, Press, 1951), p. 11.

35. Meg Greenfield, "The Truth as Fiction," *Newsweek* (August 1, 1977), p. 78.

36. James C. Thomson, "Vietnam: An Autopsy," *Atlantic Monthly* (April 1968), p. 47.

37. While serving as a staff aide in the Senate in 1975–77, I often heard Senator Humphrey use this expression in hearings held by the Foreign Relations Committee.

38. Cited by US Ambassador Robert D. Blackwill, "Engaging Iran and Building Peace in the Persian Gulf Region," *The Trilateral Committee Plenary Meeting* (April 25, 2008), Washington, DC; see also Sir Harold Nicolson, *Diplomacy* (London: Thornton Butterworth, 1939).

39. "The Administration of Foreign Affairs," from *The Operational Aspects of United States Foreign Policy*, Study No. 6 in *United States Foreign Policy: Compilation of Studies*, prepared under the direction of the Maxwell Graduate School of Citizenship and Public Affairs, Syracuse University, for the Committee on Foreign Relations, US Senate (November 1959), reprinted in Andrew M. Scott and Raymond H. Dawson, eds., *Readings in the Making of American Foreign Policy* (New York: Macmillan, 1965), p. 523.

40. Observation made to me by Martin J. Hillenbrand, former US Ambassador to West Germany (May 14, 1985), Athens, GA.

41. Hugh Heclo, *A Government of Strangers: Executive Politics in Washington* (Washington, DC: Brookings Institution, 1977), p. 111.

42. Frank Church, "Of Presidents and Caesars: The Decline of Constitutional Government in the Conduct of American Foreign Policy," *Idaho Law Review* 6 (Fall 1969), p. 12.

43. Ruhl Bartlett, testimony, "U.S. Commitments to Foreign Powers," *Hearings*, Committee on Foreign Relations, US Senate (1967), p. 20.

44. John W. Gardner, testimony, Hearings, Committee on Government Operations, US Senate (1971), quoted by Jay M. Shafritz, *The Dorsey Dictionary of American Government and Politics* (Chicago: Dorsey, 1988), pp. 148–149.

45. Loch K. Johnson, *The Threat on the Horizon* (New York: Oxford University Press, 2011).

46. Thomas L. Hughes, "The Power to Speak and the Power to Listen: Reflections in Bureaucratic Politics and a Recommendation of Information Flows," in Thomas M. Franck and Edward Weisband, eds., *Secrecy and Foreign Policy* (New York: Oxford University Press, 1974), p. 79.

47. Quoted in Roy Godson, ed., *Intelligence Requirements for the 1980s: Analysis and Estimates* (Washington, DC: National Strategy Information Center, 1980), p. 79.

48. Cited in Peter Wyden, *Bay of Pigs: The Untold Story* (New York: Simon & Schuster, 1979), p. 99.

49. Thomas Powers, *The Man Who Kept the Secrets: Richard Helms and the CIA* (New York: Knopf, 1979), p. 145.

50. Irving L. Janis, *Groupthink*, 2nd ed. (Boston: Houghton Mifflin, 1982), p. 47.

51. Steve Chan, "Intelligence of Stupidity: Understanding Failures in Strategic Warning," *American Political Science Review* 73 (March 1979), p. 178.

52. Theodore H. White, "Weinberger on the Ramparts," *New York Times Magazine* (February 6, 1983), p. 24.

53. James C. Thomson, "Vietnam: An Autopsy," *Atlantic Monthly* (April 1968), p. 50.

54. Graham H. Shepard, "Personality Effects on American Foreign Policy, 1969–84: A Second Test of Interpersonal Generalization Theory," *International Studies Quarterly* 32 (March 1988), pp. 91–123.

55. Fred I. Greenstein, "The Study of Personality and Politics: Overall Considerations," in Fred I. Greenstein and Michael Lerner, eds., *A Source Book for the Study of Personality and Politics* (Chicago: Markham, 1971), p. 14.

### Chapter 3

1. James Sterling Young, *The Washington Community: 1800–1828* (New York: Columbia University Press, 1966), p. 81.

2. *Myers v. United States*, 272 US 52, 293, emphasis added. For the views of James Madison, see *The Federalist*, Nos. 10 and 51 (New York: Modern Library, 1937), pp. 53–62, 335–341.

3. See Harold Hongju Koh, "Constitution," in Bruce W. Jentleson and Thomas G. Paterson, eds., *Encyclopedia of U.S. Foreign Relations*, Vol. 1 (New York: Oxford University Press, 1997), p. 342.

4. Louis Fisher, *Defending Congress and the Constitution* (Lawrence: University of Kansas Press, 2011), p. 273. For the Justice Department statement, see p. 252. On the *Curtiss-Wright* case, see David Gray Adler, "The Constitution and Presidential Warmaking: The Enduring Debate," *Political Science Quarterly* 103 (1988), pp. 1–36; and Michael J. Glennon, *Constitutional Diplomacy* (Princeton, NJ: Princeton University Press, 1990).

5. *Annals of Congress,* (1789), p. 439. Formally known as *The Debates and Proceedings in the Congress of the United States*, the *Annals* cover the 1st Congress through the first session of the 18th Congress, from 1789 to 1824. The *Annals* were not published contemporaneously, but were compiled between 1834 and 1856 using the best records available, primarily newspaper accounts. Today the sessions of Congress are covered in the daily *Congressional Record*.

6. J. William Fulbright, "Congress and Foreign Policy: The Constitutional Imbalance," in John C. Stennis and J. William Fulbright, *The Role of Congress in Foreign Policy* (Washington, DC: American Enterprise Institute for Public Policy Research, 1971), pp. 35–72.

7. Frank Church, "Of Presidents and Caesars: The Decline of Constitutional Government in the Conduct of American Foreign Policy," *Idaho Law Review* 6 (Fall 1969), p. 14.

8. Edward S. Corwin, *The President: Office and Powers, 1787–1957*, rev. ed. (New York: New York University Press, 1957), p. 171.

9. David Gray Adler, "Commander in Chief," in Leonard W. Levy and Louis Fisher, eds., *Encyclopedia of the American Presidency*, Vol. 1 (New York: Simon & Schuster, 1994), p. 257.

10. Arthur M. Schlesinger Jr., *The Imperial Presidency* (Boston: Houghton Mifflin, 1973).

11. Letter from Lord Acton (John Emerich Edward Dalberg-Acton) to Bishop Mandell Creighton (April 5, 1887), cited in John Bartlett, *Familiar Quotations*, 14th ed. (Boston: Little, Brown, 1968), p. 750. In an insightful modern variation on this aphorism, Nobel Peace Prize winner Aung San Suu Kyi of Myanmar remarked in 2012: ". . . it is not power that corrupts but fear. Fear of losing power corrupts those who wield it." [quoted by Thomas L. Friedman, "Hard Lines, Red Lines and Green Lines," *New York Times* (September 23, 2012), p. Wk. 13].

12. Edward A. Kolodziej," Renaissance in Security Studies? Caveat Lector!," *International Studies Quarterly* 36 (December 1992), p. 423.

13. Grant McConnell, *The Modern President* (New York: St. Martin's, 1967), pp. 52–53.

14. Louis Henkin, "Foreign Affairs: An Overview," in Leonard W. Levy and Louis Fisher, eds., *Encyclopedia of the American Presidency*, Vol. 2 (New York: Simon & Schuster, 1994), p. 654.

15. See Louis Fisher, *President and Congress: Power and Policy* (New York: Free Press, 1972).

16. See John Lehman, *Making War* (New York: Scribner's, 1992); and Rachel Maddow, *Drift: The Unmooring of American Military Power* (New York: Crown, 2012).

17. Alexander Hamilton, *The Federalist*, No. 69 (New York: Modern Library, 1937), p. 448.

18. Julian P. Boyd, ed., *The Papers of Thomas Jefferson*, Vol. 15 (Princeton, NJ: Princeton University Press, 1955), p. 397.

19. See Fisher, *Defending Congress and the Constitution*; Arthur M. Schlesinger, Jr., *War and the American Presidency (New York: Norton, 2004)*.

20. "U.S. Commitments to Foreign Powers," *Hearings*, Committee on Foreign Relations, US Senate (1967), p. 194, emphasis added.

21. James D. Richardson, ed., *Compilation of Messages and Papers of the Presidents*, Vol. 1, Joint Committee on Printing, U.S. Congress (New York: Bureau of National Literature, 1897), p. 314.

22. John Quincy Adams to Don Jose Maria Salazar (August 6, 1824), cited by Ruhl J. Bartlett, ed., *The Record of American Diplomacy*, 3rd ed. (New York: Knopf, 1954), p. 185, in "National Commitments", *Report No. 91–129*, Committee on Foreign Relations, U.S. Senate (April 16, 1969), p. 12.

23. Abraham Lincoln, Letter to William H. Herndon (February 15, 1848), in *The Collected Works of Abraham Lincoln* (New Brunswick, NJ: Rutgers University Press, 1953), Vol. 1, pp. 451–452, cited in "National Commitments," pp. 12–13, the Committee's emphasis.

24. Memorandum, Department of State (July 3, 1950), *Department of State Bulletin* 23 (July 31, 1950), pp. 173–177.

25. Senator Robert A. Taft, *Congressional Record* (Mary 19, 1971), pp. S7318–S7323, cited by Schlesinger, *The Imperial Presidency*, p. 138.

26. Testimony, "Assignment of Ground Forces of the United States to Duty in the European Area," *Hearings*, Committees on Foreign Relations and Armed Services, US Senate (February 28, 1951), p. 306.

27. Quoted by Steven V. Roberts, "Aide Cites Reagan Foreign Policy Power," *New York Times* (May 15, 1987), p. 5.

28. U.S. Senate Foreign Relations Committee, "National Commitments," *Report No. 91–129* (April 16, 1969), p. 20.

29. *Executive Sessions of the Senate Foreign Relations Committee (Historical Series)*, Committee on Foreign Relations, US Senate, Vol. 7, 1955 (Washington, DC: Government Printing Office, 1978), pp. 87, 104, cited by Senator Robert Byrd, *Congressional Record* (April 28, 1986), p. S4963.

30. Schlesinger, *The Imperial Presidency*, pp. 159–160.

31. Cited by Senator Robert Byrd, *Congressional Record* (April 28, 1986), p. S4963.

32. Cited by Senator Robert Byrd, *Congressional Record* (April 28, 1986), p. S3964.

33. *Executive Sessions of the Senate Foreign Relations Committee Together with Joint Sessions with the Senate Armed Services Committee (Historical Series)*, Committee on Foreign Relations, US Senate, Vol. 9, 1957 (Washington, DC: Government Printing Office, 1979), pp. 1, 245–246, 267.

34. *Executive Sessions of the Senate Foreign Relations Committee Together with Joint Sessions with the Senate Armed Services Committee (Historical Series)*, Committee on Foreign Relations, US Senate, Vol. 9, 1957 (Washington, DC: Government Printing Office, 1979), p. 310.

35. *Executive Sessions of the Senate Foreign Relations Committee Together with Joint Sessions with the Senate Armed Services Committee (Historical Series)*, Committee on Foreign Relations, US Senate, Vol. 9, 1957 (Washington, DC: Government Printing Office, 1979), p. 297.

36. Schlesinger, *The Imperial Presidency*, p. 162.

37. *Congressional Record* (August 6, 1964), p. 18409.

38. Church, "Of Presidents and Caesars, p. 10; for Katzenbach's testimony, see "U.S. Commitments to Foreign Powers," *Hearings*, Committee on Foreign Relations, US Senate (1967), p. 82.

39. Raoul Berger, "The Presidential Monopoly of Foreign Relations," *Michigan Law Review* 71 (1972), p. 39.

40. For an example, see Glen S. Krutz and Jeffrey S. Peake, *Treaty Politics and the Rise of Executive Agreements: International Commitments in a System of Shared Powers* (Ann Arbor: University of Michigan Press, 2009), p. 177.

41. Hollis W. Barber, *Foreign Policies of the United States* (New York: Dryden, 1953), p. 30.

42. Cited by Louis Henkin, *Foreign Affairs and the Constitution* (Mineola, NY: Foundation Press, 1972), p. 372.

43. Johnson, *The Making of International Agreements.* (New York: New York University Press, 1984).

44. See Glen S. Krutz and Jeffrey S. Peake, *Treaty Politics and the Rise of Executive Agreements.*

45. U.S. Senate Foreign Relations Committee, "National Commitments," *Report No. 91–129* (April 16, 1969), p. 27.

46. Loch K. Johnson, *The Making of International Agreements.*

47. "U.S. Security Agreements and Commitments Abroad: Laos and Thailand," *Hearings*, Subcommittee on United States Security Agreements and Commitments Abroad, Committee on Foreign Relations, pt. 6, US Senate (1969–1970).

48. U.S. Senate Foreign Relations Committee, "National Commitments," *Report No. 91–129* (April 16, 1969) p. 28.

49. Frank Church, "Of Presidents and Caesars," p. 4.

50. On the first document, see the *Washington Post* (October 14, 1976), p. A7; on the second, see "Spain and Portugal," *Hearings*, Subcommittee on United States Security Agreements and Commitments Abroad, Committee on Foreign Relations, pt. 6, US Senate (1969–1970), p. 2356.

51. U.S. Senate Foreign Relations Committee, "National Commitments," *Report No. 91–129* (April 16, 1969), pp. 28, 29.

52. For example, his remarks in Memorial Hall, Akron University, Akron, Ohio (October 21, 1964).

53. U.S. Senate Foreign Relations Committee, "National Commitments," *Report No. 91–129* (April 16, 1969), p. 23.

54. Loch K. Johnson, *A Season of Inquiry* (Lexington: University Press of Kentucky, 1985), p. 113.

55. Frank Church, "Of Presidents and Caesars," p. 11.

56. Respectively, James Risen and Eric Lichtblau, "Spying Program Snared U.S. Calls," *New York Times* (December 20, 2005), p. A1; and Ed O'Keefe, "Eric Holder 'Fast and Furious' Contempt Vote to be Held Thursday," *Washington Post* (June 25, 2012), p. A1.

57. See Allen Schick, *Congress and Money* (Washington, DC: Urban Institute, 1981).

58. Louis Fisher, *Constitutional Conflicts between Congress and the President* (Princeton, NJ: Princeton University Press, 1985), p. 238.

59. See "Kingdom of Laos," *Hearings*, Subcommittee on United States Security Agreements and Commitments Abroad, Committee on Foreign Relations, pt. 6, US Senate (1969–1970).

60. Louis Fisher, "Foreign Policy Powers of the President and Congress," *Annals of the American Academy of Political and Social Science* 499 (September 1988), p. 156.

61. James Madison, *The Federalist,* No. 51 (New York: Modern Library, 1937), p. 337.

62. For examples of Congress's uneven approach to oversight, see Loch K. Johnson, "Supervising America's Secret Foreign Policy: A Shock Theory of Congressional Oversight for Intelligence," in David P. Forsythe, Patrice C. McMahon, and Andrew Wedeman, eds., *American Foreign Policy in a Globalized World* (New York: Routledge, 2006), pp. 173–192; and James M. Lindsay, "The Senate and Foreign Policy," in Burdett A. Loomis, ed., *The U.S. Senate: From Deliberation to Dysfunction* (Washington, DC: CQ Press, 2012), pp. 220–238.

63. See Richard Rovere, *Senator Joe McCarthy* (New York: Harper Colophon Books, 1959).

64. James Madison, *The Federalist,* No. 51 (New York: Modern Library, 1937), p. 337.

### Chapter 4

1. Ernest R. May, *Imperial Democracy: The Emergence of America as a Great Power* (New York: Harcourt, Brace & World, 1961), p. 279. In addition to May's work, this case study is based on several other sources: Dexter Perkins, *The Evolution of American Foreign Policy* (New York: Oxford University Press, 1948), p. 61; David F. Trask, "Spanish-American War," in Paul S. Boyer, ed., *The Oxford Companion to United States History* (New York: Oxford University Press, 2001), p. 737; John L. Offner, "Spanish-American-Filipino War, 1898," in Bruce W. Jentleson and Thomas G. Paterson, eds., *Encyclopedia of U.S. Foreign Relations*, Vol. 4 (New York: Oxford University Press, 1997), pp. 110–114, and Offner, *An Unwanted War: The Diplomacy of the United States and Spain Over Cuba, 1895–1898* (Chapel Hill: University of North Carolina Press, 1992); and David F. Trask, *The War with Spain in 1898* (New York: Macmillian, 1981).

2. Perkins, *The Evolution of American Foreign Policy*, p. 58.

3. Frank Church, "Covert Action: Swampland of American Foreign Policy," *Bulletin of the Atomic Scientists* 32 (February 1976), p. 11.

4. Quoted in Nancy L. Hoepli, *A Cartoon History of United States Foreign Policy* (New York: Morrow, 1975), p. 1. The United States has continued to cherish these assets. As one modern essayist has put it: "Detachment—or, at the most, rare moments of engagement—is America's natural state" [Philip L. Geyelin, "The Adams Doctrine and the Dream of Disengagement," in Sanford J. Ungar, ed., *Estrangement: American and the World* (New York: Oxford University Press, 1985), p. 197].

5. Hoepli, *A Cartoon History*, p. 1.

6. Robert Wallace, "The Barbary Wars," *Smithsonian* 5 (January 1975), p. 91.

7. Louis Michael Seidman, "Let's Give Up on the Constitution," *New York Times* (December 31, 2012), p. A17.

8. Louis Fisher, *President and Congress: Power and Policy* (New York: Free Press, 1972), p. 302.

9. Caleb Crain, "Unfortunate Events," *The New Yorker* (October 22, 2012), p. 78.

10. Quoted by Thomas A. Bailey, *A Diplomatic History of the American People*, 9th ed. (Englewood Cliffs, NJ: Prentice-Hall, 1974), p. 137.

11. See Alan Taylor, *The Civil War of 1812* (New York: Knopf, 2010); and Troy Bickham, *The Weight of Vengeance* (New York: Oxford University Press, 2012).

12. James Sterling Young, *The Washington Community: 1800–1828* (New York: Columbia University Press, 1966), p. 184.

13. Bailey, *A Diplomatic History*, p. 145.

14. Bailey, *A Diplomatic History*, p. 157.

15. See Samuel Flagg Bemis, *John Quincy Adams and the Foundations of American Foreign Policy* (New York: Knopf, 1949); and Philip Coolidge Brooks, *Diplomacy and the Borderlands: The Adams-Onís Treaty of 1819* (Berkeley, CA: University of California Press, 1939).

16. Hollis W. Barber, *Foreign Policies of the United States* (New York: Dryden, 1953), p. 252; and Dexter Perkins, *Hands Off: A History of the Monroe Doctrine* (New York: Little, Brown, 1941), p. 43. Both of these sources draw on John Quincy Adams, in C.F. Adams, ed., *Memoirs of John Quincy Adams*, Vol. VI (Philadelphia; 1974–77), p. 179.

17. Cited by Richard N. Current, Alexander DeConde, and Harris L. Dante, *United States History* (New York: Scott, Foresman, 1967), p. 234.

18. John Cassidy, "Enter the Dragon," *The New Yorker* (December 13, 2010), p. 99.

19. Paul H. Bergeron, "James K. Polk," in Leonard W. Levy and Louis Fisher, eds., *Encyclopedia of the American Presidency*, Vol. 3 (New York: Simon & Schuster, 1994), p. 1185.

20. Cited in Gary A. Donaldson, *American Foreign Policy: The Twentieth Century in Documents* (New York: Longman, 2003), p. 3.

21. Quoted by Frances FitzGerald, "Reflections: Foreign Policy," *The New Yorker* (November 11, 1985), p. 112.

22. Charles O. Lerche Jr., *America in World Affairs* (New York: McGraw-Hill, 1963), p. 36.

23. Mark E. Neely Jr., *The Last Best Hope of Earth: Abraham Lincoln and the Promise of America* (Cambridge, MA: Harvard University Press, 1993).

24. Quoted in Hoepli, *A Cartoon History*, p. 27.

25. Joan Haslip, *The Crown of Mexico: Maximilian and His Empress Carlota* (New York: Holt, Rinehart and Winston, 1972).

26. Norman B. Ferris, "William Henry Seward," in Jentleson and Paterson, eds., *Encyclopedia of U.S. Foreign Relations*, Vol. 4, p. 77.

27. Lerche, *America in World Affairs*, p. 38.

28. Gaddis Smith, "The Legacy of Monroe's Doctrine," *New York Times Magazine* (September 9, 1984), p. 46.

29. Amos Perlmuter, *Making the World Safe for Democracy: A Century of Wilsonianism and Its Totalitarian Challengers* (Chapel Hill: University of North Carolina Press, 1997), p. xi.

30. John Lewis Gaddis, *Surprise, Security, and the American Experience* (Cambridge, MA: Harvard University Press, 2004), p. 13.

31. Paul Kennedy, *The Rise and Fall of the Great Powers: Economic Change and Military Conflict from 1500 to 2000* (New York: Random House, 1987). The American diplomat and scholar George F. Kennan has expressed a similar concern. Looking back on this nation's experience governing the Philippines, which the United States granted independence in 1946 chiefly because its administration had become a bother, he concluded that "the ruling of distant peoples is not our dish . . . there are many things we Americans should beware of, and among them is the acceptance of any sort of a paternalistic responsibility to anyone, be it even in the form of military occupation, if we can possibly avoid it, or for any period longer than is absolutely necessary" [George F. Kennan, *American Diplomacy, 1900–1950* (Chicago: University of Chicago Press, 1951), p. 22)].

32. Tony Smith, *America's Mission: The United States and the Worldwide Struggle for Democracy in the Twentieth Century* (Princeton, NJ: Princeton University Press, 1994), p. xiii.

33. Foster Rhea Dulles, *America's Rise to World Power: 1898–1954* (New York: Harper & Row, 1954), p. 58.

34. Daniel S. Papp, Loch K. Johnson, and John E. Endicott, *American Foreign Policy: History, Politics, and Policy* (New York: Pearson/Longman, 2005), pp. 97–98; the quote is from John Morton Blum, *The Republican Roosevelt* (New York: Atheneum, 1973), p. 127.

35. Norman Stone, ed., *The Times Atlas of World History*, 3rd ed. (Maplewood, NJ: Hammond, 1989), p. 246.

36. "Affairs in China," *Foreign Relations 1901*, Appendix (Washington, DC: U.S. Government Printing Office, 1902), p. 12.

37. For the discussion presented here of US-Japanese relations at the time, see Edmund Morris, *Theodore Rex* (New York: Random House, 2001), p. 510; James MacGregor Burns, *Roosevelt: The Soldier of Freedom, 1940–1945* (New York: Harcourt Brace Jovanovich, 1970), pp. 20, 79; and Papp, Johnson, and Endicott, *American Foreign Policy*, p. 454. On immigration matters over the years, see Roger Daniels, *Coming to America: A History of Immigration and Ethnicity in American Life* (New York: HarperCollins, 1990).

38. Morris, *Theodore Rex*, p. 414.

39. Speech at Minnesota State Fair (September 2, 1901).

40. Barbara W. Tuchman, *The Zimmermann Telegram* (New York: Ballantine, 1994).

41. W. A. White, *Woodrow Wilson* (Boston: Houghton Mifflin, 1929), p. 384, cited by Bailey, *A Diplomatic History*, p. 608.

42. *Essays and Sketches in Biography* (New York: Meridian, 1956), p. 180.

43. Alexander L. George and Juliette L. George, *Woodrow Wilson and Colonel House: A Personality Study* (New York: Dover, 1956).

44. Harriet Hyman Alonso, "Kellogg-Briand Pact," in Jentleson and Paterson, eds., *Encyclopedia of U.S. Foreign Relations*, Vol. 3, p. 3.

45. See, for example, Iris Chang, *The Rape of Nanking: The Forgotten Holocaust of World War II* (New York: Basic Books, 1997).

46. Bailey, *A Diplomatic History*, p. 708.

47. Peter McGrath, "The Lessons of Munich," *Newsweek* (October 3, 1988), p. 37. In 1991, President George H. W. Bush would justify his invasion of Iraq with the phrase, "No more Munichs." But see, also, Paul Kennedy, "A Time to Appease," *National Interest* 108 (July/August 2010), pp. 7–17, who suggests that in some circumstances a policy of appeasement can be a wise step toward defusing an incipient and unnecessary war.

48. Michael Bloch, *Ribbentrop* (London: Time Warner Books, 2003).

49. See Donald Cameron Watt, *How War Came: The Immediate Origins of the Second World War, 1938–1939* (New York: Pantheon, 1989).

50. Erik Larson, *In the Garden of the Beasts: Love, Terror, and an American Family in Berlin* (New York: Crown, 2011).

51. Arthur H. Vandenberg Jr. and J. A. Morris, eds., *The Private Papers of Senator Vandenberg* (Boston: Houghton Mifflin, 1952), p. 10, cited in Dulles, *America's Rise to World Power*, p. 198.

52. See Gordon W. Prange, with Donald Goldstein and Katherine Dillon, *Pearl Harbor: The Verdict of History* (New York: Penguin, 1991); and Burns, *Roosevelt*.

53. Bailey, *A Diplomatic History*, p. 740.

54. Bailey, *A Diplomatic History*, p. 771.

55. *The Cold War in Transition* (New York: Macmillan, 1966), p. 6.

56. Donaldson, *American Foreign Policy*, p. xii.

57. Chrystia Freeland, "America's Divided Global Outlook," *Financial Times* (June 7, 2006), p. 13.

**Chapter 5**

1. This case study is based on the following sources: David M. Barrett and Max Holland, *Blind Over Cuba: The Photo Gap and the Missile Crisis* (College Station: Texas A&M University, 2012); Max Holland, "The 'Photo Gap' that Delayed Discovery of Missiles in Cuba," *Studies in Intelligence* 49 (2005), p. 17; Gregory W. Pedlow and Donald E. Welzenbach, *The CIA and the U-2 Program, 1954–1975* (Washington, DC: Center for the Study of Intelligence, Central Intelligence Agency, 1998), pp. 199–210; Graham Allison and Philip Zelikow, *Essence of Decision: Explaining the Cuban Missile Crisis*, 2nd ed. (New York: Longman, 1995); James G. Blight, Bruce J. Allyn, and David A. Welch, *Cuba on the Brink: Castro, the Missile Crisis, and the Soviet Collapse* (New York: Pantheon, 1993); James G. Blight and David A. Welch, eds., *Intelligence and the Cuban Missile Crisis* (London: Cass, 1998); John Lewis Gaddis, *We Now Know: Rethinking Cold War History* (New York: Oxford University Press, 1997), pp. 262–263, 267, 277; Sherman Kent, "A Crucial Estimate Relived," *Studies in Intelligence* 49 (Spring 1964), p. 115; Raymond L. Garthoff, *Reflections on the Cuban Missile Crisis*, rev. ed. (Washington, DC: Brookings Institution, 1989), pp. 35–36; Michael R. Beschloss, *The Crisis Years: Kennedy and Khrushchev,*

*1960–1963* (New York: HarperCollins, 1991), pp. 544–545; James G. Blight and Janet M. Lang, "How Castro Held the World Hostage," *New York Times* (October 26, 2012), p. A27; Thomas Coffey, "The Cuban Missile Crisis Redux: Lessons from Two More Work," *Studies in Intelligence* 57 (June 2013), pp. 65–68; and my interviews with Secretary of Defense Robert S. McNamara (January 24, 1985) and Secretary of State Dean Rusk (February 21, 1985), both in Athens, Georgia.

2.  Dean Rusk, *As I Saw It*, with Richard Rusk and Daniel S. Papp (New York: Norton, 1989), p. 237.

3.  Cited by Robert C. Tucker, *Politics as Leadership* (Columbia: University of Missouri, 1981), p. x.

4.  J. Robert Oppenheimer, "Atomic Weapons and American Policy," *Foreign Affairs* 31 (July 1953), p. 529.

5.  John Mueller, "Containment and the Decline of the Soviet Empire: Some Tentative Reflections on the End of the World As We Know It," paper presented at the Annual Convention of the International Studies Association, Anaheim, CA, March 26, 1986, p. 1.

6.  On Fulbright's influence in the establishment of the UN (another example of how lawmakers can play an important role in foreign policy), see Charles B. Seib and Alan L. Otten, "Fulbright: Arkansas Paradox," *Harper's* 212 (June 1956), p. 63.

7.  Quoted by Robert D. Warth, *Soviet Russia in World Politics* (New York: Twayne, 1963), p. 320.

8.  Harry S. Truman, *Memoirs*, Vol. I (New York: Doubleday, 1955), pp. 551–552.

9.  David S. McLellan, *The Cold War in Transition* (New York: Macmillan, 1966), p. 6. For evidence that the Cold War had deeper roots, see John Lewis Gaddis, *The United States and the Origins of the Cold War: 1941–1947* (New York: Columbia University Press, 1972). On psychological aspects of the superpower rivalry, see Ralph K. White, *Fearful Warriors: A Psychological Profile of U.S.-Soviet Relations* (New York: Free Press, 1984).

10. X, "The Sources of Soviet Conduct," *Foreign Affairs* 25 (July 1947), pp. 566–582.

11. See "Containment: Forty Years Later," *Foreign Affairs* 65 (Spring 1987), p. 829.

12. John Lewis Gaddis, *Strategies of Containment: A Critical Appraisal of Postwar American National Security Policy* (New York: Oxford University Press, 1982), p. 22.

13. Quoted by Joseph M. Jones, *The Fifteen Weeks* (New York: Viking, 1955), p. 190.

14. John Lewis Gaddis, "The Long Peace," *International Security* 10 (Spring 1986), p. 130.

15. Quoted by Gaddis, *Strategies of Containment*, p. 41.

16. Henry A. Kissinger, "Mr. X," *New York Times Book Review* (November 13, 2011), p. 47.

17. Louis Menand, "Getting Real: George F. Kennan's Cold War," *The New Yorker* (November 14, 2011), p. 83.

18. Gaddis, *The United States and the Origins of the Cold War*, p. 352.

19. Gaddis, *The United States and the Origins of the Cold War*.

20. Gaddis, *The United States and the Origins of the Cold War*, p. 288.

21. See Richard H. Rovere, *Senator Joe McCarthy* (Berkeley: University of California Press, 1959); and John Earl Haynes, Harvey Klehr, and Alexander Vassiliev, with translations by Philip Redko and Steven Shadbad, *Spies: The Rise and Fall of the KGB in America* (New Haven, CT: Yale University Press, 2009).

22. Quoted by Gaddis, *Strategies of Containment*, p. 91, emphasis added.

23. Gaddis, *Strategies of Containment*, p. 130.

24. Gaddis, *Strategies of Containment*, pp. 130–131.

25. Gaddis, *Strategies of Containment*, p. 128.

26. Richard Reeves, *Daring Young Men* (New York: Simon & Schuster, 2010), p. 24.

27. See Andrei Cherny, *The Candy Bombers: The Untold Story of the Berlin Airlift and America's Finest Hour* (New York: Putnam, 2008); and Reeves, *Daring Young Men*.

28. John Lewis Gaddis, "How Relevant Was U.S. Strategy in Winning the Cold War?," *Report*, Strategic Studies Institute, U.S. Army War College (March 17, 1992), p. 5.

29. McLellan, *The Cold War in Transition*, p. 13.

30. McLellan, *The Cold War in Transition*, p. 18.

31. McLellan, *The Cold War in Transition*, p. 23.

32. Thomas C. Schelling, *Arms and Influence* (New Haven, CT: Yale University Press, 1966), p. 124, emphasis added.

33. See Nicholas Thompson, *The Hawk and the Dove: Paul Nitze, George Kennan, and the History of the Cold War* (New York: Henry Holt, 2010).

34. See Fred Kaplan, *The Counterinsurgents: David Petraeus and the Plot to Change the American Way of War* (New York: Simon & Schuster, 2012). General Petraeus served as America's military commander in Iraq and Afghanistan.

35. Michael Grow, *U.S. Presidents and Latin American Interventions: Pursuing Regime Change in the Cold War* (Lawrence: University Press of Kansas, 2008), pp. 28–56.

36. Admiral William O. Studeman, Deputy Director of Central Intelligence, "Intelligence and the Cuban Missile Crisis Symposium," remarks, CIA Headquarters (October 19, 1992), pp. 4–5 (photocopy sent to me by Adm. Studeman).

37. Larry King interview, *Larry King Live*, CNN Television (October 22, 1992).

38. Quoted by Theodore C. Sorensen, *Kennedy* (New York: Harper & Row, 1965), p. 680.

39. See Chambers M. Roberts, "The Day We Didn't Go to War," *The Reporter* (September 14, 1954), pp. 31–35.

40. Stephen E. Ambrose, *Eisenhower: The President* (New York: Simon & Schuster, 1984), p. 184.

41. Richard Reeves, *President Kennedy: Profile of Power* (New York: Simon & Schuster, 1993).

42. Peter Wyden, *Bay of Pigs: The Untold Story* (New York: Simon & Schuster, 1979), p. 100.

43. Theodore C. Sorensen, quoted in Dennis Hevesi, "Carl Kaysen," *New York Times* (February 20, 2010), p. A15. The Test Ban Treaty was also a significant environmental measure, reducing the incidence of radioactive particles in the Earth's atmosphere.

44. President Kennedy's comment to W. W. Rostow, cited in Arthur M. Schlesinger Jr., *A Thousand Days: John F. Kennedy in the White House* (Boston: Houghton Mifflin, 1963), p. 339.

45. Alan Brinkley, "Why Were We in Vietnam?," *New York Times Book Review* (September 9, 2012), p. 17, for the first statistic; and Clayton Laurie, introduction to M.H. Schiattereggia, "Counterintelligence in Counterguerrilla Operations," *Studies in Intelligence* 57 (June 2013), p. 39, for the second statistic.

46. This comparison is made by James C. Thomson Jr., "How Could Vietnam Happen? An Autopsy," *The Atlantic* (April 1968), p. 52.

47. See Stanley Karnow, "Vietnam as an Analogy," *New York Times* (October 4, 1986), p. A17.

48. Charles Figley and Seymour Levintman, eds., *Strangers at Home: Vietnam Veterans since the War* (New York: Praeger, 1980); Loch K. Johnson, "Political Alienation Among Vietnam Veterans," *Western Political Quarterly* 29 (September 1976), pp. 398–409.

49. Leslie H. Gelb and Richard K. Betts, *The Irony of Vietnam: The System Worked* (Washington, DC: Brookings Institution, 1979).

50. *White House Years* (Boston: Houghton Mifflin, 1979), p. 253.

51. Frank Snepp, *Decent Interval* (New York: Random House, 1979). Snepp was a CIA officer in Saigon at the time.

52. Alan Brinkley, "Why Were We in Vietnam?" *New York Times Book Review* (September 9, 2012), p. 17.

53. Loch K. Johnson, *America's Secret Power: The CIA in a Democratic Society* (New York: Oxford University Press, 1989).

54. Gelb and Betts, *The Irony of Vietnam*, p. 368.

55. John Spanier, *American Foreign Policy Since World War II*, 10th ed. (New York: Holt, Rinehart & Winston, 1985), p. 171.

56. Quoted by Karnow, "Vietnam as an Analogy," p. A17.

57. Quoted in the *Washington Post* (May 17, 1981), p. A14.

58. See Richard J. Barnet, *Real Security: Restoring American Power in a Dangerous Decade* (New York: Simon & Schuster, 1981), pp. 66–68.

59. Barry Blechman, "Stop at Start," *New York Times* (February 19, 2010), p. A27.

60. Lloyd C. Gardner, *A Covenant with Power: America and World Order from Wilson to Reagan* (New York: Oxford University Press, 1984), p. 213.

61. Daniel Wirls, *Buildup: The Politics of Defense in the Reagan Era* (New York: Cornell University Press, 1992).

62. William S. Cohen and George J. Mitchell, *Men of Zeal: The Inside Story of the Iran-Contra Hearings* (New York: Penguin, 1989); and Senate Select Committee on Secret Military Assistance to Iran and the Nicaraguan Opposition and House Select Committee to Investigate Covert Arms Transactions with Iran, *Hearings and Final Report* (Washington, DC: Government Printing Office, 1987).

63. Ambassador James E. Goodby, "Looking Back: The 1986 Reykjavik Summit," *Arms Control Today*, Arms Control Association (September 2006), p. 4; and Ambassador Jack F. Matlock Jr., *Reagan and Gorbachev: How the Cold War Ended* (New York: Random House, 2004), p. 134.

64. Gaddis, "How Relevant Was U.S. Strategy in Winning the Cold War?" p. 12.

65. George Bush and Brent Scowcroft, *A World Transformed* (New York: Knopf, 1998), p. 42.

## Chapter 6

1. For a gripping account of this battle, see Mark Bowden, *Black Hawk Down: A Story of Modern War* (Berkeley, CA: Atlantic Monthly Press, 1999). Also, Robert Patman, *Strategic Shortfall: The Somalia Syndrome and the March to 9/11* (Westport, CT: Praeger Security International, 2010).

2. Michael Ross, "Aspin Rejects Calls for Resignation," *Los Angeles Times* (October 8, 1993), p. A12. The appropriations bill was 107 Stat. 1475–77, sec. 8151 (1993). On these events, see Louis Fisher, *The Politics of Shared Power: Congress and the Executive*, 4th ed. (College Station: Texas A&M University Press, 1998), p. 204.

3. See Patman, *Strategic Shortfall*.

4. R. James Woolsey, testimony, *Hearings*, Select Committee on Intelligence, US Senate, 103d Cong., 2d Sess. (March 6, 1993).

5. George Bush and Brent Scowcroft, *A World Transformed* (New York: Knopf, 1998).

6. Cited in "Breakup of the Soviet Union: U.S. Dilemmas," *Great Decisions*, Foreign Policy Association (1992), p. 82.

7. This initiative was named after legislation sponsored by Senators Sam Nunn (D-Georgia) and Richard Lugar (R-Indiana).

8. "They Were Truly Idiots," interview with Mikhail Gorbachev, *Der Spiegel* (August 16, 2012), cited in Kathryn Stoner, "Whither Russia? Autocracy Is Here for Now, But Is It Here to Stay?," *Perspectives on Politics* 4 (December 2012), p. 977.

9. John Lukacs, *The End of the 20th Century and the End of the Modern Age* (New York: Ticknor & Fields, 1993), p. 21.

10. Quoted in Roger Cohen, "Cross vs. Crescent," *New York Times* (September 17, 1992), p. A5.

11. See Madeleine Albright, *Madam Secretary: A Memoir* (New York: Maramax Books, 2003); Jacqueline Sharkey, "When Pictures Drive Foreign Policy," *American Journalism Review* 15 (December 1993), pp. 14–19; and *New York Times* reporting on the Balkans during the Clinton administration, especially opinion pieces by Anthony Lewis.

12. Administration sources quoted in Elaine Sciolino, "Clinton's State Dept. Choice Backs 'Discreet' Force," *New York Times* (January 14, 1993), p. A9.

13. See Nicholas Kulish, "Recasting Serbia's Image, Starting With a Fresh Face," *New York Times* (January 16, 2010), p. A5. Also, Eric Moskowitz and Jeffrey S. Lantis, "The War in Kosovo: Coercive Diplomacy," in Ralph G. Carter, ed., *Contemporary Cases in Foreign Policy: From Terrorism to Trade* (Washington, DC: CQ Press, 2002), pp. 59–87.

14. Frank Ninkovich, *Germany and the United States* (New York: Twayne, 1995).

15. John Lehman, *Making War* (New York: Scribner's, 1992).

16. Quoted in the *Washington Post* (March 8, 1991), p. A16.

17. Rick Atkinson, *Crusade: The Untold Story of the Persian Gulf War* (Boston: Houghton Mifflin, 1993).

18. Atkinson, *Crusade*.

19. Remarks, C-SPAN television network (August 7, 1992).

20. Francis Fukuyama, *The End of History and the Last Man* (New York: Free Press, 1992).

21. Loch K. Johnson, *Bombs, Bugs, Drugs, and Thugs: Intelligence and America Quest for Security* (New York: New York University Press, 2000).

22. Enrique Peña Nieto, speech, Tijuana, Mexico, ABC *Nightly News* (February 21, 2012).

23. General Maxwell Thurman, remarks, Senior Conference XXVIII, United States Military Academy, West Point, New York (June 9, 1990), my notes.

24. David Brooks, "Where Obama Shines," *New York Times* (July 20, 2012), p. A19.

25. Rick Gladstone and Annie Lowrey, "Amid Reports of a New Massacre, Nations Seek to Step Up Pressure on Syria," *New York Times* (June 7, 2012), p. A8.

26. See John Rollins, *Al Qaeda and Affiliates: Historical Perspective, Global Presence, and Implications for U.S. Policy,* Congressional Research Service, Library of Congress (Washington, DC, January 2010).

27. Andrea Elliott, "The Jihadist Next Door," *New York Times Magazine* (January 31, 2010), p. 34. On Al Qaeda's presence in Somalia, see Mohammed Ibrahim, "Somali Rebels Vow to Send Fighters to Yemen," *New York Times* (January 2, 2010), p. A10; and Lee Jon Anderson, "The Most Failed State," *The New Yorker* (December 14, 2009), pp. 64–75.

28. "Bin Laden Determined to Strike US," *President's Daily Brief* (August 6, 2001), declassified and released to the public at the request of the Kean Commission in 2004.

29. See Loch K. Johnson, *The Threat on the Horizon* (New York: Oxford University Press, 2011).

30. See, for example, Stephen Flynn, *America the Vulnerable: How Our Government Is Failing to Protect Us from Terrorism* (New York: HarperCollins, 2004); and Johnson, *Threat on the Horizon.*

31. See the National Commission on Terrorist Attacks upon the United States (the 9/11 Commission or Kean Commission), *Final Report* (New York: Norton, 2004).

32. See Robert Jervis, *Why Intelligence Fails: Lessons from the Iranian Revolution and the Iraq War* (Ithaca, NY: Cornell University Press, 2010); Johnson, *Threat on the Horizon.*

33. Richard A. Clarke, *Against All Enemies: Inside America's War on Terror* (New York: Simon & Schuster, 2004), pp. 229, 237.

34. See Jervis, *Why Intelligence Fails*; and Johnson, *Threat on the Horizon.*

35. Bob Woodward, *Bush at War* (New York: Simon & Schuster, 2002), pp. 83–84.

36. Jane Mayer, *The Dark Side: The Inside Story of How the War on Terror Turned into a War on American Ideals* (New York: Doubleday, 2008).

37. See Louis Fisher, *The Constitution and 9/11* (Lawrence: University Press of Kansas, 2008); Walter F. Mondale, with David Hage, *The Good Fight* (New York: Scribner, 2010); and Frederick A. O. Schwarz Jr. and Aziz Z. Huq, *Unchecked and Unbalanced: Presidential Power in a Time of Terror* (New York: Basic Books, 2007).

38. For an elaboration of this thesis, see Johnson, *Threat on the Horizon.*

39. John Lewis Gaddis, *Surprise, Security, and the American Experience* (Cambridge, MA: Harvard University Press, 2005), p. 86.

40. See Steven W. Hook, *U.S. Foreign Policy: The Paradox of World Power*, 3rd ed. (Washington, DC: CQ Press, 2011), pp. 331–332.

41. See Glenn Hastedt, "Public Intelligence: Leaks as Policy Instruments—The Case of the Iraq War," *Intelligence and National Security* 20 (September 2005), pp. 419–439.

42. Dina Badie, "Groupthink, Iraq, and the War on Terror: Explaining US Policy Shift toward Iraq," *Foreign Policy Analysis* 6 (October 2010), pp. 277–296; Jervis, *Why Intelligence Fails*; and Johnson, *Threat on the Horizon.*

43. Bob Woodward, *Plan of Attack* (New York: Simon & Schuster, 2004), p. 249.

44. See Jervis, *Why Intelligence Fails*; and Johnson, *Threat on the Horizon.*

45. Paul R. Pillar, "Intelligence, Policy, and the War in Iraq," *Foreign Affairs* 85 (March/April 2006), pp. 15–28; see, also, his *Intelligence and U.S. Foreign Policy: Iraq, 9/11, and Misguided Reform* (New York: Columbia University Press, 2011).

46. George W. Bush, *Decision Points* (New York: Crown, 2010), p. 228.

47. For an account, see Graham Allison, "How It Went Down," *Time* (May 7, 2012), pp. 35–41.

48. See Barnett Richard Rubin, *The Search for Peace in Afghanistan: From Buffer State to Failed State* (New Haven, CT: Yale University Press, 1995).

49. John O. Brennan, the Obama administration's chief of counter-terrorism (and later Director of the CIA), quoted in Scott Shane, "Renewing a Debate Over Secrecy, and Its Costs," *New York Times* (June 7, 2012), p. A9.

50. Allison, "How It Went Down."

51. See, for example, the unsigned editorial, "Too Much Power for a President," *New York Times* (May 31, 2012), p. A22. Also, Loch K. Johnson, "Intelligence Analysis and Planning for Paramilitary Operations," *Journal of National Security Law & Policy* 34 (Spring 2012), pp. 481–505.

52. Scott Shane, "Senator Asks To View Files On Killings Of Americans," *New York Times* (January 15, 2013), p. A13. See, also, Louis Fisher, "What Grounds for Secrecy?" *The National Law Journal* (January 21, 2013), pp. 6–7.

53. See, for example, Gardiner Harris, "Defense Chief Shrugs Off Objections To Drones," *New York Times* (June 7, 2012), p. A9; Scott Shane, "Election Spurred A Move to Codify U.S. Drone Policy," *New York Times* (November 25, 2012), p. A1.

54. David Kilcullen, *The Accidental Guerrilla: Fighting Small Wars in the Midst of a Big One* (New York: Oxford University Press, 2009); Fred Kaplan, *The Insurgents: David Petraeus and the Plot to Change the American Way of War* (New York: Simon & Schuster, 2013).

### Chapter 7

1. On Dien Bien Phu, see Stanley Karnow, *Vietnam: A History* (New York: Viking, 1983); and Chalmers M. Roberts, "The Day We Didn't Go to War," *The Reporter* 2 (September 14, 1954), pp. 31–35. For the 1954 CIA Estimate, see Stansfield Turner (a former DCI), *Burn Before Reading: Presidents, CIA Directors, and Secret Intelligence* (New York: Hyperion, 2005), p. 79. The next year, 1954, President Eisenhower would once more reject advice, offered by the chairman of the Joint Chiefs of Staff, to use atomic bombs against an Asian nation, this time China. The President suggested to the chairman that he had to be crazy to think America's use of nuclear weapons again in Asia would be sound policy [remarks, Joseph S. Nye, Jr., *Fareed Zakaria Show*, CNN Television (July 28, 2013)].

2. Professor Laurence H. Tribe, Harvard Law School, quoted by Stuart Taylor Jr., "Reagan's Defenders Arguing He Can Defy Congress's Ban," *New York Times* (May 17, 1987), p. A1.

3. For instance, see his remarks in the *Congressional Record*, vol. 119 (1973), p. 24532.

4. Loch K. Johnson, *The Making of International Agreements: Congress Confronts the Executive* (New York: New York University Press, 1984), p. 90.

5. A chairman of the Senate Foreign Relations Committee, Alexander Wiley (R-Wisconsin), once declared that "the power of executive agreements [signed by President Franklin Roosevelt] has resulted in such catastrophes as Yalta, Potsdam, and Tehran."

[quoted by Henry Steele Commager, "The Perilous Folly of Senator Bricker," *The Reporter* 9 (October 13, 1953), p. 16].

6. Quoted in *U.S. News & World Report* (May 2, 1983), p. 29.

7. See Charlie Savage, "Obama Takes a New Route to Opposing Parts of Laws," *New York Times* (January 9, 2010), p. A9; and, for the "twice as many" statement, Charlie Savage, "Obama Disputes Detainee Limits in Defense Bill," *New York Times* (January 4, 2013), p. A1.

8. "The Rule of Law," unsigned editorial, *New York Times* (January 8, 2011), p. A18.

9. Savage, "Obama Disputes Detainee Limits."

10. Warren Christopher, "Ceasefire between the Branches: A Compact in Foreign Affairs," *Foreign Affairs* 60 (Summer 1982), p. 999.

11. While serving as an American Political Science Association Congressional Fellow in the Senate during 1969–1970, I heard Senator Fulbright make this analogy in hearings conducted by the Foreign Relations Committee.

12. Thomas E. Cronin, "Superman, Our Textbook President," *Washington Monthly* (October 1970), pp. 47–54.

13. Theodore H. White, *The Making of the President 1960* (New York: Atheneum, 1961), p. 69.

14. See, for example, Richard E. Neustadt, *Presidential Power: The Politics of Leadership from FDR to Carter* (New York: Wiley, 1980); Raymond Tatalovich and Byron W. Daynes, *Presidential Power in the United States* (Belmont, CA: Brooks/Cole, 1984); Richard M. Pious, *The American Presidency* (New York: Basic Books, 1979); Theodore C. Sorensen, *Decision-Making in the White House: The Olive Branch or the Arrows* (New York: Columbia University Press, 1963); and Richard P. Nathan, *The Administrative Presidency* (New York: Wiley, 1983).

15. Quoted in the *New York Times* (January 18, 1981), p. A3. Professor Daniel W. Drezner at Tufts University notes that "most of the time presidents don't pick the foreign policy issues they want to tackle—the issues choose them" [see his "Why Presidents Love Foreign Affairs," *New York Times* (September 21, 2012), p. A21].

16. Roberta Wohlstetter, *Pearl Harbor: Warning and Decision* (Stanford, CA: Stanford University Press, 1962).

17. Richard K. Betts, *Surprise Attack: Lessons for Defense Spending* (Washington, DC: Brookings Institution, 1982).

18. Quoted by Sorensen, *Decision-Making*, p. 30.

19. Sorensen, *Decision-Making*, p. 30.

20. Sorensen, *Decision-Making*, p. 27.

21. Sorensen, *Decision-Making*, p. 33.

22. Quoted by Neustadt, *Presidential Power*, p. 9.

23. My notes on remarks by Senator Hubert H. Humphrey (D, Minnesota), Congressional Fellows Program, American Political Science Association, Washington, DC (February 21, 1970).

24. See, for example, Scott Shane, "Senate Asks to View Filings on Killings of Americans," *New York Times* (January 15, 2013), p. A13.

25. Elie Abel, *The Missile Crisis* (Philadelphia: Lippincott, 1966), pp. 154–156.

26. John F. Lehman Jr., quoted by John H. Cusman Jr., "Ex-Insider Who Elects to Remain on Outside," *New York Times* (January 6, 1989), p. 11.

27. John F. Kennedy, in the preface to Sorensen, *Decision-Making*, p. xii.

28. Douglas T. Stuart, *Creating the National Security State: A History of the Law That Transformed America* (Princeton, NJ: Princeton University Press, 2008).

29. See Karl F. Inderfurth and Loch K. Johnson, eds., *Fateful Decisions: Inside the National Security Council* (New York: Oxford University Press, 2004); David Rothkopf, *Running the World: The Inside Story of the National Security Council and the Architects of American Power* (New York: Public Affairs, 2005).

30. Elizabeth Drew, "A Reporter At Large: Brzezinski," *The New Yorker* (July 1, 1978), p. 90.

31. Colin Powell, with Joseph E. Perisco, *My American Journey: An Autobiography* (New York: Random House, 1995), p. 352.

32. Remarks, "A Forum on the Role of the National Security Advisor," Woodrow Wilson International Center for Scholars, Washington, DC (April 12, 2001), quoted in Inderfurth and Johnson, *Fateful Decisions*, p. 142, emphasis added.

33. Remarks, Forum on National Security Advisers, Brookings Institution (1999), quoted in Inderfurth and Johnson, *Fateful Decisions*, p. 135.

34. Powell, *My American Journey*, p. 352.

35. Remarks, Forum on National Security Advisers, Brookings Institution (1999), quoted in Inderfurth and Johnson, *Fateful Decisions*, p. 138.

36. Cecil V. Crabb and Kevin V. Mulcahy, *American National Security: A President Perspective* (Pacific Grove, CA: Brooks/Cole, 1991), pp. 175–192.

37. Crabb and Mulcahy, *American National Security*, quoted in Inderfurth and Johnson, *Fateful Decisions*, p. 140.

38. Peter Baker, "A Manager of Overseas Crises, As Much as the World Permits," *New York Times* (September 24, 2012), p. A1.

39. A comparison drawn by Nicholas D. Kristof, "Make Diplomacy, Not War," *New York Times* (August 10, 2008), p. Wk. 2.

40. *U.S. Government Manual* (Washington, DC: US Government Printing Office, 2012).

41. David D. Kirkpatrick and Steven Lee Myers, "A Wave of Unrest Shows a Region Still Volatile," *New York Times* (September 13, 2012), p. A1.

42. Eric Schmitt, "Pentagon Construction Boom Beefs Up Mideast Air Bases," *New York Times* (September 18, 2005), p. A10.

43. See Winslow Wheeler, "Adventures in BabbleLand," *Time.com* (October 1, 2012); ABC *Nightly News* (January 11, 2012); and Gordon Adams and Cindy Williams, *Buying National Security: How America Plans and Pays for Its Global Role and Safety at Home* (New York: Routledge, 2010).

44. Vincent Davis, "U.S. Department of Defense," in Bruce W. Jentleson and Thomas G. Paterson, eds., *Encyclopedia of U.S. Foreign Relations* (New York: Oxford University Press, 1997), Vol. 4, p. 421. The definitive study of the Goldwater-Nichols Act is James R. Locher III, *Victory on the Potomac: The Goldwater-Nichols Act Unifies the Pentagon* (College Station: Texas A&M University Press, 2002).

45. See John Cassidy, "Enter the Dragon," *The New Yorker* (December 13, 2010), pp. 96–101, quote at p. 100.

46. Dana Priest, comments, *Booknotes*, C-SPAN Television Network (March 9, 2003); see Priest's *The Mission: Waging War and Keeping Peace with America's Military* (New York: Norton, 2003). Also see Chalmers Johnson, *The Sorrows of Empire: Militarism, Secrecy and the End of the Republic* (New York: Henry Holt, 2004); and Loch K. Johnson, *Seven Sins of American Foreign Policy* (New York: Longman, 2005).

47. Günter Bischof, "American Empire and Its Discontents: The United States and Europe Today," in Michael Gehler, Günter Bischof, Ludger Kühnhardt, and Rolf Steininger, eds., *Towards a European Constitution: A Historical and Political Comparison with the United States* (Wien, Austria: Böhlau Verlag, 2005), p. 191.

48. "Embassies as Command Posts in the Anti-Terror Campaign," *Staff Report*, Foreign Relations Committee, US Senate (December 15, 2006).

49. Ann Scott Tyson and Dana Priest, "Pentagon Seeking Leeway Overseas," *Washington Post* (February 24, 2005), p. A1.

50. See Mark Landler, "Clinton Pledges Bigger Role for Besieged State Department," *New York Times* (December 16, 2010), p. A19; ABC *Nightly News* (January 4, 2013).

51. See Loch K. Johnson, *The Threat on the Horizon* (New York: Oxford University Press, 2011).

52. Raymond Hopkins, "The International Role of 'Domestic' Bureaucracy," *International Organization* 30 (1976), p. 424.

53. James Ledbetter, "What Ike Got Right," *New York Times* (December 14, 2010), p. A27.

54. Quoted by Theodore C. Sorensen, *Kennedy* (New York: Harper & Row, 1965), p. 346.

55. Quoted by James David Barber, *The Presidential Character: Predicting Performance in the White House* (Englewood Cliffs, NJ: Prentice-Hall, 1972), p. 157.

56. From "Second Speech on Foot's Resolution," delivered in the Senate, January 26, 1830, reprinted in *The Writings and Speeches of Daniel Webster*, Vol. 6 (Boston: Little, Brown, 1903), p. 7.

57. My interview with Dean Rusk, Athens, Georgia (May 22, 1980).

58. Unsigned editorial, "Not Too Late to Curb the Filibuster," *New York Times* (May 15, 2012), p. A26. See, also, Paul

Krguman, "A Dangerous Dysfunction," *New York Times* (December 21, 2009), p. A29.

59. Walter F. Mondale (D-Minnesota), "Resolved: Fix the Filibuster," *New York Times* (January 2, 2011), p. Wk. 10. Political scientist Thomas E. Mann has referred to this misuse of the filibuster rule as the reason why "the Senate has become the most dysfunctional legislative body in the world" [interviewed by reporter Dan Rather, HDNet TV (June 10, 2012)]. For additional filibuster reform proposals, see Ezra Klein, "Let's Talk," *The New Yorker* (January 28, 2013), pp. 24–29.

60. Quoted by Vance Packard, "Uncle Carl, Watchdog of Defense,"*American Magazine* 149 (April 1950), p. 123. Wyche Fowler, a US Senator from Georgia, once observed wryly that the purpose of congressional oversight was "to keep the bureaucrats from doing something stupid" [remark to me (February 3, 1995), Washington, DC].

61. Mark Mazzetti and Scott Shane, "Senate and C.I.A. Spar Over Secret Report on Interrogation Practices," *New York Times* (July 20, 2013), p. A13.

62. My interview with CIA personnel in the Agency's Office of Legislative Affairs (March 29, 2012), Washington, DC. Robert M. Gates, deputy director of Central Intelligence at the time (and later DCI), noted in 1987 that by the mid-1970s Congress had gained "access to intelligence information essentially equal to that of the executive branch" [Robert M. Gates, "The CIA and American Foreign Policy," *Foreign Affairs* 66 (Winter, 1987), pp. 215–230, quote at p. 224].

63. Gregg Easterbrook, "What's Wrong with Congress?" *The Atlantic* (December 1984), p. 65.

64. My interview with Colby, Washington, DC (March 21, 1979); also, Carl Colby, "The Man Nobody Knew: In Search of My Father, CIA Spymaster William Colby," film (Act Four Entertainment, 2011).

65. Walter Lippmann, *Public Opinion* (New York: Macmillan, 1922), p. 183.

66. Loch K. Johnson, *A Season of Inquiry: The Senate Intelligence Investigation* (Lexington: University Press of Kentucky, 1985); and my "Accountability and America's Secret Foreign Policy: Keeping a Legislative Eye on the Central Intelligence Agency," *Foreign Policy Analysis* 1 (March 2005), pp. 99–120.

67. Merle Miller, *Plain Speaking: An Oral Biography of Harry S Truman* (New York: Berkley, 1963), p. 420.

68. Mark Shields, PBS *NewsHour* (January 11, 2012). On Shelby's "holds," see Carl Hulse, "The Rattled State of Democrats," *New York Times* (February 14, 2010), p. A12; and Julian E. Zelizer, "The Winds of Congressional Change," *The Forum*, The Berkeley Electronic Press 7 (2009).

69. Mary McGrory, *Washington Star* (March 9, 1976), p. 14.

70. Peter W. Singer, "Do Drones Undermine Democracy?" *New York Times* (January 22, 2012), p. Wk 5.

71. Stephen K. Bailey, *Congress in the Seventies*, 2nd ed. (New York: St. Martin's, 1970), p. 109.

72. Louis Fisher, "Foreign Policy Powers of the President and Congress," *Annals of the American Academy of Political and Social Science* 499 (September 1988), p. 152.

73. Michael J. Glennon, "In Foreign Policy, the Court Is Clear: President Is Subject to Will of Congress," *Los Angeles Times* (July 19, 1987), pt. V, p. 3.

74. Bernard Gwertzman, "Senate Rebukes Carter Over Ending of Taiwan Pact," *New York Times* (June 7, 1979), p. A1.

75. J. Jackson (concurring), *Youngstown Sheet & Tube Co. v. Sawyer*, p. 636, n. 2.

76. See Louis Fisher, *The Constitution and 9/11: Recurring Threats to America's Freedoms* (Lawrence: University Press of Kansas, 2008).

77. Neustadt, *Presidential Power*, p. 4.

78. Dated November 1947, Truman Archives, Truman Presidential Library.

79. Clinton Rossiter, *The American Presidency*, rev. ed. (New York: New American Library, 1960), p. 94.

80. Roy P. Basler, ed., *Abraham Lincoln: His Speeches and Writings* (New York: Da Capo Press, 1990), p. 601.

81. Tatalovich and Daynes, *Presidential Power in the United States*, p. 16.

82. Quoted by Edmund Morris, *Colonel Roosevelt* (New York: Random House, 2010), as cited in a review by Geoffrey C. Ward, "A Headlong Life," *New York Times Sunday Book Review* (November 28, 2010), p. 16.

**Chapter 8**

1. This case study is based on my firsthand observations of Representative Aspin when I served as staff director of the HPSCI Oversight Subcommittee on Intelligence. For a more detailed account, see Loch K. Johnson, *Secret Agencies: U.S. Intelligence in a Hostile World* (New Haven, CT: Yale University Press, 1989), pp. 89–94.

2. Press conference, August 26, 1983, reported in *German Press Review* (August 31, 1983), Embassy of the Federal Republic of Germany, Washington, DC,

3. John F. Kennedy, *Profiles in Courage* (New York: Harper and Row, 1956), p. 208.

4. For polling data, see Loch K. Johnson,*Seven Sins of American Foreign Policy* (New York: Pearson/Longman, 2007), pp. 56–58.

5. The passport statistic is cited in *The New Yorker* (April 16, 2012), p. 88; and the *New York Times*/CBS survey in Peter Baker, "Obama's Focus on Re-election Faces World of Complications," *New York Times* (June 18, 2012), p. A3.

6. Fred I. Greenstein, *The American Party System and the American People*, 2nd ed. (Englewood Cliffs, NJ: Prentice-Hall, 1970), p.11.

7. V. O. Key Jr., *The Responsible Electorate* (Cambridge, MA: Harvard University Press, 1966).

8. Frank Rich, "The Up-or-Down Vote on Obama's Presidency," *New York Times* (March 7, 2010), p. Wk. 10; David E. Sanger and Jodi Kantor, "Rice's Blunt Style Endeared Her to President, but Not All," *New York Times* (December 14, 2012), p. A22.

9. John Mueller, *War, Presidents, and Public Opinion* (New York: Wiley, 1973), pp. 208–213.

10. Ole R. Hosti, "American Public Opinion and Foreign Policy: Did the September 11 Attacks Change Everything?" in David P. Forsythe, Patrice C. McMahon, and Andrew Wederman, eds., *American Foreign Policy in a Globalized World* (New York: Routledge, 2006), pp. 156, 169.

11. Nelson W. Polsby, *Congress and the Presidency* (Englewood Cliffs, NJ: Prentice-Hall, 1964), p. 25.

12. Richard A. Brody and Catherine R. Shapiro, "A Reconsideration of the Rally Phenomenon in Public Opinion," in Samuel Long, ed., *Political Behavior Annual,* Vol. 2 (Boulder, CO, and London: Westview, 1989), pp. 85–86.

13. Brody and Shapiro, "A Reconsideration of the Rally Phenomenon," pp. 77–102; see, also, Richard A. Brody, *Assessing the President: The Media, Elite Opinion, and Public Support* (Stanford, CA: Stanford University Press, 1991).

14. Brody and Shapiro, "A Reconsideration of the Rally Phenomenon," p. 100, emphasis added.

15. Kennedy, *Profiles in Courage*, p. 208, emphasis added.

16. Quoted in Sir Philip Magnus, ed., *Selected Prose* (London: Falcon, 1948), p. 40.

17. Donald R. Matthews, *U.S. Senators and Their World* (Chapel Hill: University of North Carolina Press, 1960), p. 221; see, as well, *Congressional Staff Journal* 6 (November–December 1981), U.S. Congress, Washington, DC, pp.1–8. My more recent conversations from 2010 to 2012 with staff aides on key congressional committees suggest that this earlier research conclusion remains valid today.

18. Ole R. Holsti, "Public Opinion," in Bruce W. Jentleson and Thomas G. Paterson, eds., *Encyclopedia of U.S. Foreign Relations*, Vol. 3 (New York: Oxford University Press, 1997), pp. 440–447, and his *Public Opinion and American Foreign Policy* (Ann Arbor: University of Michigan Press, 2004); V. O. Key Jr., *Public Opinion and American Democracy* (New York: Knopf, 1961), p. 482; Jeffrey S. Lantis, *US Foreign Policy in Action* (New York: Wiley-Blackwell, 2013), pp. 214–216; and John C. Wahlke, Heinz Eulau, William Buchanan, and Leroy C. Ferguson, *The Legislative System* (New York: Wiley, 1962), p. 273.

19. Warren E. Miller and Donald E. Stokes, "Constituency Influence in Congress," *American Political Science Review* 57 (March 1963), pp. 45–56.

20. James M. Lindsay, "The Senate and Foreign Policy," in Burdett A. Loomis, ed., *The U.S. Senate: From Deliberation to Dysfunction* (Washington, DC: CQ Press, 2012), p. 221.

21. Lindsay, "The Senate and Foreign Policy," p. 236.

22. Thomas E. Mann and Norman J. Ornstein, *It's Even Worse Than It Looks: How the American Constitutional System Collided with the New Politics of Extremism* (New York: Perseus, 2012).

23. Walter Lippmann, *Public Opinion* (New York: Macmillan, 1922); see, for example, pp. 250–251.

24. Everett C. Ladd, "Where the Public Stands on Nicaragua," *Public Opinion* 10 (September–October 1987), p. 59.

25. Ole R. Holsti, "Public Opinion and Foreign Policy: Challenges to the Almond–Lippmann Consensus," *International Studies Quarterly* 36 (December 1992), p. 461; see, also, Hosti, "American Public Opinion and Foreign Policy."

26. Richard J. Barnet, *The Rockets' Red Glare: When America Goes to War* (New York: Simon & Schuster, 1990), p. 413.

27. Bruce W. Jentleson, "The Pretty Prudent Public: Post Post-Vietnam American Opinion on the Use of Military Force," *International Studies Quarterly* 36 (March 1992), p. 49.

28. Jentleson, "The Pretty Prudent Public," pp. 71–72.

29. Gary C. Jacobson, *A Divider, Not a Uniter: George W. Bush and the American People* (New York: Pearson/Longman, 2007).

30. See, for example, Matthews, *U.S. Senators.*; Lester W. Milbrath, *The Washington Lobbyists* (Chicago: Rand McNally, 1963); Terry M. Moe, *The Organization of Interests: Incentives and the Internal Dynamics of Political Interest Groups* (Chicago: University of Chicago Press, 1980); and Allan J. Cigler and Burdett A. Loomis, eds., *Interest Group Politics*, 7th ed. (Washington, DC: CQ Press, 2007).

31. Christine Barbour and Gerald C. Wright, *Keeping the Republic*, 5th ed. (Washington, DC: CQ Press, 2012), pp. 515, 550; Chris Good, "Citizens United Decision: Republicans Like It, Liberals Don't," *Atlantic* Online (January 21, 2010). www.theatlantic.com/politics/archive/2010/01/citizens-united-decision-republicans-like-it-liberal-don't/333935.

32. Associated Press, "China Ready to Reprocess Nuclear Fuel," *New York Times* (January 4, 2011), p. A8.

33. Zbigniew Brzezinski, "Reagan May be a Great Leader, but His Foreign Policy is a Shambles," *Washington Post* (national weekly edition, October 20, 1986), p. 23.

34. John J. Mearsheimer and Stephen Walt, *The Israel Lobby and U.S. Foreign Policy* (New York: Farrar, Straus and Giroux, 2007).

35. Lloyd Grove, "Israel's Force in Washington: The Power of AIPAC Is Respected and Resented," *Washington Post* (national weekly edition, June 24–30, 1991), p. 8. For a harsh indictment of AIPAC's influence in Washington, see Meersheimer and Walt, *The Israel Lobby*, who estimate that the AIPAC budget is more in the $40–$60 million range.

36. Organization for Economic Cooperation and Development, "Statistical Annex of the 2011 Development Cooperation Report" (Paris, OECD, 2012).

37. William B. Quandt, *Peace Process: American Diplomacy and the Arab-Israeli Conflict since 1967* (Washington, DC: Brookings Institution, 1993).

38. See Jeffrey Record, "AIPAC's Extremism Serves Israel Badly," *Los Angeles Times* (August 8, 1988), pt. II, p. 13.

39. "U.S. Plans to Sell Jet Fighters and Helicopters to Saudis," AP Report in the *New York Times* (October 21, 2010), p. A8.

40. See Randall Herbert Balmer, *God in the White House* (New York: HarperOne, 2008).

41. Scott Shane, "Groups to Help Online Activists in Authoritarian Countries," *New York Times* (June 12, 2012), p. A6.

42. Quoted in an Associated Press story, *Banner-Herald*, Athens, Georgia (September 4, 1986), p. A11.

43. See Donald G. McNeil Jr., "C.I.A. Vaccine Ruse May Have Harmed the War on Polio," *New York Times* (July 10, 2012), p. D1; and his "Pakistan Battles Polio, and Its People's Mistrust," *New York Times* (July 22, 2013), p. A1.

44. For an example of a critical inside critique, see John Kenneth Galbraith, "Staying Awake at the Council on Foreign Relations," *Washington Monthly* (September 1984), pp. 40–43. For a history of the Council, see Robert D. Schulzinger, *The Wise Men of Foreign Affairs* (New York: Columbia University Press, 1984).

45. Richard N. Haass, ABC *News Online* (January 10, 2013).

46. On the ITT-Chile case, see "Covert Action in Chile, 1963–1973," *Staff Report*, US Senate, Select Committee on Intelligence (December 18, 1975). The Nixon Administration turned down the ITT funding as unnecessary, since the CIA had already been directed by the White House to undertake covert actions against the Allende regime.

47. Robert Lindsey, "California's Tough Line on Apartheid," *New York Times* (August 31, 1986), p. 2E.

48. See Samuel Lucas McMillan, *The Involvement of State Governments in U.S. Foreign Relations* (New York: Palgrave, 2012).

49. Barnet, *The Rockets' Red Glare*, pp. 411–412.

50. For example, letter-to-the-editor, the *Atlanta Constitution* (September 7, 1986), p. A12.

51. Gillian Peele, *Revival and Reaction: The Right in Contemporary America* (New York: Oxford University Press, 1984), pp. 171–172. In the 1976 presidential elections, right-wing religious groups supported Jimmy Carter for president, viewing him as one of them: a born-again Christian. They soon turned against Carter, however, because of his "giveaway" of the Panama Canal and his support for a range of social issues anathema to the right [see Loch K. Johnson and Charles S. Bullock III, "The New Religious Right and the 1980 Congressional Elections," in Benjamin Ginsberg and Alan Stone, eds., *Do Elections Matter?* (Armonk, NY: Sharpe, 1986), pp. 155, 163, note 25].

52. "Assessing Strategic Arms Control," roundtable, MIT-Harvard Summer Program on Nuclear Weapons and Arms Control (June 27, 1985), my notes.

53. These figures are cited by Charles W. Kegley Jr. and Eugene R. Wittkopf, *World Politics: Trend and Transformation* (New York: Thomson Wordsworth, 2007), p. 170.

54. Remarks, "Sarajevo and Arms Control," *In Brief, Newsletter,* the United States Institute of Peace Newsletter, 5 (March 1989), pp. 2–3.

55. Heraclitus (540–480 BC), *Fragments* 119, from John Bartlett, *Familiar Quotations*, 14th ed. (Boston: Little, Brown, 1968), p. 77.

56. See Fred I. Greenstein and Michael Lerner, eds., *A Source Book for the Study of Personality and Politics* (Chicago: Markham, 1971).

57. Harold D. Lasswell, *Power and Personality* (New York: Norton, 1948), p. 223.

58. For instance, Alexander L. George and Juliette L. George, *Woodrow Wilson and Colonel House: A Personality Study* (New York: Dover, 1964).

59. Harold D. Lasswell, "Political Systems, Styles and Personalities," in Lewis J. Edinger, ed., *Political Leadership in Industrialized Societies: Studies in Comparative Analysis* (New York: Wiley, 1967), p. 320. In another example of father–son relationships having an effect on foreign policy (in this case, revenge on the father's behalf), in his memoir George W. Bush made this comment about one of the reasons for the US invasion of Iraq in 2003: "Saddam Hussein . . . made an assassination attempt on a former president, my father" [*Decision Points* (New York: Crown, 2010), p. 228].

60. See the account in Lewis J. Edinger, *Kurt Schumacher: A Study in Personality and Political Behavior* (Stanford, CA: Stanford University Press, 1965).

61. Karl Popper, *Conjectures and Refutations: The Growth of Scientific Knowledge* (London: Routledge, 1963).

62. The D'Souza theory on President Obama's foreign policy motivations originally surfaced in *Forbes* magazine in 2010, in a piece previewing D'Souza's forthcoming book, entitled *The Roots of Obama's Rage*; the quote used in this paragraph is cited in Maureen Dowd, "Who's The Con Man?" *New York Times* (October 15, 2010), p. A25.

63. Andrew Goldman (with quotes from Douglas Brinkley), "*His History,*" *New York Times Sunday Magazine* (November 25, 2012), pp. 26–27.

64. Stanley Hoffman, "Heroic Leadership: The Case of Modern France," in Edinger, ed., *Political Leadership,* p. 109.

65. James David Barber, *The Presidential Character*, 4th ed. (Englewood Cliffs, NJ: Prentice-Hall, 1992).

66. See, for example, David M. Barrett, *Uncertain Warriors: Lyndon Johnson and His Vietnam Advisors* (Lawrence: University Press of Kansas, 1994).

67. Robert Jervis, *Why Intelligence Fails* (Ithaca, NY: Cornell University Press, 2010); Loch K. Johnson, *The Threat on the Horizon* (New York: Oxford University Press, 2011); and Paul R. Pillar, *Intelligence and U.S. Foreign Policy* (New York: Columbia University Press, 2011).

68. David Brooks, "The Pragmatic Leviathan," *New York Times* (January 19, 2010), p. A27.

69. George E. Reedy, *Twilight of the Presidency* (New York: World, 1970), p. 4.

70. Russell Baker and Charles Peters, "The Prince and His Courtiers: At the White House, the Kremlin, and the Reichschancellery," *Washington Monthly* 3 (March 1971), p. 44.

71. Alexander L. George, "The 'Operational Code': A Neglected Approach to the Study of Political Leaders and Decision Making," *International Studies Quarterly* 13 (1969), pp. 197–200.

72. George, "The 'Operational Code,'" p. 198.

73. See Loch K. Johnson, "Operational Codes and the Prediction of Leadership Behavior: Senator Frank Church at Midcareer," in Margaret G. Hermann, ed., *A Psychological Examination of Political Leaders* (New York: Free Press, 1977), pp. 80–119.

74. See the operational-code studies of Acheson, Dulles, Fulbright, Rusk, and Vandenberg cited in Johnson, "Operational Codes," p. 102.

75. Ole R. Holsti, "The 'Operational Code' Approach to the Study of Political Leaders: John Foster Dulles' Philosophical and Instrumental Beliefs," *Canadian Journal of Political Science 3* (1970), pp. 123–155.

76. Harold D. Lasswell, *Psychopathy and Politics* (Chicago: University of Chicago Press, 1930), pp. 124, 262.

77. Graham H. Shepard, "Personality Effects on American Foreign Policy, 1969–83: A Second Test of Interpersonal Generalization Theory," *International Studies Quarterly* 33 (1988), pp. 91–123. For an illustration of emotion playing a role in the behavior of high ranking officials in the US government, see Barbara Keys, "Henry Kissinger: The Emotional Statesman," *Diplomatic History* 35 (September 2011), pp. 587–609.

78. Remarks, Professor Michael Nacht, Harvard-MIT Summer Program on Nuclear Weapons.

79. John Felton, "Testimony Sheds New Light on North's Role," *Congressional Quarterly Weekly Report* 45 (August 29, 1987), p. 66.

80. Bob Woodward, "The Man Who Wasn't There," *Newsweek* (October 5, 1987), p. 66.

81. Bob Woodward, *Bush At War* (New York: Simon & Schuster, 2002), p. 348.

82. John Stuart Mill, *On Liberty.* Harvard Classics, Vol. 25 (New York: Collier & Son, 1901), Ch. 5, p. 212 (originally published in England, 1859).

## Chapter 9

1. For a more detailed account, see Loch K. Johnson, *The Threat on the Horizon* (New York: Oxford University Press, 2011).

2. My notes on President Clinton's remarks to the CIA, Langley, Virginia (July 14, 1995).

3. CIA Booklet, *Intelligence in the War of Independence* (Washington, DC: Central Intelligence Agency, 1976), p. 11.

4. CIA Booklet, *Intelligence in the War of Independence,* p. 14; also, George Dudley Seymour, *Documentary Life of Nathan Hale* (New Haven, CT: private printing, 1941), cited by William R. Corson, *The Armies of Ignorance: The Rise of the American Intelligence Empire* (New York: Dial, 1977), p. 488.

5. On these early years of US intelligence, see Stephen F. Knott, *Secret and Sanctioned: Covert Operations and the American Presidency* (New York: Oxford University Press, 1996).

6. Robert Wohlstetter, *Pearl Harbor: Warning and Decision* (Stanford, CA: Stanford University Press, 1962).

7. Deane Potter, *Yamamoto: The Man Who Menaced America* (New York: Viking, 1963), p. 53.

8. See Edward S. Barkin and L. Michael Meyer, "COMINT and Pearl Harbor: FDR's Mistake," *International Journal of Intelligence and Counterintelligence* 2 (Winter 1988), pp. 513–532; Alvin D. Coox, "Pearl Harbor," in Noble Frankland and Christopher Dowling, eds., *Decisive Battles of the Twentieth Century* (New York: McKay, 1976), p. 148; Edwin T. Layton (with Roger Pineau and John Castello), *"And I Was There:" Pearl Harbor and Midway—Breaking the Secrets* (New York: Morrow, 1983); and Seth W. Richardson, "Why Were We Caught Napping at Pearl Harbor?," *Saturday Evening Post* (May 24, 1947), pp. 79–80.

9. Richard C. Snyder and Edgar S. Furniss, Jr., *American Foreign Policy* (New York: Rinehart, 1954), p. 229.

10. Quoted by Merle Miller, *Plain Speaking: An Oral Biography of Harry S. Truman* (New York: Berkley, 1973), p. 420, note.

11. Douglas T. Stuart, *Creating the National Security State* (Princeton, NJ: Princeton University Press, 2008).

12. Quoted by Victor Marchetti and John D. Marks, *The CIA and the Cult of Intelligence* (New York: Knopf, 1974), p. 70.

13. Johnson, *Threat on the Horizon.*

14. Steven Aftergood, *Secrecy News*, Federation of American Scientists Newsletter (October 31, 2012), p. 1. The 85 percent calculation is from *Preparing for the 21ˢᵗ Century: An Appraisal of U.S. Intelligence*, Report of the Commission on the Roles and Capabilities of the United States Intelligence Community—the Aspin-Brown Commission (Washington, DC: US Government Printing Office, March 1, 1996), p. 49. See, also, Gordon Adams and Cindy Williams, *Buying National Security* (New York: Routledge, 2010).

15. On the NSA, see Matthew M. Aid, *The Secret Sentry: The Untold History of the National Security Agency* (New York: Bloomsbury Press, 2009); and James Bamford, *The Puzzle Palace* (Boston: Houghton-Mifflin, 1984). The NSA has been referred to as "the

nation's spy warehouse," given the large capacity of its computer storage facilities in Maryland and Utah [Eric Lichtblau and Michael S. Schmidt, "Other Agencies Clamor for Data N.S.A. Compiles," *New York Times* (August 4, 2013), p. A1]. On the extent of NSA spying against Americans, see Charlie Savage, "Broader Sifting of Data Abroad Is Seen By N.S.A.," *New York Times* (August 8, 2013), p. A1, and additional references later in this book.

16. See Dana Priest and William M. Arkin, *Top Secret America: The Rise of the New American Security State* (New York: Little, Brown, 2011). For a more scholarly and less overheated examination of America's intelligence agencies, see Harry Howe Ransom, *The Intelligence Establishment* (Cambridge, MA: Harvard University Press, 1970); and Jeffrey T. Richelson, *The US Intelligence Community*, 6th ed. (Boulder, CO: Westview Press, 2012). On intelligence contract workers (the "outsourcing" of espionage), see Tim Shorrock, *Spies for Hire: The Secret World of Intelligence Outsourcing* (New York: Simon & Schuster, 2008).

17. On the CIA, see William E. Colby and Peter Forbath, *Honorable Men: My Life in the CIA* (New York: Simon & Schuster, 1978); Robert M. Gates, *From the Shadows* (New York; Simon & Schuster, 1993); Richard Helms, with William Hood, *A Look over My Shoulder: A Life in the Central Intelligence Agency* (New York: Random House, 2003); Rhodri Jeffrey-Jones, *The CIA and American Democracy* (New Haven, CT: Yale University Press, 1989); Loch K. Johnson, *America's Secret Power: The CIA in a Democratic Society* (New York: Oxford University Press, 1989), and *National Security Intelligence* (Cambridge, UK: Polity, 2012); John Ranelagh, *The Agency: The Rise and Fall of the CIA*, rev. ed. (New York: Simon & Schuster, 1987); George Tenet, with Bill Harlow, *At the Center of the Storm: My Years at the CIA* (New York: HarperCollins, 2007); Stansfield Turner, *Secrecy and Democracy: The CIA in Transition* (Boston: Houghton Mifflin, 1985); and Tim Weiner, *Legacy of Ashes: The History of the CIA* (New York: Doubleday, 2007).

18. Johnson, *National Security Intelligence* (based on extensive interviews with CIA officers periodically from 1975–2010).

19. My interview, Washington, DC (September 12, 1979). On humint, see Frederick P. Hitz, *The Great Game: The Myth and Reality of Espionage* (New York: Knopf, 2004); and Loch K. Johnson, "Evaluating 'Humint': The Role of Human Agents in U.S. Security," *Comparative Strategy* 29 (September–October 2010), pp. 308–333.

20. Loch K. Johnson, *A Season of Inquiry: The Senate Intelligence Investigation* (Lexington: University of Kentucky Press, 1985).

21. Marchetti and Marks, *The CIA and the Cult of Intelligence*, p. 90.

22. Johnson, *America's Secret Power* and *National Security Intelligence*; Marchetti and Marks, *The CIA and the Cult of Intelligence*.

23. Allen Dulles, prepared statement, "National Defense Establishment," *Hearings*, Committee on Armed Services, US Senate, Washington, DC (April 30, 1947), p. 2.

24. 50 U.S.C. 403, Sec. 102; President Truman signed the National Security Act on July 26, 1947.

25. My interview with a CIA/CI specialist, Washington, DC (December 14, 1975). See Raymond J. Batvinis, "The Future of FBI Counterintelligence through the Lens of the Past Hundred Years," in Loch K. Johnson, ed., *The Oxford Handbook of National Security Intelligence* (New York: Oxford University Press, 2010), pp. 505–517.

26. Loch K. Johnson, "James Angleton and the Church Committee," *Journal of Cold War Studies* 15 (Summer 2013). When counterintelligence fails, the consequences can be dire for the United States, as when FBI agent Robert Hanssen and CIA officer Aldrich H. Ames spied for the Soviet Union, then Russia, against the United States from inside these sensitive sanctuaries during the late 1980s and the 1990s; after more than a decade of providing top secret information to their Moscow handlers, Hanssen and Ames were finally discovered by FBI and CIA counterintelligence investigators and sent to prison for life-long terms (see Paul J. Redmond, "The Challenges of Counterintelligence," in Johnson, ed., *The Oxford Handbook of National Security Intelligence*, pp. 537–354). On other counterintelligence cases, including Jonathan Pollard, who spied for Israel against the United States, see Johnson, *National Security Intelligence*.

27. *Factbook on Intelligence*, Office of Public Affairs, Central Intelligence Agency (April 1983), p. 17.

28. Arthur S. Hulnick, "The Intelligence Producer-Policy Consumer Linkage: A Theoretical Approach," *Intelligence and National Security* 1 (May 1986), pp. 212–233; and "What's Wrong with the Intelligence Cycle?" in Loch K. Johnson, ed., *Strategic Intelligence: Vol. 2. The Intelligence Cycle* (Westport, CT: Praeger, 2005), pp. 1–22.

29. *Factbook on Intelligence*, p. 17.

30. *Report of the Secretary of Defense to the Congress on the FY 1982 Budget* (January 19, 1981), p. iii.

31. Quoted in Theodore H. White, "Weinberger on the Ramparts," *New York Times Magazine* (February 6, 1983), p. 19.

32. Unclassified CIA document, Church Committee files (September 1975).

33. Presidential press conference, White House, Washington, DC (November 30, 1978).

34. Robert M. Gates, remarks, Conference on US Intelligence: The Organization and the Profession, Central Intelligence Agency, Langley, Virginia (June 11, 1984), my notes.

35. Eric Schmitt, Mark Landler, and Andrew E. Kramer, "Copters in Syria May Not be New, U.S. Officials Say," *New York Times* (June 14, 2012), p. A7.

36. Gates, remarks, Conference on US Intelligence.

37. My interview with DNI James R. Clapper Jr., DNI Headquarters Building, Liberty Crossing, Virginia (December 2, 2011).

38. Ransom, *The Intelligence Establishment*, p. 20.

39. My interviews with intelligence officials throughout 1995, as the assistant to the Chairman of the Aspin-Brown Commission. See *Preparing for the 21st Century*.

40. Gregory W. Pedlow and Donald E. Welzenbach, *The CIA and the U-2 Program, 1954–1975* (Washington, DC: Center for the Study of Intelligence, Central Intelligence Agency, 1998); Oleg Penkovskiy, with Frank Gibney, *The Penkovskiy Papers* (Garden City, NY: Doubleday, 1965). For an excellent examination of humint and techint in the British-American efforts to monitor Soviet weapons developments during the Cold War, see Michael S. Goodman, *Spying on the Nuclear Bear: Anglo-American Intelligence and the Soviet Bomb* (Stanford, CA: Stanford University Press, 2007).

41. Thomas Powers, *The Man Who Kept the Secrets: Richard Helms and the CIA* (New York: Knopf, 1979), p. 447, note 6.

42. Robert M. Gates, former DCI, comments, conference on intelligence sponsored by the Aspin-Brown Commission, (May 4, 1995); see Johnson, *The Threat on the Horizon*. Also: Robert M. Gates, *From the Shadows* (New York: Simon & Schuster, 1996), p. 560.

43. Gary D. Brewer and Paul Bracken, "Some Missing Pieces of the C3 Puzzle," *Journal of Conflict Resolution* 28 (September 1984), p. 453.

44. In 1982, Congress passed the Intelligence Identities Act, which carries criminal penalties for anyone convicted of revealing the name of a US intelligence officer or asset. During the second Bush administration, Valerie Plame (a CIA undercover officer) had her name disclosed publicly by an aide to Vice President Cheney in retaliation against her husband, a former US ambassador to Niger who criticized the administration's claim that Iraq was buying yellow-cake uranium for the production of nuclear weapons from that African nation. The Vice President's aide perjured himself during the trail, was sentenced to prison, and then was pardoned by President George W. Bush. See Richard Leiby and Dana Priest, "The Spy Next Door: Valerie Wilson, Ideal Mom, Was Also the Ideal Cover," *Washington Post* (October 8, 2003), p. A1; Valerie Plame, *Fair Game: My Life as a Spy, My Betrayal by the White House* (New York: Simon & Schuster, 2007).

45. Gates, remarks, Conference on US Intelligence. On contemporary processing challenges (which remains chiefly the difficulty of separating out the useful from the vast amount of useless information), see Johnson, *National Security Intelligence*, pp. 53–54.

46. My interviews with intelligence officers at the National Photographic Interpretation Center (July 20, 1995), an entity initially within the organizational framework of the CIA (but at a different location), but now under the leadership of the NGA.

47. Quoted in Johnson, *A Season of Inquiry*, p. 83.

48. Vice Admiral J. M. "Mike" McConnell, quoted in my interview with a senior NSA official, Washington, DC (July 14, 1994).

49. Sherman Kent, *Strategic Intelligence for American World Policy* (Princeton, NJ: Princeton University Press, 1949), pp. 64–65.

50. *Military Review* (May 1961), cited by Ransom, *The Intelligence Establishment*, p. 147. See also Loch K. Johnson, "Glimpses into the Gems of American Intelligence: The *President's Daily Brief* and the National Intelligence Estimated," *Intelligence and National Security* 23 (July 2008), pp. 333–370.

51. Senator Bob Graham with Jeff Nussbaum, *Intelligence Matters: The CIA, the FBI, Saudi Arabia, and the Failure of America's War on Terrorism* (Lawrence: University Press of Kansas, 2008).

52. Nick Paumgarten, "Magic Mountain," *The New Yorker* (March 5, 2012), p. 53.

53. Richard K. Betts, "Analysis, War and Decision: Why Intelligence Failures Are Inevitable," *World Politics* 31 (October 1978), p. 78. See also Betts' *Enemies of Intelligence* (New York: Columbia University Press, 2010). On the intelligence mistakes related to 9/11, see *The 9/11 Commission Report* (New York: Norton, 2004); and on the Iraqi WMD errors, see Robert Jervis, *Why Intelligence Fails: Lessons from the Iranian Revolution and the Iraq War* (Ithaca, NY: Cornell University Press, 2010), and James P Pfiffner and Mark Phythian, eds., *Intelligence and National Security Policymaking on Iraq* (Manchester, UK: Manchester University Press, 2008).

54. Quoted by Loch K. Johnson, *America's Secret Power*, p. 95.

55. Gates, remarks, Conference on US Intelligence.

56. Arthur S. Hulnick, remarks, Conference on U.S. Intelligence (my notes). These same challenges linger on; see, for instance, Paul R. Pillar, *Intelligence and U.S. Foreign Policy: Iraq, 9/11, and Misguided Reform* (New York: Columbia University Press, 2011), who criticizes the George W. Bush administration for wanting only "intelligence to please."

57. Remarks of senior CIA officials, Conference on U.S. Intelligence, as well as (on the Korean airline shoot down) Seymour M. Hersh, *The Target Is Destroyed* (New York: Vintage, 1987). See also Lee H. Hamilton, "View from the Hill," in *Extracts from Studies in Intelligence* (Langley, VA: Central Intelligence Agency, September 1987), p. 68.

58. See Johnson, *Threat on the Horizon*; Pillar, *Intelligence and U.S. Foreign Policy*; and Jane Mayer, *The Dark Side* (New York: Double Day, 2008). For Tenet's perspective, see his *At the Center of the Storm*. Generally on the important topic of politicization, see Thomas L. Hughes, "The Power to Speak and Power to Listen: Reflections in Bureaucratic Politics and a Recommendation on Information Flows," in Thomas T. Franck and Edward Weisband, eds., *Secrecy and Foreign Policy* (New York: Oxford University Press, 1974), pp. 13–41.

59. Gates, remarks, Conference on U.S. Intelligence.

60. Eric Schmitt, "C.I.A. Investigates Petraeus as Lawmakers Press Inquiry Into Libya Attack," *New York Times* (November 16, 2012), p. A6.

61. Robert M. Gates, "An Opportunity Unfulfilled: The Use and Perceptions of Intelligence at the White House," *Washington Quarterly* (Winter 1989), p. 42.

62. See David M. Barrett, *The CIA and Congress: The Untold Story from Truman to Kennedy* (Lawrence: University Press of Kansas, 2005).

63. Gates, remarks, Conference on US Intelligence. See, also, Robert M. Gates, "The CIA and American Foreign Policy," *Foreign Affairs* 66 (Winter 1987), pp. 215–230.

64. My notes, Conference on US Intelligence.

65. My notes, Conference on US Intelligence. On marketing intelligence, see Loch K. Johnson, "Analysis for a New Age," *Intelligence and National Security* 11 (October 1996), pp. 657–667; and *Preparing for the 21st Century*.

66. On Clinton, see Johnson, *Threat on the Horizon*, p. 11; on Bush, see Pillar, *Intelligence and U.S. Foreign Policy*, pp. 54–55.

67. Quoted in Johnson, *Threat on the Horizon*, p. 224.

68. My notes, Conference on US Intelligence. During the Clinton administration, a newly appointed assistant secretary of state recoiled when faced with the brusque personality of a CIA analyst sent to brief him. He never allowed her in his office again. Chemistry matters—the skill with which analysts build relationships of trust with policy makers (my interview, Washington, DC, June 22, 1995).

69. Letter written by George Washington in 1777, Walter Pforzheimer Papers, Yale University, reprinted in the *Yale Alumni Magazine and Journal* (December 1983), p. 7.

70. Henry A. Kissinger, *Years of Upheaval* (Boston: Little, Brown, 1982).

71. Testimony, *Hearings*, Joint Select Committee to Investigate Covert Arms Transactions with Iran, U.S. Congress (July 21,1987), Vol. 8, p. 159.

72. Lee Hamilton, *Hearings, Joint Select Committee to Investigate Covert Arms Transactions* (July 21, 1987), Vol. 8, p. 159.

73. Johnson, *Season of Inquiry*.

74. On the abuse of the wiretap power by the administration, see James Risen and Eric Lichtblau, "Spying Program Snared U.S. Calls," *New York Times* (December 21, 2005), p. A1; and James J. Risen, *State of War: The Secret History of the CIA and the Bush Administration* (New York: Free Press, 2006).

75. On the Keating letter, see Michael S. Schmidt, "F.B.I. Said to Find It Could Not Have Averted Boston Attack," *New York Times* (August 3, 2013), p. A13; on the quest for information about the drone program, see Mark Mazzetti and Mark Landler, "Drone War Rages On, Even as Administration Talks About Ending It," *New York Times* (August 3, 2013), p. A4, as well as: Scott Shane, "U.S. Drone Strikes Are Said to Target Rescuers at Sites," *New York Times* (February 2, 2012), p. A4; Declan Walsh, Eric Schmitt, and Ihsanullah Tipu Mehsud, "Drones at Issue as U.S. Rebuilds Ties to Pakistan," *New York Times* (March 19, 2012), p. A1; and Scott Shane, "Election Spurred a Move to Codify U.S. Drone Policy," *New York Times* (November 25, 2012), p. A1.

76. Arthur M. Schlesinger Jr., *The Imperial Presidency* (Boston: Houghton Mifflin, 1973), p. 251; see also Samuel Dash, *Chief Counsel: Inside the Ervin Committee—The Untold Story of Watergate* (New York: Random House, 1976).

77. Schlesinger, *Imperial Presidency*, p. 252.

78. Schlesinger, *Imperial Presidency*, p. 252.

79. Quoted by Herb Altman, ed., *Quotations from Chairman Sam* (New York: Harper & Row, 1973), p. 1.

80. Quoted in the *New York Times* (February 26, 1976), p. A1.

81. "Fast and Furious Operation," *Joint Staff Report*, prepared for Rep. Darrell E. Issa, Chairman United States House of Representatives Committee on Oversight and Government Reform, and Senator Charles E. Grassley, Ranking Member United States Senate Committee on the Judiciary, Part 1, 112th Congress (July 31, 2012). Also in 2012, the Obama administration refused to provide lawmakers access to the Department of Justice memorandum that laid out the rationale for drone assassination targeting; not even a senior member of the Senate Select Committee on Intelligence, the third-ranking Ron Wyden (D-Oregon), was allowed to see the document [comment, Chris Anders, ACLU attorney, *NewsHour* Public Television (January 23, 2013)]. This failure to keep Congress informed makes it difficult, if not impossible, for Wyden's Committee and other panels on Capitol Hill to carry out their oversight obligations.

82. Raoul Berger, *Executive Privilege: A Constitutional Myth* (Cambridge, MA: Harvard University Press, 1974), p. 7.

83. See the firsthand account by one of the investigators: Graham with Nussbaum, *Intelligence Matters*.

84. Risen and Lichtblau, "Spying Program Snared U.S. Calls"; Eric Lichtblau, *Bush's Law: The Remaking of American Justice* (New York: Pantheon, 2008). Initially, the *Times* found out about the FISA bypass in 2004 but was asked by the administration not to publish the finding because it would harm national security; the newspapers' management bought into this argument at first, then in 2005 decided that the right of the public to know about the misuse of power trumped the administration's argument (never substantiated) that the warrantless wiretaps should remain secret.

85. John H. Glenn, "The Mini-Hiroshima Near Cincinnati," *New York Times* (January 24, 1989), p. A27.

86. On the attempts to keep the torture program details away from lawmakers, see Mayer, *The Dark Side*. On the SSCI torture report, see Mark Mazzetti and Scott Shane, "Senate and C.I.A. Spar Over Secret Report on Interrogation Program," *New York Times* (July 20, 2013), p. A13.

87. *New York Times Co. v. United States* (403 US 713 [1971]).

88. John Lofton, *The Press as Guardian of the First Amendment* (Columbia: University of South Carolina Press, 1980).

89. *New York Times Co. v. United States*.

90. Senator Daniel Patrick Moynihan, "System of Secrecy Has Served Liars Well," *Albany Times Union* (May 3, 1992), reprinted in Center for National Security Studies, *First Principles* 17 (July 1992), pp. 11–12, emphasis added.

91. Berger, *Executive Privilege*, p. 14.

**Chapter 10**

1. Quoted in Henry Steele Commager, "The Perilous Folly of Senator Bricker," *The Reporter* 9 (October 13, 1953), p. 16. See, also, Duane Tananbaum, *The Bricker Amendment Controversy* (Ithaca, NY: Cornell University Press, 1988). In 2012, Republican senators rejected a treaty that would have supported a UN ban on discrimination against people with disabilities. Backed by President Obama and former Senate Majority Leader Bob Dole (R-Kansas), the vote fell five short of the two-thirds majority necessary for approval. Dozens of Republicans in the chamber objected that the treaty would create new abortion rights and would allow State Department bureaucrats to impede the ability of people to homeschool disabled children. These allegations were "spurious," according to a former State Department attorney from the George W. Bush administration, who said further that the Senate rejection had caused "damage to our international reputation as leader in protecting the rights of the disabled." In a comment that evoke the era of the Brickerites, the attorney noted that "an increasing number of Republicans had come to view treaties in general (especially multilateral ones) as liberal conspiracies to hand over American sovereignty to international authorities" [John B. Bellinger III, "Obama's Weakness On Treaties," *New York Times* (December 19, 2012), p. A31]. The treaty was approved by most other nations in the world.

2. *Congressional Record* (February 2, 1954), p. 1106.

3. Edward S. Corwin, "The President's Treaty-Making Power," *Think* 19 (July 1953), p. 6.

4. *Congressional Record* (February 2, 1954), p. 1103, emphasis added.

5. William S. White, "Senate Defeats All Plans to Check Treaty Powers," *New York Times* (February 27, 1954), p. 15.

6. At the time, the Senate had 96 members (Hawaii and Alaska had yet to become states), and five senators missed the vote on the George Amendment; thus, 61 votes would have provided the Brickerites with the necessary two-thirds margin for success.

7. This formal definition in quotes, as well as Kennan's description, are from Norman J. Padelford and George A. Lincoln, *The Dynamics of International Politics* (New York: Macmillan, 1962), p. 340.

8. Henry A. Kissinger, *A World Restored* (Boston: Houghton Mifflin, 1957), p. 326; see also his *Diplomacy* (New York: Simon & Schuster, 1994).

9. Abba Eban, *The New Diplomacy: International Affairs in the Modern Age* (New York: Random House, 1983), p. 334. For a recent study on the nature of international negotiations, see Faten Ghosn, "Getting to the Table and Getting to Yes: An Analysis of International Negotiations," *International Studies Quarterly* 54 (December 2010), pp. 1055–1072; and for a useful examination of several different forms of diplomacy—bilateral, multilateral, summit, conference, UN, public, coercive, and nuclear—see Glenn P. Hastedt, *American Foreign Policy*, 8th ed. (New York: Pearson/Longman, 2009).

10. Hans J. Morgenthau, *Politics among Nations: The Struggle for Power and Peace*, 4th ed. (New York: Knopf, 1967; originally published in 1949), pp. 135–136.

11. David D. Newsom, *Diplomacy and the American Democracy* (Bloomington: Indiana University Press, 1988), pp. 23, 219. Newsom notes further that another valuable mission of the American diplomat is to help protect US citizens overseas. In this capacity, he or she "is a combination of parish priest and city clerk, helping to get fellow citizens out of jail, issuing replacement passports, settling citizenship problems, handling the effects of the deceased, seeking to reunite families, and registering births" (p. 199).

12. Quoted to me in correspondence from the British scholar Frank Adams (December 21, 1988).

13. Morgenthau, *Politics among Nations*, pp. 137, 139.

14. American Foreign Service Association (http://www.afsa.org/ ambassadorsgraph2.cfm), 2011.

15. George Hackett, "Notorious Ambassadors," *Newsweek* (June 5, 1989), p. 26.

16. Mami Maruko, "Envoy Puts Focus on People-to-People Ties," *Japan Times* (December 4, 2012), p. A1.

17. Morgenthau, *Politics among Nations*, pp. 540–548.

18. Morgenthau, *Politics among Nations*, p. 849.

19. Walter F. Mondale, *The Good Fight* (New York: Scribner, 2010), p. 223.

20. Leon Panetta, remarks, *This Week*, ABC News (June 27, 2010).

21. David E. Sanger, "Engage, But Move to Plan B," *New York Times* (December 5, 2010), p. Wk. 7.

22. These illustrations are drawn from the *New York Times* in a set of mostly front-page articles with the overall title of "State Secrets," published from November 29 to December 18, 2010.

23. David Kahn, "Dangerous Liaisons," *New York Times* (December 13, 2010), p. A25.

24. Council on Foreign Relations Online, "Will WikiLeaks Hobble US Diplomacy?," *Expert Roundtable* (December 1, 2010); Barney Porter, "WikiLeaks Could Have Freezing Effect on Diplomacy," *ABC News Online* (November 11, 2010).

25. Sir Crispin Tickell, remarks, University of Georgia, Athens (February 2, 1989). Abba Eban once observed that "diplomacy does not offer salvation. It moves in a world in which the stakes of diplomacy are so high that even modest progress is worthy of profound respect. Imperfect solutions have to be compared with even less perfect alternatives" (Eban, *The New Diplomacy*, p. xiii).

26. Reporting by Jo Becker and Ron Nixon, "U.S. Enriches Companies Defying the Policy on Iran," *New York Times* (March 6, 2010), p. A1, indicates that companies in South Korea, France, Brazil, and England have sometimes skirted the sanction rules.

27. "Countries Sending the Most Fulbright Students to the U.S., 2010–11," *The Chronicle of Higher Education* (October 29, 2010), p. A16. The United States was an attractive place for

many foreign students to enroll in 2009–10, with a strong surge in the number of Chinese students (127, 628, a 29.9 percent increase over the previous year), followed by India (104, 897), South Korea (72,153), and Canada. Among the other top ten countries represented on this list were, in descending order: Taiwan, Japan, Saudi Arabia, Mexico, Vietnam, and Turkey [Tamar Lewin, "China Surges Past India as Top Home of Foreign Students," *New York Times* (November 15, 2010), p. A14].

28. See Helene Cooper and Mark Landler, "White House Weighs Talks With Taliban After Afghan Successes," *New York Times* (March 13, 2010), p. A8; and Dexter Filkins, "Afghans Offer Jobs to Taliban If They Defect," *New York Times* (November 28, 2009), p. A1.

29. Steve Coll, "Sporting Chance," *The New Yorker* (August 13 and 20, 2012), pp. 65–71; Eric Schmitt and David E. Sanger, "In Sign of Normalization, Pentagon To Reimburse Pakistan $688 Million," *New York Times* (December 18, 2012), p. A6; Sabrina Tavernise, "Survey of Pakistan's Young Predicts 'Disaster' if Their Needs Aren't Addressed," *New York Times* (November 22, 2009), p. A15.

30. See Jane Perlez, "Angered by U.S. Security Measures, Pakistani Lawmakers Return Home as Heroes," *New York Times* (March 10, 2010), p. A4.

31. Salman Masood and Declan Walsh, "Pakistan Gives U.S. a List of Demands, Including an End to C.I.A. Drone Strikes," *New York Times* (April 13, 2012), p. A6. In January of 2011, the Pakistanis arrested a CIA contract worker, Raymond Davis, who had killed two Pakistani citizens whom he claimed were trying to rob him. This incident led to yet another diplomatic flap, with Davis finally released into American custody in exchange for additional foreign aid and assurances that contract officers would be removed from Pakistan.

32. The Nunn–Lugar measure is named after its creators, Senators Sam Nunn (G-Georgia) and Richard Lugar (R-Indiana), both of whom have left the Senate. The program is another illustration of the positive role Congress can play in foreign policy. So far, Nunn–Lugar has led to the deactivation of 7,600 nuclear warheads in the former Soviet Republics, as well as the destruction of 900 ICBMs, 500 missile silos, 680 SLBMs, and 900 nuclear air-to-surface missiles. The program is widely credited with the removal of all nuclear weapons from the former Soviet Republics of Ukraine, Kazakhstan, and Belarus [see Peter Baker, "Obama Calls on Russia to Renew Weapons Pact," *New York Times* (December 4, 2012), p. A10; and David M. Herszenhorn, "Russia Won't Renew Pact on Weapons with U.S.," *New York Times* (October 11, 2012), p. A10].

33. Peter Baker and Mark Landler, "Delays on Arms Control Pact Bog Down U.S. Efforts to Reset Relations with Russia," *New York Times* (March 10, 2010), p. A6.

34. Rick Gladstone, "U.S. Envoy Sees Grim Outcome for Syria," *New York Times* (May 31, 2012), p. A10.

35. Mary Elise Sarotte, "Enlarging NATO, Expanding Confusion," *New York Times* (November 30, 2009), p. A29.

36. See Herszenhorn, "Russia Won't Renew Pact"; and Peter Baker and Steven Lee Myers, "Ties Fraying, Obama Scrubs Putin Meeting," *New York Times* (August 8, 2013), p. A1.

37. Keith Bradsher, "China Uses Rules on Global Trade to Its Advantage," *New York Times* (March 15, 2010), p. A1.

38. Niall Ferguson, "In China's Orbit," *Wall Street Journal* (November 20–21, 2010), p. C2.

39. Mark Landler, "Clinton Makes Case for Internet Freedom as a Plank of American Foreign Policy," *New York Times* (January 22, 2010), p. A6.

40. Helene Cooper, "China Angered as U.S. Approves Arms Sales to Taiwan," *New York Times* (January 1, 2010), p. A5.

41. Zbigniew Brzezinski, "How to Stay Friends With China," *New York Times* (January 3, 2011), p. A19.

42. Quoted by Steven Lee Myers, "Obama Approach to Diplomacy Faces Test in China," *New York Times* (May 2, 2012), p. A11.

43. Quoted by Joseph S. Nye. Jr., "Work With China, Don't Contain It," *New York Times* (January 26, 2013), p. A19. On America's growing focus on China, see as well political scientist Kenneth Waltz, "Why Iran Should Get the Bomb," *The Diplomat* (July 8, 2012), p. 1.

44. Brian Knowlton, "Gates Sees Danger in Europe's Anti-Military Views," *New York Times* (February 24, 2010), p. A6.

45. In 2010, the Israelis announced a plan to build 1,600 new housing units in East Jerusalem, despite strong objections from the Obama administration. The Israeli government revealed this policy to the world in the middle of a trip to Israel by Vice President Joseph Biden Jr.—an embarrassing diplomatic setback for the administration.

46. Quoted by Jon Lee Anderson, "The Most Failed State," *The New Yorker* (December 14, 2009), p. 66.

47. Jeff Zeleny, "Obama Promises Continued Aid for Haiti," *New York Times* (March 11, 2010), p. A11.

48. Newsom, *Diplomacy and the American Democracy*, p. 41. According to former State Department attorney John B. Bellinger III, ". . . the Obama administration . . . has secured Senate approval of the fewest treaties in any four-year presidential term since World War II." The George W. Bush administration ratified 163 treaties over eight years, compared to Obama's nine in his first term ("Obama's Weakness on Treaties," *New York Times*).

49. Glen S. Krutz and Jeffrey S. Peake, *Treaty Politics and the Rise of Executive Agreements* (Ann Arbor: University of Michigan Press, 2009).

50. Loch K. Johnson, *The Making of International Agreements: Congress Confronts the Executive* (New York: New York University Press, 1984).

51. Krutz and Peake, *Treaty Politics*.

52. Krutz and Peake, *Treaty Politics*.

53. "Transmittal of Executive Agreements to Congress," *Senate Report No. 92–591* (January 19, 1972), pp. 3–4.

54. *Congressional Record* (June 28, 1978), p. S9996.

55. "Transmittal of Executive Agreements to Congress," *Hearings*, Foreign Relations Committee, US Senate (October 20 and 21, 1971), p. 54.

56. "Congressional Oversight of Executive Agreements," *Hearings*, Subcommittee on Separation of Powers, Senate Judiciary Committee (April 23 and 24, May 12, 18, and 19, 1972), p. 54.

57. "Executive Agreements with Portugal and Bahrain," *Hearings*, Foreign Relations Committee, US Senate (February 1, 2, and 3, 1972), p. 4.

58. John C. Stennis and J. William Fulbright, *The Role of Congress in Foreign Policy* (Washington, DC: American Enterprise Institute Press, 1971), p. 83.

59. Krutz and Peake, *Treaty Politics*, p. 187.

60. "National Commitments," *Report No. 91–129*, Committee on Foreign Relations, US Senate (April 16, 1969), p. 28.

61. "U.S. Security Agreements and Commitments Abroad: Laos and Thailand," *Hearings*, Subcommittee on United States Security Agreements and Commitments Abroad (the Symington Subcommittee, after its chairman, Stuart Symington, D-Missouri), Foreign Relations Committee, US Senate Part 6, 1969–1970.

62. "Morocco and Libya," *Hearings*, Symington Subcommittee, Part 9, 1969.

63. J. Brian Atwood, "Downtown Perspective: Lessons on Liaison with Congress," in Thomas M. Franck, ed., *The Tethered Presidency* (New York: New York University Press, 1981), p. 217.

64. Atwood, "Downtown Perspective," p. 218.

65. "Kingdom of Laos," *Hearings*, Symington Subcommittee, Part 2, p. 437.

66. "Kingdom of Laos," *Hearings*, p. 433.

67. Testimony, *Hearings*, Subcommittee on Preparedness, Committee on Armed Services, US Senate (August 25, 1966), p. 4.

68. This phrase is from *Report*, Foreign Relations Committee, US Senate (December 21, 1970), p. 4.

69. Cited in the *Washington Post* (April 9, 1975), p. A1.

70. Tad Szulc, *The Illusion of Peace* (New York: Viking, 1979), p. 212.

71. "Transmittal of Executive Agreements," *Senate Report No. 92–591*, p. 3.

72. Statement, *Congressional Record* (February 2, 1954), p. 1106.

73. Respectively, *Congressional Record* (February 26, 1954), p. 2372; *Congressional Record* (April 30, 1970), p. 13565.

74. Stephen A. Garrett, "Foreign Policy and the American Constitution: The Bricker Amendment in Contemporary Perspective," *International Studies Quarterly* 16 (June 1972), p. 213.

75. "National Commitments," *Report No. 91–129*, Committee on Foreign Relations, p. 4, emphasis added.

76. "Transmittal of Executive Agreements," *Senate Report No. 92–591*, p. 3.

77. My interview, Washington, DC (May 28, 1974).

78. David J. Kuchenbecker, "Agency-Level Executive Agreements: A New Era in U.S. Treaty Practice," *Columbia Journal of Transnational Law* 18 (1979), p. 64, note 239.

79. Joseph S. Nye Jr., "Independence and Interdependence," *Foreign Policy* 22 (Spring 1976), p. 138.

80. Kuchenbecker, "Agency-Level Executive Agreements," p. 68.

81. Marjorie Ann Browne, *Executive Agreements and the Congress*, Issue Brief No. IB-75035, Congressional Research Service, Library of Congress (February 27, 1981), Washington, DC, p. 5.

82. My interviews on Capitol Hill (June 28, 1978).

83. "International Agreements Consultation Resolution," *Senate Report No. 95–1171* (August 25, 1978), pp. 2–3.

84. "International Agreements Consultation Resolution," *Senate Report No. 95–1171*, p. 4, emphasis added.

85. Charlie Savage, "Meeting With Chinese, Official Tests Limits Set by Congress," *New York Times* (November 3, 2011), p. A21.

86. Testimony, "Treaties and Executive Agreements," *Hearings*, Judiciary Committee, US Senate (1953), p. 21.

87. Senator Frank Church, remark, *Hearings*, Committee on Foreign Relations, US Senate (1977), p. 21.

88. James T. Schollaert, "A Critique of Recent U.S. Practice of International Agreements Law," paper, annual meeting, American Society of International Law, San Francisco (April 23, 1977).

89. See John R. Bolton and John Yoo, "Restore the Senate's Treaty Power," *New York Times* (January 5, 2009), p. A19.

90. Bruce Ackerman and Oona Hathaway, professors of law at Yale and the University of California, Berkeley, respectively, letter-to-the-editor, *New York Times* (January 8, 2009), p. A26.

91. Arthur W. Rovine, "Separation of Powers and International Executive Agreements," *Indiana Law Journal* 52 (1977), p. 428.

92. Quoted in the *New York Times* (September 21, 1983), p. A1.

93. Remark, *Briefing on the Middle East*, Committee on Foreign Relations, US Senate (February 11, 1977), my notes.

**Chapter 11**

1. President Richard M. Nixon, *Presidential Talking Paper* (June 5, 1970), unclassified Church Committee files, accessed February 28, 1975 (when I served as assistant to Senator Frank Church).

2. John Lehman, *Making War* (New York: Scribner's 1992), p. 89.

3. See the *Congressional Record* from May 13, 1970, to June 30, 1970, pp. S7098–S10271.

4. President Abraham Lincoln, "Gettysburg Address," dedication of the Cemetery at Gettysburg, Pennsylvania (November 19, 1863),

reprinted in Roy P. Basler, ed., *Abraham Lincoln: His Speeches and Writings* (New York: Da Capo Press, 1946), p. 734.

5.  Paul P. Craig and John A. Jungerman, *Nuclear Arms Race: Technology and Society* (New York: McGraw-Hill, 1986), p. 8.

6.  President Ronald Reagan, news conference, Washington, DC (October 23, 1987).

7.  See, for example, Gardiner Harris, "Defense Chief Shrugs Off Objections to Drones," *New York Times* (June 7, 2012), p. A9; and unsigned op-ed, "Misplaced Secrecy on Targeted Killings," *New York Times* (January 4, 2013), p. A20.

8.  Richard Smoke, *National Security and the Nuclear Dilemma* (Reading, MA: Addison-Wesley, 1984), p. 56.

9.  Thom Shanker and Elisabeth Bumiller, "Looking Back, Gates Says He's Grown Wary of Waging 'Wars of Choice,'" *New York Times* (June 19, 2011), p. A12.

10.  For the Weinberger list, see Bernard E. Trainor, "Weinberger on Persian Gulf: Cap the Chameleon?," *New York Times* (October 9, 1987), p. A20.

11.  Colin Powell, "U.S. Forces: Challenges Ahead," *Foreign Affairs* 71 (Winter 1992/1993), pp. 32–45.

12.  Chairman Mullen quoted by Thom Shanker, "Joint Chiefs Chairman Readjusts Principles on Use of Force," *New York Times* (March 4, 2010), p. A14. This approach is closer to the venerable principles of the "just war" doctrine, which stretch back to philosophers of the Middle Ages who advocated moderation and proportionality in war fighting [see James T. Johnson, *Just War Tradition and the Restraint of War* (Princeton, NJ: Princeton University Press, 1981)]. The Dempsey statement is from *George Stephanopoulos, This Week,* ABC News (August 4, 2013), interview conducted by moderator Martha Raddatz.

13.  Quoted by Steven Erlanger, "The French Way of War," Sunday Review, *New York Times* (January 20, 2013), p. 5.

14.  See, for instance, Graham Allison, *Nuclear Terrorism: The Ultimate Preventable Catastrophe* (New York: Henry Holt, 2004).

15.  Quoted by Senator Frank Church (D-Idaho), "The SALT II Treaty," *Hearings*, Foreign Relations Committee, US Senate (July 11, 1979), p. 6.

16.  L. W. McNaught, *Nuclear Weapons and Their Effects* (London: Brassey's, 1984), p. 27.

17.  Professor George Rathjens, Harvard-MIT Summer Program on Nuclear Weapons and Arms Control, Cambridge, MA (June 17, 1985), my notes.

18.  McNaught, *Nuclear Weapons*, p. 30.

19.  P. R. Ehrlich et al., "The Long-Term Biological Consequences of Nuclear War," *Science*, 222 (December 23, 1983), pp. 145–149.

20.  Dr. Jennifer Leaning, Harvard-MIT Summer Program; see, also, Jonathan Schell, *The Fate of the Earth* (New York: Knopf, 1974); and William J. Broad, "New Advice on Unthinkable: Surviving a Nuclear Bomb," *New York Times* (December 16, 2010), p. A1.

21.  William J. Broad and Judith Miller, "Government Report Says 3 Nations Hide Stocks of Smallpox," *New York Times* (June 13, 1999), p. A1; and their "The Threat of Germ Weapons Is Rising," *New York Times* (December 27, 1999), Wk., p. E1.

22.  Ken Alibek with Stephen Handelman, *Biohazard* (New York: Random House, 1999).

23.  Quoted by Broad and Miller, "The Threat of Germ Weapons Is Rising," p. E1.

24.  Cited in Judith Miller and William J. Broad, "Clinton to Announce That U.S. Will Keep Sample of Lethal Smallpox Virus," *New York Times* (April 22, 1999), p. A12.

25.  Office of Technology Assessment, *Proliferation of Weapons of Mass Destruction: Assessing the Risks*, U.S. Congress (1993), pp. 53–54.

26.  See, for example, the essays on BMD in Chareles W. Kegley Jr. and Eugene R. Wittkopf, eds., *The Nuclear Readers: Strategy, Weapons, War* (New York: St. Martin's Press, 1985).

27.  Cited by Rathjens, Harvard-MIT Summer Program.

28.  See William Broad and David E. Sanger, "Physicists Say Weapon Failed in Missile Tests," *New York Times* (May 18, 2010), p. A1; Thom Shanker, David E. Sanger, and Martin Fackler, "U.S. Is Expanding Missile Defenses on Pacific Coast," *New York Times* (March 16, 2013), p. A1; and unsigned editorial, "A Failure to Intercept," *New York Times* (July 25, 2013), p. A22.

29.  Rathjens, Harvard-MIT Summer Program, estimated that even a comprehensive BMD system would allow the seepage of about 10 percent of attacking missiles; thus, the figure here comes from calculating 10 percent of the current Russia ICBM arsenal.

30.  Andrew E. Kramer, "Russia Tests New Missile to Counter U.S. Shield," *New York Times* (May 24, 2012), p. A8.

31.  Professor Ashton B. Carter, Harvard-MIT Summer Program.

32.  Baker Spring, "The Obama Administration's Ballistic Missile Defense Program: Treading Water in Shark-Infested Seas," *The Heritage Foundation Online* (April 8, 2010), p. 1.

33.  Thom Shanker and David E. Sanger, "Movement of Missiles by North Korea Worries U.S.," *New York Times* (January 17, 2013), p. A1; Choe Sang-Hun, "North Korean Leader Vows 'High-Profile' Retaliation Over New U.N. Sanctions," *New York Times* (January 28, 2013), p. A8.

34.  Remarks to me by Freeman Dyson, a nuclear physicist from Princeton University visiting the University of Georgia, Athens, Georgia (April 30, 1988).

35.  Carter, Harvard-MIT Summer Program.

36.  Rathjens, Harvard-MIT Summer Program.

37.  Graham T. Allison, remarks, Davidson College, Davidson, NC (November 10, 1992), my notes; Professor Allison brought this same warning up-to-date in *Nuclear Terrorism* (2004).

38.  John D. Steinbruner, "Nuclear Decapitation," *Foreign Policy* (Winter 1981–1982), p. 21. In 2012, the National Security

Archive in Washington, DC, reported finding a US government document during its historical research that authorized full-scale nuclear war against both the Soviet Union and China if the American president died or disappeared in the course of an attack against the United States. President Johnson learned about this policy in 1968 and removed the automatic provision [National Security Archives Electronic Briefing Book No. 406 (December 12, 2012)].

39. Rathjens, Harvard-MIT Summer Program.

40. David P. Barash, *The Arms Race and Nuclear War* (Belmont, CA: Wadsworth, 1987).

41. Gen. James E. Cartwright, cited by Thom Shanker, "Former Commander of U.S. Nuclear Forces Calls for Large Cut in Warheads," *New York Times* (May 16, 2012), p. A4; and unsigned editorial, "The Bloated Nuclear Weapons Budget," *New York Times* (October 30, 2011), p. Wk 10.

42. Robert S. McNamara, *The Essence of Security: Reflections in Office* (New York: Harper & Row, 1968), p. 59.

43. *Nightly News*, NBC Television (October 18, 2011).

44. Quoted by Nicholas D. Kristof, "1 Soldier Or 20 Schools?" *New York Times* (July 29, 2010), p. A23.

45. Cited by Elisabeth Bumiller, "The War: A Trillion Can Be Cheap," *New York Times* (July 25, 2010), p. Wk. 3.

46. Jill Lepore, "The Force: How Much Military Is Enough?" *The New Yorker* (January 28, 2013), p. 75; Ernest R. May, "The U.S. Government, a Legacy of the Cold War," *Diplomatic History* 16 (Spring 1992), p. 270. James Wright suggests: "There should be no military action authorized by the United States that does not include income- and corporate-tax surcharges . . . sufficient to cover all of the operation costs of the war" [*Those Who Have Borne the Battle: A History of America's Wars and Those Who Fought Them* (New York: Public Affairs, 2012), p. 214].

47. Two of America's top defense analysts posed this key question several decades ago: Alain C. Enthoven and K. V. Smith, *How Much Is Enough? Shaping the Defense Programs, 1961–1969* (Santa Monica, CA: RAND, 1971).

48. William W. Kaufmann, Harvard-MIT Summer Program.

49. "The Twenty-First Century Will Not Be a "Post-American World," *International Studies Quarterly* 56 (March 2012), p. 217.

50. In his *History of the Peloponnesian War*, Book 1, the Greek historian Thucydides wrote: "What made war inevitable was the growth of Athenian power and the fear which this caused in Sparta" (translated by Rex Warner, London: Penguin Books, 1956, p. 57).

51. David E. Sanger and Peter Baker, "Obama to Adopt Narrowed Stand on Nuclear Arms," *New York Times* (April 4, 2010), p. A1.

52. David E. Sanger and Thom Shanker, "White House Is Rethinking Nuclear Policy," *New York Times* (March 1, 2010), p. A1.

53. Louis Fisher, "Why Congress Passed the War Powers Resolution," conference paper, Center for Law and National Security,

School of Law, University of Virginia, Charlottesville (September 23,1988), p. 23.

54. Eugene Rostow, "Searching for Kennan's Grand Design," *Yale Law Journal* 87 (1978), p. 1536, note 35. Jack L. Goldsmith, a contemporary scholar known to be friendly toward executive power has argued nonetheless that working with Congress and within the rule of law are constraints that ultimately "strengthen the presidency and render it more effective" [*Power and Constraint: The Accountable Presidency after 9/11* (New York: Norton, 2012), p. xv—a viewpoint advanced, too, by another pro-executive branch scholar, Harvey C. Mansfield, Jr., *Taming the Prince: The Ambivalence of Modern Executive Power* (New York: The Free Press, 1989)].

55. Thomas Eagleton, cited in "The War Powers Act Controversy," *Congressional Digest* (November 1983), p. 276.

56. William F. Buckley Jr., remark, *Firing Line*, Public Television (December 20, 1987).

57. Pat Holt, *The War Powers Resolution: The Role of Congress in U.S. Armed Intervention* (Washington, DC: American Enterprise for Public Policy Research, 1978), p. 39.

58. Cecil V. Crabb Jr. and Pat M. Holt, *Invitation to Struggle: Congress, the President and Foreign Policy* (Washington, DC: Congressional Quarterly Press, 1984), p. 143.

59. Report No. 220, Committee on Foreign Relations, US Senate (1973), in *Senate Reports* 161, No. 13017–3, p. 4.

60. Senator Spark Matsunaga (D, Hawaii), "War Powers Legislation: Practical and Constitutional Problems," *Department of State Bulletin* 28 (June 1971), p. 834.

61. *Congressional Record* 119 (1973), p. 24532.

62. "President Nixon's Veto of War Powers Measure Overridden by the Congress," *Department of State Bulletin* 26 (November 1973), p. 662.

63. Quoted by Holt, *The War Powers Resolution*, p. 8.

64. *Congressional Quarterly Almanac* 29 (1973), p. 907.

65. Thomas F. Eagleton, *War and Presidential Power: A Chronicle of Congressional Surrender* (New York: Liveright, 1974), pp. 221, 223.

66. *Congressional Quarterly Almanac* 29 (1973), p. 916.

67. "Congress Overrides Nixon's Veto of War Powers Bill," *Congressional Quarterly Weekly Report* 31 (November 10, 1973), p. 2985; and *Congressional Record* (1973), p. 36187.

68. Sam Nunn (D-Georgia), quoted in the *Atlanta Constitution* (November 10, 1987), p. A8.

69. Michael J. Glennon, "The War Powers Resolution Ten Years Later: More Politics Than Law," *American Journal of International Law* 78 (July 1984), p. 577.

70. Louis Henkin, "Foreign Affairs and the Constitution," *Foreign Affairs* 66 (Winter 1987), p. 300.

71. For example, Stephen Solarz (D-New York), *Firing Line*, Public Television (December 20, 1987).

72. William P. Agee, "The War Powers Resolution: Congress Seeks to Reassert Its Proper Constitutional Role as a Partner in War Making," *Rutgers Law Journal* 18 (Winter 1987), pp. 405–435.

73. Glennon, "The War Powers Resolution," p. 371. See, also, Richard F. Grimmett, *The War Powers Resolution: After Thirty-Six Years*, CRS Report for Congress, 7–5700, Washington, DC (April 22, 2010).

74. Quoted by John H. Sullivan, *The War Powers Resolution: A Special Study of the Committee on Foreign Affairs*, Committee on Foreign Affairs, US House of Representatives (1982), p. 219.

75. *Congressional Record* (November 7, 1982), p. 219.

76. Barbara Hinkson Craig, "The Power to Make War: Congress' Search for an Effective Role," *Journal of Policy Analysis and Management* 1 (1981), p. 324.

77. Quoted in the *New York Times* (September 16, 1983), p. A1.

78. Quoted by Crabb and Holt, *Invitation to Struggle*, p. 147.

79. Michael J. Glennon, "Some Compromise!" *Christian Science Monitor* (October 24, 1983), p. 16.

80. Quoted by Crabb and Holt, *Invitation to Struggle*, p. 145.

81. Charles Savage and Thom Shanker, "Scores of U.S. Strikes in Libya Followed Handoff to NATO," *New York Times* (June 21, 2011), p. A8, based on interviews with US military officials.

82. Cited in Charlie Savage, "Mostly in Echo, Rivals Discuss Reach of Power," *New York Times* (December 30, 2011), p. A1.

83. Bruce Ackerman, "Legal Acrobatics, Illegal War," *New York Times* (June 21, 2011), p. A27.

84. Louis Fisher, "Parsing the War Power," *The National Law Journal* (July 4, 2011), http:www.law.com.

85. Quoted in Jennifer Steinhauer, "Senate Panel Votes in Favor of U.S. Measures in Libya," *New York Times* (June 29, 2011), p. A8.

86. Charlie Savage and Mark Landler, "Split Widens on U.S. Role in Libya," *New York Times* (June 17, 2011), p. 5.

87. Glennon, "The War Powers Resolution," p. 573.

88. Remarks, "Focus on the War Powers Act," newsletter, Center on National Policy, Washington, DC, Vol. 2 (1988), p. 6.

89. Press release, Office of Senator Sam Nunn, Washington, DC (May 19, 1988).

90. For examples of the criticism, see Louis Fisher, "Why Congress Passed the War Powers Resolution"; Henkin, "Foreign Affairs and the Constitution"; Robert A. Katzmann, "War Powers: Toward a New Accommodation," in Thomas E. Mann, ed., *A Question of Balance: The President, the Congress, and Foreign Policy* (Washington, DC: Brookings Institution, 1990); and remarks by lawmakers in the *Congressional Record* from May 20–31.

91. Katzmann, "War Powers: Toward a New Accommodation," p. 67.

92. Quoted in the *New York Times* (September 9, 1984), p. A19.

93. Quoted in the *New York Times* (September 9, 1984), p. A19.

94. Quoted in the *New York Times* (September 9, 1984), p. A19.

95. Henkin, *Foreign Affairs and the Constitution*, p. 303.

### Chapter 12

1. Drawn from Loch K. Johnson, "It's Never a Quick Fix at the CIA," *Washington Post* (August 30, 2009), Outlook Section, p. A1; and Loch K. Johnson, *National Security Intelligence: Secret Operations in Defense of the Democracies* (Cambridge, UK: Polity, 2012), pp. 77–78.

2. See David M. Barrett, *The CIA and Congress: The Untold Story from Truman to Kennedy* (Lawrence: University Press of Kansas, 2005).

3. Henry Kissinger, remark, *Evening News*, NBC Television (January 13, 1978).

4. The Intelligence Authorization Act of 1991 (50 U.S.C. 503 [e]; Pub. L. No. 102–88, 105 Stat. 441, August 14, 1991); this statue amended the National Security Act of 1947, repealed the Hughes-Ryan Amendment of 1974, and codified into law Executive Order 12333.

5. The National Security Act of 1947, Pub. L. No. 80–253, 61 Stat. 495; 50 U.S.C. 403–3(d)(5).

6. Jennifer D. Kibbe, "The Rise of the Shadow Warriors," *Foreign Affairs* 83 (2004), pp. 102–115.

7. Loch K. Johnson, "The Myths of America's Shadow War," *The Atlantic Online* (January 31, 2013).

8. My interview with a senior CIA official in the Operations Directorate, Washington, DC (February 1986).

9. B. Hugh Tovar, "Strengths and Weaknesses in Past U.S. Covert Action," in Roy Godson, ed., *Intelligence Requirements for the 1980s: Covert Action* (Washington, DC: National Strategy Information Center, 1981), pp. 194–195.

10. See George Tenet with Bill Harlow, *At the Center of the Storm: My Years at the CIA* (New York: HarperCollins, 2007); Paul R. Pillar, *Terrorism and U.S. Foreign Policy* (Washington, DC: Brookings Institution, 2003).

11. Remark to me, senior CIA operations officer, Washington, DC (July 12, 1995).

12. Quoted in *The Nation* (March 12, 1983), p. 301.

13. Frank Church, "Covert Action: Swampland of American Foreign Policy," *Bulletin of the Atomic Scientists* 32 (February 1976), pp. 7–11, quote at p. 8; reprinted in Loch K. Johnson and James J. Wirtz, *Intelligence and National Security: The Secret World of Spies*, 3rd ed. (New York: Oxford University Press, 2011), pp. 233–237.

14. These trends are based on my interviews with intelligence officers over the past three decades.

15. See, for example, Jo Becker and Scott Shane, "Secret 'Kill List' Proves a Test Of Obama's Principles and Will," *New York Times*

(May 29, 2012), p. A1; and Elisabeth Bumiller, "A Day Job Waiting for a Kill Shot a World Away," *New York Times* (July 30, 2012), p. A1.

16. See "Covert Action in Chile: 1963–1973," *Staff Report*, Select Committee on Intelligence Activities (the Church Committee), US Senate (December 1975).

17. Some authors use the term "blowback" to refer to any American foreign policy mistake abroad that comes back to haunt the United States, say, an ill-conceived attack like the one in 1975 associated with the *Mayaguez* incident in Cambodia [see, for instance, Chalmers Johnson, *The Sorrows of Empire: Militarism, Secrecy, and the End of the Republic* (New York: Henry Holt, 2004)]; the term in US government circles, though, is more narrowly defined, as in this chapter, to refer to "drifting" CIA propaganda placements than can waft back to American shores and influence an American readership.

18. Dr. Ray D. Cline, testimony, "The CIA and the Media" *Hearings*, Subcommittee on Oversight, Permanent Select Committee on Intelligence, US House of Representatives (Washington, DC: Government Printing Office, 1979), p. 90.

19. Remark by a former British intelligence officer to me, Oxford University (April 22, 2003), Oxford, England.

20. My interview with CIA official, Washington, DC (June 1984).

21. Tom Wicker et al., "C.I.A. Operations: A Plot Scuttled," *New York Times* (April 28, 1966), p. A1.

22. See Johnson, *National Security Intelligence.*

23. Eric Schmitt, "C.I.A. Said to Aid in Steering Arms to Syrian Rebels," *New York Times* (June 21, 2012), p. A1.

24. David E. Sanger, "Obama Order Set Off Wave Of Cyberattacks Against Iran," *New York Times* (June 1, 2012), p. A1—controversial reporting that led to widespread calls from Capitol Hill to stop the flow of leaks coming from the Obama administration about cyberattacks and drone assassination targeting.

25. For the Hughes–Ryan law, see Section 662 of the Foreign Assistance Act of 1974 (22 U.S.C. 2422); for the 1980 Oversight Act, Title V of the National Security Act of 1947 (50 U.S.C. 413); and for the 1991 Oversight Act: Intelligence Authorization Act, Fiscal Year 1991, Pub. L. No. 102–88, 10 Stat. 429.

26. See the Pike Committee report (House Select Committee on Intelligence, chaired by Otis Pike, D-New York), reprinted in "The CIA Report the President Doesn't Want You to Read: The Pike Papers," *Village Voice* (February 16, 1976), pp. 69–92.

27. Church Committee declassified document (May 1976).

28. Dean Rusk, Oral History No. 86, taped by Hughes Cates, Richard B. Russell Library, University of Georgia, Athens (February 22, 1977).

29. "Alleged Assassination Plots Involving Foreign Leaders," *Interim Report*, Church Committee (November 20, 1975).

30. Quoted in Douglas Martin, "Gen. Vang Pao, Laotian Who Aided U.S., Dies at 81," *New York Times* (January 8, 2011), p. A17.

31. See Theodore Shackley, *The Third Option: An American View of Counterinsurgency* (Pleasantville, NY: Reader's Digest General Books, 1981).

32. William J. Broad, John Markoff, and David E. Sanger, "Israel Tests Called Crucial In Iran Nuclear Setback," *New York Times* (January 16, 2011), p. A1; see, also, Ryan Lizza, "The Second Term," *The New Yorker* (June 18, 2012), p. 55; and Sanger, "Obama Order Set Off Wave Of Cyberattacks Against Iran."

33. "Alleged Assassination Plots."

34. Robert Wallace and H. Keith Melton, with Henry Robert Schlesinger, *Spycraft: The Secret History of the CIA's Spy Techs, From Communism to Al-Qaeda* (New York: Plume/Penquin, 2009).

35. Admiral Stansfield Turn, *Burn Before Reading: President, CIA Directors, and Secret Intelligence* (New York: Hyperion, 2005), p. 98.

36. "Alleged Assassination Plots," p. 41.

37. Stephen R. Weissman, "An Extraordinary Rendition," *Intelligence and National Security* 25 (April 2010), pp. 198–222.

38. Senator Frank Church, press conference, Washington, DC (July 19, 1975). I served as an aide to Senator Church at the time, but was surprised by this statement. An added challenge today in supervising the US secret agencies abroad is their increasing use of "outsourcing"—hiring people outside the government to carry out America's intelligence activities. These individuals often know little about the statutory boundaries for intelligence operations and can be guilty of behavior that a government bureaucrat would understand was prohibited by law or less formal congressional expectations.

39. "Alleged Assassination Plots," p. 149.

40. "Alleged Assassination Plots," p. 149.

41. Memorandum from Arthur M. Schlesinger Jr. to President John F. Kennedy (September 5, 1962), Church Committee files, US Senate, 1975.

42. "Alleged Assassination Plots," pp. 151, 154.

43. "Alleged Assassination Plots," p. 151.

44. Peter W. Singer, "Do Drones Undermine Democracy?," *New York Times* (January 22, 2012), p. Wk 5; and Scott Shane, "U.S. Drone Strikes Are Said to Target Rescuers at Sites," *New York Times* (February 6, 2012), p. A4 (based on figures from the Bureau of Investigative Journalism in Washington, DC). See also Mark Mazzetti and Salman Masood, "Cover Blown, C.I.A. Chief Is Pulled in Pakistan," *New York Times* (December 18, 2010), p. A8.

45. Scott Shane, "Election Spurred a Move to Codify U.S. Drone Policy," *New York Times* (November 25, 2012), p. A1.

46. Reported by *Der Spiegel Online* (2010).

47. *Der Spiegel Online* (2010); Shane, "U.S. Drone Strikes Are Said to Target Rescuers."

48. Michael Scheuer, *Imperial Hubris* (New York: Brassey's, 2004). For additional accounts about the CIA's early efforts to eliminate

Bin Laden (before succeeding on May 1, 2011), see Richard A. Clarke, *Against All Enemies* (New York: Free Press, 2004).

49. William E. Colby and Peter Forbath, *Honorable Men: My Life in the CIA* (New York: Simon & Schuster, 1978), p. 272; and "Gesprach mit William E. Colby," *Der Spiegel* 4 (January 23, 1978), pp. 69–115 (my translation).

50. Remarks, Pacem in Terris IV Convocation, Washington, DC (December 4, 1975).

51. My interview, Washington, DC (January 24, 1976).

52. See, for example, Richard Helm's criticism of covert propaganda operations "of no consequence" in Thomas Powers, *The Man Who Kept the Secrets: Richard Helms and the CIA* (New York: Knopf, 1979), p. 101; and his skepticism about covert action generally, p. 28.

53. Anthony Lewis, "Costs of the C.I.A.," *New York Times* (April 25, 1997), p. A19.

54. See Adam Hochschild, "An Assassination's Long Shadow," *New York Times* (January 17, 2011), p. A21.

55. For Senator Church, this was the central argument against covert action. "If we have gained little [from covert action], what then have we lost?" he once asked. His answer: "Our good name and reputation." See Church, "Covert Action: Swampland," p. 236.

56. "Gesprach mit William E. Colby," p. 101, my translation.

57. "Covert Action," *Hearings*, Church Committee (October 23, 1975).

58. "Covert Action," *Hearings*, Church Committee (December 4, 1975), emphasis added.

59. "Covert Action," *Hearings*, Church Committee (December 4, 1975), emphasis added.

60. Herman Kahn, *On Escalation: Metaphors and Scenarios* (New York: Praeger, 1965), p. 37. See also James Barry, "Covert Action Can Be Just," *Orbis* 37 (Summer 1993), pp. 375–390; and Loch K. Johnson, "On Drawing a Bright Line for Covert Operations," *American Journal of International Law* 86 (April 1992), pp. 284–309.

61. Jimmy Carter, "A Cruel and Unusual Record," *New York Times* (June 25, 2012), p. A17.

62. On the Iran-*contra* scandal and the Boland amendments, see William S. Cohen and George J. Mitchell, *Men of Zeal: A Candid Inside Story of the Iran-Contra Hearings* (New York: Penguin, 1988). In the 1980s, Representative Boland introduced seven successive amendments related to Nicaragua, all designed to reduce and eventually eliminate US covert actions against that nation. The most sweeping was the second, enacted in 1983 and often referred to as the Boland Amendment [Department of Defense Appropriations Act 1985, Pub. L. No. 98–473, 8066, 98 Stat. 1935 (1984)].

63. Title V of the National Security Act of 1947 (50 U.S.C. 413), Accountability for Intelligence Activities; the Intelligence Oversight Act of 1980 [Pub. L. No. 96–450, 407 (b), 94 Stat. 1981 (1980)].

64. See Alfred Cumming, *Sensitive Covert Action Notifications: Oversight Options for Congress*, CRS Report for Congress, Congressional Research Service, 7–5700 (July 7, 2009). See as well the Intelligence Authorization Act, Fiscal year 1991 (Pub. L. No. 102–88, 105 Stat. 441, Aug. 14, 1991).

65. See Anne Joseph O'Connell, "Intelligence Oversight," in Matthew J. Morgan, ed., *The Impact of 9//11 and the New Legal Landscape* (New York: Palgrave/Macmillan, 2009), pp.158–173; and Loch K. Johnson, *National Security Intelligence* (Cambridge, UK: Polity, 2011).

66. Jennifer D. Kibbe, "Covert Action, Pentagon Style," in Loch K. Johnson, ed., *The Oxford Handbook of National Security Intelligence* (New York: Oxford University Press, 2010), pp. 569–586.

67. My interviews with staff on the two Intelligence Committees (April 1984 and July 1986).

68. The letter was dated April 9, 1984; see the *Washington Post* (April 11, 1984), p. 170.

69. Stansfield Turner, *Secrecy and Democracy: The CIA in Transition* (Boston: Houghton Mifflin, 1985), p. 170.

70. My interviews with senior intelligence officials, Washington, DC (November 1980); see, also, Senate Select Committee on Intelligence, Annual Report No. 95–217 (May 18, 1977), p. 2; and Leslie H. Gelb, "Overseeing of CIA by Congress," *New York Times* (July 7, 1986). Former DCI Stansfield Turner has said that under congressional pressure "three times Reagan signed, then cancelled, covert action operations" [interview, WGST Radio, Atlanta, GA (July 30, 1985)], my notes.

71. My interview with staff aide, SSCI, Washington, DC (December 12, 1980).

72. See Mark M. Lowenthal, *Intelligence: From Secrets to Policy*, 4th ed. (Washington, DC: CQ Press, 2009), pp. 994–295.

73. My interview, Washington, DC (June 11, 1984).

74. My interviews with CIA officials, Washington, DC (November 17 and 18, 1980).

75. Quoted by Don Oberdofer, *Washington Post* (August 6, 1983), p. A13.

76. For Gates's remarks, see Neil A. Lewis, "Bigger Battle Awaits Clinton on Cutting the Spy Budget," *New York Times* (February 1, 1993), p. A7; for Turner, see Loch K. Johnson, "Smart Intelligence," *Foreign Policy* 89 (Winter 1992–1993), p. 67. In 2012, the SSCI held only a single public hearing, even though many aspects of this topic can be examined in an open forum (my interviews with SSCI staff members, February 7, 2013).

77. "Should the CIA Fight Secret Wars?," *Harper's* (September 1984), pp. 39, 44.

78. "Should the CIA Fight Secret Wars?," *Harper's*, p. 37.

79. Jo Becker and Scott Shane, "Secret 'Kill List' Proves a Test of Obama's Principles and Will," *New York Times* (May 29, 2012), p. A1.

## Chapter 13

1. This case study in international economics is reconstructed from WikiLeaks cables and their analysis presented in Eric Lipton, Nicola Clark, and Andrew W. Lehren, "Hidden Hand of Diplomats in Jet Deals," *New York Times* (January 3, 2011), p. A1. The United States has had an ambivalent relationship with Saudi Arabia. Seventeen of the nineteen 9/11 hijackers were radicals from this nation, and the Saudis reportedly pay the families of suicide bombers in the Middle East who target Israel; yet the Saudi royal family has ensured that its oil flows without interruption and at a reasonable price to the United States and its allies (especially Japan), and the family frequently supports Washington, DC, behind the scenes in Middle Eastern affairs. For an authoritative argument that the Saudi government may have known more about the 9/11 planning than it has conceded, see the memoir of former US Senator Bob Graham (with Jeff Nussbaum), *Intelligence Matters: The CIA, the FBI, Saudi Arabia, and the Failure of America's War on Terror* (Lawrence: University Press of Kansas, 2008).

2. Matt Bai, "The Presidency, Chained to the World," *New York Times* (September 12, 2010), p. Wk. 4.

3. Quoted by Walter F. Mondale, *The Good Fight* (New York: Scribner, 2010), pp. 284–285.

4. "Oil in America: Energy to Spare," *The Economist* (November 17, 2012), p. 63. In my experience, the number is far less than half—more like 10 percent.

5. *Nightly News*, ABC Television (November 19, 2011).

6. Warren Christopher, deputy secretary of state, "Resources and Foreign Policy," *Current Policy No. 185,* US Department of State, Bureau of Public Affairs, Washington, DC (May 28, 1980), p. 2.

7. For the 1977 figure, see Richard N. Cooper, undersecretary for economic affairs, "Economics and U.S. Security in the 1980s," *Current Policy No. 158,* US Department of State, Bureau of Public Affairs, Washington, DC (March 7, 1980), p. 2; for the 1984 figure, see *United States Trade: Performance in 1984 and Outlook,* US Department of Commerce, International Trade Administration, Office of Trade and Investment Analysis (Washington, DC: US Government Printing Office, June 1985), p. 17. The figures for Saudi oil earnings come from the *New York Times* (February 12, 1987), p. 29.

8. OPEC, *Annual Statistics Bulletin 2008* (2009), p. 13; US Energy Information Administration Website (2010); see the Deutch and Schlesinger Task Force, *National Security Consequences of U.S. Oil Dependency,* Council on Foreign Relations, Task Force Report No. 58 (2006), New York.

9. This compilation is based on Kimberly Amadeo, "Imports and Exports Components," *About.com US Economy* (2011); and *Foreign Trade,* United States Census Bureau, US Department of Commerce (November 2012).

10. For the data presented here, and the quotation, see Peter Baker, "Obama Hopes to Expand Economic Ties With Russia, but Pitfalls Exist," *New York Times* (June 23, 2010), p. A11; on the legislation regarding penalties against Russians, see David M.

11. Herszenhorn, "Bill on Russia Trade Ties Sets Off New Acrimony," *New York Times* (December 8, 2012); on the adoption prohibition, see David M. Herszenhorn and Andrew E. Kramer, "Another Rest of Relations With Russia in Obama's Second Term," *New York Times* (February 2, 2013), p. A4.

11. William Pfaff, "Reflections: Where the Wars Came From," *The New Yorker* (December 26, 1988), p. 83. On the impressive strength of the contemporary European economy, see Niall Ferguson, *Colossus: The Rise and Fall of the American Empire* (New York: Penguin, 2004).

12. See I. M. Destler, *American Trade Politics: System Under Stress*, 3rd ed. (Washington, DC: Institute for International Economics, 1995); Joseph E. Stiglitz, *Freefall: America, Free Markets and the Sinking of the World Economy* (New York: Norton, 2010).

13. Keith Bradsher, "Trade Issues With China Heating Up," *New York Times* (March 13, 2012), p. B1.

14. Reported by *Nightly News,* PublicTelevision (February 13, 2012).

15. Annie Lowrey, "Obama Vow on Exports Is on Track, With Help," *New York Times* (January 20, 2012), p. B1.

16. Keith Bradsher, "China Uses Rules on Global Trade to its Advantage," *New York Times* (March 15, 2010), p. A1.

17. *Foreign Trade,* US Census Bureau, Department of Commerce (2010).

18. Joseph E. Stiglitz, *Freefall: America, Free Markets and the Sinking of the World Economy* (New York: Norton, 2010).

19. Bradsher, "Trade Issues With China Heating Up."

20. John Cassidy, "Enter the Dragon," *The New Yorker* (December 13, 2010), p. 97.

21. Joseph Kahn, "Waking Dragon," *New York Times Book Review* (January 3, 2010), p. 14.

22. Sewell Chan, "World Trade Organization Upholds American Tariffs on Tires From China," *New York Times* (December 14, 2010), p. B3.

23. See Helene Cooper, "For Pakistan, American Aid Is all Guns, No Butter," *New York Times* (February 17, 2006), p. A27.

24. Reported by Lisa Blaydes and Drew A. Linzer, "Elite Competition, Religiosity, and Anti-Americanism in the Islamic World," *American Political Science Review* 106 (May 2012), p. 228, based on the Pew Global Attitudes Project (2009).

25. My conversation with US trade ambassador Don Johnson, University of Georgia, Athens (January 23, 2011).

26. Mortimer B. Zukerman, "What Should Make Bush Run Now," *U.S. News & World Report* (February 6, 1989), p. 70. One expert on Japan has observed that "fewer than 1,000 U.S. scientists speak Japanese, while English is a requirement for science students in Japan" [Walter Russell Mead, "Japan-Bashing, and Ugly American Tradition," *Los Angeles Times* (June 4, 1989), Sec.5, p.2].

27. For results of this test, administered by the Organization for Economic Cooperation and Development (OECD), see Sam Dillon, "Top Test Scores From Shanghai Stun Educators," *New York Times* (December 17, 2010), p. A1. Shanghai, China, came in first in science, reading, and math.

28. Keith Bradsher, "A Better Offer from China," *New York Times* (January 15, 2011), p. B1.

29. In addition to the EU, the membership includes Argentina, Australia, Brazil, Canada, China, France, Germany, India, Indonesia, Italy, Japan, Mexico, Russia, Saudi Arabia, South Africa, South Korea, Turkey, United Kingdom, and the United States.

30. Sewll Chan and Jackie Calmes, "G-20 Countries Agree to Halve Budget Deficits," *New York Times* (June 28, 2010), p. A1.

31. Helene Cooper, "Leaders Make Little Headway in Solving Debt Crisis," *New York Times* (June 20, 2012), p. A3.

32. Joan Edelman Spero, *The Politics of International Economic Relations,* 2nd ed. (New York: St. Martin's, 1981), p. 103.

33. Spero, *The Politics of International Economic Relations,* p. 110.

34. Loch K. Johnson, *America's Secret Power: The CIA in a Democratic Society* (New York: Oxford University Press, 1989), p. 22.

35. Charles Duhigg and David Barboza, "In China, the Human Costs That Are Built into an iPad," *New York Times* (January 26, 2012), p. A1.

36. Steve Coll, *Private Empire: ExxonMobil and American Power* (New York: Penguin, 2012).

37. Raymond Vernon, *Sovereignty at Bay: The Multinational Spread of U.S. Enterprises* (New York: Basic Books, 1971).

38. My interviews with former CIA officers familiar with the Angolan operation, Washington, DC (September 2 and 3, 2010).

39. Martin Hillenbrand, former US ambassador to West Germany, "Economic Diplomacy," lecture, University of Georgia, Athens (January 17, 1983).

40. Hedrick Smith, *The Power Game: How Washington Works* (New York: Random House, 1988), p. 570.

41. I. M. Destler, *Making Foreign Economic Policy* (Washington, DC: Brookings Institution, 1980), p. 215.

42. Quoted by Clyde H. Farnsworth, "Approval of Canada Trade Pact Seen," *New York Times* (May 9, 1988), p. A21.

43. Suzanne Goldenberg, "Keystone SL Pipeline: Obama Rejects Controversial Project," *The Guardian* (January 18, 2012), p. A1; John M. Broder and Clifford Krauss, "Keystone XL Pipeline, *New York Times*: http//nytimes.com (February 28, 2012).

44. I. M. Destler, *American Trade Politics: System under Stress*, 3rd ed. (Washington, DC: Institute for International Economics, 1995).

45. Binyamin Appelbaum and Jennifer Steinhauer, "Trade Deals Pass Congress, Ending 5-Year Standoff," *New York Times* (October 13, 2011), p. A1.

46. Quoted in Clifford J. Levy, "Russia Says Sanctions Against Iran Are Unlikely," *New York Times* (September 11, 2009), p. A6.

47. Andrew E. Kramer, "Russia Plan To Help Iran Challenges Sanctions," *New York Times* (August 15, 2010), p. A12.

48. Mark Landler, "Obama Aide Says Iran's Leaders Are Feeling the Strain of Sanctions," *New York Times* (November 23, 2011), p. A8.

49. Mark Landler, "Iran Face-Off Testing Obama The Candidate," *New York Times* (January 17, 2012), p. A1.

50. David E. Sanger, "New Efforts on Iran Sanctions Run Into Familiar Snags," *New York Times* (March 20, 2010), p. A6.

51. Richard N. Haass, "Economic Sanctions: Too Much of a Bad Thing," *Brookings Paper* (Washington, DC: The Brookings Institution, June 1998), p. 1.

52. Joan Hoff Wilson, "Economic Foreign Policy," in Alexander DeConde, ed., *Encyclopedia of American Foreign Policy: Studies of the Principle Movements and Ideas,* Vol. II (New York: Scribner's, 1978), p. 320.

53. Ian J. Bickerton, "Foreign Aid," in DeConde, p. 372.

54. David D. Newsom, *Diplomacy and the American Democracy* (Bloomington: Indiana University Press, 1988), p. 161.

55. Adam Entous and Siobhan Gorman, "U.S. Links Pakistani Aid to Performance," *Wall Street Journal* (August 15, 2011), p. A7.

56. Jeremy M. Sharp, "U.S. Foreign Aid to Israel," *CRS Report for Congress No. 7–5700*, Congressional Research Service (March 12, 2012), p. 1.

57. The data are from the Office of US Foreign Assistance Resources, Department of State, *Congressional Budget Justification for Foreign Operations Summary Tables* (Washington, DC: 2008 and 2012).

58. Schultz is quoted in Bernard Gwertzman, "A Citizen Pays $43 for Aid, Schultz Says, and $35 for Hairdos," *New York Times* (February 25, 1983), p. A1. The more recent comparisons come from: Michael Schaffer, "One Nation Under Dog," *Marketplace*, American Public Media (April 8, 2009), who writes that Americans spend $45 per year caring for their pets; the National Association of Confectioners, *Confectionary Industry Review* (February 2010), $30 billion on candy per year; and Jason Hardin, "The Lawn of the Future," *News & Record* (July 13, 2008), $30 billion on lawn maintenance per year. These comparisons are summarized in Oxfam, *Foreign Aid 101* (New York, 2010).

59. Steven W. Hook, *U.S. Foreign Power: The Paradox of World Power* (Washington, DC: CQ Press, 2011), p. 370. Some observers have given the Chinese higher marks than the United States for its aid programs. For example, China has focused on programs to improve drinking water and protect forests in Africa. In return, the Chinese are the beneficiaries of access to Africa's natural resources, such as oil from Sudan and Angola, along with copper from Zambia and the Democratic Republic of Congo. At the same time, the Chinese have been criticized for turning a blind eye to human rights in African and for exploiting its mineral resources [see, for example, Jane Perlez, "With $20 Billion Loan

Pledge, China Strengthens Its Ties to African Nations," *New York Times* (July 20, 2012), p. A6].

60. GNI is almost the same measure as Gross Domestic Product (GDP); but it adds income received from other countries, after subtracting comparable payments made to other countries.

61. Charles W. Kegley Jr. and Eugene R. Witkopf, *American Foreign Policy: Pattern and Process* (New York: St. Martin's, 1979), p. 93; for the 1987 data, see US Agency for International Development, "Cooperation Fosters Economic Development," *USAID Highlights* 6 (Spring 1989), p. 1.

62. Unsigned editorial, "Failing the World's Poor," *New York Times* (September 24, 2008), p. A30.

63. Alex Perry, *Lifeblood: How to Change the World One Dead Mosquito at a Time* (New York: PublicAffairs, 2011).

64. World Bank, "Millennium Development Goals Database," 2010.

65. Robert L. Heilbroner, *An Inquiry into the Human Prospect* (New York: Norton, 1975), p. 39.

66. Sabrina Tavernise, "Life Expectancy Rises Around World, Study Finds," *New York Times* (December 14, 2012), p. A4.

67. "Conference of Soviet-American Physicians," WETA Public Television, December 1984.

68. Annie Lowrey, "Extreme Poverty in Developing World Is Down Despite the Recession, Report Says," *New York Times* (March 7, 2012), p. A4.

69. Cited by Wilson, p. 287.

70. Quoted by Bickerton, p. 375.

71. Eric V. Larson, "A Diplomatic Strategy to Counter al Qaeda's Narrative," *RAND Review* (Summer 2011), p. 21.

72. Bickerton, p. 374.

73. Quoted in Bickerton, p. 375.

74. Representative Stephen Solarz (D-New York), quoted on *Washington Week in Review,* Public Television (March 14, 1986).

75. The Yemen example was cited on *The Lehrer News Hour,* Public Television (March 24, 2010); and the Afghanistan example comes from Linda Robinson, "Long Divisions," *New York Times Book Review* (September 9, 2012), p. 11, as she summarized her sense of the findings presented in Rajiv Chandrasekaran, *Little America: The War Within the War for Afghanistan* (New York: Knopf, 2012). The phrase "Ptomkin progress" is a reference to the Russian bureaucrat Grigori Potëmkin, who reputedly (the story may be apocryphal) built impressive but fake villages—merely facades—along a route traveled by Catherine the Great in 1787, trying to impress her with his ministerial abilities.

76. Cited by Jeffrey Gettleman and Neil MacFarquhar, "Somalia Food Aid Bypasses Needy, U.N. Study Finds," *New York Times* (March 10, 2010), p. A1. The new President of Egypt, Mohamed Morsi, dismissed the effectiveness of US aid with these words: "Successive American administrations essentially purchased with American taxpayer money the dislike, if not the hatred, of the peoples of the region [the Middle East]" by supporting dictatorial governments over popular opposition and Israel over the Palestinians [David D. Kirkpatrick and Steven Erlanger, "Egyptian Leader Spells Out Terms for U.S.-Arab Ties," *New York Times* (September 22, 2012), p. A1]. In July of 2013, the Egyptian military toppled President Morsi on grounds that his administration had become authoritarian. Whether this paved the way for a new try at democracy in Egypt or simply another military dictatorship remained an open question in 2013.

77. David Brooks, "The Underlying Tragedy," *New York Times* (January 15, 2010), p. A21.

78. Quoted by Neil MacFarquhar, "After Years of Plans, Haiti Is Again a Canvas for Approaches to Aid," *New York Times* (January 31, 2010), p. A12.

79. Quoted by Peter Osterlund, "Congress Tightens Foreign-Aid Screws," *Christian Science Monitor* (September 18, 1986), p. A1.

80. Bickerton, p. 378.

81. See, for example, J. Brian Atwood, M. Peter McPherson, and Andrew Natsios, "Arrested Development: Making Foreign Aid a More Effective Tool," *Foreign Affairs* 87 (November–December 2008), pp. 123–132.

82. On the 2012 figure, see unsigned editorial, "Mr. Romney Addresses Foreign Aid," *New York Times* (September 27, 2012). During the 2012 presidential election, the GOP Vice Presidential running mate, Representative Paul Ryan, advocated a cut in foreign affairs spending by 10 percent in 2013 and more in 2016 ("Mr. Romney Addresses Foreign Aid," *New York Times*). On the recent state of US foreign assistance, see also Lael Brainard, ed., *Security by Other Means: Foreign Assistance, Global Poverty, and American Leadership* (Washington, DC: The Brookings Institution, 2007); Susan B. Epstein, Marian Leonardo Lawson, and Alex Tiersky, *State, Foreign Operations, and Related Programs: FY2013 Budget and Appropriations*, Congressional Research Service Report for Congress, Library of Congress (July 23, 2012); and Steve Radelet, *Modernizing Foreign Assistance for the 21st Century: An Agenda for the Next U.S. President* (Washington, DC: Center for Global Development, 2008).

83. Carl Rowan, "American Ignorance," *Atlanta Constitution* (November 4, 1979), p. A14.

84. See Jeffrey Gettleman, "Shower of Aid Brings Flood of Progress," *New York Times* (March 9, 2010), p. A9.

85. See Esther Duflo, "Marshaling the Evidence: How Science Can Help Fight the War on Poverty," *RAND Review* (Spring 2010), p. 9; and Ian Parker, "The Poverty Lab," *The New Yorker* (May 17, 2010), pp. 79–89.

**Chapter 14**

1. These historical recollections come from Jacobo Timerman, "Reflections: Under the Dictator," *The New Yorker* (November 2, 1987), pp. 49–56.

2. See William G. Weaver and Robert M. Pallitto, "Extraordinary Rendition," in Loch K. Johnson, ed., *The Oxford Handbook of*

*National Security Intelligence* (New York: Oxford University Press, 2010), pp. 328–342.

3. David Cole and James X. Dempsey, *Terrorism and the Constitution* (New York: New Press, 2006), pp. x–xi.

4. D. K. Fieldhouse, *The Colonial Empires from the Eighteenth Century* (New York: Delacorte, 1965), photo no. 38.

5. Interview with Bob Woodward, "Secret Intelligence," Public Broadcasting System (PBS), produced by KCET Television, Los Angeles (February 13, 1989).

6. Quoted by Anthony Lewis, "Morality in Foreign Policy," *New York Times* (October 21, 1976), p. A39.

7. For a more in-depth examination of the following two cases from the Second World War, see J. E. Hare and Carey B. Joynt, *Ethics and International Affairs* (New York: St. Martin's, 1982).

8. Hare and Joynt, *Ethics and International Affairs*, p. 99.

9. Forrest C. Pogue, *George C. Marshall: Statesman, 1945–1959* (New York: Viking, 1987), p. 19.

10. Jonathan Schell, "The Spirit of June 12," *The Nation* (July 2, 2007), p. 6.

11. In this section of the chapter, I draw on lectures presented by Joseph S. Nye Jr. and others at the MIT-Harvard Summer Program on Nuclear Weapons and Arms Control, Cambridge, Massachusetts (June 1985), as well as Nye's book, entitled *Nuclear Ethics* (New York: Free Press, 1986).

12. See Michael J. Sandel, *Justice: What's the Right Thing to Do?* (New York: Farrar, Straus & Giroux, 2009).

13. J. Bryan Hehir, lecture, MIT-Harvard Summer Program (1985).

14. A phrase coined by McGeorge Bundy, "The Bishops and the Bomb," *New York Times Review of Books* (June 16, 1983), p. 4.

15. Nye, *Nuclear Ethics*, p. 17.

16. Nye, *Nuclear Ethics*, p. 17.

17. United States Catholic Conference, *The Challenge of Peace: God's Promise and Our Response* (1983).

18. J. Bryan Hehir, "There's No Deterring the Catholic Bishops," *Ethics and International Affairs* 3 (1989), p. 287.

19. Hehir, lecture, MIT-Harvard Summer Program (1985).

20. Nye, lecture, MIT-Harvard Summer Program (1985).

21. Cited by Nye, lecture, MIT-Harvard Summer Program (1985).

22. Susan Okum, "Taking the Bishops Seriously," *World Politics* 36 (July 1984), pp. 527–554.

23. Hehir, "There's No Deterring," p. 285.

24. See Keith B. Payne, "The Bishops and Nuclear Weapons," *Orbis* 27 (Fall 1983), pp. 535–543.

25. See Michael Andregg, "Ethics and Professional Intelligence," in Loch K. Johnson, ed., *Oxford Handbook of National Security Intelligence*, pp. 735–756; Ed Godfrey, "Ethics and Intelligence,"

*Foreign Affairs* 56 (1978), pp. 624–642; and the essays in *Ethics and International Affairs* 3 (1989), pp. 27–72.

26. See Loch K. Johnson, "Bricks and Mortar for a Theory of Intelligence," *Comparative Strategy* 22 (Spring 2003), pp. 1–28.

27. Cited in Victor Marchetti and John D. Marks, *The CIA and the Cult of Intelligence* (New York: Knopf, 1974), p. 167.

28. Steven Aftergood, "Secrecy News," Project on Government Secrecy, Federation of American Scientists (FAS), Washington, DC (October 31, 2012), p. 1.

29. See "The CIA and the Media," *Hearings*, Subcommittee on Oversight, US House Permanent Select Committee on Intelligence, Washington, DC (April 20, 1978).

30. Loch K. Johnson, "The CIA and the Media," *Intelligence and National Security* 1 (May 1986), pp. 143–169.

31. Loch K. Johnson, *America's Secret Power: The CIA in a Democratic Society* (New York: Oxford University Press, 1989), pp. 101–128.

32. See Robin W. Wink, *Cloak & Gown: Scholars in the Secret War, 1939–1961* (New York: William Morrow, 1987). For a sampling of criticism about CIA-academic relationships, see Gene I. Maeroff, "Harvard and CIA at Impasse Over Secret Work by the Faculty," *New York Times* (August 5, 1978), p. A7; and Robert M. Gates, "Text of Speech at Harvard by Deputy CIA Director Outlining Policy Shifts," *Chronicle of Higher Education* 31 (February 26, 1986), pp. 26–29.

33. On the 1967 inquiry, see the *Katzenbach Report* on CIA attempts to recruit US students in the National Student Association for intelligence activities overseas (prepared for President Lyndon B. Johnson by Undersecretary of State Nicholas Katzenbach), *Weekly Compilation of Presidential Documents* (April 3, 1967); the 1976 reforms resulted from the Church Committee investigation into intelligence in 1975, Select Committee to Study Governmental Operations with Respect to Intelligence Activities, *Final Report*, Vol. 1 (Washington, DC: US Government Printing Office, 1976), pp. 181–191.

34. My interviews with CIA officials, Washington, DC (March 27, 2012); see also Johnson, *America's Secret Power*, Chapter 8.

35. Joseph E. Persico, *Piercing the Reich* (New York: Viking, 1979), p. 38.

36. Loch K. Johnson, *The Threat on the Horizon* (New York: Oxford University Press, 2011), p. 249.

37. James Risen, "CIA to Issue Guidelines on Hiring Foreign Operatives," *New York Times* (June 30 1995), p. A4.

38. Johnson, *Threat on the Horizon*, p. 249.

39. Johnson, *Threat on the Horizon*, p. 249.

40. Interview with Jeffrey H. Smith conducted by Paul Schott Stevens, *National Security Law Report* 18 American Bar Association (October 1996), p. 6.

41. Reuel Marc Gerecht, "A New Clandestine Service: The Case for Creative Destruction," in Peter Berkowitz, ed., *The Future of American Intelligence* (Stanford, CA: Hoover Press, 2005), p. 118.

42. Quoted in Douglas Jehl, "An Abundance of Caution and Years of Budget Cuts Are Seen to Limit C.I.A.," *New York Times* (May 11, 2004), p. A18.

43. "Representative Porter Goss Responds to CIA Critics," *National Security Law Report*, 18 American Bar Association (December 1996), p. 11.

44. Remark made by Secretary Kissinger on October 1, 1973, cited by Larry Rohter, "The Human Rights Crowd Gives Realpolitik the Jitters," *New York Times* (December 28, 2003), Weekend Section, p. 7, based on documents acquired by the National Security Archive at George Washington University in Washington, DC.

45. Persico, *Piercing the Reich*, p. 39.

46. Frank Snepp, *Decent Interval* (New York: Random House, 1977), pp. 563–580.

47. Loch K. Johnson, "The Myths of America's Shadow War," *The Atlantic* (January 2013).

48. On the attack against Qaddafi, see Jon Lee Anderson, "Letter from Libya: King of Kings," *The New Yorker* (November 7, 2011), p. 57; the Awlaki and Bin Laden assassinations are discussed in Chapter 11 and 12.

49. For the casualty statistics, see David Carr, "Debating Drones in the Open," *New York Times* (February 11, 2012), p. B1; and Lev Grossman, "Drone Home" *Time* (February 11, 2013), pp. 28–33.

50. Ken Dilanian "CIA Nominee John Brennan No Stranger to Spycraft, Politics," *Los Angeles Times* (January 7, 2013), p. A1.

51. Scott Shane, e-mail to me (January 22, 2013).

52. Michael Isikoff, "Exclusive: Justice Department Memo Reveals Legal Case for Drone Strikes on Americans," *NBC News* (January 29, 2013).

53. James Downie, "The Justice Department's Chilling 'Targeted Killings' Memo," *Washington Post* (February 5, 2013), p. A1.

54. John McCone, press conference, US Capitol, Washington, DC (June 6, 1975), my notes.

55. The anonymous intelligence officer is quoted by Donner Day, "The Battle over US Intelligence," *Air Force* 6 (May 1978), p. 13.

56. Bob Woodward, *Veil: The Secret Wars of the CIA, 1981–1987* (New York: Simon & Schuster, 1988).

57. My conversations with British intelligence officers, Conference on Intelligence, St. Anthony's College, Oxford University (May 14, 2003); see also Roger Moorhouse, *Killing Hitler: The Plots, Assassins, and the Dictator Who Cheated Death* (New York: Random House, 2006).

58. My interview with William E. Colby, Washington, DC (March 21, 1979).

59. "Alleged Assassination Plots Involving Foreign Leaders," *Report No. 94–465*, Select Committee to Study Governmental Operations with Respect to Intelligence Activities—the Church Committee (November 20, 1975), p. 46.

60. As a staff member of the Senate Select Committee on Intelligence and of the Senate Foreign Relations Committee, I heard Helms and Kissinger make these comparisons during hearings in the 1970s.

61. My interview, Washington, DC (August 20, 1975); see also Loch K. Johnson, "National Security, Civil Liberties, and the Collection of Intelligence: A Report on the Huston Plan," in "Supplementary Detailed Staff Reports on Intelligence and the Rights of Americans," *Final Report*, Church Committee, US Senate (April 23, 1976), pp. 921–986.

62. See John Elliff, *The Reform of FBI Intelligence Operations* (Princeton, NJ: Princeton University Press, 1979); and William W. Keller, *The Liberals and J. Edgar Hoover: Rise and Fall of a Domestic Intelligence State* (Princeton, NJ: Princeton University Press, 1989).

63. Remarks, Platform Committee, Democratic National Committee, Washington, DC (June 12, 1980), mimeograph, p. 1.

64. See, for example, the depiction of Brzezinski in David S. McLellan's biography of Secretary of State Cyrus Vance— Brzezinski's idealistic counterpoint in the administration: *Cyrus Vance* (Totowa, NJ: Bowman & Allanheld, 1985).

65. Brezinski, remarks, Democratic National Committee (1980), p. 1.

66. Edmund S. Muskie, "Human Freedom: America's Vision," *Current Policy No. 208*, Bureau of Public Affairs, US Department of State (August 7, 1980), p. 3.

67. John Lewis Gaddis, *Strategies of Containment: A Critical Appraisal of Postwar American National Security Policy* (New York: Oxford University Press, 1982).

68. Muskie, "Human Freedom," p. 3. For a critical examination of inconsistencies in the approach of the Carter administration to human rights, see William F. Buckley Jr., "Human Rights and Foreign Policy," *Foreign Affairs* 58 (Spring 1980), pp. 775–796.

69. See "World Report 2012: Haiti," Human Rights Watch, New York (2013); "Haiti," Doctors Without Borders (January 31, 2012).

70. Lester R. Brown, *The Twenty Ninth Day: Accommodating Human Needs and Numbers to the Earth's Resources* (New York: Norton, 1978), p. 7.

71. Quoted in an Associated Press release (February 16, 1989).

72. Maurice Strong, Secretary General of the UN Conference on Environment and Development, held in Brazil in 1992, "40 Chernobyls Waiting to Happen," *New York Times* (March 22, 1992). p. E15.

73. J. William Fulbright, remarks, *Congressional Record* (May 17, 1966), p. 10808, cited by Randall Bennett Woods, *Fulbright: A Biography* (New York: University of Cambridge Press, 1995), p. 420.

74. Joseph S. Nye Jr., *Ethics and Foreign Policy: An Occasional Paper* (Wye Plantation, MD: Aspen Institute for Humanistic Studies, 1985), p. 24.

75. Joseph S. Nye Jr., "Superpower Ethics: An Introduction," *Ethics and International Affairs* 1 (1987), pp. 1–8.

76. Nye, *Nuclear Ethics,* p. 20.

77. Nye, *Nuclear Ethics,* pp. 91–131.

78. Stanley Hoffman, "The Rules of the Game," *Ethics and International Affairs* 1 (1987), p. 38.

79. Walter F. Mondale, speech, Commonwealth Club, San Francisco (September 5, 1980).

80. Joseph S. Nye Jr., *The Powers to Lead* (New York: Oxford University Press, 2008), p. x; and his "Recovering American Leadership," *Survival* 50 (2008), pp. 55–68; see also Ted Galen Carpenter, *Smart Power: Toward a Prudent Foreign Policy for America* (Washington, DC: CATO Institute, 2008).

81. Yan Xuetong (a political science professor at Tsinghua University in China), "How China Can Defeat America," *New York Times* (November 21, 2011), p. A23.

### Chapter 15

1. The quote is from the Senate Select Committee on Secret Military Assistance to Iran and the Nicaraguan Opposition and House Select Committee to Investigate Covert Arms Transactions with Iran (the Inouye–Hamilton Committees), *Report*, U.S. Congress (July 24, 1987), p. 158. See also William S. Cohen and George J. Mitchell, *Men of Zeal: A Candid Inside Story of the Iran-Contra Hearings* (New York: Viking, 1988).

2. See, as well, Louis Fisher, *Defending Congress and the Constitution* (Lawrence: University Press of Kansas, 2011).

3. James Risen and Eric Lichtblau, "Bush Lets U.S. Spy on Callers Without Courts," *New York Times* (December 16, 2005), p. A1.

4. Jane Mayer, *The Dark Side* (New York: Doubleday, 2008).

5. Press release, Office of Senator Feinstein, Washington, DC (February 5, 2013).

6. Cited in *Secrecy News*, Project on Government Secrecy, Federation of American Scientists (February 5, 2013).

7. Delivered on January 11, 1962.

8. Comments from a speech by the Secretary on September 8, 2010, cited by Mark Landler, "In a Speech on Policy, Clinton Revives a Theme of American Power," *New York Times* (September 9, 2010), p. A6.

9. George F. Kennan, *American Diplomacy, 1900–1950* (Chicago: University of Chicago Press, 1951), p. 79.

10. Cited by "Global Goofs: U.S. Youth Can't Find Iraq," CNN. com/education (November 22, 2002). For comparable data from earlier years, see Lee Schwartz, "We're Failing Geography 100," *Washington Post* (December 29, 1987), p. A29; Connie Leslie, "Lost on the Planet Earth," *Newsweek* (August 8, 1988), p. 3; Valerie Strauss, "History Students Going Beyond the Book," *Washington Post* (June 6, 2000), p. A13; and Gallup Organization, *Gallup Youth Survey* (May 5, 2000), p. 1.

11. Gary C. Jacobson, *A Divider, Not a Uniter: George W. Bush and the American People, the 2006 Election and Beyond* (New York: Pearson/Longman, 2007), p. 209.

12. *Geographic Literacy Study*, National Geographic-Roper Public Affairs Survey (May 2006).

13. "American Public Opinion about Islam and Muslims," Council on American-Islamic Relations (2006).

14. Data from the *Atlanta Journal and Constitution* (November 22, 1986), p. A6.

15. Stephanie Czekalinski, "Uplifting Languages," *National Journal* (January 23, 2012), p. 26. The information on Japanese versus US businesspeople comes from my interview with former US Trade Ambassador Don Johnson, School of Law, University of Georgia (February 21, 2012). A hopeful sign is the number of students in US universities who are now studying international affairs and foreign languages, their interest piqued by the nation's struggle against terrorism after the 9/11 attacks, as well as America's wars in Iraq and Afghanistan. At the University of Georgia, for instance, only a handful of students studied Arabic before the 9/11 attacks; by 2013, over 200 were enrolled in this pursuit. Language skills are vital to US diplomacy and other activities abroad. For instance, an American military patrol in Iran with a good interpreter was reportedly "10 times as valuable as one with a lousy one" [Will Bardenwerper, "For Military, Slow Progress in Foreign Language Push," *New York Times* (September 22, 2008), p. A22].

16. My interviews with State Department personnel regarding the Foreign Service; and my own experience regarding US academic institutions.

17. J. William Fulbright, "Fulbright Exchanges Enhance Our National Security," *The Chronicle of Higher Education* (December 10, 1987), p. 104. International students also contribute significantly to the American economy—more than $17.8 billion in the 2008–2009 academic year, for example [letter to me from Allan E. Goodman, President, Institute of International Education, New York (dated January 8, 2010)].

18. Fulbright Foreign Scholarship Board Annual Reports, Department of State, Washington, DC. See also William A. Adams and Donna Lind Infeld, "Fulbright Scholars in Political Science," *PS: Political Science and Politics* 44 (July 2011), p. 513, Table 3 (which has figures for the total number of Fulbrights, not just political scientists).

19. Walter F. Mondale, *The Good Fight* (New York: Scribner, 2010), p. 347. Recall, as well, former Senator Gary Hart's remarks in *Perspectives of American Foreign Policy* 14.1.

20. Quoted by William Pfaff, "If It's 'the Public Be Damned,' the Policy Is Doomed," *Los Angeles Times* (December 18, 1986), p. 11.

21. Jack Goldsmith, *The Terror Presidency: Law and Judgment Inside the Bush Administration* (New York: Norton, 2007). Goldsmith served as the assistant attorney general in the Office of Legal Counsel (OLC) during the second Bush Administration.

22. Quoted by Stuart Taylor Jr., "Reagan's Defenders Arguing He Can Defy Congress's Ban," *New York Times* (May 17, 1987), p. A14.

23. The 9/11 Commission Report, *Final Report of the National Commission on Terrorist Attacks Upon the United States* (New York: Norton, 2004), p. 420. See Loch K. Johnson, "The Church Committee Investigation of 1975 and the Evolution of Modern Intelligence Accountability," *Intelligence and National Security* 23 (April 2008), pp. 198–225.

24. See Frances E. Lee, "Senate Deliberation and the Future of Congressional Power," *PS: Political Science & Politics* 43 (April 2010), pp. 227–229.

25. Ravi Somaiya, "Republican Threatens to Block Pentagon and C.I.A. Nominees," *New York Times* (February 11, 2013), p. A10.

26. Aaron Wildavsky, "The Past and Future Presidency," *The Public Interest* 41 (Fall 1975), p. 75.

27. Susan F. Rasky, "Senators Seeking to Overhaul War Powers Resolution," *New York Times* (May 20, 1988), p. 3.

28. Quoted by Margaret Garrard Warner, "An Overture to Congress," *Newsweek* (January 23, 1989), p. 26.

29. David D. Newsom, *Diplomacy and the American Democracy* (Bloomington: Indiana University Press, 1988), p. 217.

30. Reported by Elisabeth Rosenthal, "Nigeria's Population Is Soaring in Preview of a Global Problem," *New York Times* (January 18, 2012), p. A1.

31. Paul Kennedy, "True Leadership for the Next Millennium," *New York Times* (January 3, 1993), p. E11. For contemporary statistics on global population growth, see *CIA World Factbook*, Central Intelligence Agency (Washington, DC: July 2012). Sharon L. Camp, "Population: The Critical Decade," *Foreign Policy* 90 (Spring 1993), pp. 126–144, noted that "stopping population growth by the middle of the twenty-first century at about 9 billion people will require, as a first step, the near universal availability of safe and effective birth control by the year 2000" (pp. 138–139).

32. Jack A. Goldstone, "The New Population Bomb," *Foreign Affairs* 89 (January/February 2009), pp. 31–43. In 2010, the world population included 1.57 billion Muslims.

33. Justin Gillis, "Falling Behind in Race to Feed the World," *International Herald Tribune* (June 4–5, 2011), p. 1; and Felicity Barringer, "Deforestation Hurts Energy From Rivers, Study Finds," *New York Times* (May 14, 2013), p. A8.

34. Jimmy Carter, "The United States Must Guide Third World toward Self-Sufficiency," *Atlanta Journal and Constitution* (December 3, 1988), p. A-23.

35. State of the World's Children, *United Nations Report* (2010), pp. 18–19.

36. Nicholas D. Kristof, "Postcard From Zimbabwe," *New York Times* (April 8, 2010), p. A23.

37. Quoted in George D. Moffett III, "Cuts in US Development Aid Protested," *Christian Science Monitor* (September 12, 1986), p. 8.

38. Cited by Rick Gladstone, "U.N. Presents Grim Prognosis on the World Economy," *New York Times* (December 19, 2012), p. A8.

39. Thomas J. Lueck, "57th St. Loc., 2 TVs/Rm., $400/Night," *New York Times* (January 31, 1989), p. 13; Haynes Johnson, "Let Them Eat Flowers," *Washington Post,* National Weekly Edition (March 12, 1984), p. 25.

40. Suzy Khimur, "Who Are the 1 Percent?" *Washington Post Wonkblog* (October 6, 2011).

41. For two of many critiques to this effect, see Chalmers Johnson, *The Sorrows of Empire: Militarism, Secrecy, and the End of the Republic* (New York: Henry Holt & Company, 2004); and Joseph E. Stiglitz, *The Price of Inequality: How Today's Divided Society Endangers Our Future* (New York: Norton, 2012).

42. Anthony Lewis, "When We Could Believe," *New York Times* (June 12, 1987), p. A31.

43. Brian Fishman, New American Foundation, West Point Project on Terrorism, *Newshour* Public Television (April 30, 2012).

44. Interviewed by John Hughes, "Lunch with Cap," *Christian Science Monitor* (September 12, 1986), p. 16.

45. Speech by J. Michael Kelly, reprinted in Frank R. Barnett, B. Hugh Tovar, and Richard H. Shultz, eds., *Special Operations in US Strategy* (Washington, DC: National Defense University Press, 1984), p. 223.

46. Joseph E. Stiglitz and L. Bilmes, *The Three Trillion Dollar War* (New York: Norton, 2008).

47. The figures about the Qaeda decline are widely reported CIA estimates; for example, the Afghan statistic is from journalist Bob Woodward, *Morning Joe*, MSNBC Television (January 6, 2011); in contrast, Princeton University scholar Geogary Johnsen has pointed to the growth of AQAP [*NewsHour*, Public Television (August 6, 2013)].

48. This example was provided to me by a leading European expert on counterterrorism (October 24, 2009).

49. President Ronald Reagan, quoted on *Evening News,* ABC Television (May 31, 1988).

50. Quoted by Colin Campbell, "Campaign Obscured Babbitt's Expertise in Foreign Policy," *Atlanta Constitution* (February 19, 1988), p. A6. Daniel Patrick Moynihan (D-New York), a member of the Foreign Relations Committee, noted several years before the end of the Cold War that "the one enormous fact of the third quarter of the 20th century [is] the near complete collapse of Marxism as an ideological force in the world. Nothing quite so sudden or so complete has ever happened. Economic doctrines have faded, political canons have been discarded, but here was an extraordinary world view, thought to be irresistible, maintaining a hold on sectors of opinion in all the great metropolitan centers of the world—of a sudden, vanished" ["Reagan's Doctrine and the Iran Issue," *New York Times* (December 21, 1986), p. E-19].

51. See Eqbal Ahmad and Richard J. Barnet, "A Reporter at Large: Bloody Games," *The New Yorker* (April 11, 1988), pp. 44–86; Steve Coll, *Ghost Wars* (New York: Penguin, 2004).

52. Henry A. Kissinger, "Dealing from Reality," *Los Angeles Times* (November 22, 1987), Sec. 5, p. 1.

53. "Poverty Figures by State: 2008," United States Census Bureau, Washington, DC (2008).

54. See "CDC Violence Prevention: Suicide Facts at a Glance," Centers for Disease Control and Prevention (Summer 2009). In my own community—Athens, a medium-size city in rural Georgia—the police chief has observed that the production and sale of methamphetamines has become the greatest problem for his local law enforcement officers [my interview (January 8, 2013)].

55. "Summary of Discretionary Funds, FY 2002–2011," US Department of Labor (April 2010); Richard J. Barnet, "Reflections: The Disorders of Peace," *The New Yorker* (January 20, 1992), p. 70; Rochelle L. Stanfield, "Children's Issues at a Crossroads," *National Journal* (April 17, 1993), p. 95; and Nicholas D. Kristof, "Equality, a True Soul Food," *New York Times* (January 2, 2011), p. Wk. 10.

56. Sabrina Tavernise, "Poverty Reaches a 52-Year Peak, Government Says," *New York Times* (September 14, 2011), p. A1.

57. Reported by Charles M. Blow, "America's Exploding Pipe Dream," *New York Times* (October 29, 2011), p. A17.

58. Bob Herbert, "A Word, Mr. President," *New York Times* (November 10, 2009), p. A31.

59. Sabrina Tavernise, "Study Finds Big Spike In Poorest In the U.S.," *New York Times* (November 4, 2011), p. A16.

60. *Nightly News*, ABC Television (April 19, 2012); and Adam Gopnik, "The Caging of America," *The New Yorker* (January 30, 2012), p. 73.

61. John Tierney, "Prison Population Can Shrink When Police Crowd the Streets," *New York Times* (January 26, 2013), p. A1. A report from the Congressional Research Service, Library of Congress, found that "the federal prison population has increased, on average, by approximately 6,100 inmates each year. Data show that a growing proportion of inmates are being incarcerated for immigration- and weapons-related offenses, but the largest portion of newly admitted inmates are being incarcerated for drug offenses" [cited by Steven Aftergood, *Secrecy News*, Federation of American Scientists 2013 (January 29, 2013), p. 1].

62. Unsigned editorial opinion, *New York Times* (January 11, 2013), p. A20, based on study commissioned by the National Institutes of Health (Washington, DC) in 2012.

63. Unsigned editorial opinion, *New York Times* (January 11, 2013), p. A20.

64. *Nightly News*, NBC Television (October 18, 2011).

65. Children's Defense Fund, based on Centers for Disease Control data (http://www.childrensdefense.org/child-research-data-publications/data/protect-children-not-guns-2012.pdf);

66. Mark Shields, commentator, *Newshour*, Public Television (December 20, 2012). *Newshour*, Public Television, also reported that a person is twenty times more likely to die of a gunshot wound in the United States than in any other developed country (December 17, 2012).

67. Joseph S. Nye Jr., *Soft Power: The Means to Success in World Politics* (New York: Public Affairs, 2004), p. 57.

68. George Packer, "Dead Certain," *The New Yorker* (November 29, 2010), p. 76.

69. Jimmy Carter, State of Human Rights Address 1991, a paper delivered by the former president on December 8, 1991, at the Carter-Menil Human Rights Prize ceremony, Houston, Texas, reprinted in the *Georgia Review* 46 (Spring 1992), quote at p. 4.

70. Nicholas D. Kristof, "America's Defining Choice," *New York Times* (November 12, 2009), p. A31.

71. Thomas L. Friedman, "This I Believe," *New York Times* (December 2, 2009), p. A33.

72. Aaron B. O'Connell, "The Permanent Militarization of America," *New York Times* (November 5, 2012), p. A24.

73. Stephen Flynn, *America the Vulnerable: How Our Government Is Failing to Protect Us from Terrorism* (New York: HarperCollins, 2004), p. 175. This imbalance of spending priorities occurred even though half the US veterans of the war in Afghanistan believed that the military intervention wasn't worth undertaking; and fully 60 percent of the veterans of the war in Iraq said that particular intervention wasn't worth fighting [Pew Survey, 2011, cited in Jill Lepore, "The Force," *The New Yorker* (January 28, 2013), p. 75].

74. Senator Frank Church (D-Idaho), public address, Boise, Idaho, my notes (August 6, 1972).

75. Senator Ron Paul (R-Kentucky), speech, "Containment and Radical Islam," Heritage Foundation, Washington, DC (February 6, 2013), reprinted in the *Washington Examiner* (February 6, 2013), p. 1.

76. See Daniel A. Pollock, Philip Rhodes, Coleen A. Boyle, Pierre Decoufle, and Daniel L. McGee, "Estimating the Number of Suicides among Vietnam Veterans," *American Journal of Psychiatry* 147 (June 1990), pp. 772–776; and Loch K. Johnson, "War Correlates of Political Alienation," in Charles Figley and Seymour Levintman, eds., *Strangers at Home: Vietnam Veterans Since the War* (New York: Praeger, 1980), pp. 213–228.

77. Paul Kennedy, "True Leadership for the Next Millennium."

78. Richard Critchfield, "Bring the Green Revolution to Africa," *New York Times* (September 14, 1992), p. A19.

79. OPIC press release, Washington, DC (December 14, 2012).

80. Jimmy Carter, State of Human Rights Address (1991), p. 5.

81. Josh N. Ruxin, "Pandemic Pandemonium," *National Interest* 96 (July/August 2008), p. 29.

82. Unsigned editorial, "Still Fighting Against AIDS," *New York Times* (November 28, 2011), p. A20.

83. Dr. Dennis Rosen, "Social Networks of Disease," *New York Times Book Review* (April 29, 2012), p. 17.

84. Sabrina Tavernise, "Life Expectancy Rises Around the World, Study Finds," *New York Times* (December 14, 2012), p. A4. The report was published in *Lancet*, a British medical journal, in 2012.

85. Nicholas D. Kristof, "Winning the Worm War," *New York Times* (April 20, 2010), p. A25.

86. See the Website: http://www.gatesfoundation.org/global-health/Pages/overview.aspx

87. "His Libraries, 12,000 So Far, Change Lives," *New York Times* (November 6, 2011), p. Wk. 11. An enterprising young rugby player in Canada, David Marchesseault, decided to help young Africans in Uganda stay in school by assisting them in the establishment of a school rugby club. School attendance rose and the players reportedly have more self-confidence and better social skills—all from a program that involved minimal funding [Farah Mohamed, "Using Rugby to Help Africans Win," *Toronto Globe and Mail* (November 8, 2011), p. A14].

88. On the recent effects of global warming, see in addition to the President's speech, John M. Broder, "Past Decade Was Warmest Ever, NASA Finds," *New York Times* (January 10, 2010), p. A8; Al Gore, "We Can't Wish Away Climate Change," *New York Times* (February 28, 2010), p. Wk11; and Al Gore, *The Future* (New York: Random House, 2013).

89. From *U.S. News & World Report* (February 5, 2001), as cited by Eugene R. Wittkopf and Christopher M. Jones, with Charles W. Kegley Jr., *American Foreign Policy: Pattern and Process*, 7th ed. (Belmont, CA: Thomson/Wadsworth, 2008), pp. 168–169.

90. Justin Gillis, "Global Carbon Dioxide Emissions in 2010 Show the Biggest Jump Ever Recorded," *New York Times* (December 5, 2011), p. A4.

91. *Nightly News,* ABC Television (December 4, 2009).

92. Alexei Barrionuevo, "4 Giants in Cattle Industry Agree to Help Fight Deforestation," *New York Times* (October 7, 2009), p. A7.

93. Senator Al Gore, *Congressional Record* (April 7, 1992), pp. 54872, 54874.

94. Gore, "We Can't Wish Away Climate Change."

95. Barry Bearak, "Looting Madagascar's Woodlands While the State Looks On," *International Herald Tribune* (May 25, 2010), p. 6.

96. Wendell Wood, of the Oregon Natural Resources Council, quoted in Timothy Egan, "Trees That Yield a Drug for Cancer Are Wasted," *New York Times* (January 29, 1992), p. A9.

97. See Jeffrey Gettleman, "Poachers Kill 11 Elephants In Kenyan Park," *New York Times* (January 18, 2013), p. A10.

98. *Evening News*, CBS Television (November 25, 2012).

99. Singer summarizes this research in "Kinder and Gentler," a review of Steven Pinker, *The Better Angels of Our Nature: Why Violence Has Declined* (New York: Viking, 2011), in *New York Times Book Review* (October 9, 2011), pp. 1, 12–13; quote at p. 13.

100. Quoted by John Newhouse, "The Diplomatic Round: Earth Summit," *The New Yorker* (June 1, 1992), p. 78.

101. Cited by Peter Baker, "Rice Says She Threatened to Quit Over White House Clashes,"*New York Times* (October 23, 2011), p. A20.

102. Quoted in an unsigned editorial, "Beyond Durban," *New York Times* (December 17, 2011), p. A24.

103. Cited by John M. Broder, "Climate Talks Yield Commitment to Ambitious, but Unclear, Actions," *New York Times* (December 9, 2012), p. A11.

104. Unsigned editorial, "Barack Kissinger Obama," *New York Times* (October 26, 2011), p. A25.

105. John M. Broder, "'Cap and Trade' Loses Its Standing as Energy Policy of Choice," *New York Times* (March 26, 2010), p. A13.

106. Unsigned editorial, "National Mission," *New York Times* (June 21, 2010), p. A26.

107. Unsigned editorial, "Cap and Retreat," *New York Times* (November 20, 2010), p. A18.

108. See the Websites: http://ga.water.usgs.gov/edu/gwdepletion.html; http://green.blogs.nytimes.com/2011/11/02/for-parched-times-a-new-water-calculus/; and http://www.waterfootprint.org/?page=files/GlobalWaterFootprint

109. In 2010, the House of Representatives voted 356-to-65 to reject a proposal to withdraw from Afghanistan by the end of that year; Carl Hulse, "House Rejects Plan to Leave Afghanistan By Year's End," *New York Times* (March 11, 2010), p. A6. President Obama vowed, though, to remove US forces from Afghanistan by 2014, restating this goal recently in his 2013 State of the Union Address.

# GLOSSARY

**Adams-Onís Treaty** In 1821, the United States negotiated acquisition of the Florida territory, in exchange for providing assurances to Spain that it could enjoy rule over Texas and the southwest.

**aerial terrorism** The use of airplanes to dive-bomb a target, as occurred in the 9/11 attacks.

**Al Qaeda** A terrorist movement responsible for the 9/11 attacks against the United States and centered initially in Afghanistan, whose name is derived from Arabic for "The Base" or "The Foundation."

**ambassador** The top American official in a US embassy overseas.

**American bishops' letter** A pastoral letter (document) published by the National Conference of Catholic Bishops on War and Peace in 1983 that summed up the organization's deliberations on the moral implications of nuclear deterrence.

**American foreign policy** Those decisions and actions taken by the sovereign nation of the United States with respect to other sovereign nations, as well as various international factions, groups, and organizations, in the protection of America's citizens and allies, along with the advancement of their goals and values.

**American foreign policy maxims** Key principles for the conduct of US relations abroad that include listening to other nations, helping them, setting a good example for the world, and seeking consensual solutions among nations.

**American Israel Public Affairs Committee (AIPAC)** The US Jewish community's chief lobbying arm in Washington, DC, which operates in alliance with forty-seven other organizations around the country under the umbrella of the Council of Presidents of Major American Jewish Organizations.

**analysis** The conversion of raw (unevaluated) information into "finished" (evaluated) intelligence reports for decision makers.

*ante facto* **reporting** Executive reporting to Congress in advance of a decision or an operation.

**antiballistic missile (ABM)** Developed during the Nixon administration, a precursor to the Strategic Defense Initiative and relying on nuclear-armed interceptors to destroy incoming warheads on enemy missiles before they could strike US cities or military bases.

**appeasement** A policy initially practiced by Great Britain against Nazi Germany, it became known as a futile attempt to satiate fanatics (like Hitler) by yielding to their demands.

**arms control** Efforts to achieve a balance of military weaponry among rivals, ideally at a lower inventory of warheads, to reduce the risks of war and to effect budget savings.

**assets (agents)** Foreign nationals in the secret employment of the CIA or other US intelligence agency.

**Authorization for Use of Military Force (AUMF)** A law passed in 2001 that gave the president authority to arrest or kill anyone who committed or assisted in the 9/11 attacks, or who gave safe haven to the attackers.

**balance of power** According to this perspective, if one nation becomes too dominant militarily, it will attempt to manipulate—or even conquer—other nations; therefore, vulnerable nations will form coalitions among themselves to prevent a threatening outsider from achieving military dominance over them.

**ballistic missile defense (BMD)** A more recent, generic term for the antimissile Strategic Defense Initiative proposed by the Reagan administration.

**Bay of Pigs** An ill-fated covert action attempt to overthrow the Castro regime in 1961 by landing a team of CIA-backed Cuban exiles on a beachhead at the Bay of Pigs in Cuba.

**Berlin blockade** Implemented in 1948, the Soviet Union attempted to cut off all Western supply routes to Berlin except for a narrow air corridor.

**big stick diplomacy** Brandishing the military instrument of foreign policy to nudge adversaries toward an acceptance of the US view on international disputes, as advocated periodically by President Theodore Roosevelt and others.

**bipartisanship** A willingness to support presidential foreign policy initiatives across party lines in Congress, for the sake of national unity.

**blowback (replay)** A boomerang effect whereby false information (propaganda) directed toward an adversary can find its way back home to deceive America's own citizens.

**Boland Amendment (1983)** A banning of covert action in Nicaragua, sponsored by the chairman of the House Permanent Select Committee on Intelligence, Edward P. Boland (D- Massachusetts), which led to improper covert action.

**Bosnian War** A war begun in the Balkans by a Serbian attack against Croatia and lasting from 1992 to 1995.

*Boumediene v. Bush (2008)* In this ruling, the Supreme Court gave Guantánamo prisoners an opportunity to challenge their detention by filing habeas corpus petitions, although subsequently the Court backed away from hearing additional cases on the plight of the detainees.

**Boxer Rebellion** An uprising in China in 1900 led by a zealous faction of xenophobes—the Boxers—who opposed the plans of foreigners (including the United States) to divide up their nation into spheres of influence for purposes of international commerce.

**boycott** A prohibition against imports or other forms of business cooperation with another nation.

**Bricker Amendment** In 1954, a constitutional amendment proposed by Senator John Bricker (R-Ohio) to curb the president's power over international agreement making.

**Budget and Impoundment Control Act (1974)** An effort by Congress to tighten its supervision over the executive use of impoundment to freeze government spending opposed by an administration.

**Burkean model** The pursuit of an independent stance in voting and other government activity, rising above the whims of public opinion—in the manner of the British philosopher and politician Edmund Burke.

**Bush Doctrine** In 2002, President George W. Bush released a report entitled *The National Security Strategy of the United States of America*, which outlined a US policy to strike first against terrorists and other foreign threats, even when they may not represent an immediate threat.

**Byrd-Nunn Proposal** Legislation drafted (but never enacted) in 1988 to improve the War Powers Resolution by eliminating the sixty-day clock and relying instead on executive consultation with a panel of congressional leaders to explain and defend the president's proposed use of overt force abroad.

**Camp David Accords** Negotiated in 1979 by President Jimmy Carter at the Camp David presidential compound in Maryland with the leaders of Israel and Egypt, the purpose of the agreement was to bring peace between these warring nations in the Middle East.

**cap-and-trade measures** Market-driven incentives to curb pollution that allow companies to trade special permits, designed to meet established pollution levels, by using a carbon-credits bartering system pegged to a price set for the purpose of lower greenhouse gas emissions.

**Carter Doctrine** Announced by the Carter administration in 1980 following the Soviet invasion of Afghanistan, this policy stated that "any use of outside force to try to gain control of the Persian Gulf oil area will be regarded as an assault on the vital interests of the United States and will be repelled by American military force."

**case officers (operational officers)** CIA personnel in the field who are expected to recruit local spies and secretly carry out other intelligence activities on behalf of the United States.

**Case-Zablocki Act (1972)** With passage of this law in 1972 (and its clarifying amendments in 1978), the State Department had to report to Congress on all international agreements being negotiated by the executive branch.

**Central Intelligence Agency (CIA)** One of America's leading spy organizations, with primary responsibilities for espionage and covert action.

**character** The basic personality traits of an individual.

**chief of station (COS)** The top intelligence officer serving in a foreign nation, usually with an affiliation to the Central Intelligence Agency.

**Church Committee** A Senate panel led by Frank Church (D-Idaho) that engaged in a sixteen-month probe (1975-1976) of alleged intelligence wrongdoings,

uncovering a wide array of improper spying on American citizens by their own intelligence agencies, as well as CIA assassination plots oversers.

**CINCs** Four-star officers of the separate services who head the joint specified and unified commands in the military, such as the CINCPAC (commander in chief for the Pacific theater of operations).

**citizen awareness** The degree of an individual's interest in, and understanding of, international relations, often gauged in public opinion surveys.

**congressional accountability (oversight)** An ongoing review by lawmakers of how well laws are being implemented, along with the monitoring of other aspects of the policy-making process, toward the goal of correcting mistakes and improving future initiatives.

**CNN effect** The rapid speed by which televised images of international events enter the White House Situation Room and other government offices in Washington, DC, and well as living rooms across the United States and in other nations.

**coercive diplomacy** Signaling to other nations that a diplomatic settlement may be in their best interests because the alternative could mean the introduction of military force into the equation.

**collection and analysis** The gathering and interpretation of information by intelligence officers.

**command-control-communications-and-intelligence ($C^3I$)** A nation's capacity to disseminate information and orders from decision makers to their military commanders in the field.

**compartmentation** The practice within the executive branch of maintaining operational security through the establishment of special "need-to-know" channels that sharply limit the access of individuals to intelligence across the board.

**complex interdependence** The entire intricate range of interactions among modern nations summed up also by the term "globalization," which has made transnational forces ever more important in foreign policy.

**compulsive interventionism** America's abandonment of its traditional instincts of

caution and some degree of distance from the affairs of other nations.

**confirmation power** The constitutional right of the Senate, in Article I, to either accept or reject selected presidential appointments to the executive branch.

**congressional resolution** A majority vote in both legislative chambers in support of a policy initiative.

**consequentialists** Those who elevate, ethically, the importance of the overall outcome of an act, not the objective of maintaining individual goodness while the act is carried out.

**containment doctrine** America's grand strategy for limiting the influence and expansion of the Soviet Union during the Cold War.

**conventional capabilities** Armaments that rely on nonnuclear technology, including weapons from M-16 rifles to the blast effect of chemical reactions like TNT.

**Council on Foreign Relations (CFR)** A long-established organization in the United States with foreign policy interests, and the publisher of the influential journal *Foreign Affairs.*

**counterforce** A war-fighting strategy in which the primary enemy targets are military bases and weaponry.

**counterinsurgency warfare (COIN)** Limited or low-intensity conflicts, also known as irregular wars or asymmetric wars.

**countervalue** A war-fighting strategy in which the primary enemy targets are cities with large populations, as well as industrial and communications centers.

**country desk officers** The men and women of the State Department who keep daily watch over all the major countries around the globe, reading the secret and non-secret communications that stream into Washington, DC from US embassies.

**covert action** The secret use of propaganda, political, economic, and paramilitary (war-like) activities or, defined more formally, an activity or activities of the United States Government to influence political, economic, or military conditions abroad, where it is intended that the role of the United States Government will not be apparent or acknowledged publicly.

**creeping commitments** When America's diplomatic and other foreign policy obligations are stretched beyond the original intent of Congress, or even the White House.

**Cuban missile crisis** The Soviet leader Nikita Khrushchev ordered the placement of Soviet nuclear missiles on Cuban soil in October of 1962, precipitating a dangerous confrontation between the superpowers.

**current intelligence** Information from intelligence agencies about what has happened in the world in the last twenty-four hours and what is likely to happen in the next twenty-four hours.

**cybersecurity** The protection of computer systems against attack.

**Dayton Peace Accords** In 1995, the United States brokered these agreements (signed in Dayton, Ohio) that brought an end to fighting among Croats, Bosnian Muslims, and Serbs, resulting in a division of Yugoslavia along ethnic lines.

**Defense Intelligence Agency (DIA)** One of America's top spy agencies, focusing on the analysis of military events and conditions.

**defensive warfare and offensive warfare** Respectively, the repelling of a sudden armed attack against the nation, and the use of the armed force for any purpose not directly related to the defense of the United States against sudden armed aggression.

**democratic peace hypothesis** The supposition that democracies rarely use armed forces against one another.

**demonizing adversaries** Converting potential allies into enemies through unnecessarily hostile rhetoric and behavior against them.

**détente** A period of relaxed tensions between rival nations, punctuated by arms control accords and increased trade agreements, as occurred between the superpowers during the Nixon administration.

**deterrence** The capacity to persuade other nations or terrorist organizations not to use their military forces in ways that might endanger the vital interests of the United States and its allies.

**Deutch rules** Regulations promulgated by DCI John Deutch in 1995 to prevent the recruitment by US intelligence agencies of particularly despicable agents abroad (potentially useful antiterrorist assets excluded) who were in violation of basic human rights.

**diplomacy** The art of adjusting disputes between nations and factions through formal and informal negotiations.

**diplomatic recognition** The constitutional power of the president in Article II to receive foreign diplomats, which can provide foreign nations legitimate standing with the United States that Congress might have failed to acknowledge.

**director of central intelligence (DCI)** From 1947–2004, the leader of the US intelligence community, as well as head of the Central Intelligence Agency.

**director of the Central Intelligence Agency (D/CIA)** Since 2004, the title of the leader at the Central Intelligence Agency, a change which replaced the DCI office and shifted intelligence coordination activities for the entire intelligence community to a new Director of National Intelligence (DNI).

**director of national intelligence (DNI)** An overall leadership position for America's sixteen spy agencies, created in 2004 by the Intelligence Reform and Terrorism Prevention Act (IRTPA), in hopes of strengthening US intelligence performance in the aftermath of the 9/11 intelligence failures.

**discriminating foreign policy** Instead of isolation or excessive intervention abroad, a foreign policy that achieves a more harmonious balance between realistic national goals and the availability of resources to achieve them.

**distorted perceptions** A failure of public officials to accurately comprehend events and conditions in the world around them.

**dollar diplomacy** An approach to foreign policy based on advancing private US commercial interests abroad.

**domino theory** A perspective on international affairs predicting that if one "domino" (nation) falls under the weight of a rival nation, then so will the next rival nation and the next, toppling one after another as in the child's game until, at last, the chain reaction reaches the last standing domino and the original perpetrator has conquered all rivals.

**economic (development) assistance** Help to other nations, including direct grants, technical cooperation, and loans that are either "hard" (i.e., offered at commercial bank interest rates) or, more commonly, "soft" (which are concessional, i.e., provided at low interest rates).

**economic covert action** The use of covert operations to undermine an adversary's means of production and distribution of commercial goods.

**economic statecraft** A nation's use of trade and aid—forms of diplomatic activity that rely on the commercial and financial side of foreign policy.

**Eisenhower Doctrine** In 1957, President Eisenhower asked Congress for controversial authority to use American armed force, if necessary, to protect the national sovereignty of nations in the Middle East against Soviet encroachment, which lawmakers granted—although in ambiguous language.

**electromagnetic pulse (EMP)** The gamma rays emitted in a wave when a nuclear bomb explodes, which can create atmospheric disturbances that disrupt or paralyze communications, radar operations, and early warning systems in the target nation.

**Embargo Act (1807)** Legislation enacted to prohibit the export of American goods to Britain.

**embargoes** A prohibition on exports.

**empathetic diplomacy** Genuine gestures of friendship and peace toward another nation or faction, backed by fair economic agreements.

**empire** The outcome when a nation exercises control over another sovereign territory or territories.

**espionage** The secret collection of information by spies.

**Estimate** An in-depth analysis by America's intelligence agencies on a topic of interest to policy makers, such as the likely leadership succession in China. Also known as a National Intelligence Estimate or NIE.

**ethics of ecology** A concern for the moral requirement of keeping the planet habitable for the human race now and in the future.

**ethnic cleansing** A policy of attacks against rival ethnic groups with the intent of ridding a nation or region of them.

**evasion hypothesis** The supposition that the executive branch has excluded the Congress from international agreement making.

*ex post facto* **reporting** Executive branch reporting to Congress after a decision or operation.

**exceptionalism** Belief in a mission to disperse the values of the United States around the world.

**executive agreement** An international diplomatic transaction carried out by the executive branch, usually without any meaningful consultation with either chamber of Congress—and sometimes hidden altogether from all lawmakers and even the president.

**executive fatigue** As a result of too many responsibilities and not enough time to carry them out, busy foreign policy leaders can experience a deadening effect on their ability to think clearly, or to use their imaginations and maintain a balanced sense of possibility and perspective.

**executive-legislative compact** The idea promulgated by President Carter's Undersecretary of State, Warren M. Christopher (who would later serve as Secretary of State in the Clinton administration) that Congress should allow the executive branch to manage foreign policy on a daily basis, while in return the executive should provide lawmakers with full information and consultation.

**executive privilege** An assertion by the president of constitutional authority to withhold information from the legislative and judicial branches of government.

**extraordinary rendition** The controversial CIA practice of kidnapping a suspected terrorist in another nation, then flying him or her to a location other than the United States for purposes of harsh interrogation.

**extraterritoriality** The extension of US law to American citizens who are being held by another nation on grounds of suspected criminal activity.

**finding** A formal presidential approval of a covert action, required since 1974.

**flexible response** A school of thought that emerged during the Kennedy administration, emphasizing the importance of preparations to fight at every level of combat, from guerrilla insurgencies to all-out nuclear warfare.

**foreign aid** Economic and military assistance on a government-to-government level, or through government-supported agencies or programs.

**foreign policy** A nation's pursuit of objectives in the world through relationships with other nations, international organizations, and factions.

**foreign policy instruments (means)** The methods by which the United States attempts to carry out its policy objectives in the world, including the combined or separate use of intelligence gathering, diplomacy, military force, covert action, economic statecraft, and culture and moral suasion.

**foreign policy objectives (ends)** The physical protection of a nation, its citizens, and its allies; economic prosperity; improvements in the quality of life, such as clean air and water; and the advancement of human rights, for its own citizens and people around the world.

**Foreign Service** The division of the US Department of State responsible for the day-to-day conduct of America's relations with other countries.

**form of international agreement** The three primary forms are treaties, statutory agreements, and executive agreements.

**Formosa Resolution** Unlike prior resolutions in American history, this congressional resolution adopted in 1955 at President Eisenhower's request failed either to order a specific action or even to name an enemy.

**free trade** The removal of government tariffs or other restrictions on international commercial transactions.

**(GATT) General Agreement on Tariffs and Trade** International commercial

negotiations, commonly referred to as a trade "round," where over one hundred nations have participated periodically in economic diplomacy between 1947 and 1994.

**Geneva Accords** In 1954, diplomats "temporarily" divided Vietnam at the 17th parallel and scheduled general elections for the nation in 1956 that were prevented by the outbreak of civil war.

**geopolitics** The study of how foreign policy is influenced by the number, size, strength, location, and topography of nations.

**George Amendment** A 1954 proposal that, like the Bricker Amendment of the same year, aimed at curbing executive agreements, this initiative—which failed along with the Bricker Amendment—from Senator Walter George (D-Georgia) posited that such agreements would have no effect as internal law in the United States unless enacted by Congress.

**German reunification** East and West Germany reunited in 1990 after being divided in the aftermath of the Second World War.

**global village** The capacity for modern communications—television, the Internet, and social media—for infusing a global population comprised of distant strangers with a sense of community in which the world becomes more of an intimate neighborhood.

**global warming** The gradual increase in Earth's temperature caused by the entrapment of gases inside the upper atmosphere, instead of their escape into outer space.

**globalization** The expansion of networks of interdependence around the world.

**Goldwater-Nichols Act (1986)** This statute placed the chairmanship of the Joint Chiefs of Staff in a much stronger position over the US military in the Pentagon, backed by a large professional staff, thereby strengthening unification among the armed services.

*Goldwater v. Carter* The Supreme Court held in 1979 that the president had the authority to terminate a US–Taiwan defense pact and, by implication, any of America's international agreements.

**good neighbor policy** Proclaiming a new era of friendship between the United States and Latin America in 1933, Franklin D. Roosevelt removed all US troops south of the Rio Grande (with the exception of those stationed in the Panama Canal Zone).

**Government Accountability Office (GAO)** An investigative arm of the Congress.

**grand bargain** A school of thought in the United States after the end of the Cold War in 1991 that believed a major infusion of Western capital and known-how, coupled with an insistence that the former Soviet Republics follow Western recommendations on how to revamp their economies, was the only way to avoid a Russian backslide to the old communist regime or into a civil war.

**groupthink** A tendency for individuals in some groups to cast aside a realistic appraisal of alternative courses of action in favor of high cohesiveness among the group's members.

**Gulf of Tonkin Resolution** Passed in 1964 at President Lyndon Johnson's request and allowing him wide discretion over US military powers in Vietnam.

**gunboat diplomacy** An intimidating display of military force designed to encourage another nation to negotiate rather than fight.

***Hamdi v. Rumsfeld (2004)*** The Supreme Court rejected the Bush administration's argument that terrorist detention was a purely presidential matter, above review by the courts.

**hard power** Military threats, as well as economic incentives or punishments.

**Harkin Amendment (1974)** Sponsored by Senator Tom Harkin (D-Iowa), this law placed a ban on aid to "any country which engages in a consistent pattern of gross violations of internationally recognized human rights," unless the president "determines that such assistance will directly benefit the needy people in such country and reports such determination to the Congress."

**hegemon** The situation when control of one nation over another is less sweeping than an empire relationship, but still strongly influential.

**Helsinki Accords** Declarations signed in 1975 by President Gerald R. Ford and other national leaders that encouraged respect for human rights and fundamental freedoms, improved economic and technical cooperation among the signatories, and freer movement of people, ideas, and information between the East and the West.

**honest broker** A role that has evolved for NSC advisers in which an emphasis is placed on the task of mediating disputes among the cabinet departments, and especially mollifying as much as possible the institutional tensions between State and Defense.

**Hughes–Ryan Act (1974)** A law enacted that required the president to approve all important covert actions via a "finding," and then to inform the Congress of these decisions.

**human intelligence (HUMINT)** The secret gathering of information by spies.

**human rights** The dignity of individuals around the world, including the fundamental right to freedom from repression.

**hyperpluralism** A sense that the number of power centers within a nation's government and society has become excessive, perhaps even to the point of paralysis.

**impoundment** The freezing of funds in the federal treasury by the executive branch, despite the passage by Congress of an appropriations law requiring the expenditure of the funds.

**impressment** Naval recruitment by force, as with the kidnapping of Americans to serve as sailors on British warships against the French fleet, which reached a high point during the years from 1803–1811.

**infrastructure** The CIA's worldwide network of foreign assets (agents) used for covert actions, an apparatus also known colloquially by Agency insiders as the "plumbing."

**inherent constitutional right** The claim that the president's designation as commander in chief, and the constitutional injunction that "he shall take Care that the Laws be faithfully executed," provide the holder of that top executive office with the implicit right to use US troops as he (or, one day, she) alone may wish.

**Intermediate-Range Nuclear Forces (INF) Treaty** An agreement between the United States and the Soviet Union in 1987 to remove all intermediate-range nuclear forces from West and East Europe.

**institutional comity** The condition achieved when a vigorous Congress and presidency work together, both vital pistons in the engine of democratic government meant to complement one another through constructive criticism and mutual respect.

**institutional fragmentation** The degree to which power is dispersed across a nation's government.

**instructed-delegate model** A lawmaker's following of cues from constituents on how to vote (say, from the letters they write to Washington, DC), as if he or she were a seismograph merely recording shifts in popular opinion.

**intelligence cycle** A simplified description of how intelligence is collected, analyzed, and disseminated by the United States.

**intelligence ethics** Moral considerations related to the use of secret intelligence operations.

**Intelligence Oversight Act of 1980** The most important formal measure taken by Congress to strengthen its control over America's intelligence operations, including a requirement for prior reports to the two congressional Intelligence Committees on all important secret operations.

**Intelligence Oversight Act of 1991** A formal clarification of the meaning of covert action operations, as well as a tightening of intelligence oversight procedures in Congress.

**Intelligence Reform and Terrorism Prevention Act (IRTPA)** A law signed by President Bush in 2004, designed (with only modest results) to bring greater cohesion to the nation's sixteen intelligence agencies.

**intergovernmental organizations (IGOs)** Some 245 entities worldwide that boast a wide range of nations within their memberships, such as the United Nations,

NATO, the League of Arab States (LAS), and World Health Organization (WHO).

**International Monetary Fund (IMF)** An internationally backed bank that attempts to maintain global monetary stability and provide financial support for developing nations, drawing on resources contributed by members as an initiation fee.

**international nongovernment organizations (INGOs)** These entities comprise about 90 percent of all international organizations and include the International Olympic Committee, terrorist cells, religious groups (the Roman Catholic Church, for one), professional associations (such as the global network of Doctors Without Borders), political parties, and a wide range of groups established to foster commercial relations between nations.

**interventionism** Attempts to influence the affairs of other nations, overtly or covertly.

**Iraq War** An American attack against Iraq in 2003, beginning a war that lasted until 2011 (see Operation Iraqi Freedom).

**Iraqi WMD program** In 2002–2003, the Bush administration based its main argument for war against Iraq (the Second Persian Gulf War) on a belief that this Middle East regime was likely developing weapons of mass destruction that could be used against the United States.

**iron triangles** An unofficial permanent government (sometimes known as a "subgovernment") comprised of interest groups, bureaucrats, and lawmakers whose opposition can make life difficult for a nation's chief executive officer.

**isolationism** A detachment from the affairs of other nations.

**Jay Treaty (1794)** A successful negotiation led by America's first Supreme Court Chief Justice, John Jay of New York, to restore trade relations with Great Britain after the Revolutionary War.

**Joint Chiefs of Staff (JCS)** The uniformed leadership of the US military services, answerable to the secretary of defense and equipped with authority through the JSC Chair to discipline officers who fail to participate professionally in joint-duty responsibilities assigned to them by the Chiefs.

**just war tradition** A venerable philosophy of war that advocates the right of a nation to defend itself against the unjust use of force.

**Kantians** Those who advocate, in the manner of the German philosopher Immanuel Kant, the moral purity of the individual.

**Kellogg–Briand Treaty (1928)** An international pact that renounced war as an instrument of national policy.

**Kosovo War** From 1998–1999, ethnic cleansing and fighting erupted in what was once Yugoslavia, as Muslims of Albanian heritage pushed for greater autonomy in the province of Kosovo and eventually took up arms against Serbian soldiers and police stationed there.

**law of anticipated reactions** The potential for a negative legislative reaction to a proposal from the executive branch, which may cause bureaucrats to bring their budget and other requests to Congress more in line with the likely response of lawmakers.

**leadership isolation** When a nation's leaders become cut off from reality because they lack access to vigorous debate and opinions beyond a small (and sometimes conformist) circle of top policy officials.

**League of Nations** Part of President Woodrow Wilson's "Fourteen Points" presented to US lawmakers, this international organization was meant to rely on collective action for preventing future wars, but the Senate rejected the proposal in 1919.

**Lebanon Emergency Assistance Act** A 1983 congressional resolution that gave President Ronald Reagan eighteen additional months to keep US troops in Lebanon, often used as an example of excessive presidential deference by lawmakers to the executive branch in foreign policy—even after passage of the War Powers Resolution a decade earlier, designed to curb excessive presidential control over war-making.

**legislative acquiescence** A willingness of lawmakers to give presidents free rein over the making of international agreements and other instruments of foreign policy.

**lend-lease agreement** During the administration of Franklin D. Roosevelt, the President initially used an executive agreement in 1940 to loan the United Kingdom fifty somewhat antiquated navy destroyers for the British defense against the Germans, in exchange for US leasing rights to certain naval bases in the Western Hemisphere that belonged to the British.

**liberalism (idealism)** The advocacy of resolving international conflicts by way of international law, negotiations through international organizations, and the promotion of collective security arrangements.

**Limited Test Ban Treaty (1963)** An agreement between the United States and the Soviet Union that required nuclear-weapons testing to be conducted underground.

**Lippmann school of thought on public opinion** When it came to foreign policy deliberations, such delicate matters (argued the journalist Walter Lippmann) should be left to the pros: the professional diplomats and national security experts.

**Lord Acton (on power)** According to this British statesman, "Power corrupts, and absolute power corrupts absolutely."

**McCarthyism** During the early 1950s, Senator Joseph McCarthy (R-Wisconsin) employed unfair tactics of smear and innuendo to blame the nation's foreign policy woes on unnamed communists engaged in treasonous behavior inside the government of the United States.

**Maastricht Treaty** Named after the town in Belgium where it was signed in 1992 and more formally known as the Treaty of European Union, the twelve-nation European Community (EC) pledged to establish a lasting economic and political European Union (EU).

**manifest destiny** Newspaper editor John L. O'Sullivan proclaimed in 1845 that the United States had a special and self-evident mission "to overspread and to possess the whole of the continent which Providence has given us."

**Marshall Plan** The Truman administration policy to strengthen the European economy after the Second World War through the infusion of billions of dollars in economic aid from 1948 to 1952—a policy known formally as the European

Recovery Program (ERP) and designed to thwart Soviet influence in Western Europe.

**massive retaliation** A US counterattack strategy based on using America's full nuclear arsenal—a theory of deterrence central to the Eisenhower administration. (See, also, mutual assured destruction)

**measurement-and-signatures intelligence (MASINT)** The secret collection of intelligence through the use of scientific sensory devices to determine the presence of dangerous substances, such as radioactive weaponry, lethal chemicals, and bacteriological materials.

**micromanagement** The excessive involvement in the details of policy implementations, especially by lawmakers and their staff.

**micro-states** The smaller nations of the world.

**Millennium Challenge Corporation (MCC)** A program established by President George W. Bush to provide increases in foreign aid to nations, especially in Africa, that have displayed a capacity for economic reform.

**military assistance (security assistance)** Help to other nations, including the use of military advisory groups, equipment, and defense-oriented economic support (such as funding for the construction of dock facilities and railroads).

**military-industrial complex** An informal, behind-the-scenes alliance comprised of the Pentagon, the weapons industries, and the Armed Services and Appropriations Committees in Congress.

**Monroe Doctrine (1823)** In the most heralded of all American foreign policy pronouncements, President James Monroe warned the capitals of Europe that the nations of the Western Hemisphere were "henceforth not to be considered as subjects for future colonization by any European power."

**moral and cultural suasion** Respectively, winning friends abroad by virtue of setting a good example as a vibrant democracy and by way of the attractive attributes of one's society.

**most-favored-nation (MFN)** A form of economic inducement in which one nation bestows on another nation the best available trading relationship for its imports.

**multinational corporation (MNC)** An international company with foreign subsidiaries that extends its production and marketing beyond the boundaries of any one nation.

**Munich syndrome** A situation where in a relationship between nations one side seems too weak, which might invite an attack by the other side—an allusion to the time when Hitler acted out of disdain for perceived weakness in the West and signed a false peace pact in Munich.

**mutual assured destruction (MAD)** A military doctrine that emerged after the Second World War in which each of the two "superpowers"—the United States and the Soviet Union—developed a capacity to retaliate against an attack with a massive nuclear counterresponse, thereby keeping each other at bay.

**nation** A gathering together of individuals under a common leadership, or government, in control of a well-defined territorial space.

**National Command Authority (NCA)** A nation's top political and military leaders.

**National Commitments Resolution** A statement issued by the Senate Foreign Relations Committee in 1969 that emphasized the importance of having any US national commitment abroad based on affirmative action taken by both the executive and legislative branches government, not just the executive alone.

**National Economic Council (NEC)** A White House entity, analogous to the National Security Council, created during the Clinton administration to ensure that the president's viewpoint is properly heard in domestic debates over US trade policy.

**National Geospatial-Intelligence Agency (NGA)** A US spy agency devoted to the collection of intelligence through photography ("imagery"), whether from satellites in space, reconnaissance aircraft, or spies carrying concealed cameras.

**National Intelligence Estimate (NIE)** A classified study, based on extensive research by the US spy agencies, about what is likely to happen in any nation or region, predicting as far as possible into the future.

**National Reconnaissance Office (NRO)** A US spy-satellite management agency that coordinates NSA and NGA surveillance platforms.

**National Security Agency (NSA)** America's premier spy organization for electronic communications interception, as well as for code breaking.

**National Security Council (NSC)** The most important organization in the US federal bureaucracy when it comes to foreign policy whose principal members include the president, the vice president, the secretary of state, and the secretary of defense.

**National Security Council adviser roles** Approaches to aiding the president used by national security advisers in the United States, including that of administrator, coordinator, counselor, and insurgent.

**National Security Council Memorandum No. 68 (NSC-68)** An internal memo of the Truman administration that codified the containment doctrine in 1950 and declared that "the assault on free institutions is worldwide now, and in the context of the present polarization of power a defeat of free institutions anywhere is a defeat everywhere."

**national security intelligence** The collection and analysis of information about global events and conditions as well as on the views and personalities of worldwide leaders and other individuals of significance to the United States.

**National Security Review No. 29 (NSR-29)** President George H. W. Bush's directive signed in 1991 that directed America's secret agencies to compile the most exhaustive list of US intelligence priorities since the end of the Second World War.

**NBC weapons** Nuclear, biological, and chemical armaments.

**neoclassical realism** A complex view of the world that takes into account not only the international system of nations—the number and the types of countries—but the influence of domestic politics inside each and the perceptions of world affairs held by individual national leaders.

**neoconservatism (neocons)** A group that blends liberalism and realism, promoting the spread of democracy (as do liberals) but relying on the use of military force for success (as do realists).

**neoliberalism** The advocacy of the worldwide development of democracy, open markets, and free trade through the adoption of international regimes.

**neorealism** The view that international affairs is a structured system of interacting nations, with regularities of behavior and a dependence largely on the use of hard power.

**new world order** The possible evolution toward an integrated international community that would replace the anarchy and warfare common to the current fragmented system of nations.

*New York Times Co. v. United States* **(Pentagon Papers Case)** A Supreme Court ruling in 1971 against the request of the Nixon administration to prevent the *New York Times* and other papers from publishing the Pentagon's classified, in-house history of the Vietnam War— also known informally as the Pentagon Papers case.

**9/11 attacks** The assaults by terrorists affiliated with Al Qaeda, directed against the American homeland on September 11, 2001, and specifically New York City and Washington, DC.

**Nixon Doctrine** A policy announced in 1969 by President Richard M. Nixon stipulating that nations in the developing world would be expected to use their own troops, not US soldiers, to defend themselves.

**non-state actors** Various global corporations and international organizations operating outside the framework of national governments in world affairs.

**nontariff barriers (NTBs)** Hidden obstacles to free trade with another nation, including its "buy national" campaigns; inspection requirements; customs valuation procedures; industrial and environmental standards; domestic content stipulations; and distribution intricacies, along with legal and language idiosyncrasies.

**North American Free Trade Agreement (NAFTA)** Presidents George H. W. Bush and Bill Clinton sought to improve trade ties among Canada, Mexico, and the United States and, in 1994, Clinton signed this statutory agreement into law (initiated by Bush), which lowered commercial barriers in North America.

**North Atlantic Treaty Organization (NATO)** In 1949, the United States joined with Canada and Western Europe in the creation of America's first peacetime military alliance since the early days of the Republic.

**nuclear decapitation** The use of a swift, well-coordinated nuclear strike that deprives the enemy of its top leadership in time of war.

**nuclear ethics** Moral considerations related to the use of nuclear weapons.

**nuclear winter** The possible freezing of the Earth following the detonation of large numbers of nuclear weapons during a major nuclear war—a result of soot from burning buildings rising into the atmosphere and blocking out the sun's rays.

**Nunn–Lugar Act (1991)** In 1991, Congress provided over $1 billion of initial spending to improve the security of Russian nuclear warheads and related WMD materials, out of fear that these "loose nukes" might fall into the hands of terrorists.

**Olney corollary** In 1895, Secretary of State Richard Olney informed Britain that "the United States is practically sovereign on this continent, and its fiat is law upon the subjects to which it confines its interposition"—a dramatic strengthening of the Monroe Doctrine.

**OPEC (Organization of Petroleum Exporting Countries)** A global oil cartel comprised of thirteen countries, mainly in the Middle East.

**open door policy** A view pronounced by Secretary of State Jay Hay in 1899 that each major power should have a sphere of trading influence in China that had to be honored by other nations, as well as by China.

**open source intelligence (OSINT)** The overt collection of information from non-secret sources, such as newspapers, libraries, radio broadcast, business and industrial reports, or from accredited foreign service officers—information that can comprise as much as 95 percent of intelligence reports.

**opening to China** On observing a widening of the schism between China and the Soviet Union, the Nixon administration set out in 1962 to woo China farther apart from Moscow's influence.

**Operation Desert Storm (First Persian Gulf War)** The 1990 decision by President George H. W. Bush to repel—with a massive US-led military force that quickly succeeded in 1991—an Iraqi invasion into Kuwait, a neighboring, small, oil-rich regime on the Persian Gulf.

**Operation Enduring Freedom (Afghanistan)** In the aftermath of the 9/11 attacks in 2001, the Bush administration implemented this counterattack against Al Qaeda and the Taliban regime in Afghanistan, leading to America's longest war that finally drew down in 2014.

**Operation Iraqi Freedom (Second Persian Gulf War)** The US invasion of Iraq in 2003, known informally as the Iraqi War and lasting until 2011.

**Operation Mongoose** The codename for CIA covert actions carried out against the Castro regime in Cuba from 1961–1963.

**Operation Restore Hope (Somalia)** In 1992, the United States sent troops into Somalia to provide protection for the humanitarian relief efforts of the United Nations—the largest purely humanitarian intervention abroad in America's history.

**Operation Uphold Democracy (Haiti)** In 1994, President Bill Clinton ordered a US military intervention in Haiti to stem the flow of refugees toward Florida and restore order on the poverty stricken island.

**operational code ("op-code")** A research tool for exploring individual attitudes and behavior related to foreign policy, especially by probing a leader's stated beliefs about the nature of politics and political conflict.

**opinion-leadership hypothesis** Without reliable information, individuals who might be critical of the president—say, congressional leaders in the opposition party—are in a weak position to offer a persuasive critique; therefore, they are inclined to be supportive, or at least remain quiescent.

**Oslo Accords** President Bill Clinton's diplomatic efforts in 1993 to move Israel and its neighbors closer to peace by way of negotiations, facilitated by the Norwegian government, through which the Palestine Liberation Organization (PLO) renounced terrorism and its call for the destruction of Israel in return for Israel's promise to withdraw from the Gaza Strip and the West Bank town of Jericho.

**oversight (accountability)** The ongoing review of public policy initiatives by lawmakers.

**overt-covert action** An intelligence operation designed to influence events abroad and meant to be secret but that becomes a matter of public knowledge through leaks and media reporting.

**Paramilitary covert action** Secret war-like activities, usually conducted by the CIA.

**party loyalty model** When lawmakers take cues from party leaders and vote along party lines.

**Pearl Harbor syndrome** A situation in a relationship between two nations where one side seems too strong, which might provoke an attack by the weaker side in a paranoid, last-gasp attempt at self-defense, as when Japan acted out of fear in 1941 and struck Hawaii to gain a slight advantage for what Tokyo viewed as an inevitable war with the Americans.

**Phoenix program** A CIA operation during the Vietnam War (1964–1973) designed to subdue the influence of communists in the South Vietnamese countryside (especially the indigenous Vietcong) through assassinations and other means.

**plausible deniability** The attempt to conceal any presidential ties to a US covert operation, as a means for protecting the reputation of the United States abroad.

**politicization of intelligence** The rejection by policy makers of objective intelligence, for political purposes.

**preemptive war** The rapid use of force against an adversary who is about to attack at any moment.

**President's Daily Brief (PDB)** The preeminent current intelligence document prepared by the US spy agencies for distribution to the president and a select group of other top officials in the executive branch.

**preventive war** The early use of US force against a perceived enemy state because that state might attack the United States at some future time—even if not imminently.

**prior experience** An emphasis on how the level of skill one has in a foreign policy job usually depends on one's earlier training and other life circumstances.

**prior restraint** When the government withholds the right of an unauthorized individual or group (say, the *New York Times* or a former CIA officer) to publish information about its activities.

**pluralism** The existence of multiple centers of power—primarily interest groups—within a nation.

**political covert action** Attempts to influence foreign officials through hidden channels, as with the use of secret funding for or against them.

**populist nationalism** A situation wherein people within the same nation who do not seem to agree with the reigning nationalist ideology are assigned the status of minorities, suggesting that they cannot belong within the authentic body of the national people.

**Powell Doctrine** A corollary to the Weinberger Doctrine, advocated by JCS Chairman Colin L. Powell (later a Secretary of State in the George W. Bush administration), who argued in 1992 that if America were to go to war, the nation should use overwhelming force to win quickly.

**power** A nation's ability to persuade other nations and factions to accept its policy objectives—or, at least, not to oppose them.

**power sharing** A view of American government as an array of separate institutions required by the Constitution to share authority and power in foreign and domestic policy.

**presidential deference model** The inclination of some lawmakers to defer to the president on foreign policy.

**principle of discrimination** Avoidance of the use of force against noncombatants— another way of expressing the idea of "noncombatant immunity."

**principle of noncombatant immunity** A moral prohibition against the use, or even the targeting, of weapons against civilians who are not engaged in military combat.

**principle of proportionality** The proposition that one's use of force should be roughly equivalent in scope and magnitude to that employed by a belligerent.

**professionals and amateurs** Differences in experiences and approaches to foreign policy between professional careerists and temporary amateurs ("in-and-outers" who join the government for only short periods of time, such as academicians and businesspeople) can lead to friction in the making of foreign policy decisions.

**protectionism** Support for the use of government tariffs and quotas against imports as a means of shielding US industries from foreign competition.

**psychohistory** Psychoanalytic and psychological theory applied to historical biography.

**public diplomacy** The government's projection around the world of an accurate picture of the United States through radio, television broadcasts, and other means of communications, accompanied by criticism of America's adversaries.

**rally-round-the-flag hypothesis** A perceived threat to the United States and its citizens will result in a display by the American public of strong patriotic support for the president, sending the standing of the chief executive sharply upward in opinion ratings on job performance.

**rapprochement** The establishment of cordial diplomatic relations between nations.

**Reagan Doctrine** Less a formal policy statement than a label applied by the media to the Reagan administration's new aggressiveness against the Soviets that employed the robust use of the CIA and covert action to assist nations in their resistance to communist influence from 1981 to 1989.

**realism** The philosophy that a state's external relations should rest prudently on a foundation of military and economic strength—hard power.

**realpolitik** The view that international affairs should be based not on theoretical or ethical considerations but rather on practical and material objectives.

**regimes** Written agreements entered into by states that seek mutual institutional cooperation for the benefit of all signatories, as in the case of arms control arrangements among nations; also, another term for "governments."

**reporting requirements** Statutes that mandate the delivery from the executive branch of information to various committees and subcommittees in Congress on a range of policy proposals and in a timely manner, as a means for keeping lawmakers informed of executive activities.

**rogue elephant** A description of the CIA offered by Senator Frank Church (D, Idaho) in the 1970s based on the view that this secret agency is sometimes off on a rampage of its own making without proper supervision from the president, Congress, and the courts.

**role-playing** The idea that in a government the type of office occupied by a decision maker will cause him or her to hold and implement foreign policy views traditional to the long-time practices of that particular office, as when a State Department desk officer inherits and perpetuates existing policy toward another nation.

**Roosevelt corollary** President Theodore Roosevelt issued an amendment to the Monroe Doctrine in 1904, announcing that henceforth the United States would serve as policeman to settle disputes in the Western Hemisphere.

**Rush-Bagot Agreement (1817)** In America's first significant arms control pact, the British and the Americans negotiated a removal of their naval ships from the Great Lakes.

**Rwanda genocide** The Clinton administration vacillated over whether to help bring to an end a civil war in this Africa nation in 1994, while over 800,000 people died in tribal warfare before assistance arrived from the United States and other nations.

**secret propaganda** The covert placement of materials in foreign media outlets in an attempt to persuade target nations or groups toward a certain point of view.

**second-strike capability** A nation's capacity to retaliate against a nuclear attack by using its surviving nuclear weapons.

**security dilemma** The notion that, as one nation arms itself defensively, a rival nation will grow fearful of this action and in turn further arm itself, leading to an upward spiraling of an arms race.

**self-delusion** The tendency for some officials to brush aside or bend facts that fail to conform to their preconceived worldview.

**separate institutions sharing power** A popular description of the government in the United States.

**separation of powers** A core doctrine embedded in the Constitution that seeks to avoid autocracy by spreading power across three branches of government.

**signing statements** The occasional practice of presidents when signing bills into law to issue remarks highlighting provisions in a statute that the White House believes can be properly disregarded because they supposedly amount to unconstitutional restraints on executive power.

**smart power** The ability to combine hard and soft power into an effective strategy.

**smart sanctions** Economic inducements that punish the elites in a target country rather than the average person on the street.

**Smoot–Hawley Act (1930)** A law passed by Congress in 1930 that produced a protectionist reaction worldwide that harmed international commerce, thereby contributing to the Great Depression and the outbreak of the Second World War.

**social constructivism** A school of thought that concentrates on the questions of how social norms, ideas, and images can influence international relations and the importance of how nations think of themselves and their values in comparison with other nations.

**soft power** Getting others to want what you want through the use of moral and cultural suasion. See also hard power.

**sovereignty** The legal capacity of a nation to regulate its affairs as it pleases, without permission from any outside source.

**Sparkman-Bennet letters** An understanding reached in 1978 (in an exchange of letters between the Senate and the Carter administration) that, in the future, the Department of State would inform the Foreign Relations Committee "periodically, on a confidential basis, of significant international agreements which have been authorized for negotiation."

**special operations (special ops)** Another phrase for secret paramilitary, or war-like, activities.

**statecraft** The way a leader conceives of and carries out the role of statesman, along with his or her approach to relations with followers and adversaries.

**statutory agreements** A loosely worded statute that bestows on the executive branch legislative authority to consummate an international agreement, after gaining the support of a majority vote in both chambers of Congress.

**stonewall and slow roll** When the executive branch delays, in a wide variety of ways, a response to an issue posed by lawmakers or their requests for information.

**Strategic Arms Reduction Talks (START) Treaty** Signed in 1991, this arms pact between the United States and Russia authorized dramatic cutbacks in the number of strategic nuclear warheads in both nations by some two-thirds.

**Strategic Defense Initiative (SDI)** A military defense system proposed by the Reagan administration in 1983, in which enemy missiles were to be shot down in mid-flight with US space-based laser technology.

**strategic nuclear capability** A nation's intercontinental ballistic missiles, submarine-launched ballistic missiles, and long-range bombers equipped with nuclear bombs or missiles—the so-called triad.

**Strategic Offensive Reduction Treaty (SORT)** An arms control agreement between Russia and the United States, signed in 2002, that cut the strategic nuclear arsenals of these nations to the lowest total in decades—at about 2,000 warheads each.

**Support to Military Operations (SMO)** Attention to military intelligence requirements—the top US intelligence priority for government officials, especially whenever America is at war.

**sycophancy trap** The tendency for subordinates to flatter and defer to a leader, for fear of upsetting or cutting off access to him or her.

**tactical nuclear weapons** Weaponry that rely on a nuclear reaction for their destructive force but are more limited in scope than strategic nuclear weapons and are designed for relatively small targets on the battlefield.

**Taliban regime** The regime in Afghanistan that provided a safe haven for Al Qaeda, and the target of America's war in that nation after the 9/11 attacks. (See also Operation Enduring Freedom.)

**tasking** The assignment of specific collection priorities to the intelligence agencies.

**technical intelligence (TECHINT)** The secret gathering of information by machines, such as satellites, reconnaissance aircraft, and listening devices.

**textbook presidency** A misleading image of the US presidency portrayed in some school and college books as someone who has all the information and skilled advisers necessary to make wise decisions.

**theater nuclear weapons** Though some possess the potential yield of the atomic bombs dropped on Hiroshima and Nagasaki, these weapons tend to be small in size—from backpack warheads (for use by the infantry, say, to stop a tank) and howitzer shells (with a range of twenty miles or so) to the NATO Lance battlefield-support missiles (with a range of eighty miles).

**three-dimensional ethics** The interplay between the motives of decision makers, the means they propose, and the likely consequences of their choices.

**trade promotion authority** Under this rule, congressional committees can delay trade agreements with other countries for no longer than forty-five days, once the White House submits them for congressional review—at which point Congress then must either approve or reject the deals, without amendments, within fifteen days.

**treaties** The constitutionally based form of approval by the Senate of a US international agreement, achieved by attracting a vote of two-thirds of those senators present and voting in the chamber, with subsequent ratification by presidential signature.

**Treaty of Ghent (1814)** A negotiation that ended the War of 1812 between America and Britain.

**Treaty of Guadalupe Hidalgo (1848)** A negotiation that ended the US war with Mexico and acquired for the United States all of New Mexico, California, and an extension of the Texas boundary to the Rio Grande.

**Treaty of Versailles (1919)** A negotiation that settled the terms for the end of the First World War.

**treaty provision** The constitutionally based rule stating that the president "shall have power, by and with the advice of the Senate to make treaties, provided two-thirds of the Senators present concur."

**Treaty Powers Resolution** A failed attempt by the Senate in 1978 to require that any "significant" international agreement should be cast as a treaty and submitted to senators for their advice and consent.

**triad** A strategic deterrent capability based on three types of weaponry: ground-based long-range missiles, sea-based submarine-launched missiles, and airborne intercontinental bombers.

**Truman Doctrine** President Harry Truman's proclamation of a Greek-Turkish foreign aid package in March of 1947—a important step toward the containment of communism.

**United Nations (UN)** An international organization established in 1945, designed to maintain world peace in the aftermath of the Second World War.

***United States Immigration and Naturalization Service v. Chadha*** (1983) A Supreme Court ruling that stated the legislative veto was unconstitutional, often known as the *Chadha* case.

**United States Trade Representative (USTR)** America's chief international trade negotiator.

***United States v. Curtiss-Wright Export Corporation*** (1936) In this famous law case, a lower court convicted Curtiss-Wright (an American weapons-manufacturing company) for the improper sale of machine guns to Bolivia; subsequently, opinions in the case became fodder for debate over executive-legislative relations in US foreign policy.

***United States v. Nixon*** (1974) The Supreme Court rejected the contention that a president had an absolute executive privilege; but it did give constitutional legitimacy to executive privilege for confidential communications within the executive branch, noting that great deference would be entitled to the claim if foreign policy or military secrets were involved.

**Vietnam syndrome** Restraint with respect to the military instrument of foreign policy, as well as the use of covert action, in reaction to the failed intervention in Vietnam during the 1960s.

**war power** The threatened or actual overt use of military force in the conduct of foreign policy.

**War Powers Resolution** A law enacted by the Congress in 1973 to ensure a role for lawmakers in the determination of when the United States would go to war and for how long.

**Warsaw Pact** A Moscow-led security alliance established in 1955, comprised of the Soviet Union and the nations of Eastern Europe.

**Weinberger Doctrine** A set a guidelines for future US military engagement advanced by Secretary of Defense Casper W. Weinberger in 1984 during the Reagan administration, including the prerequisite that the military action had to involve vital national interests, had to have clear-cut political-military objectives, and had to have the support of the American people.

**XYZ affair** A notorious French covert action directed against US diplomats in Paris in 1797.

**Zimmermann telegram** In 1917, German Foreign Secretary Arthur Zimmermann sent a secret telegram to his envoy in Mexico, ordering him to seek a pact of aggression with Mexico against the United States should the Americans enter the war against Germany.

**zone of twilight** A domain of authority in the law and the Constitution in which the president and Congress may have concurrent authority, or in which the proper distribution remains uncertain.

# CREDITS

# INDEX